PROCEEDINGS
OF THE
SEMINAR FOR ARABIAN STUDIES

VOLUME 38
2008

Papers from the forty-first meeting of the
Seminar for Arabian Studies
held in London, 19-21 July 2007

SEMINAR FOR ARABIAN STUDIES

ARCHAEOPRESS
OXFORD

Orders for copies of this volume of the *Proceedings* and of all back numbers should be sent to Archaeopress, Gordon House, 276 Banbury Road, Oxford OX2 7ED, UK.
Tel/Fax +44-(0)1865-311914.
e-mail bar@archaeopress.com
http://www.archaeopress.com
For the availability of back issues see the Seminar's web site: www.arabianseminar.org.uk

Seminar for Arabian Studies
c/o the Department of the Middle East, The British Museum
London, WC1B 3DG, United Kingdom
e-mail seminar.arab@durham.ac.uk

Opinions expressed in papers published in the *Proceedings* are those of the authors and are not necessarily shared by the Editorial Committee.

Typesetting, Layout and Production: David Milson

The *Proceedings* is produced in the Times Semitic font, which was designed by Paul Bibire for the Seminar for Arabian Studies.

ISSN 0308-8421
ISBN 978-1-905739-20-2

The Steering Committee of the Seminar for Arabian Studies is most grateful to

the Muḥammad bin ᶜIsā Al Jaber Foundation

for its continued generosity in making a substantial grant toward the running costs of the Seminar and the editorial expenses of producing the *Proceedings*.

Contents

Transliteration

Quotations, single words, and phrases from Arabic, or other languages written in non-Roman alphabets, are transliterated according to the systems set out below.

However, unless an author insists on a particular transliteration in all circumstances, place names and words from languages written in non-Roman alphabets which have entered English or French in a particular form (e.g. Mecca/la Mecque, Mocha, Dhofar, qadi, wadi, imam/iman), are reproduced in that form when they are part of an English or French sentence, rather than part of a quotation in the original language or of a strictly transliterated name or phrase. For example:

1. "the settlement was built in the wadi bed" BUT "the settlement in Wādī Mayfaʿah
2. "l'iman alla à Médine" BUT "Imām ʿAlī vint de al-Madīnat al-Munawwarah"

The transliteration systems are as follows:

(a) Arabic

ء	ʾ	ج	*j*	ذ	*ḏ [dh]*	ش	*š [sh]*	ظ	*ẓ*	ق	*q*	ن	*n*
ب	*b*	ح	*ḥ*	ر	*r*	ص	*ṣ*	ع	ʿ	ك	*k*	ه	*h*
ت	*t*	خ	*ẖ [kh]*	ز	*z*	ض	*ḍ*	غ	*ḡ [gh]*	ل	*l*	و	*w*
ث	*ṯ [th]*	د	*d*	س	*s*	ط	*ṭ*	ف	*f*	م	*m*	ي	*y*

Vowels: **a i u ā ī ū.** Diphthongs **aw ay.**

Note: From the next issue (PSAS 39) onwards, a modified transliteration system will be in operation. The new transliterations are shown in square brackets in the table above. Authors should note these changes when preparing their manuscripts for submission.

Initial *hamzah* is omitted

The *lām* of the article is not assimilated before the "sun letters", thus *al-shams* not *ash-shams*. The *hamzat al-waṣl* of the article is shown after vowels except after the preposition *li-*, as in the Arabic script, e.g. *wa-ʾl-wazīr, fī ʾl-bayt,* but *li-l-wazīr*.

Tāʾ marbūṭah (ة) is rendered *-ah* in pause, e.g. *birkah, zakāh,* and *-at* before a vowel, e.g. *birkat al-sibāḥah, zakāt al-fiṭr*.

(b) **Ancient North and South Arabian**
ʾ b t ṯ ḥ g ẖ d ḏ r z s^1 s^2 s^3 ṣ ḍ ṭ ẓ ʿ ḡ f q k l m n h w y.

(c) **Other Semitic languages** appear in the transliteration systems outlined in the *Bulletin of the American Schools of Oriental Research* 226 (1986), p. 3.

(d) **Persian, Urdu, and Ottoman Turkish** as for Arabic with the additional letters transliterated according to the system in the *Encyclopaedia of Islam* (New Edition) except that *ž* is used instead of <u>zh</u>.

Editors' Foreword

The Seminar for Arabian Studies is the principal international academic forum for presentation and discussion of the latest research in the humanities regarding the Arabian Peninsula (including archaeology, epigraphy, numismatics, ethnography, language, history, art, architecture, etc) from the earliest times to the present day or, in the case of political and social history, to about the end of the Ottoman Empire (1922). The Seminar has been meeting since 1968 and the 2008 seminar will be the 42nd meeting. The Seminar meets annually for three days – Thursday to Saturday – in July, and has been hosted by the British Museum since 2002. Up to 180 people attend the Seminar from all over the Middle East, Europe, and North America as well as India, Pakistan, Australia and Japan and up to 45 papers and posters are now presented each year.

The 2007 Seminar included a special invited session on the **The Palaeolithic of Arabia** which was organised by Dr Jeffrey Rose. This field is the focus of new and intensive investigation and we are delighted to have facilitated such research at the Seminar. The papers which arose from this session are included here in a separate section, together with the organiser's research objectives and a report on the round-table discussion that followed the session. We hope to continue this concept of incorporating a special research session into future programmes and the steering committee welcomes suggestions. However, we continue to also strongly encourage contributions on the latest research and results of current fieldwork, which can be delivered either as papers or posters.

Not all papers that are offered are accepted, and not all that are presented are submitted or accepted for publication. Nevertheless, the published *Proceedings* aim to give an accurate flavour of the event. Last year we expanded the editorial committee of the *Proceedings* to include a wider range of academics from around the world. We have also been making increasing use of our refereeing process in order to drive up the academic standards of the published papers. The previous editor of the *Proceedings*, Michael Macdonald, introduced a set of rigorous guidelines, Helen Knox has been a very diligent copy-editor, and the team at Archaeopress have greatly improved the appearance and quality of the *Proceedings*. We are very grateful to all of them, and to David Milson who has taken over from Paul Naish at Archaeopress, for their hard work. Final thanks are due to the authors themselves: their prompt submission of manuscripts and speedy responses to edited copy have made possible the publication of this volume in a very short time period.

For more information about the Seminar for Arabian Studies please contact: Dr. Ardle MacMahon (Secretary), Seminar for Arabian Studies, The British Museum, c/o Department of the Middle East, Great Russell Street, London WC1B 3DG. Email: seminar.arab@durham.ac.uk or visit the Seminar website at: **www.arabianseminar.org.uk**

In the meantime this is the last issue edited by ourselves and we hope you enjoy it and recommend the *Proceedings* to your colleagues, students and libraries. The next volume will be produced under the chief editorship of Janet Starkey and we hope you will give her as much support as you have given us.

St John Simpson and Lloyd Weeks

The Joint Editors

Proceedings of the Seminar for Arabian Studies 38 (2008): 1–2

Introduction: special session to define the Palaeolithic of Arabia

Jeffrey I. Rose

Scholars have long suspected that Arabia played a central role in human evolution, linking species in Africa, Europe, and Asia throughout the Pleistocene. Seventy-five years ago, renowned archaeologist Henry Field dubbed this region the "cradle" of early humans and suggested "that southwestern Asia, including the African territory, may well have nurtured the development of *Homo sapiens*" (Field 1932: 426). For an all-too-brief period following Field's remarkably prescient supposition, scientists and explorers such as St John Philby, Bertram Thomas, Gertrude Caton-Thompson, Wilfred Thesiger, and Beatrice de Cardi combed the surface of Arabia, reporting stone tools associated with relict river systems and ancient lake basins. However, due to a series of obstacles such as war, isolationism, and impenetrable geography, Palaeolithic research ground to a virtual halt during the latter half of the 20th century. Arabia has since languished in relative obscurity while more comprehensive work has been conducted in adjacent territories of the Levant and East Africa.

Notable exceptions to this were the Italian Expedition to North Yemen, Norman Whalen's work in Yemen and Oman, the Soviet Expedition to South Yemen, and the Comprehensive Survey Project in Saudi Arabia. Although few and infrequent, these projects surveyed huge tracts of land across the peninsula, recording a plethora of lithic scatters that underscore the scope of Palaeolithic habitation throughout the region. By the end of the 20th century, it had become abundantly clear that early human occupation in Arabia was extensive, yet stratified and datable Palaeolithic sites continued to elude archaeologists. Consequently, details such as the identity and chronology of these early human groups remained a mystery.

The situation changed significantly in 1999, when a team of geneticists discovered traces of one of our species' most ancient mitochondrial DNA human lineages among populations in the Horn of Africa, a lineage that was previously thought to be rooted in Asia (Quintana-Murci *et al.* 1999). Given Arabia's position as the bridge connecting East Africa and Asia, these findings heralded heightened research throughout the Arabian Peninsula by demonstrating its geographic prominence in the process of early human expansion.

As genetic research shone the Palaeoanthropological spotlight on Arabia, the pace of discovery quickened accordingly. Arabia's first datable Palaeolithic sites have finally been discovered. Recent systematic surveys permit a more comprehensive discussion of stone tool distribution across the landscape. Abundant palaeoenvironmental data allow for a reconstruction of climatic conditions over the course of the Middle and Upper Pleistocene. Genetic samples obtained from modern Arabian populations enable us to assess their position on the human family tree.

In light of these pioneering discoveries, we organized a special session of the Seminar for Arabian Studies to convene scholars from various disciplines related to early human occupation in Arabia in order to present and discuss this new information. The central theme of these papers – "defining the Palaeolithic periods in the Arabian Peninsula" – was chosen based on recent archaeological discoveries, palaeoenvironmental reconstructions, and human genetics. As the first ever symposium devoted to the Palaeolithic of Arabia, we set out to begin to articulate the prehistoric record and to assess the peninsula within a broader regional framework. Following the presentation of these data, we convened a round table discussion to assess the state of research, synthesize these findings, and examine avenues for further inquiry. A summary of the discussion can be found at the end of the papers from the Palaeolithic special session.

The symposium represented only an initial step toward a greater understanding of Palaeolithic Arabia. Hopefully, these seminal papers will engender interest in the region and set out an array of questions to be addressed in future investigations. Ultimately, these questions lead us back to the fundamental query at the heart of prehistoric research: what does this tell us about the evolution of our species? As Henry Field's "cradle of *Homo sapiens,*" Palaeolithic Arabia is an important piece of that puzzle.

References

Field, H.
1932. The Cradle of Homo Sapiens. *American Journal of Archaeology* 36/4: 426–430.

Quintana-Murci L., Semino O., Bandelt H., Passarino G., McElreavey K. & Santachiara- Benerecetti A.S.
1999. Genetic evidence of an early exit of Homo sapiens sapiens from Africa through eastern Africa. *Nature Genetics* 23: 437–441.

Author's Address
J.I. Rose, Human Origins and Palaeo-Environments (HOPE) Research Group, Department of Anthropology and Geography, Oxford Brookes University, Oxford OX3 0BP, UK.
e-mail jrose@brookes.ac.uk

Proceedings of the Seminar for Arabian Studies 38 (2008): 3–14

The "Wa^cshah method": an original laminar debitage from Ḥaḍramawt, Yemen

RÉMY CRASSARD

Summary

The discovery of several surface sites revealed the existence of an original type of lithic industry, unknown until now in Yemen, and in the rest of South Arabia. This type of debitage, called the "Waᶜshah method" is a method of laminar debitage (blade production). We announced this discovery in a former PSAS paper (Crassard & Bodu 2004), and here we develop the definition of this type of debitage in the light of recent analyses.

Keywords: lithic technology, laminar debitage, Wādī Waᶜshah, Ḥaḍramawt, Yemen

General definition and context of discovery

During surveys made by two archaeological projects, one in Wādī Waᶜshah (French Archaeological Mission in Jawf-Ḥaḍramawt — HDOR Project, directed by M. Mouton and A. Benoist) and another in Wādī Ṣanā (Roots of Agriculture in Southern Arabia — RASA Project, directed by J. McCorriston, R. Oches, and ᶜA. bin ᶜAqil), several surface sites were discovered with a new type of laminar debitage (blade production) made on local flint or chert. The discovery of a debitage modality of preferential blades constitutes a rare example of predetermined laminar debitage in the Arabian Peninsula. Sites with laminar debitage on naviform cores are known in Qatar but they are due to technical import from Levantine human groups (Inizan 1988). This type of debitage has never been found in any region of Yemen.

The debitage identified in Wādī Waᶜshah seems to be particular to South Arabia, without obvious contribution from abroad, either from East Africa, the Levant, or other areas of the Arabian Peninsula. We will name this type of debitage the "Waᶜshah method". The Waᶜshah method allows the production of pointed blades by a unidirectional laminar debitage (Fig. 1).

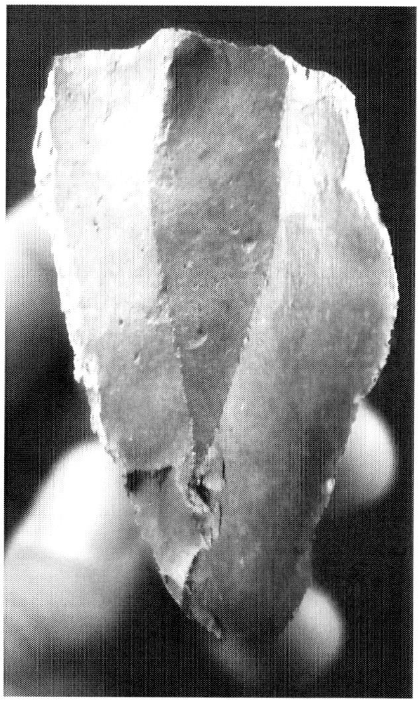

FIGURE 1. *An example of a Waᶜshah core (from Wādī Waᶜshah).*

At least ten sites in Wādī Waᶜshah and two (possibly three) sites in Wādī Ṣanā revealed a Waᶜshah industry with homogeneous characteristics (Fig. 2). In Wādī Waᶜshah, sites are especially concentrated in a 1 km perimeter, east of site HDOR 538. These geographical data, however, indicate only the surveyed zone, while this corpus could, most probably, be increased if the survey area was widened. Wādī Ṣanā also delivered some Waᶜshah debitage sites, always at the tops of the plateaus, but from surface sites, sometimes mixed with Levallois industries on axial cores with a flat debitage surface.

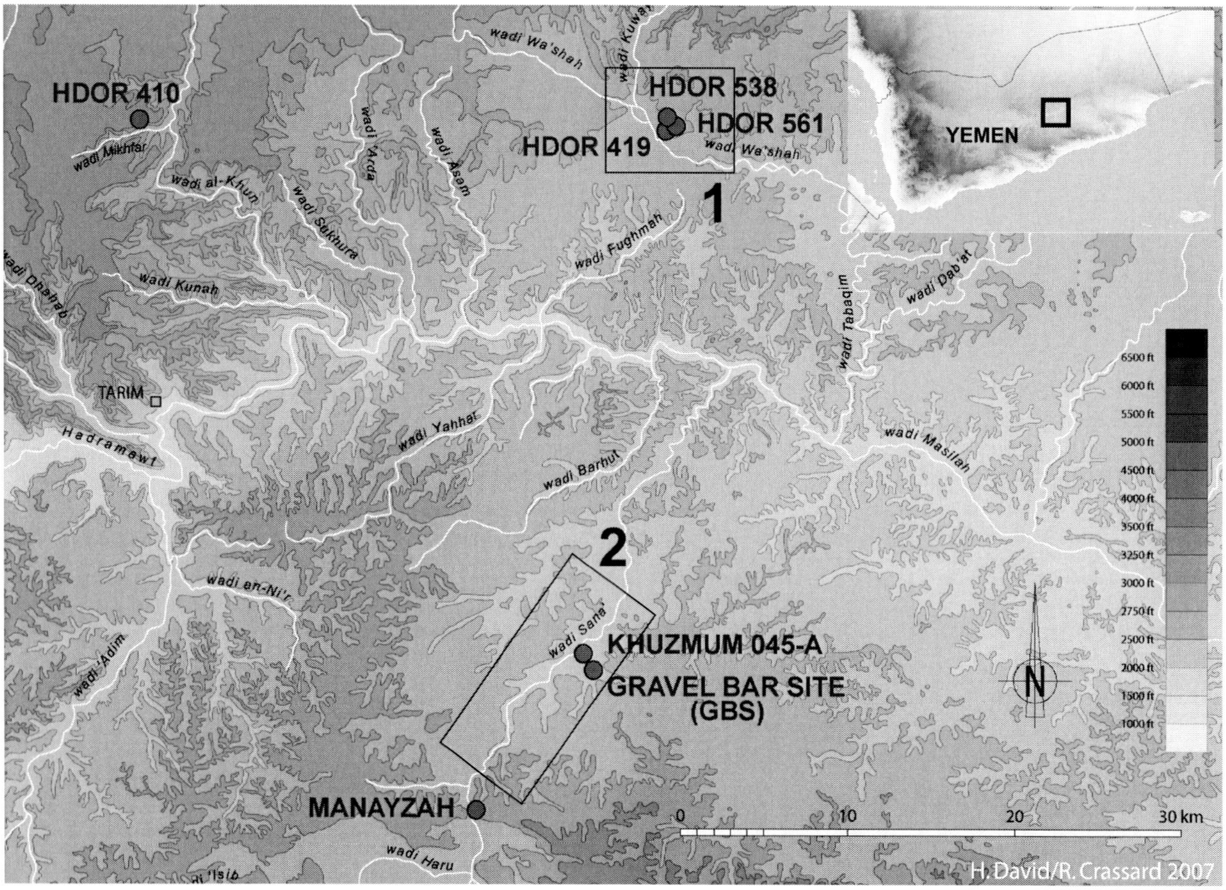

FIGURE 2. *Places of research in Ḥaḍramawt, with the names of major Early/Mid-Holocene sites: 1. Wādī Waᶜshah region (French Archaeological Mission in Jawf-Ḥaḍramawt); 2. Wādī Ṣanā region (RASA Project).*

The Waᶜshah method

We describe here a "typical" technical scheme of Waᶜshah debitage, by describing the various phases and the knapper's behaviour according to what we could observe on the archaeological artefacts. We suppose that this method of debitage has a strong chronological value, even if our understanding is still at a preliminary stage, considering the relatively low number of discovered sites (Figs 3 and 4).

phase 1

The raw material is chosen from strictly local sources, and favours naturally globular flint blocks, but the use of thick tabular flat blocks is attested. From a striking platform on a non-cortical natural surface, or after the creation of a striking platform by a transversal flake removal if a natural surface is not available, a first cortical blade is extracted (Fig. 5/1). The Waᶜshah method is carried out from a single striking platform, minimally prepared by a light abrasion of the impact zone. Blade extraction is thus only done in a unidirectional way, from a semi-turning volumetric exploitation (and not facial) on a narrow side of the core (Fig. 6).

phase 2

A first lateral blade is extracted, often semi-cortical, with a preference for plunging (*outrepassées*) blades. A second lateral blade, at the other side of the central debitage zone is obtained with the same aim of making a plunged removal (Fig. 5/2–5). The creation of guiding arrises is the goal of these preparation blades. Arrises will then be followed by the knapping shock wave. They form a strong dihedral angle on the core's surface. Therefore, the negatives' convergence of the two previous blades makes the third blank pointed.

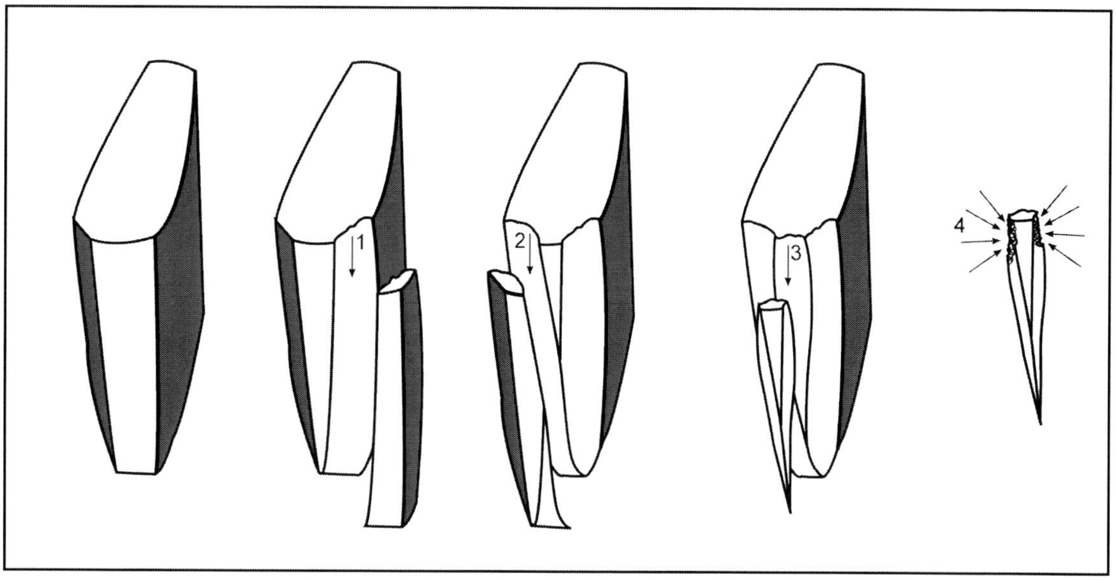

Figure 3. *A unidirectional method of predetermined pointed blades, called the "Waᶜshah method"; a first stage aims to create an acute-angled striking platform, a second one (arrows 1 and 2) prepares the pointed blade extraction (3) which comes during a third stage, before being retouched in its proximal part (4).*

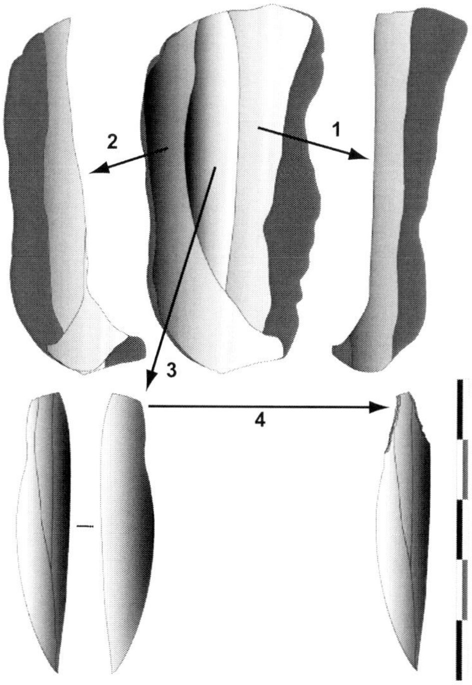

Figure 4. *A unidirectional method of predetermined pointed blades, called the "Waᶜshah method"; a theoretical reconstruction from an archaeological core.*

phase 3

The pointed blade is extracted then retouched in its proximal part on both sides by short, semi-abrupt to abrupt and direct, sometimes bifacial removals. The blade blank thus becomes a tool that we propose to call the "Waᶜshah point" (see Fig. 8; Crassard & Bodu 2004: 77).

Some possible following phases are the repetition of phases 2 and 3, if the knapper needs to do so. In fact, few archaeological cores have been strongly exploited. It reveals production of a standardized blank, but not necessarily expecting mass production of these pointed blades, while cores are not exploited to their maximum resources.

Non-pointed blades, sometimes very well made, are abandoned raw (non-retouched). They are called "second intention" blades (Fig. 7). Many of these blades are present on Waᶜshah debitage sites. A detailed analysis made on characteristic pieces indicates the intended production of pointed blades, which additionally creates a huge amount of laminar waste pieces (debris). The most distinctive are the resharpening (or rejuvenation) removals that are used to restart a debitage sequence. These removals attest to recurrent debitage production. Some of them clearly show the negatives of previous Waᶜshah point blanks (Fig. 5/5). Because the second intention blades are

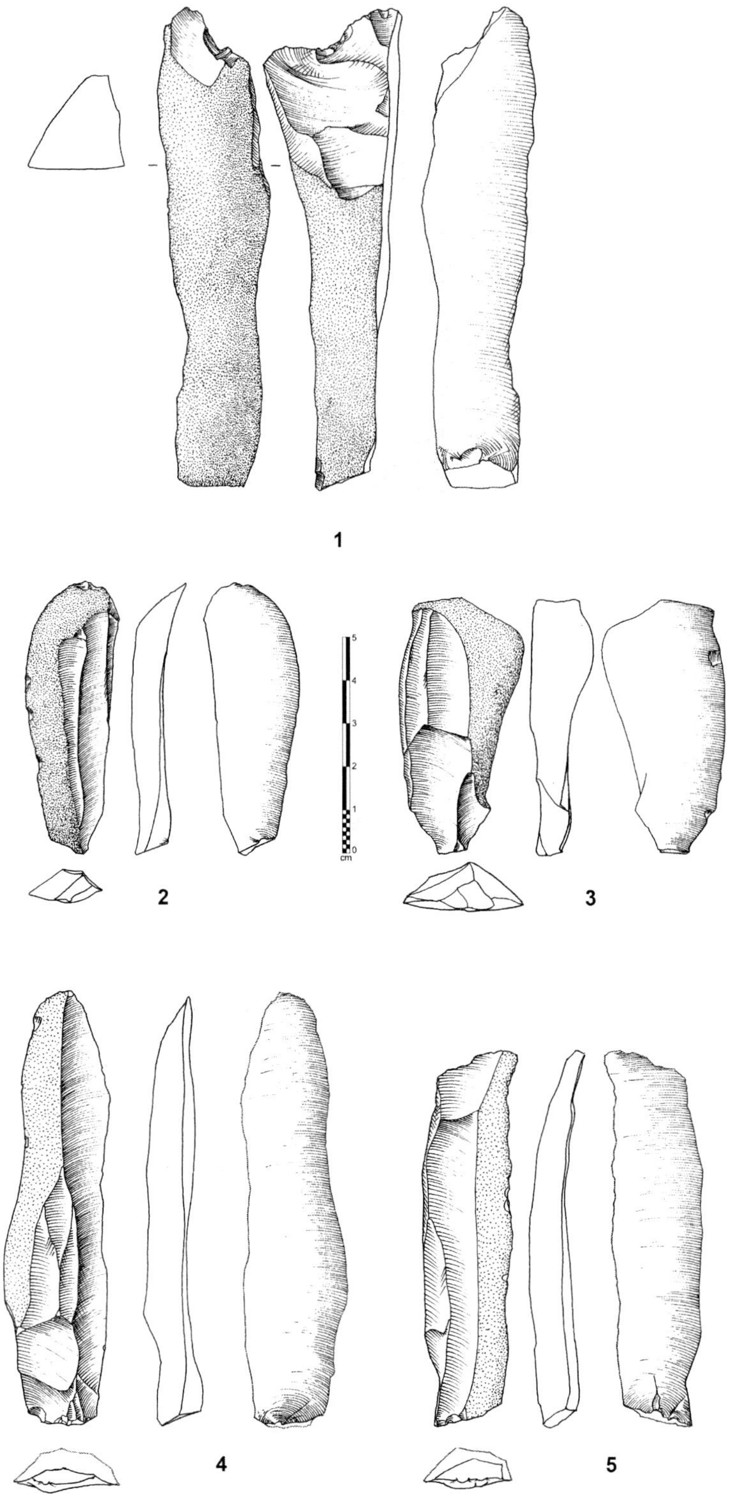

Figure 5. *Waʿshah debitage: 1. cortical blade (HDOR 571 site). 2–5. semi-cortical blades (HDOR 538 site). (Drawings by J. Espagne).*

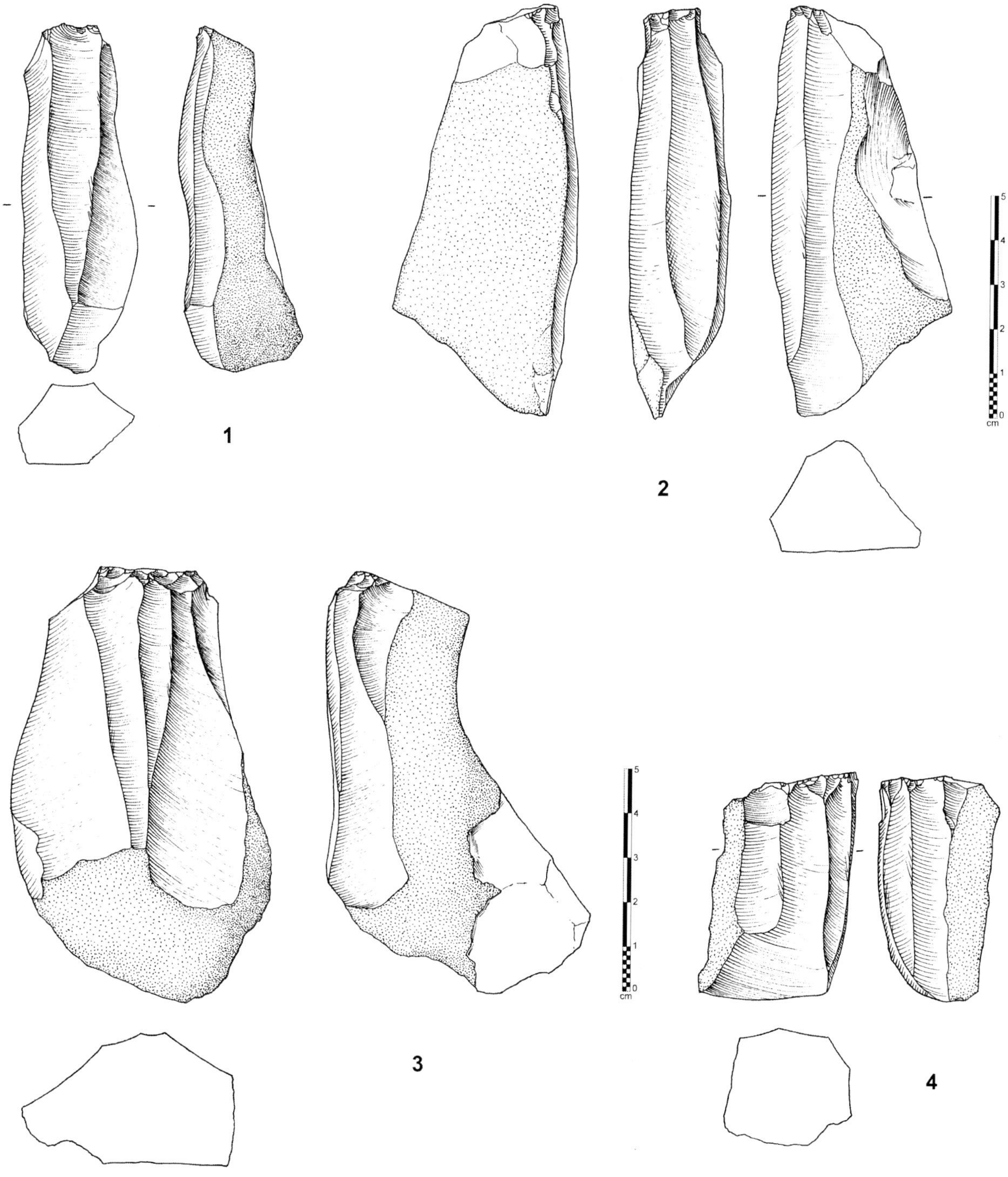

Figure 6. *Waʿshah cores: 1. from HDOR 538. 2. from HDOR 571. 3. from HDOR 567. 4. from HDOR 565. (Drawings by J. Espagne).*

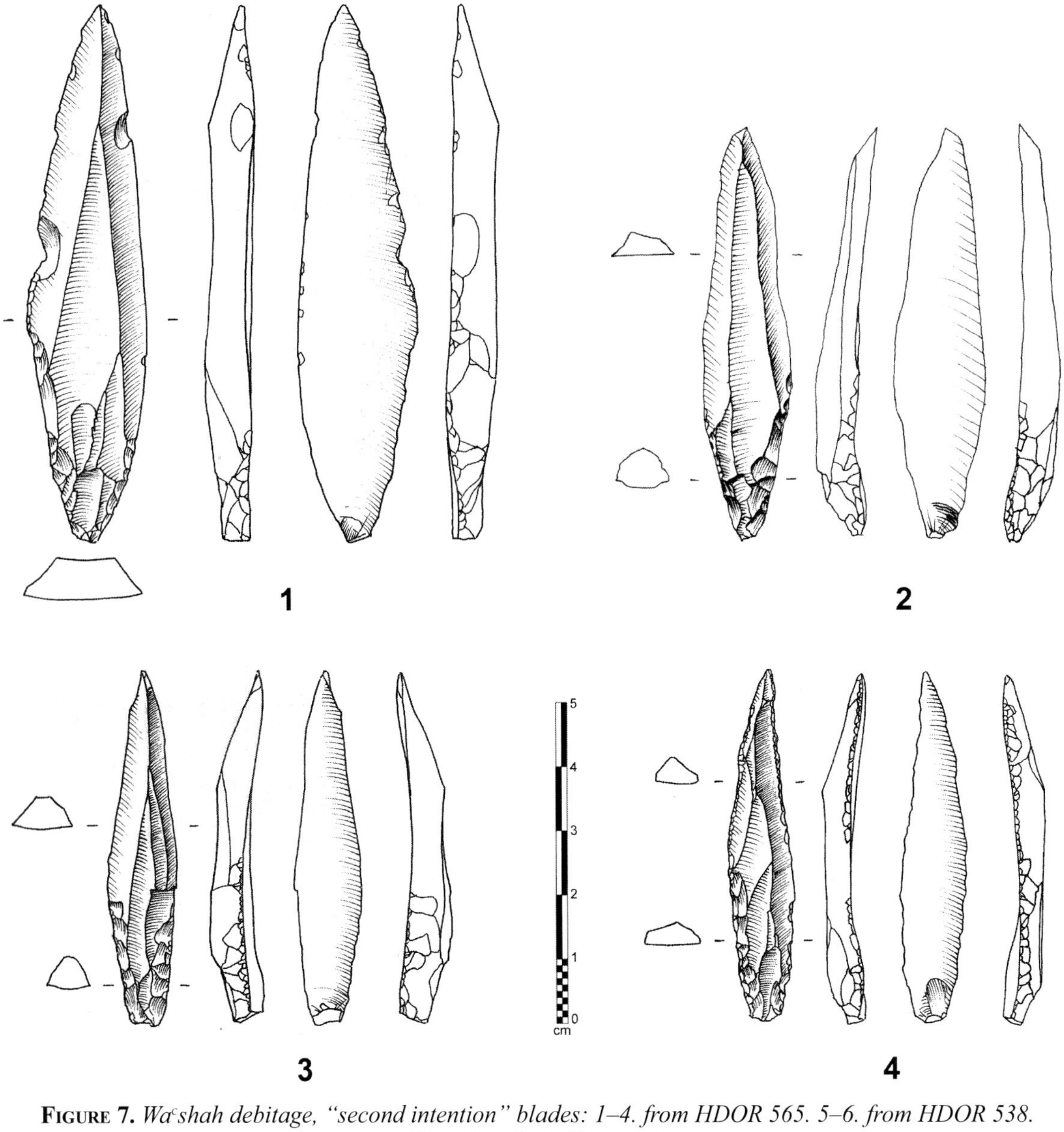

FIGURE 7. *Waᶜshah debitage, "second intention" blades: 1–4. from HDOR 565. 5–6. from HDOR 538. (Drawings by J. Espagne).*

found in large quantities, considering the near-absence of the pointed blades in debitage areas, the production of non-pointed blades does not seem to be deliberate.

The Waᶜshah points

Discoveries

Six Waᶜshah points have been found (Fig. 8), including two in a totally isolated context. Although the discovered points are scarce in number it seems that they were produced in large quantities, judging from the abundance of Waᶜshah cores. In fact, 201 blade cores, essentially resulting from Waᶜshah debitage, were discovered on the HDOR 538 site, where systematic surface collecting was undertaken. The associated products were also collected in their totality: cortical and semi-cortical blades, blades from various stages of debitage etc., with a total of 1128 pieces. Debitage is exclusively unidirectional. Neither crest preparation, nor convexity reinstallation by opposed

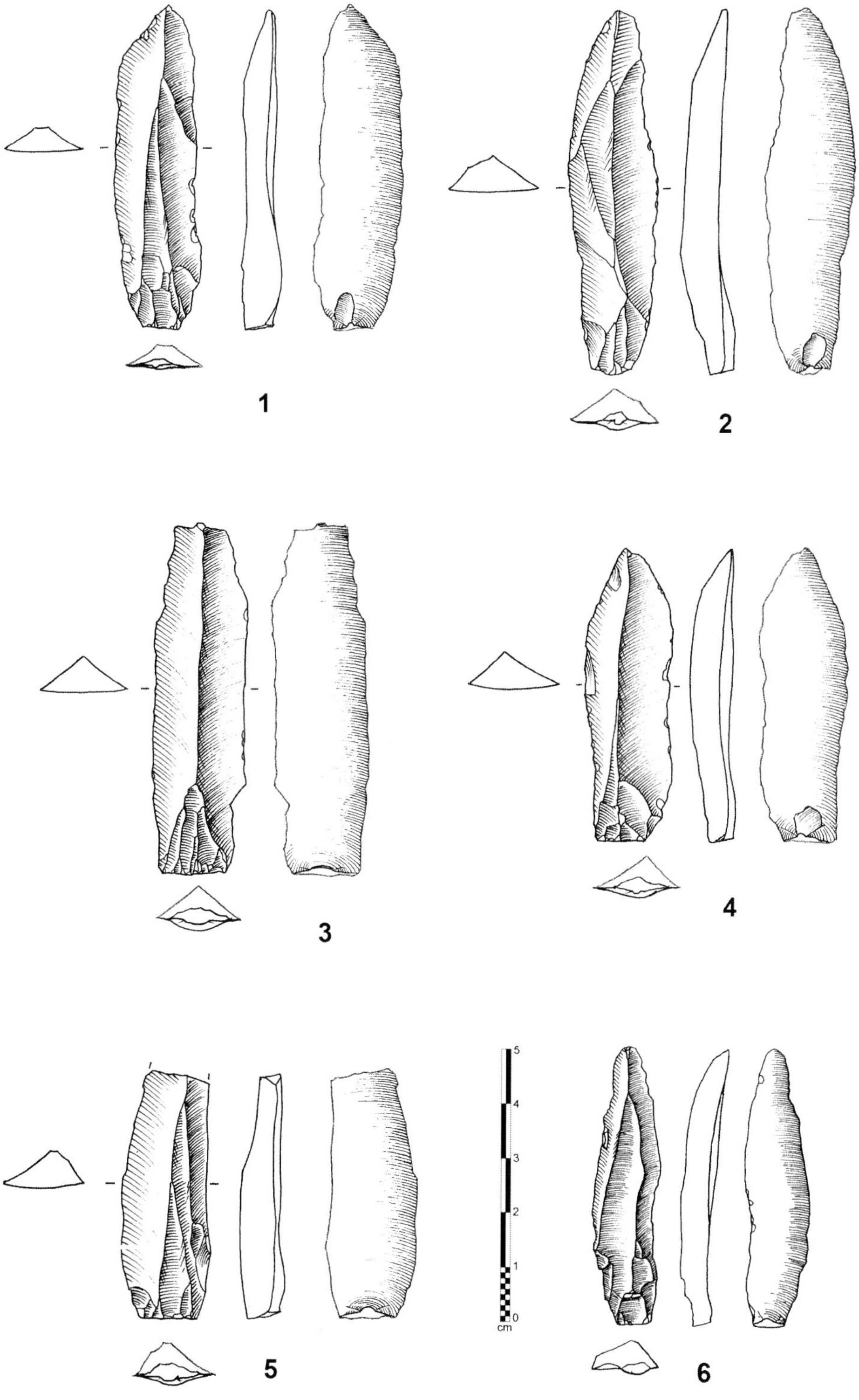

Figure 8. *Waʿshah points from HDOR 538.*
(Drawings by J. Espagne [1, 3 and 4], and R. Crassard [2]).

Point # / Condition	Site	Length	Max. width	Max. thickness
28 / Entire	HDOR 538 (-24)	51	11	7
29 / Entire	HDOR 538 (-24)	84	20	8
30 / Base-medial	Top of hill upon HDOR 566	54	16	7
31 / Entire	HDOR 538 (36B)	55	13	5
42 / Entire	HDOR 538 (2C)	64	14	7
43 / Entire	Hill upon HDOR 538	58	16	7
	Mean	61	15	7

Table 1. *Waᶜshah points dimensions (in millimetres).*

Site	Length	Width
HDOR 538 49D	51	17
HDOR 571	79	12
HDOR 538 43A	49	16
HDOR 538 47D	64	12
HDOR 561 Sd4niv3	44	15
HDOR 571	67	12
HDOR 565	45	7
HDOR 567	50	8
RASA 2004-166-1	63	17
RASA 2004-166-1	38	9
Mean	55	13

Table 2. *Dimensions observed on negatives of final pointed blades on Waᶜshah cores.*

or orthogonal removals has been observed. Pointed blades are only obtained by preparing adequate convexities thanks to *débordant* and plunging blades, during a semi-turning debitage modality centred on the extraction zone of the predefined final blade.

Dimensions

The size of the pointed blades is variable. The dimensions observed on the recovered Waᶜshah points are from 51 to 84 mm long (Table 1). Measures of the final pointed blades' negatives on the laminar cores augment the morpho-metrical corpus (Table 2), at least for the pieces' length and width, even if one cannot confirm that all of the final pointed blades were blanks for Waᶜshah points. According to the observation of eight cores, the final product has a mean length of 56 mm and a mean width of 12 mm. It is then possible to propose a "silhouette-type" (Fig. 9).

Comparisons

Thirteen points on laminar blanks are displayed in the regional museum of Sayʾūn (Crassard 2007, ii: fig. A-275). Their provenance is not known with precision, as it is only known that they come from the northern region of the Ḥaḍramawt plateaus. Two other similar pieces come from the al-ᶜAbr area, west of Ḥaḍramawt.

In addition, H. Amirkhanov has published a drawing of a typical Waᶜshah point (1997: 109–111, fig. 39/5). It comes from Wādī Ḥabak in Mahrah governorate, close to the Ḥabarūt site, on the border with Oman. The author makes only a summary typological description of it. It is 6.1 cm long, 1.1 cm wide, and retouched along 2 cm of the base on both edges. Amirkhanov considers this type of point not very important in the general lithic tools corpus found in the area. He adds that, because of the simplicity with which it was retouched, this point is a unique case in the sets of points on flakes. He finally interprets it as an arrowhead. No mention of a laminar predetermination is proposed, or any particular technical scheme which would allow placing this type of point in a broader technological context. The observation of the lithic drawing leads us to conclude the presence of the Waᶜshah method at least until the eastern limit of the Mahrah region. It is until now the only known example of a typical Waᶜshah point coming from outside the Wādī Waᶜshah area.

Discussion: chronology and perspectives

A Pleistocene date?

The originality of the Waᶜshah method raises the question of its place within the technical traditions of Arabia. It indeed represents an example, unique in the Arabian Peninsula, of a sophisticated and predetermined laminar debitage, except for one imported into Qatar (Inizan 1988). Because of this peculiarity, this debitage type does not find any regional technical pattern of comparison. Moreover, the Waᶜshah method has never been discovered in a context delivering an unquestionable date.

Two factors point to Pleistocene characteristics: (i) this method is very close in its debitage conception to

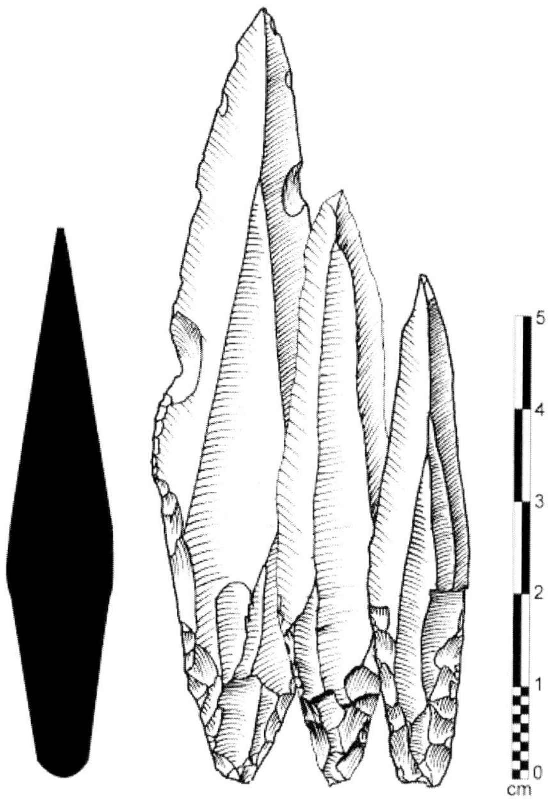

FIGURE 9. *The Waʿshah point; the silhouette-type (shaded) is deduced from the mean dimensions; the technical drawings represent one exceptional example of a long point and two others with more common dimensions.*

the production of so-called "classical" Levallois points, characterized by the preparation of unidirectional lateral convergent removals; and (ii) the use of a laminar volumetric structure refers directly to an Upper Palaeolithic-like conceptualization known in Europe and the Levant. However, no dated Upper Palaeolithic site has been discovered up to now in Yemen, whereas Levallois industries from Ḥaḍramawt are quite clearly associated with the Pleistocene (Crassard, forthcoming).

Seeing in the Waʿshah type of laminar debitage a technical manifestation datable to an Upper Palaeolithic phase (or even simply to the Pleistocene) is, however, premature: it is difficult to give a chronological assignation to this technique alone. Indeed, the laminar concept, and its innumerable variants throughout the world, is neither characteristic of a given period nor of an exclusive geographical area.

A Holocene date?

The greatest number of artefacts with Waʿshah debitage indications was discovered on the surface site HDOR 538. Numerous foliate bifacial pieces and Holocene arrowheads were discovered there, with Waʿshah cores and blades. A detailed study of the site revealed, by a spatial repartition analysis and the observation of the patinas (Crassard 2007: 171–186), that these two types of industries (bifacial and laminar) were certainly not synchronous.

Moreover, the discovery of a Waʿshah core in one of the oldest layers of HDOR 561 (2007: 187–193) would attest contemporaneity or anteriority of the Waʿshah method with some of the products typical of the Early/Mid-Holocene (bifacial shaping and pressure technique). The lack of data on the exact nature of the sedimentary deposition on this site prevents, however, reconstruction of a precise chronological frame. Indeed, HDOR 561's deposits most probably underwent significant erosion because of the flows coming from the plateau and gully erosion resulting from it. A Holocene dating is however very probable, since one date has been obtained on terrestrial shell. This date is 9045 ± 54 BP (8294–8239 cal BC [1] — laboratory ref. AA64371), but calibration is uncertain, due to the sampled material. A preliminary recalibration is nevertheless estimated at around 7300–6800 BC (2007: 191–192).

A Holocene date for the Waʿshah method is partly confirmed by the presence in layer 6 in HDOR 419 of a blade, which could be a laminar waste of a Waʿshah debitage sequence (Crassard & Bodu 2004: fig. 5/10). This layer has not been absolutely dated, but a layer just above, layer 5, gave radiocarbon dates between 7272 ± 120 BP and 6931 ± 48 BP, i.e. between 6242 and 5743 cal BC [1]. (1) A Holocene dating of the Waʿshah method thus seems more probable than a Pleistocene one, but must still be viewed with caution.

The use of indirect percussion? A technical and chronological hypothesis that remains to be tested

The observation of butts and percussion bulbs on certain pointed or not pointed blades evokes a possible use of indirect percussion, i.e. using a punch made of vegetal or animal material between striking platform and hammerstone.

Butts are most of the time plain, canted, and with a light abrasion, and present a rather acute angle, supporting impact with punch. The point of impact is often relatively far away from the core's edge and bulb scar is common, whereas the bulb's negative is well marked. These peculiarities are not exclusive to indirect percussion and can be also associated with hard percussion.

The standardization of known points (and of the supposed points from negatives on cores) however reinforces the assumption of indirect percussion use. Experimental studies to come will be devoted to the observation and comparison of the marks with archaeological pieces. If debitage by indirect percussion is confirmed, then the Wa^cshah debitage can be assigned a Holocene date, use of this technique not being known during the Pleistocene anywhere in the world.

Conclusions

The frequent occurrence of the technical scheme found on many cores throughout the studied micro-region in Wādī Waᶜshah, as well as the standardization of the points, underline the predetermination of the process and comprise a strong technical marker. Still little documented, the Waᶜshah method is only clearly evident in eastern Ḥaḍramawt (Wādī Waᶜshah and Wādī Ṣanā).

Waᶜshah laminar debitage finds its originality in the apparent simplicity of execution and in the very exclusive search for a pointed blank type. The technical scheme, however, suggests an advanced control of flint knapping. It is also remarkable by its presence in Arabia, as Arabian assemblages very seldom reveal laminar industries. Indeed, for a long time it was thought that there were no laminar industries in the Peninsula apart from those of external origin, as found in Qatar. It is significant that we now have knowledge of the Waᶜshah technical scheme, but its precise chronological frame remains unclear. Many questions around the Waᶜshah method thus remain open. At all events, the description of this method allows the application of comparative criteria to future discoveries.

Acknowledgements

Archaeological operations were supported and financed by two projects: the RASA Project and the French Archaeological Mission in Jawf-Ḥaḍramawt. I would like to thank their directors: Joy McCorriston (Ohio State University, USA), Erich Oches (University of South Florida, USA), ᶜAbd al-ᶜAziz bin ᶜAqil (GOAM, Yemen) for RASA; and Michel Mouton (CNRS, Nanterre), Frank Braemer (CNRS, Valbonne), Anne Benoist (CNRS, Lyon) for the French Mission. I also gratefully acknowledge the co-operation of the Republic of Yemen's General Organisation for Antiquities and Museums (GOAM): ᶜAbd-Allah Ba-Wazir (President), ᶜAbd al-Rahman al-Saqaf (Ḥaḍramawt GOAM branch director), and Hussein al-Aydarūs (GOAM, Sayʾūn). This work would not have proceeded without the important implication on the field and constant support of Pierre Bodu (CNRS, Nanterre). I thank Jean-François Saliège (CNRS, Paris) for having prepared samples from HDOR 419 for radiocarbon dating made by the University of Arizona AMS Facility. I also thank Julien Espagne for his drawings and advice and Marie-Louise Inizan (CNRS, Nanterre) for her comments and support. I thank also Michael Haslam (LCHES) for his kind rereading and comments.

This paper was written during a post-doctoral fellowship at the Leverhulme Centre for Human Evolutionary Studies (LCHES) directed by Prof. Robert Foley, on the invitation of Dr Michael Petraglia. I would like to thank them and the rest of the research and administrative staff for their warm welcome. Finally, I thank the Fondation Fyssen for financing my stay in Cambridge.

Notes

1 All dates were obtained by the University of Arizona AMS Facility on samples preliminarily prepared by J-F. Saliège (CNRS, Paris); see Crassard 2007: 194–202. Six dates were obtained from layer 5 and are listed below (Table 3).

Designation	Sample	d13C	Lab. ref.	age 14C BP	Calib. Age 1η BC
HDOR 419 A13 Niv 5	Charcoal	-25,6	AA64360	6931 ± 48	5872- 5743
HDOR 419 A13 Niv 5	Charcoal	-23,4	AA64359	7017 ± 52	5982- 5845
HDOR 419 A13 Niv 5	Charcoal	-25,2	AA64362	7042 ± 53	5990- 5844
HDOR 419 A14 Niv 5	Charcoal	-25,70	AA64364	7086 ± 50	6016- 5910
HDOR 419 A13 Niv 5	Charcoal	-22,12	AA64363	7169 ± 52	6071- 5995
HDOR 419 A13 Niv 5	Charcoal	-25,38	AA64361	7270 ±120	6242- 6014

TABLE 3. *Radiocarbon dates from site HDOR 419.*

References

Amirkhanov H.
1997. *The Neolithic and Postneolithic of the Hadramaut and Mahra.* Moscow: Scientific World. [In Russian].

Crassard R.
2007. *Apport de la technologie lithique à la définition de la préhistoire du Ḥaḍramawt, dans le contexte du Yémen et de l'Arabie du Sud.* (2 volumes). PhD dissertation, Paris 1 Panthéon-Sorbonne. [Unpublished].

(forthcoming). Middle Paleolithic in Arabia: the view from Ḥaḍramawt region, Yemen. In Petraglia M.D. & Rose J. (eds), *Footprints in the Sand: Tracking the Evolution and History of Human Populations in Arabia.* New York: Springer Press.

Crassard R. & Bodu P.
2004. Préhistoire du Ḥaḍramawt (Yémen): nouvelles perspectives. *Proceedings of the Seminar for Arabian Studies* 34: 67–84.

Inizan M-L.
1988. *Préhistoire à Qatar.* ii. Paris: Editions Recherche sur les Civilisations.

Author's address

Dr Rémy Crassard, Leverhulme Centre for Human Evolutionary Studies, University of Cambridge, The Henry Wellcome Building, Fitzwilliam Street, Cambridge, CB2 1QH, UK.

e-mail rc461@cam.ac.uk, rcrassard@prehistoricyemen.com, archeoremy@aol.com

Proceedings of the Seminar for Arabian Studies 38 (2008): 15–24

Into Arabia, perhaps, but if so, from where?

Anthony E. Marks

Summary

The recent discovery of *in situ* Palaeolithic sites in both Sharjah and Oman, as well as the newly postulated movement of early moderns out of Africa and into Arabia, make it important to consider the possible technological and typological relationships between the Palaeolithic in southern Arabia and adjacent areas, particularly East Africa and the Levant. Comparisons of developmental trajectories in East Africa and the Levant show that until the end of the Acheulian it will not be possible to distinguish movements from each area into southern Arabia. Starting at the end of the Acheulian, however, the developmental trajectories of the Levant and East Africa diverge markedly, particularly in their technological patterning. Thus, from about 400,000 years ago to the end of the Pleistocene, it should be possible to recognize East African versus Levantine movements into and/or influences on the southern Arabia Palaeolithic, if such took place. It is also possible, however, that much of the southern Arabian Palaeolithic resulted from local developments and will show only very general similarities to one or the other adjacent area. In addition, movements and/or influences from the east are possible but so little is known of that area that only speculation is now possible.

Keywords: southern Arabia, Palaeolithic, lithic technology, East Africa, Levant

Introduction

It has finally been clearly established that there are significant *in situ* Palaeolithic sites in southern Arabia (Rose 2004; 2006; Uerpmann *et al.* 2007). Why has it taken some seventy years, since Caton-Thompson's pioneering research in Yemen (1939), to fully establish this fact? There are many reasons: among others, there was the difficulty of working in southern Arabia, both politically and logistically (e.g. Phillips 1955); the huge areas of deflation, erosion, and sand dunes that limited the potential for Pleistocene sediment survival and exposure (al-Sayari & Zötl 1984; Jado & Zötl 1984); not to mention the almost ubiquitous spread of Neolithic arrowheads and other bifacial foliates that tended to permit attribution of virtually all post-Acheulian surface concentrations to the Neolithic (Edens 1982; Charpentier 1999). Given these factors, it is remarkable that in the past year or so, a number of *in situ* post-Acheulian Palaeolithic occurrences have been well documented: three in Sharjah (Uerpmann *et al.* 2007) and at least one in Oman (Rose 2006: 273–278). With these finds, it is likely that more and more such *in situ* occurrences will be located in the near future. Expectations have changed and there are now recognizable geomorphic settings where the prospect for *in situ* Palaeolithic occurrences is now producing positive results. Thus, it should be expected that these newly found occurrences are only the tip of the sand dune, and soon there may well be a large number of clearly pure, intact, Palaeolithic sites found in southern Arabia. In addition the presence of such sites will, without doubt, provide both credence and a temporal framework to already known surface concentrations that are typologically and technologically pre-Neolithic, but might have a Neolithic arrowhead or two in their vicinity (Rose 2006: 250–257).

How should this new reality be approached? Surely, we are beyond denial or simple conjecture as to what, at least, some of the southern Arabian post-Acheulian Palaeolithic assemblages are like. Yet our knowledge is still highly fragmentary and the challenge of constructing a coherent prehistoric framework in time and space still lies before us. Newly found assemblages must be described, dated, and placed into palaeo-environmental contexts, while previously known surface assemblages need to be re-evaluated based on these new *in situ* finds. In this manner, the Pleistocene human presence in southern Arabia will be understood both on its own terms and in the broader scope of interregional interaction. It is also very important in the construction of a prehistoric framework for southern Arabia that locally derived data take precedence over already defined and described

Palaeolithic frameworks from adjacent areas. As the new assemblages show, there is much more to the prehistory of southern Arabia than its use by early modern people as a pathway to Australia. What little we know points to a long and complex local prehistory that needs explanation within a local framework. To do so effectively, however, we must confront a number of issues that could well become problems for the development of southern Arabian prehistory and our ability effectively to construct its placement in time and space.

The most general problem we face is that there is no long-term tradition of prehistoric research in southern Arabia. To date everyone who has done any work there has come to Arabia bringing conceptual baggage from some other area. This has affected how each worker has seen the Arabian materials, what they have called it, and what significance has been given to it.

This "importation" of concepts from other areas is reflected clearly in the industry terminology found in the literature. It is all over the place. With few exceptions, workers have expected the prehistory of southern Arabia to reflect an expansion southwards of Levantine occupations. This is clearly seen in the terminology used for local southern Arabian finds (e.g. Middle Acheulian, Upper Acheulian, Mousterian, and more broadly, Middle Palaeolithic and Upper Palaeolithic). Some workers have even imported terms that traditionally are used only in western Europe (Bar-Yosef 2006: 313), such as Mousterian of Acheulian Tradition (Petraglia & Alsharekh 2004). The few exceptions brought an African perspective with them (e.g. McBrearty 1993; 1999) and, not surprisingly, used such African terms as Middle Stone Age. Others (e.g. Caton-Thompson 1954; Van Beek, Cole & Jamme 1963; Gramly 1971) all recognized a possible African connection to the bifacial foliates found in southern Arabia, particularly at Bir Khafsa (Pullar 1974), although none used specific African terminology for southern Arabian materials. Furthermore others, at different times, used both African and Near Eastern terms for their finds, such as Mode 1, Mode 2, Middle Acheulian, and Upper Acheulian (Whalen & Pease 1990; Whalen & Schatte 1997).

Are those with a Levantine bias right, or are those with an African bias more accurate? Aside from the unfortunate usage of Mousterian of Acheulian Tradition and Upper Palaeolithic — which traditionally implies a blade-based technology but, in the southern Arabian context, seems only to mean post-Middle Palaeolithic and pre-Neolithic (Inizan & Ortlieb 1987; Amirkhanov 1994) — every one of these terms might be suitable. The problem is we do not yet know whether or not they are appropriate in the context of southern Arabia. Rather than assume, *a priori*, that southern Arabian prehistory is merely an extension of either the Levant or East Africa, it would be most efficacious to develop a local terminology. Only then should detailed comparisons be made, permitting the attribution, perhaps, of none, some, or all of southern Arabian prehistory to movements into Arabia or influences from adjacent regions.

Given the geographic position of Arabia, bordered to the west by East Africa, to the north by the Levant, and to the east by Iran and the Indian subcontinent, Palaeolithic cultural developments in any or all of these areas may have played a role once, many times, or even throughout the prehistory of southern Arabia. Then again, there may well have been long periods of local development, unrelated to adjoining areas. It may be very complex and the degree of perceived complexity might well depend upon our perceptions of the changing Pleistocene environments of southern Arabia. If there really were hyper-arid periods during which human habitation was impossible, then the prehistory of southern Arabia will consist of unconnected movements into the area from one or more adjacent regions during periods of climatic amelioration, separated from each other by periods of abandonment during the hyper-arid episodes. On the other hand, all arid phases might not have been so extreme as to have precluded continued human occupation in isolated *refugia*, resulting in population continuity and, perhaps, of quite idiosyncratic cultural developments. We simply do not know.

While it would be ideal to construct the prehistory of southern Arabia wholly on its own terms and, only after doing so, look to adjacent regions for comparisons, this will not happen. The recent DNA-based proposed southern coastal route of the "Out of Africa" model (Macaulay *et al.* 2005) makes any new find in southern Arabia, particularly if only preliminarily described and/ or poorly dated, a potential argument for the model (Beyin 2006). Even the absence of data has not deterred speculation of what African industry should be found in southern Arabia (Mellars 2006). Most importantly, however, the geographic position of Arabia itself calls for the recognition of potential connections to the west, north, and east. Thus, as we construct southern Arabian prehistory, it is important that we are aware of the industrial contexts in adjacent areas through time so that reasonable postulates may be advanced as to possible, or even probable, connections.

Adjacent contexts

While it is clear that the Early Pleistocene occupation of southern Arabia, if confirmed, must have derived from Africa where it first evolved, in later periods origins and/or influences might have come from any of the adjacent regions: East Africa, the Levant, and the western edge of Iran and the Indian subcontinent. While others have considered the Cape of South Africa as a possible origin for movements into southern Arabia (Mellars 2006), the truly large distance from the Cape to southern Arabia (*c.* 6400 km), comparable to the distance from northern Germany or southern Siberia to southern Arabia, makes such a direct movement highly doubtful. Rather, East Africa is the most likely source of any population movement into southern Arabia from Africa (Bailey *et al.* 2007). Also, this paper will not consider the western edge of Iran and the Indian subcontinent simply because there have been no detailed studies of the Pleistocene prehistory of that area. On the other hand, a great deal is known of the Pleistocene prehistory of both East Africa and the Levant and this paper can only present a rather simplified view of each area. Still, it will become clear that for much of Pleistocene prehistory, East Africa and the Levant saw quite distinct developmental trajectories.

Pre-Acheulian

Since the earliest lithic industries, the Oldowan and the Developed Oldowan, evolved only in Africa, their claimed presence in southern Arabia, if confirmed, would be a clear indication of an early population movement from East Africa into southern Arabia. The problem, however, lies in the southern Arabian material, both from the surface (Whalen & Schatte 1997) and from *in situ* contexts (Amirkhanov 1994). Pre-Acheulian technology is so simple and its forms are so temporally transgressive and ubiquitous that, in and of itself, it is non-diagnostic. Its presence can only be accepted when coming from clearly datable geological contexts. Unfortunately, none of the reported assemblages, even that from al-Guza Cave comes from such a context.

Lower Palaeolithic/Early Stone Age

The Acheulian in East Africa and the Levant spans about 1 million years, from at least 1.7 million years ago to *c.* 500,000 years ago in Africa and from 1.6 million years ago to somewhat after 500,000 BP in the Levant (Bar-Yosef 1998). As expected for any techno-complex that lasted so long and over such a huge area, it exhibits a large amount of technological and typological variability, although a group of forms — bifaces, cleavers, choppers, spheroids, and polyhedrons — tends to be present at all sites to varying degrees. Most of this variability before the Late Acheulian, however, is most likely to be temporal (Gilead 1970; 1975), perhaps functional (Kleindienst 1961), if not merely stochastic (Isaac 1969), rather than cultural. This is particularly true when eastern Africa and the Levant are compared. While there are some idiosyncratic typological patterns limited to small areas, such as reported from Nubia (Guichard & Guichard 1968) where cleavers are absent, and although regional differences can be seen by the Late Acheulian (Clark 1975), for most of the million years no clear distinctions can be made between African and Levantine Acheulian assemblages. In fact, early to mid-Acheulian sites in the Levant, such as Ubeidiya (Bar-Yosef & Goren-Inbar 1993), Evron Quarry (Ronen 1991), Gesher Benot Ya'aqov (Goren-Inbar *et al.* 2000) have African links, both in their typology and, at times, in their association with some African fauna (Tchernov 1992). Thus, it is unlikely that the origin of any pre-Late Acheulian site found in southern Arabia can be traced to the Levant, or vice versa.

The Late Acheulian is another matter. In the Levant, there are Late Acheulian (Upper Acheulian) sites that exhibit a mixture of symmetric, well-made bifaces associated with well-developed Levallois technology, and at a number of sites cleavers are absent. As usual, however, many of these sites come from the surface and it is not certain that they represent homogeneous assemblages (Bar-Yosef 1998: 259), a problem that also afflicts virtually all southern Arabian "Upper Acheulian" sites (Biagi 1994; Zarins 1998; Rose 2006). Still, if assemblages are systematically collected and are large enough, there may be some potential to link Arabian materials with those in the Levant.

In East Africa, the later Acheulian exhibits a good deal of variability in the proportional occurrences of a few major tool classes but little distinction within tool class morphology (Kleindeinst 1961). Since the tool classes are very general (e.g. heavy duty tools vs light duty tools), the potential for detailed comparisons between East Africa and southern Arabia are poor. In Nubia, the Guichards defined an Upper Acheulian based on the presence of extremely well made Micoquian hand axes (Guichard & Guichard 1968: 175–179) and such an assemblage, if found in southern Arabia, might point to connections to the north-west.

Middle Palaeolithic/Middle Stone Age

About 400,000/300,000 years ago the developmental trajectories of stone tool production in East Africa and the Levant radically diverged. This bifurcation remained profound until almost the end of the Pleistocene. In some parts of East Africa, the Late Acheulian evolved into Sangoan (McBrearty & Tryon 2006), which was essentially a continuation of Late Acheulian technology with the addition of large core-axes, as well as some production of hard hammer blades, while a pattern of flake production was mainly based on discoidal cores. Yet, the Levallois method that was first seen clearly in small amounts in the Late Acheulian (McBreatry & Tryon 2006) gained in importance. In other areas, the Late Acheulian may have evolved directly into a Middle Stone Age characterized by the absence of large tools, such as hand axes, cleavers, and unifacial heavy-duty scrapers and a shift to lighter flake tools and smaller bifacial or partly bifacial tools, such as foliates, ovoids, and points. A whole range of flake tools became common, including many forms of end- and sidescrapers, perforators, burins, denticulates etc. With the shift to flake tools, there was a greater use of the Levallois and discoidal reduction methods but little emphasis was placed on the production of elongated blanks, although blades, Levallois or not, are present in small numbers in most assemblages. The Levallois method was mainly preferential or recurrent and flake shapes are mainly oval or short rectangular. While some blanks were produced by unidirectional convergent reduction or by bi-directional reduction, the vast majority were produced by classic preferential techniques. In addition, discoidal reduction was common and there was little tendency toward elongation. At Mumba Cave, Tanzania, for instance, blade blanks never account for more than *c.* 10 % of all blanks.

It has been noted that, for the first time, regional variability became recognizable during the Middle Stone Age (Clark 1988). Within East Africa, the small number of published sites hinders any attempt to define sub-regional patterns, but it appears that the MSA in the Horn of Africa (i.e. Somalia and Ethiopia) may have had a somewhat more distinct pattern and developmental trajectory (Yellen *et al.* 2005: 57–65), than was the case in Tanzania (Mehlman 1989: 183–367). While this sub-regional variability is certainly present, it is trivial when compared with the profound differences between all published East African MSA assemblages and temporally comparable assemblages from the Levant.

In the Levant, the Upper Acheulian gave way to the Mugharan Tradition (Jelinek 1981) at about 400,000/350,000 BP (Mercier *et al.* 1995; Gopher *et al.* 2005). The tradition was quite complex, having three recognized "facies": the Yabrudian, the Acheulo-Yabrudian, and the Amudian (Bar-Yosef 1998: 265). The Yabrudian and Acheulo-Yabrudian are both characterized by non-Levallois reduction, the presence of many sidescrapers, usually made on thick flakes by stepped retouch (Quina and demi-Quina), and by the presence of some asymmetric hand axes. Neither these thick Quina and demi-Quina retouched sidescrapers nor the asymmetric bifaces have been reported from East Africa. These two facies differ from each other only in the proportional occurrence of the bifaces; they are rare in the Yabrudian and reasonably common in the Acheulo-Yabrudian. Assemblages of either facies are easy to recognize even as surface concentrations but, to date, neither has been found south of Mt Carmel, Israel; therefore it is unlikely that either will be found in any part of Arabia. The associations of the thick Quina and demi-Quina retouched sidescrapers with asymmetric bifaces have never been reported from East Africa and in fact, Quina and demi-Quina retouch have not been described for East Africa.

It is the Amudian "facies", however, that is so radically unexpected in this time context. While initially thought of as a highly specialized activity facies, recent excavations at Qedem Cave, Israel, have exposed a 7.5 m sequence of Amudian assemblages dating from 380,000 to 200,000 BP (Gopher *et al.* 2005: 86), which suggests that its interpretation as a specialized activity facies needs to be rethought. Amudian technology is mainly blade production based on hard hammer, often volumetric, cores. With the exception of very rare Quina sidescrapers and even rarer asymmetric bifaces, the tools are typically Upper Palaeolithic — endscrapers, burins, backed knives, and marginally retouched blades (Gopher *et al.* 2005: 79–82). Small assemblages of the Amudian are not likely to include the rare, characteristic Yabrudian elements and differentiating such assemblages from a general Eurasian Upper Palaeolithic would not be easy. Without the asymmetric bifaces and the Quina scrapers, only the blade technology would differentiate it from the true Levantine Upper Palaeolithic in that the Amudian blades are struck with a hard hammer and the blades and blade cores exhibit no core edge preparation (Monigal 2002: 246–247).

Around 250,000 BP the Mugharan Tradition evolves into the Levantine Mousterian, which lasts in various forms until about 50,000/48,000 BP (Bar-Yosef

2007). Unlike the Mugharan Tradition, the Levantine Mousterian lacks bifacial reduction of any kind, has a strong Levallois component, and like the Amudian, has a marked tendency toward the production of elongated blanks, both Levallois and non-Levallois (Monigal 2002: 416–417, 455–460). The Levallois method in the Levant is manifest in a number of different operational chains, from classic, preferential, centripetal reduction, through recurrent centripetal, to elongate unidirectional converging. At almost any time and at any site, all of these and other specific chains can be found. Yet, the overall pattern of Levallois production from the beginning of the Levantine Mousterian to its end, with a brief exception around 150,000 BP, is the tendency toward the production of triangular blanks, most often Levallois points from unidirectional converging reduction (Meignen 1995), and then mainly elongated ones (Monigal 2002; Meignen & Bar-Yosef 2005). Associated with this tendency are large percentages of true hard hammer blades during the earliest phase, but by the end of the Levantine Mousterian virtually all elongated blanks were produced by the Levallois method. During the early part of this sequence, retouched tools included many Upper Palaeolithic forms (burins, endscrapers, backed knives), but by the end, most tools were typically Middle Palaeolithic (sidescrapers, denticulates, retouched Levallois points).

Upper Palaeolithic/Middle Stone Age

While major differences occurred in developmental trajectories of lithic industries in East Africa and the Levant during the previous period, the differences are even greater after *c.* 50,000 BP. In East Africa, essentially nothing changes. The technological and typological patterns that were well developed by 150,000 BP simply continue. There is a slight tendency for artefacts to become, on average, smaller but the main reduction strategies — Levallois, discoidal, blade and bifacial on flake blanks — continue unabated until at least 30,000 BP and, in some places, much later (Mehlman 1989: 272–367). There is a shift in that an additional reduction strategy, bipolar reduction, slowly increases in popularity but it is merely added to the repertoire of strategies, rather than replacing any. Retouched tool assemblages continue to be dominated by unifacially and bifacially retouched points and various scraper forms, denticulates, and rather informal retouched pieces. Perhaps by 50,000 BP small numbers of backed tools occur in Tanzania but their proportional occurrences are very low.

In the Levant, the Middle Palaeolithic pattern of elongate pointed blank production continues after 50,000 BP into the Initial Upper Palaeolithic. There is a change in the reduction method, so that the blades and points are no longer Levallois, although they are still struck by hard hammer and the points have the typical Levallois point arête pattern. Thus, by somewhat after 50,000 BP the Levallois method of blank production disappears from the Levant. In the Early Ahmarian (Marks 1983: 37), around 38,000 BP, there is a shift to soft hammer removals and the pointed blades and bladelets become thinner, smaller, and more standardized. In fact, virtually all blanks are now produced from a single operational chain, although there are two core sizes, one for blades and one for bladelets (Monigal 2003). The tool assemblages are dominated by semi-steeply retouched pointed blades/bladelets (El Wad points), burins, endscrapers, simple retouched blades, and an occasional backed blade. By 30,000 BP, backed tools are more common and the reduction strategies have shifted to the use of large flakes as blanks for bladelet cores (Ferring 1988). However, Ahmarian assemblages of this time are still highly laminar and semi-steep retouch on blades and bladelets dominates its assemblages until it passes into the Epipalaeolithic at about 20,000 BP (for a detailed discussion of Ahmarian development, see Coinman 2003).

At about 34,000 BP (Marks 2003: 256) there is evidence that at least one Aurignacian group moved south into the Levant, although true Aurignacian never extends south of Mt Carmel and it is highly unlikely it will be found in Arabia. To the south of Mt Carmel, however, a number of flake-based assemblages, quite distinct from the Ahmarian have been found. They are best characterized as utilizing a secondary reduction method that produces carinated cores/tools and, as a by-product, small twisted bladelets. Only one of the sites, Ein Aqev, is dated and it falls at the end of the Levantine Upper Palaeolithic, at *c.* 17,500 BP (Marks 1976: 230). Since these assemblages are not clearly and directly related to either the Ahmarian or the "classic" Levantine Aurignacian from further north, it is possible they are linked to industries outside the Levant. If so, the carinated method will be a clear diagnostic sign although, to date, no pre-Neolithic carinated method has been reported from southern Arabia.

Discussion

Although the descriptions presented above are all too brief, they do provide an introduction into the general Palaeolithic developmental patterns in the Levant and in East Africa that must form the context for any attempt to recognize either East African or Levantine incursions of people and/or the diffusion of their technological or typological elements into southern Arabia. As should be clear, the earlier the period, the less likely it is that southern Arabian materials can be differentiated from those in adjoining areas. In fact, until the very end of the Acheulian, all materials were closely linked to Africa. Whether this means a movement directly eastwards into southern Arabia from East Africa or a movement southwards from the Levant is probably unknowable.

The first realistic opportunity to distinguish East African from Levantine presence or influences in southern Arabia begins with the development of the MSA/Middle Palaeolithic about 400,000 years ago. The most obvious difference between regions is that in the Levant bifacial reduction becomes very rare, and by 200,000 BP it disappears entirely and does not appear again until the Neolithic. In East Africa, on the other hand, while hand axes disappear with the end of the Acheulian, other bifacial tools, such as core axes in the Sangoan and bifacial foliates and MSA points continue to be characteristic elements throughout the entire span of the East African Stone Age.

While in both regions the Levallois method becomes an important, almost defining characteristic, the variety of specific reduction strategies within the method (e.g. Tryon, McBrearty & Texier 2005) makes it possible to differentiate easily between the Levallois patterns of the two regions, if not by specific strategies used, then by the dominance of different strategies. The greatest difference between the regions is that in East Africa most Levallois is preferential, centripetally prepared, and results in ovoid Levallois flakes. Bidirectional, unidirectional, unidirectional converging, and recurrent types all do occur in East Africa but only as a small proportion of the Levallois production. In the Levant, on the other hand, unidirectional and unidirectional convergent strategies dominate Levallois production for virtually 150,000 years, resulting in elongated and/or triangular shaped flakes or blades (mainly Levallois points), although all other forms occur as well, in proportionately smaller numbers.

On a general technological level, there are also major differences between the East African MSA and Levantine Middle Palaeolithic. The contrast between the consistent hard hammer blade technology of the Amudian, as opposed to the mainly Levallois and discoidal reduction methods of the Early Middle Stone Age of East Africa could not be more stark. While after 200,000 BP the Levallois method dominates both regions, other reduction methods are quite distinct. In the East African MSA, there are a number of different reduction methods used in almost every assemblage: bifacial, Levallois, discoidal, volumetric blade, and bipolar. In the Levant, however, reduction strategies are almost exclusively limited to the Levallois method and to blade production from volumetric cores. While an occasional discoidal core occurs, there is no evidence for bipolar or bifacial reduction at all.

Typologically, each region exhibits comparable differences, if not so extreme. In the early to mid-MSA of East Africa, tools include bifacially retouched tools, initially core axes, but soon including bifacially and invasive, unifacially retouched points, which are unknown in the Levant. For other unifacial tools, however, both regions share a range of scraper types, denticulates, and retouched pieces. On the other hand, in East Africa there is a tendency toward points, perforators, and endscrapers, types that tend to appear much later in the Levant. Still the overlap of unifacial tool types suggests that, with the exception of bifacial tools, technology may well be a better basis for interregional comparisons than typology.

By the late MSA, beginning about 50,000 BP, there is some tendency for tools to get smaller. Yet, except for the appearance of a few backed tools (large crescents, trapezes etc.), and an increase in scaled pieces (as bipolar reduction gains in popularity), nothing much changes. Levallois and discoidal reduction still dominate; there is little increase in elongated blanks. At least at Mumba Cave the points get marginally smaller through time (Bretzke, Marks & Conard 2006: 73–80) but if anything characterizes the East African MSA it is continuity. This pattern stands in marked contrast to what was going on in the Levant with its development of fine blade/bladelet technology and the dominance of blade/bladelet tools. The difference could not be greater and it would be impossible to confuse the two.

Thus, at least from the end of the Acheulian at *c.* 400,000 BP, there should be little difficulty in distinguishing between East African and Levantine technological and even typological patterns. Yet, while helpful, it is unlikely that southern Arabian assemblages will technologically and typologically mimic any specific pattern from these adjacent areas. To do so would imply the discovery of the site left by actual initial immigrants, newly arrived in southern Arabia. It might happen, but it is more likely that southern Arabian assemblages will reflect only generally the technological and typological history of the original groups who entered southern Arabia. Most likely, southern Arabian assemblages will reflect technological and typological adjustments to local raw material distributions and quality, changes in mobility patterns reflective of local conditions, and, of course, the general drift in technological and typological proclivities that takes place over time when separated from the original immigrants' neighbours. In addition, as noted at the beginning of the paper, possible connections and influences from the north-east should not be forgotten. Until *c.* 10,000 BP there was no Persian Gulf (Lambeck 1996) and so there was a large area bordering eastern Arabia that might well have had a Palaeolithic as rich as those in the Levant or East Africa. If so, the recently discovered *in situ* Palaeolithic sites in Sharjah (Uerpmann *et al.* 2007), just on the southern rim of the Arabo-Persian Gulf Basin, might not relate directly to either the Levant or East Africa but, rather, be part of long-term local developments. Clearly, while Palaeolithic cultural characteristics in East Africa and the Levant may be found in southern Arabia as the result of diffusion or actual migration, they are not the only possible sources for southern Arabian lithic industries and care must be taken before such attributions are made. The very complexity of possible influences and local developments makes constructing the prehistory of southern Arabia a truly fascinating challenge.

References

Amirkhanov H.

1994. Research on the Palaeolithic and Neolithic of Hadramaut and Mahra. *Arabian Archaeology and Epigraphy* 5: 217–228.

Bailey G., AlSharekh A., Flemming N., Lambeck K., Momber G., Sinclair A. & Vita-Finzi C.

2007. Coastal prehistory in the southern Red Sea Basin, underwater archaeology, and the Farasan Islands. *Proceedings of the Seminar for Arabian Studies* 37: 1–16.

Bar-Yosef O.

1998. Early colonizations and cultural continuities in the Lower Palaeolithic of Western Asia. Pages 221–279 in M. Petraglia & R. Korisettar (eds), *Early Human Behaviour in Global Context*. London: Routledge.

2006. Between Observations and models: An Eclectic View of Middle Paleolithic Archaeology. Pages 305–326 in E. Hovers & S.L. Kuhn (eds), *Transitions Before the Transition*. New York: Springer.

2007. The game of dates: another look at the Levantine Middle Paleolithic Chronology. Pages 83–100 in N. Bicho & P. Thacker (eds), *From the Mediterranean Basin to the Portuguese Atlantic Shore: Papers in Honor of Anthony Marks*. Acts of the 4th Congress of Peninsular Archaeology. Faro: University of Algarve.

Bar-Yosef O. & Goren-Inbar N.

1993. *The Lithic Assemblages of Ubeidiya: A Lower Palaeolithic site in the Jordan Valley.* (Qedem, 34). Jerusalem: Hebrew University.

Beyin A.

2006. The Bab al Mandab vs the Nile-Levant: An Appraisal of the Two Dispersal Routes for Early Modern Humans Out of Africa. *African Archaeological Review* 23: 5–30.

Biagi P.

1994. An Early Palaeolithic site near Saiwan (Sultanate of Oman). *Arabian Archaeology and Epigraphy* 5: 81–88.

Bretzke K., Marks A. & Conard N.

2006. Projektiltechnologie und kulturelle Evolution in Ostafrica. *Mitteilungen der Gesellschaft für Urgeschichte* 15: 63–81.

Caton-Thompson G.

1939. Climate, irrigation, and early man in the Hadhramaut. *Geographical Journal* 93/1: 18–35.

1954. Some Palaeoliths from Arabia. *Proceedings of the Prehistoric Society* 29: 189–218.

Charpentier V.

1999. Industries bifaciales holocènes d'Arabie orientale, un exemple: Ra's al-Jinz. *Proceedings of the Seminar for Arabian Studies* 29: 29–44.

Clark D.J.G.
1975. A Comparison of the Late Acheulian industries of Africa and the Middle East. Pages 605–659 in K. Butzer & G. Isaac (eds), *After the Australopithecines*. The Hague: Mouton Publishers.
1988. The Middle Stone Age of East Africa and the beginnings of regional identity. *Journal of World Prehistory* 2: 235–305.

Coinman N.
2003. The Upper Paleolithic of Jordan: New Data from the Wadi al-Hasa. Pages 151–170 in Goring-Morris & Belfer-Cohen (eds), *More Than Meets the Eye*. Oxford: Oxbow Press.

Edens C.
1982. Towards a definition of the Rub al Khali "Neolithic". *Atlal* 6: 109–124.

Ferring R.
1988. Technological change in the Upper Paleolithic of the Negev. Pages 333–348 in H. Dibble & A. Montet-White (eds), *Upper Pleistocene Prehistory of Western Asia*. Philadelphia, PA: The University Museum.

Gilead D.
1970. Handaxe Industries in Israel and the Near East. *World Archaeology* 2: 1–11.
1975. Lower and Middle settlement patterns in the Levant. Pages 273–284 in F. Wendorf & A. Marks (eds), *Problems in Prehistory: North Africa and the Levant*. Dallas, TX: Southern Methodist University Press.

Gopher A., Barkai R., Shimelmitz R., Khalily M., Lemorini C., Heshkovitz I. & Stiner M.
2005. Qesem Cave: An Amudian Site in Central Israel. *Journal of the Israel Prehistoric Society* 35: 69–92.

Goren-Inbar N., Feibel C., Verosub K., Melamed Y., Koslev M., Tchernov E. & Saragusti I.
2000. Pleistocene Milestones on the Out-of-Africa Corridor at Gesher Benot Ya'aqov, Israel. *Science* 289: 944–947.

Goring-Morris A.N. & Belfer-Cohen A. (eds)
2003. *More Than Meets the Eye*. Oxford: Oxbow Press.

Gramly R.
1971. Neolithic flint implements assemblages from Saudi Arabia. *Journal of Near Eastern Studies* 30/3: 177–185.

Guichard J. & Guichard G.
1968. Contributions to the Study of the Early and the Middle Paleolithic of Nubia. Pages 148–193 in W. Wendorf (ed.), *Prehistory of Nubia*. i. Dallas, TX: Southern Methodist University Press.

Inizan M. & Ortlieb L.
1987. Préhistoire dans la région de Shabwa au Yemen du sud. *Paléorient* 13: 5–22.

Isaac G.
1969. Studies of early culture in East Africa. *World Archaeology* 1: 1–28.

Jado A.R. & Zötl J.G. (eds)
1984. *Quaternary Period in Saudi Arabia*. ii. Vienna: Springer-Verlag.

Jelinek A.
1981. The Middle Paleolithic in the southern Levant from the perspective of the Tabun Cave. Pages 265–280 in J. Cauvin & P. Sanlaville (eds), *Préhistoire du Levant*. Paris: CNRS.

Kleindienst M.
1961. Variability within the Late Acheulian Assemblages in eastern Africa. *South African Archaeological Bulletin* 16/62: 35–52.

Lambeck K.
1996. Shoreline reconstructions for the Persian Gulf since the last glacial maximum. *Earth and Planetary Science Letters* 142: 43–57.

Macaulay V., Hill C., Achilli A., Rengo C., Clarke D., Meehan W., Blackburn J., Semino O., Scozzari R., Cruciani F., Taha A., Shaari N., Raja J., Ismail P., Zainuddin Z., Goodwin W., Bulbeck D., Bandelt H-P., Oppenheimer S., Torroni A. & Richards M.
2005. Single, rapid coastal settlement of Asia revealed by analysis of complete mitochondrial genomes. *Science* 308: 1034–1036.

McBrearty S.
1993. Lithic Artifacts from Abu Dhabi's western region. *Tribulus: Bulletin of the Emirates Natural History Group* 3: 13–14.
1999. Earliest stone tools from the Emirate of Abu Dhabi, United Arab Emirates. Pages 373–388 in P. Whybrow & A. Hill (eds), *Fossil Vertebrates of Arabia*. New Haven, CT: Yale University Press.

McBrearty S. & Tryon C.
2006. From Acheulian to Middle Stone Age in the Kapthurin Formation, Kenya. Pages 257–278 in E. Hovers & S. Kuhn (eds), *Transitions Before the Transition*. New York: Springer.

Marks A.
1976. Ein Aqev: A Late Levantine Aurignacian Site in the Nahal Aqev. Pages 227–291 in A. Marks (ed.), *Prehistory and Paleoenvironments in the Central Negev, Israel*. i. Dallas, TX: Department of Anthropology, Southern Methodist University.
1983. The Sites of Boker Tachtit and Boker: A brief introduction. Pages 15–38 in A. Marks (ed.), *Prehistory and Paleoenvironments in the Central Negev, Israel*. iii. Dallas, TX: Department of Anthropology, Southern Methodist University.
2003. Reflections on Levantine Upper Palaeolithic Studies: Past and Present. Pages 249–264 in A.N. Goring-Morris & A. Belfer-Cohen (eds), *More Than Meets the Eye*. Oxford: Oxbow Press.

Mehlman M.
1989. *Later Quaternary archaeological sequences in northern Tanzania*. PhD thesis, University of Illinois at Urbana-Champaign. [Unpublished].

Meignen L.
1995. Levallois production systems in the Middle Paleolithic of the Near East: the case of the unidirectional method. Pages 361–380 in H. Dibble & O. Bar-Yosef (eds), *The Definition and Interpretation of Levallois Technology*. Madison, WI: Prehistory Press.

Meignen L. & Bar-Yosef O.
2005. The Lithic Industries of the Middle and Upper Paleolithic of the Levant: Continuity or Break? Pages 166–175 in A. Derevianko (ed.), *The Middle to Upper Paleolithic Transition in Eurasia: Hypotheses and Facts. Archaeology, Ethnology and Anthropology of Eurasia*. Novosibirsk: Institute of Archaeology and Ethnology Press.

Mellars P.
2006. Going East: New Genetic and Archaeological Perspectives on the Modern Human colonization of Eurasia. *Science* 313: 796–800.

Mercier N., Valladas H., Valladas G., Reyss J-L., Jelinek A., Meignen L. & Joron J.
1995. TL dates of burned flints from Jelinek's excavations at Tabun and their implications. *Journal of Archaeological Science* 22: 495–509.

Monigal K.
2002. *The Levantine Leptolithic: Blade Production from the Lower Paleolithic to the Dawn of the Upper Paleolithic*. PhD thesis, Southern Methodist University, Dallas, TX. [Unpublished].
2003. Technology, Economy, and Mobility at the Beginning of the Levantine Upper Paleolithic. Pages 118–133 in A.N. Goring-Morris & A. Belfer-Cohen (eds), *More Than Meets the Eye*. Oxford: Oxbow Press.

Petraglia M. & Alsharekh A.
2004. The Middle Palaeolithic of Arabia: implications for modern human origins, behaviour and dispersals. *Antiquity* 77/298: 671–684.

Phillips W.
1955. *Qataban and Sheba: exploring the ancient kingdom on the biblical spice routes of Arabia.* New York: Harcourt, Brace & Co.

Pullar J.
1974. Harvard Archaeological survey in Oman, 1973: flint sites in Oman. *Proceedings of the Seminar for Arabian Studies* 4: 33–48.

Ronen A.
1991. The Lower Paleolithic site Evron-Quarry in western Galilee, Israel. *Sonderveroffenlichungen, geologisches Institut der Universität zu Köln* 82: 187–212.

Rose J.
2004. The Question of Upper Pleistocene connections between East Africa and South Arabia. *Current Anthropology* 45/4: 551–555.
2006. *Among Arabian Sands: defining the Palaeolithic of southern Arabia.* PhD thesis, Southern Methodist University, Dallas, TX. [Unpublished].

al-Sayari S. & Zötl J. (eds)
1984. *Quaternary Period in Saudi Arabia.* i. Vienna: Springer-Verlag.

Tchernov A.
1992. Eurasian-African biotic exchanges through the Levantine corridor during the Neogene and Quaternary. *Courier Forschungsinstitut Senckenberg* 153: 103–123.

Tryon C., McBrearty S. & Texier P-J.
2005. Levallois Lithic Technology from the Kapthurin Formation, Kenya: Acheulian Origin and Middle Stone Age diversity. *African Archaeological Review* 22/4: 199–229.

Uerpmann H-P., Uerpmann M., Kutterer J., Händel M., Jasim S.A. & Marks A.
2007. The Stone Age Sequence of Jebel Faya in the Emirate of Sharjah (UAE). Paper presented at the Seminar for Arabian Studies 2007. [Unpublished].

Van Beek G., Cole G. & Jamme A.
1963. An archaeological reconnaissance in Hadramaut, South Arabia: a preliminary report. *Annual Report of the Smithsonian Institution* 1963: 521–545.

Whalen N. & Pease D.
1990. Variability in developed Oldowan and Acheulian bifaces of Saudi Arabia. *Atlal* 13: 43–48.

Whalen N. & Schatte K.
1997. Pleistocene sites in southern Yemen. *Arabian Archaeology and Epigraphy* 8: 1–10.

Yellen J., Brooks A., Helgren D., Tappen M., Ambrose S., Bonnefille R., Feathers J., Goodfiend G., Ludwig K., Renne P. & Stewart K.
2005. Archaeology of Aduma Middle Stone Age Sites in the Awash Valley, Ethiopia. *Paleoanthropology* 10: 25–100.

Zarins J.
1998. View from the South: the greater Arabian Peninsula. Pages 179–194 in D. Henry (ed.), *Prehistoric Archaeology of Jordan*. Oxford: BAR, International Series 705.

Author's address
Anthony E. Marks, Professor Emeritus of Anthropology, P.O. Box 5682, Santa Fe, NM, 87502-5682, USA.
e-mail amarks@mail.smu.edu

Proceedings of the Seminar for Arabian Studies 38 (2008): 25–42

Climate change and human origins in southern Arabia

A.G. Parker &. J.I. Rose

Summary

Over the past few years, prehistorians have begun to consider South Arabia with increasingly greater interest. As the corpus of genetic data grows, scholars now realize the prominent role the "Arabian Corridor" must have played in modern human origins. Unfortunately, Palaeolithic investigations throughout the peninsula have lagged sadly behind; at the time of writing there are only three dated, stratified Palaeolithic sites that fall within the Upper Pleistocene time period (Shi'bat Dihya, al-Hatab, and Jebel Faya 1). While there are meagre data to discuss the human footprint upon the landscape, we possess abundant information to describe the land itself.

This paper is intended to synthesize and present the palaeoenvironmental record throughout the late Quaternary in South Arabia, thereby presenting the landscape across which the earliest humans traversed during the initial expansion from their ancestral homeland. We present the HOPE ENV database, which is a composite sum probability curve that incorporates several hundred proxy signals used to discern ancient climatic conditions. This paper considers shifts in the terrestrial landscape morphology, as well as reconfiguration of the shorelines due to eustatic and isostatic sea levels change. We discuss how this record of environmental change might have affected human emergence, from the first appearance of anatomically modern *Homo sapiens* to the development of complex civilization in the middle Holocene.

Keywords: human origins, climate change, Arabian Peninsula, palaeoenvironment, prehistoric archaeology

Introduction

The pendulum of environmental change in Arabia has oscillated between climatic extremes throughout the Quaternary period. The landscape is riddled with evidence for ancient pluvials, apparent in the lacustrine sediments, alluvial fans and gravels, palaeosols, and speleothems (e.g. McClure 1976; Schultz & Whitney 1986; Parker *et al.* 2006; Lézine *et al.* 2007; Fleitmann *et al.* 2007). Conversely, there are numerous signals that Arabia was subjected to extremes in aridity, most obviously manifested in the expansive sand seas comprising the Nafud, Rub' al-Khali, and Wahiba deserts, as well as hyperalkaline springs (Clark & Fontes 1990) and petrogypsic soil horizons (Rose 2006).

The earliest western explorers to penetrate the Rub' al-Khali often described a series of small buttes standing out in stark white or grey against the seemingly endless wasteland of monotonous rust-coloured sand. During his pioneering journey across the desert in 1932, St John Philby recognized these features as small eroded lake basins comprised of marl terraces and hardened evaporitic crusts, noting associated freshwater shells and lithic implements scattered around the edges (Philby 1933). The occurrence of ancient stone tools near relict lake beds is ubiquitous throughout South Arabia and hints at a rich prehistoric past, one of which archaeologists have only yet encountered the tip of the iceberg.

The aim of this paper is to present the backdrop of South Arabian prehistory by providing an overview of the mosaic of shifting landscapes during the Quaternary. These data provide a useful framework for understanding the role of the climate in patterning the ebb and flow of hominin occupation across the Arabian corridor — a critical geographic zone that has recently been established as a conduit bridging early human populations in Europe, Africa, and Asia.

Geography, geology, and climate

The Arabian Peninsula is bounded on the west by the Gulf of Aqaba and the Red Sea, on the south by the Gulf of Aden and the Arabian Sea, and on the east by the Gulf of Oman and the Arabian Gulf. The subcontinent measures

2100 km from north to south along the Red Sea coast, and nearly 2000 km across at its maximum width from the westernmost region of Yemen to the easternmost point in Oman. The littoral is characterized by tropical and subtropical ecosystems, while the basin-shaped interior is dominated by alternating steppe and desert landscapes. Three major sand seas are found in Arabia: the Rub' al-Khali (600,000 km^2), Nafud (72,000 km^2), and Wahiba Sands (12,500 km^2) (Goudie 2003).

Arabia is skirted by mountainous terrain along the western, southern, and eastern edges of the peninsula. The 'Asir Highlands run along the western flank of the Kingdom of Saudi Arabia, called the Yemen Highlands where they extend into the Republic of Yemen. This mountain chain reaches nearly 4000 m above sea level in the south — the highest point on the entire peninsula; as a result, it receives up to 1000 mm of rainfall per annum. The coastal plain of southern Arabia is bounded by the Ḥaḍramawt (in Yemen) and Nejd (in Oman) plateaus. Extending north from the Dhofar escarpment, sedimentary beds rise sharply to an elevation of 1000 m above sea level, gradually levelling off northwards onto the Nejd. The entire region is comprised of uplifted Tertiary limestone that gradually slopes into the Rub al-'Khali basin. The ridge of the Dhofar escarpment marks the watershed divide; southwards-flowing drainages are seasonally active under present conditions, incising the limestone cliffs at a steep grade and creating springs and lagoons as they pool onto the coastal plain. Presently, the northwards-flowing drainages receive almost no storm flow but, during pluvial cycles, the magnitude of the monsoon was sufficient enough to produce high-energy fluvial systems.

The tectonic plate that constitutes the Arabian Peninsula is derived from Africa. For most of geological history, both landmasses formed part of a pan-Afro-Arabian continent. Then, around 30 million years ago the Arabian plate broke off from the African Shield and began to slide to the north-east, rotating in a counter-clockwise direction. This event triggered a chain reaction of seismic transformations that have had an indelible effect on the course of palaeoenvironmental and palaeoanthropological history. One significant modification was the formation of the Red Sea trough. This narrow, elongate depression is more than 2000 km long and varies in width from 180 to 300 km along the main channel. The rifting of these two plates also triggered volcanic activity along the western edge of Arabia, producing the jagged basalt peaks of the 'Asir-Yemen Highlands.

The genesis of Arabia's eastern mountain range is linked to the same tectonic movement as well. As the Arabian plate travels toward Asia, the Indian plate is sliding beneath it and forcing the ancient bed of the Tethys Sea to thrust upward. Consequently, the Hajar Mountains form the spine of south-eastern Arabia, reaching 3000 m above sea level in north-western Oman. This relatively long chain of mountains stretches from Ras al-Hadd in eastern Oman to the tip of the Musandam Peninsula at the Strait of Hormuz, a distance of over 600 km. Large, low angle alluvial fans coalesce at the mountain front, from which an extensive network of widis flow inland from the Hajar Mountains into the Rub' al-Khali, the Umm as-Samim, and the Haushi-Huqf basins.

Perhaps the most profound outcome of the African-Arabian tectonic rifting that has affected the course of human history is compression of the Arabian plate as it pushes against Eurasia. This process has led to geological subsidence throughout the eastern portion of Arabia, most notably a shallow depression that comprises the Arabo-Persian Gulf basin. In addition, buckling sedimentary strata created a series of north–south folds, thereby creating the world's largest oil reservoirs beneath the Arabian Shelf. Under the present arid climatic regime, the low-lying basins of eastern Arabia are dominated by aeolian deposition, blanketed by massive sand seas.

The Wahiba Sands are located in eastern Oman, north-east of the Haushi-Huqf Depression. This desert is comprised of linear dunes oriented on a north–south axis that run parallel to one another for several hundred kilometres. The dunes reach up to 100 m in elevation and are separated by swales 1–3 km wide (Glennie & Singhvi 2002; Preusser, Radies & Matter 2002). The most recent aeolian deposits in Wahiba formed during the last glacial maximum, at which time the emerged continental shelf provided abundant unconsolidated carbonates available for aeolian transport (Glennie 1988; Preusser, Radies & Matter 2002).

Encompassing nearly 600,000 km^2, most of the interior of southern Arabia is blanketed by the Rub' al-Khali sand sea. This massive basin slopes from an elevation of approximately 1200 m above sea level in the west to nearly sea level in the east. The dunes of the Rub' al-Khali include a variety of types, resulting from the alternating wind patterns and diverse sources of sand. The dunes are tallest in the south-western portion of the basin, as much as 200 m in height. Like the Wahiba, the extant features of the Rub' al-Khali dunes formed during the late Pleistocene, comprised primarily of reworked Pleistocene sediments above a bed of Pliocene alluvial gravels (McClure 1978).

The peninsula is subject to two different weather regimes (Barth & Steinkohl 2004). From the north come Atlantic late-winter north-westerlies, which move eastwards over the Mediterranean Sea, down the Arabian Gulf, and eventually dissipate over the Rub' al-Khali desert and Musandam Peninsula, bringing cool gentle winds and light precipitation (Parker *et al.* 2004). The second weather regime consists of summer storms brought by the south-west Indian Ocean monsoon system. From June to September, the highlands of Yemen and Oman receive relatively heavy rainfall as the mountainous terrain of southern Arabia traps moisture from the monsoon (Lézine *et al.* 1998; Glennie & Singhvi 2002). Consequently, the 'Asir and Dhofar Mountains receive between 200–1000 mm annually; while areas closer to sea level seldom collect more than 100–200 mm per year (Schyfsma 1978).

Flora and fauna

The environmental gradients across Arabia, the floral varieties in adjacent territories, and the legacy of Quaternary climate change have all had a significant effect upon the distribution of plant types throughout the subcontinent (Parker *et al.* 2004). In southern Arabia, the sparse vegetation cover is grouped within the following biotopes: coastal habitat, interior basin, 'Asir-Yemen Highlands, Dhofar Mountains, and Hajar Mountains. Flora such as *Cressa cretica* (cressa), *Nitraria retusa* (salt tree) and *Juncus maritimus* (sea rush) are found growing on the marine shores and salt flats. Wild rue, mangrove, indigo, date palms, henna, tamarinds, mistletoe, and ilb prosper around coastal wadi banks, particularly those along the Tihama (Red Sea) and al-Batinah (Gulf of Oman) coasts (Miller & Thomas 1996).

In the interior, plants such as tamarisks, poplars, acacias, and several other species of reeds, grasses, and small shrubs are found scattered near depressions and seasonal drainage systems that receive a limited degree of moisture (Hugh & Mason 1946). Due to heavy precipitation deposited by the summer monsoon, there is a wide variety of flora in the 'Asir-Yemen Highlands. Wild figs, leguminous trees, tamarisks, date palms, indigo, qat, myrrh, and a variety of flowering bushes and herbs are found along the wadi banks, while forests of juniper cover the mountain slopes between 2500 and 3000 m elevations (1946). Pollen samples taken from the wooded Yemeni highlands show a predominance of acacia, *Zygophyllum* (Syrian bean caper), and several species from the family Chenopodiaceae (goosefoot) (Lézine *et al.* 1998). A similar distribution of flora has been identified in the Dhofar Mountains and described as rolling grasslands and dense and verdant copses and woodlands, reminiscent rather of upland regions in the African savannah.

Indeed, the close resemblance of South Arabian floral varieties to that of Africa is due to the fact that many of these taxa spread eastwards from Africa. These woodland and grassland ecosystems belong to the Saharo-Sindian and Saharo-Arabian phytogeographic zones (Mandaville 1985; Ghazanfar & Fisher 1998; Ghazanfar 1999). The composition of plant communities and the morphology of endemic species suggest a close botanical relationship between Africa and Arabia throughout the Quaternary. Examples of East African-derived plant types include *Acacia* sp. (Acacia), *Ziziphus ziziphus* (Jujube), and *Apocynoideae rhazya* (dogbane).

Plant types in south-eastern Arabian (the modern territories of northern Oman and the UAE) show strong ties to the flora of Iran and south-western Pakistan (Baluchistan), comprising the Omano-Makranian sub-zone of the Nubo-Sindian centre of endemism (Mandaville 1985; Ghazanfar & Fisher 1998; Ghazanfar 1999). Floral elements that are linked to Asian taxa include *Euphorbia larica* (succulent spurge), *Prunus amygdalus* (almonds), *Ficus carica* (figs), *Lawsonia inermis* (henna), and *Indigofera tinctoria* (true indigo). These pronounced affinities in plant distribution across the Omano-Makranian sub-zone are attributed to the fact that during much of the Quaternary the basin of the Arabian Gulf was exposed, forming one continuous territory from Arabia into South Asia (Williams & Walkden 2002).

Of the large mammals, animals belonging to the family *Bovidae* are by far the most prominent on the Peninsula. These include one species of oryx, three species of *Gazella*, two species of *Capra*, one belonging to the genus *Hemitragus* (wild goat), and one of the genus *Ovis* (wild sheep). These animals typically occupy areas that receive moderate to high amounts of rainfall such as the Yemeni highlands, Dhofar, and the Hajar Mountains. Gazelle have been noted from more arid settings such as the high plateaus, while the desert-adapted oryx were once ubiquitous throughout the interior, even within the Rub' al-Khali (Harrison 1980).

Small mammals include various species from the family *Soricidae* (shrews), order *Rodentia* (rodents), and order *Chiroptera* (bats). There are carnivores such as mongooses, genets, dogs, wolves, and foxes (Harrison 1980). A variety of felines are present, including *Felis silvestris* (wild cat), *Felis margarita* (sand cat), *Caracal*

Figure 1. *Laminated lacustrine strata at Wahalah Lake, Ras al-Khaimah, UAE.*

caracal (Caracal lynx), *Panthera pardus* (leopard), and *Acinonyx jubatus* (cheetah) (Harrison & Bates 1991). Like the *Bovidae* family, these animals are typically found in and around the montane zones. There are some examples of *Lagomorpha* (rabbits, hares, and pikas) reported from the interior — on the desert plateaus and along the margins of the Rub' al-Khali (1991).

Much like the pattern of floral distributions, there are strong inter-regional links between Arabian fauna and adjacent areas. Terrestrial snails of northern Oman are primarily Palaearctic taxa, while snails found west of Dhofar have East African affinities (Mordan 1980). Fernandes *et al*. (2006) report mtDNA evidence for a recent genetic divergence between African and Arabian genets. They note several other small and medium-sized carnivores (e.g. mongooses, desert foxes, honey badger, caracal, jungle cat, golden jackal) that occur on both sides of the Red Sea that may also be genetically linked. Harrison (1980) corroborates these African and Arabian faunal connections, observing that *Crocidura somalica* (shrew) and *Genetta granti* (genet) are closely related to East African varieties.

Another indicator of faunal connections across the Red Sea is the presence of the primate *Papio hamadryas* — Sacred Baboon — in Yemen. Presently, these primates are indigenous to the rocky hill country of Somalia, Ethiopia, and Yemen. *Papio hamadryas* are arid-adapted creatures that forage protein-rich insects, hares, and other small mammals; they obtain water from shallow pools and by digging small wells in desert regions with a high water table (Nowak 1991). Analyses of *Papio hamadryas* mtDNA lineages on both sides of the Red Sea suggest that they originated in East Africa sometime between 150,000 and 50,000 years ago, and subsequently migrated into

FIGURE 2. *Relict fluvial terrace in Wadi Arah, southern Oman.*

Arabia (Wildman 2000; Wildman *et al.* 2004; Fernandes, Rohling & Siddell 2006). That the East African baboon lineage is older than the Arabian implies that there must have been a demographic bottleneck release sometime during the Upper Pleistocene.

Pleistocene and Early Holocene climate change in Arabia

Most of the precipitation that falls over Arabia is brought by the afore-mentioned south-west Indian Ocean monsoon system, considerably more so than from "north-westerly" winter storms. Consequently, the environmental fate of the region, amelioration or desiccation, rests upon the intensity of the monsoon, which has been in flux for at least the last quarter of a million years (Clemens *et al.* 1991; Muzuka 2000; Fleitmann *et al.* 2004).

Indian Ocean monsoon cycles: life and death of the South Arabian landscape

Marine cores from the Indian Ocean, Gulf of Oman, and the Arabian Sea provide a detailed history of the south-west Indian Ocean monsoon system throughout the Quaternary. Analysis of dinoflagellate cyst content from Arabian Sea deep sea cores during the last glaciation reveals an abrupt fluctuation at 12,500 years ago (Zonneveld *et al.* 1997). This spike is attributed to the disappearance of snow and ice cover over central Asia, Tibet, and the Himalayas, suggesting that one of the primary mechanisms driving monsoon fluctuations are climatic conditions at glacial-interglacial boundaries. Biogeochemical and lithogenic data from Arabian Sea cores spanning the last 350,000 years also support the notion that monsoon winds were sensitive to changing glacial climates. The retreat of ice sheets, the rise in continental albedo (solar radiation reflected off the earth's surface), and the increase of water surface temperatures in the western Indian Ocean triggered spikes in magnitude (Clemens *et al.* 1991).

Computer simulations have been used to estimate the average wind speed of the south-west monsoon during such phases of intensification. Speeds currently average around 10 m/sec, while increased periods of activity the saw wind speeds reaching 15 m/sec. Precipitation would have been 50 % greater than its present value, growing from 5 mm/day to 7.5 mm/day. Northwards-shifting insulation patterns drove the monsoons further into the Arabian Peninsula, with evidence for seasonal storms reaching as far north as Bubiyan Island in the Arabian Gulf (Sarnthein 1972; Kutzbach 1981).

Researchers have attempted to model the rate of change during shifts in monsoon magnitude. Analysis of ^{15}N isotopes was conducted on an interval of Arabian Sea

Figure 3. *Late Pleistocene dune profile at ash-Shwaib, UAE.*

core spanning the bracket of time between 43,000 and 42,000 years ago — a well-established climatic boundary. Significant changes in mean strength occurred within a span of 200 years, which is relatively instantaneous on a Pleistocene time scale (Higginson 2004). While the onset of the intensified monsoon was rapid, evidence has been presented suggesting that the shift back towards aridification was a more gradual process occurring on a millennial scale, at least during the most recent wet/dry shift (Lückge *et al*. 2001).

The stable oxygen isotope record of various planktonic foraminiferal species (i.e. *Globigerinoides ruber*, *Globigerina bulloides*, and *Neogloboquadrina dutertrei*) attests to temporal variations in marine palaeoproductivity. Analysis of species frequency distribution over the last glacial cycle shows a direct correlation between palaeoproductivity in the Arabian Sea, the strength of the monsoon, and the global oxygen isotope curve. Scholars note the onset of intensified monsoon episodes can lag up to 1000 years after shifts in glacial conditions, possibly due to the threshold necessary for sufficient amounts of snow and ice to melt and affect Indian Ocean insulation patterns (Reichart, Lourens & Zachariasse 1997; Petit-Maire *et al*. 1999; Ivanova *et al*. 2003).

Fluctuations in monsoon intensity are evidenced by a variety of signals upon and within the landscape. The most complete records come from a series of dated speleothems in the Hajar and Dhofar mountains. Pronounced pluvial conditions are also signalled by remnants of ancient lake deposits (Fig. 1), travertines, fluvial terraces (Fig. 2), and alluvial fans spreading along the piedmont regions. The expansive sand seas found throughout Arabia's desert are a testament to the hyperarid phases that have occasionally swept across the peninsula (Fig. 3).

We have compiled all of these palaeoenvironmental signals together to build a comprehensive database of

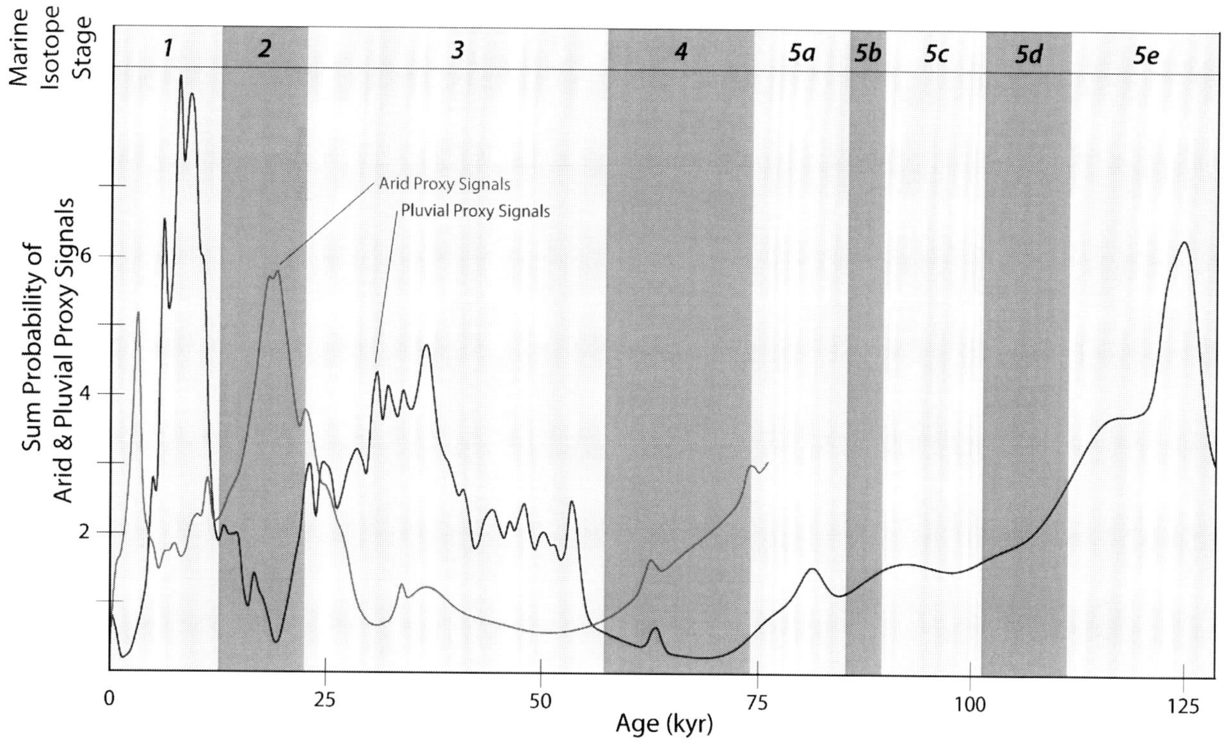

Figure 4. *HOPE ENV sum probability curve depicting wet/dry signals throughout Arabia during the Upper Pleistocene.*

climate change in Arabia, referred to as HOPE ENV. These data are derived from published sources as well as new evidence collected by the authors in the field. Based on a total of 396 absolute dates, we present a composite sum probability curve (Fig. 4) to illustrate climatic oscillations over the past 175,000 years, from MIS 6 to present. Peaks in sum probability represent periods of increased wetness, while troughs highlight drier phases. All dates are reported in calendar years BP.

Climatic conditions during the late Middle and Upper Pleistocene are of particular interest to our study, given that this span of time formed the backdrop of early human emergence from Africa. Was the climate arid enough during the last few glacial maxima to preclude hominin habitation and, conversely, were conditions humid enough to facilitate human occupation during the Last Interglacial?

Anton (1984) speculated that the environment was hyperarid during MIS 6, given that monsoon intensity roughly tracks with the global marine isotope curve. The emerging picture in Arabia indicates the situation was more varied than this initial assessment; a smattering of chronometric dates suggests there were brief pulses in precipitation. Compelling evidence for increased moisture at the MIS 7-MIS 6 interface comes from speleothems in Hoti Cave, northern Oman, where U/Th measurements exhibit an increase in growth rate between 200–180 ka (Burns *et al.* 2001). The prospect of stage 6 sub-pluvials are corroborated by optical dates on fluvial silts at Sabkha Matti (147,000 ± 12,000 BP) (Goodall 1995), two U/Th measurements from freshwater mollusca within lacustrine sediments at Mudawwara (170,000 ± 14,000 BP and 152,000 ± 8,000 BP) (Petit-Maire *et al.* 1999), optically dated fluvial silts at Falaj al-Moalla in the Wadi Dhaid, UAE (193,110 ± 30,750 BP), OSL measurements on fluvial silts recorded at the Camel Pit Site, Umm al-Qawain, UAE (174,300 ± 24,110 BP), and optical measurements on evaporitic lacustrine sediments sampled from a relict interdunal sabkha in the Liwa region of the Rub' al-Khali, UAE (160,000 ± 8000 BP) (Wood, Rizk & Alsharhan 2003).

The onset of the Last Interglacial period around 130,000 years ago was punctuated by an abrupt and drastic increase in rainfall over South Arabia that lasted until approximately 120 ka, followed by a second peak in precipitation corresponding with MIS 5a (82–74 ka). U/Th dates on palaeosols from the western piedmont of the Hajar Mountains in Oman that are correlated with isotopic stages 5e and 5a (Sanlaville 1992). Soils were also noted in the ad-Dahna Desert of northern Arabia, where late Pleistocene dunes overlie two separate pedogenic strata that could only have formed on stabilized dunes with a dense cover of vegetation (Anton 1984). There is a network of Plio-Pleistocene bas-relief gravel channels west of the Wahiba desert that is superimposed by thinner fluviatile gravels tentatively associated with particularly humid episodes during MIS 5e and MIS 5a (Maizels 1987). Stokes and Bray (2005) obtained over fifty optical dates from megabarchan dunes in the Liwa region, which lies along the eastern margin of the Rub' al-Khali. Their findings suggest a prolonged period of dune accumulation from 130 to 75 ka. This deposition was attributed to a unique combination of factors such as reduced sea levels in the Arabo-Persian Gulf that produced an abundance of sedimentary material available for transport, a rise in regional groundwater levels, and vegetation cover that stabilized the dunes. Multiple MIS 5 pluvial episodes are signalled by the aforementioned Hoti Cave speleothems, which yield U/Th dates indicating rapid growth between 135–120 ka and 82–78 ka. Researchers noted that speleothem growth was most pronounced during MIS 5e, more so than all subsequent pluvials (Burns *et al.* 1998; 2001). Most recently, we have dated a series of buried alluvial fans interstratified with fluvial sands along the western edge of the Hajar Mountains in Ras al-Khaimah, UAE. OSL ages obtained from these sediments indicate they were deposited at 117,030 ± 15,080 BP and 107,970 ± 9660 BP.

There are meagre climatic data from MIS 4 and early MIS 3 in southern Arabia. Indirect evidence from the HOPE ENV summed probability curve as well as the index of Indian Ocean Monsoon activity (Fleitmann *et al.* 2007) suggests this time frame was characterized by increasingly hyperarid conditions culminating around 70 ka, followed by a return to a more humid regime by 50,000 years ago. The only physical evidence for aridification during MIS 4 can be inferred from stratigraphic profiles in the Rub' al-Khali, which attest to a stage of aeolian accumulation sometime before 37,000 years ago. This deposition, however, is relatively minor as compared to the immense aeolian structures that accumulated during the terminal Pleistocene (McClure 1978).

Geological investigations in the heart of the Rub' al-Khali sand sea have revealed a landscape during MIS 3 that featured a series of small lakes spread across the interior (McClure 1984). Radiocarbon measurements on mollusc shells and marls indicate the lakes reached their highest levels around 37,000 BP (McClure 1976). These playas ranged from ephemeral puddles to pools up to 10 m deep, and numbered well over 1000. They are primarily distributed along an east–west axis across the centre of the Rub' al-Khali basin, covering a distance of some 1200 km (McClure 1984). Similar lake basins have been reported from the Ramlat as-Sabatayn desert in Yemen (Lézine *et al.* 1998; 2007), as well as the Nafud in northern Arabia (Garrard & Harvey 1981; Schulz & Whitney 1986).

Researchers speculate that lake-filling episodes were short-lived; these poorly drained basins would have been recharged by occasional torrential stormflow runoff and disappeared within a few years. Due to the region's wide catchment area, the Mundafan depression was the exception to this model. Arabia's thickest lacustrine deposits were recorded here, where single lake periods are estimated to have lasted at least 800 years. Fossilized faunal remains excavated within the Mundafan sediments yielded a menagerie of large vertebrates including oryx, gazelle, aurochs, wild ass, hartebeest, water buffalo, tahr, goat, hippopotamus, wild camel, and ostrich (McClure 1984). Most of these species belong to the family Bovidae, whose survival required expansive grasslands produced by light to medium rainfall distributed evenly over the Rub' al-Khali.

Ostracoda and freshwater mollusca indicative of low salinity were present at Mundafan, as well as species of foraminifera that attest to highly brackish conditions (McClure & Swain 1974). Evidence of grasses, shrubs, and herbs are indicated by both phytoliths and dikaka — thin, tubular fragments of fossilized material scattered in the aeolian sediments around the basins. These floral fossils were formed when dissolved calcium carbonate in the water precipitated onto plants as the lake evaporated. Evidence of fish remains are conspicuously absent from the Rub' al-Khali lakes, because lakes were rarely refilled and became too alkaline too quickly to develop a population (McClure 1984).

In addition to interior palaeolakes, other signals for an MIS 3 wet phase include depositional terraces in the Wadi Dhaid; although undated, their stratigraphic position suggests an age between 35 and 22 ka BP (Sanlaville 1992). Interdunal sibakh recorded in the Liwa region of the UAE have produced thirty-one dates (both uncalibrated ^{14}C as well as OSL) that cluster between 46,500 and 21,500 BP (Wood & Imes 1995;

Juyal, Singhvi & Glennie 1998; Glennie & Singhvi 2002). Palaeosols have been recorded in the ad-Dahna desert, which are stratigraphically positioned between MIS 4 and MIS 2 aeolian deposits (Anton 1984). Clark and Fontes (1990) dated calcite formations from ancient hyperalkaline springs in northern Oman, producing radiocarbon ages between 33 and 19 ka. Two soil horizons were discovered around the central plateau of the Yemeni highlands, characterized as molissols — soils that form on landscapes covered by savannah vegetation. Uncalibrated radiocarbon measurements were 26,150 ± 350 BP for the lower stratum, and 19,290 ± 350 BP for the upper horizon (Brinkmann & Ghaleb 1997).

Researchers speculate that the Terminal Pleistocene dry phase was more arid than the peninsula had experienced since the Penultimate Glaciation, if not earlier (Anton 1984). Ages obtained from dune formations in the Rub' al-Khali (McClure 1984; Goudie *et al.* 2000; Parker & Goudie, 2007), an-Nafud (Anton 1984), and the Wahiba Sands (Gardner 1988; Glennie & Singhvi 2002) all signal a major phase of aeolian accumulation between 17,000 and 9000 BP. Calcite fractures in northern Oman corroborate the evidence for increasing aridity, indicating there was considerably less moisture in the environment starting around 19,000 BP (Clark 1990). The Terminal Pleistocene hyperarid phase ended with yet another pronounced oscillation back to humid conditions. This pluvial phase period lasted until *c.* 5000 BP, at which time the present climatic regime was established (Overstreet & Grolier 1988; Cleuziou, Inizan & Marcolongo 1992; Sanlaville 1992; Brunner 1997; Wilkinson 1997; Stokes & Bray 2005; Parker *et al.* 2004; 2006*a*; 2006*b*; 2006*c*).

Shifting shorelines and human refugia

As profound as these climatic oscillations have been over the course of the Quaternary, the rise and fall of sea level has had an even greater effect on the configuration of the Arabian subcontinent. Taking into account the shallow bathymetry of the Arabo-Persian Gulf and Red Sea basins, nearly 1 million km^2 of contiguous land have been repeatedly exposed and submerged by glacio-eustatic cycles of marine regression and transgression (Fig. 5). The emergence of the continental shelf around Arabia had direct implications for prehistoric occupation, since the exposed landmass provided abundant sources of fresh water amidst a generally desiccated landscape. The role of littoral zones in the dispersal of modern humans is the crux of ongoing discussion; recent models of human emergence from Africa envision rapid coastal migration across the southern route of dispersal, facilitated by a new adaptation to aquatic resources (e.g. Stringer 2000; Mithen & Reed 2002; Mellars 2006). Evidence suggesting the importance of low-lying coastal habitats during the early and middle Holocene has been discovered by Bailey *et al.* (2007*a*; 2007*b*) around the Farasan Islands in the southern Red Sea, who report a nearly continuous line of over 1000 shell mounds along the beachfront.

Faure, Walter and Grant (2002) have identified a process of littoral freshwater upwelling they refer to as the "coastal oasis" hypothesis that may help explain the importance of coastal habitats for early humans groups. Depressed sea levels during glacial maxima caused an increase of hydraulic pressure within submarine rivers; consequently, more freshwater flowed through these aquifers. Eventually, this process led to the creation of springs in favourable loci on the emerged shelf with lithology, faults, bathymetry, and/or topography conducive to upwelling. Such a phenomenon can be observed today in the abundant submerged seeps at the bottom of the Arabo-Persian Gulf. The area around modern Qatar is the terminus of several submarine rivers that flow beneath Arabia, creating a mass of upwelling plumes once used by ancient seafarers for restocking their freshwater stores (Church 1996).

Indeed, a god known as Enki, the "Lord of the Sweet Waters", was revered by the Gulf's earliest inhabitants — a group which originated in the basin prior to its final inundation in the fourth millennium BC. Enki was believed to dwell within the "Abzu", the freshwater of the deep; in the "Myth of Enki and Ninhursag" he is credited with building canals to bring freshwater to Dilmun (Jacobsen 1987). This example taken from Sumerian mythology serves as a useful frame of reference to highlight both the availability and importance of freshwater within the Arabo-Persian Gulf basin throughout the Pleistocene and Early Holocene. The Gulf is the shallowest inland sea in the world, averaging just 40 m in depth and covering some 225,000 km^2 (Sarnthein 1972). Therefore, between 115,000 and 6,000 years ago, when sea levels were depressed below current levels, we speculate that this region served as a large refugium for local biomass (including hominins) constricted by arid conditions (for further discussion of the role of the Gulf basin in proto-history see Sayce *et al.* 1912; Barton 1929; Cooke 1987; Teller *et al.* 2000; Kennett & Kennett 2006; Sanford 2006).

Throughout the Upper Pleistocene and Early/Middle Holocene, nearly all excess runoff in south-west Asia was funnelled into the Gulf basin via submarine aquifers

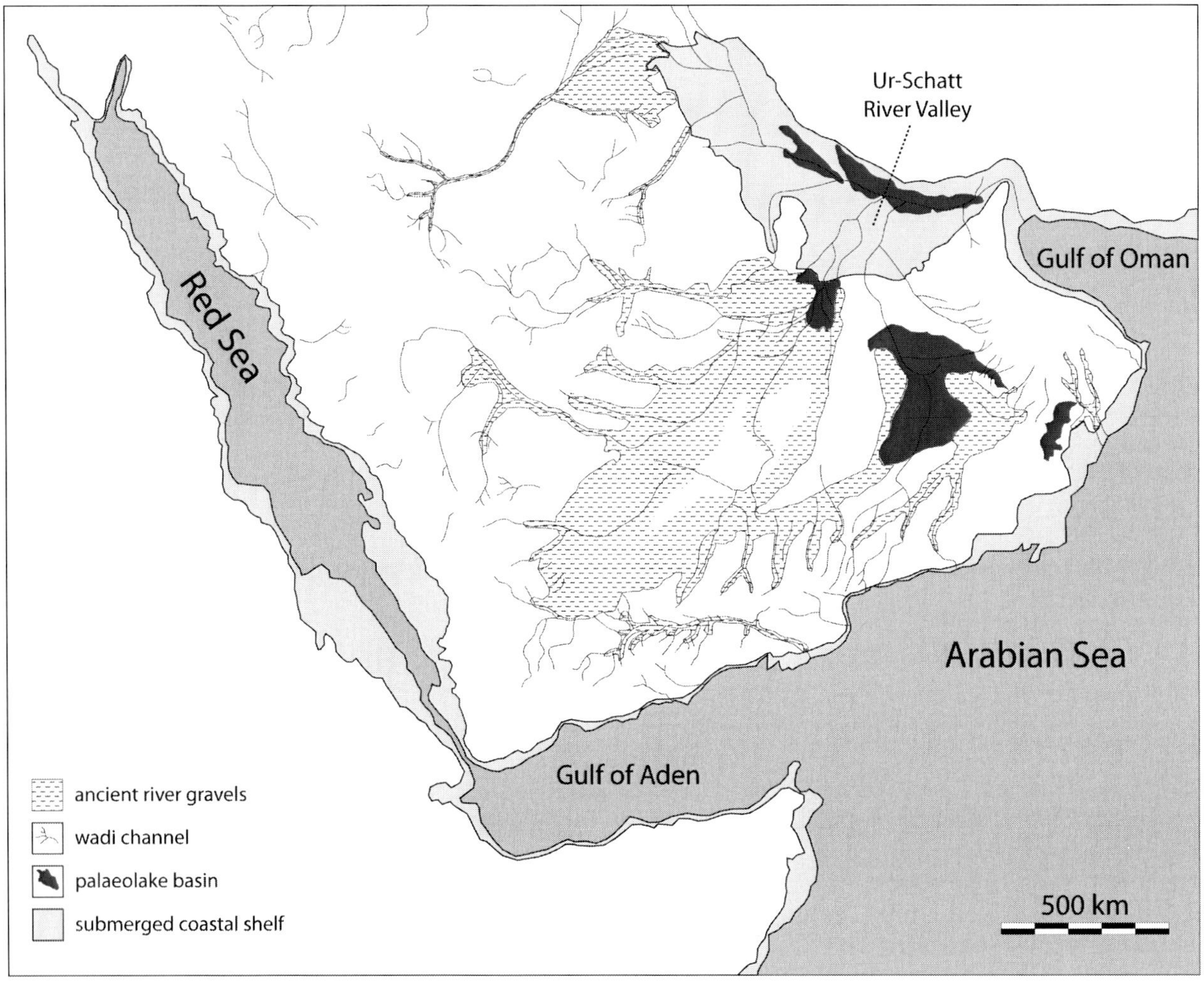

Figure 5. *Map of Arabia showing drainage channels and significant Pleistocene geomorphic features.*

flowing beneath Arabia, the Karun drainage originating in the Zagros Mountains, and the Tigris and Euphrates Rivers flowing from the Anatolian Plateau. All of these drainage systems converged within the centre of the basin, forming the Ur-Schatt River, which once traversed the entire length of the basin through a deeply incised canyon that is still evident in the extant bathymetry (Seibold & Vollbrecht 1969; Sarnthein 1972; Uchupi, Swift & Ross 1999). The most recent phase of Ur-Schatt River downcutting culminated during the Last Glacial Maximum, when global sea levels were reduced by 120 m and the basin was exposed in its entirety. Sometime around 14,000 BP, the Straits of Hormuz were breached by the Gulf of Oman, and by 12,500 BP marine incursion reached the central basin of the Gulf. This process of infilling has been relatively gradual; the waters only reached the present shoreline as recently as 6000 years ago, at which time the sea exceeded its current levels by 2 m (Bernier *et al*. 1995; Lambeck 1996; Williams & Walkden 2002).

There is freshly unearthed evidence hinting at the importance of the Gulf basin refugium throughout prehistory. One such example is the unexpectedly early presence of Ubaid-related (late Neolithic) sites clustering along the southern coastline and located on islands within the Gulf itself (Haerinck 1991; 1994; Hermansen 1993; Jasim 1996; Beech & Elders 1999; Beech, Elders & Shepherd 2000; Beech *et al.* 2005; Carter 2006). The sudden appearance of a fully-sedentary, agrarian society within this previously uninhabited niche is incongruous with the pace of local Neolithic development. Therefore, we suggest the pattern of Ubaid-related settlements in south-eastern Arabia is reason to revive the age old, unanswered debate: "from whence came the Sumerians?" (Barton 1929). This question becomes even more intriguing in light of new genetic evidence obtained from modern populations around the Gulf, who carry signature lineages from Africa, Asia, and Europe (Reguiero *et al.* 2006; Shepard & Herrera 2006). Based on these findings, Reguiero *et al.* (2006) describe the area as a "tricontinental nexus" for human dissemination.

Discussion: modelling demographic response

In considering the early human drama that unfolded amidst the backdrop of the wildly metamorphosing Arabian landscape, it is useful to consider a passage from Abd al-Qadir al-Jilani's ninth-century text *Kitab Sirr al-Asrar*, later translated into English by Sir Isaac Newton: "that which is below is like that which is above" (Dobbs, 1983). A more down-to-earth rendition of this statement might imply that demographic history in Arabia mirrors the evolution of the landscape.

This metaphor is rooted in deep geological time, when the Arabian tectonic plate split from Africa, forming the Red Sea trough. Genetic studies indicate that modern human emergence occurred in a similar manner, when a group derived from mtDNA superhaplogroup L3 branched from the ancestral population sometime prior to 75,000 BP (e.g. Metspalu *et al.* 2004), perhaps as early as 300,000 years ago (Yotova *et al.* 2007). Far from a geographic barrier, the Red Sea was a conduit for both plants and animals throughout the Quaternary. While there was no land bridge at any point during this phase (Siddall *et al.* 2002: 203–206), reduced sea levels rendered the narrow crossing at the southern extent of the Red Sea a negligible barrier. Moreover, the body of water flanking the eastern margin of the Arabian subcontinent did not exist for the majority of the Upper Pleistocene (Lambeck 1996; Uchupi, Swift & Ross 1999); the absence of this waterway was undoubtedly an integral part of the prehistoric plot. Distributions of flora and fauna across eastern Arabia — predominantly Palearctic taxa — demonstrate the region's natural Eurasian affinities. It is not surprising that Upper Pleistocene lithic industries follow the same geographic patterning (Rose 2007).

We have seen that life and death within the interior of South Arabia was dependant upon the intensity of the Indian Ocean monsoon. When global insulation patterns forced the monsoon northwards, the hinterland was transformed into a sub-tropical savannah. Conversely, when rainfall ceased during glacial maxima, the majority of the peninsula became a barren wasteland. Given these extreme fluctuations, in conjunction with its position at the intersection of Africa, Asia, and Europe, it is likely that South Arabia served a unique role in the prehistoric world: a bridge during pluvials and a barrier during arid phases.

It is only appropriate to envision these processes in the sense of long term, inter-regional genetic exchange; we do not yet possess a suitable degree of resolution within the palaeoclimatic and archaeological records to assess actual demographic events. Any statement about Upper Pleistocene human migrations out of Africa and into Arabia would be premature and grossly presumptive. There are data suggesting that certain parts of the Arabian subcontinent served as stable refugia during environmental downturns. Thus, to understand the role of the peninsula in the story of human origins, it is more productive to consider populations tethered to refugia, expanding and contracting from such habitats during cycles of amelioration and desiccation.

This paper has demonstrated that Quaternary climate change in Arabia was a complex process that produced diverse landscapes across the peninsula. For instance, while glacial events resulted in an entirely inhospitable environment within the interior, portions of the emerged continental shelf were paradisiacal gardens. Rather than a simplistic scenario of *Homo sapiens* marching across Arabia at the onset of the "human revolution", we must expect that prehistoric occupation was as complex and varied as the landscapes upon which they dwelt.

References

Ambrose S.

1998. Late Pleistocene human population bottlenecks, volcanic winter, and differentiation of modern humans. *Journal of Human Evolution* 34: 623–651.

Anderson D.E., Goudie A.S. & Parker A.G.
2007. *Global Environments through the Quaternary: Exploring Environmental Change*. Oxford: Oxford University Press.

Anton D.
1984. Aspects of Geomorphological Evolution: Paleosols and Dunes in Saudi Arabia. Pages 275–296 in A.R. Jado & J.G. Zötl (eds), *Quaternary Period in Saudi Arabia.* ii. *Sedimentological, Hydrogeological, Hydrochemical, Geomorphological, and Climatological Investigations of Western Saudi Arabia.* Vienna: Springer-Verlag.

Bailey G.N., al-Sharekh A., Flemming N.C., Lambeck K., Momber G., Sinclair A. & Vita-Finzi C.
2007*a*. Coastal prehistory in the southern Red Sea Basin, underwater archaeology, and the Farasan Islands. *Proceedings of the Seminar for Arabian Studies* 37: 1–16.

Bailey G.N., Flemming N.C., King G.C.P., Lambeck K., Momber G., Moran L.J., al-Sharekh A. & Vita-Finzi C.
2007*b*. Coastlines, Submerged Landscapes, and Human Evolution: The Red Sea Basin and the Farasan Islands. *Journal of Island & Coastal Archaeology* 2: 127–160.

Barton G.A.
1929. Whence came the Sumerians? *Journal of the American Oriental Society* 49: 263–268.

Beech M. & Elders J.
1999. An 'Ubaid-Related Settlement on Dalma Island, Abu Dhabi Emirate, United Arab Emirates. *Bulletin of the Society for Arabian Studies* 4: 17–21.

Beech M., Elders J. & Shepherd E.
2000. Reconsidering the 'Ubaid of the Southern Gulf: new results from excavations on Dalma Island, U.A.E. *Proceedings of the Seminar for Arabian Studies* 30: 41–47.

Beech M., Cuttler R., Moscrop D., Kallweit H. & Martin J.
2005. New evidence for the Neolithic settlement of Marawah Island, Abu Dhabi, United Arab Emirates. *Proceedings of the Seminar for Arabian Studies* 35: 37–56.

Bernier P., Dalongeville R., Dupuis B. & Medwecki V. de
1995. Holocene shoreline variations in the Persian Gulf: example of the Umm al-Qowayn lagoon (UAE). *Quaternary International* 29/30: 95–103.

Bray H. & Stokes S.
2004. Temporal patterns of arid-humid transitions in the south-eastern Arabian Peninsula based on optical dating. *Geomorphology* 59: 271–280.

Brinkmann R. & Ghaleb A.O.
1997. Late Pleistocene Mollisol and Cumulic Fluvents near Ibb, Yemen Arab Republic. Pages 251–258 in M.J. Grolier, R. Brinkmann & J.A. Blakely (eds), *The Wadi al-Jubah Archaeological Project:* v. *Environmental Research in Support of Archaeological Investigations in the Yemen Arab Republic, 1982 – 1987*. Washington, DC: American Foundation for the Study of Man.

Brunner U.
1997. Geography and Human Settlements in Ancient Southern Arabia. *Arabian Archaeology and Epigraphy* 8: 190–202.

Burns S.J., Matter A., Frank N. & Mangini A.
1998. Speleothem based paleoclimatic record from Northern Oman. *Geology* 26/6: 499–502.

Burns S.J., Fleitmann D., Matter A., Neff U. & Mangini A.
2001. Speleothem evidence from Oman for continental pluvial events during interglacial periods. *Geology* 29/7: 623–626.

Carter R.
2006. Boat remains and maritime trade in the Persian Gulf during the sixth and fifth millennia BC. *Antiquity* 80: 52–63.

Church T.M.
1996. An underground route for the water cycle. *Nature* 380: 579– 580.

Clark A.
1989. Lakes of the Rub' al Khali. *Aramco* 40/3: 28-33.
Clark I. & Fontes J-C.
1990. Paleoclimatic Reconstruction of Northern Oman Based on Carbonates from Hyperalkaline Groundwaters. *Quaternary Research* 33: 320–336.
Clemens S., Prell W., Murray D., Shimmield G. & Weedon G.
1991. Forcing Mechanisms of the Indian Ocean Monsoon. *Nature* 353: 720–725.
Cleuziou S., Inizan M-L. & Marcolongo B.
1992. Le Peuplement Pré- et Protohistorique du Système Fluviatile Fossile du Jawf-Hadramawt au Yemen. *Paléorient* 18: 5–29.
Cooke G.A.
1987. Reconstruction of the Holocene coastline of Mesopotamia. *Geoarchaeology* 2/1: 15–28.
Dobbs B.J.T.
1983. *The Foundations of Newton's Alchemy*. Cambridge: Cambridge University Press.
2002. The coastal oasis: ice age springs on emerged continental shelves. *Global and Planetary Change* 33: 47–56.
Fernandes C.A., Rohling E.J. & Siddall M.
2006. Absence of post-Miocene land bridges: biogeographic implications. *Journal of Biogeography* 33/6: 961–966.
Fleitmann D., Matter A., Pint J.J. & al-Shanti M.A.
2004. *The Speleothem Record of Climate Change in Saudi Arabia*. Saudi Royal Geological Society Open File Report SGS-OF-2004-8. Jeddah: Saudi Royal Geographic Society.
Fleitmann D., Burns S.J., Mangini A., Mudelsee M., Kramers J., Villa I., Neff U., al-Subbary A.A., Buettner A., Hippler D. & Matter A.
2007. Holocene ITCZ and Indian monsoon dynamics recorded in stalagmites from Oman and Yemen (Socotra). *Quaternary Science Reviews* 26: 170 – 188.
Gardner R.A.M.
1988. Aeolianites and Marine Deposits of the Wahiba Sands: Character and Palaeoenvironments. *Journal of Oman Studies Special Report* 3: 75–94.
Garrard A. & Harvey C.P.D.
1981. Environment and settlement during the Upper Pleistocene and Holocene at Jubbah in the Great Nafud, northern Arabia. *Atlal* 5: 137–148.
Ghazanfar S.A.
1999. Present flora as an example of palaeoclimate: examples from the Arabian Peninsula. Pages 263–275 in A.K. Singhvi & E. Derbyshire (eds), *Paleoenvironmental Reconstruction in Arid Lands*. Rotterdam: Balkema.
Ghazanfar S.A. & M. Fisher (eds)
1998. *Vegetation of the Arabian Peninsula*. Kluwer Academic Publishers: Dordrecht.
Glennie KW.
1998. The desert of southeast Arabia: a product of Quaternary climatic change. Pages 279–291 in A.S. Alshahan, K.W. Glennie, G.L. Whittl & G.G.StC. Kendall (eds), *Quaternary Deserts and Climatic Change*. Rotterdam: Balkema.
Glennie K.W. & Singhvi A.K.
2002. Event stratigraphy, palaeoenvironment and chronology of SE Arabian deserts. *Quaternary Science Reviews* 21: 853–869.
Goodall T.M.
1995. *The geology and geomorphology of the Sabkhat Matti region (United Arab Emirates): a modern analogue for ancient desert sediments of north-west Europe*. PhD thesis, University of Aberdeen, Aberdeen [Unpublished].

Goudie A.S., Colls A., Stokes S., Parker A.G., White K. & al-Farraj A.
2000. Latest Pleistocene dune construction at the north-eastern edge of the Rub al-Khali, United Arab Emirates. *Sedimentology* 47/5: 1011–1021.
Haerinck E.
1991. Heading for the Straits of Hormuz, an 'Ubaid site in the Emirate of Ajman (U.A.E.). *Arabian Archaeology and Epigraphy* 2: 84–90.
1994. More prehistoric finds from the United Arab Emirates. *Arabian Archaeology and Epigraphy* 5: 153–157.
Harrison D.L.
1968. *The Mammals of Arabia*. London: Ernest Benn Limited.
Hermansen B.D.
1993. 'Ubaid and ED pottery from five sites at 'An as-Sayh, Saudi Arabia. *Arabian Archaeology and Epigraphy* 4: 126–144.
Higginson M.J.
2004. A solar (irradiance) trigger for millennial-scale abrupt changes in the southwest monsoon? *Paleoceanography* 19/3: 3807–3826.
Ivanova E., Schiebel R., Singh A.D., Schmiedl G., Niebler H-S. & Hemleben C.
2003. Primary production in the Arabian Sea during the last 135 000 years. *Palaeogeography, Palaeoclimatology, Palaeoecology* 197: 61–82.
Jacobsen, T.
1987. *The Harps that once....:Sumerian Poetry in Translation*. New Haven: Yale University Press.
Jasim S.A.
1996. An 'Ubaid site in the Emirate of Sharjah (U.A.E.). *Arabian Archaeology and Epigraphy* 7: 1–12.
Juyal N., Singhvi A.K. & Glennie K.W.
1998. Chronology and paleoenvironmental significance of Quaternary desert sediment in southeastern Arabia. Pages 315–325 in A.S. Alsharhan, K.W. Glennie, G.L. Whittle & C.G.StC. Kendall (eds), *Quaternary Deserts and Climatic Change*. Rotterdam: Balkema.
Kennett D.J. & Kennett J.P.
2006. Early State Formation in Southern Mesopotamia: Sea Levels, Shorelines, and Climate Change. *Journal of Island and Coastal Archaeology* 1: 67–99.
Kürschener H.
1986. Omanish-Maranishe disjunction ein beitrag zur planzengeographischen stellung und zu den florengenetishcen bezeihungen Omans. *Englers Botanische Jahrbuch der Systematischen Pflanzengeschichte und Pflanzengeographie* 106: 541–562.
1998. Biogeography and introduction to vegetation. Pages 64–98 in S.A. Ghazanfar & M. Fisher (eds), *Vegetation of the Arabian Peninsula*. Dordrecht: Kluwer Academic Publishers.
Kutzbach J.E.
1981. Monsoon Climate of the Early Holocene: Climate Experience with the Earth's Orbital Parameters for 9000 Years Ago. *Science* 214: 59–61.
Lambeck K.
1996. Shoreline reconstructions for the Persian Gulf since the last glacial maximum. *Earth and Planetary Science Letters* 142: 43–57.
Leuschner D.C. & Sirocko F.
2003. Orbital insolation forcing of the Indian Monsoon — a motor for global climate changes? *Palaeogeography, Palaeoclimatology, Palaeoecology* 197: 83–95.
Lézine A., Saliège J., Robert C., Wertz F. & M. Inizan.
1998. Holocene lakes from Ramlat as-Sab'atayn (Yemen) illustrate the impact of monsoon activity in southern Arabia. *Quaternary Research* 50: 290–299.

Lézine A., Tiercelin J-J., Robert C., Saliège J-F., Cleuziou S., Inizan M-L. & Braemer F.

2007. Centennial to millennial-scale variability of the Indian monsoon during the early Holocene from a sediment, pollen and isotope record from the desert of Yemen. *Palaeogeography, Palaeoclimatology, Palaeoecology* 243: 235–249.

Lückge A., Doose-Rolinski H., Khan A.A., Schulz H. & Rad U. von

2001. Monsoonal variability in the northeastern Arabian Sea during the past 5000 years: geochemical evidence from laminated sediments. *Palaeogeography, Palaeoclimatology, Palaeoecology* 167: 273–286.

McClure H.A.

1976. Radiocarbonchronology of Late Quaternary Lakes in the Arabian Desert. *Nature* 263: 755–756.

1978. Ar Rub' al Khali. Pages 125–138 in S.S. al-Sayari & J.G. Zötl (eds), *Quaternary Period in Saudi Arabia.* i. *Sedimentological, Hydrogeological, Hydrochemical, Geomorphological, and Climatological Investigations in Central and Eastern Saudi Arabia.* Vienna: Springer-Verlag.

1984. *Late Quaternary palaeoenvironments of the Rub' al Khali.* PhD Dissertation, University of London, London [Unpublished].

McClure H.A. & Swain F.M.

1974. The Fresh water and Brackish Water Fossil Quaternary Ostracoda from the Rub' al Khali, Saudi Arabia. *6th African Micropalaeontological Colloquium, Tunis.*

Maizels J.K.

1987. Plio-Pleistocene raised channel systems of the western Sharqiya (Wahiba), Oman. Pages 31–50 in L. Frostick & I. Reid (eds), *Desert Sediments: Ancient and Modern. Geological Society Special Publication* 35.

Mandaville J.P.

1985. A botanical reconnaissance of the Musandam region of Oman. *Journal of Oman Studies* 7: 9–28.

Mellars P.

2006. Going East: New Genetic and Archaeological Perspectives on the Modern Human Colonization of Eurasia. *Science* 313: 796–800.

Metspalu M., Kivisild T., Metspalu E., Parik J., Hudjashov G., Kaldma K., Serk P., Karmin M., Behar D.M., Thomas M., Gilbert P., Endicott P., Mastana S., Papiha S.S., Skorecki K., Torroni A. & Villems R.

2004. Most of the extant mtDNA boundaries in South and Southwest Asia were likely shaped during the initial settlement of Eurasia by anatomically modern humans. *BMC Genetics* 5: 26.

Miller A.G. & Thomas A.

1996. *Flora of the Arabian Peninsula and Socotra.* Edinburgh: Edinburgh University Press.

Mithen S. & Reed M.

2002. Stepping out: a computer simulation of hominid dispersal from Africa. *Journal of Human Evolution* 43: 433–462.

Mordan P.B.

1980. Land Mollusca of Dhofar. Pages 103–112 in S.N. Shaw Reade, J.B. Sale, M. Gallagher & R.H. Daly (eds), *The Scientific Results of the Oman Flora and Fauna Survey 1977 (Dhofar). Journal of Oman Studies, Special Reports* 2.

Muzuka A.N.

2000. 350 ka Organic ^{13}C record of the monsoon variability on the Oman continental margin, Arabian Sea. *Proceedings of the Indian Academy Science* 109: 481–489.

Nowak R.M.

1991. *Walker's Mammals of the World.* Baltimore: Johns Hopkins University Press.

Overstreet W.C., Grolier M.J. & Toplyn M.R.

1988. *Geological and Archaeological Reconnaissance in the Yemen Arab Republic, 1985.* Wadi Al-Jubah Archaeological Project v. 4. Washington, DC: American Foundation for the Study of Man.

Parker A.G. & Goudie A.S.
2007. Development of the Bronze Age landscape in the southeastern Arabian Gulf: new evidence from a buried shell midden in the eastern extremity of the Rub' al-Khali desert, Emirate of Ras al-Khaimah, UAE. *Arabian Archaeology and Epigraphy* 18: 232–238.
Parker A.G., Wilkinson T.J. & Davies C.
2006. The early-mid Holocene period in Arabia: some recent evidence from lacustrine sequences in eastern and southwestern Arabia. *Proceedings of the Seminar for Arabian Studies* 36: 243–255.
Parker A.G., Preston G., Walkington H. & Hodson M.J.
2006. Developing a framework of Holocene climatic change and landscape archaeology for southeastern Arabia. *Arabian Archaeology and Epigraphy* 17: 125–130.
Parker A.G., Eckersley L., Smith M.M., Goudie A.S., Stokes S., White K. & Hodson M.J.
2004. Holocene vegetation dynamics in the northeastern Rub' al-Khali desert, Arabian Peninsula: a pollen, phytolith and carbon isotope study. *Journal of Quaternary Science* 19: 665–676.
Parker A.G., Goudie A.S., Stokes S., White K., Hodson M.J., Manning M. & Kennet D.
2006. A record of Holocene Climate Change from lake geochemical analyses in southeastern Arabia. *Quaternary Research* 66: 465–476.
Petit-Maire N., Burollet P.F., Ballais J-L., Fontugne M., Rosso J-C. & Lazaar A.
1999. Paléoclimats Holocènes du Sahara septentionale, Dépôts lacustres et terrasses alluviales en bordure du Grand Erg Oriental à l'extrême-Sud de la Tunisie. *Comptes Rendus de l'Académie des Sciences* 2/312: 1661–1666.
Philby H.
1933. Rub al' Khali: An Account of Exploration in the Great South Desert of Arabia Under the Auspices and Patronage of His Majesty 'Abdul 'Aziz ibn Saud, King of the Hejaz and Nejd and its Dependencies. *Geographical Journal* 81: 1–21.
Preusser F., Radies D. & Matter A.
2002. A 160,000 year record of dune development and atmospheric circulation in Southern Arabia. *Science* 296: 2018–2020.
Rampino M. & Ambrose S.
2000. Volcanic winter in the Garden of Eden: The Toba supereruption and the late Pleistocene human population crash. *Geological Society of America, special paper* 345: 71–82.
Regueiro M., Cadenas A.M., Gayden T., Underhill P.A. & Herrera R.J.
2006. Iran: Tricontinental Nexus for Y-Chromosome Driven Migration. *Human Heredity* 61: 132–143.
Reichart G.J., Lourens L.J. & Zachariasse W.J.
1997. Temporal variability in the northern Arabian Sea Oxygen Minimum Zone (OMZ) during the last 225,000. *Paleooceanography* 13: 607–621.
Rose J.I.
2006. *Among Arabian Sands: defining the Palaeolithic of southern Arabia.* PhD dissertation, Southern Methodist University, Dallas [Unpublished].
2007. The Arabian Corridor Migration Model: archaeological evidence for hominin dispersals into Oman during the Middle and Upper Pleistocene. *Proceedings of the Seminar for Arabian Studies* 37: 219–237.
Sanford W.
2006. *Thoughts on Eden, the Flood, and the Persian Gulf.* Paper presented at the Annual Meeting of the American Geological Society, Toronto, 2005.
Sanlaville P.
1992. Changements Climatiques dans la Péninsule Arabique Durant le Pléistocène Supérieur et l'Holocène. *Paléorient* 18: 5–25.

Sarnthein M.
1972. Sediments and History of the Postglacial Transgression in the Persian Gulf and Northwestern Gulf of Oman. *Marine Geology* 12: 245–266.

Sayce J.J., King L.W., Maunsell F.R. & Willcocks W.
1912. The Garden of Eden and Its Restoration: Discussion. *The Geographical Journal* 40/2: 145–148.

Schultz E. & Whitney J.W.
1986. Upper Pleistocene and Holocene lakes in the An Nafud, Saudi Arabia. *Hydrobiologia* 143: 175–190.

Schyfsma E.
1978. Climate. Pages 31–44 in S.S. al-Sayari & J.G. Zötl (eds), *Quaternary Period in Saudi Arabia. i. Sedimentological, Hydrogeological, Hydrochemical, Geomorphological, and Climatological Investigations in Central and Eastern Saudi Arabia*. Vienna: Springer-Verlag.

Seibold E. & Vollbrecht K.
1969. Die Bodengestalt des Persischen Golfs. Pages 31–56 in E. Seibold & H. Closs (eds), *Meteor Forschungsergebnisse: Herausgegeben von der Deutschen Forschungsgesellschaft*. Berlin: Gebrüder Borntraeger.

Shepard E.M. & Herrera R.J.
2006. Genetic encapsulation among Near Eastern populations. *Journal of Human Genetics* 51: 467–476.

Siddall M., Rohling E.J., Almogi-Labin A., Hemleben Ch., Meischner D., Schmelzer I., & Smeed D.A.
2003. Sea level fluctuations during the last glacial cycle. *Nature* 423: 853-858.

Stokes S. & Bray H.
2005. Late Pleistocene eolian history of the Liwa region, Arabian Peninsula. *Geological Society of America Bulletin* 117/11–12: 1466–1480.

Stringer C.B.
2000. Palaeoanthropology: coasting out of Africa. *Nature* 405: 24–26.

Teller J.T., Glennie K.W., Lancaster N. & Singhvi A.K.
2000. Calcareous dunes of the United Arab Emirates and Noah's Flood: the postglacial reflooding of the Persian (Arabian) Gulf. *Quaternary International* 68–71: 297–308.

Uchupi E., Swift S.A. & Ross D.A.
1999. Late Quaternary Stratigraphy, Paleoclimate and neotectonism of the Persian (Arabian) Gulf region. *Marine Geology* 160: 1–23.

White K., Goudie A.S., Parker A.G. & al-Farraj A.
2001. Mapping the geochemistry of the northern Rub' al-Khali using multispectral remote sensing techniques. *Earth Surface Processes and Landforms* 26: 735–748.

Wildman D.E.
2000. *Mammalian Zoogeography of the Arabian Peninsula and Horn of Africa with a Focus on the Cladistic Phylogeography of Hamadryas Baboons*. PhD dissertation, New York University, New York. [Unpublished].

Wildman D.E., Bergman T.J., al-Aghbari A., Sterner K.N., Newman T.K., Phillips-Conroy J.E., Jolly C.J. & Disotell T.R.
2004. Mitochondrial DNA evidence for the origin of Hamadryas Baboons. *Molecular Phylogenetics and Evolution* 32: 287–296.

Wilkinson T.J.
1997. Holocene Environments of the High Plateau, Yemen. Recent Geoarchaeological Investigations. *Geoarchaeology* 12/8: 833–864.

Williams A.H. & Walkden G.M.
2002. Late Quaternary highstand deposits of the southern Arabian Gulf: a record of sea-level and climate change. Pages 371–386 in P.D. Clift, D. Kroon, C. Gaedicke & J. Craig (eds), *The Tectonic and Climatic Evolution of the Arabian Sea Region*. (Special Publications, 195). London: Geological Society.

Wood W.W. & Imes J.L.
1995. How wet is wet? Precipitation constraints on late quaternary climate in the southern Arabian Peninsula. *Journal of Hydrology* 164: 263–268.
Wood W.W., Rizk Z.S. & Alsharhan A.S.
2003. Timing of recharge, and the origin, evolution, and distribution of solutes in a hyperarid aquifer system. Pages 295–312 in A.S. Alsharhan & W.W. Wood (eds), *Water Resources Perspectives: Evaluation, Management and Policy*. Amsterdam: Elsevier.
Yotova V., Lefebvre J-F., Kohany O., Jurka J., Michalski R., Modiano D., Utermann G., Williams S.M. & Labuda D.
2007. Tracing genetic history of modern humans using X-chromosome lineages. *Human Genetics* 122/5: 13.
Zonneveld K., Ganssen G., Troelstra S., Versteegh G. & Visscher H.
1997. Mechanisms Forcing Abrupt Fluctuations of the Indian Ocean Summer Monsoon During the Last Deglaciation. *Quaternary Science Review* 16: 187–198.

Authors' addresses
A.G. Parker, Human Origins and Palaeo-Environments (HOPE) Research Group, Department of Anthropology and Geography, Oxford Brookes University, Oxford OX3 0BP, UK.
e-mail agparker@brookes.ac.uk

J.I. Rose, Human Origins and Palaeo-Environments (HOPE) Research Group, Department of Anthropology and Geography, Oxford Brookes University, Oxford OX3 0BP, UK.
e-mail jrose@brookes.ac.uk

Proceedings of the Seminar for Arabian Studies 38 (2008): 43–54

Investigating Upper Pleistocene stone tools from Sharjah, UAE: Interim report

JULIE SCOTT-JACKSON, WILLIAM SCOTT-JACKSON, JEFFREY ROSE & SABAH JASIM

Summary

Initial investigations during 2006 and 2007 in Sharjah emirate (United Arab Emirates), resulted in the new discovery of Middle and Upper Palaeolithic of Arabia stone-tool manufacturing sites on a high-level limestone ridge flanking the west of the Hajar mountains in an area which correlates to a proposed "southern" route out of Africa. Although stray finds of stone tools in the Emirates have been tentatively defined as pre-Holocene, this was the first time that well-delineated and essentially *in situ* Palaeolithic sites had been found, represented by prolific surface scatters.

The clearest indicator of a Middle Palaeolithic attribution is the presence of Levallois flakes and Levallois cores. Given the uncertainty of characteristics of Stone Age industries in Arabia, a very conservative classificatory scheme was employed to determine this Levallois category. Based on the distribution of unifacial, bifacial, and heavy-duty tools, it is clear there are both Middle and Upper Palaeolithic elements represented in the various assemblages. The combined attributes of the Sharjah lithic assemblages indicate material manufactured over the course of the Middle (*c.* 250–50 ka BP) and Upper (*c.* 50–10 ka BP) Palaeolithic periods.

Keywords: Middle Palaeolithic, Upper Palaeolithic, UAE, southern route, Arabian Peninsula.

Introduction

The discovery of three Palaeolithic of Arabia (Upper Pleistocene) stone-tool manufacturing sites in 2006 on a high-level limestone ridge flanking the western anticlines of the Hajar mountains in the east of Sharjah emirate (UAE), followed a desk-based assessment of the general area and discussions with others (see Scott-Jackson, Scott-Jackson & Jasim 2007; http://users.ox.ac.uk/~padmac /). As the limestone areas of the UAE are karstic environments, a desk-based assessment procedure was used that had proved successful in the past as an initial method of investigation in other karstic environments having associated chert/flint inclusions. Karstic environments which are characterized by a set of landforms resulting largely from the action of chemical weathering processes have the potential to yield *in situ* Palaeolithic sites which may be retained in fissures and depressions in the limestone that have formed by the process of dissolution. We are always mindful however, that although this predictive analysis is focused on limestone ridges with chert outcrops (ridges such as these extend throughout the UAE and south into Oman), other high-level areas with different knappable materials may have also been utilized by Palaeolithic people.

The Arabian Gulf Palaeolithic "problem"

A Palaeolithic presence in the Arabian Gulf region has been the subject of acceptance, rejection, and dispute since the 1950s. The pioneering Danish workers in Qatar during the 1950s and 1960s believed that the Arabian Peninsula had been inhabited for some 55,000 years (Kapel 1967). This view was strengthened with the publication of the *Atlas of the Stone Age Cultures of Qatar* (*ibid.*). In this the prehistorian Holger Kapel classified a large number of stone tools from various sites into four groups, namely A, B, C, and D. Group A which he considered to be the earliest included massive primitive-looking hand axes, whereas Group D included finely-made tanged arrowheads — this happy state of Palaeolithic chronology lasted until 1976.

Then, from 1976 to 1978, a French team conducted a number of excavations at the prolific stone-tool hilltop site of Al Khor, on the east coast of Qatar (a site which had previously been investigated by Kapel and assigned to type D). Finds dated by C^{14} included a hearth at 6290 ± 100 BP and two shells, one at 6560 ± 120BP and the

Figure 1. *Site ESF06A and the surrounding area.*

other at 6240 ± 100BP. It is also recorded that in an area covered in flint tools and flakes, an excavation revealed three clearly defined levels of occupation. It is at this point that the Arabian Palaeolithic "problem" begins, as a reassessment of Kapel's Group A, B, C, and D classification was made by the French team. The French concluded that, as "Group A" and "Group C" were found together in the same layer, together with a fragment of Mesopotamian Ubaid pottery, the tool-making industry of "Group A" could not be earlier than the other groups and was therefore not Palaeolithic. The French team's re-evaluation of the Qatar type A as Neolithic (Inizan 1980), which Kapel (1967) had previously tentatively assigned to the Palaeolithic, seems to have been interpreted as demonstrating a general absence of Palaeolithic in the Gulf. Consequently, the resulting assumption that any lithics from the area would almost certainly be of a later date, severely limited Palaeolithic research in the region for two decades. For example, prolific surface sites in Oman, first noted by Pullar (1974), were assigned to the Holocene period until recent analysis by Rose (2006) suggested a much earlier date for some Omani finds.

Fieldwork during 2006 in the Fili area of Sharjah, UAE

Against the background of general confusion regarding the Arabian Palaeolithic but inspired by the hypothesis of a "southern" migration route of hunter-gatherers out of Africa to the Far East during the Middle Palaeolithic (see e.g. Petraglia & Alsharekh 2003; Forster & Matsumura 2005), Dr Julie Scott-Jackson and Dr William Scott-Jackson conducted field investigations in the Fili area of Sharjah (UAE) during March 2006.

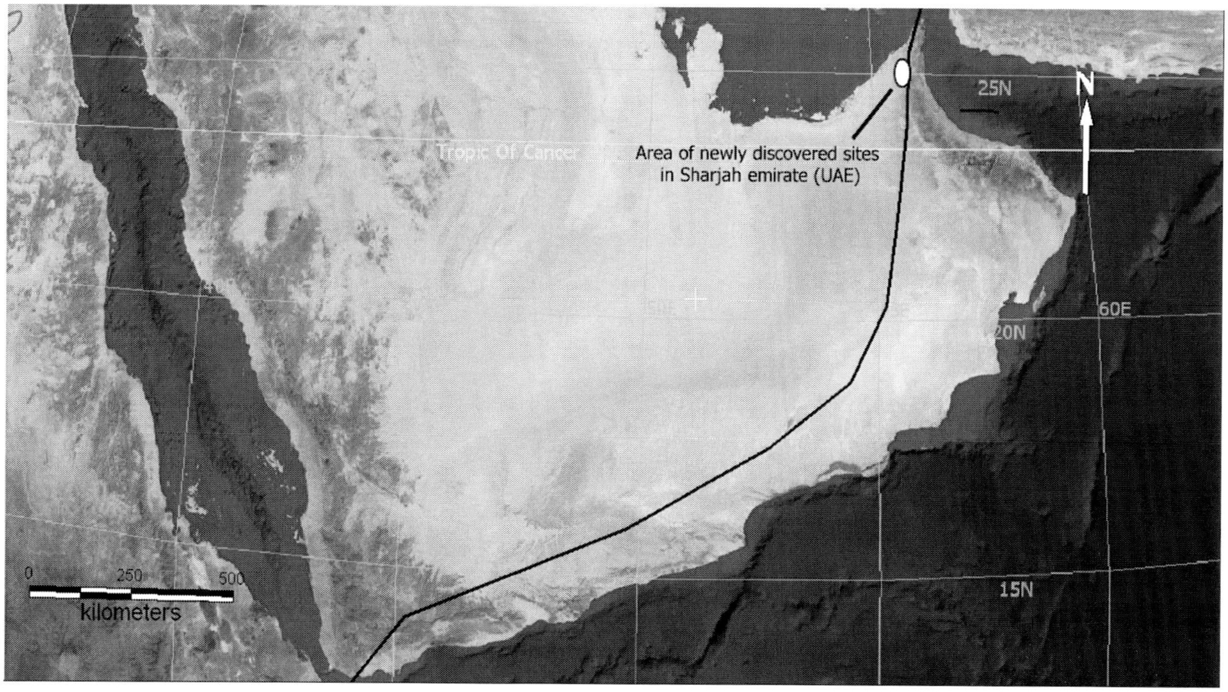

Figure 2. *A topographic map showing the relationship between the locations of newly discovered Upper Pleistocene manufacturing sites in Sharjah emirate, UAE and the proposed southern route out of Africa. (After Forster & Matsumura 2005).*

On a limestone ridge with outcroppings of red chert they discovered three high-level Palaeolithic sites (ESF06A, B, and C).

Sites ESF06A, B, and C

The prolific stone-tool manufacturing site at ESF06A (Fig. 1) is on the highest part of the ridge (on top of the hill) at *c.* 279 m above mean sea level (AMSL). Although the ridge has been subject to a certain amount of slope erosion, attested by extensive lithic scatters on the slope, this site is essentially *in situ.* ESF06B at *c.* 263 m AMSL and ESF06C at *c.* 264 m AMSL are discrete lithic scatters on lower terraces to the east of ESF06A. All three lithic assemblages are made from red chert. The chert outcrops clearly provided a readily available source of good knappable raw material for Palaeolithic people. High up on the hilltop they would be ideally positioned to monitor the movements of animals (and perhaps other hunters) in the wadis below, whilst making their stone tools. Similar topographic locations of Middle Palaeolithic sites have been recorded for other areas of the Arabian Peninsula (e.g. Amirkhanov 1994; Smith 1977; Rose 2004).

The importance of the Fili sites (ESF06A, B, and C) is twofold. Firstly, they represent a Middle Palaeolithic of Arabia (Upper Pleistocene) presence in the UAE and secondly, they are closely aligned to the proposed "southern" migration route of hunter-gatherers out of Africa to the Far East during the Middle Palaeolithic (Fig. 2), a hypothesis suggested by several authors (e.g. Petraglia & Alsharekh 2003; Forster & Matsumura 2005). It is also important to note that, as the combined attributes of the various Sharjah lithic assemblages indicate material manufactured over the course of the Middle (*c.* 250–50 ka BP) and Upper (*c.* 50–10 ka BP) Palaeolithic periods (see Chronology below), the sites may also represent evidence of other patterns of migration, including that of Palaeolithic people coming back into the Arabian Peninsula, from all points east.

To date, the only recorded finds by others in the general area of Fili are those by Stephen Green and Gary Feulner who in 1990 found a lithic scatter made from chert in a derived context on low rounded hills to the north of Fili, an area approximately 2 km from the ESF06 sites described here. By contrast, on the other side of the Al Madam Plain, approximately 18 km west from the

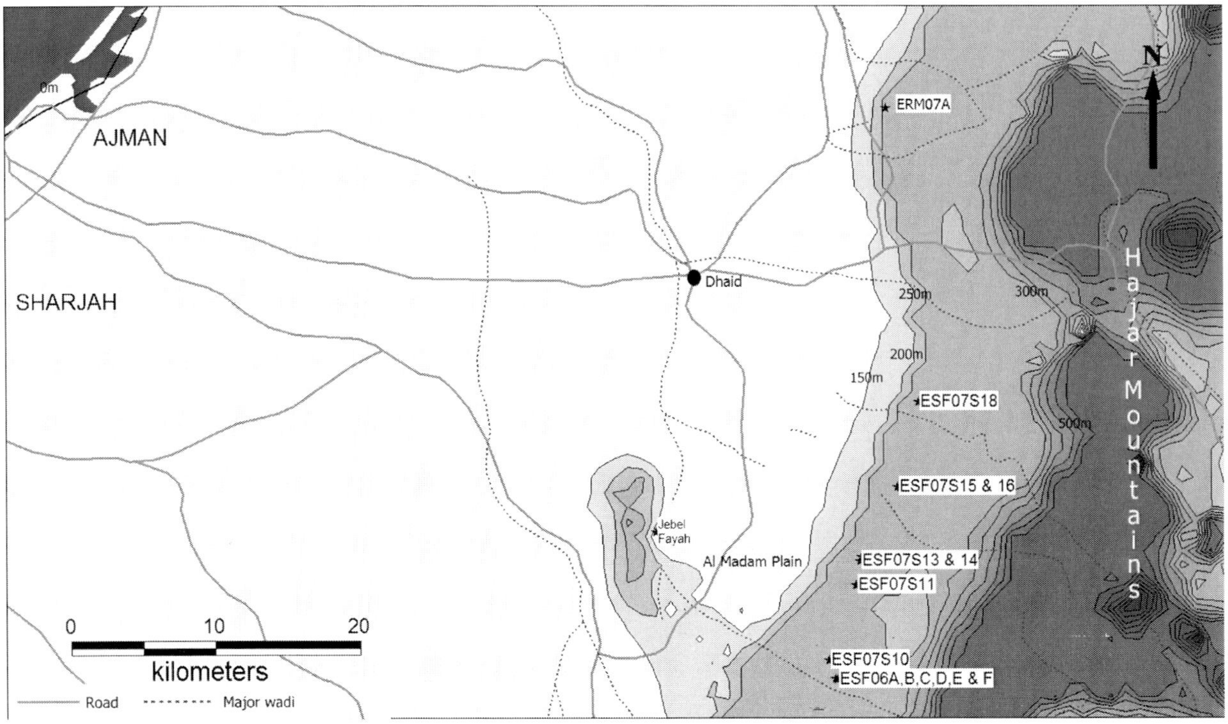

FIGURE 3. *Comparable topographic locations of the newly discovered sites in Sharjah and Ras Al-Khaimah emirates (UAE).*

ESF06 sites at Fili, Prof. Hans-Peter Uerpmann and his team have been excavating a multi-period rock shelter at Jebel Faya (Uerpmann *et al.* 2007).

Fieldwork 2007 — aims and methodology

Following the 2006 discovery of ESF06A, B, and C, a decision was taken in 2007 to extend the desk-based assessment northwards but still within the vicinity of the western foothills of the Hajar mountains and the limestone ridges with associated seams of red chert, and also to investigate specific areas near the ESF06 sites, with the hope that if more Palaeolithic high-level sites were found, we could then begin to construct a distribution pattern. The next stage of the investigations would require geological, sedimentological, pedological, and geomorphological investigations of these high-level sites and an analysis of the associated lithics. Then, by combining the results of this research with that of data derived from other investigations (e.g. low-level excavated Palaeolithic sites) a framework could be created that would allow us to begin to build a picture of Palaeolithic peoples' use of the landscape as whole.

As the proposed 2007 area of investigation was extensive, the team led by Dr Julie Scott-Jackson and Dr William Scott-Jackson drew on the expertise of Gary Feulner and other members of the Dubai Natural History Group to carry out the initial geological field surveys. Specific sedimentological advice was provided by Dr Adrian Parker and Dr Helen Walkington and contributory artefact analysis by Dr Sarah Milliken.

Results

The 2007 field investigations resulted in the following Palaeolithic discoveries (see Figs 3–4): Sites ESF06D; ESF07F; ES07S14. Eroded site: ES07S15. Lithic scatters: ESF07E; ES07S10; ES07S11; ES07S13; ES07S16; ES07S18 and ERM07A, all of which are briefly described below (sites ESF06A and ESF06D provide geographical reference points).

ESF06D

The ESF06D site in the Fili area of Sharjah (identified 2006 — investigated 2007) is *c.* 276 m AMSL and on

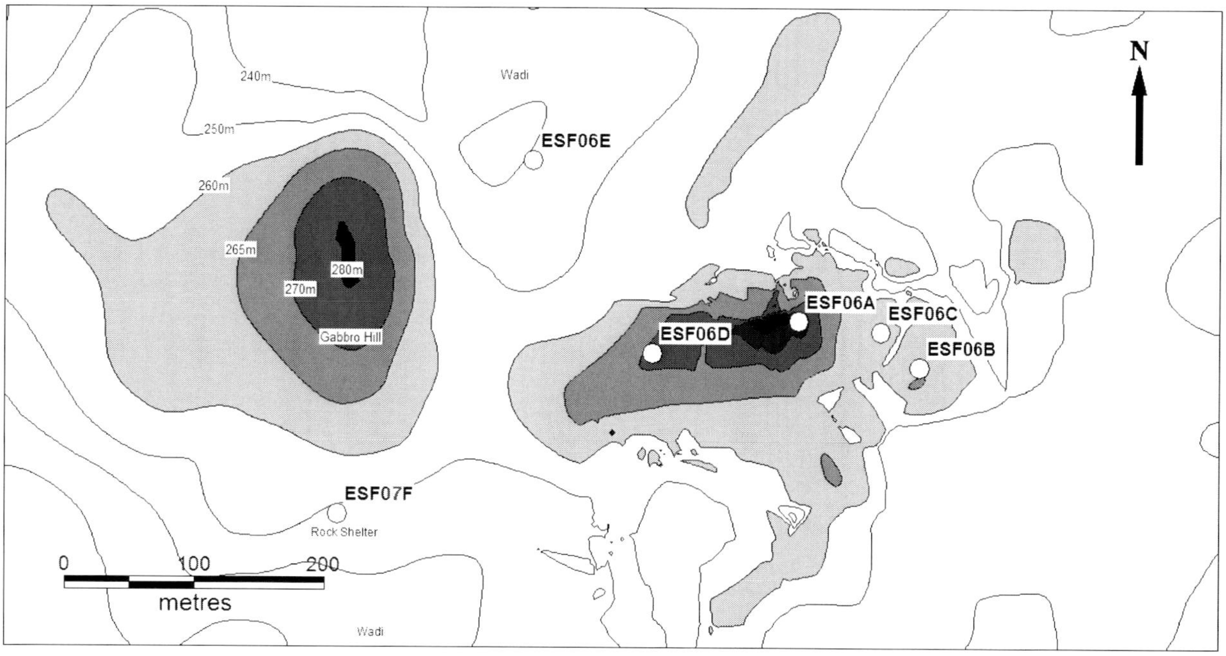

FIGURE 4. *Sites in the locale of ESF06A and ESF06D.*

a prominent hilltop that has steep sides. It is situated on the same ridge as ESF06A (at *c.* 260 m AMSL) but approximately 100 m to the west of this site and separated from ESF06A by a low eroded section of the ridge. For Palaeolithic people it was an ideal location to make stone tools from the readily available red chert and to observe the movements of animals, as there are long views (to a distance of *c.* 10 km) across the Al Madam plain to the west, the foothills of the Hajar mountains in the east, and into the wadis below.

The ESF06D site *per se* covers an area of *c.* 8 m x 5 m, which is composed of large red chert boulders that outcrop from a sandy silt deposit. Numerous lithics made from red chert litter the surface of this high-level site and on the slopes directly below. At some time in the past, the western edge of the site has been disturbed. Stones and lithics have been pushed away from an area of *c.* 2 m in diameter exposing a smooth, sandy silty surface. Also, lying on a rock next to this area was a single, very sharp small flint flake. This flake contrasts with the red chert Palaeolithic assemblage in that it is made from what appears to be black flint (the source of which is yet to be found) and lacks both patination and weathering. The typology and condition of the flake is suggestive of a more recent date of manufacture but how and why it came to be on this site cannot be answered.

ESF07E

A distinctive glossy dark red-brown lithic scatter designated ESF07E was observed on a low wadi terrace *c.* 249 m AMSL. In this area the wadi is *c.* 1 km wide with a narrow incised channel winding through it. The lithics were in a discrete concentration on the south-east side of the channel. This wadi terrace site is approximately 267 m to the north-west of the high-level sites ESF06A and ESF06D.

ESF07F

Site ESF07F (Fig. 5) is situated on a rocky outcrop at *c.* 252 m AMSL above a small cave. The site is so positioned to overlook a large wadi immediately to the south and smaller wadis to the east and west. The assemblage from this site is characterized by blades and blade cores made of red chert. Chert outcrops in the immediate vicinity show possible signs of large flakes being removed for the manufacture of stone tools. The site of ESF07F is *c.* 300 m to the south-east of ESF06A and ESF06D and on the lower slopes of the large rounded foothill which run north–south (orthogonal to the ESF06A and ESF06D ridge). To the north, the hill rises to *c.* 279 m AMSL and is covered with a black gabbro boulder train. Amongst the boulders, occasional chert lithics were observed, but no

FIGURE 5. *The ESF07F site area and a small cave.*

sign of chert raw material. This scatter is *c.* 200 m to the north of the main site.

ES07S10

Lithic scatters made of chert (ES07S10) were found in a derived context at various locations on rounded hills (height range 230–250 m AMSL) north of Fili. The 2007 investigation encompassed an area previously explored in 1990 by Stephen Green and Gary Feulner, who also found chert lithics in a derived context on low rounded hills. This area, north of Fili, is *c.* 2 km north-west of ESF06A and ESF06D.

ES07S11

Lithic scatters made of chert (ES07S11) were found at *c.* 252 m AMSL on a low rounded hill; these lithics are on heavily eroded slopes and not *in situ.* ES0711 is approximately 8 km north of ESF06A and ESF06D.

ES07S13

An extensive lithic scatter made of chert (ES07S13) was found at a height of *c.* 240 m AMSL on a low rounded hill; these lithics are on heavily eroded slopes and not *in situ.* ES07S13 is approximately 2 km north-east of ES0711.

ES07S14

The prolific site of ES07S14, which appears to be an *in situ* manufacturing site, is centred on a small plateau on the top of a limestone ridge at *c.* 238 m AMSL. Just below the site there is an outcrop of good quality chert. The lithics observed here were mainly large flakes made from chert; there was also a small gabbro boulder (*c.* 25 cm

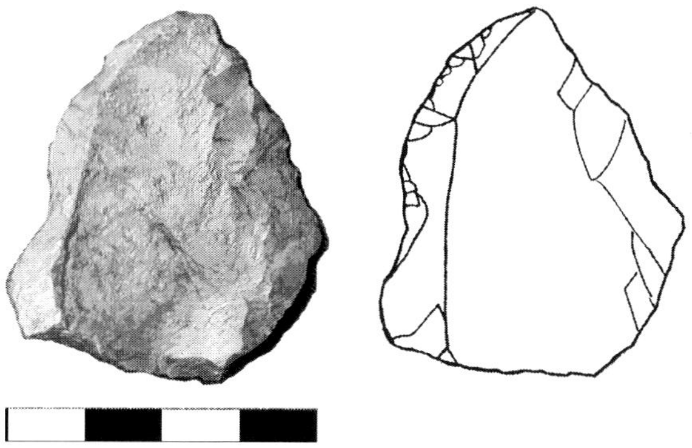

Figure 6. *A Levallois flake from site ESF06C.*

in diameter) that exhibited wear consistent with use as a hammer stone. There is no source of gabbro on the hill or in the immediate vicinity. Slope erosion has resulted in extensive lithic scatters on the slopes and on the track at the base of the hill. This site has similarities to ESF06A and ESF06D both of which are *c.* 9.2 km south–south-west. ES07S14 is *c.* 370 m to the north of ES07S13.

ES07S15

The site of ES07S15 was once at a height of at least 256 m AMSL. The heavily eroded hilltop is now a narrow ridge (*c.* 2 m maximum) made up of chert boulders with very little deposit. No lithics were seen on the ridge but the slopes directly below the ridge are covered with an enormous number of chert lithics that are clearly derived directly from the ridge above. The site overlooks a major wadi to the east; also there are long views to the south and east. ES07S15 is *c.* 14 km north of ESF06A and ESF06D.

ES07S16

A chert lithic scatter (ES07S16) was found at a height of *c.* 242 m AMSL on a low rounded hill adjacent to the ES07S15 hill and south of the ES07S15 site. ES07S16 is *c.* 14 km north of ESF06A and ESF06D.

ES07S18

A discrete chert lithic scatter (ES07S18) was found at a height of *c.* 227 m AMSL on a rounded hill. The site is just south of the Sharjah/Fujairah border and *c.* 20 km north–north-east of ESF06A and ESF06D.

ERM07A

A discrete chert lithic assemblage (ERM07A) was found at a height of *c.* 213 m AMSL on a rounded hill with red chert outcrops in the south of Ras al-Khaimah, UAE (in an area drawn to our attention by Prof. A. Goudie and Dr A. Parker (personal communication). Chert lithics also litter the heavily eroded sides of this isolated hill. Destruction of the site has been exacerbated by military activity. This site, like those in Sharjah, is situated on the western foothills of the Hajar mountains. To the west there are long views over the desert and to the south across a gravel plain. This site is directly north of site ES07S18 and *c.* 40 km north–north-east of ESF06A and ESF06D.

Chronology

The number and size of Palaeolithic lithic assemblages observed at the various sites in Sharjah during our 2006 and 2007 field investigations exceeded all our expectations. Therefore, the most characteristic tools and debitage, now briefly described, represent a very small percentage indeed of the total of Palaeolithic artefacts examined in these assemblages.

The analyzed assemblage is comprised of 441 pieces of chipped stone material, manufactured on a reddish-brown chert of variable quality. The artefacts have a dark reddish-brown patina (Munsell colour 2.5 yr 3/4) or strong brown patina (Munsell 7.5 yr 5/6). When newly fractured, the chert is a light reddish-yellow colour (Munsell 7.5 yr 7/6). One testament to the antiquity of these artefacts is the heavy weathering observed on most of the pieces within the assemblage. The edges and arêtes have been rounded by aeolian abrasion and a thick reddish-brown patina has accumulated on most surfaces.

While patina is a poor indicator of age, in this case it is useful to demonstrate the antiquity of the assemblage relative to a handful of other collected lithics that have only minimal to moderate patina.

The clearest indicator of a Middle Palaeolithic attribution is the presence of twenty-five (9 %) Levallois flakes and seventeen (33 %) Levallois cores (Fig. 6). Given the uncertainty of characteristics of Stone Age industries in Arabia, a very conservative classificatory scheme was employed to determine this Levallois category. Pieces labelled Levallois exhibited a set of characteristics including: faceted striking platforms, radial, bidirectional, or convergent dorsal scar patterns, and flat longitudinal cross sections. Of particular interest in this analysis is the presence/absence of faceted striking platforms, which

Figure 7. *Retouched flakes (refitting) from site ESF06D.*

is a characteristic that until now has been practically unknown among Arabian lithic assemblages. Among the 288 unifacial pieces in this assemblage, fifty-eight (20 %) exhibited faceted platforms, while an additional seventeen (6 %) were dihedral.

There is a range of specific techniques (see Usik 2003) among the Levallois pieces recorded in this assemblage. Six of the cores are classified as centripetal Levallois with radial preparation to establish convexity along the working surface, four show short flake removals along a supplementary distal platform, two demonstrate convexity maintenance from a supplementary lateral platform, and five exhibit a unipolar-convergent technique to produce triangular-shaped Levallois points.

Given this range of techniques, many of the assemblages are probably palimpsests and may represent a series of repeated occupations over the course of the late Middle and Upper Pleistocene periods.

The distribution of tool types corroborates this claim, as most of which can be considered typical of the European Middle Palaeolithic. A total of 180 tools were recorded, which can be generally categorized into three different groups: unifacial tools, bifacial tools, and heavy-duty tools.

Unifacial tools include sidescrapers (twenty-five), retouched flakes/blades (twenty) (Fig. 7), endscrapers (thirteen), perforators (nine), denticulates (eight), notches (six), truncations (six), retouched Levallois points (four), dejete scrapers (three), thumbnail scrapers (three), and a burin (one). Bifacial tools are comprised of foliates (eleven) (Fig. 8), miscellaneous fragments (eleven), backed bifaces (five), bifacial scrapers (three), and bifacial hand axes (two). Among the heavy-duty tool category there are backed knives (twenty-one), naturally backed knives (nineteen), chopping-tools (nine) (Fig. 9), and a tranchet (one).

Based on the distribution of these types, it is clear there are both Middle and Upper Palaeolithic elements represented in the various assemblages. One diagnostic indicator is the foliate category, a few of which are considered Khasfian Foliates (see Rose 2004) that have been found in archaeological deposits dating to MIS 3. The combined attributes of the various Sharjah and

Figure 8. *A bifacial foliate from site ESF06A.*

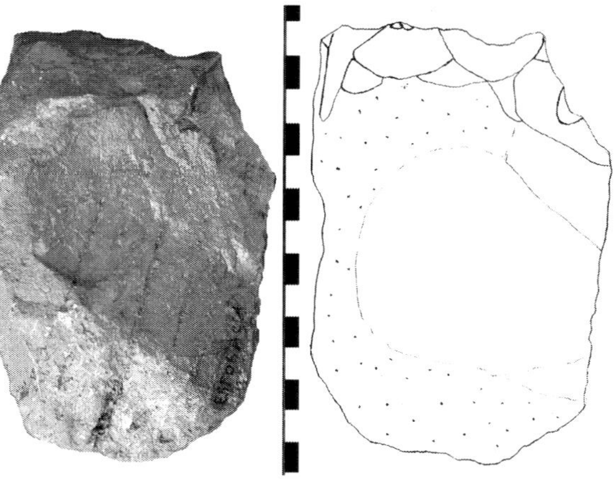

FIGURE 9. *A chopping tool from site ESF06A.*

Ras al-Khaimah lithic assemblages indicate material manufactured over the course of the Middle (*c.* 250–50 ka BP) and Upper (*c.* 50–10 ka BP) Palaeolithic periods.

Discussion

The discovery of Middle and Upper Palaeolithic artefacts in Sharjah and Ras al-Khaimah provides the foundations of a framework for Palaeolithic research in the UAE. Inevitably, the results of this research will regenerate many of the queries associated with a Palaeolithic presence in the Arabian Peninsula — but that is how it should be.

Clearly, high-level Palaeolithic sites in karstic environments provide important evidence of Palaeolithic occupation and land use in the UAE. However, their investigation presents many challenges especially from the perspective of traditional archaeological methodology. The deposits are often decalcified, resulting in the loss of organic environmental evidence, which in turn makes dating difficult but not impossible if methods such as Optically Stimulated Luminescence (OSL) are used. Also, although the deposits often appear unstratified, this may not be so. When analysing any desert landforms it is essential to remember that many of the features seen today may have been inherited from earlier humid climates. Site-specific investigations are therefore required to understand a particular site formation and the context in which the Palaeolithic artefacts were found. For example, particle-size analysis may be used to determine sedimentological and pedological processes; geophysical techniques to model sub-surface features; photogrammetry to model, in three dimensions, the orientations of individual lithics, the detailed topography of the site itself, and the interrelationship of sites in their wider context.

The integrity of Palaeolithic scatters on high-level sites is somewhat different to many of those found at low levels. For although these scatters may represent different occupations over long periods of time, they are not in a derived context. They are essentially *in situ*, i.e. it is clearly the place where Palaeolithic people made these stone tools.

The sites that still exist on the top of the highest parts of the limestone ridges are retained in deposits held in depressions and fissures. Features such as these are the product of simultaneous geomorphological processes (both chemical and mechanical) operating on the limestone over geological time. For example, dissolution of the underlying limestone; surface weathering often by the action of water; aeolian processes, which include erosion, transport, and deposition of materials by the wind.

Over time the Palaeolithic assemblages may become incorporated into the deposits and then, perhaps later, exposed once again by deflation. This is an erosional process whereby fine-grained material is removed from a site by wind and water leaving a lag deposit of the heavier material behind. Consequently, when this finer material has been removed, the stone tools originally contained in deposits from separate successive occupations can now be found together within the same assemblage. Previous work by Scott-Jackson (e.g. 2000) however, has demonstrated that in karstic environments, high-level lithic scatters have, in many instances, been indicative of underlying embedded *in situ* Lower and Middle Palaeolithic sites. The geomorphological processes operating in karstic regions work both for, and against, the survival of a Palaeolithic site. On the one hand, depressions, fissures, and caves are formed and deepened, so retaining sites. On the other hand, the destabilizing of the slopes by erosional processes results in the loss of material from the sides of the hills and ridges. Over time the highest areas of the hills and ridges change shape and are reduced in size, the consequence of which is often the loss of part or all of the *in situ* Palaeolithic sites.

Currently, the greatest threats to these high-level Palaeolithic sites are hunting and military activity in the form of digging fox-holes; the twenty-first-century demands for building materials and new housing; complacency to their value and place in the archaeology of the Palaeolithic of Arabia; and perhaps also climate change.

Acknowledgements

These investigations and research were carried out under the directions of His Highness Dr Shaikh Sultan Bin Mohammad Al Qasimi, Member of the Supreme Council and Ruler of Sharjah, Emirate, and under the patronage of the Culture and Education Department in Sharjah. We are greatly indebted to Dr Sabah Jasim, Director of Antiquities in Sharjah for his unfailing support. We would also like to thank Prof. Hans-Peter Uerpmann (University of Tübingen, Germany) and his team for sharing their extensive experience of the region's lithics and for inviting members of the PADMAC Unit (University of Oxford) to visit his excavations at Jebel Faya. The authors wish to acknowledge the most valuable contribution made to the 2007 field surveys by Gary Feulner, Angela Manthorpe, Stephen Manthorpe, and David Palmer (all of the Dubai Natural History Society). Also to Stephen Green (together with Gary Feulner) for sharing the results of their earlier field surveys. Helpful advice and practical assistance was provided by Eisa Abbas of the Sharjah Directorate of Antiquities, and this was much appreciated, as were site visits from Dr Adrian Parker, Dr Helen Walkington (Oxford Brookes University, UK), and the contribution to the artefact analysis by Dr Sarah Milliken of the Institute of Archaeology (University of Oxford). Thanks are also due to Prof. Andrew Goudie (University of Oxford) and Dr Adrian Parker for drawing our attention to the Ras al-Khaimah site, and to Dr Christian Velde of the Ras al-Khaimah Department of Antiquities and Museums for kind permission to investigate the area.

References

Amirkhanov H.
1994. Research on the Palaeolithic and Neolithic of Hadhramaut and Mahra. *Arabian Archaeology and Epigraphy* 5: 217–228.

Forster P. & Matsumura S.
2005. Did Early Humans Go North or South? *Science* 308: 965–966.

Inizan M.L.
1980. Premiers résultats des fouilles préhistoriques de la région de Khor. Pages 51–97 in J. Tixier (ed.), *Mission Archéologique Française à Qatar.* Doha: Dar al-Uloom.

Kapel H.
1967. *Atlas of the Stone Age Cultures of Qatar.* Aarhus: Aarhus University Press.

Petraglia M.D. & Alsharekh A.
2003. The Middle Palaeolithic of Arabia: Implications for modern human behaviour and dispersals. *Antiquity* 77/298: 671–684.

Pullar J.
1974. Harvard archaeological survey in Oman, 1973: flint sites in Oman. *Proceedings of the Seminar for Arabian Studies* 4: 33–48.

Rose J.I.
2004. The Question of Upper Pleistocene connections between East Africa and South Arabia. *Current Anthropology* 45/4: 551–555.
2006. *Among Arabian Sands: Defining the Palaeolithic of Southern Arabia.* PhD dissertation, Southern Methodist University. [Unpublished].
2007. The Arabian Corridor Migration Model: archaeological evidence for hominin dispersal into Oman during the Middle and Upper Pleistocene. *Proceedings of the Seminar for Arabian Studies* 37: 219–237.

Scott-Jackson J.E.
2000. *Lower and Middle Palaeolithic artefacts from deposits mapped as Clay-with-flints — a new synthesis with significant implications for the earliest occupation of Britain.* Oxford: Oxbow Books.

Scott-Jackson J.E., Scott-Jackson W.B. & Jasim S.A.
2007. Middle Palaeolithic — or what? New sites in Sharjah, UAE. *Proceedings of the Seminar for Arabian Studies* 37: 277–279.

Smith G.H.
1977. New prehistoric sites in Oman. *Journal of Oman Studies* 3: 71–81.
Uerpmann H-P., Uerpmann M., Kutterer J., Handel M., Jasim S.A. & Marks A.
2007. *The Stone Age Sequence of Jebel Faya in the Emirate of Sharjah (UAE).* Paper presented at the Seminar for Arabian Studies 2007. [Unpublished]
Usik V.
2003. The variants of Levallois method of Middle Palaeolithic industries of Ukraine. Pages 32–62 in L. Kulakovska (ed.), *The Middle Palaeolithic Variability on the Territory of Ukraine*. Kiev: Shliakh.

Authors' addresses

Dr Julie Scott-Jackson, Director, PADMAC Unit, University of Oxford, Institute of Archaeology, 36 Beaumont St, Oxford, OX1 2PG, UK.
e-mail juliescott-jackson@arch.ox.ac.uk

Dr William Scott-Jackson, PADMAC Unit, University of Oxford, Institute of Archaeology, 36 Beaumont St, Oxford, OX1 2PG, UK.
e-mail williamscott-jackson@arch.ox.ac.uk

Dr J.I. Rose, Human Origins and Palaeo-Environments (HOPE) Research Group, Department of Anthropology and Geography, Oxford Brookes University, Oxford OX3 0BP, UK.
e-mail jrose@brookes.ac.uk

Dr Sabah Jasim, Director, Department of Antiquities, PO Box 5119, Sharjah, UAE.
e-mail sjasim@archaeology.gov.ea

Proceedings of the Seminar for Arabian Studies 38 (2008): 55–64

Barakah: a Middle Palaeolithic site in Abu Dhabi Emirate

Ghanim Wahida, Walid Yasin al-Tikriti & Mark Beech

Summary

Recently collected lithic artefacts from Jebel Barakah, the well-known Late Miocene fossil locality situated in the Western Region of Abu Dhabi Emirate, provide clear evidence for a Middle Palaeolithic presence in the region. The artefacts come from three localities around Barakah: one lies to the west of the jebel, the other to the south and south-west, and the third to the east. The three cluster sites represent a single techno-typological industry. Most artefacts were collected from locality BRK1 (on the western side of the jebel), that lies between the sea cliffs and the first line of ridges, some 40 m from the sea, which may be the site described by McBrearty. The presence of a Levallois flake core, a Levallois point flake, two broken bifaces/hand-axes, and the centripetal radial or discoid form and the prepared Levallois technique of manufacturing flakes, place the Barakah assemblage in the Middle Stone Age. The total absence of blade implements further points to a Middle Palaeolithic industry. Previous reporting on the Barakah material had suggested several possible dates for the Barakah assemblage, ranging between Middle Pleistocene, Acheulian or Middle Stone Age, and mid- to Late Holocene. The Barakah material complements the recent discovery of Palaeolithic material elsewhere in the UAE and in Oman.

Keywords: Jebel Barakah, Middle Palaeolithic, lithics, Levallois, Acheulian, Abu Dhabi Emirate, United Arab Emirates

Introduction

Until recently, our knowledge of the Palaeolithic period in Arabia has been fairly limited. A number of Palaeolithic tools have been collected and reported early in the last century, such as a Lower Palaeolithic hand-axe from central Arabia (Cornwall 1946). In addition geological teams have reported a number of Acheulean implements from Arabia (Field 1971; Overstreet 1973). In the late 1970s, archaeologists began a five-year comprehensive programme to survey Saudi Arabia. A large number of archaeological sites from various periods were discovered throughout the country. Nearly 200 Acheulean sites of the Middle Pleistocene and even more sites of the Middle Palaeolithic were discovered in the central, western, and south-western Provinces (Parr *et al.* 1978; Zarins *et al.* 1980; Zarins, Murad & al-Yish 1981). Of special importance were three older sites, namely Shuwayhitiya in the north, another near Najran in the south end, and Tathlith in the south-west of Saudi Arabia. These sites belong typologically to an early part of the Pleistocene (Whalen & Pease 1992). Research into another possible Lower Palaeolithic site is currently under way in central Saudi Arabia (Petraglia & Alsharekh 2003; Alsharekh 2007).

The first *in situ*, datable Middle Acheulean site excavated in Arabia so far is that of Saffaqah near Ed-Dawadmi in central Saudi Arabia (Whalen *et al.* 1983; Whalen, Siraj-Ali & Davis 1984). Uranium-thorium dating has demonstrated that the site dates to more than 200,000 years BP (Whalen & Pease 1992).

Work on the Palaeolithic of the Arabian Gulf started in the early 1990s. A number of international expeditions began to discover Pleistocene sites in Abu Dhabi Emirate (McBrearty 1993; 1999) and in Sharjah in the United Arab Emirates (Uerpmann 2007; Scott-Jackson, Scott-Jackson & Jasim 2007), as well as in neighbouring Oman (Rose 2004; 2005). Five pre-Acheulean sites were also discovered in the Ḥaḍramawt mountains of southern Yemen (Whalen & Pease 1992). Genetic studies have recently been introduced to the study of Palaeolithic Arabia and evolutionary geneticists have begun to appreciate the major role that Arabia must have played in the origin of modern humans. New genetic evidence has highlighted the significance of the Arabian Peninsula as a corridor for early human migration to and from Africa (James & Petraglia 2005; Abu-Amero *et al.* 2007). The new Palaeolithic evidence now emerging from the Arabian Gulf promises to provide a wealth of data to explore questions surrounding Lower and Middle Palaeolithic

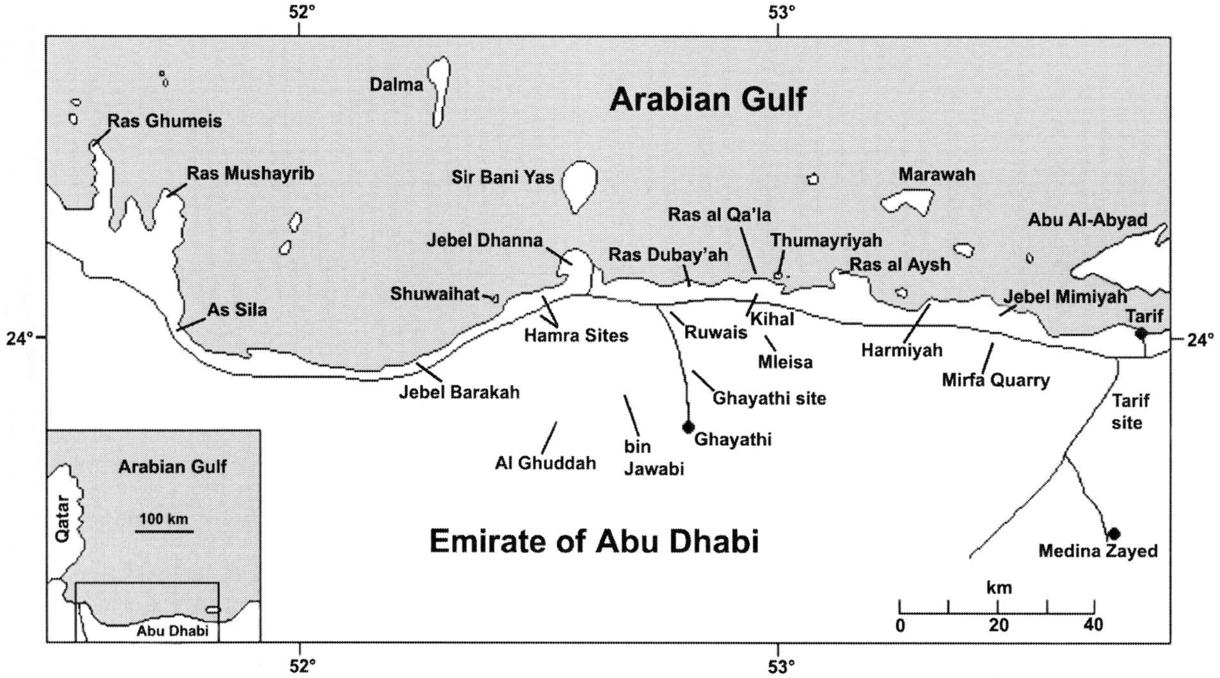

FIGURE 1. *The location of Jebel Barakah in the Western Region of Abu Dhabi Emirate (after Whybrow and Hill eds 1999).*

occupation on the Arabian Peninsula. It should be noted that a previous synthesis of Middle Palaeolithic sites in Arabia largely drew a blank for the Arabian Gulf region (Potts 1990; Petraglia & Alsharekh 2003).

Jebel Barakah

Jebel Barakah is located on the coast of Abu Dhabi Emirate, between Jebel Dhannah and the Qatar peninsula (Fig. 1). The coastline of Abu Dhabi is generally low and dominated by sabkha with occasional sand hills and low grass vegetation. Jebel Barakah at 62.6 m is the highest point along this stretch of coastline. It is an isolated outcrop composed of red sandstone (originally wind-blown sand) and thin bands of conglomerate (originally water-transported, wadi pebbles). The outcrop occupies the north-western part of a much wider plateau, and its oval peak overlooks the sea. The international highway (Abu Dhabi–Sila) cuts the southern part of the plateau, quite a distance from the jebel itself (Fig. 2). The jebel is the last elevated area as you head westwards prior to the Sabkha Matti.

Before the recent archaeological discoveries, Jebel Barakah was probably best known for its Late Miocene fossil remains (Whybrow & Hill 1999). Part of the sea cliff contains the type section for the Baynunah Formation, which covers the Shuwaihat Formation (Whybrow 1989; Whybrow & Hill 1999). At most outcrops of the Baynunah Formation, the sequence is capped by a thick layer of resistant tabular chert/flint (cryptocrystalline siliceous rocks produced by diagenetic solution). This provides the ever-lasting raw material for Abu Dhabi's earliest toolmakers.

As mentioned above, the lithic material from Jebel Barakah was first reported upon by McBrearty (1993; 1999). She noted that a large number of artefacts occurred on the level bluffs on the southeast side of the jebel (1999: 378). The artefacts lie directly on Baynunah Formation rocks; upslope they are overlain by a thin superficial layer of soft unconsolidated sediment derived from the exposures of the Baynunah Formation above. McBrearty also reported that the Barakah artefacts demonstrate a very consistent and formalized flaking method, being composed almost entirely of radial cores and the flakes derived from them. There was no trace of any blade element. All sixteen cores collected by McBrearty are radial or high-backed radial forms.

The aim of this paper is to introduce some new data collected from Jebel Barakah, which will typologically confirm its Middle Palaeolithic affinity.

Figure 2. *Jebel Barakah looking north. The view from the Abu Dhabi–Sila highway.*

Three localities around the jebel

The lithic material currently under study by Dr Ghanim Wahida was collected on several visits to the jebel by staff members of the former Department of Antiquities and Tourism in Al Ain, now the Abu Dhabi Authority for Culture and Heritage (ADACH).

The lithic material came from three localities around Jebel Barakah (Fig. 3). Locality 1, known by the site code BRK0001, lies on the north-west and western side of the jebel between the sea cliffs and the first line of ridges up the slope, a distance of about 300 m. Most of our material comes from this location. Artefacts were scattered on a thin layer of soft soil derived from the exposure of the Baynunah Formation outcrops. Much of the archaeological material along the cliffs would have been eroded away to the Arabian Gulf through substantial erosion processes over the millennia. McBrearty's description of her site does agree with the above description of Locality 1. Unfortunately, it contradicts with the co-ordinates provided in her report (1999), which plot the site location on the north-west side of Barakah, in proximity to Locality 3.

Locality 2, known by the site code BRK0002, is situated on the south and south-western side of the jebel. This site has produced a small number of artefacts.

Locality 3, known by the site code BRK0003, lies to the eastern side of the jebel.

A key point, however, is that the three cluster sites represent a single techno-typological industry. To all intents and purposes they appear to be all inter-related.

The lithic assemblage

It should be stressed here that the study of the Barakah assemblage is still in its preliminary stages and further analysis has been planned with more material to be added. Test pits will be considered if needed. This forthcoming analysis will include, among other details, a discussion of the economy and way of life indicated by the tools.

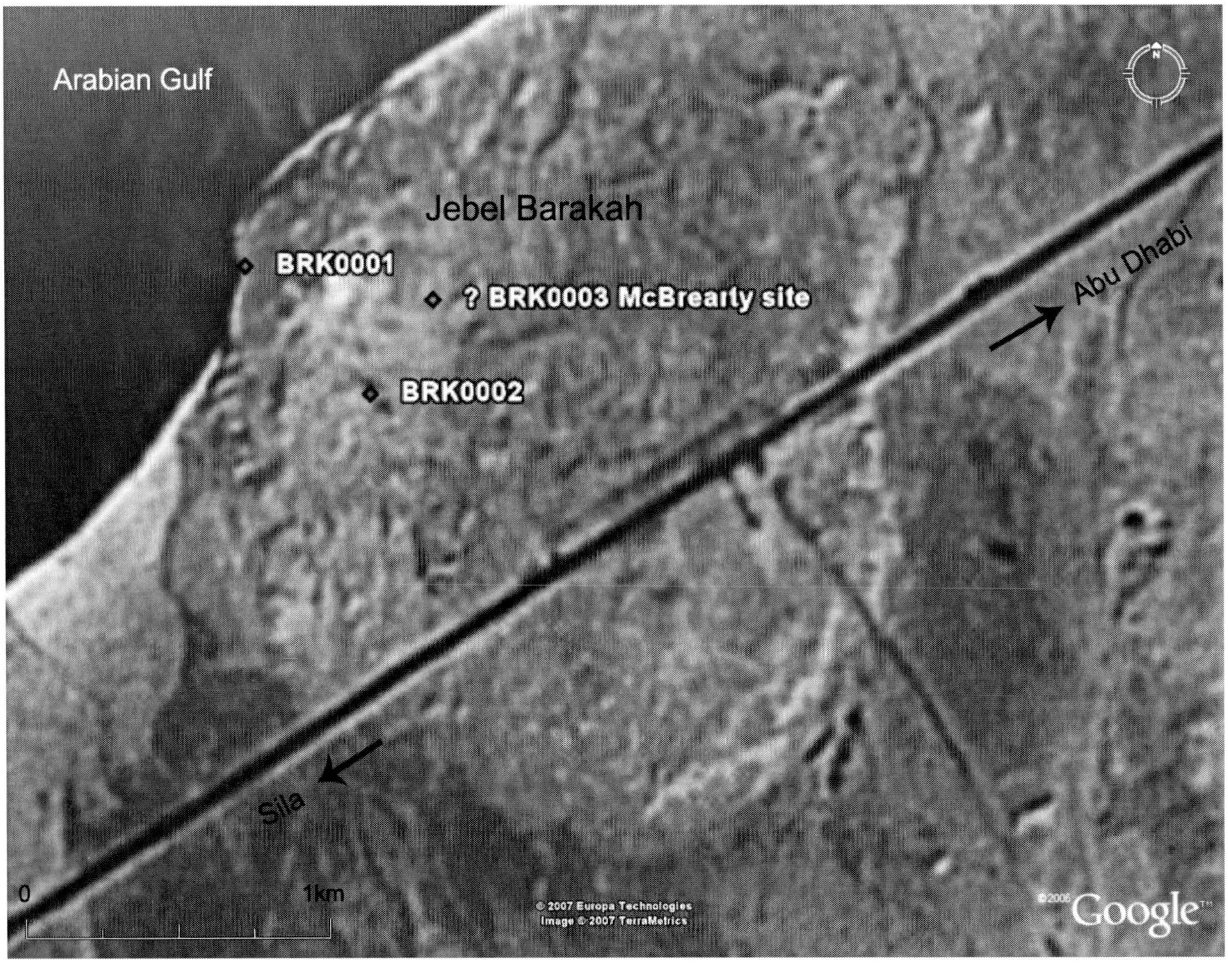

FIGURE 3. *The location of the lithic scatters at Jebel Barakah. Note the summit of the jebel (height = 62.6 m above sea level), which is the whitish-coloured spot visible immediately below the label BRK0001. (Source: Google Earth 2007).*

The Barakah artefacts were made of fairly good quality flint, some of it very good indeed, with a black to blue black patina. They were unlike those McBrearty found and more numerous, with several tool types which can provide more appropriate dating. Beyond the radial cores mentioned above, McBrearty also collected 218 objects of which only eight were artefacts. McBrearty suggested several dates for the Barakah assemblage, ranging between the Middle Pleistocene, Acheulean, Middle Stone Age, and mid- to late Holocene. The first three dates were based on the presence of radial and high-backed radial cores from which the flakes originated. The last date was probably based on the presence of two broken implements: one a bifacial tip, the other a fragment flake with unifacial trimming. McBrearty should be given credit for her achievement as the limited collection of tool types gave her no space for other conclusions to be drawn. Indeed, McBrearty offered in her article an excellent outline of the palaeo-environment of the Western Region of Abu Dhabi Emirate, including Barakah to which there is little for us to add (1999).

Technology

Two techniques of core reduction were available to the Barakah flint knappers. One is the centripetal radial, high radial, or the discoid form, and the convergence of some of the flakes into actual tools (Figs. 4 and 5). The other was the prepared core technique known as the Levallois. This

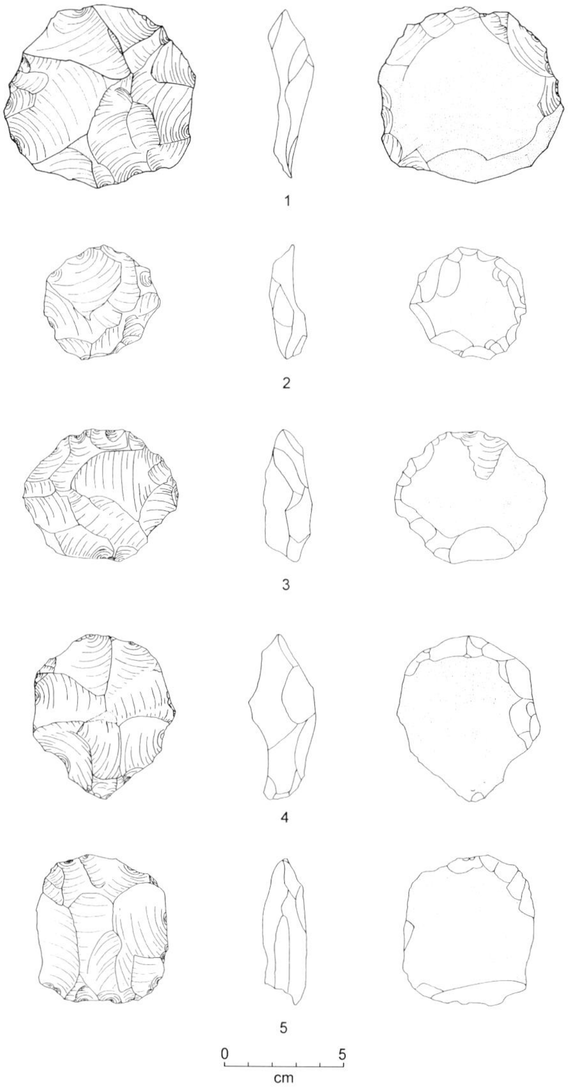

FIGURE 4. *Radial cores partially bifacial (1-3). Pointed radial core (4). Square-shaped partially bifacial core (5).*

technique, which requires the surface of the core to be specially prepared beforehand, allowing a predetermined flake size and shape to be detached, was evolved in the Levant during Middle Acheulean times (Copeland & Hours 1978) and is characteristic of many Mousterian industries in Africa, Europe, and the Near East. Of course, flint knappers of any period had to apply some form of preparation to the cores if reasonable-sized flakes were to be obtained. The Barakah flint knappers seem to have adopted a tendency towards a centripetal core manufacturing strategy, which was the technology during the transition from the Middle to Upper Pleistocene.

Typology

The lithic assemblage, randomly collected, numbered eighty-four objects with no debitage or debris; among these fifty-one are actual tools (Table 1) including cores, with thirty-three plain flakes. The assemblage has been divided into three categories: cores (11); tools including cores (47); and primary flakes (33). Among the cores category were one Levallois flake core, radial cores and semi-discoid cores, and one undecided. The tools category included some diagnostic elements of the Middle Palaeolithic assemblages, including two broken bifaces/hand-axes (Fig. 6) and one Levallois point flake (Fig. 7).

TOOL TYPE	NO.	%
Radial / discoid Core	11	21.57
Levallois flake Core	1	1.96
Levallois point Flake	1	1.96
Bifacial / hand-axe (broken)	2	3.92
Unifacial	3	5.88
Possible Core	1	1.96
Notch	16	31.37
Denticulate	1	1.96
Borer	2	3.92
Possible Chopper	2	3.92
False Burin	2	3.92
Retouched Implement	8	15.69
Slug-shaped Implement	1	1.96
Total	51	100

TABLE 1. *The number and percentage of tool types found at Barakah.*

Apart from the diagnostic implements, the majority of the tools category comprised the usual non-diagnostic types, including notches and denticulates (Fig. 8), retouched blanks, and borers.

Although these are non-diagnostic implements, they must have been important components within the Barakah assemblage. A number of microwear and refitting studies have indicated that similar tools had one or more functions in the daily life of hunter-fisher-gatherers (Keeley 1977; 1980; Cohen, Keely & van Noten 1979). These included woodworking, splitting bone for the extraction of marrow

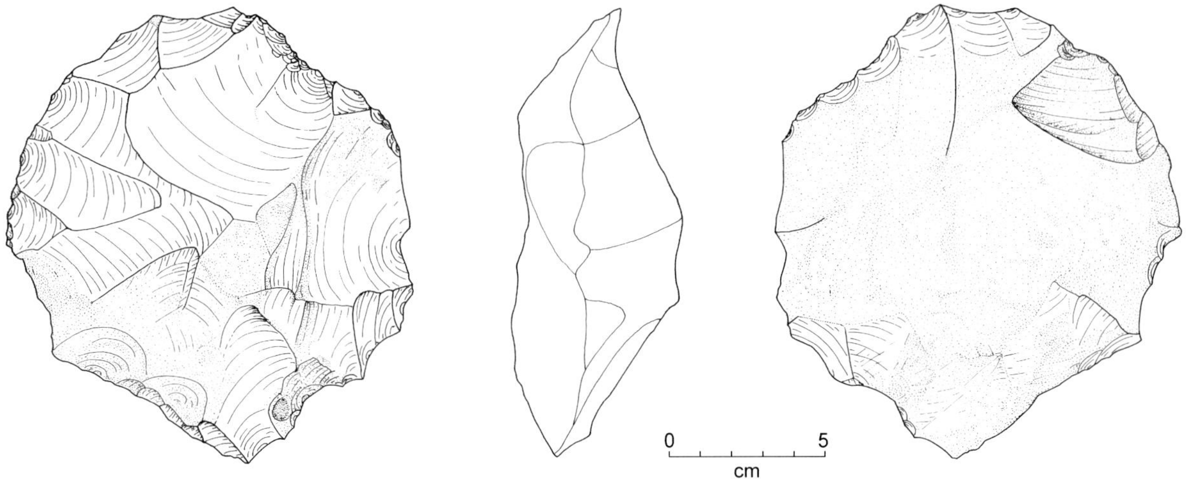

Figure 5. *Large discoid core.*

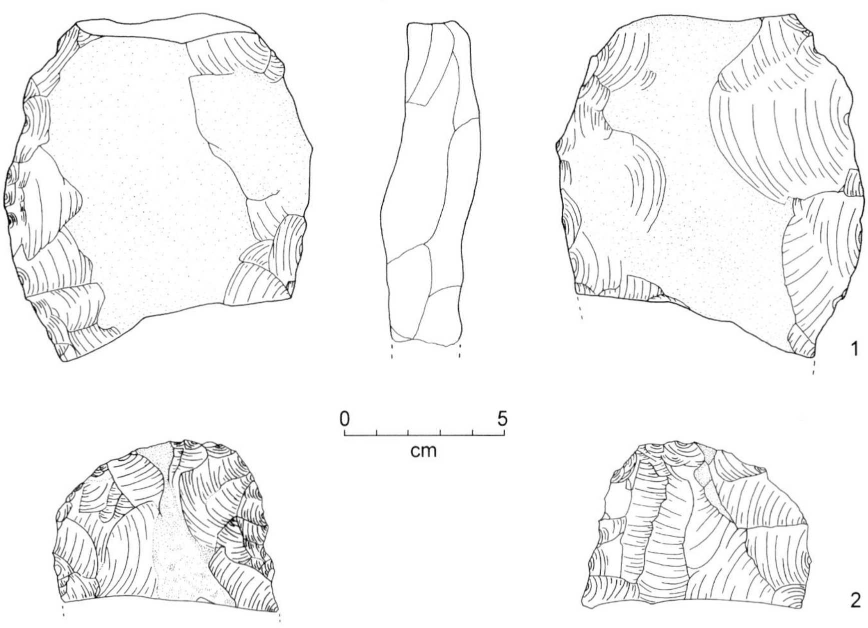

Figure 6. *Biface/handaxes (1-2).*

and fashioning bone tools, hide cutting and piercing, butchering of animals, and the preparation of plant food. They also showed that discoid or radial cores were used for woodworking and for this reason they were classified as tools in Table 1.

The "primary flakes" category included specimens that lack any trace of deliberate working in the form of retouch, on either side of the blank. Among this category there are flakes with sharp edges or wide distal end suitable for cutting or scraping, and others that might be termed false burins. It should be noted here that the majority of the blanks in this and the tools categories were broken.

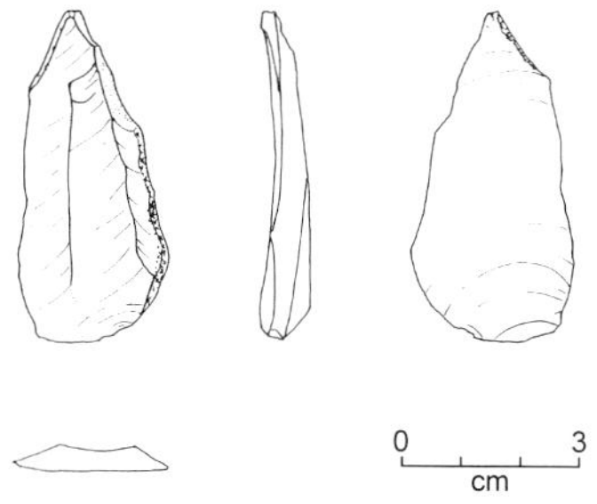

Figure 7. *Levallois point flake.*

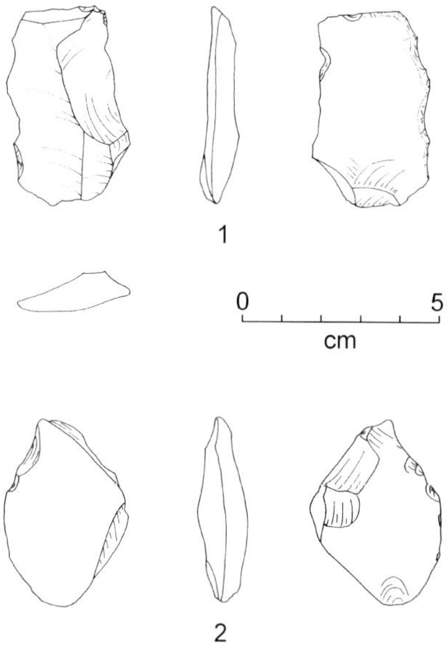

Figure 8. *Notches and denticulates (1-2).*

As mentioned above this present study of the assemblage aims to set it within its broad framework and further detailed analysis is to be carried out at some future date.

Conclusion and perspectives

The Barakah assemblage can confidently be assigned typologically to the Middle Palaeolithic in the Arabian Peninsula. This conclusion is supported by the presence of one Levallois flake core, a Levallois point flake, two broken bifaces/hand-axes, together with the presence of the radial and Levallois techniques of tool manufacturing. Missing at Barakah were blades and the blade manufacturing techniques. The Barakah assemblage may therefore be dated roughly to around 200,000 years ago, or marine oxegene-isotope stage (MIS) 5, (Rose 2004; 2008; Van Peer *et al.* 2007). Typical Upper Acheulean tools like well-balanced, thin, symmetrical bifaces were absent at Barakah. Also missing are large Acheulean cleavers, choppers, and axes. Thus the material cannot be dated other than to the Middle Palaeolithic. The Barakah assemblage complements the recent discovery of Middle Palaeolithic material elsewhere in the UAE and Oman. The exciting discovery of stratified materials of an unknown Palaeolithic industry at Jebel Fayah in Sharjah Emirate (Uerpmann 2007), and the expected OSL dating of their associated sediments, will, it is hoped, shed some light on the approximate date of movement of Palaeolithic communities through the United Arab Emirates.

The early sites of southern and northern Arabia complement the migration theory of *Homo erectus* from Africa into Asia along two possible routes. In the south of Arabia, the importance of the Lower Palaeolithic tool sites of Najran and Tathlith, and those in the Ḥaḍramawt area of Yemen, lie in their geographical locations. If these sites were vestiges of the early migrants, this evidence supports the short crossing route theory across the Bab al-Mandab Straits into Asia.

Evidence in support of a longer migration route from Africa to Asia is provided by the Shuwayhitiya site in northern Saudi Arabia. This site's existence suggests a passage through Egypt and the Rift Valley of northern Arabia. This theory is further supported by several well-known sites in the Levant, such as Ubeidiya in Palestine and Sitt Markho and Khattab in Syria, and others in Lebanon and Jordan.

At Barakah, the material did not come from excavations, so there is therefore no way of assessing the long-term presence of hunter-fisher-gatherers on the site. This problem can only be resolved by excavation, thus determining a stratigraphic presence, if any. Stratified deposits at Barakah would mean a sequence of long-term occupation, i.e. a base camp. *In situ* material would permit functional interpretations of the way the site was used. Such functional analysis has been carried out at the stratified site of Saffaqah in Saudi Arabia, where animal bones were absent (Whalen, Siraj-Ali & Davis 1984). Similar analysis has been also carried out at Torralba and Ambrona in Spain, where animal bones and some plant remains were found associated with the lithic artefacts (Howell 1966; Freeman 1975; 1978).

As mentioned above, the three Barakah localities

had suffered heavily from erosion and that would leave a slim chance, if any, for the Palaeolithic deposits to be preserved.

The strategic position of Jebel Barakah overlooking the eastern edge of the Sabkha Matti must have attracted Middle Palaeolithic hunters following their prey along the ancient river courses. Water may have certainly flowed along the Sabkha Matti, draining down into the Arabian Gulf basin. Palaeo-environmental conditions from southern Arabia indicate that at least three pluvial conditions were associated with MIS 5e, 5a, and 3 (Rose 2004), providing habitable conditions for hunter-fisher-gatherers to the region. It should be noted here that the Arabian Gulf during the time in question was a huge river-valley system and the Barakah people were living in a world completely different from today.

The Abu Dhabi Authority for Culture and Heritage (ADACH) is currently striving to protect important archaeological and palaeontological sites throughout the Abu Dhabi Emirate. The discovery of the first Middle Palaeolithic material in the Abu Dhabi Emirate places Jebel Barakah, with its already known fossil-rich Late Miocene deposits, as a site deserving the highest degree of protection by the authorities.

Acknowledgements

Thanks go to Mr Mohammed Khalaf Al Mazrouie, Director-General of the Abu Dhabi Authority for Culture and Heritage (ADACH), Dr Sami El-Masri, Director of the Strategic Planning Office (ADACH) and Mr Mohamed Amer al-Neyadi, Director of Historic Environment (ADACH) for supporting our work.

Thanks also to Drs Julie and William Scott-Jackson for kindly sharing their thoughts and ideas concerning the Barakah lithic material.

Finally, thanks go to Dr Jeffrey I. Rose (Oxford Brookes University, UK) for organizing this special session on the Palaeolithic in Arabia and for inviting us to participate.

References

Abu-Amero K.K., Gonzales A.M., Larruga J.M., Bosley T.M. & Cabrera V.M.

2007. Eurasian and African mitochondrial DNA influences in the Saudi Arabian population. *BMC Evolutionary Biology* 7: 32.

Alsharekh A.

2007. *An early Lower Palaeolithic site from central Saudi Arabia*. Poster presented at the Seminar for Arabian Studies 2007. [Unpublished].

Cohen D., Keeley L.H. & van Noten F.L.

1979. Stone Tools, Toolkits, and Human Behavior in Prehistory. *Current Anthropology* 20/4: 661–683.

Copeland L. & Hours F.

1978. La séquence Acheuléenne du Nahr el Kebir Région Septentrionale du Littoral Syrien. *Paléorient* 4: 5–31.

Cornwall P.B.

1946. A Lower Palaeolithic Hand-Axe from Central Arabia. *Man* 46: 144.

Field H.

1971. *Contribution to the Anthropology of Saudi Arabia*. Miami, FL: Field Research Project.

Freeman L.G.

1975. Acheulean Sites and stratigraphy in Iberia and the Maghreb. Pages 661–743 in K.W. Butzer & G.L. Isaac (eds), *After the Australopithecines: Stratigraphy, Ecology, and Culture Change in the Middle Pleistocene*. The Hague/Paris: Mouton Publishers.

1978. The analysis of Some Occupation Floor Distributions from Earlier and Middle Paleolithic Sites in Spain. Pages 57–116 in L.G. Freeman (ed.), *Views of the Past*. The Hague: Mouton Publishers.

Howell F.C.

1966. Observations on the Earlier Phases of the European Lower Palaeolithic. *American Anthropologist* 68/2–2): 88–201.

James H.V.A. & Petraglia M.D.

2005. Modern human origins and the evolution of behavior in the later Pleistocene record of South Asia. *Current Anthropology* 46 (Supplement): 1–27.

Keeley L.H.
1977. The Functions of Palaeolithic Flint Tools. *Scientific American* 237/5: 108–26.
1980. *Experimental Determination of Stone Tool Uses. A Microwear Analysis.* Chicago: University of Chicago Press.
McBrearty S.
1993. Lithic artefacts from Abu Dhabi's Western Region. *Tribulus (Bulletin of the Emirates Natural History Group)* 3: 12–14.
1999. Earliest Tools from the Emirate of Abu Dhabi, United Arab Emirates. Pages 373–388 in P. Whybrow & A. Hill (eds), *Fossil Vertebrates of Arabia — With Emphasis on the Late Miocene Fauna, Geology, and Palaeoenvironments of the Emirate of Abu Dhabi, United Arab Emirates*. New Haven, CT/London: Yale University Press.
Overstreet W.C.
1973. *Contributions to the Prehistory of Saudi Arabia*: Miami, FL: Field Research Projects.
Parr P., Zarins J., Ibrahim M., Waechter J., Garrard A., Clarks C., Bidmead M. & al-Badr H.
1978. Preliminary Report on the Second Phase of the northern Province Survey 1397/1077. *Atlal* 2: 29–50.
Petraglia M.D. & Alsharekh A.
2003. The Middle Palaeolithic of Arabia: Implications for Modern Human Origins, Behaviour and Dispersals. *Antiquity* 77/298: 671–684.
Potts D.T.
1990. *The Arabian Gulf in Antiquity*. i. Oxford: Oxford University Press.
Rose J.I.
2004. The question of Upper Pleistocene connections between East Africa and South Arabia. *Current Anthropology* 45/4: 551–555.
2005. Archaeological investigations in the Sultanate of Oman, 2004. *Archaeological researches in Ukraine* 2003/04: 339–342. [Co-authored; in Russian].
2007. The Arabian Corridor Migration Model: archaeological evidence for hominin dispersals into Oman during the Middle and Upper Pleistocene. *Proceedings of the Seminar for Arabian Studies* 37: 219–237.
Scott-Jackson J.E., Scott-Jackson W.B. & Jasim S.
2007. Middle Palaeolithic or what? New sites in Sharjah, United Arab Emirates (UAE). *Proceedings of the Seminar for Arabian Studies* 37: 277–279.
Uerpmann H-P.
2007. Excavations at different sites along the eastern slopes of the Jebel Faya. Online source: *http://www.urgeschichte.uni-tuebingen.de/index.php?id=292*
Van Peer, P. & Vermeersch, P. M.
2007. The Place of Northeast Africa in the Early History of modern humans: New Data and interpretations on the middle Stone Age. In Mellars P, Boyle K, Bar-Yosef O & Stinger C. *Rethinking the human revolution*. McDonald Institute for Archaeological Research.
Whalen N.M. & Pease D.W.
1992. Early Mankind in Arabia. *Saudi Aramco World*: 16–23. Online source: http://ww.saudiaramcoworld.com/issue/199204/early.mankind.in.arabia.htm
Whalen N.M., Siraj-Ali J & Davis W.
1984. Excavation of Acheulean Sites near Saffaqah, Saudi Arabia, 1403 AH/1983. *Atlal* 8: 9–24.
Whalen N.M., Sindi H., Wahida G. & Sirag-Ali J.
1983. Excavation of Acheulean Sites Near Saffaqah in Ad-Dawadmi 1402 AH/1982. *Atlal* 7: 9–21.
Whybrow P.J.
1989. New stratotype; the Baynunah Formation (Late Miocene), United Arab Emirates: Lithology and palaeontology. *Newsletters on Stratigraphy* 21: 1–9.
Whybrow P.J. & Hill A. (eds).
1999. *Fossil Vertebrates of Arabia — With Emphasis on the Late Miocene Faunas, Geology, and Palaeoenvironments of the Emirate of Abu Dhabi, United Arab Emirates*. New Haven, CT/London: Yale University Press.
Zarins J., Murad A. & al-Yish K.S.
1981. Comprehensive Archaeological Survey Program: A — The second preliminary report on the southwestern province. *Atlal* 5: 9–42.

Zarins J., Whalen N., Ibrahim M., Murad A. & Khan M.
1980. Saudi Arabian Reconnaissance 1979: preliminary report on the central and southwestern province survey. *Atlal* 4: 9–36.

Authors' addresses
Dr Ghanim Wahida, 106 Barton Road, Cambridge, CB3 9LH, UK.
e-mail ghanimwahida@hotmail.com

Dr Walid Yasin al-Tikriti, Head of Division — Archaeology, Abu Dhabi Authority for Culture and Heritage (ADACH), PO Box 15715, Al Ain, UAE.
e-mail wyasin11@yahoo.com

Dr Mark Beech, Head of Division — Cultural Landscapes, Abu Dhabi Authority for Culture and Heritage (ADACH), PO Box 2380, Abu Dhabi, UAE.
e-mail mark.beech@cultural.org.ae

Proceedings of the Seminar for Arabian Studies 38 (2008): 65–70

Defining the Palaeolithic of Arabia? Notes on the Roundtable Discussion

J.I. Rose & G.N. Bailey

List of Participants

Geoff Bailey (moderator), Abdullah Alsharekh, Mark Beech, Rob Carter, Rémy Crassard, Richard Cuttler, Francesco Fedele, Nic Flemming, Michael Harrower, Lamya Khalidi, Johannes Kutterer, Anthony Marks, Sarah Milliken, Garry Momber, Adrian Parker, Ashley Parton, Diana Pickworth, Kathryn Price, Jeffrey Rose, Julie Scott-Jackson, William Scott-Jackson, Henry Thompson, Hans-Peter Uerpmann, Simon Underdown, Ghanim Wahida, Helen Walkington, Alex Wasse

Introduction

Unlike Palaeolithic studies in other parts of the world, which have developed slowly and concurrently over time, Arabian prehistory has remained (pardon the pun) in the Stone Age. That is not to say it has been ignored – theories and predictive models abound, offering a cornucopia of conjecture as to the role of the subcontinent in human biological and cultural evolution (e.g. Lahr and Foley 1994; Stringer 2000; Petraglia and Alsharekh 2003; Mellars 2006). Yet most of these theoretical scenarios are based on inadequate archaeological data. Even now, there are too few dated Pleistocene assemblages to hold a meaningful conversation concerning prehistoric events in Arabia. Thus, the purpose of this roundtable discussion is *not* to establish any sort of consensus; rather, it is to pool research strategies, calibrate common questions, and discuss avenues for further inquiry. The discipline has abruptly matured and we find ourselves in the unique position of being able to address epistemological and taxonomic issues with a clean slate, before the babble of competing nomenclatures threatens to topple our Tower of Babel.

Whither the Weather?

The best place to build the foundation of this metaphorical tower is upon the landscape, nested within regional variability and oscillating palaeoenvironments. Of the Arabian climate, Thesiger observed "a cloud gathers, the rain falls, men live; the cloud disperses without rain, and men and animals die" (Thesiger 1959: 1). On a broad scale, this environmentally deterministic behaviour is theorized to have been the primary mechanism that drove Palaeolithic occupation in Arabia (e.g. Rose 2007; Parker and Rose, this volume). The problem, however, is just that – it is theoretical and broad. This type of generalisation is only adequate for a crude characterization of prehistoric habitation, but severely limits our scope of understanding by glossing over questions of localized variability and magnitude. In other words, how wet was wet, how dry was dry, and where/when did these climatic changes occur?

As we proceed forward, we must wean ourselves from overly simplified scenarios and work toward greater resolution on a regional scale. This will enable us to address climate and corresponding occupation in Arabia as a dynamic system rather than just a yes or no proposition. For instance, Rose (2006) has suggested periodic *tabula rasa* events rendered South Arabia uninhabitable, precluding autochthonous development. In actuality, the prehistoric occupation may be far more complex and varied across the landscape, linked to topographic relief and localized climatic regimes. During some arid phases, populations may not necessarily have left Arabia, rather, contracted into favourable refugia such as the Dhofar Mountains, Yemeni Highlands, the Arabo-Persian Gulf basin, or the now submerged coastal lowlands of the southern Red Sea basin. Our investigations should work toward identifying if such core zones do exist, and determining to what extent hunter-gatherers expanded and contracted from these niches. At what point and under what conditions did a given area become uninhabitable?

From this question, we can then address the extent of behavioural elasticity among early humans in Arabia, which, in part, is a function of resource predictability. In the 'coastal oasis hypothesis,' Faure et al. (2002) show that depressed sea levels led to amelioration in littoral zones due to freshwater upwelling. Did the coastlines running along the fringe of the Arabian Peninsula provide predictable sources of freshwater and adequate biomass? If so, how did these stable resources affect mobility patterns? To what extent was hominin occupation and transhumance shaped by variable geography? To this end, the work of Bailey et al. (2007) provides a useful model for coastal exploration.

One of the most troublesome deficiencies in our knowledge of the Arabian Palaeolithic stems from a dearth of absolute dates. Surface scatters of lithic artefacts are everywhere, yet datable contexts are elusive. Only in the last year have the first stratified Palaeolithic archaeological sites been discovered and dated (Delagnes et al. 2008; Rose et al. nd). One efficient way around this obstacle is to seek guidance from previous geological studies that have been carried out throughout the Peninsula. There are numerous relict Pleistocene landscapes that have been analyzed and even dated, including travertines (e.g. Clark and Fontes 1990), palaeosols (e.g. Sanlaville 1992), lacustrine deposits (e.g. Parker et al. 2006), aeolianites (e.g. Gardner 1988), speleothems (e.g. Burns et al. 2001), and wadi gravels (Parker and Rose, this volume).

Using previously-studied geomorphic zones such as these to locate archaeological sites: (1) should enable us to build upon known research and immediately correlate archaeological remains with palaeoenvironmental and geographic data. Pleistocene depositional environments (e.g. the marls from Lake Mundafan reported by McClure 1976) may yield preserved faunal material, a line of evidence that is hitherto unknown in Arabia. These data, in turn, are instrumental for understanding hominin interaction with the landscape. We can also evaluate taphonomic processes and learn from the successes of prior research. For example, Uerpmann's excavations at Jebel Faya have demonstrated the presence of *in situ*, stratified Pleistocene material at the front of a rockshelter; Palaeolithic artefacts were found far below the sterile layer that was the lower boundary of the previous team's investigations at the site. So, we now know to dig deeper, beyond the eboulis and gravel that often underlie such Holocene occupations.

That is not to say we should only focus on buried sites. The peninsula is dominated by erosional contexts; as such, the majority of the Pleistocene archaeological record is lying exposed on the surface. The exponentially increasing rate of construction projects and oil exploration poses a growing threat to these pristine landscapes and the archaeological heritage resting upon them. Therefore, equal attention must be given to surface survey projects that mitigate the permanent loss of data. This strategy will also provide a more comprehensive understanding of site distribution across different zones, otherwise any consideration of prehistoric landscape usage patterns will be skewed toward those places we have chosen to investigate.

The perception of Arabia as a discrete geographic region is flawed, to say the least. The Arabian Peninsula is formed by a mosaic of jagged mountain ranges, upland plateaus, myriad networks of incised drainage channels, sandy deserts, gravel pavements, and coastal plains. This last category comprises not only the presently exposed littoral, but also includes the submerged continental shelf along the Red Sea, Arabian Sea, as well as the entire Arabo-Persian Gulf basin. How were these different landscapes exploited by prehistoric inhabitants? To what extent does geography pattern variability in the material record? As our incipient discipline develops, one reasonable way forward is to frame archaeological data sets within regional stratigraphic contexts. In turn, these units can be used to articulate and assess variability over time and space.

What's in a Name?

Undoubtedly, this temporal-spatial approach to categorizing archaeological assemblages will produce countless organizational units. A few have already sprung up such as "Wa'shah" (Crassard, this volume), "Khasfian" (Rose 2004), "Nejd Leptolithic" (Rose 2006), and "Sibakhan" (ibid.). At the onset of what promises to be a naming bonanza, we must consider that "all generalisations are dangerous unless we understand from the very beginning that they are generalisations" (Goodwin 1946: 74). As long as we are mindful of the *class* of arbitrary data that any given temporal-spatial unit represents, our Tower of Babel will hold firm no matter how many industrial bricks are piled upon it.

To this end, the nomenclature appearing in Bishop and Clark (1967) is recommended as a useful foundation, which presents and appraises efforts to systematize Palaeolithic taxonomies in Africa. Conceptual categories such as facies, industry, tradition, and culture are addressed in order to define meaningful units for analysis. Given these delineations, we should remember "Wa'shah" is a well-described core reduction strategy from Hadramaut, "Sibakhan" is a suite of technologies associated with palaeolakes in central Oman, "Nejd Leptolithic" encompasses a variety of blade production methods found throughout the Nejd Plateau in Dhofar. None can yet be called an industry.

There is consensus that the names of discrete archaeological units should be based upon their geographic-palaeoclimatic associations: in other words, from the ground up. Conversely, to examine lithic technological variability, generalised patterns in reduction must first be recognized and described. These observations should be sufficiently broad to allow us to assess the extent of technological continua versus geographically or temporally conscribed, unique reduction methods. For example, if we are to assess blade technologies throughout southern Arabia, we must first describe the full range of coeval varieties. Are the Sibakhan, Nejd Leptolithic, and Wa'shah methods of producing blade-proportionate blanks simply different aspects of a single continuum? If so, that continuum must be articulated to determine its geographic and temporal range.

Each region that surrounds the Arabian Peninsula employs a different set of names to describe its archaeological phases: East Africa uses Early, Middle, and Late Stone Age; the Levant follows the traditional European taxonomy of Lower, Middle, and Upper Palaeolithic; archaeologists working in South Asia have recently introduced the term Late Palaeolithic (James and Petraglia 2005). Each of these areas is characterized by markedly different lithic trajectories; therefore, the names chosen to describe archaeological phases in Arabia carry connotations that insinuate regional affinities. This is problematic because we do not yet have enough data to make such a decision, techno-typological links to other regions may vary over time and in different parts of the peninsula, and there may be associations with all three surrounding areas. To avoid this potential source of confusion, it is suggested that temporal terminology should be linked to climatic episodes.

The Road Ahead

As Arabian Palaeolithic archaeology emerges from obscurity, we must be mindful of the limits set by the current paucity of data. It is tempting to envision modern humans marching across Arabia, wielding foliates, microliths, leptoliths, baryliths, or any combination thereof. This kind of precocious modelling is akin to asking an infant to run before it can crawl; our discipline is not yet at a stage when it can be expected to perform such tasks. Rather, we should investigate known Pleistocene geomorphic zones, work toward contextualizing assemblages within a localized palaeoenvironmental framework, and describe the range of variability amongst lithic technologies. At the beginning of this conference we set out to seek a definition of the Arabian Palaeolithic. At its conclusion, the only concrete entity to have emerged is ourselves. Hence, the participants of this symposium resolve to establish a collaborative network for the purposes of organizing future meetings, sharing data, discussing findings, and facilitating cooperative research.

We are afforded the unique opportunity at the inception of this discipline to augment our progress by harnessing the internet. One suggested application is to build a web-based, interactive, cooperative research framework, where data input might resemble that of a wiki. This would serve three primary functions: 1) to record, in one central location, a resource assessment that presents new developments in research and a comprehensive database of our findings; 2) to provide a real time forum for discussion; 3) to share evolving research objectives that highlight successful methodologies and target areas threatened by infrastructural developments. This final point is perhaps the most important. While we cannot define the Arabian Palaeolithic at this stage, we can safely say occupation throughout the peninsula reaches far back in time to the dawn of our species. The destruction of unrecorded archaeological sites in Arabia threatens to rob us of information essential to understanding human origins.

References

Bailey G.N., Flemming N.C., King G.C.P., Lambeck K., Momber G., Moran L.J., al-Sharekh A. & Vita-Finzi C. 2007. Coastlines, Submerged Landscapes, and Human Evolution: The Red Sea Basin and the Farasan Islands. *Journal of Island & Coastal Archaeology* 2: 127–160.

Bishop, W.W. & J.D. Clark
1967. *Background to Evolution in Africa*. Chicago: University of Chicago Press.

Burns S. J., D. Fleitmann, A. Matter, U. Neff & Mangini A.
2001. Speleothem evidence from Oman for continental pluvial events during interglacial periods. *Geology* 29(7): 623–626.

Clark I. & Fontes J.-C.
1990. Paleoclimatic Reconstruction of Northern Oman Based on Carbonates from Hyperalkaline Groundwaters. *Quaternary Research* 33: 320–336.

Crassard, R.
2008. The "Waᶜsha method": an original laminar debitage from Ḥaḍramawt, Yemen. *Proceedings of the Seminar for Arabian Studies* 38: 3–14.

Delagnes, A., R. Macchiarelli, J. Jaubert, S. Peigne, J.-F. Tournepiche, P. Bertran, R. Cassard, L. Khalidi, C. Tribolo, C. Hatte, N. Mercier, E. Messager, A. Meunier, E. Abbate, M. Al Halbiy & Mosabi A.
2008. Middle Paleolithic Settlement in Arabia: First Evidence From a Stratified Archaeological Site in Western Yemen. Paper presented at Meeting of the Palaeoanthropology Society, Vancouver, British Columbia, March 25-26, 2008.

Faure H., Walter R.C. & Grant D.R.
2002. The coastal oasis: ice age springs on emerged continental shelves. *Global and Planetary Change* 33: 47–56.

Gardner, R.A.M.
1988. Aeolianites and marine deposits of the Wahiba Sands: character and palaeoenvironments. *Journal of Oman Studies, Special Report* 3: 75–94.

Goodwin, A.J.H.
1946. *The loom of prehistory; a commentary and a select bibliography of the prehistory of southern Africa*. Cape Town: South African Archaeological Society Handbook No. 2, pp. 151.

James H. V. A. & Petraglia M. D.
2005. Modern human origins and the evolution of behavior in the later Pleistocene record of South Asia. *Current Anthropology* 46: S1–S27.

Lahr, M.M. & Foley R.A.
1994. Multiple dispersals and modern human origins. *Evolutionary Anthropology* 3: 48-60.

McClure H.A.
1976. Radiocarbonchronology of Late Quaternary Lakes in the Arabian Desert. *Nature* 263: 755–756.

Mellars P.
2006. Why did modern humans populations disperse from Africa *ca.* 60,000 year ago? A new model. *Proceedings of the National Academy of Sciences* 103(25): 9381–9386.

Parker A.G., Goudie A.S., Stokes S., White K., Hodson M.J., Manning M. & Kennet D.
2006. A record of Holocene Climate Change from lake geochemical analyses in southeastern Arabia. *Quaternary Research* 66: 465–476.

Parker, A.G. & J.I. Rose
2008. Climate change and human origins in southern Arabia. *Proceedings of the Seminar for Arabian Studies* 38: 25–42.

Petraglia, M.D. & Alsharekh A.
2003. The Middle Palaeolithic of Arabia: implications for modern human origins, behaviour and dispersals. *Antiquity* 77: 671–684.

Rose J.I.
2004. The question of Upper Pleistocene connections between East Africa and South Arabia. *Current Anthropology* 45(4): 551–555.
2006. *Among Arabian Sands: defining the Palaeolithic of southern Arabia.* PhD dissertation, Southern Methodist University, Dallas [Unpublished].
2007. The Arabian Corridor Migration Model: archaeological evidence for hominin dispersals into Oman during the Middle and Upper Pleistocene. *Proceedings of the Seminar for Arabian Studies* 37: 219–237.

Rose, J.I., Usik, V.I., as-Sabri, B., al-Asmi, K., Parker, A.G., Schwenniger, J.-L., Clark-Balzan, L., Oppenheimer, S.J., Parton, A., Underdown, S., Petraglia, M., Foley, R., & Lahr, M.
[nd.] Archaeological Evidence for Modern Humans in Southern Arabia during the Last Glacial Maximum. In preparation.

Sanlaville P.
1992. Changements Climatiques dans la Péninsule Arabique Durant le Pléistocène Supérieur et l'Holocène. *Paléorient* 18: 5–25.

Stringer, C.B.
2000. Palaeoanthropology: coasting out of Africa. *Nature* 405:24–26.

Thesiger W.
1959. *Arabian Sands*. New York: E.P. Dutton and Company, Inc.

Authors' addresses
Dr J.I. Rose, Human Origins and Palaeo-Environments (HOPE) Research Group, Department of Anthropology and Geography, Oxford Brookes University, Oxford OX3 0BP, UK.
e-mail jrose@brookes.ac.uk

Prof. G.N. Bailey, Department of Archaeology, University of York, The King's Manor, York, YO1 7EP, UK.
e-mail gb502@york.ac.uk

Proceedings of the Seminar for Arabian Studies 38 (2008): 71–74

Relative clauses in the dialect of Rijal Alma' (south-west Saudi Arabia)

Yahya Asiri

Summary
This paper examines relative clauses in the dialect of Rijal Alma', a province 45 km to the west of Abha, capital city of the region of Asir in south-west Saudi Arabia (Fig. 1). This dialect is well known throughout Saudi Arabia because of tourism in the area. There are about 100,000 native speakers of the dialect, but this number is now decreasing gradually. It is very important to examine this dialect and record its most distinctive features before they are lost as a result of the social and economic changes affecting its speakers. The dialect has a number of phonetic and morphological features that distinguish it from other Arabic dialects both in Saudi Arabia and in other Arabic countries. The objective of this paper is to examine the construction of relative clauses in the dialect. This dialect has four relative pronouns ḏa, ta, ma, and wula which, in contrast to modern Arabic dialects, agree with a definite antecedent in terms of gender and number. It also exhibits an apparent lack of inflectional agreement in the verb within a definite relative clause, but full verbal agreement within an indefinite relative clause. The apparent archaic features within this language variety may shed light on the development of Arabic within the Arabian Peninsula.

Keywords: Rijal Alma', relative pronouns, demonstratives, definiteness, anaphora

1. Introduction

Rijal Alma' has four relative pronouns: ḏa for a masculine singular antecedent, ta for a feminine singular antecedent, wula for a human plural or dual antecedent whether feminine or masculine, and ma for a non-human plural antecedent. These relative pronouns are only used when the antecedent is definite as no relative pronoun is used when the antecedent is indefinite. In the vast majority of Arabic dialects, the relationship between the relative clause and the antecedent is expressed by an anaphoric pronoun in the relative clause (al-rājiᶜ or al-ᶜāid). This is not the case in Rijal Alma': where the subject of the relative clause is identical to the antecedent, the verb in the relative clause does not agree for (feminine) gender or, generally, for plural number. Where the object of the relative clause is coreferential with the antecedent, the object pronoun may be omitted. However, when the antecedent is coreferential with a possessive pronoun in the relative clause, the possessive pronoun must be expressed (see 3.1d, 3.1 e and 3.2a). For Sabaic, it has also been mentioned that the only time an anaphoric pronoun is obligatory in the relative clause is when it functions as a possessive pronoun (Beeston 1984).

2. Demonstrative pronouns

There are similarities between demonstrative pronouns and relative pronouns in Rijal Alma' (Asiri 2006). The dialect has nine demonstrative pronouns depending on gender and number:

1. ḏīh "this" for the singular, masculine near the speaker.

ḏīh waladin ṭayyibin — "This is a good boy"

2. tīh "this" for the singular, feminine near the speaker.

tīh bintin ṭayyibatin — "This is a good girl"

3. ḏahnah "that" for the singular, masculine at a distance from the speaker.

ḏahnah waladin ṭayyibin — "That is a good boy"

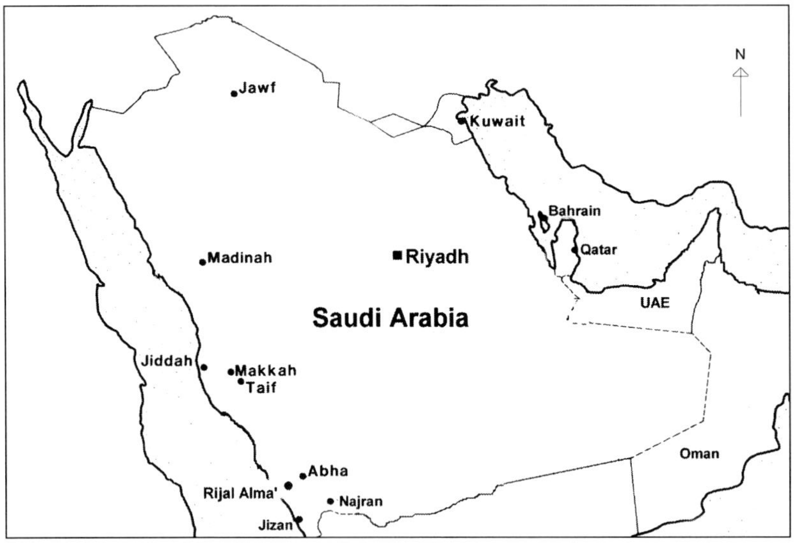

Figure 1. *The position of Rijal Alma' in south-west Saudi Arabia.*

4. tahnah "that" for the singular, feminine at a distance from the speaker.

tahnah bintin ṭayyibatin "That is a good girl"

5. wulīh "these" for the human plural near the speaker.

wulīh banātin ṭayyibāh "These are good girls"

6. wulahnah "those" for the human plural at a distance from the speaker.

wulahnah ʾawlādin ṭayyibīn "Those are good boys"

7. wulāx̣ "those" for the human plural at a distance from the speaker.

wulāx̣ banātin ṭayyibāh "Those are good girls"

8. mahnīh "these" for non-human plural near the speaker.

mahnīh ğanamin ḥalāh "These are good sheep"

9. mahnah "those" for non-human plural at a distance from the speaker.

mahnah bagarin ḥalāh "Those are good cows"

The relative pronouns in Sabaic, most particularly in late Sabaic, are very similar to those in Rijal Alma', namely ḏ for masculine singular, t- for feminine singular and ʾl- for plural (Beeston 1984).

3. Relative pronouns with definite antecedent

3.1 *ḏa (s.m.)*

a. antah rayta m-walad ḏa šarad

"have you seen the boy who ran away?"

b. anti samaʿtī m-rajil ḏa yamšī ʿilayn

"have you heard the man who is walking upstairs?"

c. iftaḥ im-bāb ḏa yadḫil im-majlis

"open the door that leads to the sitting-room"

d. sāfara m-rajil ḏa šarayt sayyāratūh

"the man, whose car I bought, travelled"

e. waštari m-bayt ḏa yabīʿ jārna

"I'll buy the house that our neighbour is selling"

We note in example e the absence of an anaphoric object pronoun in the relative clause, whereas in example d the anaphoric pronoun is expressed in the possessive pronoun.

3.2 *ta (f.s.)*

a. antu raytu m-šajarat ta gaṭaᶜaw

"have you seen the tree that they cut?"

b. gābalt im-brat ta lisa yasmaᶜ

"I met the girl who couldn't hear"

c. ᶜali ištara m-lāy ta yāx̣il im-zarᶜ

"Ali bought the cow that eats the crops"

d. ištara m-sayyārat ta gid ẖarb

"he bought the car that had broken down"

In examples b, c, and d we see that the verb in the relative clause does not agree in gender with the antecedent, although the subject of the relative clause is coreferential with the antecedent. In example a we see the absence of an anaphoric object pronoun in the relative clause.

3.3 *wula (human plural)*

In the case of the plural relative pronoun wula, the verb and its antecedent have two alternative agreement possibilities: they may or may not agree in number, but lack of agreement is more common:

a. gābalt im-ᶜuwāl wula saragu m-maḥall ~ gābalt im-ᶜuwāl wula saraga m-maḥall

"I met the boys who stole from the shop"

b. ᵓaḥmad ḏa wadda m-niswat wula jāš ᵓams ~ ᵓaḥmad ḏa wadda m-niswat wula jāwš ᵓams

"Ahmad is the one who gave a lift to the women who visited you (f.s.) yesterday"

c. widdī ᵓasmaᶜ im-ṭālbayn wula yagil innihim yabḡānī ~ widdī ᵓasmaᶜ im-ṭālbayn wula yaglūn innihim yabḡūnnī

"I would like to hear from the two pupils who want to see me"

d. gilu lim-niswat wula yabḡa jamšī yaẖrijūn ~ gilu lim-niswat wula yabḡawūn jamšūn yaẖrijūn

"tell the women who want to leave to come out"

3.4 *ma (non-human plural)*

ma introduces a definite relative clause with a non-human plural antecedent. Lack of an anaphoric pronoun in the relative clause is as common in this case as in the case of wula.

a. anta rayta m-sayyārāt ma ẖarb ~ anta rayta m-sayyārāt ma ẖarban

"have you seen the cars that broke down?"

b. im-bagar ma bāᶜ ~ im-bagar ma bāᶜaha

"the cows that he sold"

c. im-maḥāll ma bana ~ im-maḥāll ma banāha

"the houses that he built"

4. Relative clauses where the head noun is indefinite

If the antecedent is indefinite, there is no relative pronoun. In an indefinite relative clause, the verb must agree with the antecedent.

a. ana rayt ibratin šaradan

"I saw a girl running away"

b. ana rayt niswatin jaww

"I saw some women coming"

c. waštarī baytin yabīᶜūh jārna

"I'll buy a house our neighbour is selling"

5. Language change

In the dialect of Rijal Alma', the use of the relative pronoun illī is becoming increasingly noticeable and frequent nowadays due to contact with other dialects and the mass media. It is mainly used by younger people.

When illī is used, the anaphoric pronoun in the relative clause is obligatory, irrespective of its syntactic function. In parallel with the use of illī we also find that the definite article il- is used in place of im- and the frequent use of borrowed words. Consider the following examples:

a. ant šift il-sayyārah illī ʿaddat

"have you (m.s.) seen the car that passed?"

b. samaʿit il-bint illī tamšī fawg

"I heard the girl who is walking upstairs"

6. Conclusion

The dialect of Rijal Alma' has four relative pronouns: ḏa for a masculine singular antecedent, ta for a feminine singular antecedent, wula for a human plural or dual antecedent whether feminine or masculine, and ma for a non-human plural antecedent. These relative pronouns are only used when the antecedent is definite as no relative pronoun is used when the antecedent is indefinite. There are obvious similarities between relative pronouns and demonstratives in Rijal Alma', and between the relative pronouns in Rijal Alma' and those recorded for late Sabaic.

Acknowledgements

I would like to thank my supervisor, Professor Janet Watson, whose consistent patience and encouragement, advice and suggestions for the improvement of this paper have all been the main source of this work. I owe Prof. Watson a great debt for editing, proofreading, and rereading this paper.

References

Asiri Y.M.
2006. Aspects of the Phonology and Morphology of the Dialect of Rijal Alma' (south-west Saudi Arabia). Paper presented at the 7th Congress of the Association Internationale de Dialectologie Arabe, 5–9 September 2006, Vienna. [Unpublished].

Beeston A.F.L.
1984. *Sabaic Grammar*. Manchester: University of Manchester.

Author's address
Mr Yahya Asiri, School of Languages, University of Salford, Maxwell Building, Salford, Greater Manchester M5 4WT, United Kingdom.
e-mail y.asiri@pgr.salford.ac.uk, yahyama@hotmail.com

Proceedings of the Seminar for Arabian Studies 38 (2008): 75–88

Ancient irrigation in Wādī Jirdān

Ueli Brunner

Summary

Wādī Jirdān is one of the few valleys at the eastern fringe of the Ramlat as-Sabᶜatayn. It is located 50 km south of Šabwa, the ancient capital of Ḥaḍramawt. The most important archaeological sites in the valley are al-Barīra and al-Bināʾ. Construction of the Yemen LNG pipeline project offered the opportunity to study the small oasis of Darbas in detail and to map two impressive canals, Naqb and Nuqayb, that were cut into the surrounding hills of Wādī Ṣaᶜdah. An ancient field wall that is covered by the spoil of Nuqayb but runs over the hewn-out material of Naqb allowed a relative dating, according to which Nuqayb is older than Naqb. Naqb itself can be placed in the ancient South Arabian period following the discovery there of a short inscription of that period.

The oasis of Darbas is a clearly defined irrigation unit of 120 ha. The ancient irrigation led to silt accumulations of up to 7 m. Two different irrigation schemes can be detected. The stone structures of the two schemes which served to divide the flow of the canals show a different architecture. The layout of the system on the higher level can be traced almost completely and allows a functional interpretation. Further signs of the former irrigation include tree impressions, ploughing furrows, and field walls on the surface of the silt sediments and canal structures within them.

This research into the small irrigation oasis of Darbas adds another piece in the reconstruction of the puzzle of the South Arabian hydraulic civilisations. Comparative material exists from many large wadis of Yemen such as Jawf, Ḏana, Jūba, Bayḥān, Marḫah, or ʾIrma. The comparison shows that the irrigation scheme of Darbas is closest to that in Wādī Marḫah.

Keywords: Darbas, irrigation, Yemen, Wādī Jirdān, South Arabia, archaeology

Introduction

The geographical centre of the ancient South Arabian cultures was the Ramlat as-Sabᶜatayn. Many fertile valleys drain into this sand desert. Only two of them reach it from the east, i.e. from the limestone plateau of the Jawl. These are the Wādī ᶜIrma, on whose border the capital of the Kingdom of Ḥaḍramawt, Šabwa, is located and to the south, the Wādī Jirdān. Von Wissmann (1962: pl. 3) has given an accurate geomorphological map of the lower Wādī Jirdān on the basis of aerial photographs and two journeys made many years before his publication. He also drew attention to several large waterworks and the presence of silt sediments accumulated through irrigation. Two archaeologists later visited this valley and provided brief descriptions of the two ancient sites of al-Barīra and al-Bināʾ (Lankester Harding 1964: 32–37; Doe 1971: 190–215) but neither mentions the intervening site which von Wissmann called Hajar Ṣaᶜdah.

The geology of this region is quite complex. The wadi has cut deeply into the early Tertiary limestone plateau of the Jawl. Many scattered black basaltic mounds, especially in the south of the valley, bear witness to Quaternary volcanic activity. The wadi has accumulated a large gravel fan at the fringe of the Ramlat as-Sabᶜatayn. In the middle of the fan rises a longitudinal hill with an old gravel surface, most likely the product of an underlying salt dome that has pushed the overlying sediments upwards. Such salt domes are very well known in the larger surroundings, for instance at Šabwa and Sāfir, and the salt of some of these is exploited to this very day.

The Project of the Yemen Liquefied Natural Gas Company (YLNG Co.) to build a pipeline through this part of the Wādī Jirdān allowed a German-French team to carry out a new reconnaissance study of this region. (1) Some preliminary results have already been published

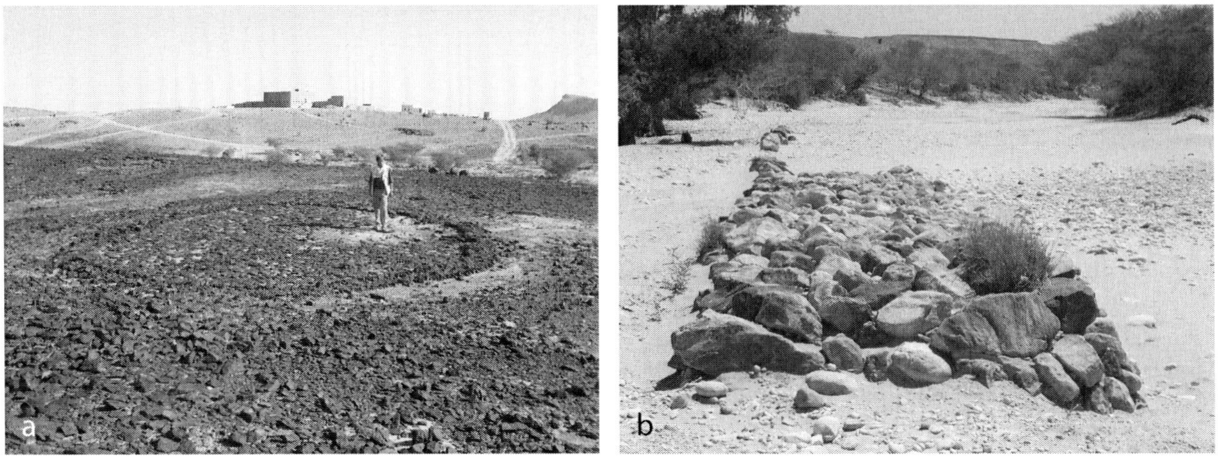

Figure 1. *a. A threshing place in al-Ḥammah. It is bordered by a double ring with standing stone plates; b. An ancient deflector dam in al-ᶜAṭfah. It stretches up to the wadi border in the background. The flood arrived on the right side from the far end.*

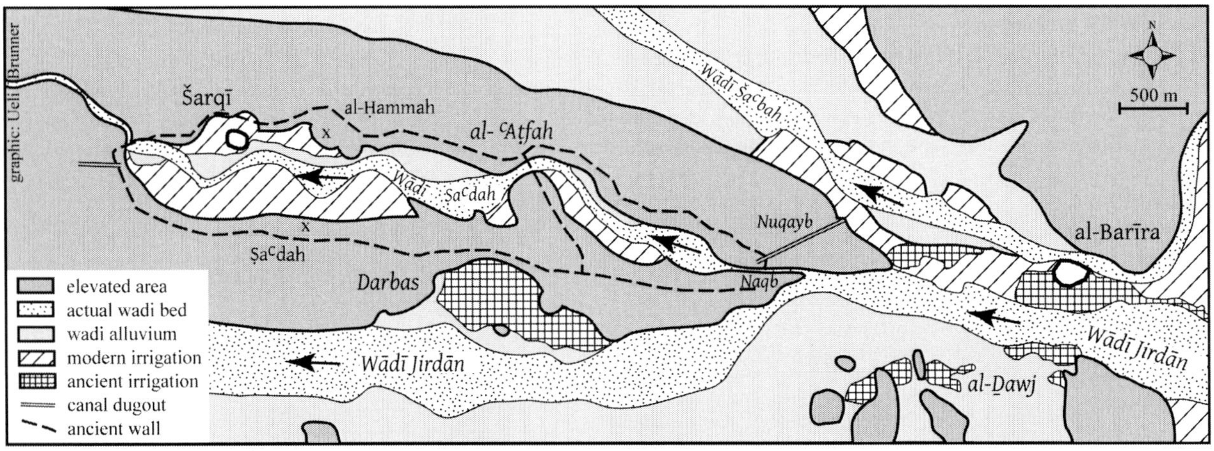

Figure 2. *A geomorphological map of the central part of Wādī Jirdān and Wādī Ṣaᶜdah.*

(Crassard & Hitgen 2007). My fieldwork concentrated on evidence for ancient agriculture, particularly irrigation and related structures.

The Wādī Ṣaᶜdah

Von Wissmann (1962: 185) reported the ancient site of Hajar Ṣaᶜdah on the northern side of the valley, opposite the modern village of Ṣaᶜdah, which was visited by D. van der Meulen and A. J. Drewes in 1952. The site seemed rather large, but new houses were built in Islamic times on top of the old foundations. Von Wissmann (1962: pl. 3) localized the site north of modern Ṣaᶜdah on a gentle hill. The local people call this black hill Ḥammah, which means volcano. Although it does resemble the remains of a volcano, it actually consists of a hard ferracious sandstone whose dark desert varnish gives the impression of basaltic rock. The slopes of this hill are totally free of any ancient remains except for a well-preserved threshing place. This has a diameter of about 8 m (Fig. 1a). The floor is covered with horizontal sandstone plates, and it is surrounded by a ring, about 0.5 m wide, where the plates stand in an upright position. The layout, size, and desert varnish point to an old date, most likely South Arabian.

The site of Hajar Ṣaᶜdah itself lies 800 m to the west on a rocky hill (Fig. 2). Some modern houses form the village of Šarqī. A few inscriptions and rock carvings as well as stairways, pottery, mud-brick structures, and the

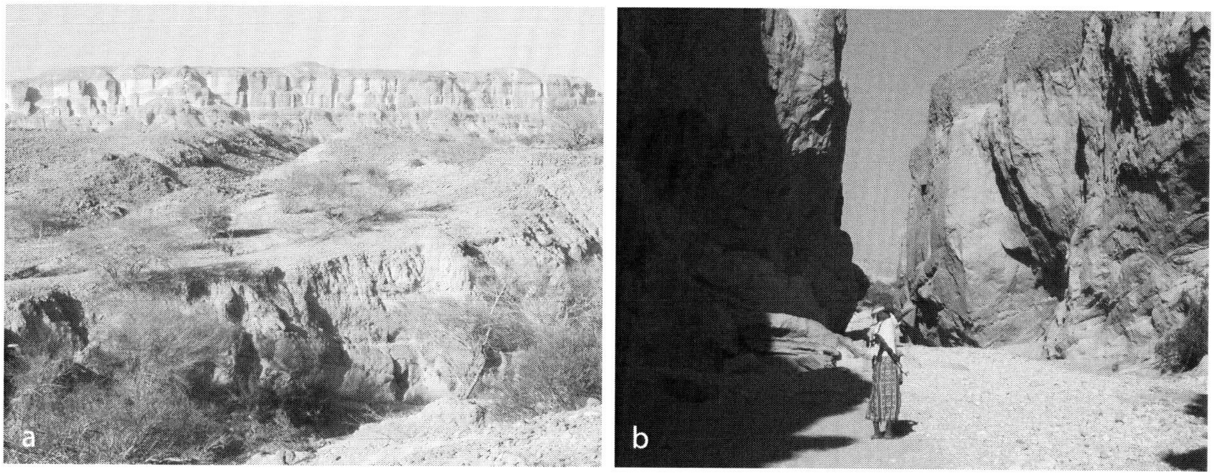

Figure 3. *a. The two canal dugouts Naqb (in the foreground) and Nuqayb at the entrance of Wādī Ṣaʿdah seen from the south-west; b. Naqb near the outlet into Wādī Ṣaʿdah. The Mesozoic sediments are covered by Pleistocene gravel. The vertical walls in the middle are the result of a man-made cutting.*

large quarries at the foot of some of the houses indicate an ancient settlement. It is most likely that Šarqī is the site of Hajar Ṣaʿdah.

There is a wall all around the Wādī Ṣaʿdah. It is 10.9 km long and mostly follows the top of the flat hill, so to this day this well-preserved wall is very clearly visible from all points. The wall is 80 cm across and survives to a height of up to 90 cm. The construction method is always the same. On the outer side hand-sized stones are placed one on top of the other with the intervening space filled with smaller stones and pebbles. There is no indication of covering slabs. A connecting wall, 1 km long, divides the upper part of Wādī Ṣaʿdah from the lower one at al-ʿAṭfah. The wall therefore attains a total length of almost 12 km. The height of the wall indicates that it did not have a defensive character. Its purpose was instead to indicate the presence of a flourishing agricultural community centred on a fertile oasis in this hidden valley.

The central part of the raised fan is formed by a longitudinal depression that had no natural entrance or outlet. Nevertheless today this depression is watered by a side branch of the Wādī Jirdān. Modern fields cover an area measuring 77 ha, 14 ha of which are located upstream of al-ʿAṭfah, 53 ha downstream on the left side of the wadi, and 10 ha on the right side. The dense tree covering on the whole valley floor is striking. It is an indication of a good groundwater table and forms the basis for the honey industry in Wādī Jirdān, which is well known all over Yemen. The fields are cultivated by the Yemeni floodwater irrigation or *sayl* (Brunner 2000: 53). Long deflector dams deflect part of the *sayl* into large fields which are flooded to knee height. The height of the threshold of an outlet defines the amount of water given to the field. This outlet may lead to another field or back to the wadi. A single flooding is enough to achieve a yield.

At al-ʿAṭfah, on the left side, a modern canal is dug into the solid rock. An ancient stone structure is found just after the narrowest point (Fig. 1b). Altogether it is 90 m long and runs from north–north-east to south–south-west. Its width varies between 3.5 m at the northern end and 3 m at the southern end. The kerbstones are from local sandstone quarries and measure an average 0.6×0.4×0.3 m. The intervening space is filled with up-ended limestone boulders. The height of the wall remains undefined owing to the accumulation of gravel in the wadi. At the northern end the wall forms a step consisting of at least two stone layers that stand a little over 0.5 m. After a few metres it reaches the firm rock. The direction of the wall, which forms an angle of 120° to the arriving flood, indicates its function as a well-built deflector dam. The height of the wall determined the amount of water entering the main canal, which then conducted the water to the fields on the left side of the broad valley. This is exactly the arrangement we see today and the only difference is that the modern deflector dam is located upstream of the gorge. Exact dating of the ancient wall is not possible but the level and method of construction indicate an ancient South Arabian date.

The modern Wādī Ṣaʿdah is a very good example of how water is divided into different branches. It starts with

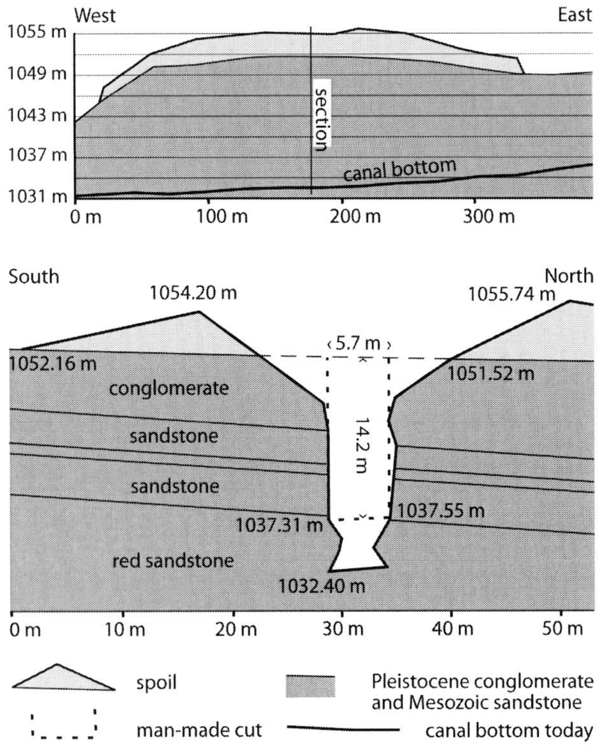

Figure 4. *A longitudinal and cross section of Naqb.*

a very low ridge of loose gravel stones somewhere in the wadi. This ridge becomes larger and larger until it is a real wall constructed with all kinds of material. At this stage the wall has reached the edge of the wadi and forms a canal between it and the hill slope. Stone structures, similar to the ones in Darbas, bring the water to the fields. These fields are comparable in size to the ancient ones. It is interesting to note that one main canal can bring water for an oasis almost the size of Darbas. In conclusion it can be said that the Wādī Ṣaᶜdah showed much useful comparative material for the understanding of the ancient situation in Darbas. (2)

Naqb and Nuqayb, two rock cuttings

The Wādī Ṣaᶜdah forms a closed longitudinal unit in the middle of the oval gravel hill. It is most likely that in prehistoric times the valley did not have a tributary, so that when the people wanted to use this valley for irrigated agriculture they had to open it towards the main wadi. In fact there are two man-made cuttings at the beginning of the valley (Wissmann 1962: pl. 3; Doe 1971: 194–195). The shorter but deeper and therefore more impressive one is called Naqb (Fig. 3). This term is well-known from Naqb al-Hajr, the ancient Mayfaᶜat, where a similar watercourse cutting exists (Doe 1971: 189–190). In Arabic the verb *naqab* means "to drill through", "to dig", or "to perforate". The Naqb leads water from the Wādī Jirdān into the Wādī Ṣaᶜdah. It stretches from east to west. The artificial cutting is 350 m long. The modern gorge is 20 m deep and its width varies between 5 m and about 20 m according to the hardness of the rock.

The *sayl* of Wādī Jirdān still enters the gorge because its bottom lies deeper than that of Wādī Jirdān. In my opinion this situation has lead to the large triangular structure in Wādī Jirdān that von Wissmann (1962: 183–184) interpreted as an immense man-made "Buhne" or deflector dam, but survey along this still existing terrace in the wadi bed did not provide any evidence of an artificial structure. It seems to be the result of the ongoing erosion of the main watercourse due to the lower level of the outflow into Naqb. The second rock cutting is called Nuqayb, literally a small Naqb. It measures 740 m in length and hence is more than twice as long as Naqb. Nevertheless it is less impressive because it is not very deep. Today it seems to represent only a small amount of the original cutting, as it has been heavily infilled following the rains. What can still be seen is a funnel measuring 3–6 m in depth and 20 m across at the top. It was built to bring *sayl* water from the Wādī Šaᶜbah into the Wādī Ṣaᶜdah. The bottom of the canal now lies 5 m higher than the fields in Wādī Šaᶜbah, so it is unclear if Nuqayb ever functioned.

Let us start the discussion by considering Naqb (Fig. 4). The gorge exposes the geological formations. At the top there is a layer of Pleistocene gravel 6–8 m in thickness and partly cemented to a conglomerate. It lies discordant on well-stratified Mesozoic sediments. The layers bend north–south and fall towards the east at an angle of approximately 30°, and for this reason the layers appear almost horizontal in the cross section on Figure 4 and appear to be concordant with the overlying conglomerate. The rock varies a great deal and soft marl layers change to hard sandstone banks. Ripple marks and petrified wood offer further information about the environmental conditions at the time of their origin. The width of the gorge reveals different types of rock: where the gorge cuts through hard sandstone it is narrow, but where it passes through soft stones such as marl it opens up into a rather wide valley. Within the hard parts the original traces of cutting of the canal can still be seen. It is obvious that the modern bottom of the gorge lies much deeper than the bottom of the artificial cutting, which was at about 1037.5 m above sea level. The erosion is in the order of 3 m at the beginning of the gorge and 5 m at the end. The width of the artificial cutting varies between 5 and 6 m, and the height between 7 and 15 m. If we therefore take average measurements of 5.5 m for the width, 13 m for the height and 350 m for the length, an estimated total of 25,000 m³ of material had to be hewn out. About half of this was conglomerate and the rest Mesozoic rocks, mostly hard sandstone. A great deal of this material can still be observed above the gorge in long spoil hills, although since its construction much of this material has been washed into the gorge and transported away with the *sayl*.

The spoil is helpful for dating the cutting. On the southern side of the gorge the wall that surrounds the whole valley of Ṣaᶜdah is covered by the spoil and on the northern side the buried wall can be detected in the profile, but a new wall stands on top of the spoil built of the hewn-out material. These facts show that the wall is older than the Naqb but that it was still in use at the time the Naqb was constructed. Iris Gerlach found an inscription on the old surface at the southern wall of the gorge near its end. It has four clearly readable South Arabian letters, W Ḥ Š M, with possibly a fifth letter at the end. The Naqb can therefore be dated at least as early as the ancient South Arabian period. The wall also helps to date the Nuqayb in relation to the Naqb as it crosses the Nuqayb, but no traces of it can be found beneath the spoil. It goes up to the top of the spoil and shows precisely the same deep desert varnish as the rest of the wall, and thus appears to be younger than the Nuqayb. This means that we can hypothesize the following sequence: first, the Nuqayb was built in order to bring water into the Wādī Ṣaᶜdah. Second, the surrounding wall was constructed and the third stage involved the hewing of the Naqb out of the rock. All of this work was done at least as early as the ancient South Arabian period.

The question then arises as to why did they build two labour-intensive canal dugouts into the Wādī Ṣaᶜdah? As the modern situation illustrates, there can be no doubt that one would have been sufficient. A possible answer might be that in early times the main wadi, i.e. Wādī Jirdān, flowed to the north of the gravel hill. This situation would also change the location of al-Barīra. This important city would then be at the border of the most important wadi of the region, as indeed are all South Arabian cities. Later, upstream of al-Barīra, the wadi broke through to the left and took the course south of Wādī Ṣaᶜdah, which is the course that it still takes today. After this far-reaching event the community of Ṣaᶜdah were obliged to dig a new canal through the rock in order to bring water to their fields.

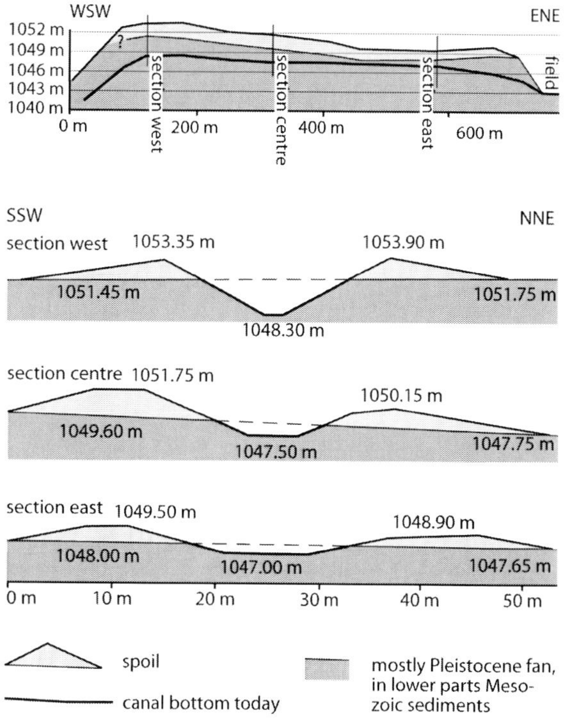

Figure 5. *A longitudinal section and three cross sections of Nuqayb.*

A second possibility is that Nuqayb was constructed in order to connect the Wādī Ṣaᶜdah with the Wādī Šaᶜbah. Perhaps the builders thought that the *sayl* of this wadi would be sufficient for irrigation in Wādī Ṣaᶜdah and that it was less dangerous to tap a smaller wadi; after some time, as they realized that this *sayl* was uncertain and less frequent than the one in Wādī Jirdān, they dug the second cutting in the direction of the main wadi.

The Nuqayb is much less spectacular than the Naqb (Fig. 5). The depth of the canal in comparison to the surface of the fan is a maximum of 3 m, and often no more than 1 m, whereas the quantity of the spoil is much greater than the small hollow would suggest, as large hills composed of hewn-out material stretch along the sides of the canal. This contrast cannot be explained at present. If the canal filled up, the material to do this would have come from the spoil. The solution to this mystery needs further investigation through excavation. Most of the hollow was dug into the gravel and only at the highest point of the canal, in the west, does sandstone appear in the spoil. However, because accumulation is faster than erosion the border between gravel and rock could not be

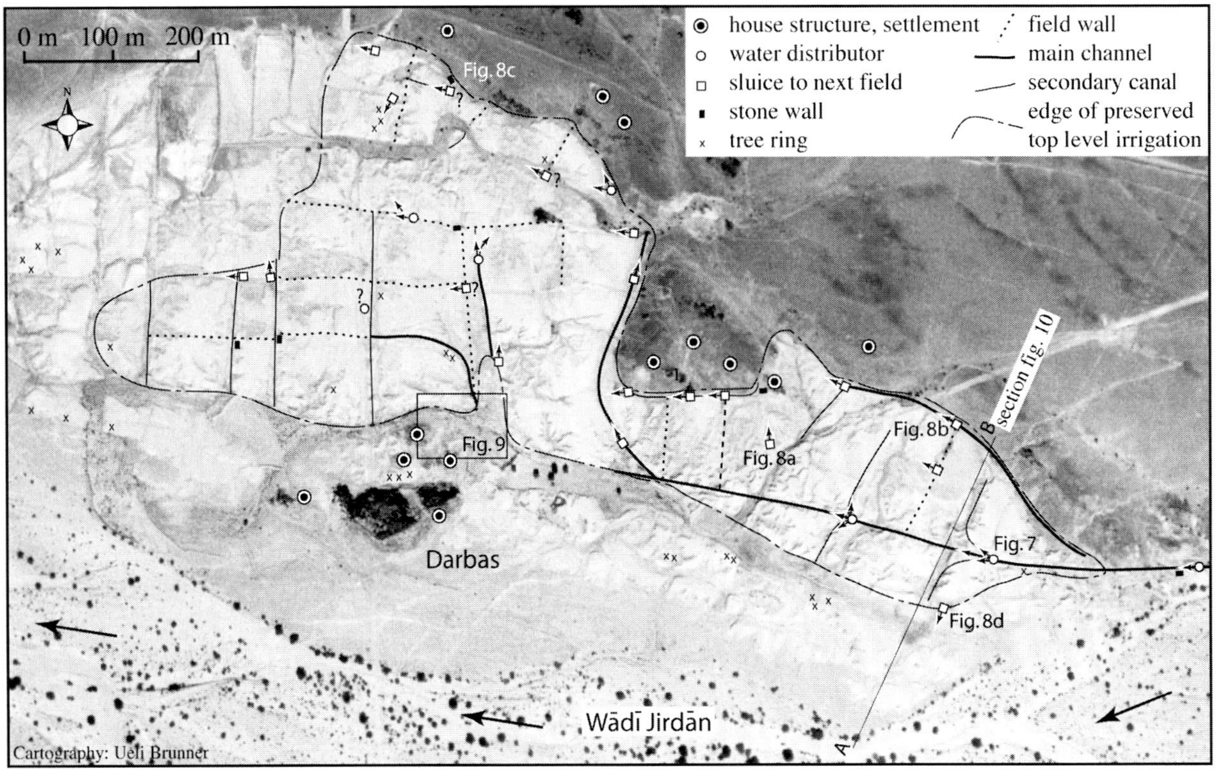

Figure 6. *An aerial photograph of Darbas with all the remaining structures of the ancient irrigation on the higher level.*

detected *in situ*. The present situation with the high level of the canal bottom leads to the impression that Nuqayb was never finished.

At the western end of the Wādī Ṣa^c^dah the situation is also quite complex (Fig. 2). The *sayl* leaves the wadi at a right angle via a narrow gorge 987 m above sea level. Another cutting exists where the main wadi course extends in a straight line. Its bottom is 998 m above sea level. This is 3 m higher than the surface of the nearby ancient irrigation sediments. The canal was cut into the gravel and all the spoil was thrown onto the northern side. The canal is 315 m long and approximately 25 m wide but is presently a mere 2–3 m deep. At its end the bottom lies 3 m lower than at its start. Many myrrh trees grow along this depression. The possible interpretation of these findings at the end of Wādī Ṣa^c^dah is as follows: there might have been a natural outlet close to where the water leaves the valley today. Its level was higher than it is today and its location 100 m further to the east. In order to protect the fields from erosion the ancient South Arabian farmers constructed a dam at this point. The highest preserved part reaches a level of 998 m above sea level, which is exactly the level of the canal. Perhaps the outlet of the wadi was also on a level too low to reach the underlying fields and that is why they started to dig the canal into the gravel plateau. Everywhere in southern Arabia, artificial conduits show a very low gradient, close to one out of a thousand. If the end of the canal is 995 m above sea level, the start will have been at almost the same level and that corresponds very well to the surface of the ancient irrigation sediments. However, status of the canal gives the impression that it was not finished and that this canal was therefore never used.

The irrigation system in Darbas

The ancient oasis of Darbas is located in a niche of the Pleistocene fan plateau, 1.3 km east-south-east of Ṣa^c^dah on the right side of the Wādī Jirdān. Twin hills composed of granite, gneiss, and sandstone outcrops at the edge of the wadi emphasize its well-defined area of about 120 ha (Fig. 6). The oasis is marked by irrigation sediments

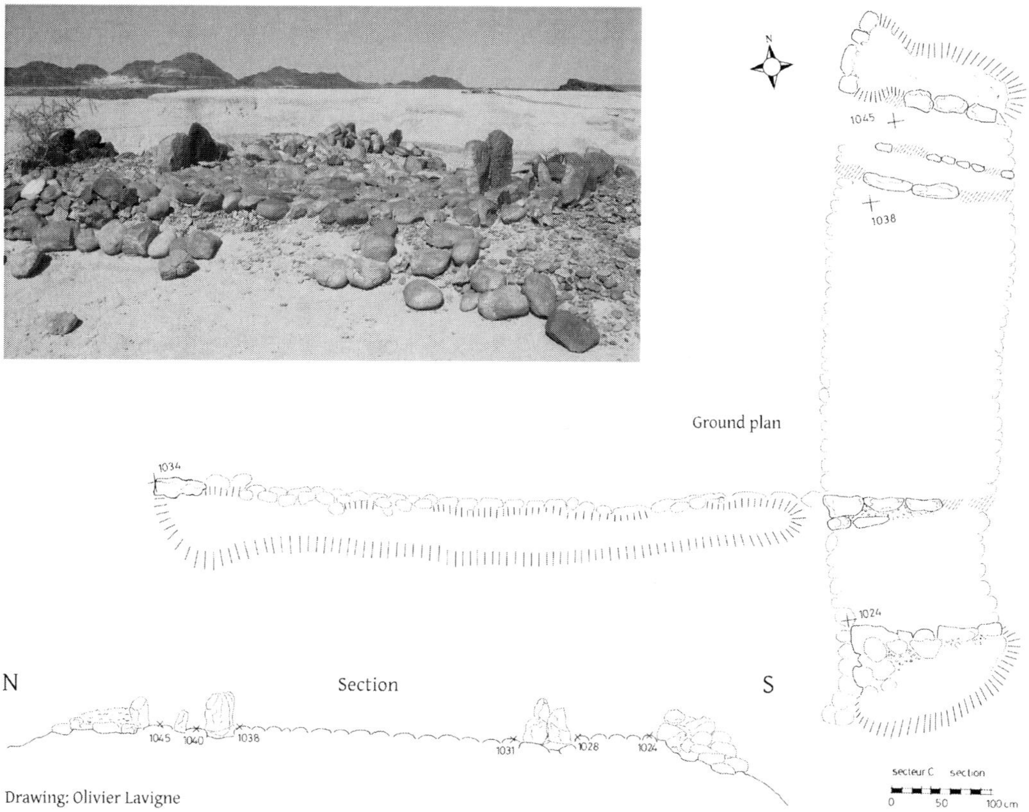

FIGURE 7. *A section and ground plan of a well-preserved water distributor on the highest level and a photograph of the same structure seen from the east. (For the location see Fig. 6).*

with a characteristic rectangular erosion pattern on their surface (Brunner 2000: 53). These irrigation sediments do not cover the entire niche as they are missing in the western part where gravels form the surface. The irrigation sediments show three different levels: the highest level can be found in the eastern part, a middle level in the centre, and the lowest level in the western part.

There are two possible explanations for these terraces. They could be the result of erosion or of accumulation. If the terraces are the result of erosion, this means that the surface of the highest terrace represents the youngest fields and the lowest represents the oldest fields. If the terraces are the result of accumulation, the surfaces of all three terraces could be the same age, the lowest could even be the youngest or the highest the oldest. There is no doubt that a lateral strip along the wadi was eroded by floodwaters. Some small local runoffs have cut through the irrigation sediments but there is not even a hint of denudation. The desert varnish on outcrops reaches the modern surface of the silt accumulations. Furthermore the irrigation-related structures are located only a fraction of a metre higher than the present surface. These facts clearly show that erosion of the fields since their abandonment was almost nil, and this is further evidence that these terraces already existed during the agricultural use of this oasis. In addition the modern irrigated area in the Wādī Ṣaᶜdah shows similar terraces between the fields. It seems that the western part, where the irrigation sediments are missing, was never used as fields.

The irrigation system on the higher level is better preserved. It can be traced from its beginning at the border of the wadi until its end in the fields. It is laid out on the highest and middle level. The main canal started its course in a corner of the gravel plateau where it was safe from being washed away by flash floods, and just 1 km downstream of Naqb. A slightly visible terrace stretches 440 m to a cut in the rocks. This was the bottleneck of the system (Crassard & Hitgen 2007: fig. 9). The cross section of the canal reveals the following figures, which are helpful in calculating the capacity of the system:

Figure 8. *a. A short conduit that helped to overcome a level of 0.6 m; b. A water distributor of the lateral canal; c. A protection wall of the lateral canal; d. A conduit from a higher to a lower level. (For the locations see Fig. 6).*

height on the hillside	1.9 m
width at bottom	3.2 m
height on wadi side in rock	0.9 m
preserved height of stonework	0.5 m
total height on wadi side	1.4 m
width on top	4.4 m
cross section	*c.* 6 m^2

The velocity of the water in the canals is mostly below 2 m/sec. The capacity at this point therefore will have been in the order of about 10 m^3/sec. This means that the whole oasis of 120 ha could theoretically be flooded by half a metre of water in less than a day. A few metres further on, several terrace walls show that the main canal was divided into two canals. One of these followed the contour of the plateau, whereas the other continued straight on for 170 m where it met a water distributor. This structure is very well preserved and shows the way the water was divided (Fig. 7). The water distributor had three outlets, of which the central one was the largest at 3 m wide. The left one was 1 m wide, and the right one was 0.7 m across. This small outlet was further divided by two upright plates into two sections measuring 0.2 m and 0.4 m across. The corresponding canals can be seen a few metres further on where they lead, orthogonally to the main canal, to the fields.

The main canal continues in the direction of the two sandstone outcrops where the small settlement was located (Crassard & Hitgen 2007: 53). For 300 m it cannot be seen because erosion has lowered the level and bulldozers

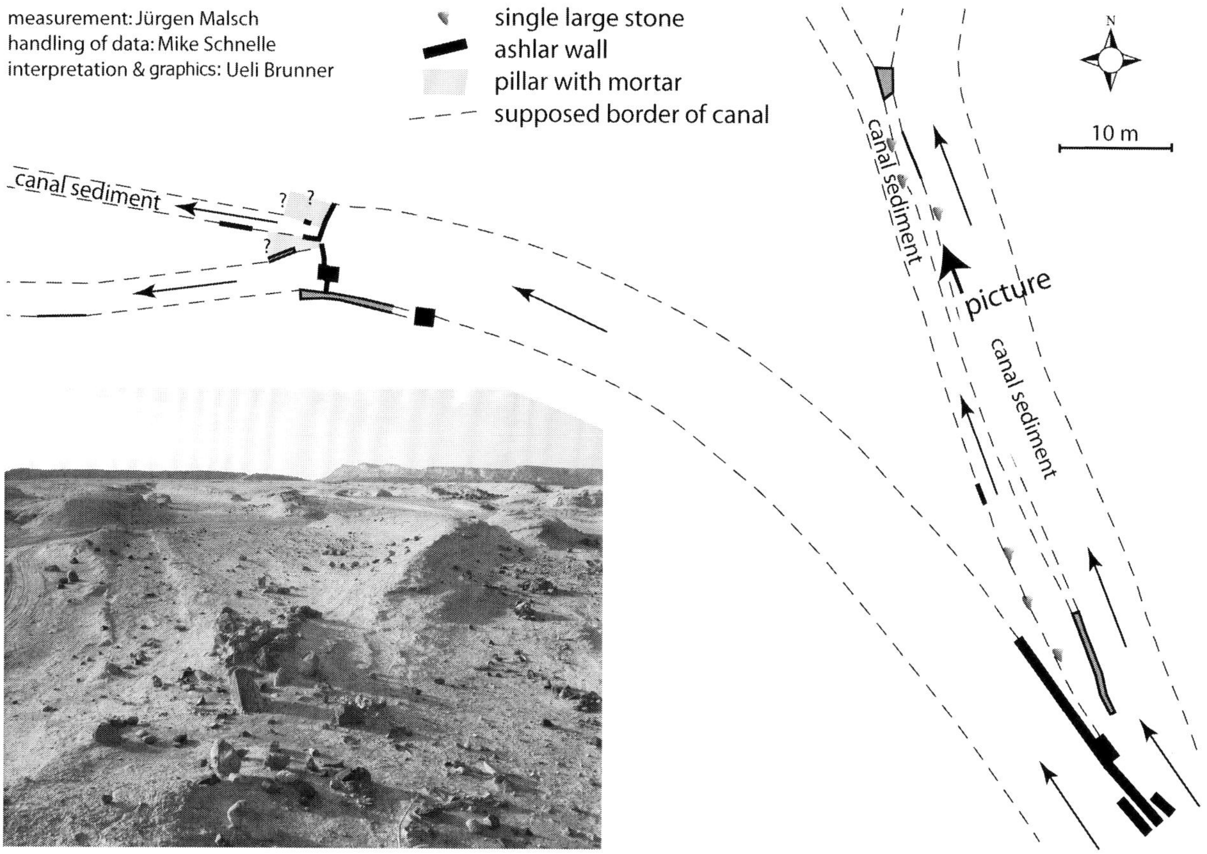

Figure 9. *A ground plan of an arrangement of water distributors on the lower level with an interpretation of possible canals belonging to these structures. (The direction view of the photograph is marked above; for the location see Fig. 6).*

have flattened the whole area in order to establish new fields; thus the principal division of the main canal no longer exists. Nevertheless it is clear where it was and in which direction the ongoing canals led: one turned to the north-west to reach the fields at the inner end, and the other one continued to the west and fed all the canals turning off at an angle of 90° to the north.

Within the distribution system we find different water-related stone structures (Fig. 8). The aim of a water distributor was to divert water from the canal into another canal or directly into the field. A water conduit directed the water safely from one field to the next, which mostly lay on a lower level, so a terrace had to be overcome without erosion. Other water-related structures are stone walls built in order to protect the fields or canal banks from being eroded or to prevent surface flow from the adjacent hills washing the canal away. The method of construction of all these stone structures on the top level is always very similar. The bottom was laid out with limestone boulders from the wadi bed. The foundation of the walls was built with medium-sized quarry stones of quartzite or sandstone standing in an upright position. Quite often these ashlars stand in a double row so there is still an intervening space, which was filled with a variety of small stones and gravel. Mortar could not be found at any site. All of these structures have a clear function, are of simple construction, and are quite short.

This is in contrast to the irrigation system on the lower level where quite long and complicated structures prevail. In this system the water was conducted by walls that continued for over 50 m (Fig. 9). Often there are so many walls that it is hard to determine their function. The walls are built of large ashlars of hard quartzite, which stand upright one behind the other forming a line. When

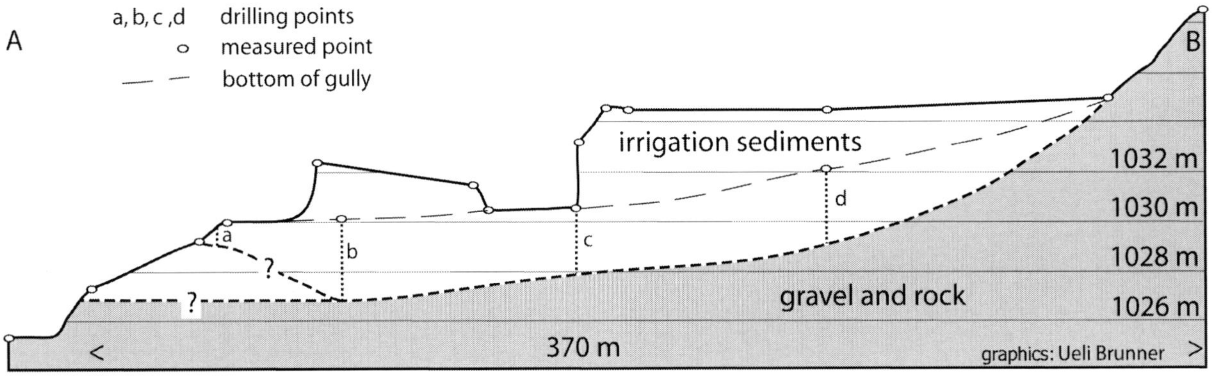

Figure 10. *A cross section of the sediments of the oasis of Darbas in its eastern part. (For the location see Fig. 6).*

smaller quarry stones were used for construction, they were held together by a greyish mortar consisting mostly of silt and clay and some ash. All of the aforementioned characteristics — long stone walls, large ashlars, and use of mortar — lead us to suppose that the water flowed in this canal system with a higher velocity than in the rectangular system on the higher level. Unfortunately this supposition could not be confirmed by the grain size of the corresponding irrigation sediments, as there is no difference in the sediments between the lower and the upper level.

The sediments show the characteristic grain size distribution of all the irrigation sediments in southern Arabia (Brunner 1983: 18). They consist mostly of silt with a high content of clay and a little fine sand. Coarser material is completely absent. Proof of their artificial origin are the missing layers and all the irrigation-related structures in the accumulations such as canals, field walls, tree impressions, furrows, and the high content of very fine root holes. The canal sediments are the only well-stratified sediments. The height of the sediments was looked for in a cross section at the eastern part. Four drillings enabled us to detect the original surface of the terrain before irrigation (Fig. 10). It emerged that it was rather flat. The situation close to the wadi was unclear. After less than 1 m the drill got stuck on hard gravel, so it is not clear if this is only a thin layer of gravel overlying the irrigation sediments or whether there was a natural hill formed by accumulation. The maximal height for the irrigation sediments is 6.6 m. The sedimentation rate in floodwater-irrigated fields in southern Arabia is around 1.1 cm per year (Brunner 1983: 65). Hence in Darbas there was irrigated agriculture for at least 600 years. This time period corresponds very well with the history, which could be established by archaeological survey and excavations. According to initial results, Darbas was settled from about the middle of the first millennium BC to the first century AD (Crassard & Hitgen 2007: 56–57). In the meantime a series of radiocarbon dates from the settlement of Darbas point to the fact that it was in use longer than so far suggested. The oldest sample dates from the tenth century BC, the latest one from the seventh century AD.

Some indications exist for a relative chronology of the two irrigation systems. The upper system was situated on the surface of the high and middle level, whereas the lower system bypassed the high level and used the low level as well as some parts of the middle level as fields. Nowhere was an intermingling of the irrigation sediments to be observed. So the first idea, that the lower system is the older one that was once sedimented by irrigation and then exposed through erosion, could not be supported by the findings in the field. The second idea was that the lower system could have been arranged on a lateral erosion terrace of the oasis, which means it would be younger than the upper one. Comparison of the building material and style of the waterworks suggests this may be correct. The structures on the high level are characterized by their regular layout, small size, boulders, and the absence of mortar. These regularities point to planned engineering work, as was customary in ancient South Arabia in the centuries BC. The arrangement on the lower level appears arbitrary. The building technique and material changes from one place to the other. The lack of precision during building is compensated by the use of mortar. Even if the mortar is not the real Qaddād with volcanic supplements, it points to a date in the first centuries AD (Brunner 1989: 39). Gentelle (1991: 14) reports a similar system in Šabwa.

Two samples gathered for radiocarbon dating from

the irrigation sediments give an idea of their age. The first sample is charcoal from a fireplace, 90 m north of the western settlement of Darbas (Fig. 6). It was embedded 80 cm below the surface of the higher level. The sample (Poz 21856) was dated to 2100±40 BP, which corresponds with a certainty of 68 % to 180–50 BC. This means that irrigation on the higher level stopped shortly after this period. The second sample from the fields is a snail of Melanidae sp., which was found 3.3 m below the surface at 1031.14 m above sea level. It was located 400 m east of Darbas and dated to 3785±35 BP (Poz 21843) which corresponds with a certainty of 95 % to 2340–2120 BC. This result is surprising. Two explanations are possible. Firstly, the basis of the silts in Darbas has accumulated naturally. Secondly, there was incipient irrigation in the late third millennium. The first of these possibilities is rather unlikely. All indications — such as grain size, structures in the sediment, or missing stratification — point to irrigation sediments. This therefore seems to be a further clue for dating the start of irrigated agriculture in southern Arabia to the late third millennium BC (Brunner 1997: 80).

The history of irrigation in Darbas may be outlined as follows: irrigation started in Darbas in the second half of the third millennium BC. After a rather short period, the oasis was abandoned. Sometime during the first millennium BC irrigation restarted. A normal rectangular system was applied. Water was taken from the *sayl* of the Wādī Jirdān by an upstream deflector dam. The division of the water was effected by short well-constructed distributors. This kind of irrigation was successful and lasted for several hundred years. During this time the level of the fields, especially those in the east that were flooded first, rose above 6 m. Due to the high level of these fields, irrigation became more and more labour-intensive. At the beginning of the first millennium AD, when the region was already in decline, a new irrigation scheme was applied. It bypassed the highest fields and shifted the oasis more to the west. Long wall-like structures conducted the water into the small canals and into the fields. Mortar helped to strengthen these easily built distributors. This system lasted perhaps only a century or two, and the oasis of Darbas was abandoned in the middle of the first millennium AD.

Darbas may also be set in relation to al-Barīra and al-Bināʾ. Both sites are considered to date to the middle of the first millennium BC (Doe 1971: 193). Around al-Barīra, which is located 4 km upstream of Darbas, the irrigation sediments are interesting. The cliff facing the Wādī Jirdān still stands at a height of 9 m. The layout of the fields is clearly visible. Their size, an average 60×55 m, is smaller than in Darbas where they normally measure 100×70 m. The numerous signs of tree impressions on the surface indicate a dense bush vegetation, as it exists on modern fields. What is surprising is the absolute lack of any stone structures in the whole area of the ancient irrigation sediments although it is deeply dissected by gullies. The only exception is a small longitudinal hill, 100 m outside al-Barīra, which is covered by boulders. The same can be said of the irrigation sediments on the south side of Wādī Jirdān, in al-Ḏawj. Judging from an aerial photograph, it is possible that the canals from al-Barīra were related to the ones at al-Ḏawj and thus formed a common irrigation unit. This would be further evidence to support the theory that the Wādī Jirdān once flowed north of al-Barīra out onto the plain.

Wādī Jirdān in comparison with other ancient South Arabian irrigation systems

Bowen (1958), followed by Brunner & Haefner (1990) with a quantitative study, was the first to show the wide distribution of ancient irrigation across southern Arabia. The area covered by the remaining irrigation sediments in Wādī Jirdān — less than 1000 ha — is small in comparison with other valleys, especially Wādī Marḫah, where they cover an area of 12,000 ha (Brunner & Haefner 1990: 151). It is interesting to note that the same method — namely the Yemeni floodwater irrigation — was used in all the wadis (Gentelle 2003: 109). In Maʾrib the irrigation system was centralized with the Great Dam as the only water collection (Brunner 1983: 96–99). Two main canals delivered the water from the dam sluices to the beginning of the two oases, where many feeder canals started. Conduits led the water from the canal into the fields or from one field to the next. In Šabwa as in most other valleys such as Jawf, Bayḥān, or Marḫah the agricultural land use consisted of several independent units (Gentelle 1991: 19; Bowen 1958: fig. 35; Brunner 1997: 76). The same can be stated for Wādī Jirdān, as the present paper shows. There were small irrigation units in Wādī Ṣaʿdah and Darbas and possibly larger ones around al-Barīra and al-Bināʾ. All the surfaces of ancient irrigation sediments in Wādī Jirdān show the rectangular erosion pattern indicating the Sabaean geometric influence of a well-planned rectangular arrangement of the canal system. On the other hand, Šabwa (Gentelle 1991: 14) and the lower Wādī Marḫah (Brunner 1997: 79–83) show a different arrangement with a hand-like system and irregularly arranged fields.

The technique of constructing water-related structures in Wādī Jirdān is very simple. Untreated quarry stones and natural boulders were usually used for building distributors or conduits. This is in contrast to the oases where the capitals of the ancient South Arabian kingdoms were located and where limestone ashlars were prepared for the construction of sluices, thus forming perfect walls. Examples of these can be found at Šabwa (Gentelle 1991: 31), Maʾrib (Brunner 1983: table 18), and Raybūn (Sedov 1988: fig. 8). Similar distributors to those at Darbas are known from Šabwa (Philby 1939: 112; Gentelle 1991: 44) or from the lower Wādī Marḫah (Brunner 1997: 78). It therefore seems that Darbas was a peripheral place where people did not expend much energy in carefully cutting the stones. The style of the water distributors is similar to the one in Wādī Marḫah and Ḥaḍramawt but different from that in Maʾrib and Jawf. The labour-intensive work to produce an oasis in Wādī Ṣaʿdah indicates a special interest on the part of the central power to settle people in this lateral outpost. The cuttings of Naqb and Nuqayb and the construction of a 12 km-long wall all around the valley support this argument.

Notes

1 The work was financed by YLNG Co Ltd. The project management and the organization lay in the hands of the German Archaeological Institute (DAI Ṣanʿāʾ, Iris Gerlach) and the French Centre for Archaeology and Social Science in Ṣanʿāʾ (CEFAS, Jean Lambert). I would like to thank these institutions for their great support as well as the General Organization of Antiquities and Museums (GOAM, Dr ʿAbd Allah Bā Wazīr, President and Ḫayrān Moḥṣin al-Zubaydī, director of Šabwa branch) for their effort in setting up the project in the tribal region. Very helpful information and co-operation was given during the fieldwork by Rémy Crassard, Iris Gerlach, Holger Hitgen, Sarah Japp, Olivier Lavigne, Jürgen Malsch, Mike Schnelle, Moḥammad ʿAmīn, and Rabiaʿ ʿAbd Allah al-Baṭfur. Finally the author would like to express his gratitude to Holger Hitgen for reading and correcting this paper.

2 Unfortunately, because of tribal problems it was not possible to study the modern irrigation in detail.

References

Bowen R. LeB.
1958. Irrigation in Ancient Qatabân (Beihân). Pages 43–131 in R. LeB. Bowen & F.P. Albright, *Archaeological Discoveries in South Arabia*. Baltimore, MD: The Johns Hopkins Press.

Brunner U.
1983. *Die Erforschung der antiken Oase von Mārib mit Hilfe geomorphologischer Untersuchungsmethoden*. (Archäologische Berichte aus dem Yemen, 2). Mainz: Philipp von Zabern.
1989. Bausteine der Sabäer. *Münchner Beiträge zur Völkerkunde* 2: 27–42.
1997. The history of irrigation in Wādī Marḫah. *Proceedings of the Seminar for Arabian Studies* 27: 75–85.
2000. The Sustainability of the Ancient Great Dam of Maʾrib in Yemen. *International Commission on Irrigation and Dams Journal* 49/4: 49–61.

Brunner U. & Haefner H.
1990. Altsüdarabische Bewässerungsoasen. *Die Erde* 121: 135–153.

Crassard R. & Hitgen H.
2007. From Ṣāfer to Bālḥāf — rescue excavations along the Yemen LNG pipeline route. *Proceedings of the Seminar for Arabian Studies* 37: 43–59.

Doe B.
1971. *Southern Arabia*. London: Thames and Hudson.

Gentelle P.
1991. Les irrigations antiques à Shabwa. Fouilles de Shabwa II. *Syria* 68: 5–54.
2003. *Traces d'Eau — Un géographe chez les archéologues*. Paris: Editions Belin.

Lankester Harding G.
1964. *Archaeology in the Aden Protectorates*. London: Her Majesty's Stationery Office.

Philby H.St.J.B.
1939. *Sheba's Daughter. Being a Record of Travel in Southern Arabia*. London: Methuen & Co. Ltd.

Sedov A.
1988. Raybūn, a complex of archaeological monuments in the lower reaches of Wādī Dauʾan and certain problems of its protection and restoration. Pages 61–66 in S.Y. Bersina (ed.), *Ancient and Mediaeval Monuments of Civilization of Southern Arabia*. Moscow: Nauka.

von Wissmann H.
1962. Al-Barîra in Girdân im Vergleich mit anderen Stadtfestungen Alt-Südarabiens. *Le Muséon* 75: 177–209.

Author's address
Dr Ueli Brunner, Gündisauerstrasse 2, 8330 Hermatswil, Switzerland.
e-mail ueli_brunner@bluewin.ch

Proceedings of the Seminar for Arabian Studies 38 (2008): 89–92

Stone vessels from KHB-1, Ja'lān region, Sultanate of Oman (Poster)

Fabio Cavulli & Simona Scaruffi

Keywords: stone vessels, KHB-1, Ja'lān, Oman

The site of KHB-1 is located on the coast of the eastern Ja'lān region (Sultanate of Oman) and lies about 1.5 km north of the village of Khabbah and less than 1 km from the Ra's al-Khabbah headland. It is situated on a ridge next to a marine erosion terrace that starts at the promontory, continues northwards and stops 3 km south of the village of Ra's al-Hadd. The terrace varies in width between 150 and 1200 m and lies about 35 m above sea level. In the past this natural feature separated the sea from the inner palaeo-lagoon to the west. The lagoon must have been fed both by the sea and the wadi given the presence of *Terebralia palustris* shell fossils (Berger *et al.* 2005; Coltorti 1989; Cremaschi 2001; Zaffagnini 1999). The site is a multi-stratified fishing settlement with some evidence for domesticated animals, and has been dated between the end of the fifth and the beginning of the fourth millennium BC (Biagi 1988: 276–279; 1994; Magnani *et al.* 2007). Occupation of the site was probably seasonal and the community who lived in KHB-1 may have been of nomadic character, with seasonal movements between the internal mountain ranges and the coastal area where fish are abundant during winter. The stratigraphic excavation of the site has revealed the presence of five phases of occupation and three of these are associated with dwelling structures (Cavulli 2004; 2005a; 2005b; forthcoming).

One of the most distinctive groups of artefacts found at KHB-1 is represented by ten fragments of stone vessels. The majority were found on the surface in the western part of the site (area C), and only one was uncovered through excavation in trench D. Despite their fragmented condition, almost all have diagnostic elements.

All were made of calcarenite containing rounded granular bioclasts and all are carved. Nonetheless, the crumbly and powdery nature of the stone does not allow recognition of traces of the working processes such as pecking or polishing.

Some fragments were conserved with a solution of Paraloid B-72 and acetone in order to rehydrate and consolidate the stone; (1) the reconstructable pieces were glued together with Mecosan S. In some cases the stone

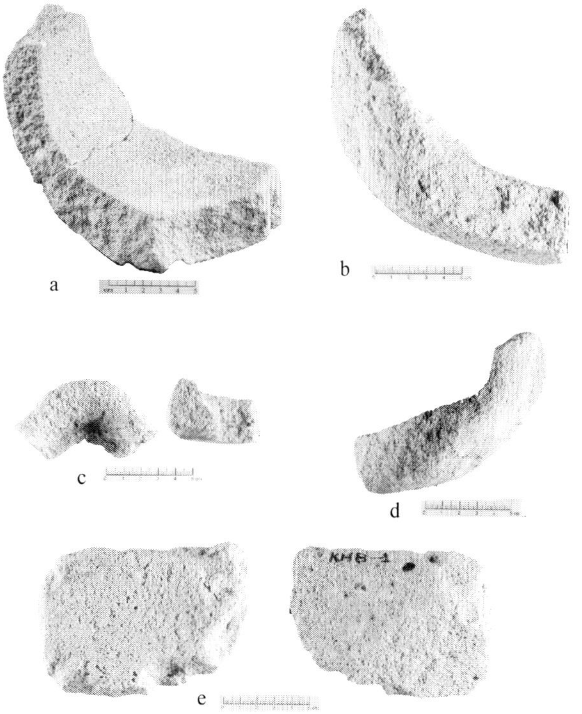

Figure 1. *Class 1, basins with no clear distinction between sides and the bottom: a (DA 12527), b (DA 14220), d (DA 12528); Class 3, shallow quadrangular bowl: c (DA 12529); Class 4, quadrangular plate-like vessel: e (DA 14022).*

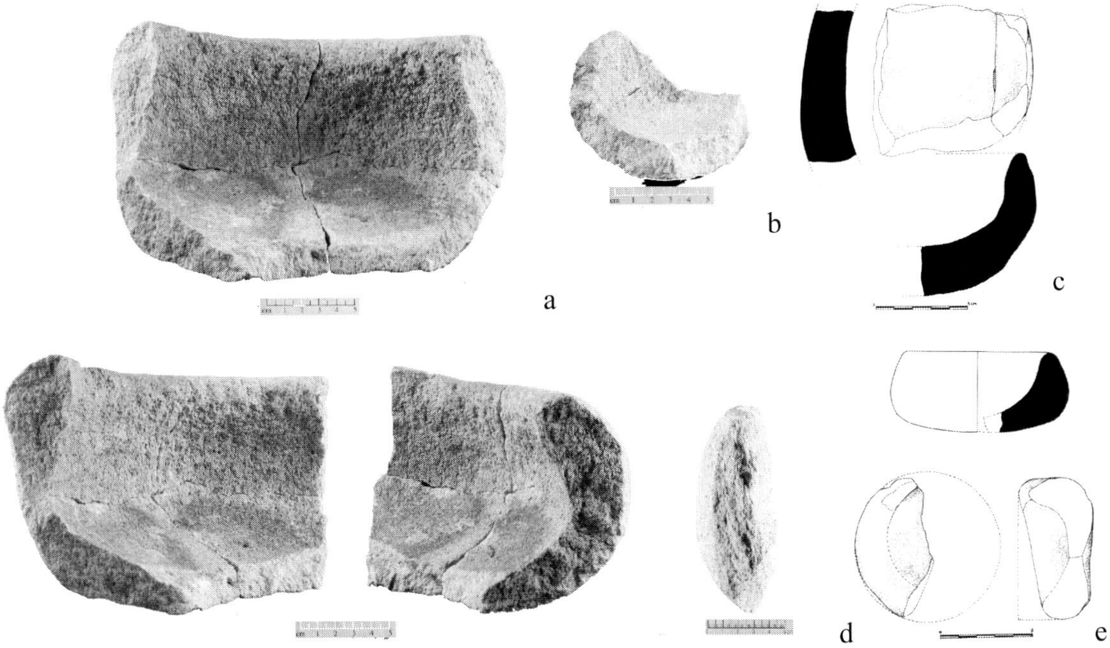

FIGURE 2. *Class 2, bowl with a distinction between sides and bottom: a (DA 18245), b-c (DA 15323), d (DA 18301), e (DA 15139).*

changed colour from grey to soft pink or orange following treatment owing to the dehydrated condition of the stone. As with all findings, a detailed description of these artefacts was entered into a database purposely created for this excavation (the main table with the general data, i.e. number, measurements, source, etc., is linked to more specific tables for each class of materials, divided into wide categories, such as adornments, lithic elements, and stone tools).

Four main shape classes were recognised following typological analysis. The first class consists of a basin-like form, with no clear distinction between the sides and bottom (Fig. 1/a–b, d). There are three examples, with a height of 15.9 cm, length of 11 cm, and thickness of 3.5 cm. The well–preserved example of a vase, made up of four joining fragments, also belongs to this class (Fig. 2/a). As a considerable portion of this vase survives, it is possible to estimate a maximum diameter of approximately 38–39 cm.

The third class corresponds to a single fragment belonging to a shallow quadrangular–like vessel bowl with a very eroded or thin base and which measures 8.4 cm high, 3.9 cm across and 2.7 cm thick (Fig. 1/c).

The fourth class is represented by a single fragment belonging to a quadrangular plate–like vessel measuring about 12.1 cm high, 8.1 cm long and 3.1 cm thick (Fig. 1/e). It has one right angle and a flat, rather concave, shape which was probably worn through heavy use. Another fragment is not attributable to any of these categories as it is a simple piece of a vessel rim (DA14020).

The stone vessels uncovered at KHB-1 belong to an interesting class of finds found elsewhere in eastern and southern Arabia. Similar examples are known from the United Arab Emirates (including Dalma island), Yemen, and Oman, and the majority was found in surface collections associated with Ubaid and Mid-Holocene contexts (Edens 1988: 30; Inizan 1988: 72; Kallweit 2001: 126; Kallweit, Beech & Al-Tikriti 2005: 103–104; Zarins 2001: 45). The common interpretation is that these objects could have been used as a type of mortar for grinding food, which is in accordance with several similar artefacts found across the Near East and dated as early as the Epipalaeolithic and Neolithic periods (Wright 1991; 1994). However, a different interpretation might be proposed for the finds from the Arabian coastal Middle Holocene sites. The presence of large hearths associated with burnt shells at KHB-1 and the ethnographic comparisons with local traditions suggests that the sandstone vessels might have been used to grind burnt shells and produce a waterproof powder, which would have been applied to plant-fibre fishnets.

Notes

[1] Restored by Thomas Conci – THC Design and Exhibit

Acknowledgements

* The authors' contribution is equal. The authors would like to thank the directors of the Joint Hadd Project: M. Tosi and S. Cleuziou, and Mark Tomasi for correcting the English.

References

Berger J-F., Cleuziou S., Davtian G., Cattani M., Cavulli F., Charpentier V., Cremaschi M., Giraud J., Marquis P., Martin C., Méry S., Plaziat J-C. & Saliège J-F.

2005. Evolution paléogéographique du Ja'alan (Oman) à l'Holocène moyen: Impact sur l'évolution des paléomilieux littoraux et les stratégies d'adaptation des communautés humaines. *Paléorient* 31/1: 46–63.

Biagi P.

1988. Surveys along the Oman coast: preliminary report on the 1985–1988 campaigns. *East and West* 38: 17–291.

1994. A radiocarbon Chronology for the aceramic shell-middens of coastal Oman. *Arabian Archaeology and Epigraphy* 5: 17–31.

Cavulli F.

2004. Khabbah 1: un villaggio di pescatori raccoglitori del V millennio a.C. *Scoprire. Gli scavi dell'Università di Bologna, Catalogo della mostra*, 18 maggio–18 giugno 2004: 225–229.

2005a. L'insediamento di KHB-1 (Ra's al-Khabba, Sultanato dell'Oman): lo scavo, i resti strutturali e i confronti etnografici. *Ocnus* 12: 37–48.

2005b. Problemi stratigrafici relativi allo scavo di sedimenti sciolti in ambiente arido. *Ocnus* 12: 49–62.

forthcoming. Problems of stratigraphy relating to the excavation of loose sediment in dry environments: a case study of KHB-1, Ra's al Khabbah, Sultanate of Oman. *Journal of Archaeological Method and Theory*

Coltorti M.

1989. Geomorphological characteristics of the Ra's al-Junayz area (Sultanate of Oman). Pages 79–96 in P.M. Costa & M. Tosi (eds), *Oman Studies. Papers on the archaeology and history of Oman*. (Serie Orientale Roma, 63). Rome: Istituto Italiano per il Medio ed Estremo Oriente.

Cremaschi M.

2001. *Aggiornamento su: l'evoluzione olocenica delle lagune costiere comprese fra Ras al-Hadd ed Assila – Il fattore paleoclimatico*. Rome: Istituto Italiano per l'Africa e l'Oriente. [Unpublished manuscript].

Edens C.

1988. The Rub' al-Khali "Neolithic" Revisited: the view from Nadqan. Pages 11–43 in D.T. Potts (ed.), *Araby the Blest. Studies in Arabian Archaeology*. (Carsten Niebuhr Institute Publications, 7). Copenhagen: Museum Tusculanum.

Inizan M.L. (ed.)

1988. *Préhistoire à Qatar. Mission archéologique française*. ii. Paris: Éditions Recherche sur les Civilisations.

Kallweit H.

1996 [2001]. *Neolithische und Bronzezeitliche Besiedlung im Wadi Dhahr, Republik Jemen. Eine Untersuchung auf der basis von Geländebegehungen und Sondagen. Inaugural-Dissertation der Philosophischen Fakultäten der Albert-Ludwigs-Universität zu Freiburg i. Br.* URL: www.freidik.uni-freiburg.de/volltexte/270/ [Unpublished].

Kallweit H., Beech M. & Al-Tikriti W.Y.

2005. Kharimat Khor al-Manahil and Khor Al Manahil — New Neolithic sites in the south-eastern desert of the UAE. *Proceedings of the Seminar for Arabian Studies* 35: 97–113.

Magnani G., Bartolomei P., Cavulli F., Esposito M., Marino E.C., Neri M., Rizzo A., Scaruffi S. & Tosi M.
2007. U-series and radiocarbon dates on mollusc shells from the uppermost layer of the archaeological site of KHB-1, Ra's al Khabbah, Oman. *Journal of Archaeological Science* 34: 749–755.

Wright K.I.
1991. The Origins and development of ground stone assemblages in Late Pleistocene Southwest Asia. *Paléorient* 17/1: 19–45.
1994. Ground-Stone Tools and Hunter-Gatherer Subsistence in Southwest Asia: implications for the Transition to Farming. *American Antiquity* 59/2: 238–263.

Zaffagnini F.
1999. *Laguna di Ra's al-Khabbah.* Rome: Istituto Italiano per l'Africa e l'Oriente. [Unpublished manuscript].

Zarins J.
2001. *The Land of Incense. Archaeological work in the Governatorate of Dhofar, Sultanate of Oman 1990–1995.* The Project of the National Committee for the supervision of Archaeological survey in the Sultanate, Ministry of Information (Sultan Qaboos Publication, Archaeology & Cultural Heritage Series, 1). Sultanate of Oman: Al Nahda.

Authors addresses
Fabio Cavulli, Laboratorio di Preistoria "B. Bagolini", Dipartimento di Filosofia, Storia e Beni Culturali, University of Trento, Corso 3 Novembre, 132, I-38100, Trento, Italy.
e-mail Fabio.Cavulli@lett.unitn.it

Simona Scaruffi, Dipartimento di Archeologia, University of Bologna, Department of Archaeology, Piazza San Giovanni in Monte, 2, I-40124, Bologna, Italy.
e-mail simonascaruffi@yahoo.it

Proceedings of the Seminar for Arabian Studies 38 (2008): 93–116

Hunter-gatherers of the "empty quarter of the early Holocene" to the last Neolithic societies: chronology of the late prehistory of south-eastern Arabia (8000–3100 BC)

VINCENT CHARPENTIER

Summary
The data from recent excavations in the Oman peninsula, especially in the Ja'alan and the Jebel Qara (Sultanate of Oman) enable us better to refine certain cultural entities and to define new ones, to help determine the chronology of a part of the late prehistory of south-eastern Arabia. To begin with, the "empty quarter of the early Holocene" is half full: "Fasad facies" characterizes one of the earliest Holocene hunter-gatherers occupation in Oman (8000–7500 BC). Today we possess data from several stratified sites, enabling definition of two quite distinct Neolithic techno-facies, which appear in succession: the trihedral points facies (Habarut facies) between 6500 and 4500 BC, and the facies of the points with diamond-shaped section (Suwayh facies) between 4500 and about 3800–3700 BC.

Keywords: prehistory, early and middle Holocene, Neolithic, chronology, Arabia, Oman peninsula.

Introduction

In a seminal article published in 1992, Margaret Uerpmann laid the basis for the chronology of the late prehistory of the Oman peninsula (1992). Fifteen years later, most of these questions remain with us. The identification of the hunter-gatherer societies of the beginning of the early Holocene, the role of autochthonous cultures in the appearance of the first producer societies, and the influence of the PPNB of the Levant in the emergence of the Neolithic in the Oman peninsula are indeed themes that remain crucial for research.

The Saruq facies identified by M. Uerpmann has included up to the present all Neolithic cultures with developed lithic industries in the Oman peninsula (Uerpmann M 1992; Uerpmann & Uerpmann 2003: 142–162). The aim of this article is to take up the question of these bifacial industries, in order to present two different techno-facies based on controlled stratigraphic data: the Habarut facies (6500–4500 BC), which is followed by the Suwayh facies (4500–3800/3700). The presence of other categories of artefacts besides these two lithic facies demonstrates that two cultural entities can be defined.

The data from recent excavations between the Gulf and the Arabian Sea are still rare for these periods: along the Gulf (Dalma, Marawah, Akab), inland within the UAE (Buhais, Jebel Faya) and in the Sultanate of Oman, especially in the Ja'alan and the Jebel Qara (Dhofar). However, they enable us better to refine certain cultural entities and to define new ones, to help determine the chronology of a part of the late prehistory of south-eastern Arabia.

The Ja'alan: twenty years of looking for stratigraphy

The Ja'alan is the eastern extremity of the Arab world and covers about 3000 km^2. Commencing in 1985, archaeological research has concentrated on the early Bronze Age (Hafit and Umm an Nar periods) in this region and between Ra's al-Jins and Ra's al-Hadd. From the beginning of the project, a survey centred on the environment and the resources of past populations enabled identification of the first Neolithic flint-knapping workshops on the Jebel Saffan (Charpentier 1986; 1988). Considered to be a zone of intensive study, this province was surveyed several times, intensively on its coast (Biagi 1988*a*; 1988*b*; 1994; Biagi & Maggi 1990; Charpentier 1986; 1988; 2001; Usai 2000), but less so in the interior, or for specific reasons (research on tethering stones, for example) (Edens 1988*a*; Cavallari 2004). Some experiments with intra-site spatial analysis and

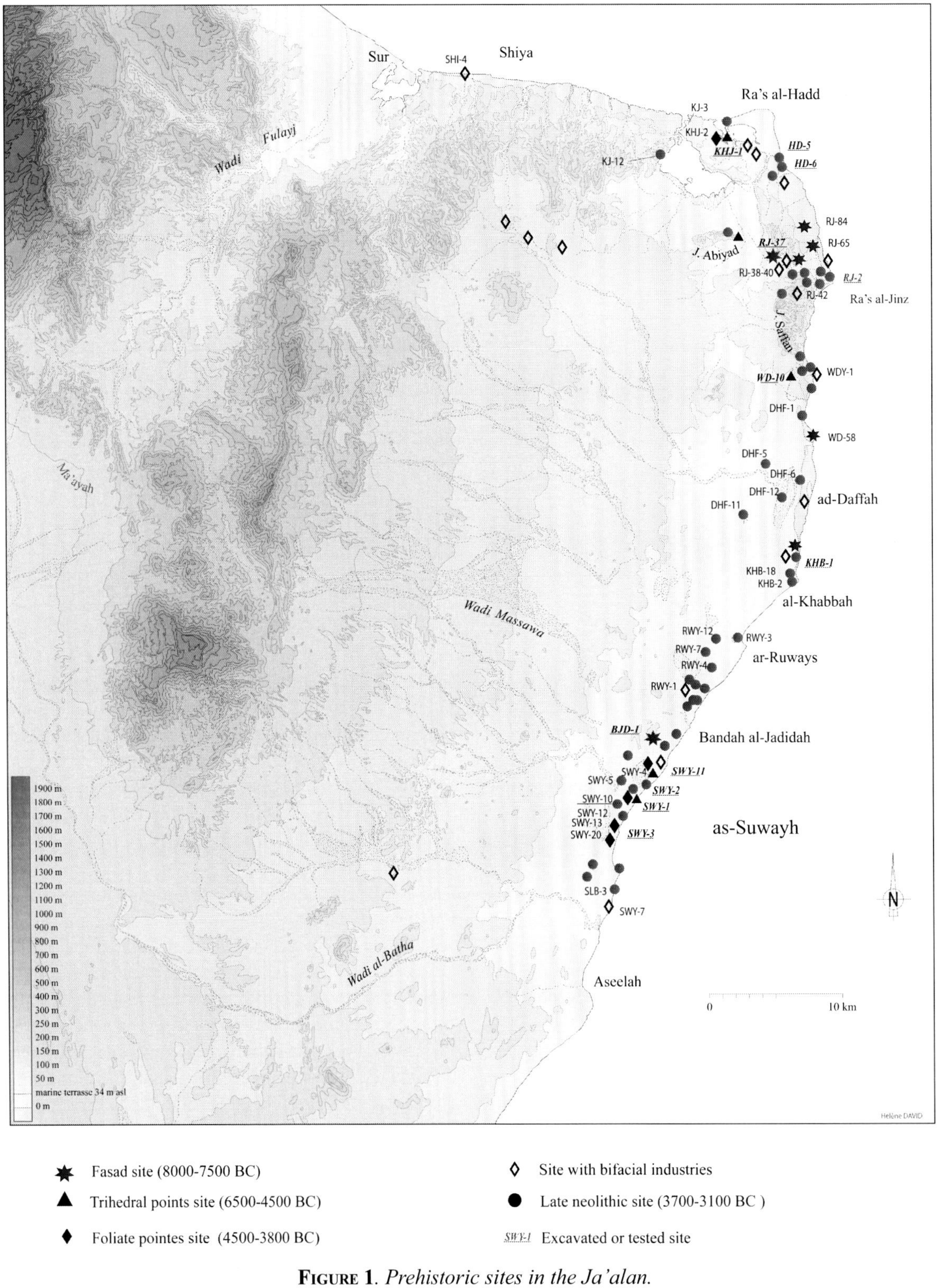

Figure 1. *Prehistoric sites in the Ja'alan.*

exhaustive collecting were carried out in parallel, but sometimes without sufficiently taking into account the strong deflation which affects most of the surface sites, and therefore having implications for understanding their chronology (Gzeis, Ra's Wudayyah WD-10) (Giraud *et al.* 2005; Putzolu 1999).

At the heart of the project, the search for stratified Neolithic settlements was a major consideration. This was not easy, and the thin Neolithic levels of Ra's al-Jins RJ-2 (4990±100 BP, 4430±60 BP) long remained the only elements of this period available to researchers. The first excavations at Suwayh SWY-2, the test trenches at SWY-3 and SWY-10, and at Ra's al-Hadd HD-2 and 5, the excavations at HD-6 (Period I), and finally those at Ra's al-Khabbah KHB-1, provide us today with quality documentation for the fourth millennium (Fig. 1). However, the earlier periods remain to be discovered. Between Ra's al-Khabbah and the Wahiba Sands, the Pleistocene valleys of coastal erosion were repeatedly invaded by marine transgressions of the Holocene: the early human occupations are today submerged (Berger *et al.* 2005; Cremaschi 2001; Lézine *et al.* 2002). Thus, the shores of the Ja'alan are not propitious for understanding occupation during the Pleistocene or the early Holocene. The test trench at Suwayh 11, then the excavation of the Suwayh SWY-1 settlement during three campaigns, have nevertheless brought to light the earliest stratified human occupation in the Ja'alan (middle of the sixth millennium BC), and enable us to push back the chronology of this region more than two millennia.

Today four lithic facies pre-dating the Bronze Age are now identifiable in this region. The "empty quarter of the early Holocene" is henceforth half full!

"Fasad": a group of early Holocene hunters (8000–7500 BC)

The "Fasad facies", with an industry having points of the same name, characterizes the earliest human occupation found today in the Ja'alan. Eight sites from this period have been discovered: Ra's al-Jins RJ-37, 36, 44, 65, 85, Ra's Wudayyah WD-58, Ra's al-Khabbah KHB-1, and Al-Haddah BJD-1 (Charpentier 1991; 1996; Charpentier, Cremaschi & Demnard 1997; Usai 2000). These settlements are situated in various environments: the top of a knoll (RJ-37), the foot of a jebel (RJ-44), terraces overlooking the sea (RJ-65, 84, KHB-1), or next to a spring (BJD-1). In spite of several test trenches at Ra's al-Jins (RJ-37) and Al-Haddah (BJD-1), and to a lesser extent at Ra's al-Khabbah (KHB-1), none of these sites have produced stratified levels. This is also true for all the open-air sites known for this period in Arabia. Since the early Holocene, they have been subjected to strong deflation by wind or violent erosion by streaming water. There should nonetheless be deposits buried under thick accumulations of alluvia, which remain to be identified. In 1996, Mauro Cremaschi and I had the project of seeking these deposits along the fringes of the Wahiba Sands and on the piedmont of the inland jebels. Engaged in other programmes (Suwayh, Khor Rhori), we were not able to carry out this research in the Ja'alan, but M. Cremaschi has discovered levels of this type in the rock shelters of Wadi Genikermat, in the Jebel Qara (Cremaschi & Negrino 2002; 2005).

The lithic assemblage

The elements characteristic of this assemblage are projectile points made on blanks of flakes that are thin or sometimes thick; blade products are rarer. The tang is generally fashioned by bifacial retouch, sometimes simply direct or inverse, rarely alternately. The distal extremity of these points is naturally sharp and not retouched, although some are sometimes reworked by a series of short marginal retouching (Charpentier 1991; 1996). With more than sixty points, the series from al-Haddah is one of the most important in Oman (Fig. 2). Aside from the variety of materials in which they were made, the diversity of forms of the blanks is very surprising: flake with central vein, blade flake but also blade product with three faces, reminiscent of the Washʿah technique defined by R. Crassard and P. Bodu in Yemen (2004), without however strictly belonging to this technique. Except for these "Fasad points" — it is not known whether they were used with a bow — our knowledge of the lithic assemblage was almost nil a short time ago. The industries from the levels of rock shelters KR213 and KR108 of the Jebel Qara (Dhofar) enable us to comprehend them.

Blade debitage is not totally absent from the assemblage, and several blade flakes are blanks for tools (Cremaschi & Negrino 2002: fig. 5/1–3, 10–12). For Fabio Negrino, the tanged points made on thick flakes, from KR213 and KR108, are related to the "Fasad points" (Cremaschi & Negrino 2002: fig. 5/4, 8/3), which I can confirm. Those on blade flakes appear to be even more characteristic (2002: KR213 fig. 5/2; KR108 fig. 8/3; KR98 fig. 8/1; KR96 fig. 8/2; KR143 fig. 8/10). Side-scrapers, notches, and denticulation produced by direct-scaled retouch dominate the tools. A backed point

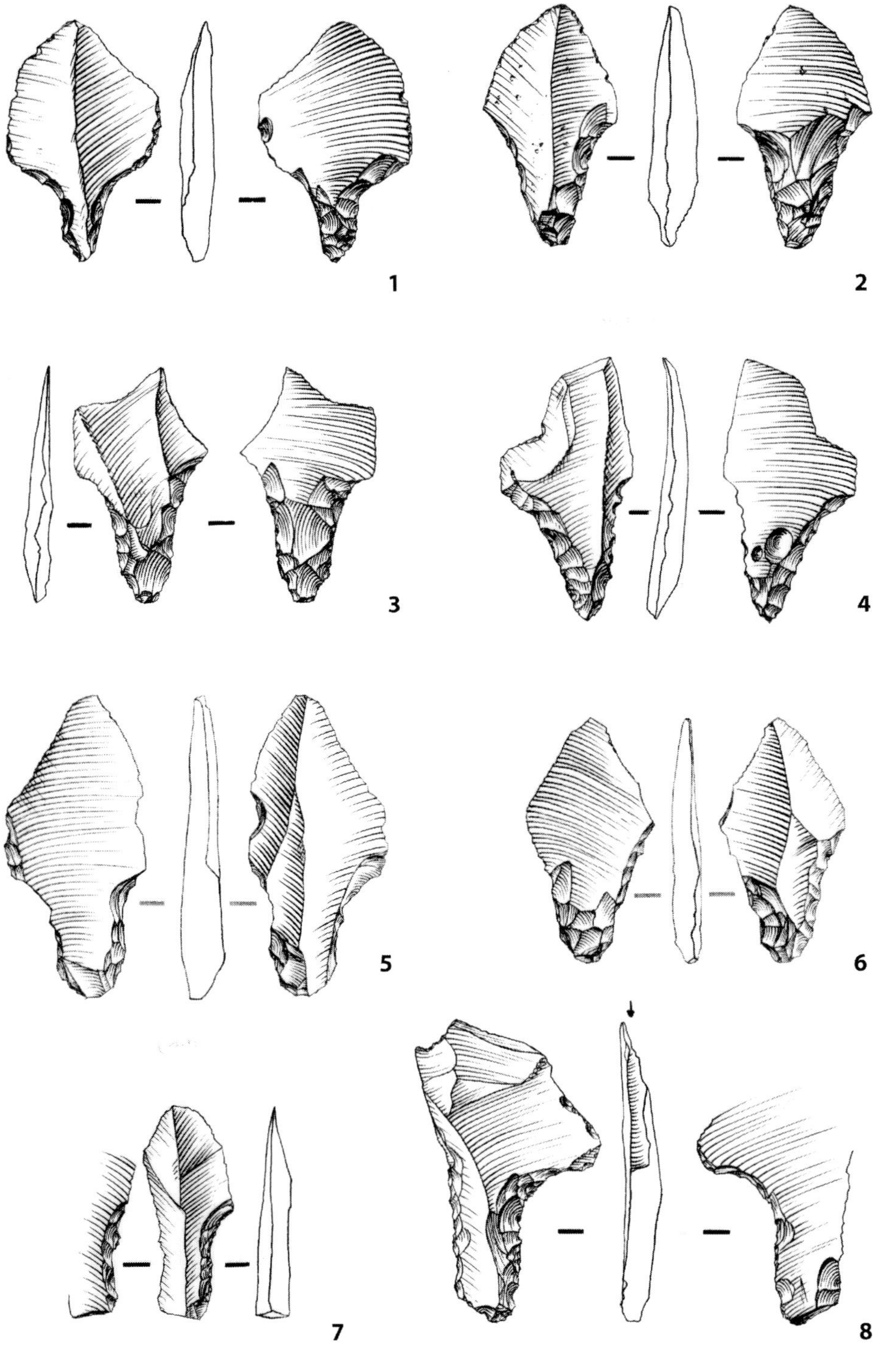

Figure 2. *Fasad points. Bandar al-Jadidah/Al-Haddah BJD-1 (c. 8000–7500 BC). (Drawings by G. Devilder).*

on a burin spall is present, a type of object also found at al-Haddah (Charpentier, Cremaschi & Demnard 1997). There are no drills in the assemblage.

Chronology

Only a few rare datings at Wadi Wuttaya and Zebrit (9280 ± 210 BP) have recently provided evidence of human presence in Arabia for this period, to the point that M. Uerpmann has evoked an "empty quarter of the early Holocene" (Amirkhanov 1996; Uerpmann M 1992; Zarins 2001). Up to the present, the chronology of the lithic facies of Fasad was based on conjectures, a date in the seventh–sixth millennia often being proposed (e.g. Charpentier, Cremaschi & Demnard 1997; Usai 2000). A single dating, based on shell material from Ra's al-Jins RJ-37, has provided a date of 6070 ± 70 (4479–4211 2 sigma) which I judged ten years ago to be too late to characterize this facies (see below) (Charpentier 1996). Today, datings from the rock shelters of KR108 (8750 ± 50 yr BP; 7910–7690 cal. BC) and KR213 (8720 ± 60 yr BP; 7740–7590 cal. BC) (Cremaschi & Negrino 2002) enable the attribution of the Fasad facies to the first half of the eighth millennium, a period of high precipitation on the southern fringe of Jebel al-Qara, which can be correlated with the south-west monsoon record (2002: 330).

The trihedral points facies (6500–4500 BC)

A new chrono-cultural entity developed between the seventh and the fifth millennia over the whole of Oman and the UAE, a part of Yemen and Saudi Arabia (Charpentier 2004; Crassard 2007). Its lithic industry is particularly characterized by projectile points that are not bifacial but trifacial: "the trihedral points" (Charpentier 2004). This Neolithic facies is not however the oldest, as certain earlier Yemeni sites have produced industries of Neolithic character (Khuzmum, HDOR 538 & 561, etc.) (Crassard 2007).

Nearly 100 sites corresponding to this group have been identified in the Arabian Peninsula. Since their recent inventory (Charpentier 2004), a few new surface deposits have been discovered in the UAE and in Oman, including Marawah 11 in the Emirate of Abu Dhabi and Jebel Faya in the Emirate of Sharjah (Beech *et al.* 2005: fig. 5; Uerpmann H-P *et al.* 2007), al-Thabiti in the oasis of Ibra (Schreiber 2005: 265, fig. 14), but also sites around Qalat (M. Tosi, personal communication), in the Wahiba Sands at al-Hadd (ALHD-1), and at Maysar (M4T23). (1) In the Ja'alan, besides Khor al-Hajar (KHJ-1) and Suwayh 1, two surface sites have produced this type of point: Ra's Wudayyah (WD-10) and Jebel Abiyad (2) (Charpentier 1991; Charpentier & Inizan 2002).

In the Sultanate of Oman, only the sites of Wadi Wutayya, Khor al-Hajar, Suwayh 1 and 11 have stratified levels for this period, while Marawah MR.1 and MR.11 are the only stratified sites with trihedral points in the UAE (Beech *et al.* 2005; Charpentier 2001; 2004; Charpentier *et al.* 2000; Uerpmann M 1992; Uerpmann & Uerpmann 2003: 142–162). The sequence of Suwayh 1 is at the present time the most developed and serves here as a reference for defining this lithic facies in Oman (Fig. 3).

The bifacial and trifacial industry

The majority of the points of Period 1 of Suwayh 1 are trihedral (Fig. 4/1–8), sometimes "fluted" (Charpentier & Inizan 2002; Charpentier 2004). Other points which are pressure-retouched but bifacial are present but fewer in the assemblage: foliated bifacial point with biconvex section, rare barbed and tanged points (Fig. 4/9–13). Bifacial pieces with parallel edges are associated with this complex (Fig. 4/19).

Many piercing tools are associated with these pressure-retouched tools, such as rare points with backed edge (Fig. 4/14), drills on bladelets (Fig. 4/15–17), as well as tools on micro-lithic flakes, especially side-scrapers. Tools made from nodules are characteristic of this period. Pebbles are worked by scalariform bifacial retouch, leaving at one extremity a point or a beak of polygonal section (Fig. 4/18).

Chronology

The chronology of this facies has recently been clarified (Charpentier 2004; Crassard 2007). It would cover two millennia, as it emerges very early in certain sites of the Ḥaḍramawt, Manayzah in particular, at about 6500, and disappears at Suwayh 1 and Wadi Wutayya in about 4500 BC (Charpentier 2004; Charpentier *et al.* 2006; Crassard 2007; Uerpmann M 1992; Uerpmann & Uerpmann 2003: 142–162). At Suwayh 1, it characterizes the early occupation (Period I) of the site — which is located directly on the fossil beach, 7245 ± 55 BP (5554–5307 cal. BC) — and fades out in the middle of the fifth millennium BC.

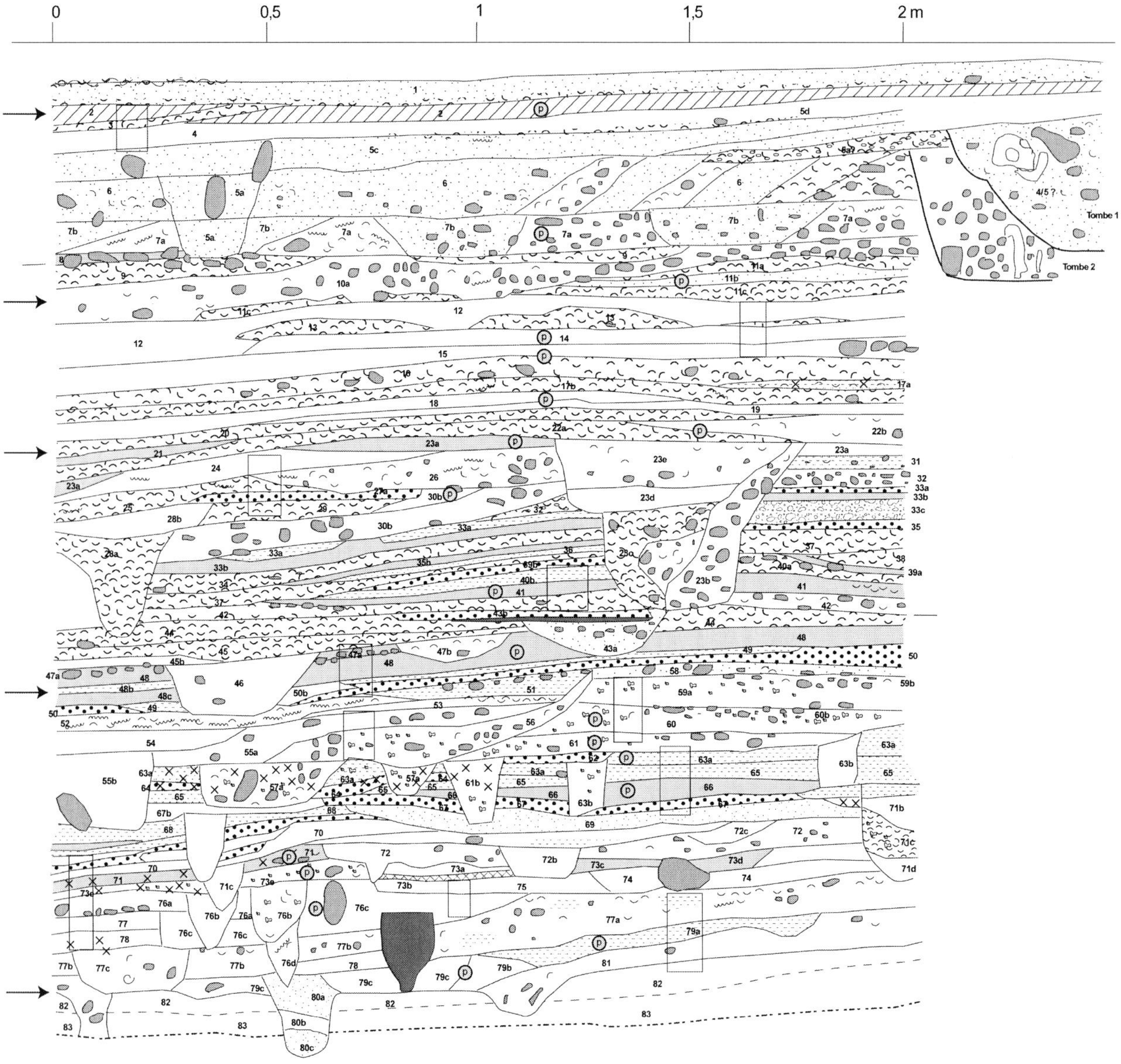

FIGURE 3. *Suwayh SWY-1 section 2. (Drawing by J-F. Berger & G. Davtian [Cepam CNRS]).*

A new cultural entity: Suwayh and the fusiform foliated points (4500–c. 3700 BC)

At about 4500 cal. BC, a new cultural entity emerges, which I propose calling the Suwayh culture. Coming from the "trihedral points facies", its material culture is manifested by the appearance of several innovations, some of which affect the lithic industry. Although a number of tools still have the same typological characteristics, the trihedral points henceforth make way for new forms of very slender projectile points, with an often fusiform silhouette and a diamond-shaped or lozenge-shaped section. Pressure working is at its peak and fluting is probably still in use, while a new technical process seems to emerge: the plunging process (Inizan & Tixier 1978; Charpentier 2003). Finally, knapped blade products on semi-turned nuclei are part of the assemblage.

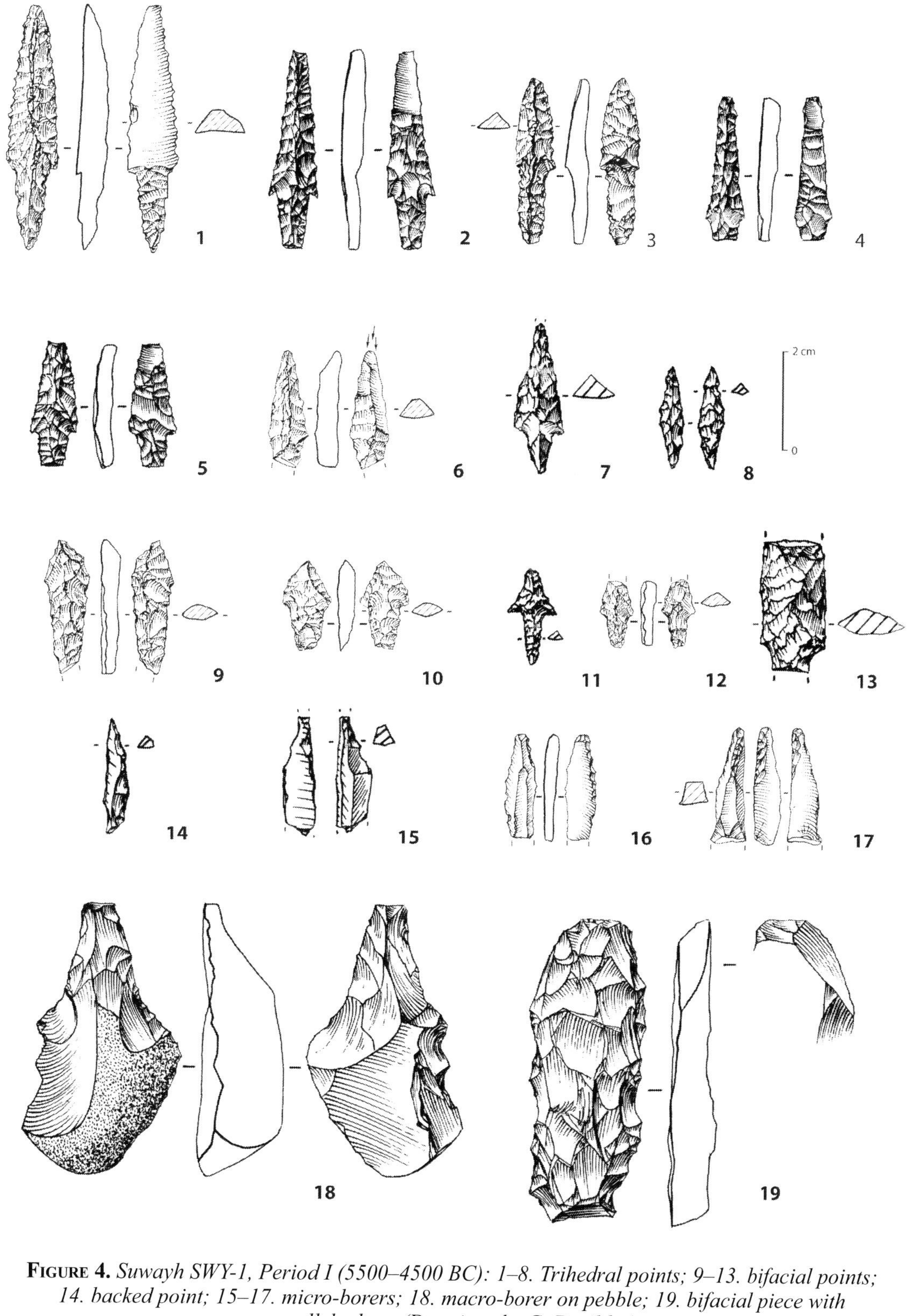

Figure 4. *Suwayh SWY-1, Period I (5500–4500 BC): 1–8. Trihedral points; 9–13. bifacial points; 14. backed point; 15–17. micro-borers; 18. macro-borer on pebble; 19. bifacial piece with parallel edges. (Drawings by G. Devilder).*

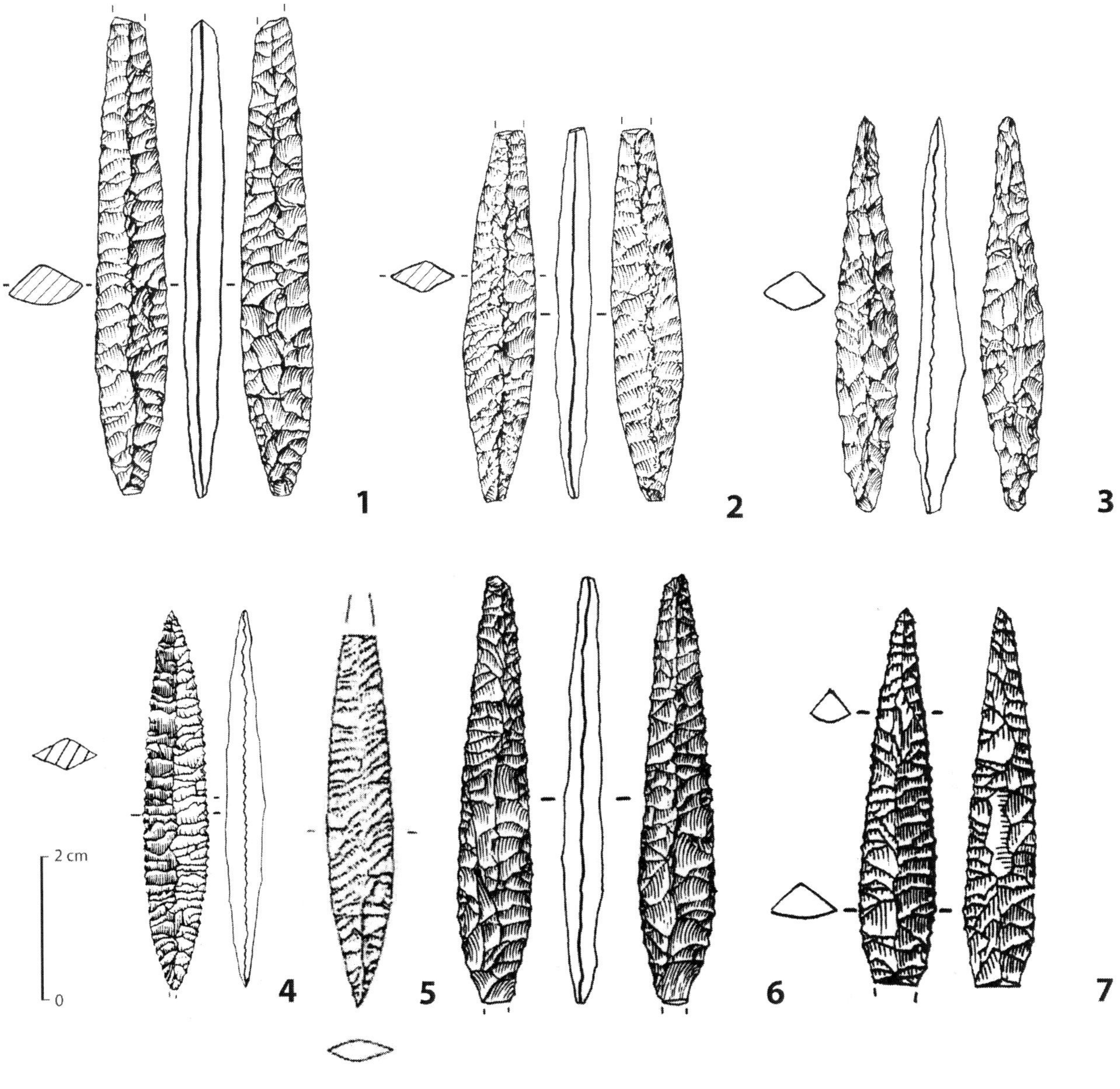

Figure 5. *Very slender fusiform points, lozenge-shaped or diamond-shaped section (4500–3700 BC): 1–3. Suwayh, Period II, sections 2 and 5; 4. al-Madar (S69) Umm al-Qaiwain Emirate (after Boucharlat et al. 1991); 5. Ra's Shaqallah 1, (after Biagi 1988b); 6. Suwayh SWY-3; 7. Sharjah Tower, Sharjah Emirate (after Millet 1988). (Drawings by G. Devilder).*

Bifacial tools

This covers a wide range of tools, projectile points but also small "daggers", and perhaps small thick heart-shaped or oval bifacial pieces. The use of pressure retouch is not automatic and is used for the most delicate pieces, at the end of the technical process.

The fusiform foliated pieces

These bifacial points have two pointed extremities. Their section is biconvex, often diamond-shaped, and more rarely asymmetrical. The bifacial retouch is total, sometimes ordered (transverse parallel or oblique parallel). Micro-denticulations are more rarely found on

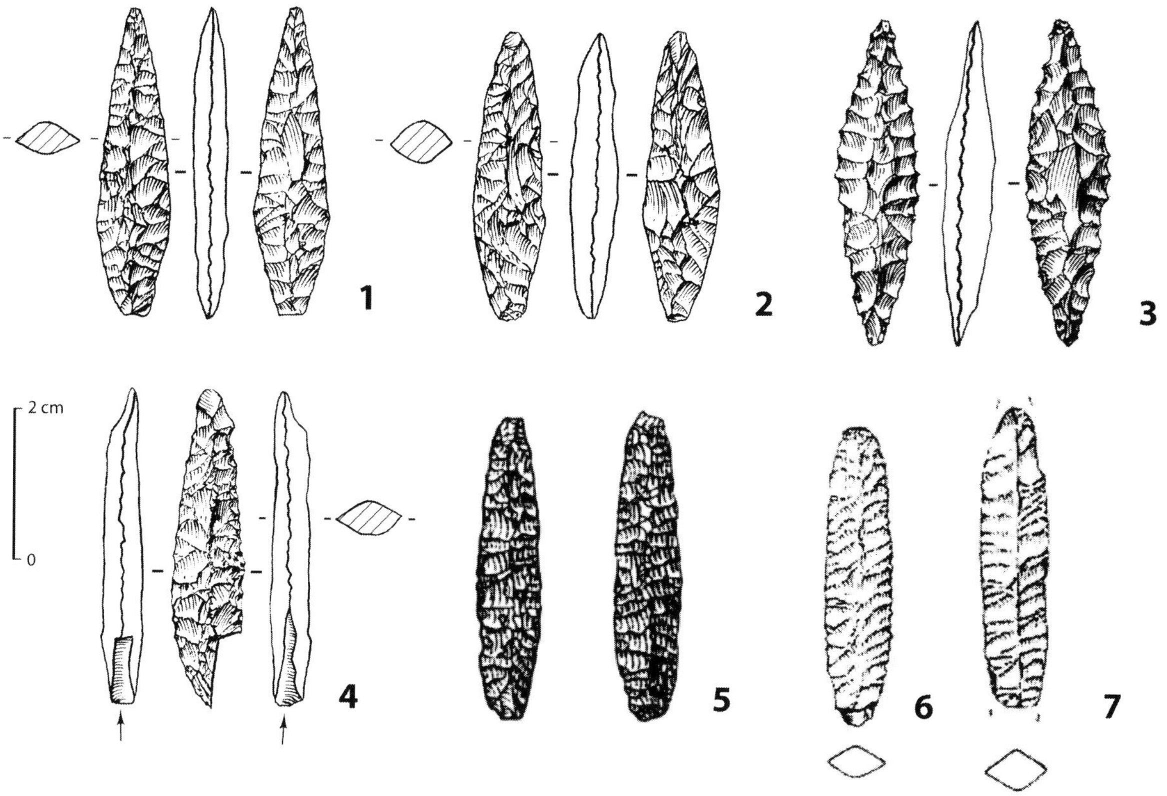

FIGURE 6. *Fusiform points: 1–2. Suwayh SWY-1 section 5; 3. Ruwayz RWY 1b4; 4. Suwayh SWY-1; 5. Ra's al Hamra RH-5, HWE/B, DA 7686 (courtesy of the Italian archaeological mission in Oman); 6–7. Ra's Shaqallah 1 (after Biagi 1988b). (Drawings by G. Devilder).*

the edges of the points. This group of projectile points includes many sub-types, listed here as follows:

Type 1.A. Very slender fusiform points

These large points, which can be longer than 57.5 mm, have parallel or slightly convergent edges. The base is sometimes straight convergent, the section usually diamond-shaped (Fig. 5). These points are found at Suwayh 1 and Ra's Shaqallah 1 in Oman, and at Yahar, in the Emirate of Abu Dhabi (Biagi 1988*b*: fig. 12/1; Hellyer 1998: 22). Certain points with V-shaped bases come from Suwayh 3, but also from Sharorah in the Rub' al Khali, from Sharjah Tower and from al Madar (S69) in the Emirates of Sharjah and Umm al-Quwain (Cauvin & Calley 1984: fig. 9/4–5; Edens 1982: pl. 101, B 25; Millet 1988: fig. 8/1).

Type 1.B. Short thick fusiform points

These are much more bulky pieces (Fig. 6/1–2). The section is biconvex, diamond-shaped, even pentagonal, the edges straight convergent, the base V-shaped. Examples are present at Suwayh 1 and at Mundafin in the Rub' al Khali (Edens 1982: pl. 101, B. 18).

Type 1.C. Wide fusiform points

Already known from the early levels at Suwayh 1, this type of foliated point with biconvex section continues in the Suwayh facies. Rare in Yemen and in the Ḥaḍramawt, where they are dated to 5750 BC (Crassard 2007), they appear more frequent in the Ja'alan (Suwayh-1 Period I, Khor al-Hajar 1, Jebel Abiyad, Ruwayz 1B4 (Fig. 6/3), Ra's Shaqallah 1) (Biagi 1988*b*: fig. 12/2).

Type 2.A. Foliate points with convex base

These projectile points with biconvex section have parallel or slightly convergent edges. The base is especially convex. They have been identified in particular at Suwayh 1, at Ra's al-Hamra RH-5 and in the Rub' al Khali, at

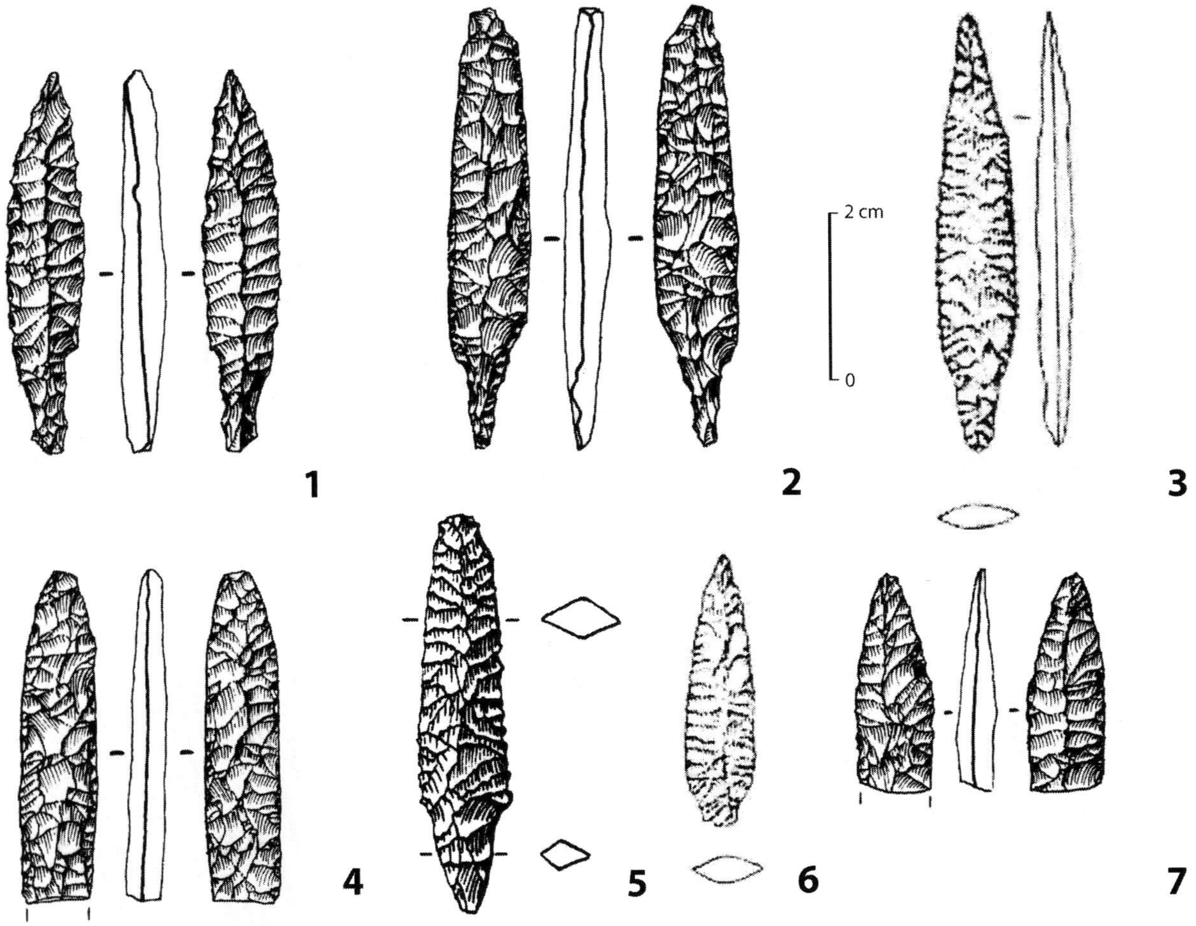

Figure 7. *Slender tanged points with parallel edges: 1. Suwayh SWY-4; 2. Suwayh SWY-1; 3 & 6. Ra's Shaqallah 1, after Biagi 1988b; 4 & 7. Suwayh 11; 5. Sharjah Tower (after Millet 1988). (Drawings by G. Devilder).*

Jiledah and at Sharorah (Edens 1982: fig. 101, B) (Fig. 6/4–7). Other more slender forms exist, especially in the Rub 'al Khali (Field 1958).

Type 2.B. Foliated points with convergent edge and convex base

This type of short thick point with diamond-shaped section has never been found in a stratigraphic context, but could probably be attributed to this period. An example was found on the surface of the occupation at Ra's al-Jins RJ-44, another on the surface of Saruq (Charpentier 1999: fig. 5/4; Uerpmann & Uerpmann 2003: fig. 5/12.3).

Type 3.A. Slender tanged points with parallel edges

These slender points with parallel or slightly convex edges and biconvex or diamond-shaped section have a short tang with convergent edges. At Suwayh 1, 4, and 20, most of the tangs, sometimes the distal extremity, were worked by a much less fine alternate retouch than most of the pieces, an operation which most certainly occurred after production of the arms (Fig. 7/1–2). They have been found at Suwayh 1, 4, 20, Khor al Hajar 2 and perhaps Ra's al-Jins 37. They have also been identified in southern Oman at Ra's al-Shaqallah (SAQ-1) (Fig. 7/3,

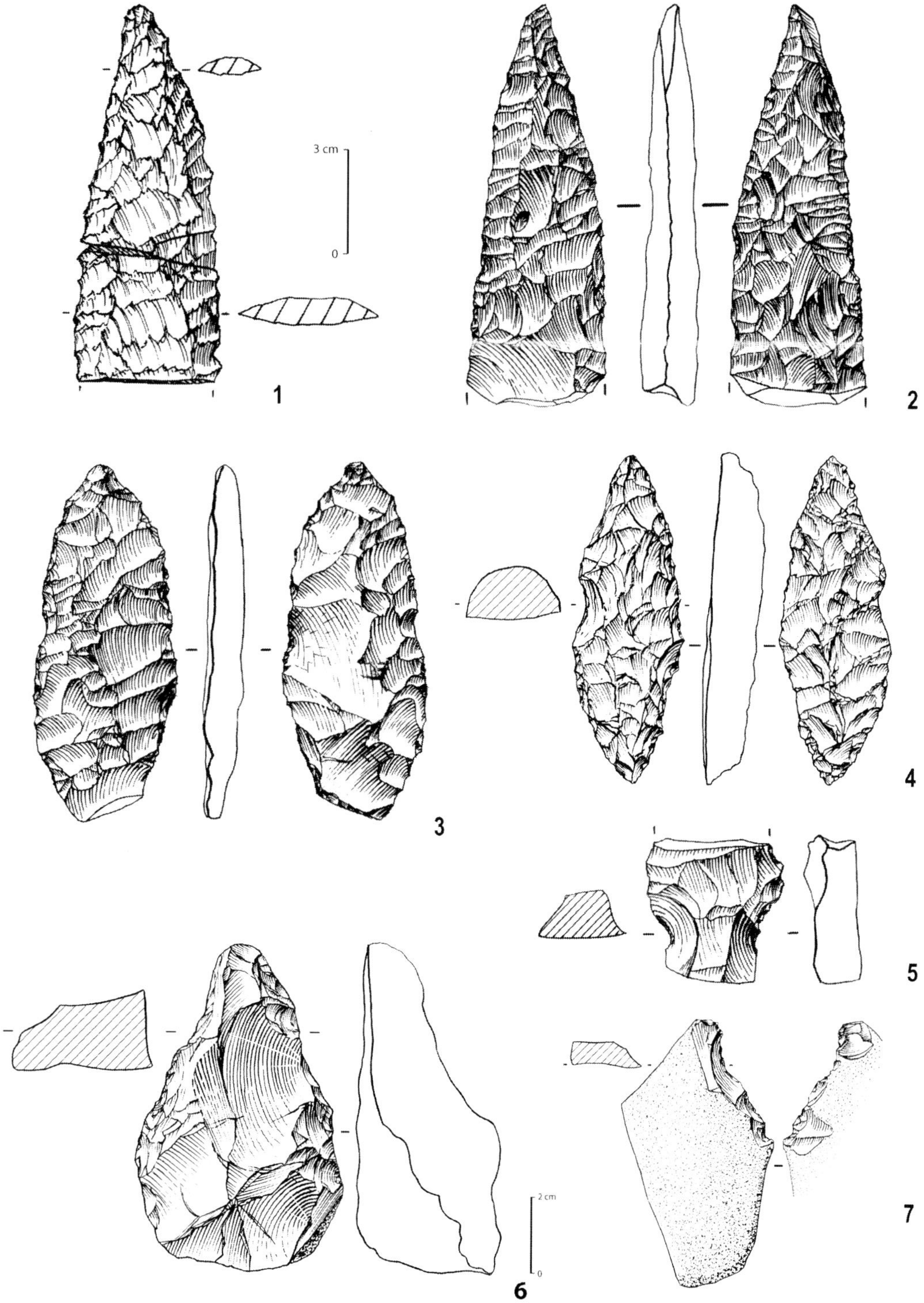

Figure 8. *Bifacial tools (4500–3700 BC): 1, 4–5. "daggers", Suwayh SWY-1; 2. Suwayh SWY-7; 3. bifacial foliate, Suwayh SWY-1; 6. macro-borer on pebble, Suwayh SWY-1; 7. tile knife, SWY-1. (Drawings by G. Devilder).*

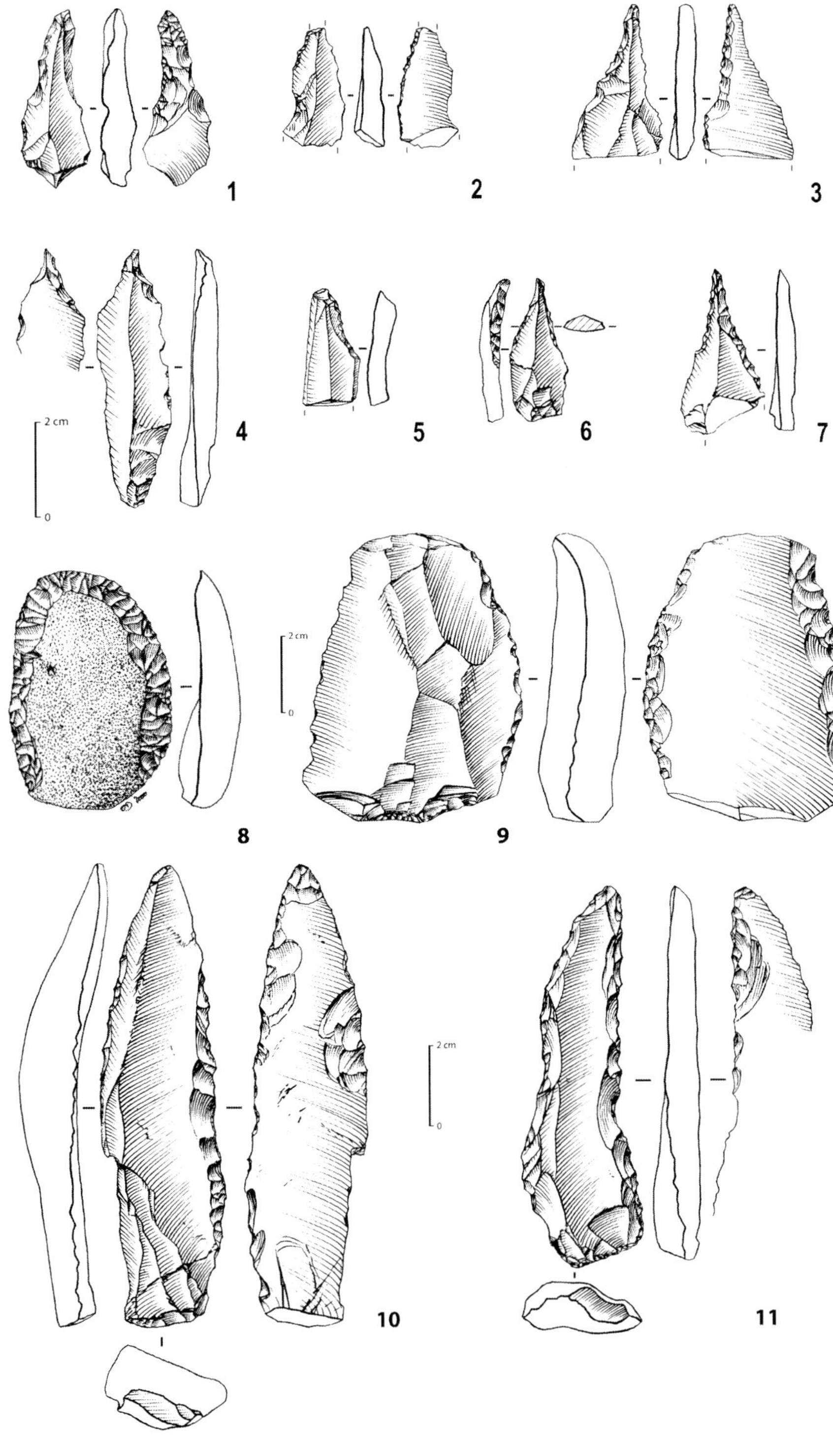

FIGURE 9. *Suwayh SWY-1 period II (4500–4200 BC): 1–3, 5 & 7. micro-borers; 4. bec; 6. Suwayh SWY-2 Period I (level 28) micro-borer; 8. end-scraper; 9. side-scraper; 10–11. retouched blades.*

6) al-Hadd (ALHD-1), but also in the Emirate of Sharjah (Sharjah Tower) (Fig. 7/5) (Biagi 1988*a*: fig. 52/1–3; 1988*b*: fig. 12/1–9; Charpentier 1991: fig. 4/11; 2001: fig. 3/4; Millet 1988: fig. 8/15).

Type 4 A. Barbed and tanged points

These projectile points are in the minority in the assemblages of the Ja'alan, but are much more frequent in the UAE. Associated with the trihedral points in the early and late levels of Suwayh 1, they are only known at Ruwayz RWY-1 and at Suwayh 3. That of SWY-3 has a particularly long body, straight convergent, and is related to the points found at ar-Ramlah 6 and al-Madar (S69) (Boucharlat *et al*. 1991: fig. 1/2; Uerpmann & Uerpmann 1996: fig. 4).

The little "daggers", foliated pieces, and small bifaces

With straight sides, sometimes slightly convex with pointed extremities, the "daggers" have a biconvex section that is sometimes diamond-shaped (Fig. 8/1–2, 4–5). Frequent at Suwayh 1, they are well attested in the occupations of Suwayh 7 and 20, Ra's Jibsh and al-Hadd (ALHD-1), but especially in the specialized workshops such as Ra's al-Jins (RJ-38) and Ra's Wudayyah (WD-10) (Cavallari 2004; Charpentier 1999: fig. 6/2). Small bifaces are known at Saruq and have been found at Ra's al-Jins 25, 34, 38–39 (Charpentier 1999; Uerpmann & Uerpmann 2003: fig. 5/12.16).

Tools with bifacial retouch on pebbles

Tile knives are characteristic tools of the Neolithic period in the Gulf, but have already been noted on certain Omani sites, particularly at Saruq (Uerpmann & Uerpmann 2003: fig. 5/13.3). The occupation of Suwayh 1 produced a single example (Fig. 8/7). On the other hand, pieces with bifacial retouch with convergent edges, made on pebbles, which are related to the "macro-drills", are frequent at Suwayh 1 (Fig. 8/6) and have been identified at SWY-20.

Tools on flakes

Small drills are always more numerous and are produced on thin flakes but also on bladelets (Fig. 9/1–6). End-scrapers are much in evidence. Some of them are pressure-retouched (Fig. 9/7). Side-scrapers (Fig. 9/8) on large blanks with inverse retouch are present and also attested at Saruq (2003).

A new blade production

One of the major characteristics of this new industry is the appearance of blade blanks, which are thin and relatively large in size (Fig. 9/9–10). These blades are produced by unipolar debitage on a turning nucleus, and worked by continuous direct retouch, which is usually scalariform. The leptolithic character of this facies is not unique to the Ja'alan as it is also present in the Gulf (Uerpmann & Uerpmann 1996).

A new facies that goes beyond the Oman peninsula

In the Ja'alan, the Suwayh facies is well represented at Suwayh 1, 4, 11, and 20, at Khor al-Hajar 2, at Ra's al-Jins RJ-37, 44, etc. (Fig. 10). It is also attested in the south, in the Wahiba Sands (al-Hadd ALHD-1, Ra's al-Shaqallah SAQ-1) and in the Dhofar (site 93.42), but especially in certain sites of the Rub' al Khali such as Jiledah, Sharorah, and Mundafin, or Ramlat as-Sahmah (Biagi 1988*b*: fig. 12/1–9; Edens 1982: pl. 101; 1988*b*: fig. 3/12–13; Gotoh 1981: fig. 2/11; Smith P 1961: fig. 1/h; Zarins 2001: fig. 19/42p). It is also present in the north, at Ra's al-Hamra 5, Saruq, Miskin, Sayq, and in the Wadi Suq (Pullar 1985: fig. 6/1; Smith GH 1976: fig. 3/6; 1977: fig. 4/21; Uerpmann & Uerpmann 2003: fig. 5/12.1). It is the same in the UAE, at Sharjah Tower, al-Madar (S69), Umm al-Qaiwain UAQ-1, Mleiha, Jazirat al-Hamra, but also at Jebel Buhais (BHS-18) and on several sites around al Ain, including Ayar (3) (Boucharlat *et al*. 1991; Charpentier 2004: fig. 3/2–3; Hellyer 1998: fig. 22; C.S. Phillips. personal communication 2007; Uerpmann *et al*. 2007).

Chronology

Following the facies with trihedral points, the facies found at Suwayh begin to develop at about 4500 and disappear about 3700 BC. At Suwayh, it is present in all the late levels of SWY-1 (4500–4200 cal. BC) and in the earliest levels of SWY-2–3, beginning in 4200 BC (4228–4144 cal. BC). The occupation at Ra's Shaqallah SAQ-1 (6040 ±60 BP) is related to this group (Biagi 1994), as are several sites of the Gulf, including al-Madar (S69) (5890±170 BP), Jazirat al-Hamra (5955±100 BP), and ar-Ramlah 6 (6181±50) (Boucharlat *et al*. 1991; Uerpmann & Uerpmann 1996). The foliated or diamond-shaped points of Jebel al-Buhais (BHS-18) should belong to the end of the occupation of the settlement and the necropolis, dated to 4300 BC (Uerpmann, Uerpmann & Jasim 2000).

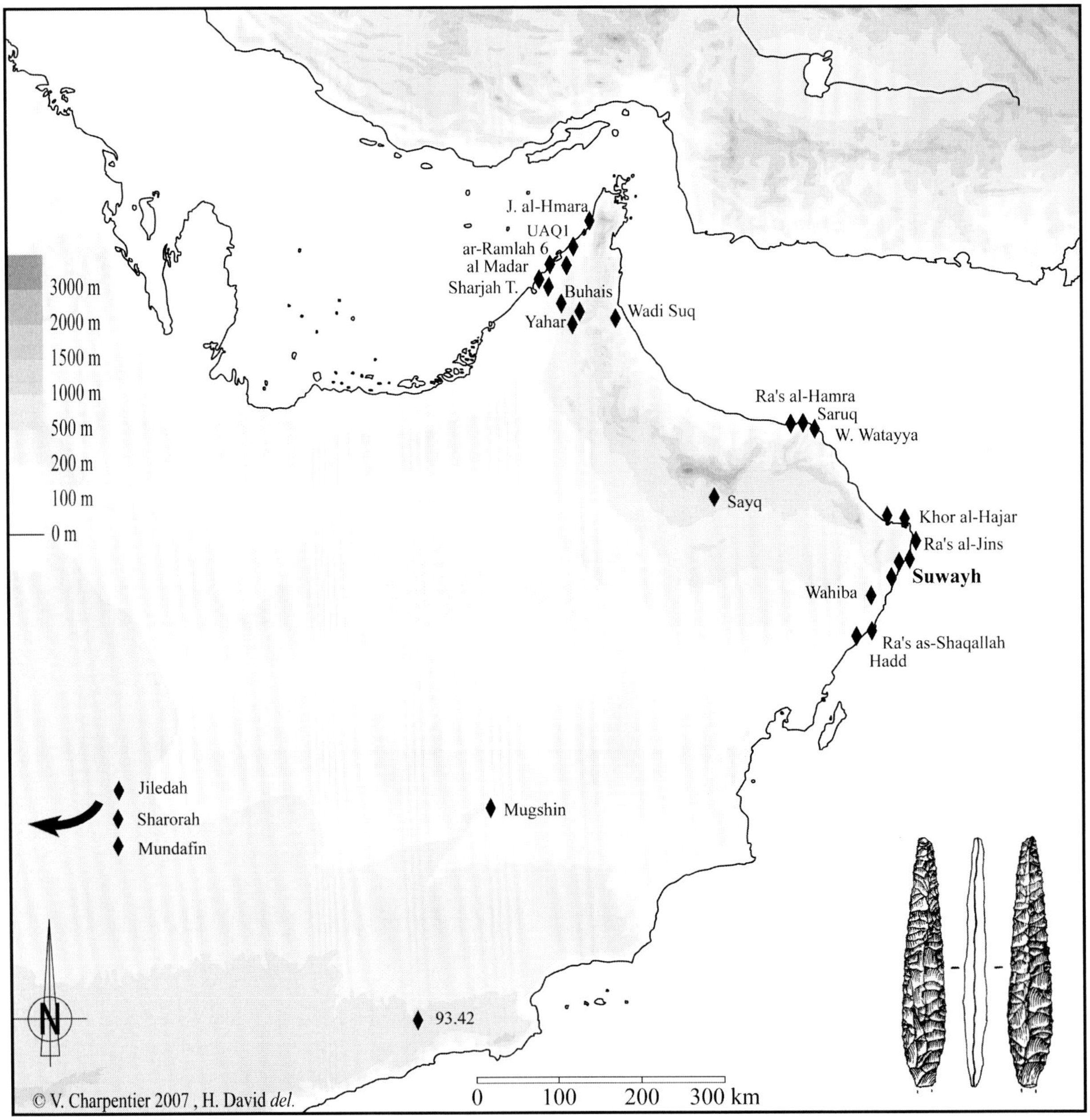

Figure 10. *Fusiform and diamond-shaped points in the Oman peninsula.*

The end of this culture remains imprecise, as it has been found only in the test trenches of Suwayh 2 and 3, the earliest horizons of the latter site being dated to 3942–3838 cal. BC. A very worn piece found at Ra's al-Hamra RH-5 comes from a pit and is very probably related to the first horizons of the site (about 4000–3750 BC) (D. Usai, personal communication 2003). From 3700–3600 BC onwards, the characteristic lithic assemblage of the Suwayh facies is no longer in evidence. This is the case especially for Khor Milkh, Ra's al-Khabbah 1, Wadi Shab 1, the levels of Period II of Suwayh 2 and those of Period 1 at Ra's al-Jins 2.

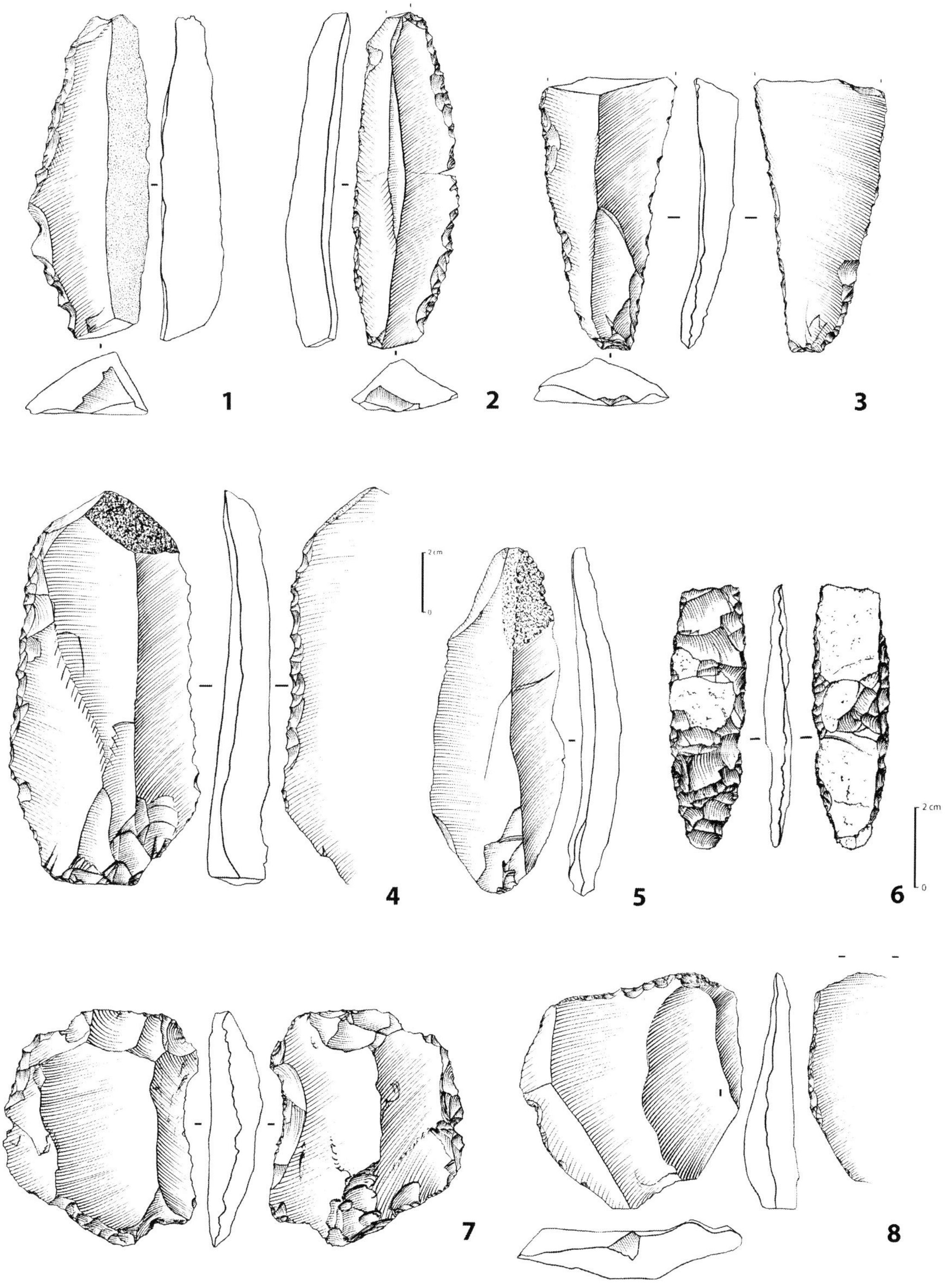

FIGURE 11. *Suwayh (3700–3100 BC): 1–3, 5–8. Suwayh SWY-2; 4. Suwayh SWY-5. 1–5. blades and retouched blades; 6. bifacial point; 7–8. scrapers. (Drawings by G. Devilder).*

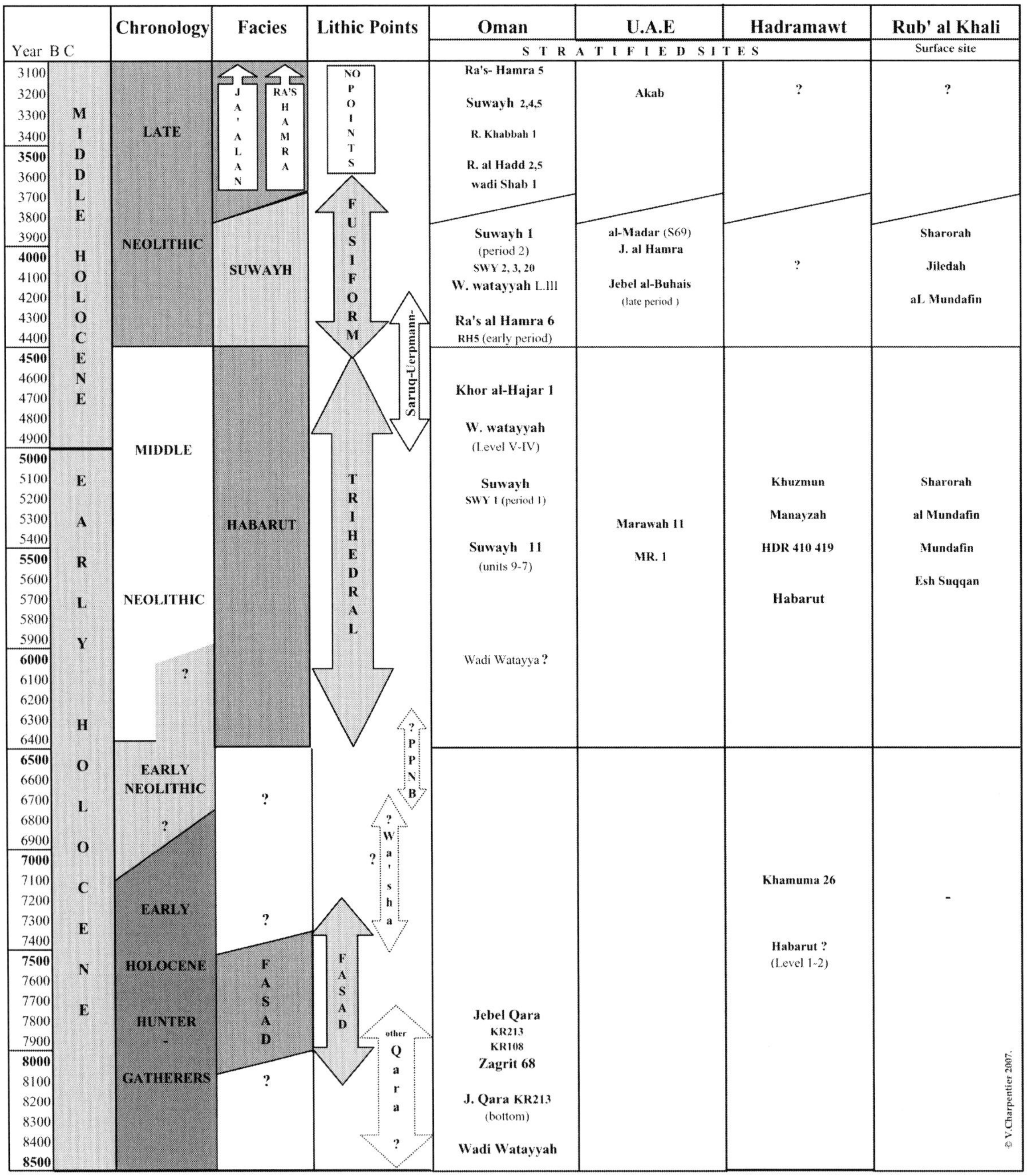

Figure 12. *The chronology for late prehistory in the Oman peninsula.*

The end of the Neolithic (c. 3700–3100)

In the Ja'alan, the sites attributable to the end of the Neolithic are the most numerous and those whose material culture we know best, in spite of the small number of publications concerning their lithic industry. More than fifty sites of this period were found, mainly on the coastal side, and several excavations or test trenches were made, at Ra's al Hadd (HD-2.5, HD-6 Period I), Ra's al-Jins RJ-2 (Period I), Suwayh (SWY-2–3, 10), and Ra's al-Khabbah (KHB-1).

The lithic tools of the end of the Neolithic are made up of end-scrapers, side-scrapers and denticulated pieces (Fig. 11/7–8), products usually made on very large blanks (Biagi *et al.* 1984: fig. 4/6; Cattani & Tiscornia 1988; Charpentier 2001: figs 4–5; Uerpmann & Uerpmann 2003: figs 7/14, 7/25; Tosi & Usai 2003: 6/4). A new type of unipolar blade appears which is quite wide or quite thick, and is represented in all the specialized workshops of the Jebel Saffan (Fig. 11/1–5). The diffusion of these blades, over a distance of more than 100 km, is part of a complex trade network.

This period also sees the end of the use of the pressure technique. Thus, only two projectile points dated to this period have been found in the Ja'alan. The first, greatly burnt (Fig. 11/6), is clearly pressure-retouched. It comes from a horizon of Suwayh 2, which is dated to 3360–3240 cal. BC, but could in reality come from earlier horizons of the site (3900–4200). The second is a barbed and tanged point from Ra's al-Jins 2, which was worked using a hard percussion tool and of which only the extremities were retouched.

From 3700 onwards, and in the last centuries of the Neolithic, a strong regionalization seems to have operated in the Oman peninsula, which has been noticed by several authors (Biagi 2004; Uerpmann M 1992; Usai 2005). Thus, the industries of Ra's al-Hamra 5 are for example very different from those found in the region of the Ja'alan. This aspect (Ra's al Hamra and Ja'alan facies) will not be developed here.

Discussion

Are we able today to put into place a chronology for late prehistory in the Oman peninsula? M. Uerpmann attempted to do this with a certain degree of success fifteen years ago, but the exercise remains perilous, as our knowledge is still only partial for the early periods of the early Holocene in the Oman peninsula, and even absent for the second half of the eighth and all of the seventh millennia. Moreover, certain very important questions remain unanswered: the influence of the PPNB/Qatar B on the Oman peninsula, the possible extension of the Washᶜah points of the Ḥaḍramawt in the same region, the date and the manner of the emergence of the Neolithic, and also the role played by autochthonous groups. The synthesis which follows is thus schematic (Fig. 12) and should be completed, even renewed in the future.

The chronology which I propose is based only on the data which come from stratified deposits, supported by radiometric dating and of which the lithic industry includes in particular good chrono-typological markers. Levels VIII–VII of Wadi Wutayya, which characterize the facies of the same name, do not thus appear, M. Uerpmann (1992) having written that she found "a relatively undifferentiated stone tool-using facies".

The "empty quarter of the early Holocene" is half full

We know henceforth that the "Fasad" facies developed during the first half of the eighth millennium BC and probably persisted beyond that period. Its spatial distribution covers in particular the whole of Oman and the UAE. It is represented in the Marha and the Ḥaḍramawt, but less so, while other points on prepared blanks, the "Washᶜah points", perhaps appear from this period onwards in this part of Yemen (Charpentier 1996; Crassard 2007; Crassard & Bodu 2004). The techno-facies of "Fasad" and that of "Washᶜah" are henceforth partially defined, but other facies remain to be identified. The base of the rock shelter of KR213 in the Jebel Qara (Oman) has industries dated to 9130 ± 290 yr BP (8600–7700 cal. BC), of which the tools are characterized by lunate pieces and by unipolar blade knapping where the "Fasad points" and the "Washᶜah points" are absent (Cremaschi & Negrino 2002). While the Palaeolithic of Arabia is debated today, in a context where stratigraphic research is cruelly lacking, (4) the societies that follow it are often called "post-Palaeolithic", "epi-Palaeolithic", even "Mesolithic" and "pre-Neolithic", without a reason always being given (Crassard 2007). The idea of hunter-gatherer societies of the early Holocene seems more appropriate to me. As for the Palaeolithic, the acquisition of stratigraphic data is urgent for this period.

The Habarut culture or the appearance of the middle Neolithic?

All the Neolithic bifacial industries of the Oman peninsula were grouped together fifteen years ago as the "Saruq facies", then considered to be a local variant of the Arabian bifacial tradition (Uerpmann M 1992; Uerpmann & Uerpmann 2003: 142–162), defined in 1982 by C. Edens. The site of Wadi Wutayya, which is a stratified site, characterizes another earlier lithic facies, dated to the beginning of the second quarter of the Holocene and whose lithic industry, still not very characteristic, would have been contemporary with Qatar B (Uerpmann

M 1992). Today we possess data from several stratified sites, enabling the definition of two quite distinct techno-facies, which appear in succession: the trihedral points facies between 6500 and 4500 BC, and the facies of the fusiform points with diamond-shaped section between 4500 and *c.* 3800–3700 BC. A non-stratified surface site, Saruq belongs to that of the fusiform points with diamond-shaped section.

Following H. Amirkhanov, I propose that the group of trihedral points be named the "Habarut facies", (5) as this stratified site, situated between Yemen and the Sultanate of Oman (which was one of the first discoveries and studied by many researchers) is one of its best illustrations (e.g. Amirkhanov 1994; 1996; 1997; Paynes & Hawkins 1963). I believe that this "Habarut facies" corresponds to a fully Neolithic culture, a production society which had mastered domestication and formed strong groups in the form of coastal villages principally oriented towards production related to fishing. Technologically, it was an innovating society, devising trifacial projectiles, fluting of certain points, sophisticated fishing kit, etc.

As an indication of new social relations, the creation of trade movement, especially over very long distances, is regarded as one of the characteristics of Neolithicization. In Arabia, it is during this period that complex networks of long-distance trade developed, internal to Arabia and reaching to distant lands such as the Horn of Africa (Inizan & Francaviglia 2002). The materials traded in these networks included precious materials, such as exotic marine shells in the Rub' al Khali and clastic rocks such as obsidian in Yemen and Saudi Arabia, and possibly opalescent flint in the Oman peninsula. In the Emirates, it was the populations corresponding to the "Habarut facies" who made the first contact with the Ubaid 1 and 2–3 society and were to assimilate goods and artificial materials (pottery, plaster, bitumen) (Méry, Blackman & Beech, in preparation).

The Suwayh culture; the emergence of the late Neolithic

Less easy to perceive than the preceding one, the "Suwayh facies" covers a much more reduced period: 4500–3800/3700 BC. It emerged during a phase of great aridification (Lézine *et al.* 2002; Parker, Davis & Wilkinson 2006).

Very few stratified sites which characterize it have been excavated or simply tested: Suwayh 1, Wadi Watayya (levels V–IV), the trial trenches of the Jazirat al-Hamra and al-Madar, certain levels of Ra's al-Hamra 6, (6) and the earliest horizons of RH-5. The site of Thumama could be its most north-western expression.

New shapes of points appear out of the "Habarut facies". Within the assemblage a true blade production is manifested, as much in Oman as in the UAE. Along the Arabian Sea, fishing equipment becomes standardized and new tools are henceforth fabricated. It is during this period, even a little earlier, that the open sea is conquered, with tuna fishing in the Sea of Oman and in the Arabian Gulf (cf. Dalma, Akab, Ra's al-Hamra 6, etc.: Beech 2004; Uerpmann & Uerpmann 2003: 142–162; Méry, Charpentier & Beech, 2008).

The trade networks for precious products persisted during this period, the diffusion of ornaments in soft rocks (chlorite and chloritite, serpentinite, talc, schist) appearing to intensify. Besides the introduction of new raw materials, there are new categories of finished goods which are distributed, such as axes and adzes made from metamorphic rocks, the study of which is still to be done. The Suwayh facies constitutes the first phase of the late Neolithic in the Oman peninsula.

At about 3800–3700, the second phase of this late Neolithic period signals the end of the vast trade networks related to the lithic industry. The distribution of obsidian appears to decline in most of Arabia, except perhaps for Yemen where the south-Arabian societies made late use of it in the production of geometric microlithic pieces. In the Gulf, the end of trade with Ubaid 4–5 groups occurred at around 3700 and that region entered into what M. Uerpmann (2003) has called the "dark millennium": the fourth millennium, of which certain vestiges are well known in the Sultanate of Oman. Indeed, this period constitutes a field entirely open to discovery and exploration on the Gulf side.

Conclusion

Present in the northern Levant from about 8200 BC, PPNB and naviform debitage are attested in the Gulf in Qatar (Inizan & Lechevallier 1994) during the seventh millennium BC, and this allochthonous technical tradition marks the introduction of a pastoral economy in this part of the Gulf. The role of these industries of Levantine origin in the Neolithicization of the Oman peninsula remains to be defined today, and it is not certain that the PPNB constituted the first wave of Neolithicization in this zone of Arabia. Might it not rather have been a new Neolithic "surge" in a milieu that would have already transferred to a production economy? I incline more towards this hypothesis, but it must be recognized that research has not yet produced definitive answers to these questions, crucial as they are for the understanding of Arabia's past.

Defined in 1992 by M. Uerpmann, the "Saruq facies" appeared during the first half of the fifth millennium BC and covered all the Neolithic cultures that developed the bifacial industries of Oman. At present two distinct lithic facies can be defined on stratigraphic bases: the Habarut and the Suwayh facies. In both cases, their area of extension exceeds the Oman peninsula, covering a part of the Rub' al Khali for the Habarut and Suwayh cultures, the Marha and the Ḥaḍramawt for the Habarut culture. This distribution is probably still wider and the present lack of data is clearly related to the low investment of the archaeological community for this period; in any case, the Oman peninsula was not isolated at this period, far from it. No excavation concerning the fifth millennium or the beginning of the fourth millennium BC has taken place so far in the Ḥaḍramawt or the Ramlat as-Sabat'ayn, even less so in the Rub' al Khali. Large areas of Arabia (Nejd, Hejaz, etc.) are still unexplored, and future research will certainly reveal other lithic facies.

The association with other categories of artefact (ornaments, fishing equipment, etc.) shows that besides the two lithic facies, there are two cultures here, at least in the Oman peninsula (Charpentier *et al.* 2006). But this goes beyond the present paper and will be the subject of a future publication.

Notes

1 Maysar M4T23 was discovered by the German archaeological mission. In April 2004, G. Weisgerber and I found a trihedral point in opalescent flint, several flakes transformed into small nuclei, and a few flakes in various materials (brown-orange radiolarites, brown cherts, etc.).

2 The lithic industry of this site, identified by J. Giraud and called Khor 10 (locus 2) contains a debitage of bladelets, small drills, an unfinished trihedral point worked by hard percussion tool, and a "wide fusiform" point with biconvex section worked by pressure.

3 Kept at the archaeological museums of Sharjah, Ra's al-Khaimah, and from the Rothfeld collection of the museum of al Ain. We thank W. Yasin al-Tikriti for access to the collections of the museum of al Ain and C. Velde for the documentation of the Museum of Ra's al-Khaimah.

4 Except for certain deposits in Yemen and possibly the Emirate of Sharjah.

5 Also called "early south Arabian Neolithic" (Amirkhanov 1994; 1996).

6 The base of Ra's al-Hamra 6 is dated to 6360±60 BP (Level 14), 6140±70 BP (Level 9) and is thus contemporary to the late levels at Suwayh 1. Few lithic tools show a relation to this industry of "fusiform and diamond-shaped points" except for some micro-drills, a few well-made end-scrapers, and a point or "dagger" with biconvex section (Biagi 1999; Maggi 1990: fig 5/1–6, 18–19).

References

Amirkhanov H.

1994. Research on the Palaeolithic and Neolithic of Hadramaut and Mahra. *Arabian Archaeology and Epigraphy* 5: 217–228.

1996. Bilinear cultural parallelism in the Arabian early Neolithic. Pages 16135–16139 in G. Afanasev, S. Cleuziou, R. Lukacs & M. Tosi (eds), *The Prehistory of Asia and Oceania.* Colloquium XXXII: Trade as a Subsistence Strategy, Post-Pleistocene Adaptations in Arabia and Early Maritime Trade in the Indian Ocean. XIII International Congress of Prehistoric and Protohistoric Sciences. Forli: Abaco.

1997. *The Neolithic and post-Neolithic of Hadramaut and Mahra.* Moscow: Scientific World. [In Russian].

Beech M.

2004. *In the land of the Ichthyophagi. Modelling fish exploitation in the Arabian Gulf and Gulf of Oman from the 5th millennium BC to the Late Islamic period.* Abu Dhabi Islands Archaeological Survey, Monograph 1. (British Archaeological Reports, International Series, 1217). Oxford: Archaeopress.

Beech M., Cuttler R., Moscrop D., Kallweitt H. & Martin J.
2005. New evidence for the Neolithic settlement of Marawah Island, Abu Dhabi, United Arab Emirates. *Proceedings of the Seminar for Arabian Studies* 35: 37–56.
Berger J.F., Cremaschi M., Cattani M., Cavulli F., Charpentier V., Davtian G., Giraud J., Marquis P., Martin C., Méry S., Plaziat J.C., Saliège J-F. & Cleuziou S.
2005. Evolution paléogéographique du Ja'alan (Oman) à l'Holocène moyen: impact sur l'évolution des paléomilieux littoraux et les stratégies d'adaptation des communautés humaines. *Paléorient* 31/1: 46–63.
Biagi P.
1988*a*. Prehistoric survey carried out in winter 1986/1987 along the Oman coast. Pages 56–63 in S. Cleuziou & M. Tosi [eds] *The Joint Hadd Project, Summary Report on the Second Season*. Naples: IUON. [Mimeographed].
1988*b*. Surveys along the Oman Coast: Preliminary Report on the 1985–1988 Campaigns. *East and West* 38/1–4: 271–291.
1994. A radiocarbon chronology for the aceramic shell-middens of coastal Oman. *Arabian Archaeology and Epigraphy* 5: 17–31.
1999. Excavations at the shell-midden of RH-6 1986–1988 (Muscat, Sultanate of Oman). *Al-Râfidân* 20: 57–84.
2004. Survey along the Oman Coast: A review of the prehistoric sites discovered between Dibab and Qalhat. *Adumatu* 10: 29–50.
Biagi P. & R. Maggi
1990. Archaeological surveys along the Oman coast: preliminary results of five years of research (1983–1987). Pages 543–553 in M. Taddei (ed.), *South Asian Archaeology 1987, Proceedings of the Ninth International Conference*, *Venice*. (Serie Orientale Roma, 64). Rome: Istituto Italiano per il Medio ed Estremo Oriente.
Biagi P., Torke W., Tosi M. & Uerpmann H-P.
1984. Qurum: a case of coastal archaeology in Northern Oman. *World Archaeology* 16/1: 43–61.
Boucharlat R., Haerinck E., Phillips C. & Potts D.
1991. Note on an Ubaid-pottery site in the Emirate of Umm al-Qaiwain. *Arabian Archaeology and Epigraphy* 2: 65–71.
Cattani M. & Tiscornia I.
1988. *Preliminary report on the excavation of the aceramic phases at RJ-2: Excavation season 1988*. Rome: Istituto Italiano per l'Africa e l'Oriente. [Unpublished report, mimeographed].
Cauvin M.C. & Calley S.
1984. A survey in Sharjah Emirate — U.A.E. *Preliminary report on the lithic material First Report (March 5–14 1984)*: 16–19 & 30–33. [Unpublished].
Cavallari A.
2004. Joint Hadd Project: Campagna di ricognizione 2003–2004, Sultanato dell'Oman, regione del Ja'alan: risultati prospettive per una comprensione del popolamento nomade nel Medio Olocene. *Ocnus* 12: 27–35.
Charpentier V.
1986. Studies on the lithic industries of Ra's al-Junayz. Pages 43–44 in S. Cleuziou & M. Tosi [eds] *The joint Hadd Project. Summary report on the First Season*. Naples: IUON. [Mimeographed].
1988. Short preliminary report on the lithic artefacts on Ra's al-Junayz. Pages 48–50 in S. Cleuziou & M. Tosi [eds] *The joint Hadd Project. Summary report on the Second Season*. Naples: IUON. [Mimeographed].
1991. La fouille du campement préhistorique de Ra's al-Junayz 37, (RJ37) — Sultanat d'Oman. *Paléorient* 17/1: 127–141.
1996. Entre sables du Rub' al Khali et mer d'Arabie, Préhistoire récente du Dhofar et d'Oman: les industries à pointes de «Fasad». *Proceedings of the Seminar for Arabian Studies* 26: 1–12.
1999. Industries bifaciales holocènes d'Arabie orientale, un exemple: Ra's al-Jinz. *Proceedings of the Seminar for Arabian Studies* 29: 29–44.

2001. Les industries lithiques de Ra's al-Hadd. *Proceedings of the Seminar for Arabian Studies* 31: 31–45.

2004. Trihedral points: a new facet to the "Arabian Bifacial Tradition". *Proceedings of the Seminar for Arabian Studies* 34: 53–66.

Charpentier V. & Inizan M-L.

2002. Diagnostic Evidence of the Fluting Technique in the Old World: the Neolithic Projectile Points of Arabia. *Lithic Technology* 27/1: 39–46.

Charpentier V., Cremaschi M. & Demnard F.

1997. Une campagne archéologique sur un site côtier du Ja'alan: Al-Haddah (BJD-1) et sa culture matérielle (Sultanat d'Oman). *Proceedings of the Seminar for Arabian Studies* 27: 99–111.

Charpentier V., Angelucci D., Méry S. & Saliège J-F.

2000. Autour de la mangrove morte de Suwayh, l'habitat VIe–V^{e} millénaires de Suwayh SWY-11, Sultanat d'Oman. *Proceedings of the Seminar for Arabian Studies* 30: 69–85.

Charpentier V., Berger J.F., Marquis P., Méry S., Pellé E., Saliège J-F. & Tengberg M.

2006. *Between sea, mangrove and lagoon: Suwayh SWY-1, a 5500–4200 BC cal settlement.* Paper delivered at the Seminar for Arabian Studies 2006. [Unpublished].

Crassard R.

2007. *Apport de la technologie lithique à la définition de la Préhistoire du Hadramawt, dans le contexte du Yémen et de l'Arabie du Sud.* Thèse de Doctorat, Université de Paris 1 (Panthéon-Sorbonne). [Unpublished].

Crassard R. & Bodu P.

2004. Préhistoire du Hadramawt (Yémen): nouvelles perspectives. *Proceedings of the Seminar for Arabian Studies* 34: 67–84.

Cremaschi M.

2001. *Aggiornamento su: l'evoluzione olocenica delle lagune costiere comprese fra Ra's al-Hadd ed Assila — Il fattore paleoclimatico.* Rome: Istituto Italiano per l'Africa e l'Oriente. [Unpublished report].

Cremaschi M. & Negrino F.

2002. The Frankincense of Sumhuram: palaeoenvironmental and prehistorical background. Pages 325–363 in A. Avanzini (ed.), *Khor Rori report 1.* (Arabia Antica, 1). Pisa: Edizioni Plus — Università di Pisa.

2005. Evidence for an abrupt climatic change at 8700 ^{14}C yr B.P. in rockshelters and caves of Gebel Qara (Dhofar-Oman): Palaeoenvironmental implications. *Geoarchaeology* 20/6: 559–579.

Edens C.

1982. Towards a Definition of the Western ar Rub' al-Khali "Neolithic". *Atlal* 6/3: 109–123.

1988*a*. Preliminary Archaeological Survey of the Ja'alan Interior. Pages 64–74 in S. Cleuziou & M. Tosi [eds] *The Joint Hadd Project. Summary Report on the Second Season.* Naples: IUON. [Mimeographed].

1988*b*. Archaeology of the Sands and Adjacent Portions of Sharqiyah. Results of the Royal Geographical Society in the Scientific Oman Wahiba Sands Project 1985–87. *The Journal of Oman Studies, special report* 3: 107–110.

Field H.

1958. Stone Implements from the Rub' al Khali, Southern Arabia. *Man* 120–121: 93–94.

Giraud J., Bernigaud N., Martin C., Gernez G., Davtian G. & Berger J-F.

2005. Etude de l'organisation spatiale et fonctionnelle du site protohistorique de Gzeis (Ja'alan, Oman). Pages 399–404 in J-F. Berger, F. Bertoncello, F. Braemer, G. Davtian & M. Gazenbeek (eds), *Temps et espaces de l'Homme en société, analyses et modèles spatiaux en archéologie.* XXVe rencontres internationales d'archéologie et d'histoire. Antibes: Editions APDCA.

Gotoh T.

1981. A Stone Age Collection from the Rub' al Khali desert. *Bulletin of the Ancient Orient Museum* 3: 1–15.

Hellyer P.

1998. *Hidden Riches, an archaeological introduction to the United Arab Emirates.* Abu Dhabi: Emirates Printing Press/Ministry of Information and Culture.

Inizan M-L. & Francaviglia F.V.
2002. Les périples de l'obsidienne à travers la Mer Rouge. Pages 11–19 in F. Le Guennec Coppens & S. Méry (eds), Afrique-Arabie, d'une rive à l'autre en mer Erythrée. *Journal des Africanistes* 72/2.
Inizan M-L. & Lechevallier M.
1994. L'adoption du débitage laminaire par pression au Proche-Orient. Pages 23–32 in H.G. Gebel & S.K. Kozlowski (eds), *Neolithic chipped Stone Industries of the Fertile Crescent, Studies in Early Near Eastern Production, Subsistence, and Environment 1*. Berlin: ex Oriente.
Inizan M-L. & Tixier J.
1978. Outrepassage intentionnel sur des pièces néolithiques du Qatar (Golfe Arabo-Persique). *Quaternaria* 20: 29–40.
Lézine A.M., Saliège J-F., Mathieu R., Tagliatela T.L., Méry S., Charpentier V. & Cleuziou S.
2002. Mangroves of Oman during the late Holocene: Climatic Implications and Impact on Human Settlements. *Vegetation History and Archaeobotany* 11/3: 221–232.
Maggi R.
1990. The Chipped stone Assemblage of RH6 (Muscat, Sultanate of Oman). Some considerations on technological aspects. *East and West* 40/1–4: 293–300.
Méry S., Blackman J. & Beech M.
(in preparation). An interesting Ubaid-related pottery vessel from MR11, Marawah island, United Arab Emirates. *Arabian Archaeology and Epigraphy.*
Méry S., Charpentier V. & Beech M.
2008. First evidence of shell fishhook technology in the Gulf. *Arabian Archaeology and Epigraphy* 19: 15-21.
Millet M.
1988. Survey of the Sharjah Coast. *Sharjah Archaeology* 4: 21–30.
Parker A., Davis C. & Wilkinson T.
2006. The early to mid-Holocene moist period in Arabia: some recent evidence from lacustrine sequences in eastern and south-western Arabia. *Proceedings of the Seminar for Arabian Studies* 36: 243–255.
Paynes J.C. & Hawkins S.
1963. A Surface Collection of Flints from Habarut in Southern Arabia. *Man* 63: 185–188.
Pullar J.
1985. A Selection of Aceramic Sites in the Sultanate of Oman. *Journal of Oman Studies* 7: 49–87.
Putzolu C.
1999. *Survey activities in the Ra's al-Wuddaya area. A preliminary report, The Joint Hadd Project, 1998–1999.* Rome: Istituto Italiano per l'Africa e l'Oriente. [Mimeographed].
Schreiber J.
2005. Archaeological survey at Ibra' in the Sharqîyah, Sultanate of Oman. *Proceedings of the Seminar for Arabian Studies* 35: 255–270.
Smith G.H.
1976. New Neolithic sites in Oman. *The Journal of Oman Studies* 2: 189–198.
1977. New Prehistoric sites in Oman. *The Journal of Oman Studies* 3/1: 71–81.
Smith P.
1961. Two "Neolithic" Collections from Saudi Arabia. *Man* 17 (1962): 21–22.
Tosi M. & Usai D.
2003. Preliminary report on the excavations at Wadi Shab, Area 1, Sultanate of Oman. *Arabian Archaeology and Epigraphy* 14: 8–23.
Uerpmann M.
1992. Structuring the Late Stone Age of Southeastern Arabia. *Arabian Archaeology and Epigraphy* 3: 65–109.
2003. The dark Millennium — Remarks on the final Stone Age in the Emirates and Oman. Pages 74–81 in D. Potts, H. Al Naboonah & P. Hellyer (eds), *Archaeology of the United Arab Emirates.* Proceedings of the First International Conference on the Archaeology of the U.A.E. London: Trident Press.
2006. *Grabungsprojekte/V.A.E./al-Buhais 18/Lithics. Distribution of bifacial flint artefacts in BHS18.* Tübingen: Eberhard Karls Universität web site.

Uerpmann H-P. & Uerpmann M.
2003. *The Capital Area of Northern Oman: Stone Age Sites and their Natural Environment*. Part 3. Beihefte zum Tübinger Atlas des vorderen Orient. Reihe A (Naturwissenschaften), Nr. 31/3. Wiesbaden: Dr Ludwig Reichert.

Uerpmann M. & Uerpmann H-P.
1996. Ubaid pottery in the eastern Gulf — new evidence from Umm al-Qaiwain (U.A.E.). *Arabian Archaeology and Epigraphy* 7: 125–139.

Uerpman M., Uerpmann H-P. & Jasim S.A.
2000. Stone Age nomadism in SE-Arabia — palaeo-economic considerations on the Neolithic site of Al-Buhais 18 in the Emirate of Sharjah, U.A.E. *Proceeding of the Seminar for Arabian Studies* 30: 229–234.

Uerpmann H-P., Uerpmann M., Kutterer J., Handel M., Jasim S.A. & Marks A.
2007. *The Stone Age Sequence of Jebel Faya in the Emirate of Sharjah (UAE).* Paper delivered at the Seminar for Arabian Studies 2007. [Unpublished].

Usai D.
2000. New prehistoric site along the Oman coast from Ra's al-Hadd to Ra's al-Jins. *Arabian Archaeology and Epigraphy* 11: 1–8.
2005. Chisels or perforators? The lithic industry of Ra's al-Hamra 5 (Muscat, Oman). *Proceeding of the Seminar for Arabian Studies* 35: 1–9.

Zarins J.
2001. *Dhofar: land of incense. Archaeological work in the Governorate of Dhofar, Sultanate of Oman 1990.* (Archaeology and Cultural Heritage Series). Muscat: Sultan Qaboos University Publications.

Author's address
Vincent Charpentier, Inrap, UMR 7041 ArScan du CNRS, Maison de l'Archéologie et de l'Ethnologie, 21 allée de l'Université, 92023 Nanterre cedex, France.
e-mail vincent.charpentier@mae.u-paris10.fr, vincent.charpentier@inrap.fr

Proceedings of the Seminar for Arabian Studies 38 (2008): 117–136

A Neolithic settlement near the Strait of Hormuz: Akab Island, United Arab Emirates

V. CHARPENTIER & S. MÉRY

Summary
Three excavation campaigns on the island of Akab have brought to light a large Neolithic settlement dating to 4700–3600 BC cal. The Neolithic populations largely exploited the resources of the surrounding lagoon, but also fished for tuna in the open ocean. Structures built on posts were revealed. The material culture of Akab includes Mesopotamian pottery (Ubaid) and several types of characteristic beads. In particular the occupants of Akab produced discoid beads in *Spondylus sp.*, to the extent that this site may be termed one of specialized production.

Résumé
Trois campagnes de fouille sur l'île d'Akab viennent de mettre au jour un important habitat néolithique daté de 4700–3800 BC cal. Les populations néolithiques ont largement exploité les ressources de la lagune environnante, mais ont aussi pratiqué la pêche au thon en haute mer. Une architecture sur poteaux porteurs a été mise en évidence. La culture matérielle d'Akab comprend de la poterie mésopotamienne (Obeid) et plusieurs types de perles caractéristiques. Les occupants d'Akab ont notamment produit des perles discoïdes en *Spondylus sp.*, au point que l'on peut parler d'un site de production spécialisé.

Keywords: Neolithic, Arabian Gulf, United Arab Emirates, Akab, settlement, fifth millennium BC, fishing

Introduction

For geomorphologists, climatologists, and prehistorians, the study of the lagoon of Umm al-Qaiwain serves as a reference for the Arabo-Persian Gulf. Its wild mangrove, although reduced today, is one of the last surviving between Ra's al-Khaimah and Abu Dhabi (Fig. 1). Akab, Tell Abraq, ed-Dur, al-Madar, and numerous other archaeological sites border this vast lagoon, which includes several islands. The site of Akab faces the city of Umm al-Qaiwain, capital of the Emirate that occupies the great lagoonal bar west of the lagoon (Fig. 2).

Edged with mangrove trees (*Avicenna marina*), the island of Akab is today deserted and includes in its south-west part a hillock of wind-blown sand of Pleistocene origin, on which Neolithic populations settled 6500 years ago. In 1989 a team of the French Archaeological Mission to Umm al-Qaiwain discovered an important concentration of dugong bones (*Dugong dugon*) along with objects characteristic of the fifth and fourth millennia BC. This concentration of dugong bones was partially excavated in the early 1990s, and Akab was interpreted as a site for slaughtering or butchering (Prieur & Guérin 1991; Jousse *et al.* 2002). However, archaeological understanding of the site was limited, as only the concentration of dugongs was investigated, without seeking to verify whether it was part of a larger and more complex site. The chronological range revealed by radiocarbon dating (4700–3050 BC) was very wide, without any phases being differentiated on the site.

The French Archaeological Mission to the UAE resumed excavation at Akab in 2002 with the following hypothesis: the exceptional concentration of marine mammal bones found on the site must represent a specialized area which was part of a settlement. The latter was still to be identified and defined. It was also necessary to verify whether distinct levels, dated to the fifth and fourth millennia BC, were preserved in the stratigraphy, as well as to seek traces of Neolithic dwelling structures. This had not been carried out during earlier excavations at Akab. The aim was to establish the actual presence of Neolithic occupations *in situ* as well as to determine the extent, stratigraphy, and chronology of the site.

Test trenches and excavation

The island of Akab was subjected to a landscaping project several decades ago. Its shores were remodelled and its

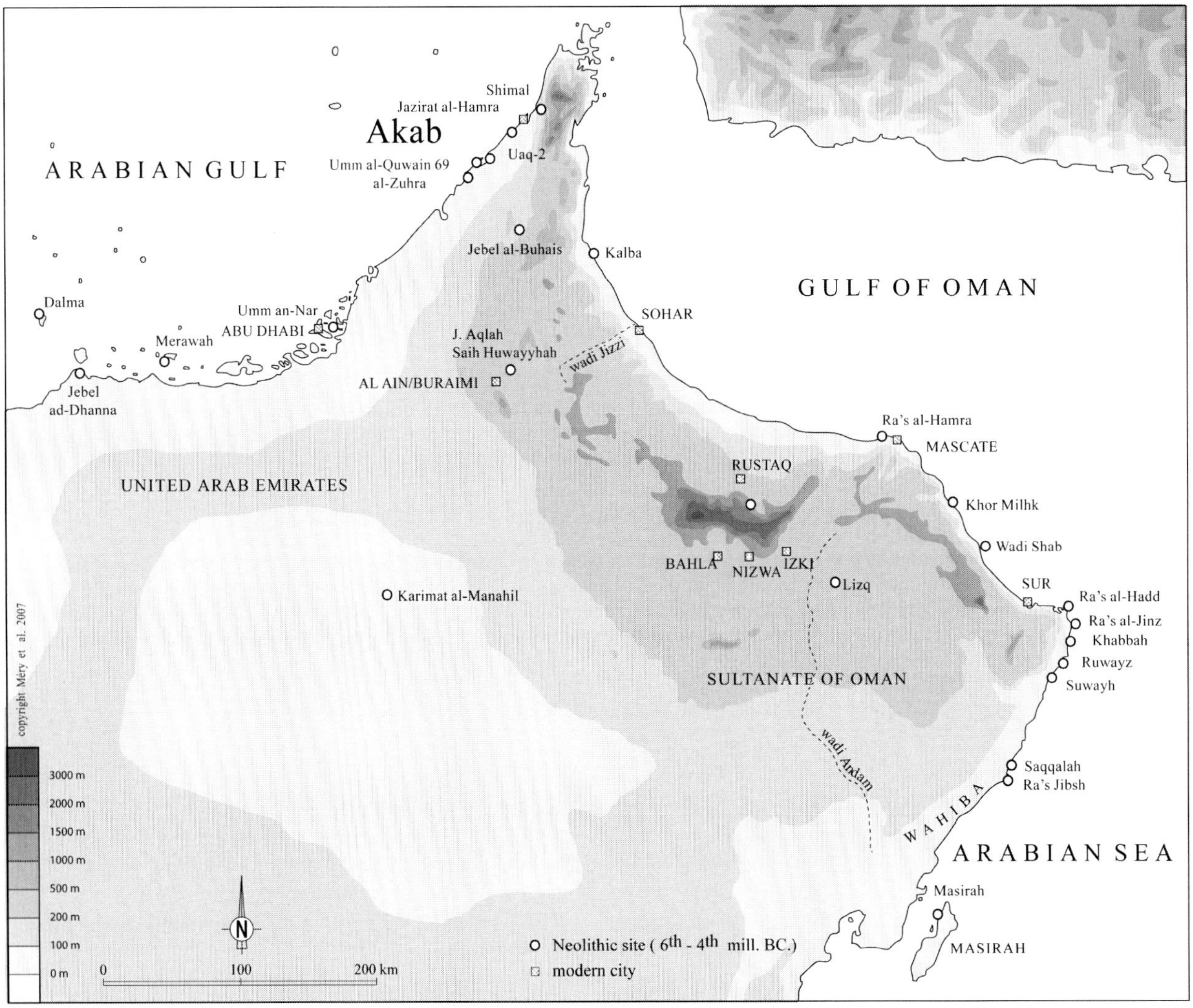

Figure 1. *A map of Neolithic sites in the United Arab Emirates and the Sultanate of Oman. Drawing by H. David.*

surface levelled using machinery, but a hillock of wind-blown sand of Pleistocene origin was preserved intact in the south-west part of the island. It is on this low hillock that the Neolithic site is located. The vestiges of human occupation are spread over a surface of about 1 ha and cover a sterile dune.

In 2002, a series of six 2×4 m test trenches were dug to the south and the north of the dugong mound (Fig. 3). Test trenches TT.4 and TT.6, which are sterile, enabled definition of the extent of the ancient site. Test trenches TT.1 and TT.3, which produced human occupation levels at 10 cm and 30 cm respectively below the present surface, were enlarged in order to acquire a better spatial insight into the organization of the archaeological material. The upper levels of TT.1, which are poorly preserved, date to the fourth millennium.

Test trenches TT.2 and TT.5 revealed levels dated to the fifth millennium. In TT.2, a layer of wind-blown sand 1.2 m thick covers the human occupation levels, at the base of which post holes and a basin-shaped hearth were discovered. The lower level, dated to 6275 $\pm$ 50 BP (calibrated to 4748–4441 BC at 2 sigma — see below), represents the oldest occupation of Akab, not found elsewhere on the site. Test trench TT.5, situated north of the mound of dugongs, produce well-stratified horizons, sealed by a wind-blown deposit which is less thick than

FIGURE 2. *An aerial photograph of the site of Akab and its mangrove. (© T. Sagory, French archaeological mission in the UAE).*

that of TT.2. Excavation was opened in 2006 based on this test trench (Sector 1), with two new extensions in 2007 (Sectors 2 and 4). The surface of Sectors 1, 2, and 4 cover a total of 72 m^2, and only Sector 4 has not yet been excavated down to virgin soil. The soil removed was sieved entirely with a mesh of 2–3 mm; tests were carried out with a 0.4 mm mesh to recover the smallest elements.

Stratigraphy of Sectors 1 and 2

Sectors 1 and 2, which cover a surface of 48 m^2, were excavated down to virgin soil. The archaeological levels developed to a thickness of 25 to 35 cm, directly on a deposit of Pleistocene wind-blown sand. They are very homogenous, made up of grey-brown sandy sediments rich in organic materials (shell, fish bones, etc.). The levels of occupation contain a succession of floors characterized by an abundant spread of *Marcia hiantina*, concentrations of oysters (*Saccostrea cucculata*) and murexes (*Murex kusterianus*), articulated fish skeletons and crab carapaces, as well as various burnt or trampled materials, and also empty spaces (Figs 4–6). No wind-blown fine sandy horizon is present between the archaeological levels, which suggest the absence of lengthy phases of abandonment. Finally, at the base of all the horizons, the negatives of post holes are visible in the contact zone between the last archaeological level and the sterile sediment.

The top of the archaeological levels is disturbed by the tunnelling of foxes and the nests of seagull colonies which occupied the site after its abandonment. The eggs are

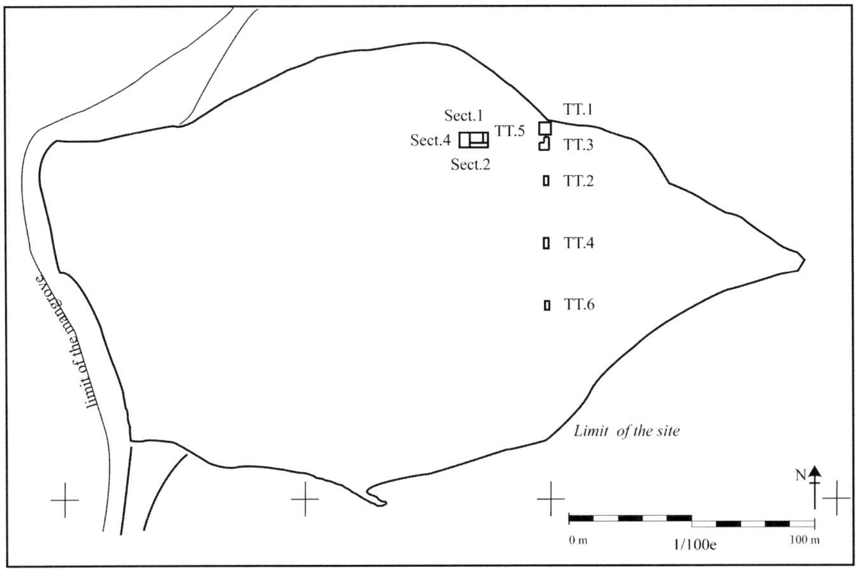

Figure 3. *A sketch of the location of the test trenches and the excavations 222-2007. (© French archaeological mission in the UAE).*

Figure 4. *Concentration of food waste (*Saccostrea cuccullata*). (© French archaeological mission in the UAE).*

Figure 5. *Concentration of food waste (broken* Terebralia palustris*).*
(© French archaeological mission in the UAE).

Figure 6. *Concentration of broken crab pincers, thrown away in pairs. Settlement of Akab, fifth-millennium levels. (© French archaeological mission in the UAE).*

generally very little broken and belong to brown seagulls. Such remains have also been discovered at Marawah MR11 where they are probably evidence of reoccupation by marine birds of isolated or insular archaeological sites. The levels are sealed by a deposit of wind-blown sand 65 cm thick. This layer is sterile or only very slightly affected by human activity, and corresponds to a phase of unfavourable climatic conditions which brought on aridification.

The dating of the early levels: Akab in its local context

AKAB	Lab. no.	Spec.	BP	1η BC	2η BC	ʌR
S2 L6	Pa 2355	Marcia	6275 ± 50	4674-4516	4748-4441	163 ± 40 BP
Sect 1 base	Pa 2440	Marcia	5970 ± 35	4320-4246	4357-4198	163 ± 15 BP
S5 L6	Pa 2356	Marcia	5900 ± 50	4303-4135	4331-4033	163 ± 40 BP
A/B/C/21	Pa 2439	Marcia	5710 ± 30	4019-3945	4081-3906	163 ± 15 BP

Table 1. *Radiocarbon dates of marine shells from Akab settlement. Calibration program: M. Stuiver and P.J. Reimer (1986-2005). ʌR is the marine reservoir effect in Qatar (Saliège et al. 2005: fig. 1).*

The early occupation of Akab, which is the subject of this article, covers the last seven centuries of the fifth millennium and the first two centuries of the fourth millennium BC (4748–3906). The earliest level of the site was identified at the base of test trench 2 (level 6) and dates to 6275 ± 50 BP (4748–4441 cal. BC, 2 sigma) (Table 1). This level has not been found elsewhere on the site. The occupation of sector 1 is a little later according to the three dates established: 5970 ± 35 BP (4357–4198 cal. BC); 5900 ± 50 BP (4331–4033 cal. BC); 5710 ± 30 BP (4081–3906 cal. BC).

Comparison with the uncalibrated dates of other regional sites shows that the early levels of test trench 2 are slightly earlier than the levels at Al Ramlah 6 (6181 ± 50 BP), and contemporary or a little later than those of Dalma DA-11 (6395 ± 60; 6220 ± 45; 6165 ± 55; 5830 ± 55). The levels of Sector 1 are contemporary to those of Al Qassimimiya (5960 ± 120/5800 ± 110 BP), of Jazirat al-Hamra 1 (5955 ± 100 BP) and 2 (5845 ± 105), of Al Madar S69 (5890 ± 170 BP), and of Al Ramlah 6 (5713 ± 50 BP), but earlier than the latest levels at Marawah 11 (5630 ± 50 BP) or those of Al Ramlah 3 (Beech 2004; Boucharlat *et al.* 1991; Uerpmann & Uerpmann 1996: 132).

Settlement structures of Sectors 1 and 2

Sectors 1 and 2 were excavated in a total of six units to virgin soil. The thickness of these units was defined according to the main archaeological floors, indicated in particular by the presence of *Marcia*.

Post-hole negatives were discovered in section and during the course of the excavation of the grey-brown levels of Sectors 1 and 2, but they were especially clear in the level of sterile sand in contact with the earliest horizons in this zone. In March 2007, 175 post-hole negatives were excavated over a surface of about 40 m^2. They are located for the most part in the western part of the excavated zone (Fig. 7). These post holes have various diameters and depths and their fill consists of materials from the horizon with which they are associated (black-brown sediments, remains of fish, crabs, and especially shells). Determination of the architecture based on the analysis of these post holes is a complex operation, and is in progress at the present time, but we can already stress the extensive and recurrent setting-up of successive structures in this zone of the site. We also observe that very dense zones contrast with others that are nearly empty (north-east angle of Sector 1).

It should be kept in mind that no circular structure identical to that of Dalma or the late levels of Suwayh 1 (Sultanate of Oman) was immediately apparent during excavation, the only evidence that appears to indicate the location of architecture of this type being post holes of varying depth and diameter. This evidence is found in the south-east part of the excavation, in a zone which is not very dense in post holes.

On the other hand, several groups composed of four or five identical post holes (i.e. with similar diameter, depth, and fill) are clearly visible and could be hypothetically interpreted as awnings, a type of structure which has not so far been found on a Neolithic site in Arabia. Akab is thus, with Dalma, the only Neolithic site in this part of the Gulf which has produced architecture with carrier posts. Its excavation emphasizes the essential fact that the Neolithic shell middens of eastern Arabia are stratified and structured features in which structures in the negative are perceptible if they are excavated with this in mind.

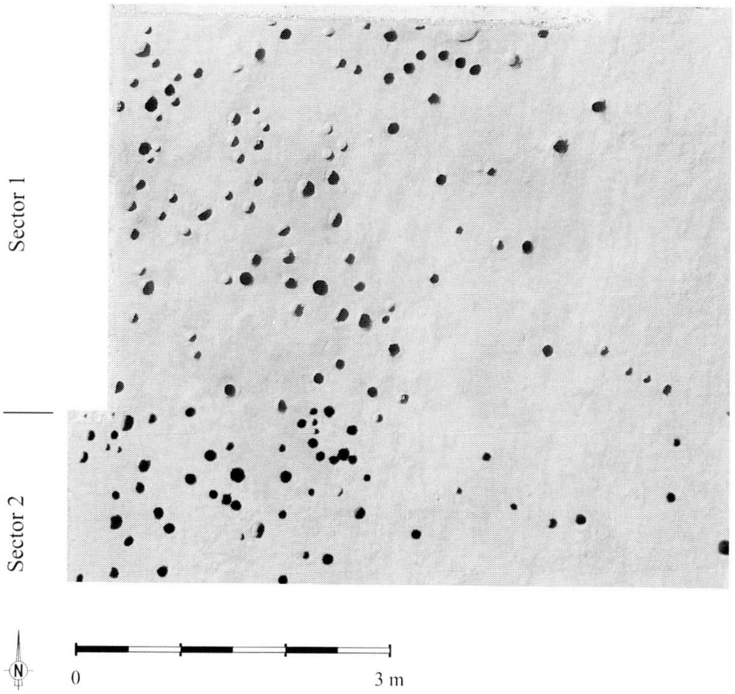

Figure 7. *An aerial view of post holes of Sectors 1 and 2. Settlement of Akab, base of fifth-millennium levels. (© M. Pons and T. Sagory, French archaeological mission in the UAE).*

The hearths

Several ashy zones were excavated in the settlement of Akab (TT.2; Sectors 1, 2, and 4), but proper hearths are difficult to discern and probably correspond to non-constructed flat zones. They differ from hearths of the same period in the Sultanate of Oman where several types of structures are in evidence, always well constructed and easily found in the excavation. It should be pointed out that rock materials are absent in the environment of Akab.

Material culture

Fishing equipment

At Akab, net sinkers are made from hard rocks that do not come from the site itself but from the shores of the lagoon or beyond. All are worked by notching or picking and correspond to a type of net sinker with a transverse groove, well known in the Gulf and on the shores of the Sea of Oman and the Arabian Sea in the sixth–fifth millennia BC (Fig. 8/1–8). The kind of sinkers found at Akab are not specific to the Gulf, as they are also found in Oman, but conversely, a certain Omani type is not found at Akab or other Gulf sites. This Omani type is characterized by a preferential choice of material (i.e. calcites), working by notching or longitudinal grooving, and a tendency towards uniform size and shape of the objects.

The fish hooks in mother-of-pearl are well represented in the settlement, whether as pre-forms, rough forms, or finished products (Fig. 9/6–9) (see also Méry, Charpentier & Beech 2008: fig. 2). They constitute one of the main discoveries made since 2002 on the site of Akab, and their existence refutes a widespread idea. Several scholars have put forward the hypothesis that mother-of-pearl fish hooks were not used on the Gulf coast during the Neolithic, because the waters are shallow and the shores are sandy (Cleuziou 2005). According to these archaeologists, the Gulf would have been more favourable for fixed traps (net enclosures, of the *ḥaḍrah* or *maskar* type), while the deep waters of the Indian Ocean would be more favourable for line fishing and the mother-of-pearl fish hook, to capture tuna at the edges of the deep-sea zone. The discovery at Akab of the remains of fish hooks in different stages of fabrication shows that this technology is well represented

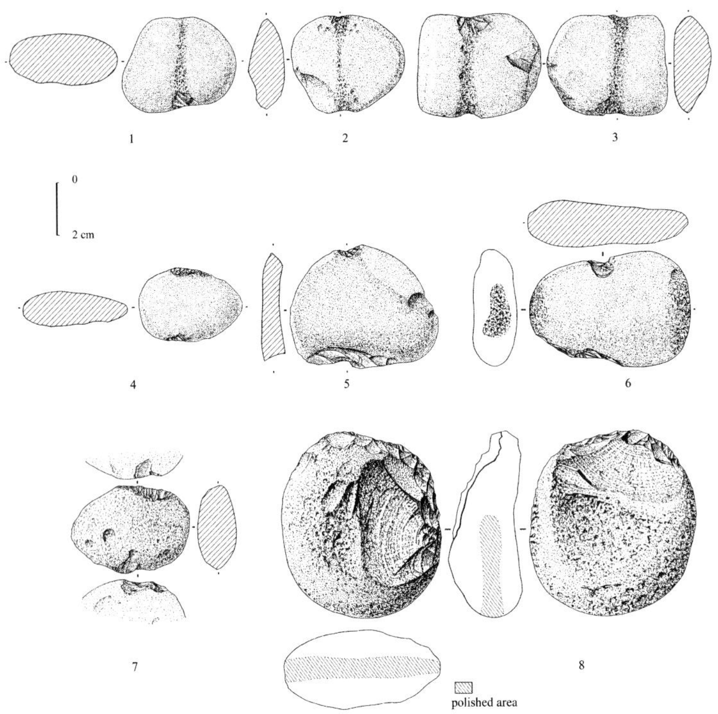

Figure 8. *1–8. Net sinkers; 9. crushing stone. Settlement of Akab, fifth-millennium levels. (Drawing by G. Devilder, French archaeological mission in the UAE).*

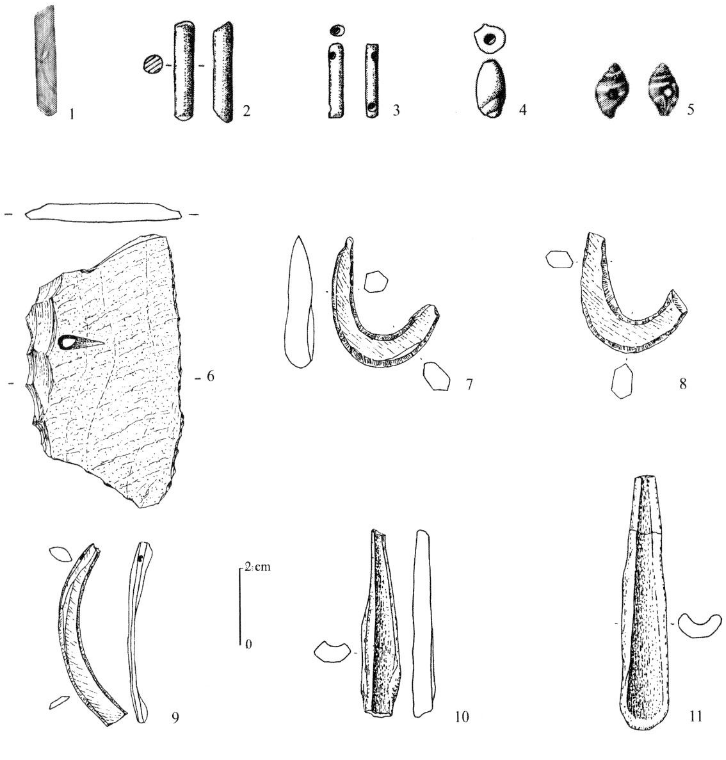

Figure 9. *1–3. beads of "Akab type"; 4–5. other shell beads; 6. ébauche of Pinctada margaritifera fish hook; 7–9. fish hooks; 10–11. bone points. Settlement of Akab, fifth-millennium levels. (Drawing by G. Devilder and S. Eliès, French archaeological mission in the UAE).*

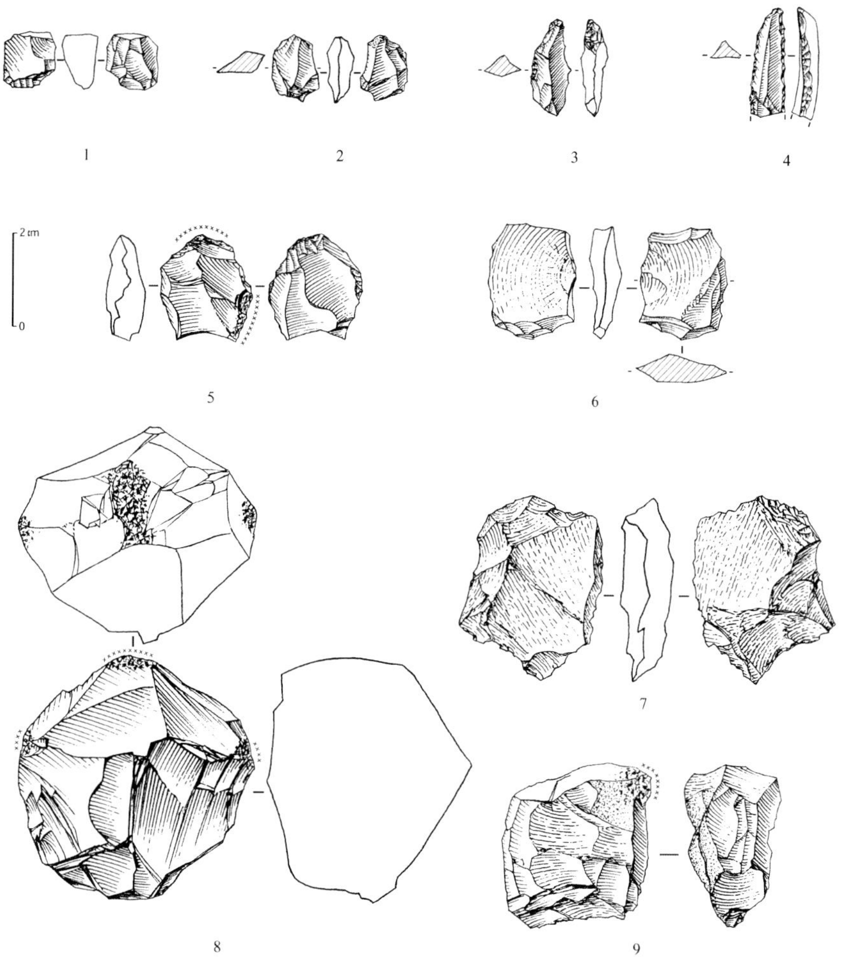

FIGURE 10. *1–2, 5–6, 7, 9. pièces esquillées; 3. borer; 4. double backed bladelet; 8. core. (Drawing by G. Devilder, French archaeological mission in the UAE).*

on the shores of the Gulf. It is thus an element of material culture common to the coastal populations of the Oman peninsula (Méry, Charpentier & Beech 2008).

Other tools

Lithic material is generally not abundant on the coastal sites of the UAE, and is particularly lacking at Akab, but the raw materials present are not of such bad quality on the whole. Translucent or opaque brown flints are found in coastal contexts, and it appears that the population of Akab had access, although probably indirectly, to very good material, in particular a black flint present in very small quantities in many coastal settlements of the UAE (Marawah 1, Abu Dhabi airport, etc.) (Hellyer 1998: 28).

Most of the tools are *pièces esquillées* which are sometimes microlithic (Fig. 10/1–2), and a few drills are also present (Fig. 10/3); these two types of tool are used in the local fabrication of beads from *Spondylus* shells. A small bifacial piece shows that pressure working was mastered at Akab, and it would not be surprising to find slender points one day in this settlement, as these are found on contemporary neighbouring sites (al-Madar S69, ar-Ramlah, UAQ-1 and 2, Jezirat al-Hamra, etc.) (Millet 1988; Phillips 2002; Uerpmann & Uerpmann 1996).

A crushing stone dating to the fifth millennium was also discovered at Akab in the upper levels of the excavation. It is a fairly flat discoid pebble, marked by a small depression on each face (Fig. 8/9). The two faces of this object were used as an anvil, and one side as a percussion tool; its edges are straight along the main

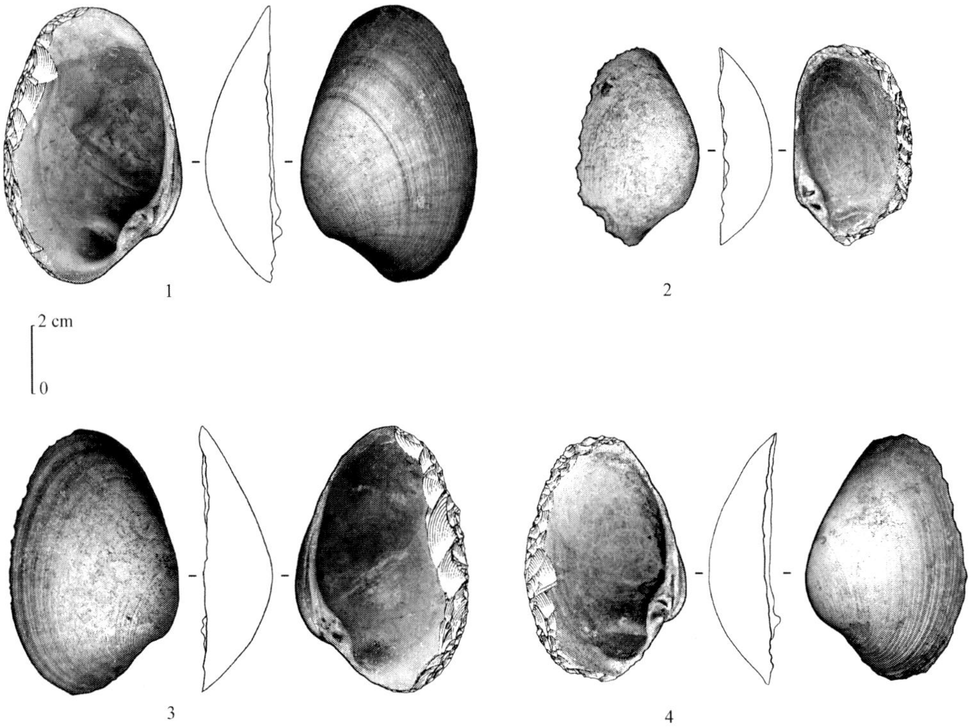

Figure 11. *Verenidae side-scrapers. (Drawing/scan by G. Devilder and R. Douaud, French archaeological mission in the UAE).*

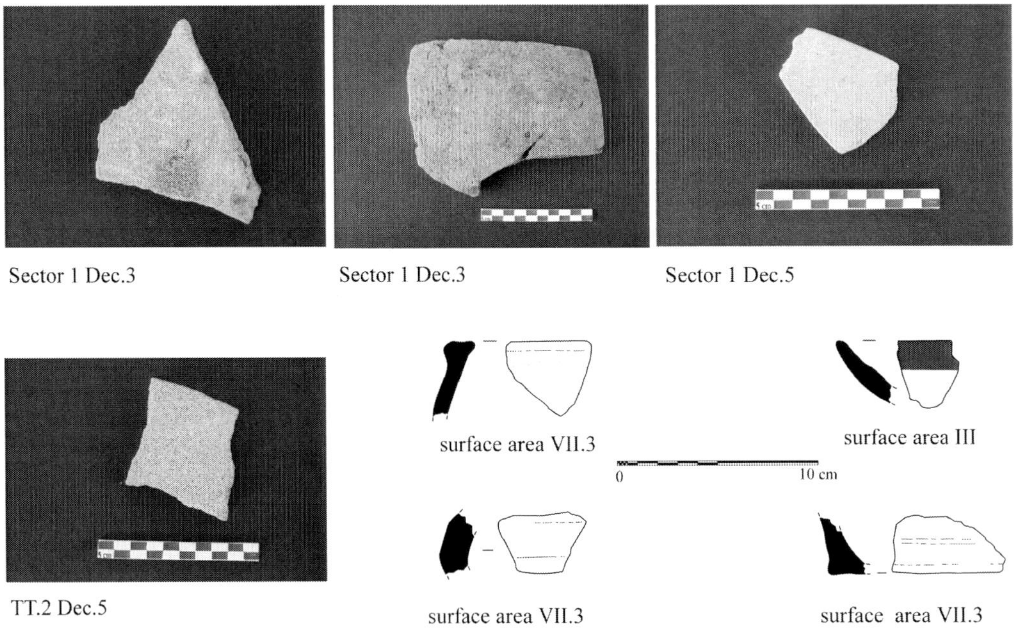

Figure 12. *Pottery sherds. Settlement of Akab. (© French archaeological mission in the UAE).*

axis of the stone. This type of tool is generally related to the presence of *Terebralia palustris*, as for example at Umm an-Nar, UAQ-2, and Jezirat al-Hamra in the Gulf (Frifelt 1995: 209, fig. 300; Vogt 1994; C. Phillips, personal communication); it would have been used to break the shells. Crushing stones are also frequent in the assemblages of the Omani coastal sites (Ra's al-Hamra, Ja'alan), especially in Dhofar (Rassek HSK-1 and HBM2; M. Tosi, personal communication) where they can make up the majority of the archaeological objects as at Ad-Dhariz, one of the fossil mangroves of Salalah. This tool is however found in several Neolithic settlements where *T. palustris* is absent, at Shagra (Qatar) for example (Inizan 1988: fig. 55/2). In any case, crushing stones are poor chronological markers, as they persist in the Gulf up to the Iron Age, as at Tell Abraq and Muweilah (Potts 2000; P. Magee, personal communication 2002).

For the mineral materials, ochre is present on the site in the form of small friable nodules, a material already reported in the Gulf and the Oman peninsula for the fifth–fourth millennia (Inizan 1988; Salvatori 2007).

The tools in hard faunal materials consist of bone points (Fig. 9/10–11), but no straight-throated fish hooks, a type known on other contemporary sites in the Oman peninsula. With fifty-four examples, the knives and side-scrapers in Veneridae (*Callista erycina* and *Amiantis umbonella*) constitute the commonest type of tool at Akab. Their shells were used locally in the production of knives made by "inverse" retouch, convex or rectilinear; the removals can include all of the ventral edge of the shell or be limited to a particular area (Fig. 11). The rarity of unworked shells of *C. erycina* and *A. umbonella* in the excavation indicates that the collection of these shells was exclusively intended for the production of tools, as was also the case in Oman (Charpentier, Méry & Phillips 2004).

The pottery

Several Neolithic sites in Umm al-Qaiwain have already produced Mesopotamian pottery sherds of the Ubaid 3-4 period: UAQ2, ar-Ramlah 3, and al-Madar S69 (Boucharlat *et al.* 1991; Phillips 2002; Uerpmann & Uerpmann 1996). In Akab, Ubaid pottery (Ubaid 4, when diagnostic) is present in fifth-millennium BC stratified horizons and at the surface of the site (Fig. 12).

The ornaments

Beads represent the great majority of the objects found in the settlement of Akab since 2002. They are made from different types of shell, such as *Pinctada margaritifera*, *Ancilla sp.* (Fig. 9/4), and immature *Conus sp.*, but the most highly represented species by far is *Spondylus*. The working of beads in the mother-of-pearl of *P. margaritifera* is attested on the site by outlines and finished products as well as by quantities of related waste bits, and by the fabrication of fish hooks.

FIGURE 13. *A fine pearl. Settlement of Akab, fifth millennium BC. (© French archaeological mission in the UAE).*

Pearl

A small fine non-perforated pearl from *Pinctada radiata* was discovered in Sector 1 (level 2) (Fig. 13). This pearl, which measures 3.42 x 3.26 mm, was very little altered, still retaining a beautiful lustre. It is the oldest pearl bead discovered in the context of a settlement in the Oman peninsula; the fine pearls found previously were discovered in the Neolithic burials of Buhais BHS-18, Umm al-Qaiwan UAQ-2, and Suwayh SWY-1 for the fifth millennium, and also in the later necropolises of Ra's al-Hamra (RH-5, RH-10) (Charpentier, Marquis & Pellé 2003; Phillips 2002; Salvatori, 2007; 1996; Santini 1987). It is rarer to discover a pearl in a settlement, as at Suwayh 1 in levels dating to 4200 BC (unpublished), and at Khor Milkh 1 for the fourth millennium (Shöler 2003; Uerpmann & Uerpmann 2003: 142–162). In the north of the Gulf, a pierced pearl is known from the settlement of As-Sabiyah in Kuwait (Carter & Crawford 2002; forthcoming).

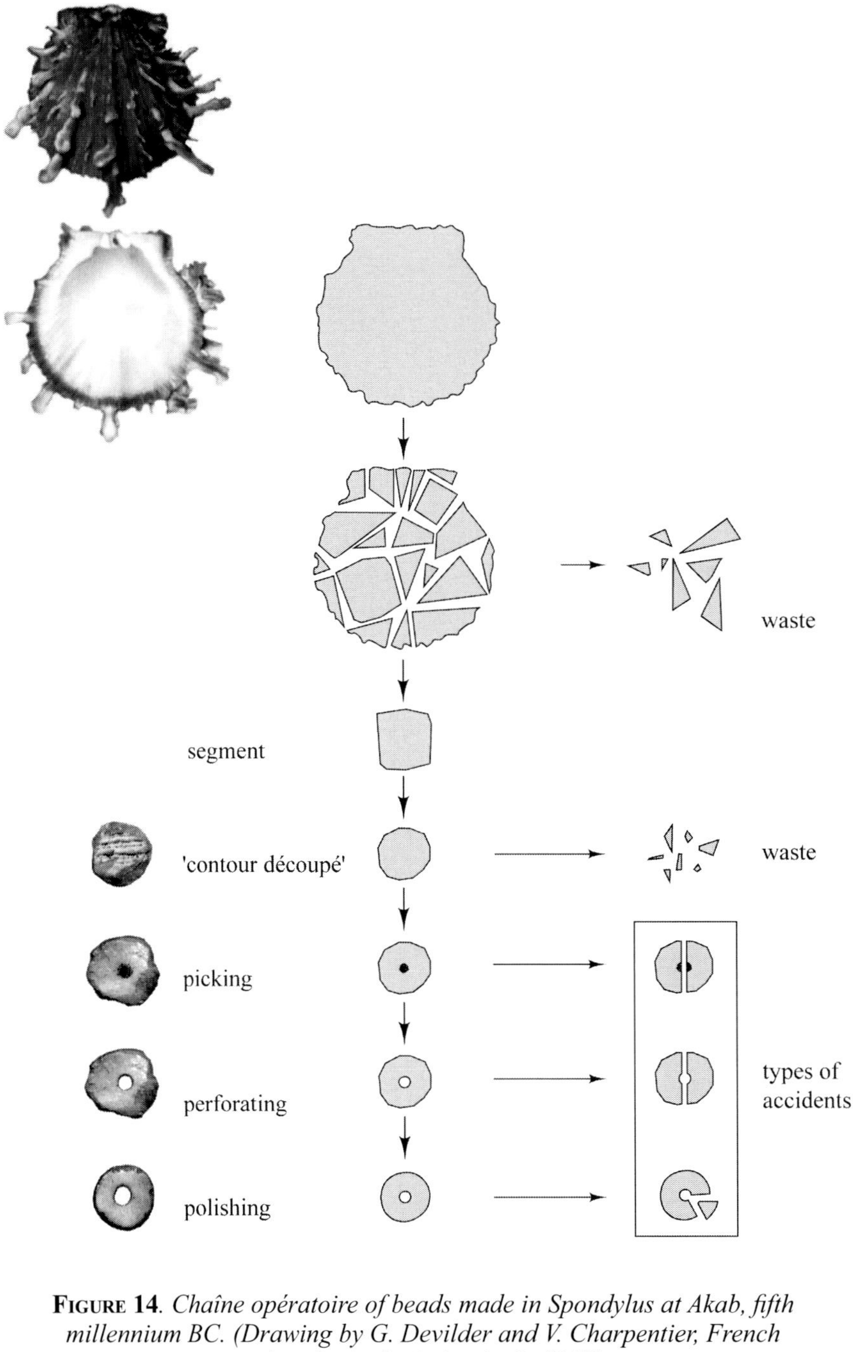

Figure 14. *Chaîne opératoire of beads made in Spondylus at Akab, fifth millennium BC. (Drawing by G. Devilder and V. Charpentier, French archaeological mission in the UAE).*

Engina mendicaria beads

The discovery of beads made from *E. mendicaria* is certainly of interest (Fig. 9/5) as these shells are not local, but found today on the rocky coast, in particular at the junction of the Gulf with the Sea of Oman. These shells, which have also been identified in a Neolithic context at Dalma, offshore from Abu Dhabi, were most probably traded over moderate to long distances, beginning in the fifth millennium.

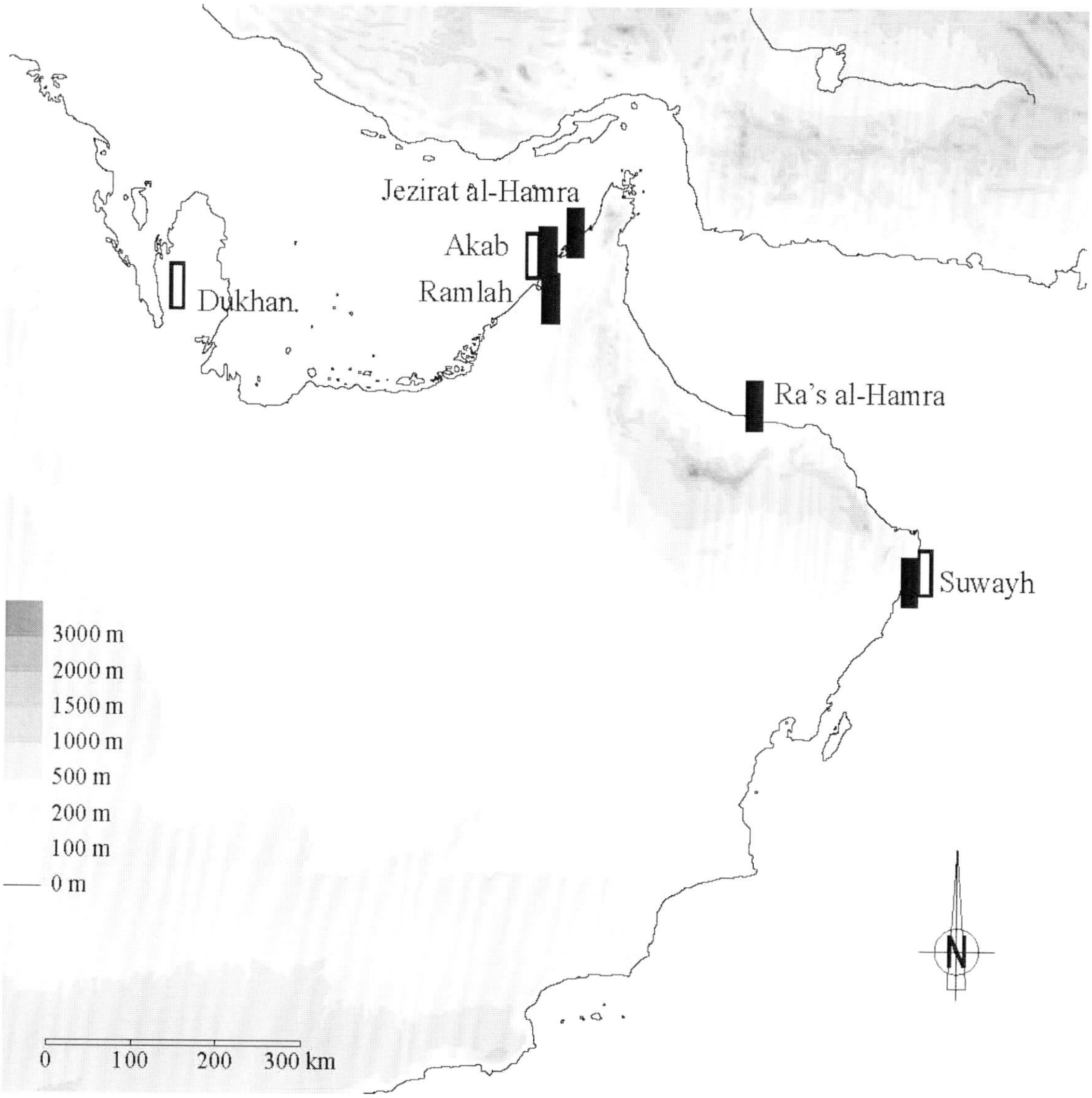

FIGURE 15. *Distribution map of tubular "Akab type" beads in the Gulf and in the north of the Indian Ocean.*

Spondylus beads

Spondylus shells were locally collected, and hundreds of beads and roughed-out forms as well as much waste from fabrication were found at Akab on habitation floors (Fig. 14). They appear as small concentrations of objects and not in specialized areas devoted to them. The discovery of hundreds of unfinished beads and waste indicates both the importance and the recurrence of this activity, suggesting a certain specialization of the site in the production of this type of ornament.

All the elements in the fabrication sequence were found in place. The shells were first cut into small squares or hexagons using a *pièce esquillée*, and then perforated with a drill; these two types of flint tool were found on the site of Akab. The phase of biconical perforation is one of the most delicate phases of work, and in the excavation many roughed-out forms of beads were found broken at this stage. The last phase of fabrication corresponds to the *calibration* of the beads, i.e. finishing, by polishing to reduce down to a uniform shape and size, e.g. with a limestone polisher. No tool of this type has been found at Akab or any other Gulf site except H3, As-Sabiyah (Carter & Crawford 2002: 3), but the fourth-millennium settlement of Ra's al-Khabbah in Oman has produced one (excavations by G. Trapani, unpublished).

Tubular beads of "Akab type"

These are long tubular beads, which measure 30 x 2 mm and are produced in two different materials. The first is soft rock (steatite or chlorite), which is not native to the Gulf shores but probably originated in the foothills of the Oman mountains. The others, in marine shell, are fashioned in the columella of Murcidae (Madsen 1961: 195; Prieur & Guérin 1991). Two models are differentiated at Akab, as much by the form of the extremities as by their perforation technique. The first, in stone or shell, has a double distal perforation which is angled, the first perforation following the axis of the object and the second following one of its rays, which creates a very original means of attachment and assemblage. Other beads in shell have a single extremity of this type, the other extremity being bevelled with a central biconical perforation. No bead in green rock has this form. One shell bead, which is a non-perforated rough form, has both extremities bevelled.

The fifth-millennium settlement of Akab (Sector 1) has produced three complete examples of these beads in three different levels: two come from the two oldest archaeological levels (AK. 438, removal 5, square F2; AK. 439, removal 6, square E2), the last from an upper level (AK. 437, removal 2, square K1). Two of these beads were made from a murex columella (AK. 437 and AK.438), the third in soft stone (AK. 439). Example AK. 438 (Fig. 9/1 and 2) is a non-perforated rough form measuring 25.5×4.8 mm and the only known bead of "Akab type" whose two extremities are bevelled. Bead AK. 437, of which the two extremities have a double angled distal perforation, measures 25.2 mm x 3.4 mm. Finally, AK. 439 (Fig. 9/3), which measures 19.2 mm x 2.9 mm, has two angled distal perforations, but these are not opposite each other.

Beads of "Akab type" are mostly found in the coastal settlements of the northern UAE, especially Akab, where thirty-four examples were found at the beginning of the 1990s (Prieur & Guérin 1991) (Fig. 15). They are found in the Sultanate of Oman only on the site of Suwayh SWY-2 (Charpentier, Blin & Tosi 1998: figs 9–5). Other beads of the same type come from al-Madar (S69) in the south of the coastal band of Umm al-Qaiwain, and from Ramlah 2 at the far end of its lagoon, and also from Jazirat al-Hamra in the Emirate of Ra's al-Khaimah (Uerpmann M 2003: fig. 3; Vogt 1994). The only bead found outside the Oman peninsula comes from a surface site in Qatar, the site of Dukhan (Madsen 1961: fig. 18).

The association of chlorite and murex tubular beads of "Akab type" is so far found only at Akab in fifth-millennium levels, and at Suwayh 2 in the levels dated to 3360–3240 cal. BC. The other chlorite beads of "Akab type" come from sites generally dated to the end of the fifth or the beginning of the fourth millennium, such as Jazirat al-Hamra or Ramlah-2. The bead in serpentine from Ras al-Hamra RH-6, attributable to the fifth millennium and which has the same type of attachment, is very singular in its form and unusual length (61 mm) (Biagi 1999: fig. 15/3). The bead found at Qatar, of a size equivalent to the Akab beads, is quadrangular in section (Madsen 1961: 195).

The beads of "Akab type" are cultural markers rather than the markers proposed by other authors (Uerpmann & Uerpmann 2003: 258). As these beads are absent in the necropolis of Buhais 18, which dates to the fifth millennium, M. and H-P. Uerpmann proposed that they were chronological markers for the fourth millennium, interpreted as late imitations of the tubular beads with longitudinal perforation from Buhais. The recent discoveries at Akab show that beads of "Akab type" were already present by 4300 BC and that they are a type of bead which is distinct from that known at Buhais, although contemporary. So far identified only in the coastal settlements, they disappear at the end of the fourth millennium. J. Benton and D.T. Potts (1994: fig. 71/30) believed that they had found them in Tomb I at Jabal al-Emalah, dated to the beginning of the third millennium, but the beads from this collective burial have a quadrangular section and biconical distal perforations; this type is very different from that of Akab, highly characteristic of the Hafit period (i.e. the beginning of the local early Bronze Age) and found in abundance at Ra's al-Hadd HD-6 (Zaros 2004).

The discovery at Akab of a tubular bead in bevelled but non-perforated murex moreover enables confirmation of what was observed at the fifth–fourth millennia coastal sites of Ja'alan, Ra's al-Khabbah, and especially Suwayh, namely the possible arrival of semi-finished products on settlement sites (in this case unfinished earrings in soft stone). The discovery of an unfinished bead at Akab is of much interest: determining trade in semi-finished products is especially difficult in the Neolithic as most of the artefacts found in the settlements and particularly the necropolises were used; they are thus worn, broken, and sometimes repaired. The unfinished bead from Akab may thus be a new indicator of this type of trade in the fifth millennium.

Fauna

On the whole the animal bones are well preserved at Akab as they are highly mineralized, a frequent natural phenomenon on the Neolithic sites of the Umm al-Qaiwain lagoon and already reported by other researchers. The land animals are particularly well represented in the fifth-millennium levels of the settlement, compared to other coastal sites in the UAE and considering the high aridity of the ancient environment of Akab. According to Dr M. Beech from ADACH-Abu Dhabi and E. Pellé, from CNRS-Paris, the domestic fauna found at Akab includes goat (*Capra hircus*), sheep (*Ovis aries*), cow (*Bos sp.*), and dog (*Canis familiaris*). The hunted fauna are represented by *Gazella gazella* and wild donkey (*Asinus africanus*).

While the green turtle (*Chelonia mydas*) is rare in the settlement, the dugong is represented in all levels in the form of vertebrae and broken ribs. Ribs and vertebrae, with scapulae, also represent the main dugong bones found at other Neolithic settlements of the Gulf, including Marawah 11, Dalma, Jazirat al-Hamra, and Al-Markh (Beech 2000; Beech *et al.* 2005; Beech & Kallweit 2001; Roaf 1974).

Besides the shellfish, fish represent most of the faunal remains: needlefish, grouper, jack/trevally, tuna/mackerel, and catfish. The discovery of many headless fish skeletons indicates local preparation of fish. According to M. Beech (2005), who studied the fish bones found at Akab in 2002, "fishing largely took place in shallow water habitats. Whilst the majority of the fish could have been caught in the neighbouring Umm al-Qaiwain lagoon, tuna were probably caught outside the lagoon in open waters". These results differ from the observations made by other researchers at Ramlah, at the far end of the lagoon of Umm al-Qaiwain, as well as at Akab by the team of C. Guérin. The fishing was described as practised exclusively in shallow water, with "no indication that boats or any refined technology were used for fishing" (Uerpmann & Uerpmann 1996: 134). For the same reasons, the results of the new excavations at Akab do not follow the first conclusions made by J. Desse (2002), based on a small sample of fish remains from earlier excavations of the dugong mound at Akab.

Concentrations of crab remains from consumption were also often recovered *in situ* in the fifth-millennium BC levels of Sectors 1 and 2 at Akab, the crabs' pincers having been clearly broken and thrown away in pairs in certain cases. Several species of crab are represented, *Portunus sp.* first of all, but also mangrove crabs such as *Scylla serrata*. Two fragments of cuttlefish carapace were found in Sector 1; Umm al-Qaiwain 2 has already produced an example (C. Phillips, personal communication).

The large majority of consumed shellfish recovered at Akab are characteristic of a sandy-silty lagoonal environment, but a few species, such as *Lunella coronata*, come from rocky shores. Concentrations of shells whose contents were eaten were often found in situ. The gastropods *T. palustris* and *Murex kuesterianus* were usually found broken and some carried traces of fire. In the shell assemblages, *M. kuesterianus*, *M. hiantina*, and *S. cucculata* are predominant, followed by *Strombus decorus persicus*, *T. palustris*, and *Pinctada radiata*. Other species are rare, even exceptional.

Conclusion

The three excavation campaigns carried out by our team have shown that the settlement of Akab had multiple occupations beginning in 4750 BC, and that most of the levels excavated so far date to the fifth millennium. It is definitely the site of a settlement, whose surface area covers about 1.5 ha, and which contains archaeological deposits with no trace of major discontinuity for more than half a millennium. The site contains many vestiges of structures on carrier posts, which were implanted successively and repeatedly. The activities of its occupants were largely oriented towards exploitation of the lagoon, but they also practised tuna fishing in the open sea, which demanded sophisticated equipment. The discovery of workshops for the production of beads made from *Spondylus* in all levels of the settlement indicates that certain sites in the Gulf could have already been specialized in the production of craft objects in the fifth millennium. We have no evidence of a local production of tubular beads of "Akab type", but the discoveries made in the settlement of Akab show that they should not be regarded as a chronological marker of the end of the fourth millennium (they appear at about 4600 BC).

Instead, they better represent a cultural marker of the Neolithic populations in the Oman peninsula, together with other types of personal ornaments of the fifth–fourth millennia, e.g. laurel-leaf pendants in *P. margaritifera*, composite bracelets carved from large Conidae, or soft-stone earrings. In the Arabian Peninsula, the distribution of tubular beads of "Akab type" extends from Qatar

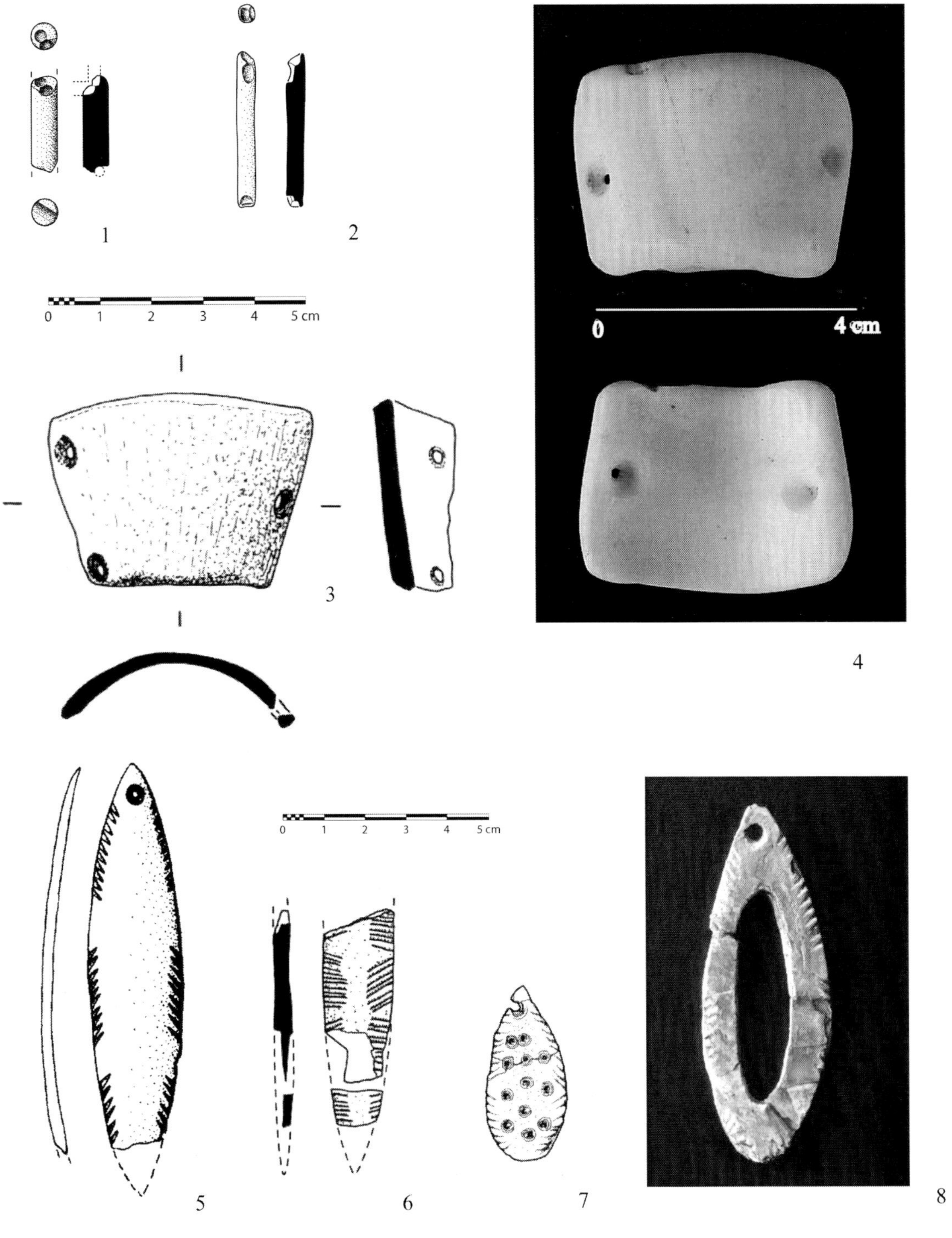

Figure 16. *"Akab beads" from Suwayh SWY-2: 1. murex; 2. steatite. Composite bracelets carved from large Conidae: 3. Suwayh SWY-2; 4. Hili 8 surface 2005. Examples of laurel-leaf shapes in P. margaritifera: 5. Ra's al-Hamra RH-5 (after Salvatori 1996); 6. Suwayh SWY-2; 7. Ra's al-Hamra RH-5 (after Salvatori 1996); 8. Ra's al-Hamra RH-10, grave 122 (after Santini 1987).*

to Oman (Fig. 15). It is the first time that such a wide distribution of Neolithic ornamental elements can be observed in the region. Except for Qatar, this distribution is the same as that of laurel-leaf shapes and composite bracelets (Fig. 16). All the elements of ornament under consideration (pendants and bracelets in the UAE and the Sultanate of Oman, earrings in the Sultanate of Oman) share the same types of decoration (indentations, series of rays and chevrons for the earrings; indentations and series of rays for the pendants in the form of a laurel leaf; series of rays for the bracelets) (Kiesewetter, Uerpmann & Jasim 2000; Méry & Charpentier forthcoming; Salvatori 2007). Elements of bracelets in Conidae are frequently found in the settlements and necropolises of the Sultanate of Oman from 4200 BC to the very beginning of the third millennium, and certain tombs of Hafit type still contained them (Santini 1992). They are more rare but known in the UAE, at Umm al Qaiwain 2, and also at Hili 8 (surface find 2005 by S. Méry, unpublished). The pendants in mother-of-pearl, found in the Sultanate of Oman and in the UAE, are of three types: the first type is laurel-leaf-shaped, the second has a convex base and is small in size, the third has a convex base and a hollowed-out central part (Ra's al-Hamra RH-4, 5–10; Suwayh 2 (unpublished), Buhais 18, al-Ain) (Durante & Tosi 1977: fig. 9; Kiesewetter, Uerpmann & Jasim 2000: figs 3 & 6; Salvatori 1996: fig. 6; Santini 1987; Stoel 1990; Uerpmann M 2003: fig. 3).

All these observations support the hypothesis of a recognizable cultural entity spread over the Oman peninsula in the fifth and fourth millennia, as indicated by the common elements of material culture. This hypothesis is not contradicted by the fact that the study of the arrowheads enables the definition of two distinct chronological cultures for the period 6500–3800 BC (Charpentier 2008; this volume).

Acknowledgements

The excavations of the French Archaeological Mission in the UAE at Akab are organized under the aegis of the Museum of Umm al-Qaiwain. We warmly thank His Highness Mohammed bin Rashid al Muala, Sheikh Khalid bin Humaid al Mualla, General Director of the Department of Antiquities and Heritage in the Emirate of Umm al-Qaiwain, and Ms Alyaa Al Ghafly, Director of the Museum of Umm al-Qaiwain, for their strong support.

We also thank the Sous Direction de l'Archéologie et de la Recherche en sciences sociales du Ministère des Affaires étrangères et européennes (Paris) for their funding as well as the French Embassy in Abu Dhabi for its support. Dr M. Beech (ADACH-Abu Dhabi) kindly gave his agreement to the publication of some preliminary results of the fauna analysis. The French mission is also the beneficiary of generous aid from Gulf Marine Service Abu Dhabi. The authors also wish to thank warmly P. Paoli and R. Chaffort (Ambassade de France), M. Pierre (Ministère des Affaires étrangères), Dr J-F. Jarrige (Président de la Commission des Fouilles), and J. Desplaces (GMS-Abu Dhabi).

References

Beech M.

2000. Preliminary report on the faunal remains from an 'Ubaid settlement on Dalma island, United Arab Emirates. Pages 68–78 in M. Mashkour, A.M. Choyke, H. Buitenhuis & F. Poplin (eds), *Archaeology of the Near East IV (B). Proceedings of the fourth international symposium on the archaeozoology of southwestern Asia and adjacent areas*. Groningen: ARC Publicatie 32.

2004. *In the land of the Ichthyophagi. Modelling fish exploitation in the Arabian Gulf and Gulf of Oman from the 5th millennium BC to the Late Islamic period.* Abu Dhabi Islands Archaeological Survey, Monograph 1. (British Archaeological Reports, International Series, S1217). Oxford: Archaeopress.

2005. Preliminary report on the shells, crabs, fish and mammal bones from the 2002 excavations on Akab Island, Umm al Qaiwann, United Arab Emirates. Pages 11–22 in V. Charpentier & S. Méry (eds), *Akab island (Umm al-Qaiwain) Archaeological Season 2002, Field Report.* Paris : Mission archéologique Française aux Emirats Arabes Unis.

Beech M. & Kallweit H.
2001. A note on the archaeological and environmental remains from JH57, a 5th–4th Millennium BC shell midden in Jazirat al-Hamra, Ra'as al-Khaimah. *Tribulus* 11/1:17–20.

Beech M., Cuttler R., Moscrop D., Kallweit H. & Martin J.
2005. New evidence for the Neolithic settlement of Marawah Island, Abu Dhabi, United Arab Emirates. *Proceedings of the Seminar for Arabian Studies* 35: 37–56.

Benton J. & Potts D.
1994. Jabal al-Emalah. *Report compiled for the Department of Culture and Information, Government of Sharjah.* [Mimeographed].

Biagi P.
1999. Excavations at the shell-midden of RH-6 1986–1988 (Muscat, Sultanate of Oman). *Al-Râfidân* 20: 57–84.

Boucharlat R., Haerinck E., Phillips C., & Potts D.
1991. Note on an Ubaid-pottery site in the Emirate of Umm al-Qaiwain. *Arabian Archaeology and Epigraphy* 2: 65–71.

Carter R. & Crawford H.
2002. The Kuwait-British Archaeological Expedition to As-Sabiyah: Report on the Fourth Season's Work. *Iraq* 64: 1–13.
(forthcoming). Small finds. In Crawford H. & Carter R. (eds), *Maritime interactions in the Arabian Neolithic, the evidence from H3, an Ubaid-related site in Kuwait.*

Charpentier V.
2008. Hunter-gatherers of the "empty quarter of the early Holocene" to the last Neolithic societies: chronology of the late prehistory of south-eastern Arabia (8000–3100 BC). *Proceedings of the Seminar for Arabian Studies* 38: 93-116.

Charpentier V., Blin O. & Tosi M.
1998. Un village de pêcheurs néolithiques de la péninsule d'Oman: Suwayh 2 (SWY-2), première campagne de fouilles. *Proceedings of the Seminar for Arabian Studies* 28: 21–38.

Charpentier V., Marquis P. & Pellé E.
2003 La nécropole et les derniers horizons Ve millénaire du site de Gorbat al-Mahar (Suwayh, SWY-1, Sultanat d'Oman): premiers résultats. *Proceedings of the Seminar for Arabian Studies* 33: 11–19.

Charpentier V., Méry S. & Phillips C.
2004. Des coquillages … outillages des Ichtyophages? Mise en évidence d'industries sur Veneridae, du Néolithique à l'âge du Fer (Yémen, Oman, EAU). *Arabian Archaeology and Epigraphy* 15: 1–10.

Cleuziou S.
2005 Pourquoi si tard ? Nous avons pris un autre chemin. L'Arabie des chasseurs-cueilleurs de l'Holocène au début de l'Age du Bronze. Pages 123–148 in J. Guilaine (ed.), *Aux marges des grands foyers du Néolithique. Périphéries débitrices ou créatrices?* Paris: Errance.

Desse J.
2002. Note sur l'échantillon d'ichtyofaune de Akab (Emirats arabes unis). *Paléorient* 28/1: 58–60.

Durante S. & Tosi M.
1977. The Aceramic Shell Middens of Ra's al-Hamra: a Preliminary Note. *Journal of Oman Studies* 3/2: 137–162.

Frifelt K.
1995. *The island of Umm an-Nar.* ii. *The third Millennium settlement.* (Jutland Archaeological Society Publications, 26/2). Aarhus: Moesgard.

Hellyer P.
1998. *Hidden Riches, an archaeological introduction to the United Arab Emirates.* Abu Dhabi: Union Natinoal Bank.

Inizan M-L.
1988. *Préhistoire à Qatar, mission archéologique française à Qatar.* ii. Paris: Editions Recherche sur les Civilisations.

Jousse H., Faure M., Guérin C. & Prieur A.
2002. Exploitation des ressources marines au cours des Ve–IVe millénaires: le site à dugongs de l'Île d'Akab (Umm al-Qaiwain, EAU). *Paléorient* 28/1: 43–58.

Kiesewetter H., Uerpmann H-P. & Jasim S.A.
2000. Neolithic jewellery from Jebel-al Buhais 18. *Proceedings of the Seminar for Arabian Studies* 30: 137–146.

Madsen H.J.
1961. En Flintplads i Qatar. *Kuml*: 185–201.

Méry S. & Charpentier V.
(forthcoming). Rites funéraires du Néolithique et de l'Age du bronze en Arabie orientale. In J. Guilaine (ed.), *Sépultures et sociétés*. Paris: Errance.

Méry S., Charpentier V. & Beech M.
2008. First evidence of shell fish hooks in the Gulf. *Arabian Archaeology and Epigraphy* 19: 15-21.

Millet M.
1988. Survey of the Sharjah Coast. *Sharjah Archaeology* 4: 21–30.

Phillips C.S.
2002. Prehistoric Middens and a Cemetery from the Southern Arabian Gulf. Pages 169–186 in S. Cleuziou, M. Tosi & J. Zarins (eds), *Essays on the Late Prehistory of the Arabian Peninsula.* (Serie Orientale Roma, 93). Rome: Istituto Italiano per l'Africa e l'Oriente.

Potts D.T.
2000. *Ancient Magan, the secrets of Tell Abraq*. London: Trident Press.

Prieur A. & Guérin C.
1991. Découverte d'un site préhistorique d'abattage de dugongs à Umm al-Qaiwain (Emirats Arabes Unis). *Arabian Archaeology and Epigraphy* 2/2: 72–83.

Roaf M.
1974. Excavations at Al Markh, Bahrain: a fish midden of the fourth millenium BC. *Paléorient* 2/2 : 499–501.

Saliège J.-F., Lézine A.-M., Cleuziou S.
2005. Estimation de l'effet reservoir 14C marin en Mer d'Arabie. *Paléorient* 31/1 : 64–69.

Salvatori S.
1996. Death and ritual in a population of coastal food foragers in Oman. Pages 205–222 in G. Afanas'ev, S. Cleuziou, R. Lukacs & M. Tosi (eds), *The Prehistory of Asia and Oceania.* Colloquium XXXII, Trade as a Subsistence Strategy, Post-Pleistocene Adaptations in Arabia and Early Maritime Trade in the Indian Ocean. XIII International Congress of Prehistoric and Protohistoric Sciences. Forli: Abaco.
2007. The Prehistoric graveyard of Ra's al-Hamra 5, Muscat, Sultanate of Oman. *Journal of Oman Studies* 14: 5-353.

Santini G.
1987. Site RH-10 at Qurum and a preliminary analysis of its cemetery: an essay in stratigraphic discontinuity. *Proceedings of the Seminar for Arabian Studies* 17: 179–198.
1992. *Analisi dei caratteri dominanti per la definizione del rituale nelle necropoli preistoriche e protostoriche della Penisola di Oman.* Doctoral thesis, Istituto Universitario Orientale, Naples. [Unpublished].

Shöler S.
2003. Mineralogical and petrological examination of some objects found at Khor Milkh, Sultanate of Oman. Pages 142–162 in H-P. Uerpmann & M. Uerpmann (eds), *Stones Age Sites and their Natural Environment — The Capital Area of Northern Oman Part III.* (Beihefte zum Tübinger Atlas des Vorderen Orients. Reihe A (Naturwissenschaften), 31/3). Wiesbaden: Reichert.

Stoel P.
1990. Al-Hair Archaeological Site Emirates. *Emirates Natural History Group Bulletin* 41: 22–24.

Uerpmann M.
2003. The dark Millennium: remarks on the Final Stone Age in the Emirates and Oman. Pages 73–81 in D.T. Potts, H. al Naboodah & P. Hellyer (eds), *Archaeology of the United Arab Emirates, Proceedings of the First International Conference on the Archaeology of the U.A.E.* London: Trident Press.

Uerpmann H-P. & Uerpmann M.
2003. *Stones Age Sites and their Natural Environment — The Capital Area of Northern Oman Part III.* (Beihefte zum Tübinger Atlas des Vorderen Orients. Reihe A (Naturwissenschaften), 31/3). Wiesbaden: Reichert.

Uerpmann M. & Uerpmann H-P.
1996. Ubaid pottery in the eastern Gulf — new evidence from Umm al-Qaiwain (U.A.E.). *Arabian Archaeology and Epigraphy* 7: 125–139.

Vogt B.
1994. In Search for Coastal Sites in Pre-Historic Makkan: mid-Holocene "shell-eaters" in the coastal desert of Ras al-Khaimah, U.A.E. Pages 113–128 in J.M. Kenoyer (ed.), *From Sumer to Meluhha: Contributions to the Archaeology of South and West Asia in Memory of Georges F. Dales, Jr.* (Wisconsin Archaeological Reports, 3). Madison, WI: Prehistory Press.

Zaros D.
2004. *La produzione artigianale delle perline ornamentali dai contesti di Abitato (HD-6) e di Necropoli (HD-10) a Ra's al Hadd, Sultanato d'Oman.* Degree thesis, Facoltà di conservazione dei beni culturali, University of Bologna. [Unpublished].

Authors' addresses
Vincent Charpentier, Inrap, UMR 7041 ArScan du CNRS, Maison de l'Archéologie et de l'Ethnologie, 21 allée de l'Université, 92023 Nanterre cedex, France.
e-mail vincent.charpentier@mae.u-paris10.fr, vincent.charpentier@inrap.fr

Sophie Méry, CNRS, UMR 7041 ArScan du CNRS, Maison de l'Archéologie et de l'Ethnologie, 21 allée de l'Université, 92023 Nanterre cedex, France.
e-mail sophie.mery@mae.u-paris10.fr

Proceedings of the Seminar for Arabian Studies 38 (2008): 137–140

Some reflections on human-animal burials from pre-Islamic south-east Arabia (poster)

Aurelie Daems & An De Waele

Keywords: burials, camelids, equids, south-east Arabia

Presented here is an excerpt of our poster on human burials directly connected with the burial of large animals, namely camelids and equids. In addition to reporting on the main characteristics and the chrono-geographical spread of the phenomenon, we have focused on the inter-dependency of humans and animals, looking also at the possible motivations for the occurrence of this specific burial form.

The phenomenon of interring large animals in close association with a human being has been occasionally documented in the south-eastern Arabian record between the third millennium BC and the late seventh century AD. Since it is occasional and thus seemingly restricted to some individuals, it is worthwhile analysing it in more detail, as we are currently doing at the South-east Arabia Archaeology Unit of Ghent University, Belgium.

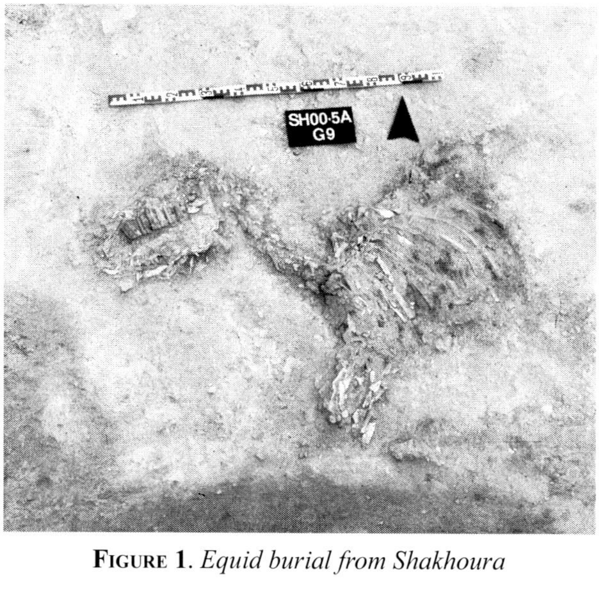

Figure 1. *Equid burial from Shakhoura*

Our research draws partly on previous work published by Vogt (1994), Mashkour (1997), Jasim (1999), and H-P. Uerpmann (1999), and proposes some additional considerations on possible modes of interaction between animals and humans in the mentioned time and space. Since this is work in process, our discussion of the phenomenon should be seen as preliminary.

Human-animal burials of the kind we assess have been reported in Bahrain, Qatar, Saudi Arabia, the UAE, Oman, and Yemen. While some are dated to the Bronze Age, the majority comes from the turn of the first millennium BC to the first millennium AD. The animals were either buried alone next to a human grave, as seen at e.g. Shakhoura (Daems & Haerinck 2001: 94), Mleiha (Jasim 1999), Ali (Bent 1890: 16) and al-Buhais (Uerpmann & Uerpmann 1999: 458) or with other animals, as seen at e.g. ed-Dur (Haerinck 2001: 49) and Mleiha, where at least one camelid and equid were buried together (Jasim 1999). Either the animals are deposited next to a main grave and covered by a tumulus, e.g. at Shakhoura (Daems & Haerinck 2001: 92); located in the entrance chamber to a grave, e.g. at ed-Dur (Haerinck *et al.* 1993: 184) and al-Buhais (Uerpmann & Uerpmann 1999: 457); or deposited directly into a rectangular pit, next to a human grave. Occasionally burial gifts accompany them in the form of pilgrim flasks, beads, pendants, arrowheads, or rarer, a harness with bit. According to Vogt (1994: 286) most associated gifts are connected to the ritual killing of the animal, but the evidence from Mleiha (Jasim 1999) and ed-Dur (O. Lecomte and C.S. Philips, personal communication), where mainly "non-lethal" artefacts seem to have been found, probably contradicts this statement.

The human-"large animal" burials we review surely must have been special, particularly as they do not occur on every contemporary burial ground in the region, and when they do they are connected mainly with the most sumptuous graves of each site. Thus this burial practice must have been an act reflecting the status of the deceased, in life and after death. Camelids were of great importance as beasts of burden and mounts in the long-distance trade in copper ore, frankincense, and myrrh (Retsö 1991) for which southern Arabia held an age-long monopoly. These animals would thus probably have been carefully tended, and perhaps regarded as tokens of pride and a means to accumulate wealth through e.g. bartering. Equids seem to have been used more sporadically (Uerpmann & Uerpmann 1997). Because of their poorer resistance to extreme heat and more limited lactating capacities, their use was mostly restricted to that of mounts during hunting and raiding (Mashkour 1997: 734).

H-P. Uerpmann (1999: 116) has interpreted the Mleiha burials as probably related to the funeral of a noble family, while Vogt (1994: 280) and Mashkour (1997: 734) say the practice of killing camels upon someone's death may be linked to an ancient Arabian myth that ordered camels to be used as mounts upon resurrection of the deceased.

Other understandings can also be considered for this specific burial custom. We cannot exclude that these animals were for instance seen as the personal estate of the deceased, of which the value decreased with the death of the master or mistress. Alternatively, they may have been gifts offered by other persons of similar esteem upon the death of a social equal. Whatever the motivation, we can assume that the animals used for burial were extremely valuable and carefully selected, "chosen" ones. Indeed for Mleiha, the camelids killed were either female dromedaries or camel hybrids, the latter seemingly having been status animals because they are larger, stronger, and faster than their parents (Uerpmann H-P 1999: 108, 111). These animals do not appear in the record of consumed animal bones on this particular site and seem to have been killed at a time when they had great economic value as beasts of burden or when they were ripe for breeding and riding (1999: 116). This implies that these animals must have been closely linked to and partly responsible for the deceased's success and failure in life, through death and in the special burial that followed.

References

Bent J.T.

1890. The Bahrein Islands, in the Persian Gulf. *Proceedings of the Royal Geographical Society and Monthly Record of Geography*. New Monthly Series 12/1: 1–19.

Daems A. & Haerinck E.

2001. Excavations at Shakhoura (Bahrain). *Arabian Archaeology and Epigraphy* 12: 90–95.

Haerinck E.

2001. *The University of Ghent South-East Arabian Archaeological Project. Excavations at ed-Dur (Umm al-Qaiwain, United Arab Emirates). Volume II. The Tombs.* Leuven: Peeters.

Haerinck E., Phillips C.S., Potts D.T. & Stevens K.G.

1993. Ed-Dur, Umm al-Qaiwain (U.A.E.). Pages 183–193 in U. Finkbeiner (ed.), *Materialien zur Archäologie der Seleukiden- und Partherzeit im südlichen Babylonien und im Golfgebiet. Ergebnisse der Symposien 1987 und 1989 in Blaubeuren (Deutsches Archäologisches Institut, Abteilung Baghdad).* Tübingen: Ernst Wasmuth Verlag.

Jasim S.A.

1999. The Excavation of a Camel Cemetery at Mleiha, Sharjah, U.A.E. *Arabian Archaeology and Epigraphy* 10: 69–101.

Mashkour M.

1997. The Funeral Rites at Mleiha (Sharja-U.A.E.), the Camelid Graves. *Anthropozoologica* 25/26: 725–736.

Retsö J.

1991. The Domestication of the Camel and the Establishment of the Frankincense Road from South Arabia. *Orientalia Suecana* 40: 187–219.

Uerpmann H-P.

1999. Camel and Horse Skeletons from Protohistoric Graves at Mleiha in the Emirate of Sharjah (U.A.E.). *Arabian Archaeology and Epigraphy* 10: 102–118.

Uerpmann H-P. & Uerpmann M.

1999. The Camel Burial of al-Buhais 12 (Sharjah, U.A.E.). Pages 455–462 in C. Dobiat & K. Leidorf (eds), *Historia Animalum Ex Ossibus. Festschrift für Angela Von den Driesch*. Rahden: Verlag Maria Leidorf GmbH.

Uerpmann M. & Uerpmann H-P.

1997. Animal Bones from Excavation 519 at Qala'at al-Bahrain. Pages 235–262 in F. Højlund & H.H. Andersen (eds), *Qala'at al-Bahrain. Volume 2. The Central Monumental Buildings*. (Jutland Archaeological Society Publications, 30/2). Moesgaard: Jutland Archaeological Society.

Vogt B.

1994. Death, Resurrection and the Camel. Pages 279–290 in N. Nebes (ed.), *Arabia Felix. Beiträge zur Sprache und Kultur des vorislamischen Arabien. Festschrift Walter W. Müller zum 60. Geburtstag*. Wiesbaden: Harrassowitz Verlag.

Authors' addresses
Dr Aurelie Daems, Dept. of Languages and Cultures of the Near East and North Africa, Ghent University, St. Pietersplein 6, B-9000 Ghent, Belgium.
e-mail aurelie.daems@ugent.be

An De Waele, Dept. of Languages and Cultures of the Near East and North-Africa, Ghent University, St. Pietersplein 6, B-9000 Ghent, Belgium.
e-mail an.dewaele@ugent.be

Proceedings of the Seminar for Arabian Studies 38 (2008): 141–152

Derniers résultats, nouvelles datations et nouvelles données sur les fortifications de Shabwa (Ḥaḍramawt)

Latest results, new dating, and recent evidence for the fortifications of Shabwa (Ḥaḍramawt)

Christian Darles

Summary
The research undertaken since 2002 on the urbanism and fortifications of Shabwa allows a better understanding of the relationships between the occupation of the town, the domestic architecture and the three lines of curtain walls. The first curtain enclosed the *intra-muros* town with its high-status buildings and was originally constructed on a flat site. The area measuring 15.5 ha is enclosed by a wall 1.6 km long. The most ancient inscription found in the curtain wall, Sh VI/76/89, dates from the seventh century BC according to the "high chronology" but from the fourth century BC according to Jacqueline Pirenne's studies (1990: 121–123). From the seventh to the sixth century BC this wall enclosed pre-existing and independent fortified structures, which were grouped together since the second millennium BC. Dating shows that mortar was present before the fourth century BC in temple 44, and they are also in the wall foundations near gate no. 6 with a ^{14}C date of the fourth century BC. The wall then later expanded to include an important extra-mural building under the later royal palace, this latter only acquiring its status once it became part of the town. The second lies within the line of the first. Its over-large wall circuits measuring 3535 m were difficult to defend and do not seem to have been designed to counter a specific threat, but rather to repel brigands and nomads. Thus this line protected herds and caravans within an area measuring 53.9 ha and 2.6 km of perimeter. Later still, the citadel, which had hitherto been independent, became part of a third circuit which extended up the valley to the south. This new area, measuring 3.7 ha, is enclosed by a wall 850 m long.

Keywords: South Arabian antiquities, Yemen, architecture, fortification

Shabwa, une ville riche ouverte sur l'extérieur qui protège ses habitants et ses activités

Décrite par les auteurs classiques comme la tête de pont du commerce de l'encens, Sabota ou Sabbatha, l'actuelle ville de Shabwa, est dotée par ses habitants d'un ensemble complexe de fortifications. Elle est aujourd'hui en totalité abandonnée par ses habitants qui se sont installés à quelques distances. Le site est recouvert par trois petits villages tribaux partiellement en ruine: Mathnā, Miʾwan et al-Hagar. L'étude du rempart entamée dès 1977 et continuée en 1980 et 1981, puis reprise en 1998, 2000 et 2002 n'a cependant porté majoritairement que sur des prospections de surface et des dégagements sommaires. Si deux chantiers ont été ouverts (le secteur occidental — Ch VI — et la porte sud — Ch I), il faut cependant regretter l'absence de fouilles extensives pour l'étude de son urbanisme et plus particulièrement celle de ses systèmes défensifs.

La situation géographique de Shabwa n'a eu de cesse de surprendre les chercheurs. Eloignée de la vallée éponyme, la capitale du royaume antique de l'Ḥaḍramawt est située de surcroît au débouché d'une vallée où les crues sont rares (Fig. 1). Pourtant il est raisonnable de penser que la richesse de cette cité est due autant à ses ressources agricoles — la ville est entourée de toutes parts par une zone irriguée de près de 2000 ha en cumulé — qu'à son rôle de plate-forme, à la frange du désert, pour différents échanges commerciaux (Breton 1988: 99).

La ville s'est principalement développée au centre d'un vaste triangle de collines soulevées par un dôme de

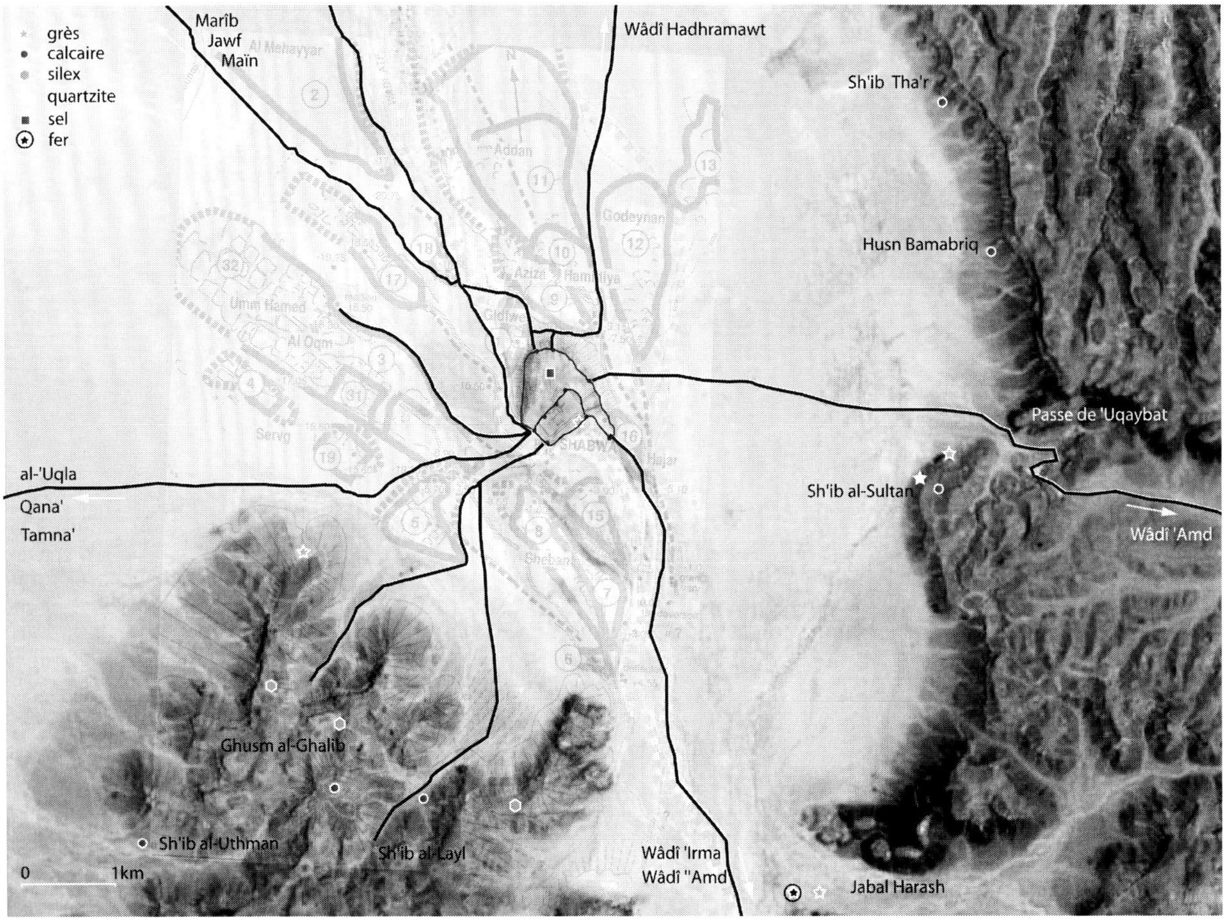

Figure 1. *Shabwa: le territoire, les carrières et les pistes.*

sel gemme qui partage le cours du Wādī Irma en deux branches, le Wādī Maʾshar à l'ouest et le Wādī ᶜAtf à l'est. Elle n'a jamais occupé l'ensemble de la dépression dont l'altitude oscille autour de 700 m et où affleurent plusieurs mines de sel (Fig. 2). Les constructions, dont le nombre peut être estimé à près de 200 à l'apogée de la cité ont, depuis les premiers temps de la ville, été installées contre le versant nord de l'éperon d'al-ᶜAqab (Fig. 3). La ville a aussi dépassé la crête des collines de Qārat al-Ghirān et Qārat al-Burayk en venant coloniser son versant oriental avec des quartiers extra-muros dont les bâtiments, construits en terre, sont principalement destinés à des activités artisanales (Ch XIII et Ch XIV). Rapidement l'agglomération chercha à se doter d'un système défensif urbain qui alla en se complexifiant au fil des siècles (Darles 2003: 215–227). La partie la plus densément occupée est entourée d'un ample rempart percé de cinq portes puis les collines sont couronnées par une nouvelle ligne de fortifications réalisée en deux temps (Breton 1992*a*: 59–75).

Les différentes enceintes sont percées par dix passages qui mettent en relation, d'une part, les différentes parties entre elles et, d'autre part, la ville avec son territoire périurbain d'où partent les pistes permettant de rejoindre les autres contrées de la région (Breton 1994: 128–130). Les portes nº 1 et nº 6 s'ouvrent autant vers des terrains agricoles que vers les routes qui mènent au port de Qana ou vers Timnaʾ en Qataban. Elles donnent également vers le Ghusm al-Ghalib où de nombreuses carrières ont été identifiées. Ces deux portes ouvrent aussi en direction du piton rocheux d'al-ᶜUqla, lieu sacré où furent investis de nombreux rois du Ḥaḍramawt. Les portes nº 7 et nº 8 sont orientées en direction du désert qui sépare Shabwa de Marīb et du Jawf; elles permettent d'atteindre un quartier artisanal, les grands domaines irrigués du nord de la ville et les lieux de pâturage qui bordent le Wādī Maʾshar et

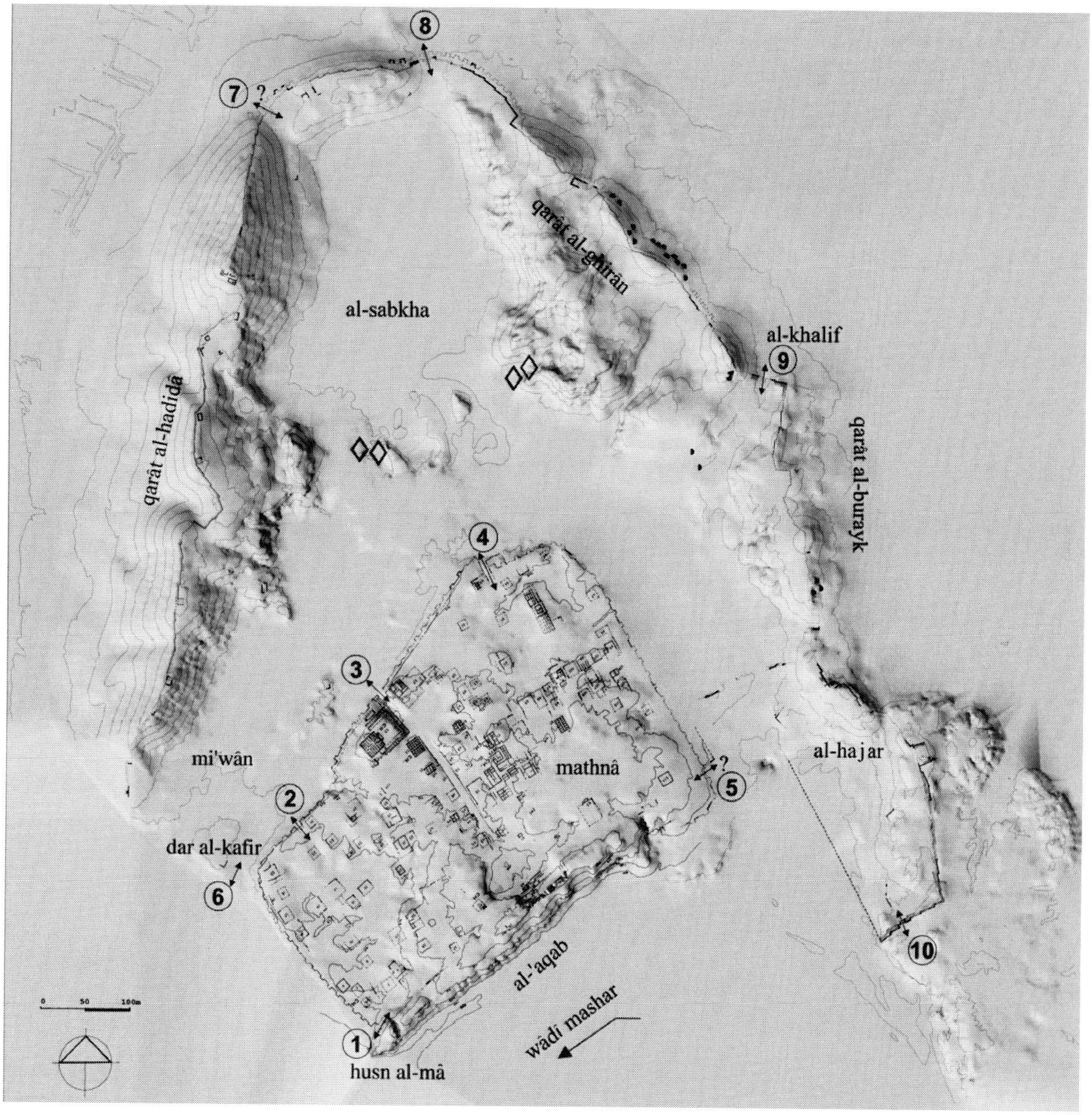

Figure 2. *Un plan général de Shabwa.*

le Wādī ᶜAtf. Par ces deux portes, on peut également rallier les carrières du piémont occidental du Jawl et, en le longeant, atteindre la vallée du Wādī Ḥaḍramawt. La porte nº 9, entre les collines de Qārat al-Ghirān et de Qārat al-Burayk, donne vers la passe d'ᶜUqayba qui permet aux caravanes de rejoindre la vallée du Wādī Ḥaḍramawt en traversant le plateau tabulaire du Jawl (Pirenne 1990: 51–54). Cette porte permet également de rejoindre les quartiers extra-muros de l'est de Shabwa et dessert une nécropole hors les murs et différentes zones de pâturages. La porte nº 10 s'ouvre vers l'amont du Wādī Maʾshar et donne accès aux territoires irrigués et aux grands aménagements hydrauliques de captage des eaux de la crue. Il s'agit d'un accès direct à l'oasis, planté

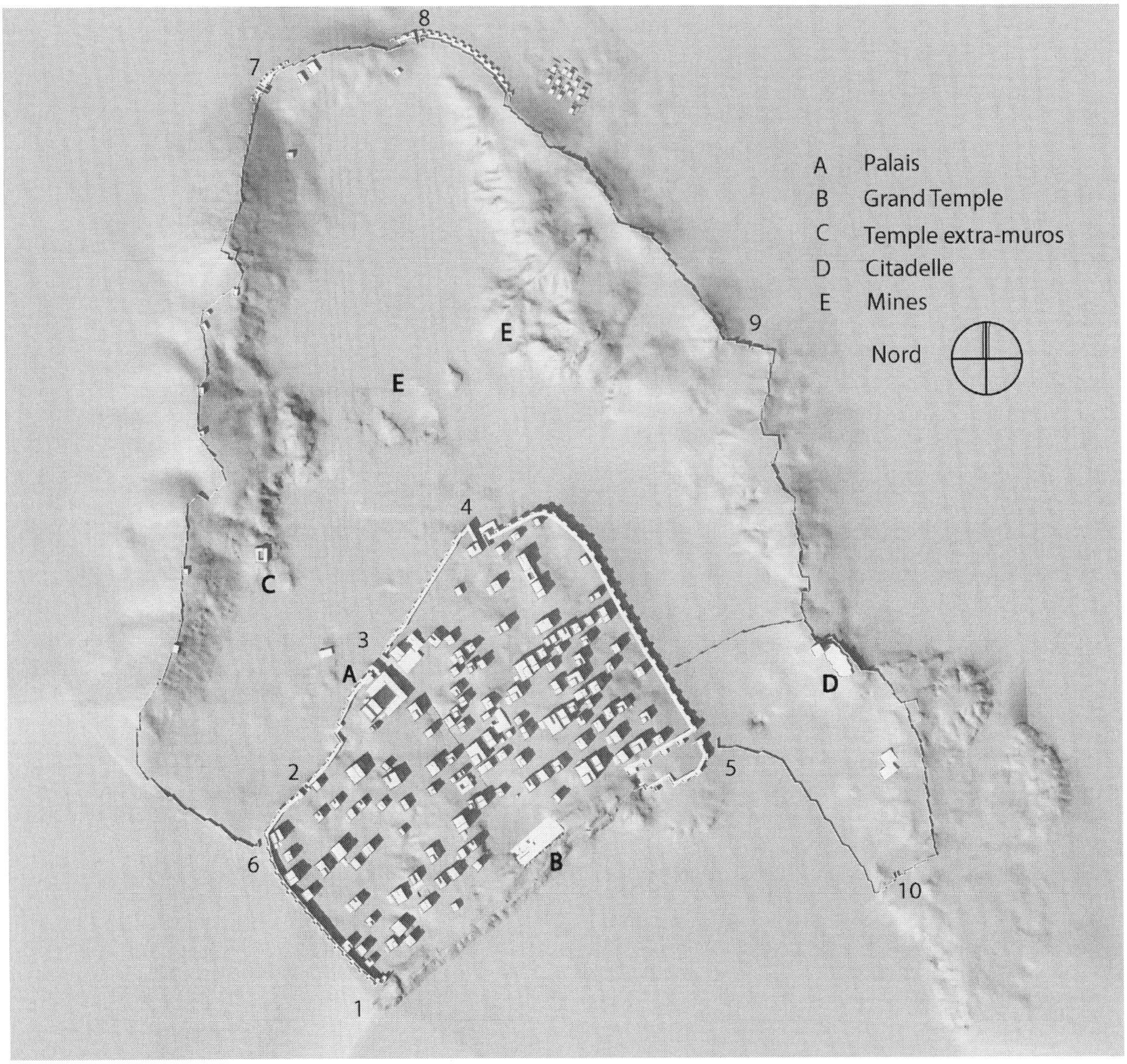

Figure 3. *Une restitution du plan de la ville.*

de jujubiers, d'acacias et de palmiers. Enfin la porte n° 5, mal connue, située à proximité d'un lieu d'extraction de blocs de grès, met en relation la ville avec les différents puits au sud de la colline d'al-ᶜAqab d'une part et les zones irriguées du sud-ouest d'autre part.

Hypothèses sur le développement urbain et la chronologie des fortifications

La relative pauvreté des données chronologiques nous amène à proposer un schéma de développement hypothétique de la ville de Shabwa, avant tout fondé sur les interprétations des données recueillies sur le terrain ainsi que sur des approches comparatives avec les autres villes des basses terres (Fig. 4).

Deux sondages stratigraphiques ont été réalisés. Le premier, de 1976 à 1981, a atteint le substrat géologique, il a été publié par Leila Badre (1992: 229–314), le deuxième en 2000 et 2002 n'est pas terminé à ce jour. Il a permis de reconnaître une séquence stratigraphique de 8.20 m de dépôts archéologiques entre la cote 706.40 m et la cote 714.60 m du sol actuel; il doit faire l'objet d'une

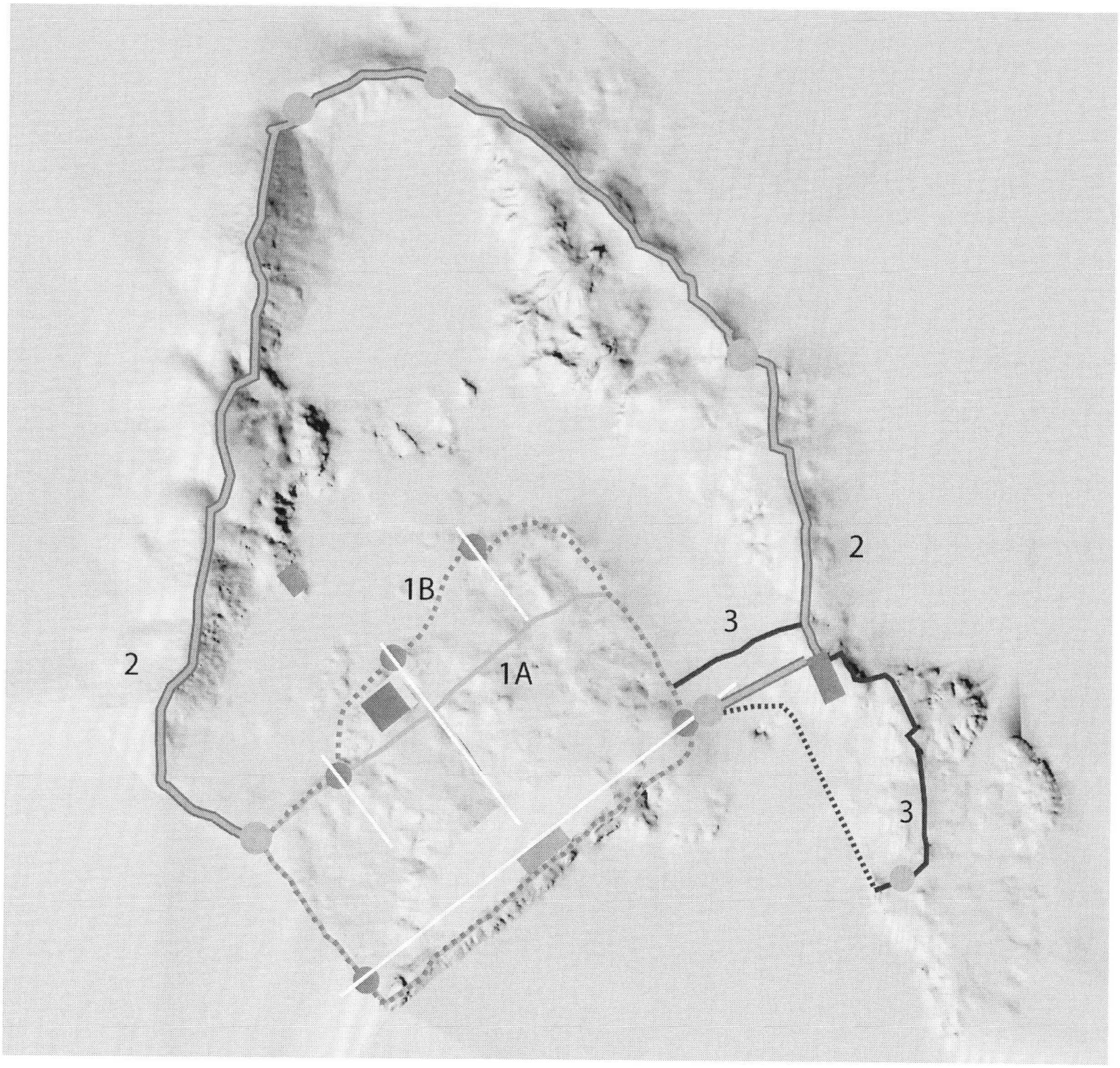

Figure 4. *Les phases de construction du système défensif.*

prochaine publication (Breton, Darles & Roux, à paraître). Les résultats sont concordants. Les premières occupations apparaissent sur le terrain plat de la dépression centrale, contre le flanc nord de l'arête d'al-ᶜAqab, durant la première moitié du IIe millénaire av. J.-C. et vont donner naissance au premier noyau urbain. A cet emplacement, au sommet du tell, à une altitude de 715 m, sous le village actuel de Mathnā et dans ses environs immédiats, l'épaisseur des couches archéologiques dépasse les dix mètres.

Les premières séquences stratigraphiques du sondage le plus récent, mais malheureusement pas les plus anciennes, (1) sont datées du XIVe s. av. J.-C. Elles prouvent que les premières constructions — séquences 1 à 3 — sont uniquement réalisées en terre, soit en adobes (briques de terre crue) soit en bauge (terre massive). L'architecture de pierre ou composite, à ossature en bois, n'apparaît pas avant le IVe s. avant notre ère. Peut-on pour autant parler d'une ville en terre sous la ville de pierre? Ainsi l'aspect du paysage actuel de Shabwa, avec ses nombreux socles

Figure 5. *La porte nº 3, vue vers l'ouest.*

de pierre, qui intriguèrent tant les voyageurs, doit faire place, durant le Ier millénaire av. J.-C., à l'image d'un village ordonné bâti d'édifices en terre.

Aux alentours du Xe s. av. J.-C., au changement de millénaire, un grand bâtiment est édifié au milieu de la dépression d'as-Sabkha, face aux premières constructions. Il est construit sur un puissant massif de briques crues (Breton 2001: 38; 2002; 2003; Breton & Roux 2005: 95–113; Darles, à paraître, *a*). Un édifice monumental en pierre pourrait avoir été édifié au-dessus de ce massif de fondation. En témoigneraient plusieurs monolithes imposants réutilisés dans le palais. L'un d'eux (Darles 2005: 151–171), situé sous l'accès monumental et doté de plusieurs feuillures, n'est pas sans rappeler les grands monolithes des temples du Jawf ou de Marīb.

Jaqueline Pirenne date la plus ancienne des inscriptions mentionnant l'édification d'une courtine, Sh VI/76/89, de type paléographique B, des environs du IVe s. av. J.-C (1990: 59). La chronologie basse défendue par J. Pirenne est aujourd'hui controversée et contredite par de nombreuses découvertes. Cette inscription trouvée durant la fouille du rempart occidental pourrait être, à la lumière des progrès de l'épigraphie sud arabe, datée du VIIe s. av. J.-C. (Schiettecatte 2006: 275). Ce rempart primitif, doté d'une ou de plusieurs portes, (2) entourait de manière lâche le noyau primitif de la future capitale. A cette époque apparaissent les premières inscriptions faisant part du rôle politique de Shabwa.

Une autre inscription trouvée dans le Shiʾb al-Layl, au pied du Ghusm al-Ghalib, à l'ouest de Shabwa, de style C, selon la chronologie paléographique établie par Jaqueline Pirenne, et datée par elle du IVe s. av. J.-C., pourrait également être plus ancienne d'un ou deux siècles. Le texte inscrit mentionne la construction du palais Shabaʾan par ʿAlyafaʾ Dubyan, fils du roi ʿAmdahar. Doit-on penser que ce palais se substitue au grand édifice précédent? Les preuves archéologiques sont réduites et la question trouvera peut-être un jour une réponse rationnelle.

Une datation ^{14}C donne pour la construction du rempart, à l'emplacement de la porte nº 6, le IVe s. av. J.-C. (3) Il pourrait s'agir d'une réfection de la fortification primitive du VIIe siècle qui englobe alors le palais et l'intègre au

Figure 6. *Le rempart extérieur sur les crêtes de Qarāt al-Hadidā.*

sein de la ville. En effet, la face nord de l'enceinte initiale est totalement transformée, peut-être en plusieurs temps, au moins à partir de la porte n° 2 jusqu'à la face orientale. Nous pensons que la première enceinte était préalablement dotée, sur cette face nord, d'un seul franchissement, la porte n° 3 (Fig. 5); ce serait à la suite de la modification du tracé que les portes n° 2 et n° 4 sont créées et la porte n° 3 avancée et déplacée vers le nord. Le nombre de portes est fonction du développement du site (Fig. 4).

Ce rempart, long de 1585 m, est réalisé et transformé en utilisant une maçonnerie monumentale en grand appareil liaisonné avec un mortier de qualité. Ce mode constructif a très bien pu préexister dans le rempart primitif que nous avons beaucoup de mal à distinguer de ses transformations ultérieures, qui ne cesseront pas jusqu'au IIe s. de notre ère. Ce mode de construction se retrouve utilisé dans la citadelle, dont un angle est encore debout sur plus de 6 m de hauteur au sommet de la colline d'al-Hagar, à une altitude de 720 m. Même s'il est toujours difficile et délicat de tenter des approches chronologiques d'après des techniques de construction, nous proposons d'attribuer une même datation pour l'édification de ces deux ensembles disjoints. Cinq portes sont connues, trois sur la face nord-ouest (portes n° 2, n° 3 et n° 4), une à la jonction de la pointe sud de l'éperon d'al-ᶜAqab, Husn al-Maᵓ, et de la face sud-ouest (porte n° 1) (4) et une à l'angle est (porte n° 5). Une première structuration de l'espace intra-muros est alors en train de naître avec la structuration de la rue qui relie la porte n° 3, au pied du palais, et le grand édifice considéré jusqu'à aujourd'hui encore comme le temple majeur dédié au dieu Sayᵓin. Si l'on en croit une datation de son escalier oriental, le socle du palais pourrait également dater du IVe s. av. J.-C. (5) Les niveaux les plus profonds du «Grand Temple» sont également datés du IVe–IIIe s. av. J.-C. (Breton 1988: 95–152). Est-ce également à cette période qu'est édifié le temple extra-muros (1998: 157–161)?

En l'absence de données archéologiques et chronologiques précises, il est difficile de dater la construction du rempart qui couronne le triangle de collines

Figure 7. *La tour de Dar el-Kafir et la porte n° 6, vue vers le sud.*

dominant la dépression où est construite l'agglomération initiale. Ce rempart constitué d'un glacis de galets et de courtines disposées en crémaillère, correspond plus à un enclos de protection qu'à un ouvrage réellement défensif (Fig. 6). Il mesure 2160 m de long et comporte des tours et des bastions régulièrement espacés. A l'emplacement des cols et des zones les plus sensibles il est également redoublé par des ouvrages avancés qui protègent quatre portes supplémentaires. Cette deuxième ligne de fortifications s'appuie d'une part contre le rempart existant (porte n° 6 de Dar el-Kafir) d'autre part il s'adosse à la citadelle en transformant de manière radicale le système défensif de la ville intra-muros (Fig. 7). La porte n° 1 donne-t-elle alors toujours à l'extérieur de l'espace urbain, son rôle diminuant grâce à la présence de la porte n° 6 au pied de la tour de Dar el-Kafir? Les recherches archéologiques ont bien montré qu'à une certaine époque, ce passage fut condamné et muré. La date de cette réfection n'est pas connue. Les portes n°s 2, 3 et 4 permettent de passer de la ville densément peuplée à la dépression d'al-Sabkha, non bâtie et peut-être destinée à accueillir caravanes, voyageurs et troupeaux. Une nouvelle importance est donnée aux portes de la deuxième enceinte (portes n°s 6, 7, 8 et 9) qui vont servir de seuil entre la capitale et son territoire, en s'ouvrant vers les champs cultivés, vers les pâturages et vers les grandes pistes du trafic commercial. La présence du hameau actuel de Mathnā, là où la puissance des couches archéologiques semble être maximale, n'a pas pu permettre la réalisation des sondages qui auraient donné des informations précises sur les différents emplacements de la porte n° 5, située à la rencontre de plusieurs lignes de fortification (Darles, à paraître, *b*). Nos hypothèses de restitution de ce secteur se fondent uniquement sur les prospections de surface.

Quelque temps plus tard, à l'emplacement de l'actuel hameau de al-Hagar, une troisième ligne de fortification est édifiée alors que la seconde est localement rectifiée. La citadelle est totalement englobée à l'intérieur d'une enceinte qui se développe vers le sud. Son périmètre est estimé à 820 m environ dont 685 m reconnus (une partie de la muraille a été emportée par les crues du wadi) et la surface circonscrite est proche de 5 ha dont 3.7 ha au sud de al-Hagar. La citadelle, véritable pivot et initialement isolée de la ville sur une hauteur, devient alors partie prenante du réseau défensif. Aucune fouille archéologique n'a pu être menée dans ce quartier aujourd'hui recouvert par les ruines du village qui était encore occupé, il y a quelques décennies. L'implantation de cette enceinte complémentaire a sans nul doute transformé le secteur défensif situé aux alentours de la porte n° 5 qui devint une des articulations du système. A l'extrémité sud de ce quartier clos, en éperon entre le Wādī ʿAtf et le Wādī Maʾshar, une nouvelle porte n° 10 s'ouvre vers le sud-est, (6) l'oasis et les réseaux irrigués de l'amont de la vallée.

Conclusion

La capitale du royaume de Ḥaḍramawt, excentrée par rapport au cœur de son territoire centré autour de la vallée de la rivière éponyme, a su bâtir un système de défense diversifié. Outre sa position stratégique au pied du grand plateau calcaire du Jawl et au milieu du débouché d'une vallée qui la met à l'abri d'attaques-surprises, la ville a été installée au centre d'un triangle de collines qui lui assurent une première protection.

Trois types d'architecture garantissent sa sécurité. Tout d'abord l'édification de maisons tours construites sur de hauts soubassements de pierre (Breton & Darles 1995: 449–457; Darles 1998: 3–26). Ces bâtiments fortifiés, dont l'accès se situe «à l'étage», forment une protection à ses habitants qui peuvent s'y replier et soutenir momentanément un siège. (7)

La réalisation de plusieurs lignes continues de fortifications permet de garantir la sécurité de trois zones distinctes: une zone densément peuplée — «Shabwa intra-muros» —; un vaste espace vide — la dépression d'al-Sabkha — manifestement destiné à des occupations temporaires et à l'exploitation des mines de sel (Breton, à paraître, *a*); enfin un quartier «sud», autour et au sud de la citadelle. Distinct des deux autres entités, nous n'en connaissons ni la densité d'occupation ni ses particularités morphologiques. Ces trois lignes de rempart ne sont pas construites sur le même modèle. La première enceinte consiste en une suite de saillants et de rentrants. La deuxième, qui couronne les collines, comprend une paroi maçonnée à crémaillère à l'abri d'un large glacis de galets. Elle est renforcée par des bastions d'appuis, ou des redoutes, qui dominent les champs irrigués et d'où l'on peut surveiller très loin jusqu'aux dunes de sable du Ramlat as-Sabataynʾ. Ce rempart est épisodiquement redoublé par une deuxième ligne de courtines et de saillants munis de flanquements. La troisième ligne de fortification est construite avec un large massif de briques crues protégé à l'extérieur par un mur parfaitement parementé en moyen appareil.

La citadelle est un édifice initialement isolé qui sera, dans un deuxième temps, rattaché aux remparts. Elle domine la vallée et le secteur sud-est de la ville en direction du plateau de l'Ḥaḍramawt. Le bâtiment, long d'une quarantaine de mètres et totalement enfoui sous le village d'al-Hagar, n'est que partiellement visible. Il n'a jamais fait l'objet de fouilles archéologiques.

Le traitement de l'ensemble des données recueillies sur les fortifications de Shabwa permet aujourd'hui de proposer des hypothèses de restitution du système défensif ainsi que des séquences d'un développement urbain qui n'est pas sans rappeler celui d'autres cités d'Arabie du nord (Breton 2000: 850–853; Breton, à paraître, *b*).

Notes

1. Suite à une incompréhension scientifique, ce sondage n'a pas pu être totalement terminé en 2003.
2. Nous proposons comme hypothèse de travail la présence des portes n° 1, n° 3 et n° 5. La porte n° 3 mènerait par une voirie directement aux premiers établissements où sera installé, lors d'une phase ultérieure, le grand temple. Les portes n° 1 et n° 5 sont reliées par un passage qui longe l'éperon d'al-ʿAqab.
3. Des fragments de charbon découverts dans le mortier de la tour de Dar al-Kafir ont pu être datés. Beta 189252, Dar al-Kafir, 2200 ± 40 BP, 360–190 BC en datation calibrée 1 sigma, et 380–160 BC en 2 sigma.
4. La porte n° 1 a fait l'objet d'une campagne de fouilles par R. Audouin en 1976–chantier VI. Cette fouille a été suivie, en 1978, par des dégagements menés par Ch. Darles et J. Seigne. Les résultats apparaîtront dans l'ouvrage monographique qui sera, en 2009, consacré aux «Fortifications de Shabwa, analyse structurelle et approches comparatives» par Ch. Darles.
5. 2270 ± 50 BP soit 389–382 BC (Breton 2000: 861).
6. La porte n° 10 a fait l'objet d'une campagne de fouilles durant l'hiver 1974–1975 par P. Gouin — chantier I. Les résultats apparaîtront dans l'ouvrage monographique cité en note 4.
7. Aux alentours de l'an 230 de l'ère chrétienne, le palais Shaqarʾ a été investi par les sabéens, il subira alors un long siège par les habitants de la ville. Assoiffés et prêts à se rendre à leurs assaillants, ils sont libérés par le roi sabéen Shaʾr Awtar. L'inscription de Mārib (al-Iryāni 13) relate également que la ville est alors entièrement

incendiée. L'inscription Ja 949 (RES 4912), gravée sur un rocher au pied du piton d'al-ᶜUqla, mentionne la reconstruction du palais royal Shaqarᵓ ainsi que celle du temple (Breton 2003: 208–209).

Références

Badre L.

1992. Le sondage stratigraphique de Shabwa. Pages 229–314 in J-F. Breton 1992*b*.

Breton J-F.

1988. Les villes d'Arabie méridionale. Pages 95–107 in J-L. Huot (éd.), *La ville neuve, une idée de l'Antiquité?* (Les cahiers du groupe scientifique Terrains et Théories en archéologie). Paris: Éditions Errance.

1992*a*. Le site et la ville de Shabwa. Pages 59–75 in J-F. Breton 1992*b*.

1992*b*. (éd.) *Fouilles de Shabwa II, Rapports préliminaires.* (Institut Français du Proche-Orient, Publication Hors Série, 19). Paris (= Extrait de *Syria* 68, 1991: 5–462).

1994. *Les fortifications d'Arabie méridionale du VIIe au Ie siècle avant notre ère.* (Archäologische Berichte aus dem Yemen, 8) Mainz: von Zabern.

1998. (éd.) *Fouilles de Shabwa III. L'architecture civile et religieuse.* (Bibliothèque archéologique et historique, 154). Beyrouth: Institut Français d'Archéologie du Proche-Orient.

2000. Shabwa (Yémen): traditions sémitiques, influences extérieures (IIIe s. av.–IIIe s. ap. J.-C.), *Comptes Rendus de l'Académie des Inscriptions et Belles-Lettres*: 849–882.

2001. Recherches archéologiques dans la région de Shabwa. *Orient-Express*: 37–38.

2003. Preliminary notes on the development of Shabwa. *Proceedings of the Seminar for Arabian Studies* 33: 199–213.

(à paraître, *a*). De Shabwa à Palmyre: questions d'urbanisme in J-F.Breton, à paraître, *b*.

(à paraître, *b*). (éd.) *Fouilles de Shabwa IV: L'environnement culturel et historique*. Ṣanᶜāᵓ: CEFAS.

Breton J-F. & Darles C.

1995. La maison tour et ses origines. Pages 449–457 in P. Bonnenfant (éd.), *Sanaa, architecture domestique et société*. Paris: CNRS.

Breton J-F. & Roux J-C.

2005. Preliminary report on new excavations in Shabwa. Pages 95–113 in A.M. Sholan, S. Antonini & M. Arbach (éds), *Sabaean Studies. Archaeological, Epigraphical and Historical Studies in Honour of Yūsuf M. ᶜAbdallāh, Alessandro de Maigret, Christian J. Robin on the Occasion of Their Sixtieth Birthdays.* Naples: Yemeni-Italian Centre for Archaeological Researches/Ṣanᶜāᵓ: University of Ṣanᶜāᵓ and Centre français d'archéologie et de sciences sociales de Ṣanᶜāᵓ.

Breton J-F., Darles C. & Roux J-C.

(à paraître). *Sondage stratigraphique dans la ville antique de Shabwa (Yémen). Le chantier XV (XIVe s. av. n. è.–IIIe s. de n. è.)* Arabia 4.

Darles C.

1998. Etude typologique de l'architecture civile intra-muros. Pages 3–26 in J-F. Breton (éd.), *Fouilles de Shabwa III. L'architecture civile et religieuse*. (Bibliothèque archéologique et historique, 154). Beyrouth: Institut Français d'Archéologie du Proche-Orient.

2003. Les fortifications de Shabwa, capitale du royaume antique de Ḥaḍramawt. *Proceedings of the Seminar for Arabian Studies* 33: 215–227.

2005. Hypothèses de restitution du dispositif d'entrée du Palais de Shabwa. Pages 151–172 in A.M. Sholan, S. Antonini & M. Arbach (éds), *Sabaean Studies. Archaeological, Epigraphical and Historical Studies in Honour of Yūsuf M. ᶜAbdallāh, Alessandro de Maigret, Christian J. Robin on the Occasion of Their Sixtieth Birthdays.* Naples: Yemeni-Italian Centre for Archaeological Researches/Ṣanᶜāᵓ: University of Ṣanᶜāᵓ and Centre français d'archéologie et de sciences sociales de Ṣanᶜāᵓ.

(à paraître, *a*). A restitution of ancient Shabwa. *Acts of the VIth International Conference on Yemeni Civilization, Aden, May 2007.*

(à paraître, *b*). Les portes fortifiées de Shabwa, analyse et comparaisons. *Raydan* 8.

Pirenne J.
1990. *Fouilles de Shabwa I. Les témoins écrits de la région de Shabwa et l'histoire*. (Bibliothèque archéologique et historique, 134). Paris: Geuthner.

Schiettecatte J.
2006. *Villes et urbanisation de l'Arabie du Sud à l'époque préislamique*. Thèse de doctorat d'université, volume 1, Université de Paris-Panthéon Sorbonne. [Non publiée].

Author's address
Pr. Christian Darles, Ecole nationale supérieure d'architecture de Toulouse, 83 rue Aristide Maillol, BP 10629, F 31106 Toulouse Cedex 1, France.
e-mail christian.darles@toulouse.archi.fr

Proceedings of the Seminar for Arabian Studies 38 (2008): 153–172

Wādī aṯ-Ṯayyilah 3, a Neolithic and Pre-Neolithic occupation on the eastern Yemen Plateau, and its archaeofaunal information

FRANCESCO G. FEDELE

Summary
The stratified site WTH3, located at an altitude of 2025 m in the upper drainage of the Wādī aṯ-Ṯayyilah on the eastern highlands of Yemen, was found during surveys in 1984 and partially studied through detailed excavation in 1984–1986, within the activities of the Italian Archaeological Mission. This work confirmed its tentative attribution to the Neolithic and revealed a virtually unknown manifestation of the mid-Holocene occupation of highland Yemen. This Neolithic culture is aceramic (pottery makes its appearance on the Yemen Plateau during the Bronze Age) and is characterized by the occurrence of small-tool lithic components in association with certain recurrent stone features, including "enclosure" alignments and oval or elliptical "huts". The occupation at WTH3 is associated with mid-Holocene sediments that can be dated to the sixth–fifth millennia BC on the basis of pedology as well as a ^{14}C measurement on the soil's organic acids. A pilot study of the abundant lithic collection and the zooarchaeological analysis of the fauna has been completed, while the collation of the field records towards final publication is in progress. In this paper an up-to-date appraisal of the site and excavations is given, including a particular account of Neolithic economy as derived from the archaeofaunal information. WTH3 and similar sites on the eastern Plateau appear to be connected with cattle pastoralists, a picture that accords well with a milder, moister, greener mid-Holocene landscape.

Keywords: Yemen Plateau, Wādī aṯ-Ṯayyilah, Neolithic, mid-Holocene, pastoralism

Introduction

The purpose of this paper is to summarize and update information on the research programme carried out at Wādī aṯ-Ṯayyilah 3 (WTH3), (1) a Neolithic and Pre-Neolithic site in the eastern sector of the Yemen Plateau, between 1984 and 1986. Full publication of work conducted at the site has long been delayed, unfortunately, and only short interim reports and cursive evaluations have appeared in print (Fedele & Zaccara 2005, with references). However, WTH3 remains to this date one of the very few Neolithic settlements investigated on the Yemen Plateau in general, and continues to be mentioned in the occasional publications on the Neolithic of highland Yemen (e.g. Kallweit 1996). In addition, the site was excavated and recorded with exacting procedures, and as a consequence generated a very large controlled collection of lithic finds and a valuable sample of archaeofaunal material, the latter never reported in any detail. These facts and characteristics suggest that WTH3 still deserves to be brought to the consideration of a wider community of interested scholars. (2)

The Wādī aṯ-Ṯayyilah basin is located in the region of Khawlān at-Tiyāl, which together with Al-Hadā formed the core study area of the Italian Archaeological Mission between 1980 and 1990 (Fig. 1). The region includes a mosaic of mountains and small intermontane plains, with average annual precipitation of around 200 mm, as well as more dissected and barren fringes nearer the edge of the Plateau, above 2000 m in altitude. These uplands are scarred by wadis that eventually cut through the margin of the Plateau and disappear from escarpments into the vast stretches of semi-desert and desert to the east. The largest wadi system draining this part of the eastern Plateau is the Wādī Ḏanah, the very river course that flows down to Mārib and facilitated the florescence of the ancient Sabaean capital on the desert border. Both Wādī aṯ-Ṯayyilah and a fossil furrow nearby, An-Najd al-Abyad or "white valley", belong to the Wādī Ḏanah drainage.

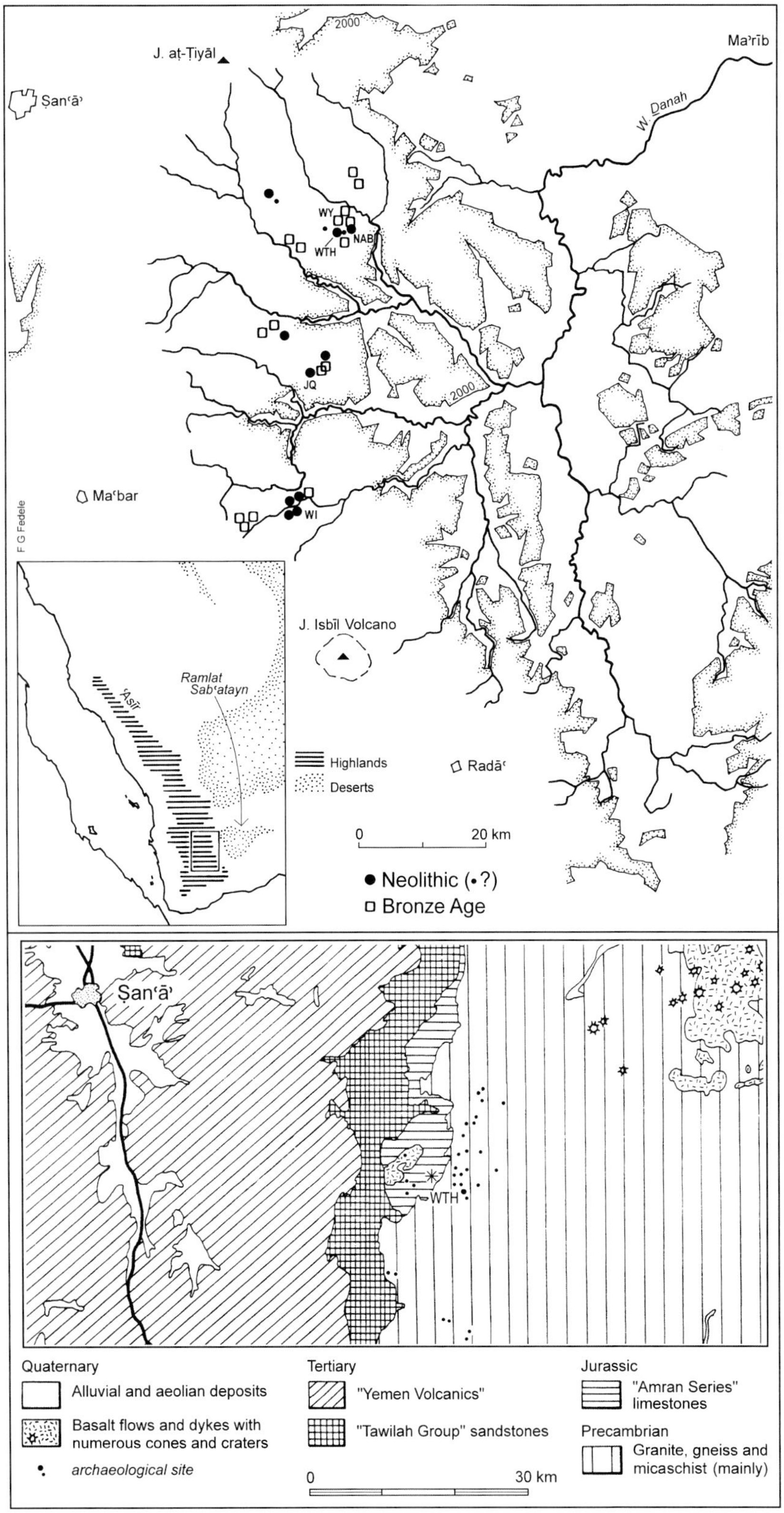

FIGURE 1. *Above: a map of the central part of the eastern Plateau, emphasizing the Wādī Ḏanah basin and the 2000 m contour line. The main Neolithic sites include JQ = Jebel Qutrān, NAB = Wādī an-Najd al-Abyad, WI = Wādī al-ᶜIšš, WTH = Wādī aṭ-Ṭayyilah. Below: a simplified geological map of the Khawlān at-Tiyāl. (Redrawn after B. Marcolongo, geological data derived from Grolier & Overstreet 1978). WTH as above; the asterisk is Jebel al-ᶜArqūb.*

Historiography of research

WTH3 was found by Alessandro de Maigret and co-workers during a late stage of their general archaeological survey of the Italian study area in September 1984 (de Maigret 2002). This was one of a number of sites represented by particular block-and-boulder structures combined with substantial scatters of chipped stone artefacts on the ground, with pottery strangely lacking. The eastern Plateau was *terra incognita* as far as prehistoric archaeology was concerned. On the basis of structures above ground, rock patination, and perceived affinities of lithic types, a "Neolithic" label was assigned to such occurrences, although no archaeological association was available, strictly speaking, and the food economy was obviously unknown.

By that time, in the same district of the Khawlān, de Maigret had been able to identify a later prehistoric manifestation, which included pottery and was based on a different kind of settlement features and locational choices, which he called the Yemeni Bronze Age (de Maigret 1990). In 1984, a stratigraphic confirmation that the so-called "Neolithic" preceded this ceramic tradition came from a test excavation at An-Najd al-Abyad site 7 (NAB7), where a level with scanty Neolithic material appeared below a surface layer with Bronze Age structures (de Maigret *et al.* 1984). WTH3 nearby seemed to offer comparable conditions. Later that year, when I was asked to join the Italian Mission with the task of developing the Neolithic and its palaeo-economic aspects (de Maigret 2002: 120–126), I examined the "Neolithic" sites and eventually selected WTH3 for a specific excavation programme.

The choice of WTH3 for detailed excavation was dictated by a need for context. Only buried occupations that afforded reliable contextual evidence could advance the definition and understanding of the presumed, aceramic Neolithic of the Khawlān. WTH3 appeared to be notable for surface area, indications of sizeable buried portions, and richness in lithics. Furthermore, by 1984 a certain difference had been perceived between the stone-tool composition of most Khawlān "Neolithic" sites, as gleaned from surface sampling, and a supposed Neolithic site at Jebel Qutrān (GQ1; "JQ" in Fig. 1), to the south of the study area, which had been tested for two days late in 1983 (de Maigret 1983). An assessment of the variation and peculiarities of the Plateau "Neolithic" had thus become an additional reason for undertaking a specific Neolithic programme.

WTH3: setting, stratigraphy, and organization

Site setting and general stratigraphy

WTH3 (44°39'58" E, 15°10'00" N) is a stratified site located in a semi-desert environment at an altitude of 2025 m in the upper Wādī aṯ-Ṭayyilah drainage, 60 km south-east of Ṣanᶜāᵓ (Fig. 2). The drainage is almost completely set within the Precambrian granites at the foothills of the limestone tableland of Jebel al-ᶜArqūb (cf. Fedele 1990*a*). Half buried on the rock-strewn hillside, the site occupies a shallow depression between rocky hillocks and covers an estimated area of 0.53 ha (1.3 acres), within a rectangle of about 70×90 m (Fig. 3). The settlement coincides with a mildly sloping terrace in proximity of a watercourse, a standard location among the Neolithic sites of the Khawlān. The present-day wadi runs eastwards about 100 m north of the site and is flanked by a series of alluvial terraces; the third and topmost possibly indicates the margin of the mid-Holocene riverbed. Some amount of rainwater flows across the site during the monsoonal season, but actual erosion tends to be low due to the diffuse pattern of runoff.

A generalized litho- and pedo-stratigraphy of what we may call the Najd al-Abyad-Ṭayyilah area — in view of its uniform environmental record — is summarized in Figure 4. Detailed profiles and cultural horizons from site WTH3 can be correlated rather easily to the local depositional sequences of the area. Above the decayed granite bedrock there are 40 to 80 cm of colluvial and aeolian sediments, predominantly silty-sandy in texture, due to prolonged but discontinuous slope deposition. This trend was punctuated by one major phase of soil formation, simultaneously identified at WTH3 (horizon "G", for grey); (3) (de Maigret *et al.* 1984: 431–437; Fedele 1985) and by the Italian geologists in the Najd al-Abyad-Ṭayyilah area (Marcolongo & Palmieri 1986). On qualitative data this fossil soil was designated the "Thayyilah Palaeosol" (Fedele 1986; 1987; 1988; 1990*b*); quantitative data have subsequently improved the identification (Marcolongo & Palmieri 1988; de Maigret *et al.* 1989). This palaeosol was traced to the north during a brief survey in the Suhmān (Fedele 1990*c*; and unpublished data).

The Thayyilah Palaeosol is a local expression of a mid-Holocene soil which appears to represent a useful pedo-stratigraphic marker over a wide area of Yemen and south-western Arabia, having been reported from an

FIGURE 2. *Above: the confluence of Wādī aṯ-Ṯayyilah and Wādī an-Najd al-Abyad, a panoramic view from the Jebel al-ᶜArqūb escarpment; site WTH3 is within inset frame. Below: site WTH3 from across Wādī aṯ-Ṯayyilah.*

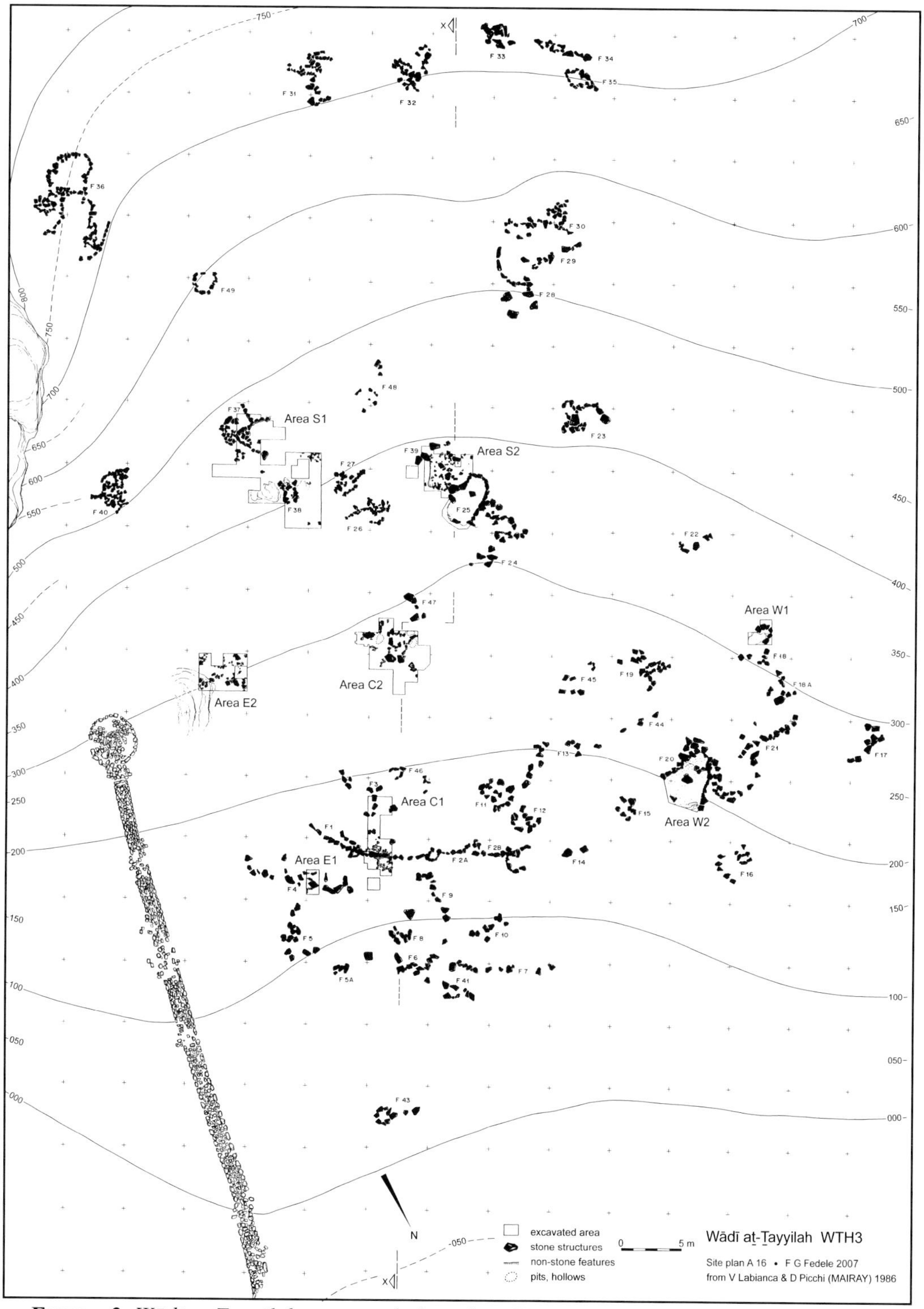

FIGURE 3. *Wādī aṯ-Ṯayyilah: a general plan of site WTH3. Excavations and above-ground features of the prehistoric site are shown; the large structure to the east is a later tomb, unrelated to the Neolithic and Pre-Neolithic occupations.*

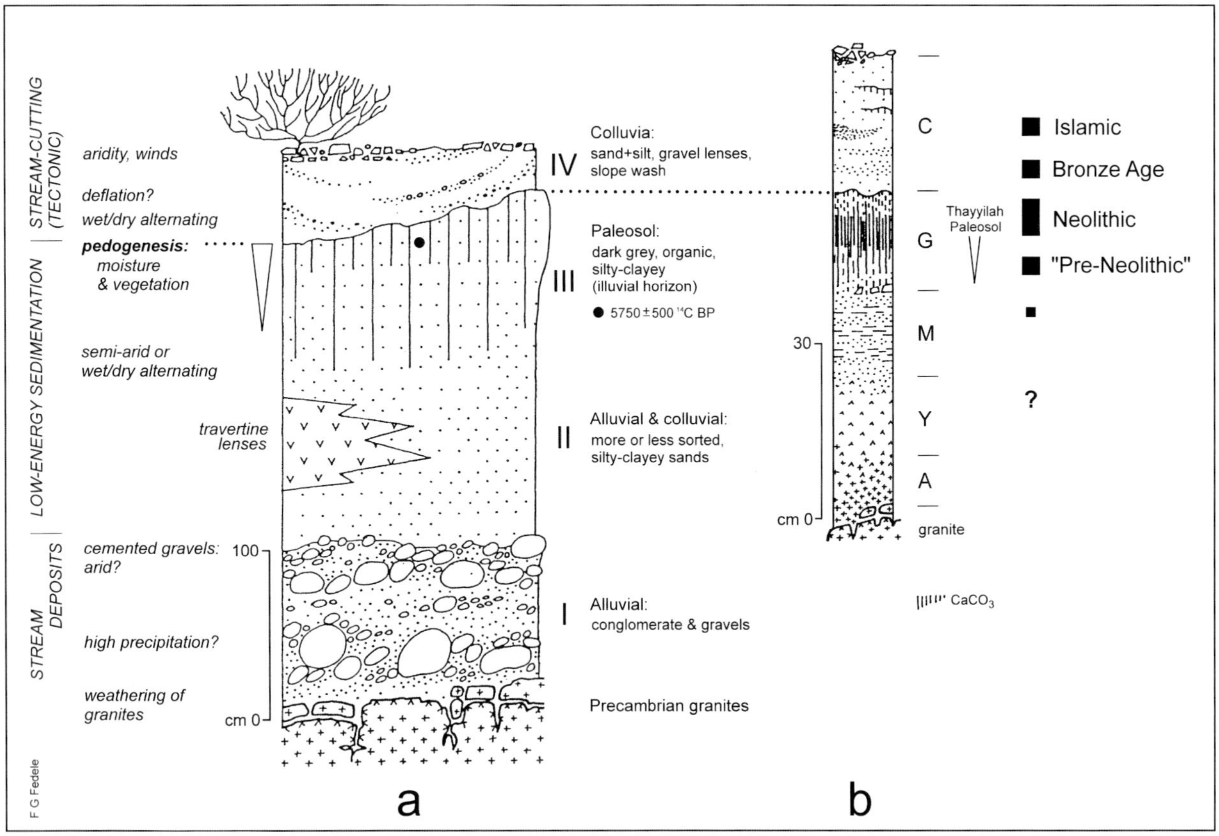

FIGURE 4. *Late Quaternary depositional sequences in the eastern Yemen Plateau, NAB-WTH area (cf. Figs 1–2). a. a generalized lithostratigraphy and palaeoenvironmental sequence. (After Marcolongo & Palmieri 1986; 1988). The radiocarbon date is from the Rome laboratory and is unpublished. (Reported in Marcolongo & Palmieri 1986); b. the stratigraphy of site WTH3 according to the 1984–1986 excavations: litho- and pedostratigraphic units on the left, cultural horizons or "ethnostratigraphy" on the right.*

increasing number of locations at different altitudes (e.g. Bintliff & van Zeist 1982; Overstreet, Grolier & Toplyn 1988; Overstreet & Grolier 1996; Garcia *et al.* 1991; Wilkinson 1997; Lézine *et al.* 1998; McCorriston 2000; French 2003; Parker, Davies & Wilkinson 2006). On the basis of correlation to similar pedogenetic bodies, and a radiocarbon determination on the soil's organic acids that calibrates to *c.* 5300–4000 BC (Fig. 4.a), the Thayyilah Palaeosol can be dated to the sixth–fifth millennia cal. BC. This soil is bounded by a well-defined upper limit and was truncated in places by deflation or erosion. Subsequently in the series only aeolian silts and exfoliation debris can be seen, linked to recent aridity.

The Thayyilah Palaeosol has environmental significance for the Neolithic of the eastern Plateau (cf. Fedele 1988). Site topography, soil and sediment evidence, and a palynological test (Lentini 1988; Fedele 1990*b*: fig. 4), strongly suggest the presence of some vegetation cover, high water table conditions, and scattered ponds in many upland basins. An ecosystem with woodland vegetation and well-watered districts can also be inferred from the incidence of bovine husbandry in the Neolithic, as suggested below. The connection of widespread soil formation with a period of milder and moister oscillations, plausibly resulting from higher rainfall (e.g. Wilkinson 2005), is generally accepted, hence the frequent designation of Mid-Holocene Pluvial. Widespread geomorphic stability contributed to this kind of landscape on the eastern Plateau. By the beginning of the third millennium BC such conditions gave way to a new cycle of severe desiccation, exacerbated by riverbed erosion induced by tectonic uplift, which changed the landscape and brought to an end the Neolithic lifeways (Fedele 1990*b*).

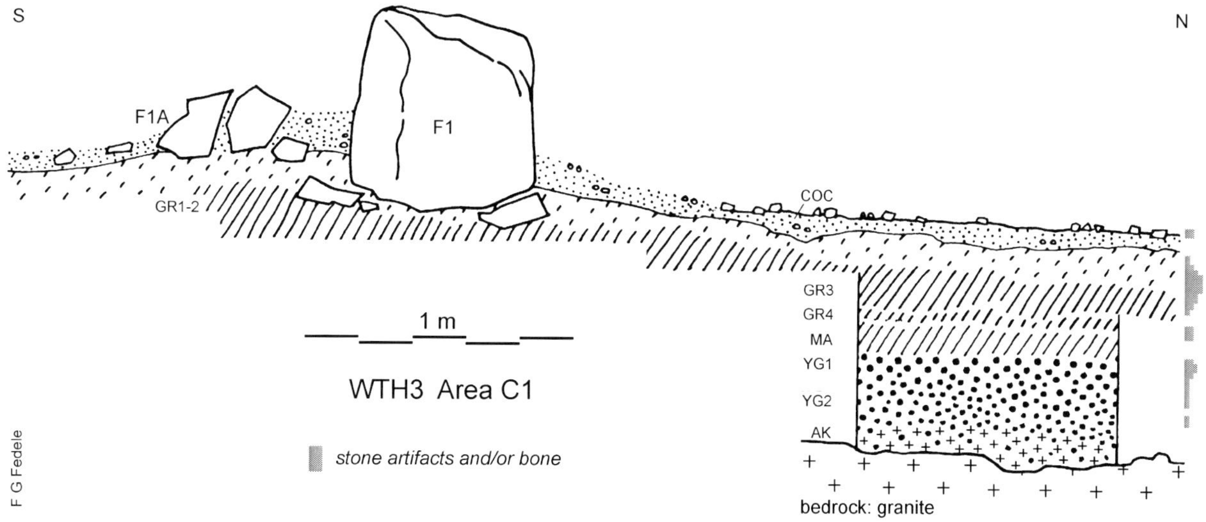

FIGURE 5. *Site WTH3: south–north stratigraphic profile in Area C1, across alignment F1, showing one of the soundings down to the bedrock (1984 excavations) and the vertical distribution of cultural material.*

Site components

Site WTH3 was studied through detailed excavation during three intensive seasons. A total of approximately 120 m² were excavated, amounting — in spite of the effort — to perhaps 5% of the site. In order to sample the internal variation eight excavation areas were opened (Fig. 3); area code letters stand for central, eastern, western, and southern, these being conventional partitions only. We managed to employ tight spatial control and very detailed recording criteria, unprecedented on the Plateau, encompassing both cultural evidence and geo-archaeological context. All sediments were dry screened with a 4 mm mesh and expertly hand picked for artefacts and ecofacts. Deposits from particular contexts were bagged for water sieving in Ṣanᶜāʾ.

Site WTH3 is stratified and up to 1 m thick in places. Already during the initial testing in 1984 it turned out to possess some evidence of earlier material in addition to the principal and more conspicuous component. Two main cultural strata were eventually recognized in some parts of the settlement (Fig. 4.b): a rich "Neolithic" assemblage associated with fully domesticated animals; and a lower and earlier component, only detected in small portions of the site, particularly in Area C2 and through soundings in Areas S1 and C1 (Fig. 5). This latter component is here labelled "Pre-Neolithic", an explicitly noncommittal designation, and provisionally equated with the Pre-Pottery Neolithic B of the Levant on the basis of pedo-stratigraphy — as it appears to antedate the formation of the Thayyilah Palaeosol — and owing to some peculiar finds.

A partial figurine made of hardened, unfired clay (Fig. 8.n), which may represent a female torso — or two closely facing figures — is currently understood to be the oldest piece of portable "art" in Yemen (Fedele 1986: fig. 28; Fedele & Zaccara 2005: fig. 5). The nearest parallels are probably to be found in the PPNB of Jordan (e.g. Kuijt & Chesson 2005: figs 8.2, 8.4), and according to this hypothesis a date in the seventh millennium BC is tentatively proposed. The figurine was found within a deep feature in Area S1, an erosional furrow containing a pocket of dark ashy silts and piled stones, probably from a nearby hearth. The same locus gave a small group of bone remains from rather large bovids, possibly wild (see below). Other features from this lower horizon include stone clusters set inside pits in Area C2. We may be dealing with ephemeral human occupation by essentially mobile groups, such as those found near Saᶜdah to the north (Garcia *et al.* 1991; Garcia & Rachad 1997); its classification as "Mesolithic" might in future turn out to be appropriate.

Spatial organization

The main Neolithic cultural stratum will be briefly described. As elsewhere on the eastern Plateau, the defining features of the settlement typically comprise "enclosure" alignments and oval or elliptical "huts" (Fig. 6). These are simply shorthand terms for partly

FIGURE 6. *Site WTH3: a. the large-stone alignment F1–F2 from the west; b. elliptical "hut" F25 and its inside hollow during excavation in 1986.*

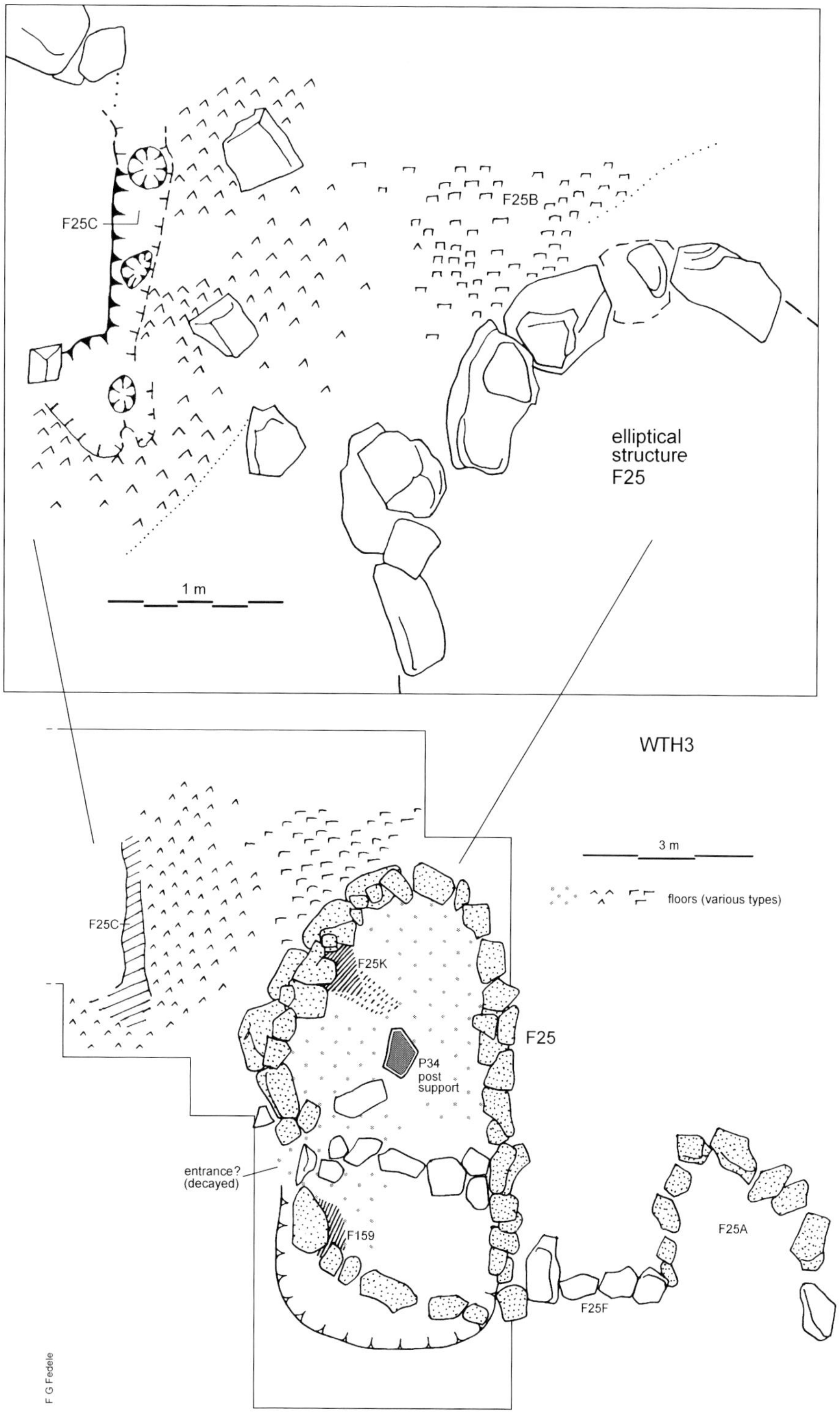

FIGURE 7. *Site WTH3: a simplified plan of elliptical "hut" F25 and its accessory structures. The annexe shown in the enlarged plan, above, is bounded by F25C, which can be recognized as the base of a light wall probably made of stakes and branches.*

buried, dry-stone constructions of varying shape, size, and preservation. The most conspicuous structures are made of large stone blocks and lie apparently scattered. In addition, as already mentioned, most Neolithic sites are consistently located on gently sloping ground near watercourses or silted-up alluvial flats. At WTH3 there is a curved boulder alignment in the lower half of the site, F1–F2, and about six elliptical "huts". Although obviously scattered, these elliptical structures are all located in the western half of the site and appear to share the main axis orientation (south-west–north-east, curiously diagonal to the slope).

Two large elliptical structures were excavated and studied within their surrounding context (F20 and F25) (Fig. 7). They measure about 4×7 m and 3×5 m respectively, and are typically built of large unfashioned blocks. Cultural refuse suggests that they should be considered houses, or rather, part of house compounds. Two heavily eroded hearths were found inside F25. The ellipses have a slightly sunken floor, often paved with cobbles and angular broken stones; near the centre stood a flat stone that may have supported a post (Fig. 6.b). It appears that the stone-built part of the house was the base, while the upper walls and the roofing were made of perishable or other material (hides? mud?); the smaller stones that litter the site today may have been walling material as well. Some ideas about the original plan of certain elliptical "houses" were gleaned from better-preserved above-ground examples occasionally to be seen elsewhere among the Neolithic sites of the Khawlān. Useful suggestions towards the reconstruction and interpretation of some structures were also derived from elements of contemporary rural villages in the Khawlān at-Tiyāl and Al-Hadā.

In addition, alignment F1 was studied. The fact that its juxtaposed boulder faces show a kind of façade in a downslope direction may support the hypothesis that it was an enclosure. An alternative possibility is to interpret F1 as a "divider", an activity-area divider in particular; or else it may have been for the control of surface runoff. Work at WTH3 was insufficient to resolve the functional interpretation of such an alignment.

The above-ground features, as excavation has shown, only bear a vague resemblance to their buried counterparts. WTH3 is a dilapidated site, whose structures were robbed of their stones during later prehistoric and historical times (witness to this is the construction of the large cairn-and-ray tomb, possibly Bronze Age in date; Fig. 3). Furthermore, an emphasis on large-stone elements alone would give a biased picture of the site. Substantial stone buildings were only a small part of the settlement. There are several small-stone features that are difficult to interpret. There are floored sectors in the open and, often, higher densities in lithic artefacts appear to be mutually exclusive with them. The main occupation at WTH3 represents an open-air village in which substantial stone "houses" and flimsy structures appear to have existed side by side. Light structures built from wood and other organic materials were recognized, particularly in Area S1 (Fig. 7). Parts of the site, which on the surface appeared to be empty, were shown to be occupied by inconspicuous features made without stones.

This summary suggests the coexistence of several types of habitation and non-habitation elements, a complex settlement organization and a rather varied village life. The agricultural capacity of these groups is not known, but their integration into a tropical high-plateau ecosystem appears to have been efficient, largely on the basis of cattle breeding (see below). WTH3 and the florescence of these Neolithic groups in general can be attributed to the sixth–fourth millennia BC on the basis of their correlation to the Thayyilah Palaeosol. (4) The archaeological map for the Neolithic, although very incomplete, would point to high population densities in several areas of the eastern highlands (cf. also Fedele 1990*c*), whereas the region is characterized today by very low population densities, both of humans and animals. The recent depopulation thus contrasts sharply with the situation during an earlier part of the Holocene.

WTH3: small finds, particularly lithic artefacts

WTH3 is an aceramic lithic site. Stone artefacts comprise, by far, the single most abundant class of archaeological evidence, as is common throughout the Neolithic of the Plateau. The WTH3 lithic collections derive from both excavation and surface sampling and amount to over 15,000 items, including manuports. (5) About 98% is represented by chipped stone artefacts; polished stone is virtually nonexistent. Small finds and lithic typology will be mentioned only very briefly in this article. More information can be found in a pilot study recently published in advance of final reports (Fedele & Zaccara 2005), with lithic analysis particularly aiming at a dynamic, behavioural understanding of stone-working technology. The initial surface collections from 1984 were examined in typological fashion by Di Mario (1992).

On the basis of the excavated assemblages a "Thayyilah

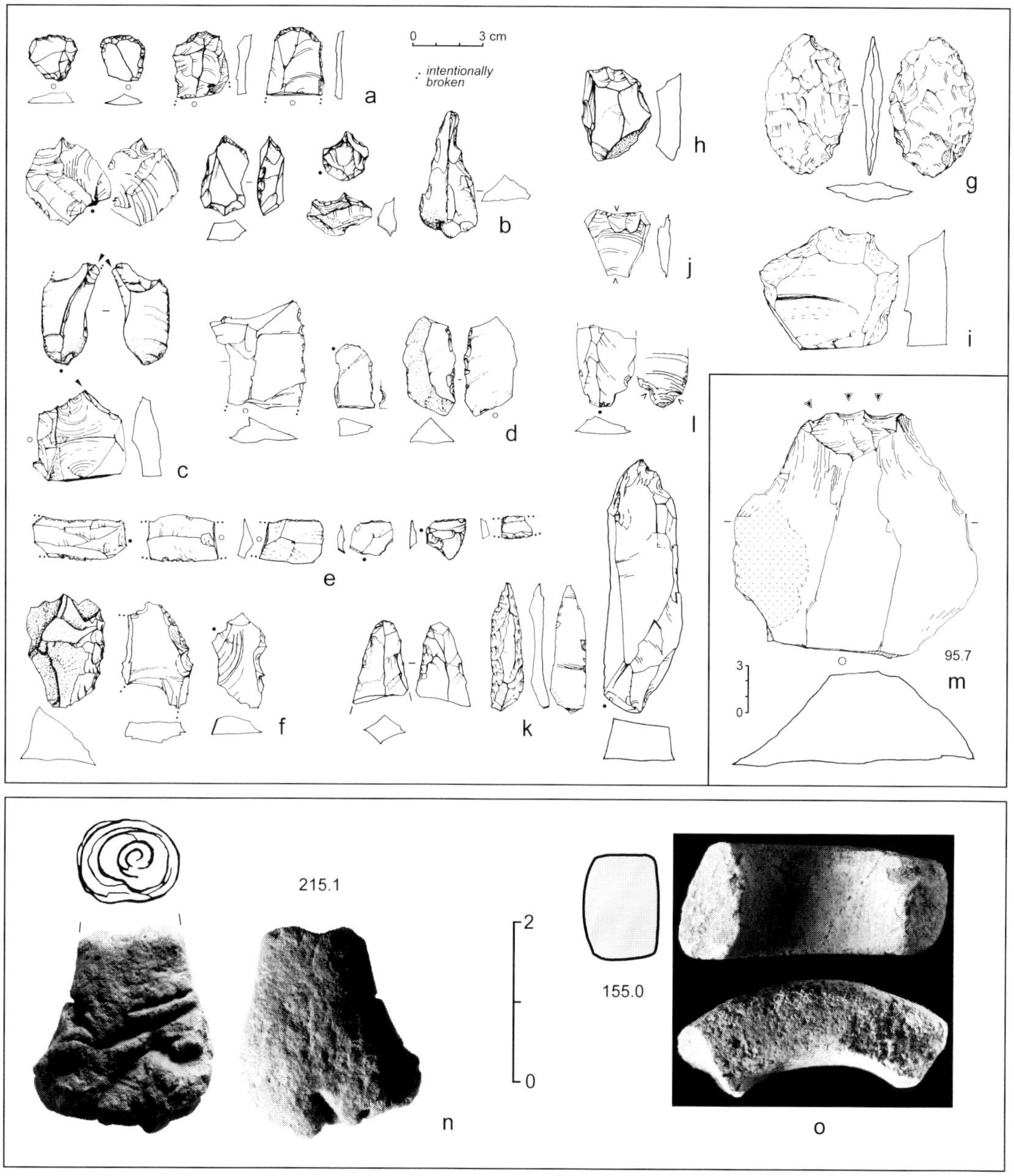

FIGURE 8. *A sample of chipped lithic tools representing artefact types in the Thayyilah industry, from WTH3: a. endscrapers; b. borers; c. burins; d. naturally backed knives; e. a series of "segments" as mounted on a reaping knife or sickle; f. scrapers; g. a foliate; h. rabots; i. denticulate core-tool; j. a pièce esquillée; k. stout unifacial points; l. contracting-stemmed pieces; m. a macrolith, a large granite chopper. Special finds: n. a Pre-Neolithic partial figurine made of unfired clay; o. a Neolithic stone bracelet fragment.*

industry" can be defined. The prehistoric users were interested in the geometry of the lithic piece and utterly indifferent to reduction categories and blank orientation in the archaeological sense (cf. Andrefsky 1998: 197). Fundamental aspects of morphology were thus controlled by blank choice in terms of size, proportions, and edge articulation. Concurrent characteristics are scant interest in formal blades, expedient utilization of blanks, and an authentic passion for intentional breakage by snapping ("segmentation"; Fedele 1987). At least 50% of actual tools are not retouched at all, but simply obtained by deliberate segmentation. Hafting and the composite-tool component were highly developed. Obsidian (cf. Francaviglia 1990) accounts for about 25% on average, but the main raw material is chert from the limestone belt (cf. Fig. 1).

Toolkits are dominated by various kinds of scraping, boring, and cutting implements reflecting a way of life in which grass cutting and skin- and plant-material processing had gained importance. Ordinary-sized tools include — in decreasing frequency — naturally backed cutting tools, endscrapers, perforators and borers, rabots, burins, discoid core-tools, stout unifacial points, truncated tablets, *pièces esquillées*, stemmed pieces, and scrapers (Fig. 8). Hafting by insertion or binding is amply indicated on a number of different types, and utilized blades and "segments" were often mounted as a series on reaping knives or sickles. In addition to ordinary-sized tools there are frequent and well-made macroliths, including granite choppers and large denticulates, which point to the relevance of heavy-duty equipment.

Foliates and foliate fragments are extraordinarily rare, an estimated 0.2%. Often crudely made, they include broad ovate bifaces (Fig. 8.g), bifacial drills and tanged bifacial arrowheads. This paucity stands in contrast to the frequency of foliates not only in the southern Khawlān and al-Hadā regions, including Jebel Qutrān and perhaps Wādī al-ᶜIšš, but in most Neolithic inventories of Yemen and southern and central Arabia in general (e.g. Edens 1982; 1988; Di Mario *et al.* 1989; Edens & Wilkinson 1998; Kallweit 1996). Richness in foliates and arrowhead types is fundamental to the definition of an Arabian Bifacial Tradition or "Rubᶜ al-Khali Neolithic" centred on the lowlands and desert. Although Qutrān remains essentially unique to this day, its inventory is clearly reminiscent of this latter tradition. WTH3 seems to represent a different kind of Neolithic, also lacking e.g. polished adzes and gouges. In light of such compositional attributes, I have argued for a distinction between two Neolithic industries on the eastern Plateau, provisionally named "Thayyilah" and "Qutran" (Fedele 1988; de Maigret, Fedele & Di Mario 1988; Fedele & Zaccara 2005; cf. Wilkinson, Edens & Gibson 1997; Edens & Wilkinson 1998), but on present evidence their actual identity and space-time articulation are impossible to assess.

Worth noting among WTH3's small finds are some unique objects specifically coming from house floor contexts. A cache of entirely natural calcarenite manuports with evocative shapes was preserved within structure F20. Similarly, elliptical structure F25 gave a fragment of a white marble bracelet (Fig. 8.o). It closely matches finds from the Neolithic occupation of Shaabat Sulaiman 1 in the Wādī Ḏahr (Kallweit 1996: 123, pl. 20), and can be compared in a more general way with finds from the Ramlat Sabᶜatayn (Di Mario *et al.* 1989) and other parts of Arabia, the Levant and predynastic Lower Egypt.

On lithic evidence, the Neolithic and Pre-Neolithic manifestations appear to be phases of a single continuum, in spite of the very small size of the Pre-Neolithic sample. There is also the impression of similarities with the East African sequence rather than the Fertile Crescent, which would incline towards adopting an eastern African terminology. If so, the lithic phases above could be grouped under a designation such as "Late Stone Age" of the Yemen Plateau (cf. Uerpmann M 1992 for a similar terminology in the context of south-eastern Arabia). Further exploration of this issue is clearly necessary.

Archaeofaunal information

Neolithic and Pre-Neolithic WTH3

Recovery of bone material in the field is problematic in the drier parts of Yemen, as a result of the loss of organic substance, mechanical abrasion, and splitting. Most faunal finds from WTH3 were very badly preserved and had to be block-lifted within their matrix for laboratory processing after consolidation in the field: samples had to be generated, not just collected (Fig. 9). This painstaking procedure resulted in a larger collection — about 400 pieces — and ensured that more finds became amenable to faunal identification. What follows is an account of Neolithic and Pre-Neolithic economy as derived from the archaeofaunal information (cf. Fedele 1991; 1992: 69–76). Anatomical measurements are given in millimetres.

Totalling about 265 individual pieces, the archaeofauna from Neolithic WTH3 (Table 1) is represented by 73% domestic cattle and 16% domestic caprines, in terms of number of identified specimens; no caprine could be identified to species. A calculation of the minimum number of individuals might indicate rather more cattle, although small sample size suggests caution. Adults predominate, with adult-to-juvenile ratios of about 15:1 in cattle and 4:1 in caprines. The remaining 11% is represented by wild or possibly wild species, notably a small equid (Fig. 9.b), accounting for a theoretical 5%. A diaphysis of *Bos* points to a larger animal than normal, domestic or wild. Two fragments can apparently be attributed to gazelle and

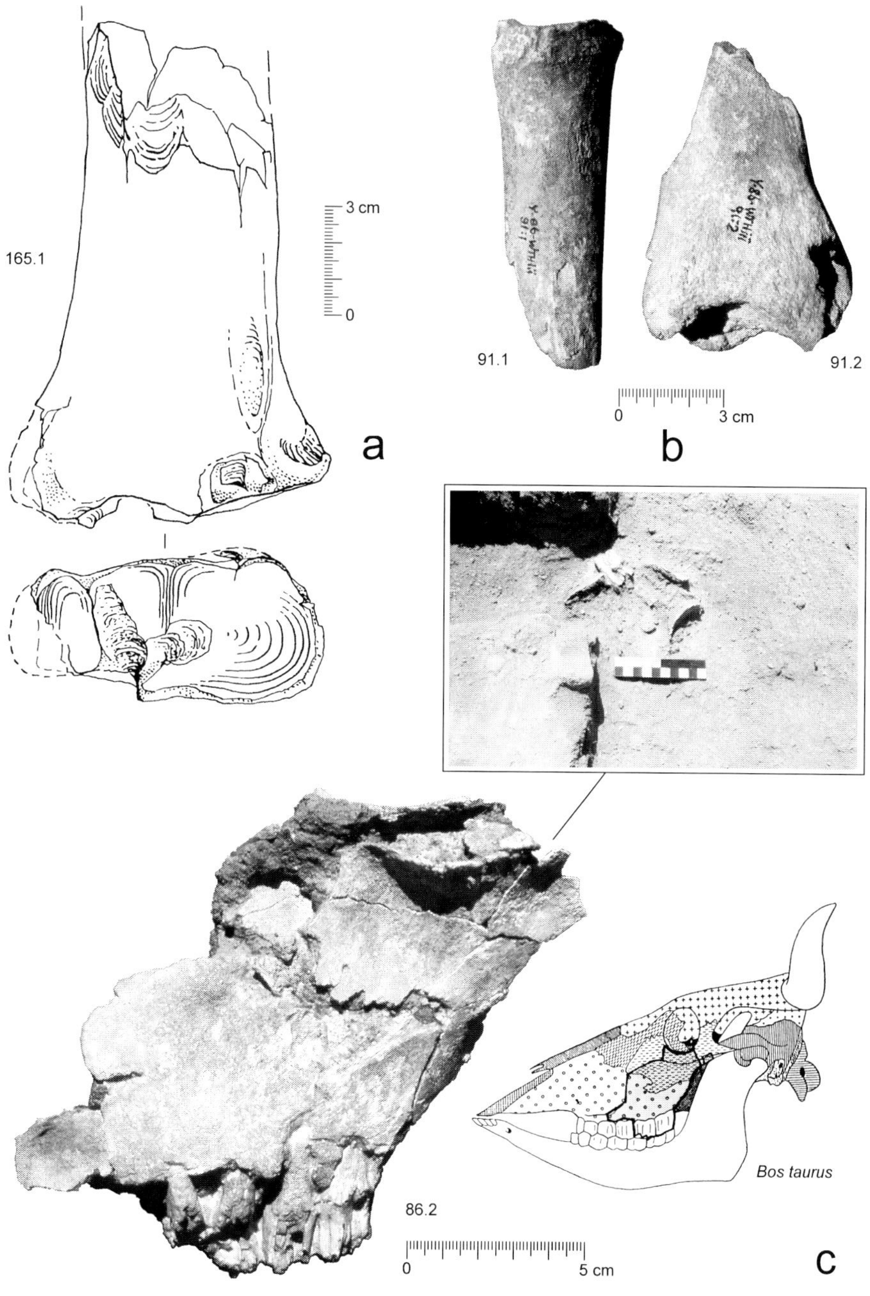

FIGURE 9. *Faunal remains from WTH3: a. Pre-Neolithic,* Bos sp.*, proximal radius intermediate between wild and domestic cattle; b. Neolithic,* Equus sp.*, metatarsal and tibia; c. Neolithic,* Bos taurus*, jugal-maxillary portion of a skull (and the find* in situ *in Area C2).*

a cervid, and there is in addition a freshwater clam.

As to cattle, most material is compatible with diminutive, domesticated *Bos*, very plausibly the common western Eurasian cattle; the water buffalo should be excluded. An outstanding find is a lateral skull piece from Area C2 (Fig. 9.c), which includes the maxilla and jugal with a part of the orbital rim, its hollow sinus exposed, and the two distal molars. It belongs to an aged adult

	WTH3: Neolithic	WTH3: Pre-Neolithic	An-Najd al-Abyad NAB7	Jebel Qutrān GQ1
Total number of specimens	c. 265 (identified 44)	c. 140 (identified 6)	18+ (identified 4)	280 (identified 49)
Domestic species				
Bos taurus, cattle	32		1	12
Capra hircus, goat				3
Ovis aries, sheep				4
Ovis/Capra, domestic caprines	7		2	19
Wild species				
cf. Gazella, possibly gazelle	1	2		
?*Cervid*	1			
Bos cf. primigenius, ?aurochs				7
Capra ibex, ibex				1
Equus sp., ass or hemione	2			
Equus sp., small equid				2
freshwater clam	1			
Meriones sp., jird			1	
Only identified to size				
caprine-gazelle size group	c. 50	c. 20		
cattle-equid size group	c. 70	c. 45		
Indeterminate status				
Bos sp., possibly wild	1	4		
Carnivore: *Canis cf. familiaris,* ?dog				1

TABLE 1. *Archaeofauna from excavated Neolithic sites: species composition and number of identified specimens. The sites include WTH3 (Neolithic and Pre-Neolithic), NAB7, and GQ1 (Analysis of Jebel Qutrān after Bökönyi 1990). + indicates an indeterminate quantity of comminuted debris from bones and teeth.*

individual (crown height of M^3 ~ 17; length of M^3 = 28 and of M^2–M^3 ~ 55). This piece raises the question of the zebu, *Bos indicus*, being represented among our finds. (7) However, the diagnostic criteria do not substantiate this possibility (Grigson 1976; 1980; cf. Marshall 1989): our find presents sharp, converging borders to the lower angle of orbital rim and an apparently prominent orbit, and the cheek is proportionally high as in *Bos taurus* (distance from molar tip to orbit rim = 119).

Identification of the equid fragments — a proximal metatarsal and a distal tibia — is difficult. The bones are slightly worn, particularly the medial malleolus of the tibia which is important for determination (Uerpmann H-P 1991: 24); morphology is thus inconclusive. Metrically the tibia (Bd = 55, Dd = 38) exactly falls at the boundary between wild or early domestic ass, *Equus (Asinus) africanus*, and hemione, *E. (hemionus) hemionus* (e.g. Fedele 1990*d*: fig. 165; a Bronze Age donkey from Wādī Yanāʿim has Bd = 54 and Dd = 37). H-P. Uerpmann has long attracted attention to the distribution of wild ass in the Arabian Peninsula, and has aptly predicted that its mountainous margins may have provided suitable habitats for *E. africanus*, which is adapted to the same sort of stony and arid environment on the other side of the Red Sea (Uerpmann H-P. 1987; 1991: 29–30). My preferred interpretation is to consider the species from WTH3 to be African ass, although slightly smaller than the equivalent examples from eastern Arabia reported by Uerpmann.

The Pre-Neolithic samples come from deep contexts in Areas S1 and E2 and total about 140 pieces (Table 1). Preservation was mildly favoured by rapid burial and slight charring, as in the locus of the clay figurine in Area S1, which yielded bone remains from rather large bovids. An adult radius (Fig. 9.a) is metrically intermediate between wild and domestic cattle. The estimated width of proximal radius is Bp = 94 ± 1, so its logarithmic difference from the animal assumed as standard by Grigson — a European *Bos primigenius* female — is ~ -0.030: it means that although large the WTH3 radius could be either wild or domestic (Grigson 1989: fig. 5; and *in litteris* 26.07.1988). Other relevant measurements are BFp ~ 85, Fp depth = 38, maximum proximal depth = 43; a proximal radius from the Neolithic occupation has Bp = 73.5, and an associated distal humerus has BT = 73.

Since all the materials from the Pre-Neolithic horizon appear to derive from large bovids and gazelle-sized animals, with domesticates not clearly present, I would suggest that we are dealing with a wild fauna in which the aurochs may be dominant. However, one should take into account the report of mid-Holocene wild buffalo from an occupation at Saᶜdah ("*Pelorovis antiquus* = *Bubalus arnee*"; Garcia *et al.* 1991; Garcia & Rachad 1997); depictions of the same species do indeed appear on a rock surface nearby. The Pre-Neolithic occupations of WTH3 can be equally interpreted as campsites where hunting groups would bring butchered game.

Faunal data from other Neolithic sites

Neolithic faunal samples only come from two other sites in the Italian study area: Jebel Qutrān GQ1 and NAB7 lower layer (Table 1). Neolithic NAB7 only gave scanty remains of domestic cattle (a proximal femur) and caprines (permanent upper molars, one diaphysis from a juvenile), all identical to WTH3 in size. A femur from a jird is considered ancient rather than intrusive, due to its physical appearance and adhering matrix identical with the rest of the fauna: anatomically *Meriones* (Fedele 1990*d*: 161–162), it may be the king jird, the most characteristic "sand rat" of the south-western Arabian highlands.

The chance sample from Qutrān, examined by Bökönyi (1990), would vaguely confirm the picture from WTH3; domestic caprines are slightly dominant over cattle, however. As Bökönyi states, "both cattle and caprovine remains point to comparatively large domestic individuals"; in addition, "four tooth fragments and [a] humerus fragment are really large even by European standards, thus they are solid proofs of wild cattle". These contentions cannot be checked, (8) but the identification of wild cattle should be approached with caution. Apart from the presumed aurochs the wild fauna is very scanty. "A left proximal tibia fragment and a distal metatarsus fragment come from a small equid species"; ibex is indicated by a third phalanx with GL = 36.5, and the dog is "only probable".

Obviously we know very little, and the above is a rough approximation to the economies on the eastern Plateau. However, what we get is probably a picture of cattle pastoralists (Fedele 1992: 74–77; Grigson 1996: 48), which would accord well with a milder, greener mid-Holocene landscape, very different from the arid conditions of today. Grigson (1996: 65) postulated long ago a correlation between summer rainfall regime and dominance of cattle, not caprines. It is encouraging to observe that the faunal composition of WTH3 is replicated at mid-Holocene sites in the Wādī Ḏahr, north-west of Ṣanᶜāʾ, admirably studied by Kallweit (1996: 133; analysis by A. von den Driesch). The Neolithic groups at Ḏahr were most likely pastoral nomads breeding cattle, sheep, and goat, and occupying small seasonal camps situated on the flanks of the wadi.

Conclusions

Elsewhere I speculated (Fedele 1988; 1991) that most of the eastern Plateau Neolithic might represent a regional tradition, somewhat specific to the high plains and distinct from desert and coastal cultures (cf. Tosi 1986; Durrani 2005). Such an "upland Neolithic tradition" would be associated with highland settlement by early cattle herders who co-adapted to this severe landscape — albeit under climatic optimum conditions — using pastoralism and particular toolkit inventories. This tradition remains a hypothetical construct. However, if the idea is correct, it may have more in common with the parallel and broadly coeval developments in the Ethiopian Highlands, or elsewhere around the Horn of Africa, than with the Neolithic of the Near East. Yemen ought perhaps to be viewed as the southern periphery of a cultural continuum specific to the West Arabian uplands. During the subsequent Bronze Age, in the third millennium BC, the Neolithic life ways were superseded by a caprine-and-sorghum farming economy. The pastoralists of the highlands can be contrasted with the hunting groups that were active alongside the desert, where hunting presumably remained a persistent way of life and disappeared from the arid lowlands only recently.

Acknowledgements

Special thanks are due to Alessandro de Maigret for his substantial support within the Italian Archaeological Mission to Yemen. Permission for fieldwork was granted by the General Organisation of Antiquities, Manuscripts and Museums (Ṣanᶜāᵓ), then headed by Dr Yūsuf ᶜAbdallāh. The excavations were carried out with the assistance of Francesco Di Mario and the participation of Yemeni archaeologists from GOAMM and Italian students and technical staff. I am grateful to Jill Morris and particularly Daniela Zàccara for laboratory assistance, and to Mark Beech, Jeffrey A. Blakely, Ueli Brunner, Robert Carter, Joy McCorriston, Christopher Edens, Michel-Alain Garcia, Caroline Grigson, Marie-Louise Inizan, Heiko Kallweit, and Tony J. Wilkinson (among others) for literature or comments, although the use here made of this information is my sole responsibility.

Notes

1 The spelling of the place name was obtained from residents and checked with the assistance of Yemeni officers. WTH3 was initially coded WTHiii.

2 Work towards the full publication of WTH3 was resumed in 2002 after a long interruption. The archaeological collections from the site are housed at the National Museum in Ṣanᶜāᵓ, except for two small lithic assemblages temporarily exported to the University of Naples through an official agreement.

3 Stratum G in the WTH3 standard profile (Fig. 4.b; cf. units GR1 to GR3 in Fig. 5) normally represents the lower part of a distinctive "A" soil horizon, typically enriched in humus due to ecosystemic conditions and prolonged geomorphic stability.

4 Although sedimentary indications of former hearths were found (e.g. within "house" F25) well-preserved charcoal was very rare at WTH3; and, alas, several charcoal samples for radiocarbon were misplaced in Rome after preparation for shipping to the dating laboratory. Only a return to the site would allow a dating programme to be performed.

5 Unfashioned natural elements brought to the site by people (after Leakey 1971).

7 Grigson (1996: 46) remarks that, in western Arabia, "although most cattle today are zebu, there are small unhumped cattle in the mountainous part of the Yemen and it is possible that these were once more widely distributed". Unhumped taurine cattle are certainly common in the Khawlān.

8 The present whereabouts of the Qutrān collection are unknown.

References

Andrefsky W. Jr.
1998. *Lithics. Macroscopic Approaches to Analysis*. Cambridge: Cambridge University Press.

Bintliff J.L. & van Zeist W. (eds)
1982. *Palaeoclimates, Palaeoenvironments and Human Communities in the Eastern Mediterranean Region in Later Prehistory*. (British Archaeological Reports, International series, 133). Oxford: British Archaeological Reports.

Bökönyi S.
1990. Preliminary report on the animal remains of Gabal Qutrān (GQi) and Al-Masannah (MASi). Pages 145–148 in A. de Maigret (ed.), *The Bronze Age Culture of Hawlān at-Tiyāl and Al-Hadā (Republic of Yemen): A First General Report*. (IsMEO Reports and Memoirs, 24). Rome: Istituto Italiano per il Medio ed Estremo Oriente.

de Maigret A.
1983. Activities of the Italian Archaeological Mission in the Yemen Arab Republic (1983 campaign). *East and West* [N.S.] 33: 340–344.
2002. *Arabia Felix: An Exploration of the Archaeological History of Yemen*. London: Stacey International.

de Maigret A., Azzi C., Marcolongo B. & Palmieri A.M.
1989. Recent pedogenesis and neotectonics affecting archaeological sites in North Yemen. *Paléorient* 15: 239–243.

de Maigret A., Bulgarelli G.M., Fedele F.G., Marcolongo B., Scerrato U. & Ventrone G.
1984. Archaeological activities in the Yemen Arab Republic, 1984. *East and West* [N.S.] 34/4: 423–454.
de Maigret A., Fedele F. & Di Mario F.
1988. Lo Yemen prima del regno di Saba. *Le Scienze* 40/234: 12–23.
Di Mario F.
1992. L'industria "neolitica" di Wadi Ath-Tayylah, sito 3 (Repubblica dello Yemen): studio della collezione litica di superficie. *Yemen. Studi archeologici, storici e filologici sull'Arabia meridionale* 1: 55–77.
Di Mario F., Costantini L., Fedele F.G., Gravina F. & Smriglio C.
1989. The western ar-Rubᶜ al-Khālī "Neolithic": new data from the Ramlat Sabᶜatayn (Yemen Arab Republic). *Annali, Istituto Universitario Orientale* 49: 109–148.
Durrani N.
2005. *The Tihamah Coastal Plain of South-West Arabia in its Regional Context c. 6000 BC–AD 600.* (Society for Arabian Studies Monographs, 4). Oxford: Archaeopress.
Edens C.
1982. Towards a definition of the western ar-Rubᶜ al-Khālī "Neolithic". *Atlal* 6/3: 109–123.
1988. The Rubᶜ al-Khālī "neolithic" revisited: the view from Nadqan. Pages 15–43 in D.T. Potts (ed.), *Araby the Blest: Studies in Arabian Archaeology*. (Carsten Niebuhr Institute Publication, 7). Copenhagen: Museum Tusculanum.
Edens C. & Wilkinson T.J.
1998. Southwest Arabia during the Holocene: recent archaeological developments. *Journal of World Prehistory* 12/1: 55–119.
Fedele F.G.
1985. Research on Neolithic and Holocene paleoecology in the Yemeni highlands. Pages 369–373 in A. de Maigret *et al.*, Archaeological activities in the Yemen Arab Republic, 1985. *East and West* [N.S.] 35: 337–395.
1986. Neolithic and Protohistoric cultures. Excavations and researches in the eastern Highlands. Pages 396–400 in A. de Maigret et al., Archaeological activities in the Yemen Arab Republic, 1986. *East and West* [N.S.] 36: 376–470.
1987. *Research on the Neolithic and the Holocene of the Yemen Highlands, 1987.* Naples: Institute of Anthropology, University of Naples. [Unpublished circulated report for MAIRAY].
1988. North Yemen: the Neolithic. Pages 34–37 in W. Daum (ed.), *Yemen. 3000 Years of Art and Civilisation in Arabia Felix*. Innsbruck/Frankfurt am Main: Pinguin.
1990*a*. Fossil volcanism and archaeology: the North Yemen Highlands. Pages 11–23 in C. Albore Livadie & F. Widemann (eds), *Volcanology and Archaeology. Proceedings of the European Workshops of Ravello, November 1987 and March 1989.* (PACT, 25). Strasbourg: Conseil de l'Europe, European Study Group on Physical, Chemical, Biological and Mathematical Techniques Applied to Archaeology.
1990*b*. Man, land and climate: emerging interactions from the Holocene of the Yemen Highlands. Pages 31–42 in S. Bottema, G. Entjes-Nieborg & W. van Zeist (eds), *Man's Role in the Shaping of the Eastern Mediterranean Landscape*. Rotterdam/Brookfield: A.A. Balkema.
1990*c*. *Prehistoric Archaeology and Ecology in the Eastern Highlands of North Yemen. Report of Activities Conducted in February 1990.* Naples: Laboratory and Museum of Anthropology, University of Naples. [Unpublished circulated report for MAIRAY].
1990*d*. Bronze Age faunal collections from North Yemen. Pages 149–185 in A. de Maigret (ed.), *The Bronze Age Culture of Hawlān at-Tiyāl and Al-Hadā (Republic of Yemen): A First General Report*. (IsMEO Reports and Memoirs, 24). Rome: Istituto Italiano per il Medio ed Estremo Oriente.
1991. Holocene Man-animal Relations in the Yemen Highlands. Paper presented at the "Arabia Antiqua" International Conference, May 1991, Rome, *IsMEO*. [Unpublished circulated paper].
1992. Zooarchaeology in Mesopotamia and Yemen: a comparative history. *Origini. Preistoria e protostoria delle civiltà antiche* 16: 49–93.
Fedele F.G. & Zaccara D.
2005. Wādī at-Ṭayyila 3: a mid-Holocene site on the Yemen Plateau and its lithic collection. Pages 213–245 in A.M. Sholan, S. Antonini & M. Arbach (eds), *Sabaean Studies. Archaeological, Epigraphical and*

Historical Studies in Honour of Yūsuf M. ᶜAbdallāh, Alessandro de Maigret, Christian J. Robin on the Occasion of Their Sixtieth Birthdays. Naples: Yemeni-Italian Centre for Archaeological Researches/ Ṣanᶜāʾ: University of Ṣanᶜāʾ and Centre français d'archéologie et de sciences sociales de Ṣanᶜāʾ.

Francaviglia V.
1990. Obsidian sources in ancient Yemen. Pages 129–136 in A. de Maigret (ed.), *The Bronze Age Culture of Hawlān at-Tiyāl and Al-Hadā (Republic of Yemen): A First General Report.* (IsMEO Reports and Memoirs, 24). Rome: Istituto Italiano per il Medio ed Estremo Oriente.

French C.A.I.
2003. The Dhamar region, central highlands, Yemen. Pages 224–234 in C. French (ed.), *Geoarchaeology in Action. Studies in Soil Micromorphology and Landscape Evolution.* London: Routledge.

Garcia M-A. & Rachad M.
1997. *L'Art des Origines au Yémen.* Paris: Éditions du Seuil.

Garcia M., Rachad M., Hadjouis D., Inizan M-L. & Fontugne M.
1991. Découvertes préhistoriques au Yémen, le contexte archéologique de l'art rupestre de la région de Saada. *Comptes rendus de l'Académie des Sciences de Paris* 313/2: 1201–1206.

Grigson C.
1976. The craniology and relationships of four species of Bos. 3: Basic craniology: Bos taurus L. sagittal profiles and other non-measurable characters. *Journal of Archaeological Science* 3: 115–136.

1980. The craniology and relationships of four species of Bos. 5: Bos indicus L. *Journal of Archaeological Science* 7: 3–32.

1989. Size and sex: evidence for the domestication of cattle in the Near East. Pages 77–109 in A. Milles, D. Williams & N. Gardner (eds), *The Beginnings of Agriculture.* (British Archaeological Reports, International series, 496/Symposia of the Association for Environmental Archaeology, 8). Oxford: British Archaeological Reports.

1996. Early cattle around the Indian Ocean. Pages 41–74 in J. Reade (ed.), *The Indian Ocean in Antiquity.* London: Kegan Paul International/The British Museum/New York: Kegan Paul International.

Grolier M.J. & Overstreet W.C.
1978. *Geologic Map of the Yemen Arab Republic (Ṣanᶜāʾ).* (US Geological Survey Miscellaneous Investigations Series, Map I-1143-B). Reston, VA: US Geological Survey.

Kallweit H.
1996 [2001]. *Neolithische und Bronzezeitliche Besiedlung im Wadi Dhahr, Republik Jemen. Eine Untersuchung auf der basis von Geländebegehungen und Sondagen.* Inaugural-Dissertation der Philosophischen Fakultäten der Albert-Ludwigs-Universität zu Freiburg i. Br. [Unpublished].

Kuijt I. & Chesson M.S.
2005. Lumps of clay and pieces of stone: ambiguity, bodies, and identity as portrayed in Neolithic figurines. Pages 152–183 in S. Pollock & R. Bernbeck (eds), *Archaeologies of the Middle East. Critical Perspectives.* Oxford: Blackwell.

Leakey M.D.
1971. *Olduvai Gorge, 3: Excavations in Beds I and II, 1960–63.* Cambridge/London: Cambridge University Press.

Lentini A.
1988. Preliminary pollen analysis of paleosoil [sic] horizon in the Yalā area. Pages 52–53 in A. de Maigret (ed.), *The New Sabaean Archaeological Complex in the Wādī Yalā (Eastern Hawlān at-Tiyāl, Yemen Arab Republic). A Preliminary Report.* Rome: Istituto Italiano per il Medio ed Estremo Oriente.

Lézine A-M., Saliège J-F., Robert C., Wertz F. & Inizan M-L.
1998. Holocene lakes from Ramlat as-Sabᶜatayn (Yemen) illustrate the impact of monsoon activity in southern Arabia. *Quaternary Research* 50: 290–299.

McCorriston J.
2000. Early settlement in Hadramawt: preliminary report on prehistoric occupation at Shiʾb Munayder. *Arabian Archaeology and Epigraphy* 11/2: 129–153.

Marcolongo B. & Palmieri A.M.
1986. Palaeoenvironmental conditions in the areas of Wādī at-Tayyilah and Baraqiš: preliminary report. Pages 461–464 in de Maigret et al., Archaeological activities in the Yemen Arab Republic, 1986. *East and West* [N.S.] 36: 376–470.
1988. Environmental modification and settlement conditions in the Yalā area. Pages 45–51 in A. de Maigret (ed.), *The New Sabaean Archaeological Complex in the Wādī Yalā (Eastern Hawlān at-Tiyāl, Yemen Arab Republic). A Preliminary Report*. Rome: Istituto Italiano per il Medio ed Estremo Oriente.

Marshall F.
1989. Rethinking the role of Bos indicus in Sub-saharan Africa. *Current Anthropology* 30/2: 235–240.

Overstreet W.C. & Grolier M.J.
1996. Summary of environmental background for the human occupation of the al-Jadidah basin in Wadi al-Jubah, Yemen Arab Republic. Pages 337–429 in M.J. Grolier, R. Brinkmann & J.A. Blakely (eds), *Environmental Research in Support of Archaeological Investigations in the Yemen Arab Republic, 1982–1987*. Washington, DC: American Foundation for the Study of Man.

Overstreet W.C., Grolier M.J. & Toplyn M.R.
1988. *The Wadi al-Jubah Archaeological Project, 4: Geological and Archaeological Reconnaissance in the Yemen Arab Republic, 1985*. Washington, DC: American Foundation for the Study of Man.

Parker A., Davies C. & Wilkinson T.
2006. The early to mid-Holocene moist period in Arabia: some recent evidence from lacustrine sequences in eastern and south-western Arabia. *Proceedings of the Seminar for Arabian Studies* 36: 243–255.

Tosi M.
1986. The emerging picture of prehistoric Arabia. *Annual Review of Anthropology* 15: 461–490.

Uerpmann H-P.
1987. *The Ancient Distribution of Ungulate Mammals in the Middle East*. (Beihefte zum Tübinger Atlas des Vorderen Orients, Reihe A 27). Wiesbaden: Dr. Ludwig Reichert Verlag.
1991. *Equus africanus* in Arabia. Pages 12–33 in R.H. Meadow & H-P. Uerpmann (eds), *Equids in the Ancient World*. ii. (Beihefte zum Tübinger Atlas des Vorderen Orients, Reihe A 19/2). Wiesbaden: Dr. Ludwig Reichert Verlag.

Uerpmann M.
1992. Structuring the Late Stone Age of southeastern Arabia. *Arabian Archaeology and Epigraphy* 3: 65–109.

Wilkinson T.J.
1997. Holocene environments of the high plateau, Yemen, recent geoarchaeological investigations. *Geoarchaeology, an International Journal* 12/8: 833–864.
2005. Soil erosion and valley fills in the Yemen highlands and southern Turkey: integrating settlement, geoarchaeology, and climate change. *Geoarchaeology, an International Journal* 20/2: 169–192.

Wilkinson T.J., Edens C. & Gibson McG.
1997. The archaeology of the Yemen High Plains: a preliminary chronology. *Arabian Archaeology and Epigraphy* 8: 99–142.

Author's address
Francesco G. Fedele, Chair and Laboratory of Anthropology, University of Naples "Federico II", via Mezzocannone 8, 80134 Naples, Italy.
e-mail ffedele01@yahoo.it

Proceedings of the Seminar for Arabian Studies 38 (2008): 173–186

Nineteenth century settlement patterns at Zekrit, Qatar: pottery, tribes and territory

Alexandrine Guérin & Faysal ᶜAbdallah al-Naᵓimi

Summary

In 2002 the French archaeological mission in Qatar commenced a research programme dealing with the Islamic period in Qatar. The first phase treated the methods of establishment in the desert and posed the problem of the description of tribal territories and the phenomenon of sedentarization during the modern period. The site of Zekrit offers the possibility of testing these questions. Three excavation campaigns were carried out from 2002 to 2005, followed by a study season in 2006.

The site is located at the southern end of the bay of Zekrit, which skirts the small peninsula next to the town of Dukhan, up to 40 m from the shore of the Arabian Gulf. The entire site covers some 18,000 m^2 (200×90 m) and includes two built structures, namely a fort and a *madbassa* close to the shore. The fort is quadrangular, measuring about 50 m on each side, and has circular or quadrangular towers. A third zone of investigation is related to an area of encampment between the fortress and the *madbassa*.

The importance of this study lies firstly in the short duration of occupation of the site as it was only occupied for about a century, and secondly in the information it gives on the local plain ware assemblage of pottery. Few publications deal with this type of material and the traditional chronological discussions are based on the so-called "luxury wares" (either glazed or porcelain), whereas studies devoted to "common wares" in this region are virtually unknown.

Keywords: Qatar, nineteenth century, tribes, territory, fortress, *madbassa*, encampment, pottery

Introduction

First known from the surveys of B. de Cardi in 1973–1974, the fort at Zekrit (Fig. 1) is dated to the recent era through the surface ceramics and is comparable in plan with other forts of this period in Qatar — i.e. the end of the eighteenth and beginning of the nineteenth centuries — for example at Al-Huwaylah and Zubara. The ceramic assemblage is comparable with those found at these sites. It includes Chinese imports (blue and white porcelain, maroon or black glazes), and other glazed ceramics (blue and white, brown and olive) which are characteristic markers of the nineteenth century (Fig. 2) (Garlake 1978*a*; Hardy-Guilbert 1980; 1991).

The fort of Zekrit is mentioned briefly in English sources: "There are in this place 12 wells built with the ruins of a fort built by Rahmat B Jabayr at the beginning of the 19th century" (Lorimer 1970, ii/B: 1576). It would seem that this fort might have been built at the beginning of the nineteenth century when Rahmat b. Jabayr seized Zubara in 1809 and installed his hegemony over this part of Qatari territory at the northern end of the peninsula. Zekrit represents the southernmost point of the territorial expansion of this tribal head, but this superiority was short-lived since in 1811 the town of Zubara was once again seized by the tribe of Al-Thani. Rahmat b. Jabayr retreated to the town of Damman at the time of his eviction from Zubara. One cannot know from the current state of research if the fort of Zekrit became a retreat zone for the troops of Rahmat b. Jabayr, or if the abandonment was total. The known acts of piracy of one member of this clan as late as 1841 raise the possibility of the continuing use of this coastal fort as a base or place of refuge, as it was located in an inlet with difficult access. The documentary sources do not inform us as to the possible destruction of the fort by the ruling power, which could be contemporary with the destruction of the fleet of Jasim b. Jabayr in 1841. It would seem that the fortress was reoccupied at the beginning of the twentieth century, and the sheikh of the modern village of Zekrit claims to have seen the fortress still standing as late as the 1920s. The complete destruction of the site as one can see it today is due not only to wind erosion but also to its dismantling for reuse of the stone by the local inhabitants.

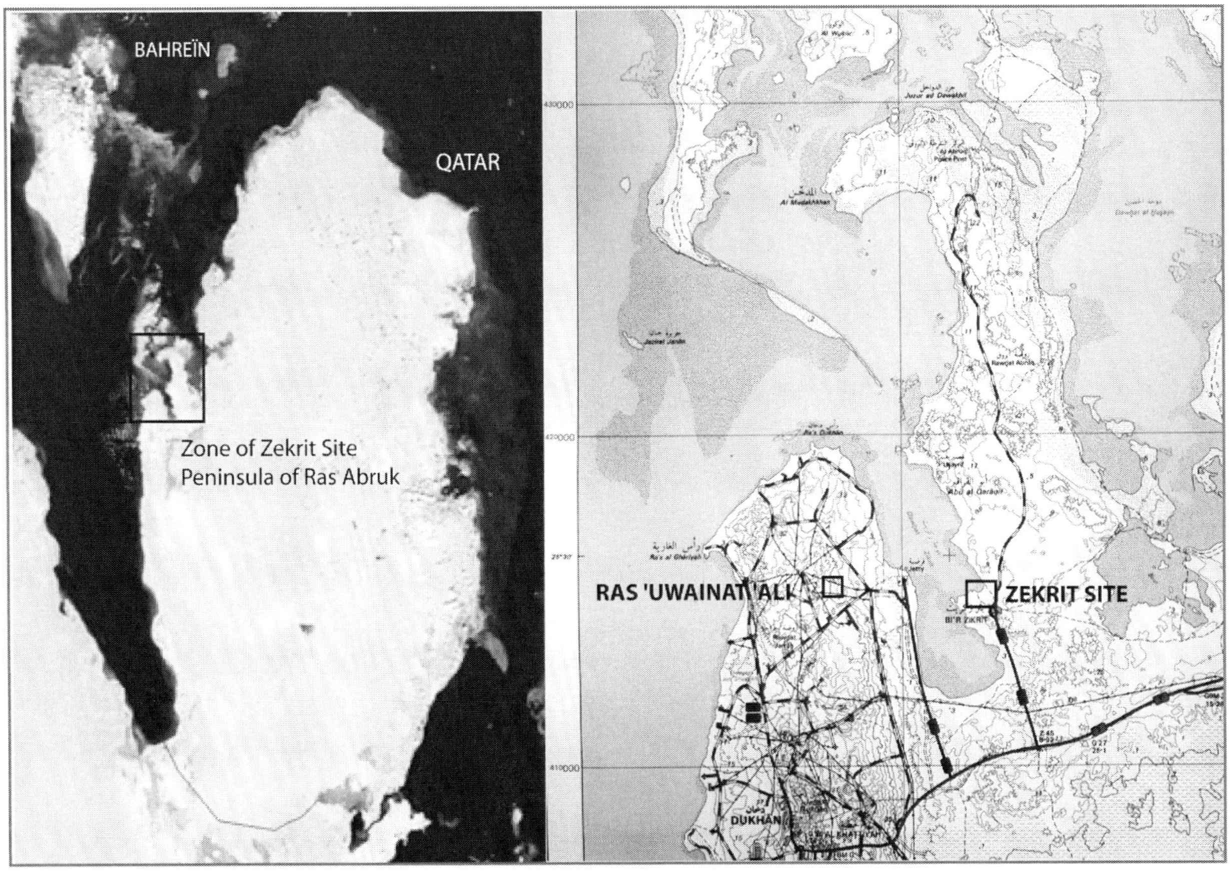

Figure 1. *The location of Zekrit, Qatar.*

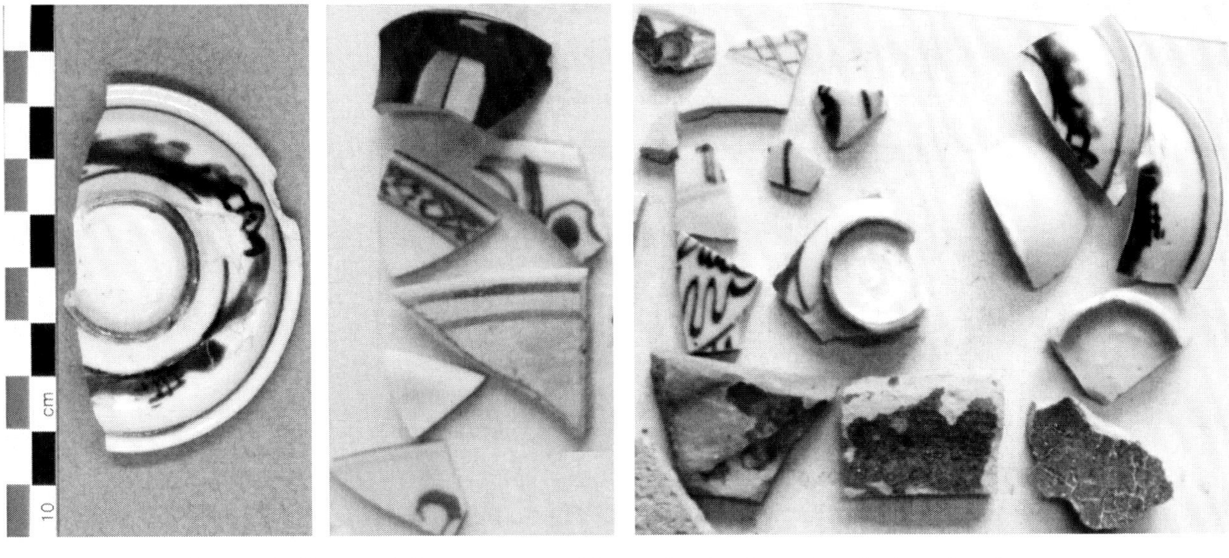

Figure 2. *Imported Chinese pottery (blue and white, brown) and other glazed wares from Zekrit, all datable to the 19th century.*

The investigations carried out during the three archaeological seasons enabled a comprehensive study of the archaeological site and show intensive occupation of different types. The fortress does not seem to have been a particularly sophisticated piece of defensive architecture but it corresponds to a place of surveillance of the desert territories, controlling the zone of Ras-Abaruk with its protected anchorages and control of maritime territories.

The English and Arab documentary sources confirm the construction of this fortress by Rahmat b. Jabayr, who was a significant character as he was head of the tribe and led various expeditions against the ruling powers at the beginning of the nineteenth century. This fortress would also represent a mark of tribal territory. During this period, other tribes close to the government also seemed well endowed with fortresses on the northern coast of the Qatar peninsula, but the Zekrit zone would have been under the authority of an opponent, Rahmat b. Jabayr. The presence of a *madbassa* (date-syrup factory) of some size and so close to the sea suggests there was trade between Qatar and Bahrain at the beginning of the nineteenth century: there are no palm plantations along this broad zone of the western coast and we therefore suppose the dates were imported by sea. These exchanges were facilitated by the privileged relations that Rahmat b. Jabayr maintained with some of the tribes of Bahrain. The surveys carried out in the intermediate zone reveal traces of occupation, doubtless from temporary encampments.

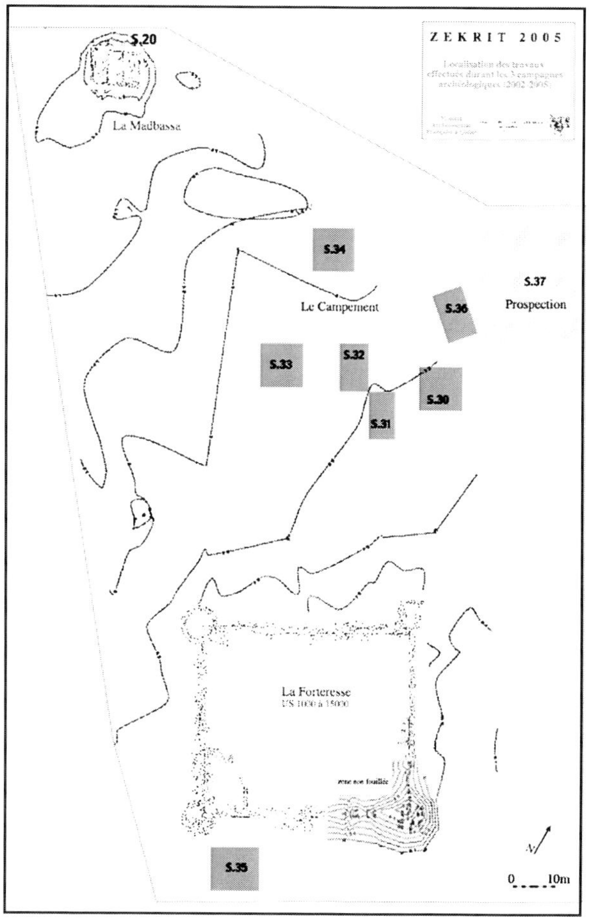

FIGURE 3. *The site.*

The site of Zekrit

The fortress

The Zekrit fortress is 52.20 m long and 45 m across (Fig. 3). Two gates allowed access: the south gate is 6.50 m wide and was perhaps the main entrance whereas the second opening is a small northern door, measuring only 1.40 m across, which gave access to the *madbassa* and faced the sea.

A circular or quadrangular tower was added to each corner. The circular towers were not joined to the curtain walls at ground level, at least not in the two excavated cases, whereas the rectangular tower was constructed at the same time as the curtain walls. The towers were built to a height of one or two storeys.

The ruins measure between 0.80 m and 2.35 m high. The walls of the fort are preserved up to 2.20 m high, and 3.80 m above sea level. The south-western tower reaches a total height of 4.28 m at its centre and its external walls are preserved at a height of 2.35 m. The uppermost parts of the structure are buried in a layer of stones and sand, beneath which there is a layer of gypsum of uneven thickness (measuring between 0.10 and 0.52 m). Beneath these destruction horizons we come to the level of occupation. It is very difficult to distinguish the phases of construction and occupation. Interior installations are perceptible and include several 4 m-wide by 3 m-deep cells with benches and partitions, and a number of hearths. An in-depth survey also revealed some turquoise blue glazed ceramics of the Abbasid period (ninth century) but no traces of structures belonging to this period were found, suggesting that there was a temporary encampment on the site contemporary with the nearby extensive site of Uwaynat ʿAli, located on the opposite side of the bay of Zekrit. This last site currently lies within the zone of oil drillings of the Qatar Petroleum Company but was catalogued by the British team during their 1973 survey.

Investigation zones at Zekrit	Fortress	Madbassa	Encampment	Survey (extension of the encampment)	Total Zekrit Site
Total no. diagnostic sherds	226	16	446	179	867
Total no. non-diagnostic sherds	1563	48	2497	1834	5942
Total no. sherds	1789	64	2943	2013	6809

Table 1. *Frequency of pottery in the different excavation areas and surface survey collection.*

The *madbassa*

A *madbassa* is a structure intended for the transformation of dates into syrup. During its operation, the *madbassa* consisted of three adjacent rooms. The openings were all built in the central axis of each room; those in the eastern and western rooms measured 1.50 m across whereas the central room had a slightly narrower opening measuring 1.40 m across. Insets on either side of this door restricted access to no more than 1 m. No traces of door sockets were found and it is unclear whether the doors were single or double-leaved. The interior of each room was filled with a gypsum-coated structure containing various numbers of drains intended to collect the date syrup. These furrows were orientated north-east–south-west, parallel with the longest sides of the building and dipping down to the south-west in order to facilitate the flow of the syrup. They joined a transverse drain dug to the south of the structure; another drain, dug in the eastern part, allowed the flow of the date extract towards an earthenware jar placed below. The gradient of the longest drains varied from 3.5 cm to 4.5 cm per metre. The dip of the transversal drains varied from 1.5 cm per metre to 3 cm per metre.

A second and domestic phase of use of the *madbassa* is represented by an abundance of hearths with large scatters of ash inside and outside the rooms. Four coral-built hearths were located in the west (diameter of hearth A: 0.75 m), one in the south (0.50 m from the door of the central room; diameter of double hearth B: 1.50 m), and two further hearths measuring 2 m and 1.40 m across were situated 1 m to the east.

The western room had hearths directly installed on the ground, including a larger one with an area of ash rake-out in the north-eastern corner. The central room also contained four hearths built directly in the soil of the occupation area. Two of these occupied almost half of the surface of the room. The eastern room did not include any such remains and the two door casings are flat with no evidence for door sockets. This room seems to have been abandoned during this phase and its function is unclear. We do not presently know if this phase pre-dates the abandonment of the fortress between the beginning of the twentieth century and *c.* 1920, or whether it was contemporary with the first abandonment of the fortress in the middle of the nineteenth century. No ceramics or other evidence for dating were found belonging to this phase.

The encampment

The encampment was the third zone of investigation and corresponds to the "empty" area between the northern enclosure of the fortress and the *madbassa* situated on the shore. This 127 m-long zone also makes it possible to fill a gap observed at the time of excavation of the fortress. Indeed, the fort has very few interior installations. It does not seem that there was an intensive occupation of the construction area. At the time of prior excavations we had highlighted a wide room in the south-western corner of the fortress, as well as five small cells along the internal face of the eastern enclosure wall. Despite the investigations that we carried out both inside and outside and close to the fortress, we must conclude that there were no other traces of building. The seven surveys, numbered from 30 to 36, were carried out in quincunxes and in areas containing a strong density of ceramic material close to the hearths.

Finally, along and across the modern thoroughfare leading to Ras-Abaruk at the northern end of the Zekrit peninsula and skirting the site on its eastern face, a survey was undertaken over an area measuring 90 m x 40 m. A specific collection pick-up was carried out over an area measuring 26×31 m.

The ceramics

Methodology and research strategy

The ceramic materials discovered at Zekrit come from all three areas of excavation (fortress, *madbassa*, and encampment) and the surface survey collection. Sampling amounts to 7093 items (diagnostic and undiagnostic sherds) divided into 6809 items (diagnostic and undiagnostic sherds) of common ceramics and 284 pieces (diagnostic and undiagnostic sherds) of glazed earthenware and porcelain (Tab. 1). This last group accounted for only 4% of the total material found and will be the subject of a future study in order to determine their sources. Our objective here is to present an analysis of the common wares which were classified according to ware and form. The study concludes by linking these dual classifications with the results of the archaeological investigations, and discusses their find spot, function, and relative quantity per sector.

The importance of this study lies firstly in the short duration of occupation of the site as it was only occupied for about a century, and secondly in the information it gives on the local plain ware assemblage of pottery. Few publications deal with this type of material and the traditional chronological discussions are based on the so-called "luxury wares" (either glazed or porcelain), whereas studies devoted to "common wares" are virtually unknown. (2) This thorough catalogue of the pottery from Zekrit attempts to fill this gap as far as possible for the period from the end of the eighteenth or beginning of the nineteenth to the beginning of the twentieth centuries. Moreover this corpus will find an echo in archaeological investigations carried out by Qatari teams and focused on the sites of fortresses and towns of the early modern period. For some fifteen years teams have been investigating the site of Zubara, a fortified city founded in the middle of the eighteenth century, and since 2004 excavations have been underway at the site of the fortress and *madbassa* at Frayhat. The study and analysis of the ceramics from these two contemporary sites will give a significant insight into the material culture in Qatar in these periods and for which equivalent published sources are sadly lacking. The ceramic corpus of Zekrit was thus compiled from the point of view of a work of co-operative venture with our Qatari colleagues.

Ware typology

Methodology

After an initial visual sort of all the sherds, a macroscopic description was conducted in order to define a classification of all the wares present. (3) The following categories were detailed:

- the colour and hardness of the ware (from 1 – very crumbly, to 7 – very hard)
- the nature of the inclusions (clay nodules, quartz, gypsum, volcanic rock)
- the size of the inclusions (in mm)
- the shape of the inclusions (from very round to very angular) and the abundance of additives (in %)
- the granulometric distribution of additives (from very good to dispersed).

The descriptive cards were supplemented with photographs at various scales, the internal and external faces of the sample, and the cross-section. For the restricted corpus at Zekrit, ten wares were given (assigned letter codes A to J). The definition of these wares also makes it possible to include all the non-diagnostic sherds (totalling 5942 from all sectors).

Results

Among the ten distinguished wares, only one lacks any gypsum inclusions: this is ware D, which looks laminated whereas all the other wares contain nodules or slivers of gypsum. Without confirming a local production source for all these wares, it should be noted that the local peninsula of Ras-Abaruk, where Zekrit is located, is rich in gypsum deposits.

Wares A, B, and C (Fig. 4) comprise inclusions of small quartz sizes as well as gypsum but in a smaller quantity than the other wares (1 to 3%). These wares are usually used as table ware (wide bowls and dishes) and for storage (jars or jugs).

Wares E, F, and H (samples 1 and 2) have the same inclusions but in a more significant proportion (5 to 7%) and of a larger size (Fig. 5). The majority of these wares carry traces of burning and seem intended for the kitchen.

Wares H (sample 3), I, and J (Fig. 6) also contain gypsum and quartz inclusions, but a third type of inclusion defines the ware, viz. possible iron nodules, fragments of volcanic rock which could be basalt (very frequently found in the area of Ras-Abaruk), and orange gypsum concretion. Some earthenware jars of large diameter (18 cm or larger) are manufactured with wares H (3) and I; ware J seems to be a coarse ware, possibly intended for cooking (standard F122).

Ware G is a single item: it is an earthenware storage or transport jar with the remains of a pair of handles and a "button" base; the neck was not found. The jar was discovered *in situ* in the *madbassa* at the base of the date-syrup drains. No other sherds of this ware were discovered at the site. All things considered, we propose

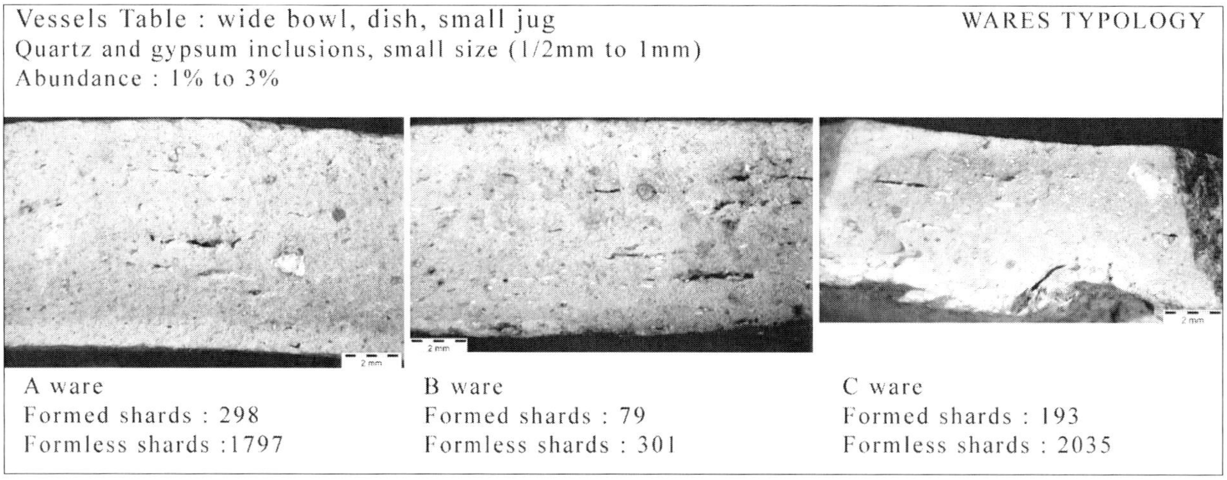

FIGURE 4. *Ware typology: photomicrographs of a bowl, a dish, and small jug.*

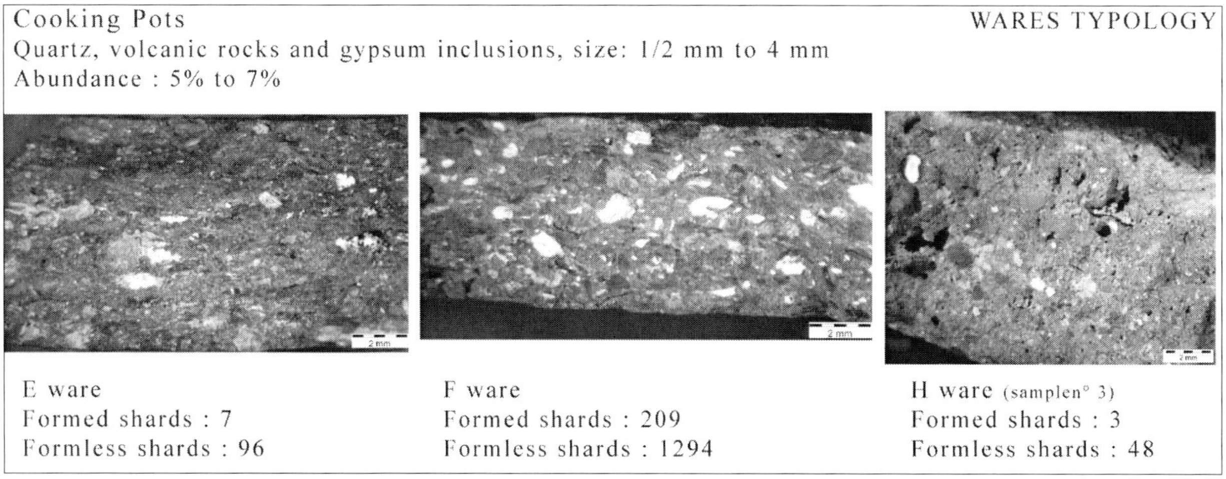

FIGURE 5. *Ware typology: photomicrographs of cooking vessels.*

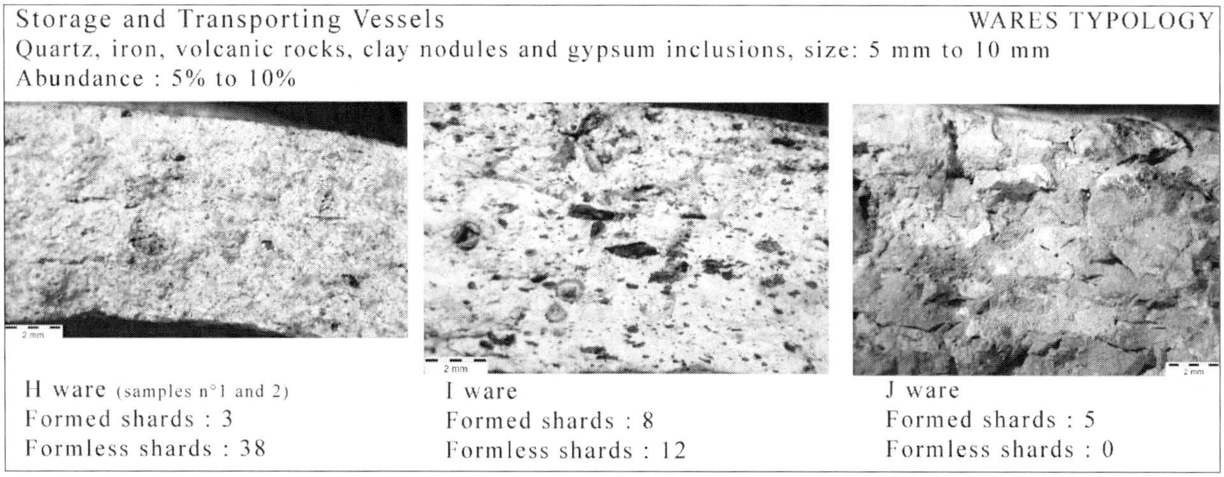

FIGURE 6. *Ware typology: photomicrographs of storage and transport vessels.*

Ware	A	B	C	D	E	F	G	H	I	J	Total no. diagnostic sherds	Total no. sherds
Diagnostic/non-diagnostic	100/ 535	- -	85/ 658	2/ 22	- -	39/ 348	- -	- -	- -	- -		
Total no. sherds	635		743	24		387					226	1,789
% diagnostic/total by ware	16%		11%	8%		10%						Diagnostic sherds/total 13%

Table 2. *Frequency of pottery wares from the fortress.*

Ware	A	B	C	D	E	F	G	H	I	J	Total no. diagnostic sherds	Total no. sherds
Diagnostic/non-diagnostic	7/12	0/5	5/22	- -	- -	3/9	1/0	- -	- -	- -	16	66
Total no. sherds	19	5	29			12	1					
% diagnostic/total by ware	36%	-	17%	-	-	25%	-	-	-	-		Diagnostic sherds/total 23%

Table 3. *Frequency of pottery wares from the madbassa.*

Ware	A	B	C	D	E	F	G	H	I	J	Total no. diagnostic sherds	Total Pottery sherds Of the Encampment
Diagnostic/non-diagnostic	121/ 607	63/ 125	85/ 854	50/ 266	3/ 63	115/ 531	- -	4/44	0/7	5/0		
Total no. sherds	728	188	939	316	66	646		48	7	5	446	2943
% diagnostic/total by ware	16%	33%	9%	16%	5%	18%	-	8%	-	100%		Formed sherds/total 15%

Table 4. *Frequency of pottery from the encampment.*

Ware	A	B	C	D	E	F	G	H	I	J	Total Formed Sherds	Total Pottery sherds of the Survey
Diagnostic/non-diagnostic	70/ 643	16/ 171	18/ 500	9/ 32	4/ 33	52/ 406	- -	2/44	8/5	- -		
Total no. sherds	713	187	518	41	37	458		46	13		179	2,013
% diagnostic/total by ware	10%	8,5%	3%	21%	10%	11%	-	4%	13%	-		Formed sherds/total 9%

Table 5. *Frequency of pottery from the survey of the encampment.*

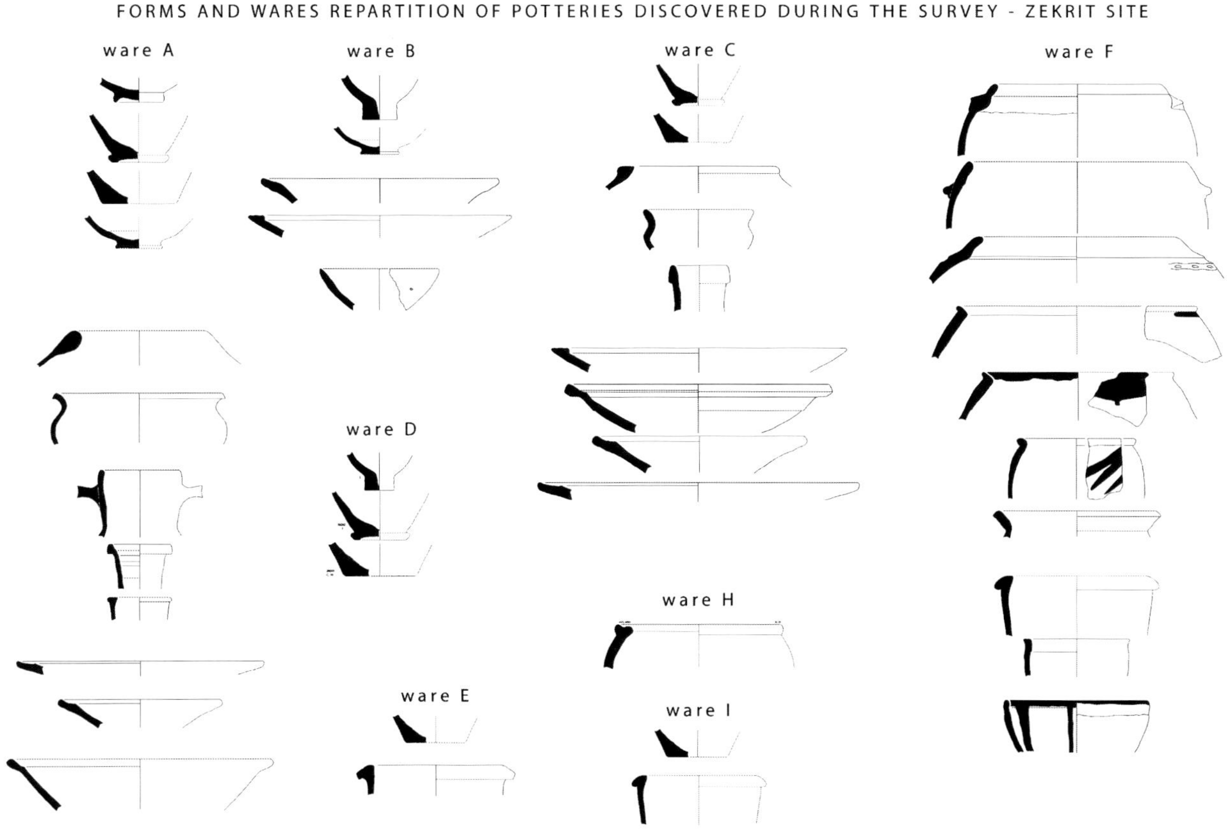

Figure 7. *Forms and wares discovered during the Zekrit site survey.*

that this is an import, perhaps from Bahrain whence the dates possibly came.

Wares A, C, and F are the most frequent amongst the material found at Zekrit. Ware A totals 2095 sherds (31% of the total), Ware C totals 2229 sherds (33% of the total), and Ware F 1503 sherds (22% of the total). Wares B, D, E, G, H, I, and J comprise the remaining 14% of the pottery.

Form typology

Methodology

The total number of the diagnostic sherds from Zekrit comes to 867 pieces including the closed shapes (F), the open shapes (O), and the bases (B). Handles and spouts were too rare to be categorized by form. From this sample of 867 pieces, eighty-three types were defined and classified (Figs. 7 and 8).

Results

The closed shapes (F) — the cooking pots without necks, included in the type "F1" — have a single inward-facing lip and horizontal handles placed on the top of the body. The earthenware storage or transport jars have lips with a surface that is more or less flattened and if the handles are present, they are arranged vertically on the body. Type "F2" — a cooking pot with a short neck — is very well represented, firstly by a series of parts with a frayed lip or a short flat surface and secondly by another series with a rising fine lip with an interior ledge-rim lid support. These types are exclusively made from ware F, are sometimes decorated with red paint (vertical bands on the interior of the neck), and have a completely rounded or flat base. Only three types are manufactured with a different ware (wares A, C): these have the characteristic of a slightly sloped lip with an inward bevelled rim or a more or less flattened rim.

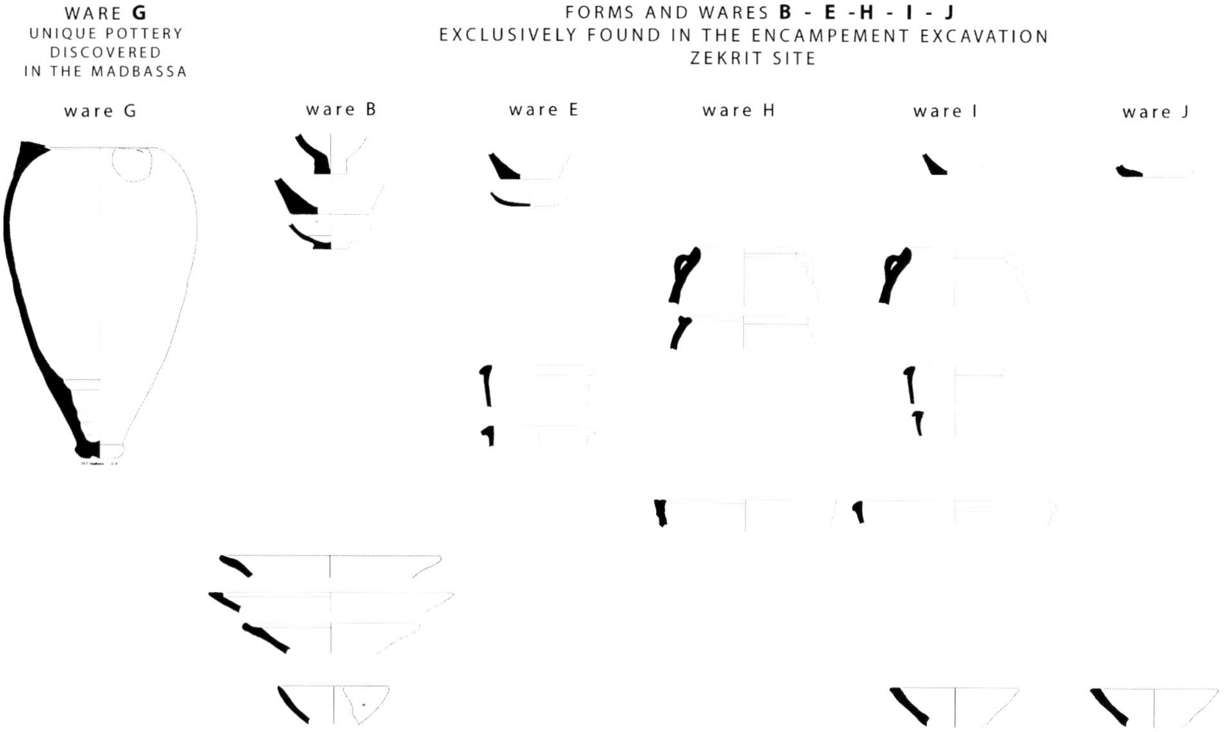

FIGURE 8. *Forms and wares found in the encampment excavation during the Zekrit site survey.*

The pots with a very wide opening compared with the body were intended for storage and the conservation or preparation of food (F3). Exclusively produced from wares A and C, except for one case in particular (F372 in ware F), they have a frayed and rounded or bevelled lip. Two types have an interior ridge.

The jars and jugs have the constant feature of a high neck and straight wall (F4). The lip has a rounded rim but most of the pieces have a partly flat surface lip with a certain number of variations, i.e. more or less flattened, projecting, or bevelled. A single specimen of a padded lip and two specimens of a flat rim complete the sample.

The open vessels (O) — the kitchen series, ware F — are represented in a series of bowls or deep "salad bowls" whose walls are either straight or slightly convex. They are the type with a round rim and a fine padded rim, which sometimes have red painted decoration inside and outside. Two other types with a lip, whose rim is a partly flat surface either on the interior or the exterior, are wares A and I.

The bowls and very wide dishes can be divided into pieces whose lips finish with a *marli* (O2) and pieces whose lips are marked with a pronounced interior projection (O3). All these pieces are manufactured from wares A and C, some rare B (O211 and O261a), and D (O331). Some large dishes with convex walls supplement this category of "open-vessels" (ten specimens, seven types), whose wares for the broadest diameters (24 to 28 cm) are H, I, and F. While for the narrowest diameters (10 to 14 cm), the wares are similar to those that are indexed for the bowls and deep salad bowls (wares A and C). Four of the types have a flat rim (F491 with F494).

The bases (B) are indexed in five types with their variations. The high circular bases and "button" bases are wares A, B, C, and D and are to be joined to the shaped earthenware storage jars or transporting jars (F131, F161, F172, and F191). The annular base, which is more or less oblique (B22 and B23), corresponds to either the small jug or the bowls and dishes. They are for the most part manufactured from ware A, some specimens are in wares C and D, and there is only one example of ware F. Finally the flat and disc bases are rather common, although they are not very discernible because they are fragmented. The disc bases are associated with the earthenware storage or transport jars, generally in wares A and C, while the flat bases are associated with the kitchen pots in ware F.

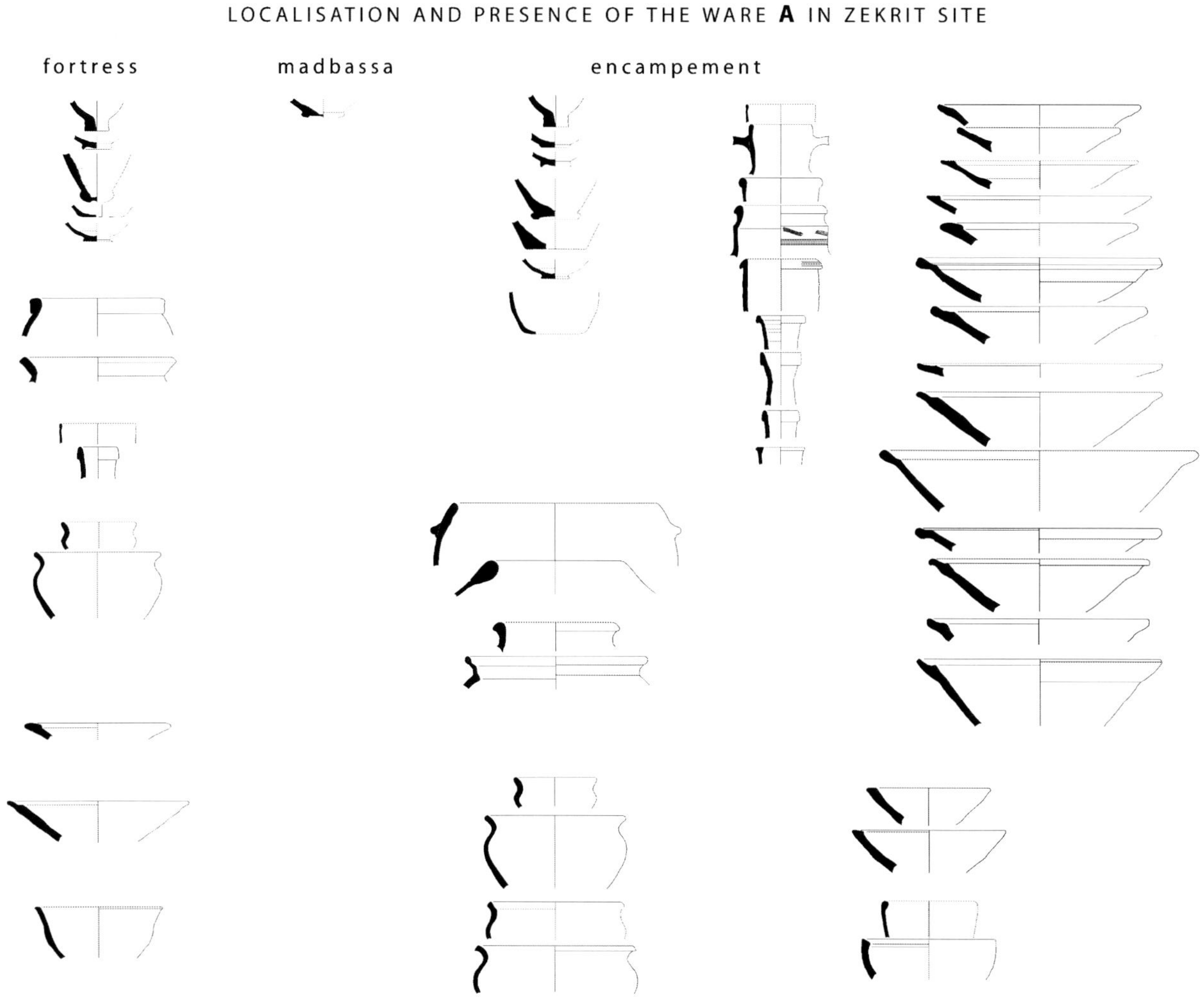

FIGURE 9. *Localisation of Ware A at Zekrit.*

Comparison of classifications by ware and form

Methodology

Each illustration links the presence of a ware (i.e. A, B etc) with its spatial distribution (Figs. 9-11). The survey zone is treated separately because the stratigraphic and space data are not comparable.

Results

The complete inventory of the ceramics shows the quantitative distribution of ceramics across the three zones of occupation at the site. The encampment is particularly rich and 61% of the pottery was discovered in this area (2013 sherds including 446 shapes found among the total of the material discovered in the excavation — 4796 sherds). The material of the fortress represents 37% (1789 sherds including 226 shapes) while the *madbassa* was particularly poor: only sixty-four sherds were discovered here, representing sixteen shapes. This quasi-absence of material is specific to all "work-zones", which implies a seasonal activity (period of transformation of dates after their harvest). In addition, the lack of direct stratigraphic relation between the fortress (dated from the beginning of the nineteenth century) and the *madbassa* does not make it possible to determine the utilization period of this artisanal zone.

Finally, the prevalence of the material in the

Figure 10. *Localisation of Ware C at Zekrit.*

encampment shows an intense occupation in this area without permanent buildings. In the fortress, despite its great number of rooms, only four wares are present (A–D, F).

With A, C, and D characteristic wares, the table vessels and jugs account for 78% of the material of the fortress while the kitchen ware (F) only represents 22%. The fortress was not a place with prevalence for preparation and cooking, but the consumption of food, and the reception of it were more significant. We observe an identical proportion of the above wares in the *madbassa* area. Indeed, in addition to the quasi-complete earthenware jar and a single specimen of ware G, table wares and jugs comprise 82% while kitchen ware F reaches 18%. In the encampment zone all of the wares are present. The wares allotted to the table ware (A, C) account for 57% of the material, the kitchen ware (F, E) accounts for 24%, and the storage vessels account for 19% (B, D, I, J). Formal sampling is also complete in the zone of the encampment.

The inventory of the items coming from this survey present, with some minor variations (table: 61%, kitchen: 25%, storage: 15%), an identical distribution of the wares and thus of the functions of the pottery present

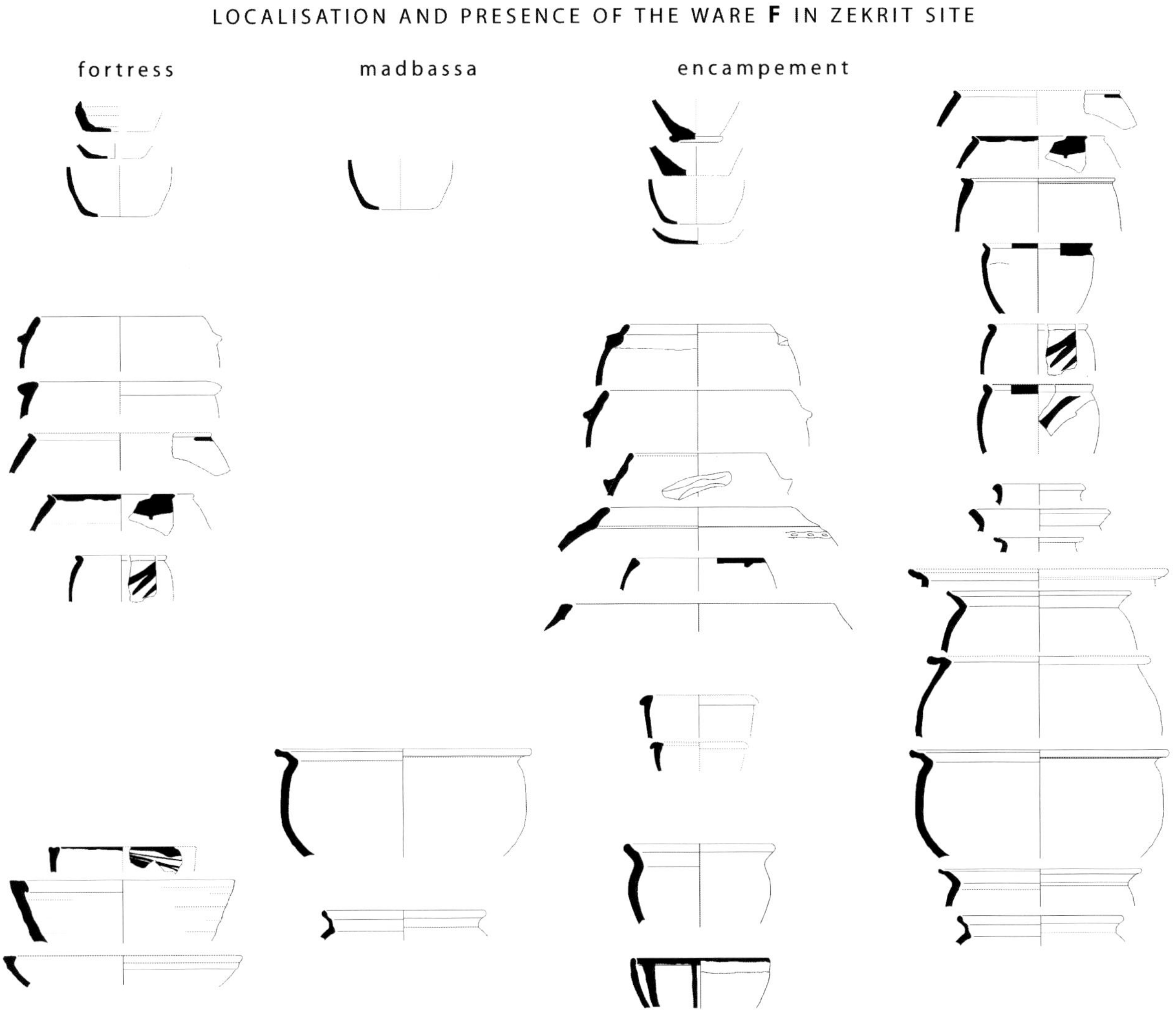

FIGURE 11. *Localisation of Ware F at Zekrit.*

in the excavated zone of the encampment. This zone of survey is located on the eastern edge of survey 36 (zone of encampment) and seems to be only one extension of the latter. Only the proportion of shapes is less than half of that found in the stratigraphic context (15% of shapes in the encampment, 8% of shapes in the survey).

Lastly, the observation of the source of glazed items and the porcelains, generally of Chinese import, repeat exactly the same pattern of space distribution of the table vessels: 21% of the material as discovered in the fortress, 47% in the zone of encampment, and 32% come from the survey. These observations show a significant occupation of the zone of encampment as a place of transformation of food (kitchen and cooking) and an area of consumption of these preparations. Part of the preparation and the cooking of food seem to be intended for the population of the fortress, but this zone is not only an additional kitchen for the fortress, it is in fact a place of production, consumption, and storage. Sampling is complete in this zone. Life was organized in structures which where not fixed and perhaps varied in a temporary and/or seasonal way. Indeed, the artisanal zone of the *madbassa* functioned only for a few months each year and the population diversified its economy with an occupation related to cattle (goats, sheep, and dromedaries) or to its geographical context, i.e. the coast. The harvest of pearl-bearing oysters is attested by a significant deposit of shells close to the *madbassa* and the protected situation of this complex at the end of the inlet allowed strategic protection as well as specific sorties in the Gulf (fishing, trade of coastal traffic, acts of piracy?).

The study of the coarse wares proves the intense occupation of a zone that was not composed of fixed structures. This area was possibly also a seasonal encampment closely associated with a fortress and an artisanal zone, which would also have been seasonal.

Notes

1 This programme is supported by the French Ministry of Foreign Affairs and the Maison de l'Orient et de la Méditerranée-Jean Pouilloux (Lyon). The director of the French Team would like to express profound gratitude to H.E. Sheikha Al-Mayyassah b. Hamad b. Khalifa Al-Thani, Minister for the Culture of Qatar and H.E. Sheikh Hassan b. Mohammad b. Ali Al-Thani, Vice Chairperson of Qatar Museum Authority. It is authorized by the National Council for Culture, Arts and Heritage and by the Qatar Museum Authority. The French team appreciated the full support of the Department of Archaeology and is particularly grateful for the total co-operation on the scientific field and for all administration of the excavations. The ceramic drawings are by C. Mani.

2 Concerning Qatar, one can consult the two contributions by P.S. Garlake in the volume of B. de Cardi: Garlake (1978*a*) publishes ceramics from a 3 x 3 m survey of an encampment, and fig. 2, p. 168 relates to pottery collected on the surface; Garlake (1978*b*) discussed the architecture of the fortress and the village, and fig. 2, p. 175, relate to the potteries collected on the surface (cf. also Hardy-Guilbert 1991: figs 9–12).

3 These observations took place at the laboratory "Archéométrie et Archéologie", UMR 5138, Lyon.

References

Garlake P.S.

1978*a*. Year Encampment of the seventeenth to nineteenth centuries on Ras Abaruk, Site 5. Pages 164–171 in B. de Cardi (ed.), *Qatar Archaeological Report: Excavations 1973*. Doha/Oxford: Oxford University Press.

1978*b*. Fieldwork at Al-Huwailah, Site 23. Pages 172–179 in B. de Cardi (ed.), *Qatar Archaeological Report: Excavations 1973*. Doha/Oxford: Oxford University Press.

Hardy-Guilbert C.

1980. Recherche sur la période islamique au Qatar. Pages 111–128 in J. Texier (ed.), *Mission archéologique Française à Qatar*. Ministry of Information, State of Qatar, Dar al-Uloum, Doha.

1991. Dix ans de recherche archéologique sur la période islamique dans le Golfe (1977–1987). Bilans et perspectives. Pages 131–192 in Y. Ragheb (ed.), *Documents de l'Islam médiéval, Nouvelles perspectives de recherches*. TAEI n°29, IFAO, Le Caire.

Lorimer J.G.

1908–1915. *Gazetteer of the Persian Gulf, 'Oman and Central Asia*. Calcutta. England: Dar Gharnit lil-Nashr, 1995. [Reprinted 1970].

Authors' addresses

Alexandrine Guérin, 5 rue Audran, 69001 Lyon, France.
e-mail alexandrine1g@free.fr

Faysal ʿAbdallah al-Naʾimi, Head of Antiquities, Qatar Museums Authority, P.O. Box 2777, Doha, Qatar.
e-mail falnaimi@qma.com.qa

Proceedings of the Seminar for Arabian Studies 38 (2008): 187–202

Mapping and dating incipient irrigation in Wadi Sana, Ḥaḍramawt (Yemen)

Michael J. Harrower

Summary
The irrigation systems of Yemen's ancient states have attracted considerable research attention but far less is known about their smaller-scale predecessors. Agricultural constructions are notoriously difficult to date and in areas with millennia of agricultural land use archaeologists face many challenges in distinguishing modern and historic from very ancient systems. Confirming comparable dates in western Yemen, radiocarbon assays place the earliest irrigation in Wadi Sana during the fourth millennium BC. A satellite imagery-derived Digital Elevation Model (DEM) used to model surface water flow sheds new light on techniques employed, and associated results of the Roots of Agriculture in Southern Arabia (RASA) Research Project help illustrate the long-term societal contexts in which locally tailored irrigation originated.

Keywords: irrigation, agriculture, Geographic Information Systems, south-west Arabia, Yemen

Introduction

The impressive flash floodwater irrigation systems of Yemen's ancient states required advanced knowledge to design and considerable labour for construction, operation, and maintenance, yet the technological and social precursors of these large-scale systems remain scantly known. While research on south-west Arabian irrigation has traditionally concentrated around major state capitals (e.g. Bowen 1958; Brunner 1997*a*; 1997*b*; 2000; Brunner & Haefner 1986; Coque-Delhuille 1998; Francaviglia 2000; 2002; Gentelle 1991; Hehmeyer 1989; Vogt 2004), investigations through a broader spatio-temporal range have begun to shed new light on irrigation's early development (Darles 2000; McCorriston & Oches 2001; Mouton 2004; Vogt, Buffer & Brunner 2002; Wilkinson 1999; 2005; 2006). This paper summarizes the results of archaeological survey concentrating on small-scale irrigation along Wadi Sana, Ḥaḍramawt, as part of the Roots of Agriculture in Southern Arabia (RASA) Project research. While quantitative results of Geographic Information Systems-based modelling are to be published in more detail elsewhere, this report utilizes a Digital Elevation Model (DEM) extracted from the two stereo bands of ASTER satellite imagery for largely qualitative assessments of hydrology, and concentrates on results of archaeological survey, specifically efforts to establish the spatial and chronological contexts of irrigation in the area (see also Harrower 2006; Harrower, McCorriston & Oches 2002; McCorriston & Harrower 2005).

The 3600 km^2 Wadi Sana watershed is a landscape of deeply cut canyons, arid channels, and expansive rocky plateaux, which today receives approximately 70 mm of precipitation per annum (1) and flows north emptying into Wadi Masila (Fig. 1). The area has long been a sparsely populated hinterland. Since the mid-Holocene archaeological remains including hearths, habitation, and irrigation structures are unusually well preserved, the area offers a unique opportunity to explore the technical foundations of incipient irrigation and related culture change.

Field mapping, test excavation, and radiocarbon dating

RASA Project investigations in 1998 and 2000 identified check dams, water diversion channels, and earthen-banked fields in a number of locales along Wadi Sana (McCorriston *et al.* 2002; McCorriston & Oches 2001). While these efforts, including test excavations of two structures, generated approximate dates via Optically Stimulated Luminescence assays (see below), they raised

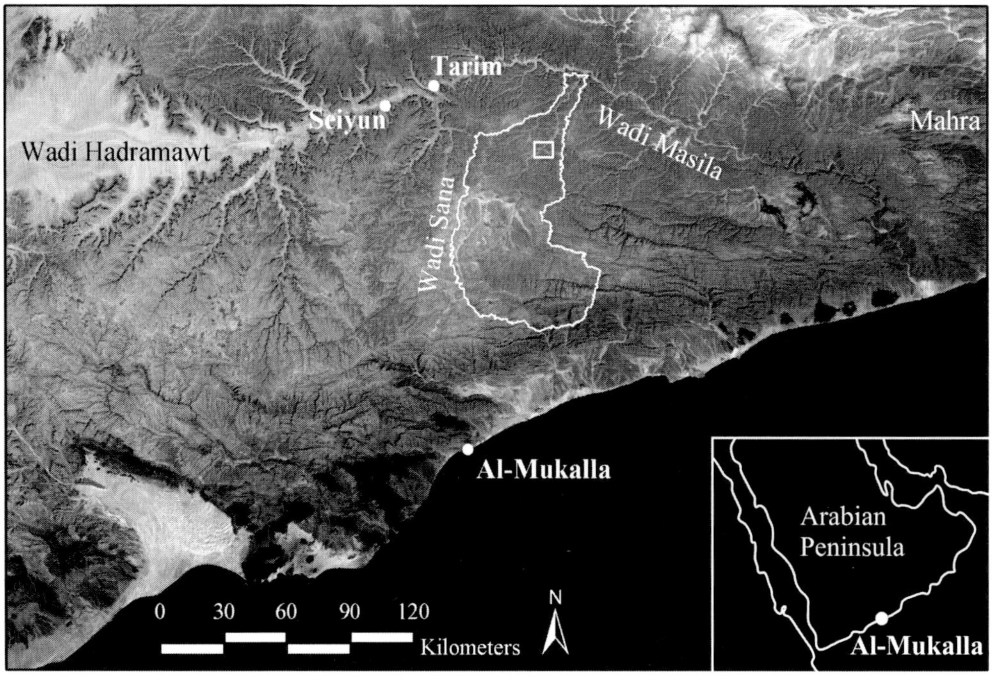

FIGURE 1. *A MODIS satellite image map of the Ḥaḍramawt region showing the teardrop-shaped Wadi Sana watershed (the white box shows area depicted in Fig. 2).*

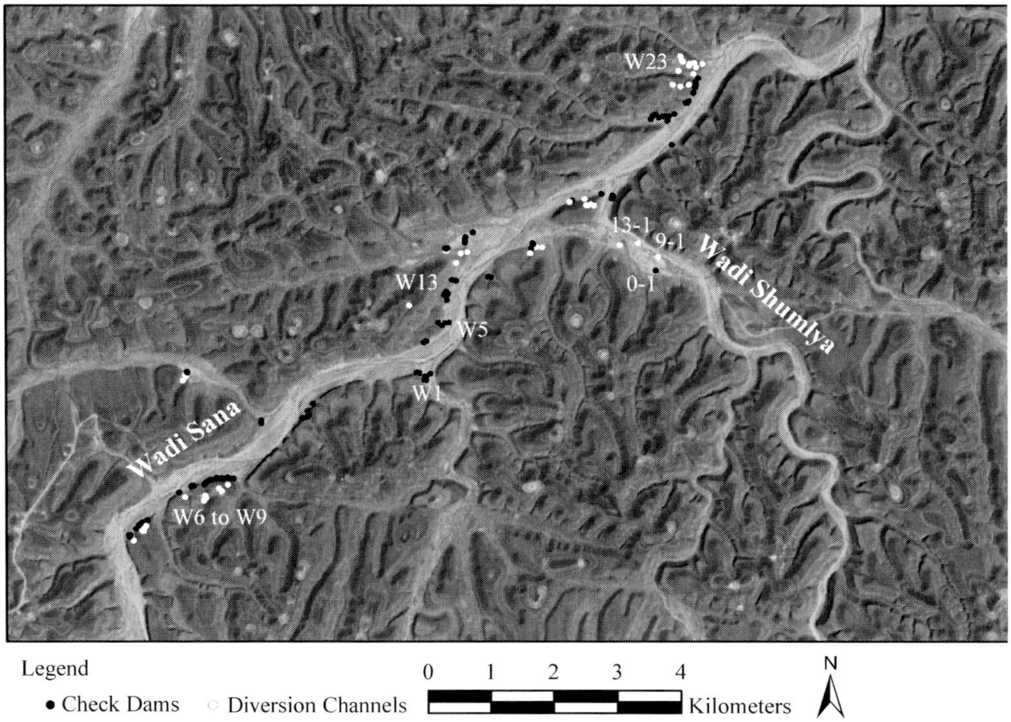

FIGURE 2. *An ASTER satellite image map showing the middle Wadi Sana area where most of the ancient irrigation structures were found.*

Figure 3. *A typical* shrūj *diversion channel (84-1, left) and a typical* shrūj *check dam (W5-3A, right).*

important questions that could only be answered by further landscape oriented fieldwork. When — more precisely — did irrigation begin in the area? What techniques were used and how did they change over time in conjunction with environmental and social change?

Dissertation fieldwork initiated in 2004 combined results of the RASA Project survey, including random sampling along the main channel of Wadi Sana (McCorriston, Harrower *et al.* 2005), with judgemental sampling specifically targeting irrigation. A bilingual (Arabic-English) water management form was completed for each irrigation structure or clustered group of structures and each structure was delineated as a line vector using a Trimble GPS backpack. The collective sample from work in 1998, 2000, and 2004 consists of 174 irrigation structures along the main channel and tributaries of Wadi Sana (Fig. 2). Aside from a few earthen dams constructed during the last few decades (which, according to locals, never yielded crops), there is presently no irrigation farming along middle Wadi Sana where most ancient irrigation structures were identified. Survey encountered a number of small natural springs seeping from the limestone bedrock along Wadi Sana, but no ancient wells, human-made cisterns, or other water collection features were identified. Although such structures may have existed once and since been destroyed, natural springs seeping from bedrock likely provided the primary ancient and historic source of water for domestic consumption and animals.

Most ancient irrigation structures along middle Wadi Sana capture run-off from low infiltration limestone hillslopes and illustrate a type of irrigation locally known as *shrūj*. Although the term *shrūj* has a variety of meanings throughout south-west Arabia, variously referring to small channels or small-scale irrigation (Maktari 1971: 58, 63; Serjeant 1988: 143), in Ḥaḍramawt it describes hillslope run-off irrigation as opposed to water harnessed from *ghayl* springs or more powerful *sayl* flash floods (see Ba-Qhaizil, Saeed & Ghawth 1996: 85; al-Khanbashi & Badr [n.d.]: 91). In Wadi Sana ancient *shrūj* systems consist of two basic types of structures: 1) diversion channels that redirect run-off; and 2) check dams that slow run-

#	Sample #	Sample	Context	Lab #	Age for	C^{14} yr BP	cal BC/AD	Med. Prob.
1	2004- W5-1-T1-6	char. plant debris	burnt layer overlaying dam	AA60247	*terminus ante quem* for W5-1	293 ± 39	1481 1792	AD 1568
2	2004- 9-1-T3-7	wood char.	sediment above diversion channel	AA60245	*terminus ante quem* for 9-1	4471 ± 42	3348 3020	3195 BC
3	2004- 9-1-T1-2	wood char.	sediment above diversion channel	AA59569	*terminus ante quem* for 9-1	4475 ± 36	3342 3027	3214 BC
4	2004- W23-1-H1-1	wood char.	hearth in silt immediately below diversion channel	AA60251	*terminus post quem* for W23	5637 ± 44	4548 4360	4469 BC
5	2004- W13-1-H1-1	wood char.	hearth in silt section 9m from check dam	AA60250	*terminus post quem* for W13-1	5783 ± 44	4764 4506	4635 BC
6	2004- W6-1-H2-1	wood char.	hearth in silt section 11m from check dam	AA60249	*terminus post quem* for W6-1	5923 ± 44	4931 4709	4798 BC
7	2004- W1-4-H1-1	wood char.	hearth on silts 17m from dam	AA60246	*terminus ante quem*? for W1-1	6168 ± 51	5293 4986	5122 BC
8	2004- W5-3A-3	wood char.	hearth in silt section 51m from check dam	AA60248	*terminus post quem* for W5-3A	6232 ± 45	5309 5057	5210 BC

TABLE 1. *Radiocarbon dates for irrigation in Wadi Sana. Assays in bold taken 26 m apart from sediments above structure 9-1 are most significant as they provide independent terminus ante quem dates that place the earliest irrigation during the mid-fourth millennium BC. Calibration ranges were calculated with CALIB v5.02 using IntCal04 data (Reimer et al. 2004); values are listed at the 2-sigma (95 %) confidence interval. The median probabilities produced by CALIB and shown in the right-hand column are used in the text.*

off (often from the aforementioned diversion channels) distributing moisture and nutrients on arable sediments (Fig. 3).

In addition to field recording and mapping, test excavations were dug in five locales. Eight radiocarbon assays clarify the chronological sequence of irrigation's appearance and development from about 5500 years ago (Table 1). While these dates provide information for only a small handful of documented structures, attention to natural and cultural landscape contexts further assists in illustrating the chronology of irrigation in the area (*cf.* Doolittle, Pool & Neely 1993; Wilkinson 2003: 49–51, 66–70). Diagnostic artefacts were seldom found in association with irrigation features in ways that could facilitate dating, yet reconstructions of geomorphological history led by RASA Project geologist E.A. Oches along with archaeological features found in association with irrigation, including high circular (cairn) tombs, help illustrate the timing and contexts of irrigation's local genesis.

The earliest conclusively dated irrigation structure, a 74m long rock-bordered canal designated 9-1, is the single most important structure for understanding the origins of irrigation in Wadi Sana. This small canal located along the Wadi Shumlya main channel (Fig. 2) was first identified during the RASA survey in 1998 and subsequently published in a short report (McCorriston & Oches 2001). Although it was originally interpreted as a check dam, subsequent investigations revealed that it is better interpreted as a water diversion channel or more specifically a small rock-bordered canal. Two lines of small boulders are visible on the surface for 41m, after which the stones enter a silt bank (natural section) cut by a small wash that dissected the structure (removing sediments but leaving dislodged stones stranded in a shallow gully). In 1998 the RASA team cleaned and examined this natural section, and excavated a 3×0.5m test unit approximately 5m north-west of the section that confirmed the irrigation structure continued as a buried feature. The team collected a sample for Optically Stimulated Luminescence (OSL) dating from the section approximately 0.5 m below the structure. This OSL assay yielded an age of 7300 ± 1500 years ago (McCorriston & Oches 2001). Given the age of sediments determined by radiocarbon assays on hearths embedded in sediments nearby (see below), it was suspected that the actual age probably fell at the younger end of the error range. In 2004 more rigorous attempts were made better to establish the age and original extent of 9-1. The test trench excavated in 1998 was expanded in 2004 to 1×3 m and two additional test trenches were excavated down the length of the structure to determine if it continued further than had been identified in 1998 (Fig. 4). These efforts revealed the full preserved length of the structure (74 m). The structure runs at a bearing of approximately 332°. From the south-east, remains of the structure are visible on the surface for 41 m and then enter the aforementioned naturally-cut section and continue under the present surface for 33 m where the canal terminates at an approximately 5 m drop carved by the modern Wadi Shumlya main channel. Although the stones are somewhat scattered in the gully area, two distinct lines of stones embedded or buried in silt are evident in six locations (Fig. 4). Two radiocarbon samples from sediments immediately above the stones of the structure 26 m apart yielded ages of 3195 and 3214 cal BC (Table 1).

Numerous lines of evidence indicate 9-1 was a rock-bordered canal constructed before 3200 BC. Examinations of the naturally cut section show that prior to construction the area was part of an active fluvial channel (the Wadi Shumlya main channel or a meander) where successive layers of silt and gravel were laid during periods of alternating flow intensity. The structure was most likely constructed of two earthen banks approximately 1 m apart, each supported on the outside edge by a line of small boulders. Sometime near 3200 BC these earthen banks were destroyed by flood waters. The small boulders shifted slightly and were buried approximately 50 cm deep by homogenous silt. The two dated wood charcoal fragments probably originated from the burning of vegetation in the area upstream from the structure. Burned surfaces are common in silts along Wadi Sana and many contain similar charcoal fragments. Although there is a possibility these fragments may have come from vegetation that died prior to construction of the structure and was subsequently washed in during burial of the structure long after 3200 BC (i.e. the structure is actually much younger than the dates), RASA Project geomorphological reconstructions make this possibility unlikely. Of the thirty-nine radiocarbon samples buried in silt and dated by RASA since 1998, all but two yielded ages older than those obtained on charcoal above 9-1 (Harrower 2006: 109–110). RASA reconstructions show that middle Wadi Sana silt deposition took place predominantly during the early Holocene and largely ceased near the end of the fourth millennium when increasingly arid conditions (e.g. Burns *et al.* 1998; Fleitmann *et al.* 2007; Parker *et al.* 2006) resulted in a local shift from sedimentary aggradation to an erosive hydrological regime (Oches *et al.* 2001; Anderson 2007). RASA has not found silts beds in the middle Wadi Sana deposited after 3200 BC, providing good reason to conclude that the dates obtained for 9-1 provide an accurate *terminus ante quem* for the structure, i.e. it was constructed, destroyed, and buried before the end of the fourth millennium. Indeed, two dates collected in 1998 from natural silt sections along the path cut by Wadi Shumlya just north of 9-1, yielded ages of 4744 and 4753 cal BC. (2) The former comes from a bell-shaped pit 24 m away and 3.54 m below 9-1. Given the position of 9-1 relative to the pit, this equals an average of 2.3 mm per year of sediment accumulation over 1549 years, an estimate generally consistent with measurements of accumulation on spate irrigated fields (Brunner 1983; Tesfai & Sterk 2002). Although the precise elevation of the latter date from a nearby hearth could not be determined relative to 9-1 in 2004 because of subsequent erosion since 1998 along the 5 m drop cut by Wadi Shumlya, it lies approximately 10 m away from the irrigation structure and its early age similarly supports the accuracy of assays taken above 9-1.

To evaluate further the interpretation that 9-1 was a rock-bordered canal, elevations along its length were measured in 2005 (using a Wild theodolite). The wide areal pattern of silt deposition indicates that Wadi Shumlya previously meandered across a span of up to 400 m between limestone bluffs (Fig. 2). In contrast to the modern location of the Wadi Shumlya main channel north of 9-1, local patterns of silt deposition and the orientation of 9-1 suggest that the Wadi Shumlya main channel was previously south of 9-1 and that water travelled along the small canal from south-east to north-west. To evaluate this interpretation, elevation readings were taken in all six locations where embedded or buried boulders were found along the 74 m length of the structure. Elevations show a consistent decrease from south-east to north-west. In total, elevation drops 53 cm in 74 m giving a slope of 0.7 %. This is roughly consistent with gradients for small earthen canals that generally vary between 1 and 3 % (Charles 1988: 34). Collectively, findings support the conclusion that 9-1 was a rock-bordered canal constructed before 3200 BC, making it one of the oldest dated agricultural constructions in south-west Arabia (*cf.* Ghaleb 1990; Wilkinson 1999; 2005; 2006).

Two structures near 9-1 further clarify the nature of

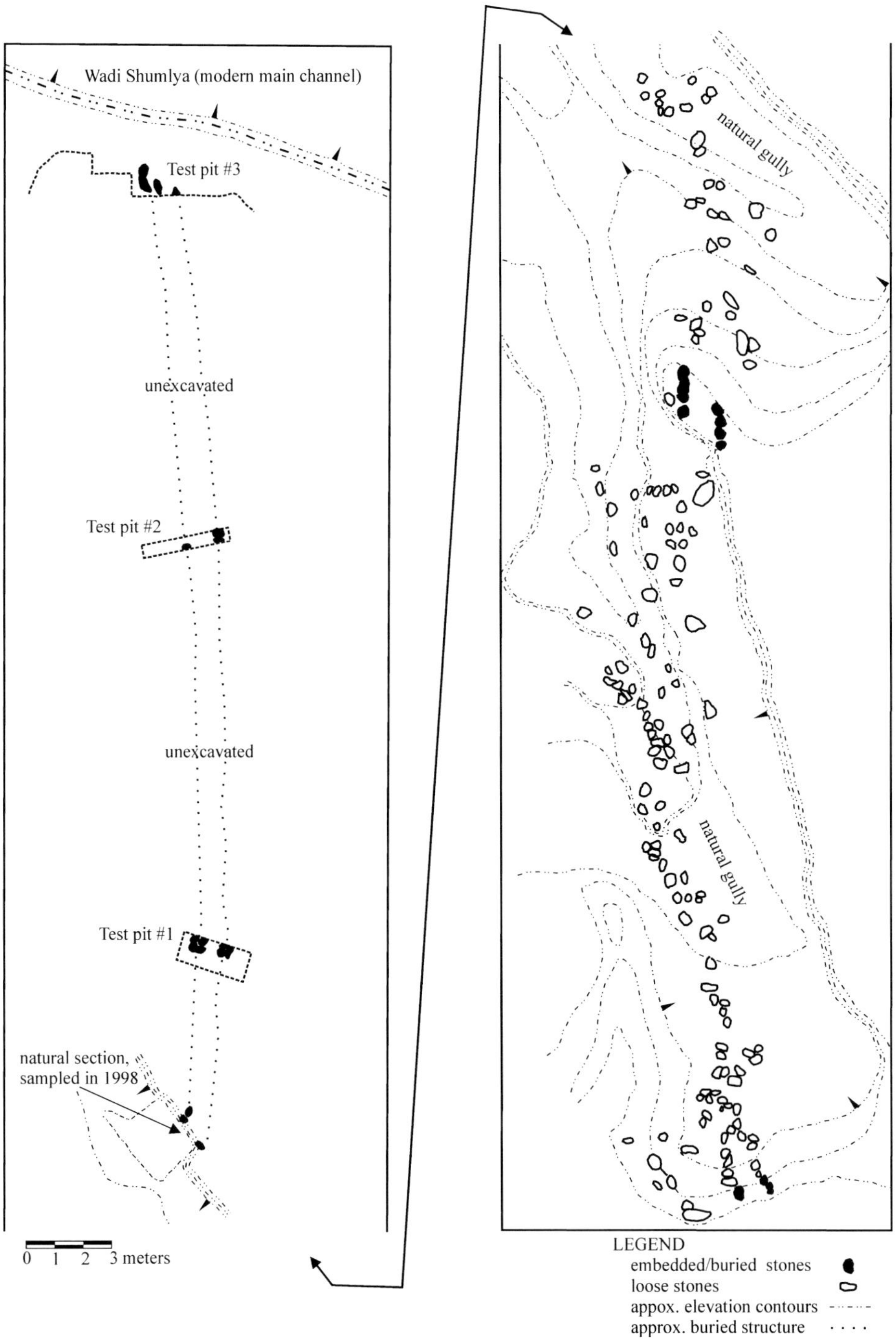

Figure 4. *A plan map of rock-bordered canal 9-1. The box on the left aligns with the box on the right to extend a total distance of 74 m. Radiocarbon dates nos 2 and 3 in Table 1 were taken from test pit no. 3 and test pit no. 1 respectively.*

irrigation near the mouth of Wadi Shumlya. The first was discovered in 1998 in an area known as the Gravel Bar Site (0-1) 195 m south of 9-1 (Fig. 2). The surface of the site is covered by a dense scatter of Arabian Bifacial Tradition (ABT) lithics already published in a short report (Walter, McCorriston & Oches 2000). Three test trenches were excavated in 1998 to determine if sub-surface lithics were present and investigate a series of limestone slabs protruding from the surface. Although lithics did not extend any significant depth below the surface, their very high density and the fact that they did not exhibit evidence of water-transport damage suggest that they remain *in situ*. The limestone slabs, interpreted as the remains of an ancient check dam, were discussed in the aforementioned report by McCorriston and Oches (2001). Since 1998 no further work has been conducted at this location. As discussed by McCorriston and Oches (2001: 675), these slabs have no *in situ* natural source. They are too large to have been water-transported and therefore must have been carried from a nearby bedrock outcrop by ancient irrigators who aligned them on end to construct a check dam. Both an OSL date of 10,400 ± 4500 years ago from below the slabs and the approximately 8000–4000-year-old ABT lithics capping the structure suggest it was constructed at least 4000–6000 years ago, near in time to 9-1. Although the precise water flow patterns when the structure was constructed are difficult to determine because of subsequent erosion and road construction, the structure lies below a small 27 ha catchment that likely supplied waters slowed by the dam.

The second test-excavated structure near 9-1 is a water diversion channel (13-1) with a preserved length of 14 m first discovered in 1998. It is located on a raised area of stranded silts along the main channel of Wadi Shumlya 340 m downstream from 9-1 (Fig. 2). The structure is only preserved at the highest point of a small (approximately 20 m^2) raised area of silt. Although 13-1 must have extended further than 14 m, most of it was likely destroyed as sediments in the surrounding area eroded. In 2004 a 1×0.5 m trench was excavated to determine the depth of the structure and to search for datable materials. The structure is shallowly buried, extending only 10 cm below the surface. Below it a loose sandy deposit containing snail shells (*Melanoides tuberculata*) suggests that the structure was built in a moist, fluvially active or slack water area (al-Safadi 1991; Brown & Gallagher 1985; Radies *et al*. 2005).

Three kilometres upstream from the confluence of Wadi Sana and Wadi Shumlya an area designated WATER1 (W1) offered promising opportunities for dating but yielded circumstantial dates for irrigation that we suspect may be too early to be accurate. Located near the mouth of a small Wadi Sana tributary, W1 consists of seven structures in a shallow gully eroded from surrounding silt beds. Two 50×50 cm units were excavated in the largest (and we suspect the oldest) structure, W1-1, a curvilinear dam. Excavations revealed the apparent height and breadth of the structure to be an illusion caused by erosion. The structure was originally a curved wall approximately 50 cm high. As silt beds around it eroded, its small boulders and cobbles slid downslope to cover and protect immediately surrounding sediments and today it therefore appears much higher and wider than it was originally. Fourteen hearths on a low silt knoll 16 to 39 m south of the structure offered opportunities for radiocarbon dating (Fig. 5). It was hypothesized that since they are upstream and at approximately the same height as the original base of the structure, these hearths must post-date its use since they would have been washed away if placed there during times of fluvial activity in the area. Two hearths were sampled, the single sample submitted for dating yielded an age of 5122 cal BC (Table 1). Although we originally hypothesized that this would be a *terminus ante quem* for the structure, such an early age for the dam is difficult to accept. The assay on the hearth is most probably accurate. There has been very little silt accumulation during the past 5000 years along middle Wadi Sana and charcoal samples from shallowly buried hearths have yielded similarly early dates. Moreover, two Fasad projectile points were found 58 m and 93 m away, further confirming a relatively early time frame of human activity in the area (see Charpentier 1996). But this indirect date suggests a surprising and perhaps unreasonably early age for irrigation. Precise elevation measurements were made in 2005 with a Wild theodolite. The dated hearth lies 0.5 cm above the level of the basal stones of the dam in one test unit, and 19.5 cm below the basal stones in the other test unit, so it is indeed at approximately the same height as the dam. Although it is difficult to explain how hearths could be upstream and at approximately the same height as the dam without being destroyed when the dam was used, it is equally difficult to accept an age this early for the dam (at least 1000 years older than any other present evidence for irrigation or crop agriculture in south-west Arabia). Perhaps the hearths were very shallowly buried when the dam was in use. Alternatively, irrigation could be substantially earlier than most present evidence suggests, but this possibility

Figure 5. *A hearth radiocarbon dated to 5122 cal BC on a low knoll (foreground) immediately upstream of check dam W1-1 (background).*

requires independent confirmation before such an early time frame for irrigation could be accepted.

A group of structures designated WATER5 similarly held potential for clarifying the beginnings of irrigation in Wadi Sana. Located approximately 2.7 km upstream from the Wadi Shumlya, W5 consists of three check dams and a 75 m long water diversion/retention wall. The check dams are distributed for 200 m down the length of a small tributary of Wadi Sana that drains a small 28 ha catchment. They would have slowed sediment-laden waters in the gully and provided an irrigated area of approximately 0.5 ha. The wall, still in an excellent state of preservation, blocked waters from an adjacent hillslope to prevent erosion of silts along the margins of the gully. Based on its preservation, and the general lack of desert varnish on its stones, the wall was thought to have been no more than approximately 1000 years old, but we speculated that some of the check dams might have been older. The final check dam (constructed of mounded sediment backed by a wall of small boulders) was breached on its northern end allowing examination of it in section. Once cut back by shovel and trowel, this section revealed four major strata, including the sediments used to construct the dam, and a layer of charred plant debris that washed over the dam. A radiocarbon sample from the charred debris layer yielded an age of AD 1568 indicating that this layer was deposited relatively recently. An additional radiocarbon sample retrieved from a hearth embedded in silts before down-cutting of the W5 gully yielded a *terminus post quem* age for the gully of 5210 cal BC (Table 1). While the former date does not necessarily demonstrate that the final check dam (W5-1) was constructed or used as recently as 1568, it is possible that some efforts to irrigate in Wadi Sana continued during the Islamic era.

FIGURE 6. *A gully between stranded silt beds and bedrock cliffs along the margins of Wadi Sana. This gully area, designated WATER8, is typical of eroded gullies along middle Wadi Sana, many of which contain check dams. Hearths in silt sections along these gullies must have been deposited before gully incision began, and therefore radiocarbon dates from such hearths (including nos 5, 6, and 8 in Table 1) provide* terminus post quem *dates for gullies and the irrigation structures they contain.*

While radiocarbon dates for 9-1 place the earliest irrigation during the mid-fourth millennium BC, the precise ages of many structures in the sample of 174 remain somewhat uncertain. Since RASA geomorphological reconstructions show that middle Wadi Sana silt aggradation largely ceased after the late fourth millennium (Anderson 2007), surveys aimed to find structures buried in silt that might provide opportunities for further *terminus ante quem* dating. Although some structures may be so deeply covered that they would require subsurface remote sensing to identify them, no structures other than 9-1 were found buried (or partially buried) in more than a few centimetres of silt. In many areas diversion channels directed water from plateaux and low bedrock terraces into gullies eroded in silt beds along the margins of Wadi Sana (Fig. 6). These gullies provide convenient capture points, but would have only started to form after middle Wadi Sana had shifted from a mode of predominantly aggradation to degradation and incision. Two radiocarbon assays from hearths embedded in silt sections along the sides of such gullies yielded *terminus post quem* ages for gullies and the irrigation structures they contain of 4798 and 4635 cal BC, and another assay of 4469 cal BC taken from a hearth immediately below a diversion channel further suggests irrigation originated after the mid-fifth millennium (Table 1). In one location

(W9) a diffuse scatter of Arabian Bifacial Tradition tools was found in and around diversion channels but these lithics could pre- or post-date the channels. In another location a diversion channel was constructed using the stones of a pre-existing trilith monument presumably constructed near the cusp of the Common Era (al-Shahri 1991: 193; Cremaschi & Negrino 2002: 342; de Cardi, Doe & Roskams 1977: 28; Zarins 2001: 134). Irrigation thus may have continued for thousands of years after the fourth millennium but there is only sparse evidence for human activity along middle Wadi Sana during the last 4000 years. In four field seasons RASA has found Old South Arabic graffiti and triliths along middle Wadi Sana but less than fifty pottery fragments; and of fifteen dated hearths, weak palaeosols, and burned surfaces, only one date falls after the fourth millennium (McCorriston *et al.* 2002: 68). If the most intense period of human activity along middle Wadi Sana from the seventh to the third millennia BC is applied as a guide (2002), most *shrūj* diversion channels and check dams most plausibly fall near the end of this interval during the late fourth and third millennium, but some structures may date to the first millennium BC or later.

The natural and cultural contexts of irrigation in Wadi Sana

Wadi Sana exemplifies natural and cultural contexts shaping irrigation's origins. Circumstances undoubtedly varied across south-west Arabia. Rain-fed farming may have been feasible in parts of highland western Yemen, which today receive much higher rainfall, but even in areas with marginally enough rain for dry-farming, irrigation would have mitigated the impacts of inter-annual variability. Indeed, studies of global rainfall variability have consistently shown that inter-annual variability generally increases as mean annual rainfall decreases (e.g. Dewar & Wallis 1999) making subsistence flexibility particularly important in arid regions. In Mahra (eastern Yemen) and Dhofar (western Oman), ethnographic agro-pastoral nomads moved frequently, including from the coast to the highlands (ElMahi 2001; Janzen 1986; 2000; Zarins 1992) and an analogous pattern of transhumance likely prevailed in many areas (including in and around Wadi Sana) during ancient times. Towns eventually grew in areas where *ghayl* springs and/or *sayl* floodwaters could be harnessed and these more complex irrigation systems encountered allocation and management challenges that undoubtedly contributed to differential intra-community power and social change (cf. Varisco 1983).

Hydrologically, the spatial distribution of irrigation structures in Wadi Sana helps illustrate how patterns of land and water use shifted in concert with changing climates and local geomorphology. A 15 m DEM extracted from the two stereo bands of ASTER satellite imagery facilitates assessment of run-off patterns (Harrower 2006). Only a small handful of preserved structures, including 9-1 and 13-1, captured water from the main channel of a major wadi — in this case near the mouth of the 164 km^2 Wadi Shumlya watershed. These early structures were operable before full culmination of mid-Holocene ardification when greater precipitation and more vegetation would have contributed to lower velocity, longer-duration flows along primary wadi channels. They captured only a tiny portion of available water that sustained slack-water areas as demonstrated, for instance, by the abundance of snail shells (*Melanoides tuberculata*) found in sediments at the confluence of Wadi Sana and Shumlya. As precipitation waned during the late fourth and third millennia, flow along higher-order channels would have become more abrupt and precarious. Early irrigators shifted their efforts to much smaller 10 to 40 ha (0.1–0.4 km^2) tributary catchments where even brief rainfall episodes on hillslopes devoid of sediment would have generated low-energy, easier to manage water flows (cf. Shanan 2000). Preliminary assessments show run-off to run-on ratios of approximately 40:1, a figure comparable to those reported for western Yemen (Eger 1987; Wilkinson 2006) and in the Negev Desert (Shanan 2000). Once precipitation fell to contemporary levels near or below 70 mm per annum, hillslope run-off irrigation was no longer tenable along middle Wadi Sana (cf. Yair 2001: 301) and cultivators concentrated instead on flash flood (*sayl*) water irrigation techniques in other areas that eventually sustained south-west Arabian towns, then cities and ancient states.

In tandem with hydrology, culture history and social contexts are vital to understanding irrigation's local genesis. During the fifth millennium, forager-herders built widely scattered, circular, stone-foundation houses (McCorriston *et al.* 2002) and a ring of more than forty cattle skulls near the confluence of Wadi Sana and Wadi Shumlya (McCorriston, Heyne *et al.* 2005). As populations became less mobile demands for human food and animal forage would have intensified, favouring development of irrigation. Early irrigation structures were likely designed and operated at the household level, perhaps with kin groups holding clusters of irrigated land much like *Hamum badu* hold grazing rights along Wadi Sana today. High circular (cairn) tombs built along ridge lines were visible to anyone passing through the area marking territorial claims to land, water, and irrigated areas reinforced through reference to ancestry. By the first millennium the rise of state societies along the Ramlat as-Saba'tayn Desert's margins sparked demands for incense. Itinerant trades-people must have passed through Wadi Sana perhaps carrying local cargo or commodities from Mahra and Dhofar. Triliths may have marked passageways or ritual stopping points, and Old South Arabic graffiti at rock shelters occupied travellers' imaginations. As a comparatively vegetation-rich conduit, Wadi Sana became one of many important travel corridors. By the first few centuries AD, the fortified Himyarite period hillfort of Qalat Habshiya stood prominently on high cliffs at the entrance of Wadi Sana proper, exerting authority as a gateway to and from Wadi Sana and beyond (Beeston 1962: 41–42).

Concluding remarks

As a critical element of ancient sustenance, the breadth of irrigation's economic and social significance in ancient Yemen is difficult to ignore. Caton-Thompson and colleagues in the Ḥaḍramawt (Caton-Thompson & Gardner 1939) and Bowen (1958) in Wadi Beihan long ago pioneered a geo-archaeological mode of investigating irrigation that remains relevant today. As offspring of these early studies, landscape methods including GIS analyses of hydrology are particularly well suited to clarify technological dimensions of irrigation's development. Yet, even with the far wider scope of expository instruments of the radiocarbon age, studies of irrigation still face a variety of obstacles. Sedimentation, erosion, and subsequent land use obscure ancient practices, and efforts to indirectly establish the age of agricultural systems through links with geomorphology and/or nearby archaeological evidence are sometimes the only means of dating available (Doolittle, Pool & Neely 1993; Wilkinson 2003).

In conjunction with research on technical and hydrological elements of irrigation, continued investigations of social contexts and operational logistics of irrigation are necessary better to understand irrigation's millennia-long role as an instigator and reflector of social change. Irrigators' early experiences with run-off and terrace agriculture, now dated as early as the fourth millennium in both western and eastern Yemen, contributed to new social dynamics as populations grew and understandings of space and territory changed. Wadi Sana contributes to knowledge of hinterland run-off techniques that formed part of emerging agro-pastoralism. Operation of these and other small-scale systems was likely accomplished without supra-household co-ordination, but design, operation, and maintenance tasks posed increasing management challenges as the scale and complexity of irrigation expanded. Considerable research documents large-scale state irrigation technologies but their intermediate-scale antecedents are arguably the least well known and possibly most important for understanding irrigation's long-term development. After many years of interest, irrigation remains a topic of central significance poised to make continuing contributions to understanding the long-term trajectories of ancient south-west Arabian societies.

Acknowledgements

This research draws on Roots of Agriculture in Southern Arabia (RASA) Research Project investigations in Wadi Sana and adjacent areas since 1998. In particular directors Joy McCorriston, Eric Oches, and Abdalaziz bin 'Aqil deserve many thanks. Thanks are also due to the General Organization of Antiquities and Museums directors and staff, the American Institute for Yemeni Studies, and Canadian Nexen Inc. In addition to general RASA Project funding from the National Science Foundation (NSF) and other sources, support specifically for research on irrigation included Social Sciences and Humanities Research Council of Canada (SSHRC), Doctoral and Post-Doctoral Fellowships, and a NSF Dissertation Improvement Grant (BCS–0332278).

Notes

1. Precipitation data for Seiyun (1981–2002) provided by the Southern Governates Rural Development Project Office, Seiyun.
2. These dates of 5870 ± 45 and 5880 ± 55 C^{14} yr BP were originally reported by McCorriston *et al.* (2002: 68).

References

Anderson J.M.
2007. *Climatic and Structural Controls on the Geomorphology of Wadi Sana, Highland Southern Yemen.* MSc thesis, University of South Florida. [Unpublished].

Ba-Qhaizil S.A., Saeed I.A. & Ghawth M.S.
1996. *A documentary study of the forms of traditional irrigation systems and methods of water harvesting in the governates of Hadramawt and Shabwa* Council of Environmental Protection Technical Secretariat — Aden Branch. [In Arabic].

Beeston A.F.L.
1962. Epigraphic and Archaeological Gleanings from South Arabia. *Oriens Antiquus* 1: 41–52.

Bowen R.L.
1958. Irrigation in Ancient Qataban (Beihan). Pages 43–89 in R.L. Bowen & F.P. Albright (eds), *Archaeological Discoveries in South Arabia.* Baltimore, MD: Johns Hopkins University Press.

Brown D.S. & Gallagher M.D.
1985. Freshwater snails of Oman, South Eastern Arabia. *Hydrobiologia* 127: 125–149.

Brunner U.
1983. Die Erforschung der antiken Oase von Ma'rib mit Hilfe geomorphologischer Untersuchungsmethoden. *Archaologische Berichte aus dem Yemen* 2. Mainz: von Zabern.
1997*a*. Geography and Human Settlements in Ancient Southern Arabia. *Arabian Archaeology and Epigraphy* 8: 190–202.
1997*b*. The History of Irrigation in Wadi Marhah. *Proceedings of the Seminar for Arabian Studies* 27: 75–85.
2000. The Great Dam and the Sabean Oasis of Ma'rib. *Irrigation and Drainage Systems* 14: 167–182.

Brunner U. & Haefner H.
1986. The Successful Floodwater Farming System of the Sabeans: Yemen Arab Republic. *Applied Geography* 6: 77–86.

Burns S.J., Matter A., Frank N. & Mangini A.
1998. Speleothem-based paleoclimate record from northern Oman. *Geology* 26: 499–502.

Caton-Thompson G. & Gardner E.W.
1939. Climate, Irrigation, and Early Man in the Hadramaut. *The Geographical Journal* 93: 18–38.

Charles M.P.
1988. Irrigation in Lowland Mesopotamia. Pages 1–39 in J.N. Postgate & M.A. Powell (eds), *Irrigation and Cultivation in Mesopotamia, Part I.* Cambridge: Sumerian Agriculture Group.

Charpentier V.
1996. Entre sables du Rub' al Khali et mer d'Arabie, Préhistoire récente du Dhofar et d'Oman: les industries à pointes de "Fasad". *Proceedings of the Seminar for Arabian Studies* 26: 1–12.

Coque-Delhuille B.
1998. Contrôle des Périmètres d'Irrigation Antiques. Pages 87–94 in J-F. Breton, J.C. Arramond, B. Coque-Delhuille & P. Gentelle (eds), *Une vallée aride du Yémen antique: le Wadi Bayhan*. Paris: Editions Recherches sur les Civilisations.

Cremaschi M. & Negrino F.
2002. The Frankincense road of Sumhuram: paleoenvironmental and prehistorical background. Pages 325–363 in A. Avanzini (ed.), *Khor Rori Report I*. Pisa: Edizioni Plus.

Darles C.
2000. Les structures d'irrigation du Wadi Surban au Yemen. *Proceedings of the Seminar for Arabian Studies* 30: 87–97.

de Cardi B., Doe B. & Roskams S.P.
1977. Excavation and Survey in the Sharqiyah, Oman, 1976. *Journal of Oman Studies* 3: 17–33.

Dewar R.E. & Wallis J.R.
1999. Geographical Patterning of Interannual Rainfall Variability in the Tropics and Near Tropics: An L-Moments Approach. *Journal of Climate* 12: 3457–3466.

Doolittle W.E., Pool M.D. & Neely J.A.
1993. Method for distinguishing between prehistoric and recent water and soil control features. *Kiva* 59: 7–25.

Eger H.
1987. *Run-off Agriculture: A Case Study About the Yemeni Highlands*. Wiesbaden: Reichert.

ElMahi A.T.
2001. The traditional pastoral groups of Dhofar, Oman: a parallel for ancient cultural ecology. *Proceedings of the Seminar for Arabian Studies* 31: 131–143.

Fleitmann D., Burns S.J., Mangini A., Mudelsee M., Kramers H., Vila I., Neff U., Al-Subbary A., Buettner A., Hippler D. & Matter A.
2007. Holocene ITCZ and Indian monsoon dynamics recorded in stalagmites from Oman and Yemen (Socotra). *Quaternary Science Reviews* 26: 170–188.

Francaviglia V.M.
2000. Dating the Ancient Dam of Ma'rib (Yemen). *Journal of Archaeological Science* 27: 645–653.
2002. Some Remarks on the Irrigation Systems of Ancient Yemen. Pages 111–144 in S. Cleuziou, M. Tosi & J. Zarins (eds), *Essays on the Late Prehistory of the Arabian Peninsula*. Rome: Istituto Italiano per L'Africa e l'Oriente.

Gentelle P.
1991. Les Irrigations Antiques à Shabwa. *Syria* 68: 5–54.

Ghaleb A.O.
1990. *Agricultural Practices in Ancient Radman and Wadi Al-Jubah (Yemen)*. PhD Dissertation, University of Pennsylvania. [Unpublished].

Harrower M.
2006. *Environmental versus social parameters, landscape, and the origins of irrigation in Southwest Arabia (Yemen)*. PhD Dissertation, The Ohio State University. [Unpublished].

Harrower M., McCorriston J. & Oches E.A.
2002. Mapping the Roots of Agriculture in Southern Arabia: the Application of Satellite Remote Sensing, Global Positioning System and Geographic Information System Technologies. *Archaeological Prospection* 9: 35–42.

Hehmeyer I.
1989. Irrigation Farming in the Ancient Oasis of Marib. *Proceedings of the Seminar for Arabian Studies* 19: 33–44.

Janzen J.
1986. *Nomads in the Sultanate of Oman: tradition and development in Dhofar*. Boulder, CO: Westview Press.
2000. The destruction of resources among the mountain nomads of Dhofar. Pages 160–176 in M. Mundy & B. Musallam (eds), *The Transformation of Nomadic Society in the Arab East*. Cambridge: Cambridge University Press.

al-Khanbashi S.U. & Badr A.A.
[n.d.]. *Traditional sayl irrigation systems in Do'an: technologies, laws, and features*. Mukalla, Yemen: Al-Manar. [in Arabic].

McCorriston J. & Harrower M.
2005. Annales history, Geographic Information Systems, and the analysis of landscape in Hadramawt, Yemen. Pages 31–41 in J-F. Berger, F. Bertoncello, F. Braemer, G. Davtian & M. Gazenbeek (eds), *Temps et Espaces de l'Homme en Société, Analyses et Modèles Spatiaux en Archéologies*. Antibes: Éditions APDCA.

McCorriston J. & Oches E.
2001. Two Early Holocene Check Dams from Southern Arabia. *Antiquity* 75: 675–676.

McCorriston J., Harrower M.J., Oches E.A. & Bin 'Aqil A.
2005. Foraging Economies and Population in the Middle Holocene Highlands of Southern Yemen. *Proceedings of the Seminar for Arabian Studies* 35: 143–154.

McCorriston J., Oches E.A., Walter D. & Cole K.L.
2002. Holocene Paleoecology and Prehistory in Highland Southern Arabia. *Paléorient* 28: 61–88.

McCorriston J., Heyne C., Harrower M., Patel N., Steimer-Herbet T., al-Amary I., Barakany A., Sinnah M., Ladeh R., Oches E.A., Crassard R. & Martin L.
2005. Roots of Agriculture (RASA) Project 2005: A Season of Excavation and Survey in Wadi Sana, Hadramawt. *Yemen Update: Bulletin of the American Institute for Yemeni Studies* 47: 23–28.

Maktari A.M.A.
1971. *Water rights and irrigation practices in Lahj; a study of the application of customary and Shari'ah law in south-west Arabia.* Cambridge: Cambridge University Press.

Mouton M.
2004. Irrigation et Formation de la Société Antique dans les Basses-Terres du Yemen: un essai de modèle. *Syria* 81: 81–104.

Oches E.A., McCorriston J., Harrower M. & Devogel S.
2001. Middle Holocene Human-Environment Interactions in Southern Arabia. *Geological Society of America Abstracts with Programs, Vol. 33, No. A295.*

Parker A.G., Goudie A.S., Stokes S., White J.W., Hodson M.J., Manning M. & Kennet D.
2006. A record of Holocene climate change from lake geochemical analyses in southeastern Arabia. *Quaternary Research* 66: 465–476.

Radies D., Hasiotis S.T., Preusser F., Neubert E. & Matter A.
2005. Paleoclimatic significance of Early Holocene faunal assemblages in wet interdune deposits of the Wahiba Sand Sea, Sultanate of Oman. *Journal of Arid Environments* 62: 109–125.

Reimer P.J., Baillie M.G.L., Bard E., Bayliss A., Beck J.W. *et al.*
2004. IntCal04 Terrestrial radiocarbon age calibration, 26-0 ka BP. *Radiocarbon* 46: 1029–1058.

al-Safadi M.M.
1991. Freshwater macrofauna of stagnant waters in Yemen Arab Republic. *Hydrobiologia* 210: 203–208.

Serjeant R.B.
1988. Observations on irrigation in Southwest Arabia. *Proceedings of the Seminar for Arabian Studies* 18: 145–153.

al-Shahri A.A.A.M.
1991. Grave types and "triliths" in Dhofar. *Arabian Archaeology and Epigraphy* 2: 182–195.

Shanan L.
2000. Run-off, erosion, and the sustainability of ancient irrigation systems in the Central Negev desert. Pages 75–106 in M.A. Hassan, O. Slaymaker & S.M. Berkowicz (eds), *The Hydrology-Geomorphology Interface: Rainfall, Floods, Sedimentation, Land Use* (IAHS Publication # 261). Jerusalem: IAHS Publications.

Tesfai M. & Sterk G.
2002. Sedimentation rate on spate irrigated fields in Sheeb area, eastern Eritrea. *Journal of Arid Environments* 50: 191–203.

Varisco D.M.
1983. Sayl and Ghayl: The Ecology of Water Allocation in Yemen. *Human Ecology* 11: 365–383.

Vogt B.
2004. Towards a new dating of the great dam of Marib: preliminary results of the 2002 fieldwork of the German Institute of Archaeology. *Proceedings of the Seminar for Arabian Studies* 34: 377–388.

Vogt B., Buffa V. & Brunner U.
2002. Ma'layba and the Bronze Age irrigation in coastal Yemen. *Archäologische Berichte aus dem Yemen* 9: 15–26.

Walter D., McCorriston J. & Oches E.A.
2000. Shumlya GBS — an Arabian Bifacial Tradition Assemblage from the Hadramawt Province, Yemen. *Neolithics* 2: 12–14.

Wilkinson T.J.
1999. Settlement, soil erosion and terraced agriculture in highland Yemen: a preliminary statement. *Proceedings of the Seminar for Arabian Studies* 29: 183–191.
2003. *Archaeological Landscapes of the Near East*. Tucson, AZ: The University of Arizona Press.
2005. Landscape dynamics in SW Arabia and the Fertile Crescent: Integrating settlement, geoarchaeology and climate change. *Geoarchaeology* 20: 169–192.
2006. From Highland to Desert: The Organization of Landscape and Irrigation in Southern Arabia. Pages 38–70 in J. Marcus & C. Stanish (eds), *Agricultural Strategies*. Los Angeles: Cotsen Insitute of Archaeology, University of California.

Yair A.
2001. Water-Harvesting Efficiency in Arid and Semiarid Areas. Pages 289–302 in S-W. Brecklem (ed.), *Sustainable Land Use in Deserts*. Berlin: Springer-Verlag.

Zarins J.
1992. Pastoral nomadism in Arabia: ethnoarchaeology and the archaeological record — a case study. Pages 219–240 in O. Bar-Yosef & A. Khazanov (eds), *Pastoralism in the Levant, Archaeological Materials in Anthropological Perspectives*. Madison, WI: Prehistory Press.
2001. *The Land of Incense: Archaeological Work in the Governorate of Dhofar, Sultanate of Oman, 1990–1995*. Muscat, Oman: Sultan Qaboos University Publications.

Author's address
Michael J. Harrower, Department of Anthropology, University of Toronto, 19 Russell St., Toronto ON, M5S 2S2, Canada.
e-mail: m.harrower@utoronto.ca

Proceedings of the Seminar for Arabian Studies 38 (2008): 203–214

A field methodology for the quantification of ancient settlement in an Arabian context

Nasser Said al-Jahwari & Derek Kennet

Summary
Most field surveys apply systematic methodologies of field walking and surface survey sampling techniques in order to quantify settlement in a way that allows inter-period and inter-regional comparisons to be made. These methods, which were mostly developed for the ploughed fields of northern Europe, the Mediterranean, and Mesopotamia, depend on a systematic, probabilistic approach that allows the collection of statistically valid data and the ability of the archaeologist to define and to count "sites". In many parts of Arabia, particularly the cultivated areas of the Arabian Gulf, it is difficult to apply these techniques because of the nature of the geography and agriculture. This paper describes a survey methodology that is capable of taking into consideration the landscape peculiarities of the Oman peninsula and allows the quantification of ancient settlement intensities in an unbiased and testable way. The paper describes a case study survey carried out using this method in the Wadi Andam in the al-Sharqiyah region of the Sultanate of Oman. It sets out the method used, and presents a preliminary indication and discussion of the results achieved.

Keywords: Oman peninsula, Wadi Andam, settlement history, archaeological survey

Introduction

One of the prime objectives of archaeological field survey is to quantify settlement in a way that allows inter-period and inter-regional comparisons to be made. To this end systematic methodologies of sampling, field walking, and defining and counting sites have been developed (e.g. Bintliff & Sbonias 1999; Francovich, Patterson & Barker 2000; Wilkinson TJ 2003: 37–39). Such methodologies have led to a much clearer understanding of settlement history in many parts of the world including the Near East: for example, the seminal work of Adams in Mesopotamia (1965; 1981) has identified periods of growth, intensification, and decline of settlement over long periods of time, adding enormously to our understanding of the history of settlement in that region (Fig. 1).

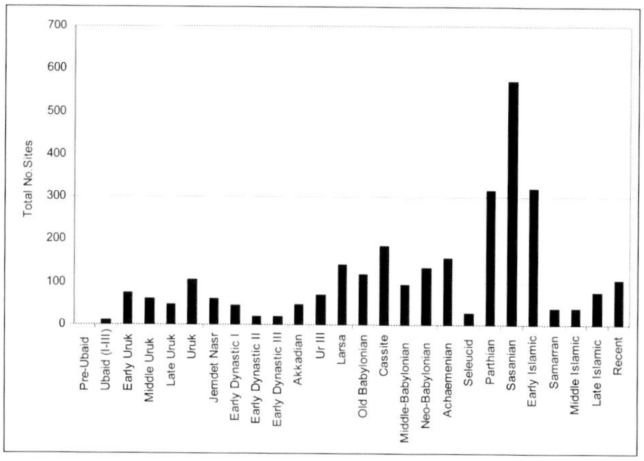

Figure 1. *A graph showing the total number of recorded sites by period in southern Iraq (from Adams 1981).*

Most of these methods depend on two methodological assumptions. Firstly a systematic, probabilistic approach that allows the collection of statistically valid data and secondly the ability of the archaeologist to define and to count "sites", i.e. discreet and definable areas of archaeological scatter or mounding with a discreet and definable period of occupation. This concept of a "site" was developed in the relatively flat, ploughed fields of northern Europe, the Mediterranean, and Mesopotamia where it is, for the most part, easily applicable. However, the concept is not universally applicable because of regional differences in the nature of ancient occupation, surface geography, and agricultural techniques, all of which may have affected the preservation and recovery of archaeological deposits in a variety of ways.

FIGURE 2. *A typical wadi village on the banks of the Wadi Andam.*

The situation in many parts of Arabia presents particular difficulties for the definition of sites and thereby for the quantification of ancient settlement. This paper describes these difficulties in the specific circumstances of the al-Sharqiyah region of the Sultanate of Oman and presents a field methodology that attempts to overcome them and thereby permit the quantification of ancient settlement intensities in an unbiased and testable way.

Peculiarities of the Arabian environment

The arid landscape of the al-Sharqiyah region, as in much of the Oman peninsula, is characterized largely by high, rugged mountains and rocky hills with very steep slopes and little or no soil cover. These are intersected by wadis which are narrow and steep in their upper reaches and broader in their lower reaches where they are associated with flat, rolling, arid interfluves that have only limited soil cover. Very little of this environment is suitable for agricultural settlement, being too steep, too narrow, lacking in soil cover, or lacking in water. There are only a few places in the landscape that are suitable for agricultural settlement and these are generally found on the banks of the larger wadis in the parts where sufficient space is present between the wadi channel and the hill slopes (Fig. 2). These locations therefore tend to have been occupied repeatedly, later occupation and agricultural activity having disturbed and obscured the remains of earlier settlements and, for the most part, rendered impossible the definition of sites with a limited chronological or spatial extent (see below). Instead of the landscape presenting a broad canvas onto which a settlement pattern can be drawn, it presents a very limited number of potential locations that have, in many cases, been constantly or repeatedly occupied. This means that single or short-period occupation sites can only rarely be identified and site counting is not possible. This problem has already been noted and discussed by various field workers in the region (e.g. Costa & Wilkinson 1987; Kennet 2002: 154; Wilkinson TJ 1974: 123–132).

This situation is replicated in many other parts of the Arabian Peninsula where a similar geography prevails and where settlements are concentrated in wadis and mountainous areas.

Traditional survey methods

Numerous archaeological surveys have been carried out in the al-Sharqiyah and surrounding regions (e.g. Humphries 1974; Hastings, Humphries & Meadow 1975; de Cardi, Collier & Doe 1976; de Cardi, Doe & Roskams 1977; Doe 1977; Weisgerber 1980; 1981; Yule

& Weisgerber 1988; Orchard & Stanger 1994; 1999; Ibrahim & Gaube 2000; Häser 2000; 2003; Schreiber 2004; 2005; 2007) but none of them have been concerned specifically with collecting quantified data on settlement. They have instead, for the most part, set out to locate, explore, and describe areas or settlements or to answer specific research questions. Many of them provide excellent descriptive data on settlement and, when their results are viewed together, it is possible to gain a picture of longer-term regional trends in the growth and decline of settlement intensity. Unfortunately, however, the lack of systematic, probabilistic methodologies means that such trends are unverifiable and are potentially biased and misleading. Some surveys working in similar environments have attempted to use methodologies that give statistically valid data, but they are in the minority (e.g. Costa & Wilkinson 1987; de Cardi, Kennet & Stocks 1994; Kennet 2002). No tried and tested methodology of quantifiable field survey has yet been established for the region.

Wadi agriculture

Before developing a quantified method that is capable of taking into consideration the nature and peculiarities of this landscape, it is important to understand the most significant post-depositional processes that have affected the archaeological evidence. As has already been noted, the relatively limited number of locations where agricultural settlement is possible appears to have been a major constraining factor in the settlement pattern. It has meant that many locations have been repeatedly occupied through many archaeological periods. This, in turn, has meant that the remains of older settlements will have been disturbed or destroyed by later occupation as well as the natural processes of alluviation and erosion. More importantly, as will be shown below, the high degree of land disturbance caused by traditional practices used in date-palm agriculture destroys, obscures, and disturbs archaeological material creating a confused surface scatter of pottery in which all periods of occupation are represented, although in a very mixed state.

To understand these processes, the various stages of what can be called the "cycle of wadi agriculture" have been mapped out in Figure 3. This shows the fictional example of a settlement consisting of a number of mud-brick buildings that was established during the Umm an-Nar period on the lower hill slopes above the wadi bed (Fig. 3/1). Once the settlement was abandoned its structures and the pottery-containing deposits associated with them eroded and spread down the slopes and out onto the wadi channel, where they became partly buried by alluvium (Fig. 3/2 & 3). At a later time date-palm groves were established, involving excavation into the alluvium to facilitate irrigation and necessitating the piling up of the excavated earth into bunds and clearance mounds (Fig. 3/4). The bunds and clearance mounds would include traces of buried archaeological materials resulting from the earlier Umm an-Nar settlement, in particular pottery. Temporary abandonment of the settlement will result, in turn, in the date-palm groves and bunds being eroded and buried by alluvium (Fig. 3/5). In due course the cycle will repeat itself with each subsequent abandonment and reoccupation (Fig. 3/5 & 6).

This cycle destroys and obscures archaeological remains and leaves only very limited and fragmentary evidence, such as tombs on the fringes of occupied areas and perhaps occupation deposits in the sections of wells dug into the alluvium. However, the process does have one important advantage for the archaeologist: the constant churning of the mixed alluvium and archaeological deposits caused by the agricultural cycle will bring to the surface buried archaeological material resulting from earlier periods of occupation. This will present itself as a very mixed surface scatter, which is likely to contain some traces of all periods during which the site has been occupied, even if only in very limited quantities.

Large-scale pottery collection

In order to exploit the archaeological potential of these pottery scatters, large-scale surface pottery collection is necessary. This is a method that has already been used in this region, for example, at Siraf (Wilkinson TJ 1974), Suhar (Costa & Wilkinson 1987) and in Ras al-Khaimah (de Cardi, Kennet & Stocks 1994; Kennet 2002). It was further developed, tested and perfected by one of the present authors (N.S. al-Jahwari) during the course of his PhD research in the Wadi Andam (below).

The method is very simple: on arrival at a settlement location, which in most cases is also the site of a modern wadi village with ongoing occupation and agriculture, the first step was to make a rough sketch plan of the entire location, using a few fixed points from a hand-held GPS for increased accuracy (Fig. 4). This sketch plan could potentially be combined with a geo-corrected satellite photograph if available. The locality was then divided on the sketch plan into a number of arbitrary pottery collection areas (PCAs) of varying shape and up to about 4 ha in size, each of which was numbered (Fig. 5). The

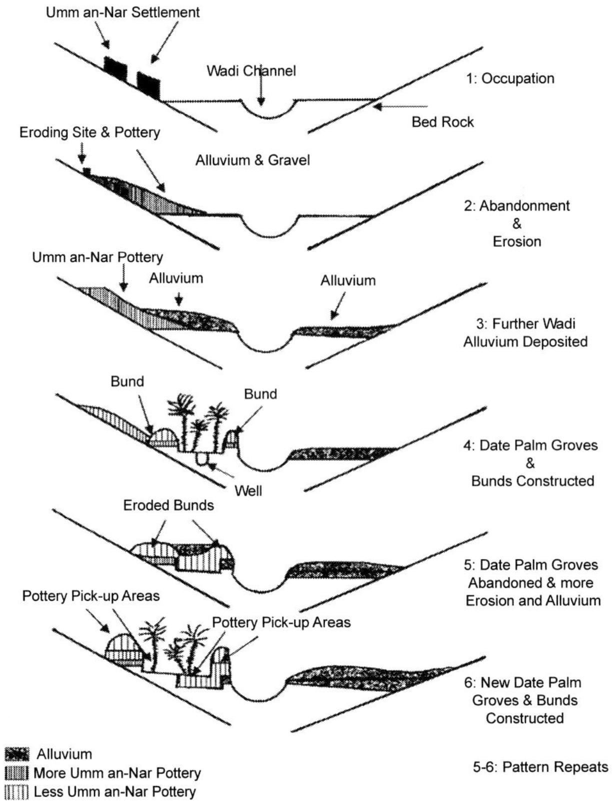

Figure 3. *The "cycle" of wadi agriculture*

PCAs are normally irregularly shaped because features such as tracks and field boundaries were used to delimit them. In theory pottery from the entire location could be collected and mixed together but the PCAs offer the opportunity to locate surface collections with a slightly higher degree of precision, and also allow a limited degree of spatial comparison across the wadi village location.

A large collection of surface sherds was then made from each of the PCAs; normally pottery was collected by one individual for between twenty and thirty minutes, picking up all visible ceramics. This resulted in large sherd collections of up to about 600 sherds from a single PCA in some cases. The pottery was then taken back to base camp, washed, sorted, and identified by ware and archaeological period. All sherds were recorded on an electronic database to facilitate interrogation and analysis of the data. In order to gain a quantifiable impression of the amount of activity or settlement, two approaches can be taken: counts can be made of the number of sherds of each archaeological period in the assemblages, either from individual PCAs, from individual wadi villages, or from all or a number of wadi villages, in order to give an impression of the changing levels of activity. It is also possible to use what might be termed a "ubiquity" or "presence-or-absence" analysis to count the PCAs or wadi villages at which sherds of any particular archaeological period were found.

In order to illustrate the method and to present some preliminary data, a summary of the work and the results of two seasons' work in the Wadi Andam are briefly described below.

A test case: the Wadi Andam survey

Methodology

In the winter of 2004–2005 and 2005–2006, a survey was carried out in the Wadi Andam in the al-Sharqiyah region of the Sultanate of Oman. This wadi lies approximately between 22° 45' N and 57° 98' E, and is one of the major wadis crossing the Wilayat al-Mudaybi and Sinaw,

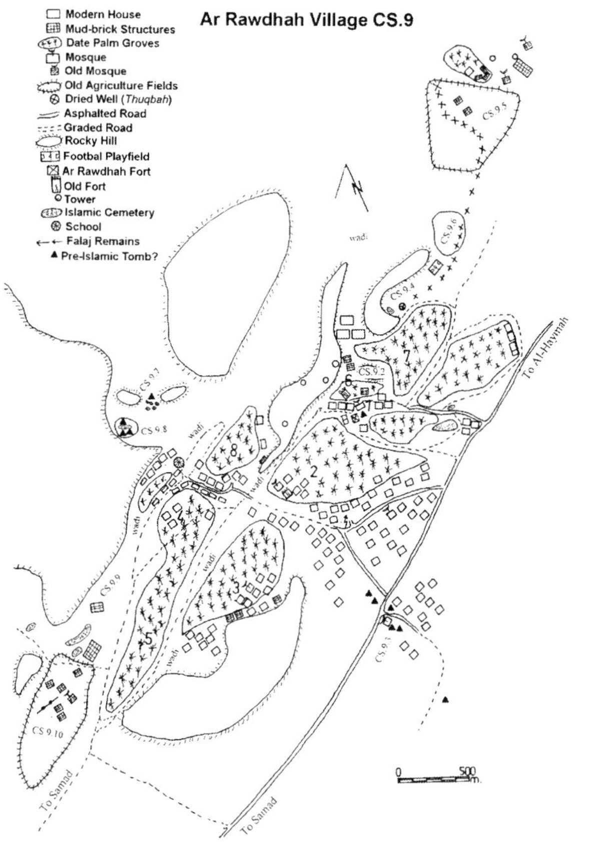

Figure 4. *A sketch plan of the wadi village al-Rawdah.*

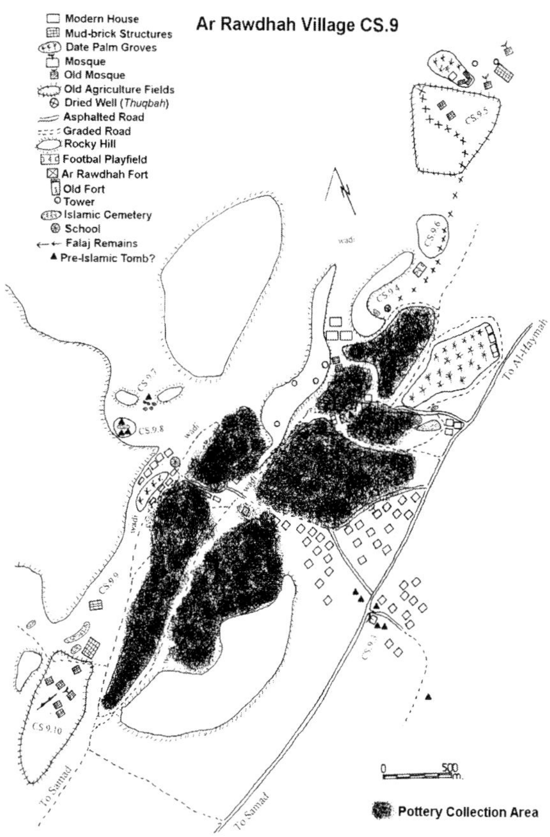

Figure 5. *A sketch plan showing the Pottery Collection Areas in the wadi village al-Rawdah.*

extending for hundreds of kilometres in the Sharqiyah region (ElMahi & al-Jahwari 2005: 57). It passes most of the villages in al-Mudaybi and runs into the Wadi Halfayn basin, reaching the Arabian Sea close to the Hijj area in Wilayat Mahuwt in the south. There are several tributary wadis joining the Wadi Andam, all of which are dry for most of the year but, along with the Wadi Andam, these tributary wadis are the only locations with surface and subsurface water in the area (2005: 57). The survey transect measures 40 km x 100 km and covers four geographical zones: 1) watersheds and upper wadi in the far north; 2) lower wadis; 3) gravel hills and broad wadis; and 4) gravel flat interfluves zone in the south (Fig. 6).

The first archaeological investigations in the Wadi Andam occurred during the early 1970s when the Harvard Archaeological Expedition carried out a rough survey using a traditional methodology with the aim of locating early settlement sites, particularly those dated to the third millennium BC (e.g. Pullar 1974; Humphries 1974; Hastings, Humphries & Meadow 1975; Meadow, Humphries & Hastings 1976). Other investigations were carried out in this wadi by the British Archaeological Mission (e.g. de Cardi, Collier & Doe 1976; de Cardi, Doe & Roskams 1977; Doe 1977) as well as the work carried out by the German Archaeological Mission in the al-Sharqiyah region, mainly the Samad-Maysar area (e.g. Weisgerber 1980; 1981; Yule & Weisgerber 1988; Yule & Kazenwadel 1993; Yule 1993; 2001). The latter project focused on recording specific types of sites, namely Late Iron Age/Samad tombs in order to understand the distribution and chronology of activity of this period. It is important to indicate, therefore, that at least two of these surveys were focused principally on recording sites of a specific archaeological period, which may lead to a biased picture of settlement history if the results are used in a quantified way.

The aim of carrying out the Wadi Andam survey was to employ a rigorous, probabilistic sampling technique in order to collect data that is free from period bias, testable and suitable for quantified analysis, and that in turn allows analysis of activity and settlement intensity over time. To achieve this, the Wadi Andam survey involved surveying six selected wadi village locations along the banks of the wadi and its tributaries, each representing at least one of the wadi's geographical zones (Fig. 6). (1)

A number of control surveys of around 5 km^2 were carried out by car and on foot in randomly selected locations away from wadi villages, in order to check for evidence of different types of occupation in locations other than those under discussion here. Next, a preliminary "surrounding survey" was carried out by car and on foot around each selected wadi village to a distance of between 1 and 2 km^2, in order to check for peripheral archaeological features and to collect pottery. This included checking all agricultural areas, and areas of land disturbance such as wells.

Each wadi village was then divided into pottery collection areas (PCAs) and pottery was collected exactly according to the method described above. All areas of the village, including date-palm groves and modern occupation, were included.

Results

A total of 19,240 sherds were collected from the whole survey, of which 9,702 come from thirty-six PCAs in six wadi villages. It was thought that a sample this large would be necessary in order to increase the possibility of finding pottery from periods which are not generally well represented, such as the Wadi Suq period.

Figure 7 shows the total number of sherds by period from all sites recorded by the survey, i.e. the wadi villages as well as the control surveys and other locations visited by the survey. (2) It shows that the majority of sherds are from the Islamic period, mainly the Late Islamic period. Among the pre-Islamic sherds, Late Iron Age/Samad sherds are the most common, followed by the Umm an-Nar period. This figure also shows that there are very few sherds from the Wadi Suq and Sasanian/Early Islamic periods. Table 3 shows the sherd counts only from the PCAs from the six surveyed wadi villages. It shows the same trends as the whole survey, i.e. that the most common sherds are those dated to the Late Islamic period. To have a clearer idea of the pre-Islamic periods, Table 4 shows sherds only from these periods from the PCAs in the six wadi villages. It shows that sherds of the Umm an-Nar period are by far the most common, followed by the Late Iron Age/Samad, while the least common are sherds of the Wadi Suq, Early Iron Age and Sasanian/Early Islamic periods.

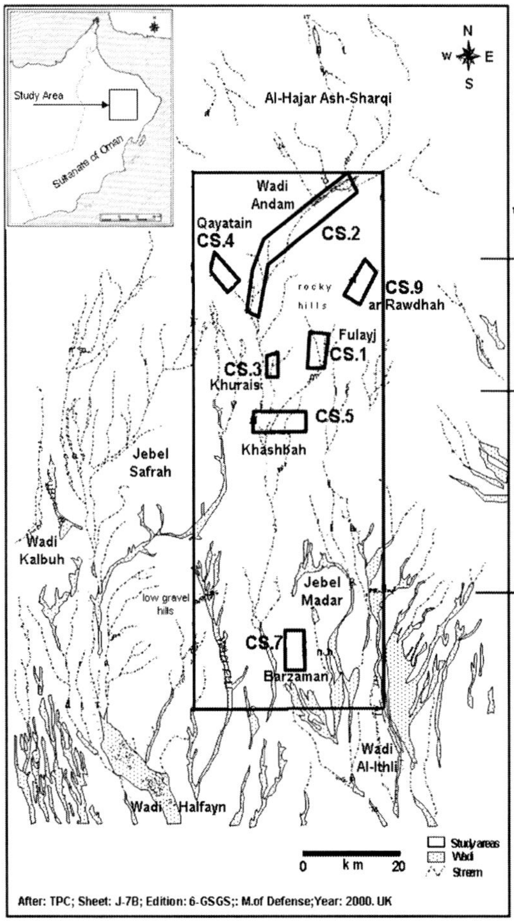

FIGURE 6. *A map showing the survey transect and the location of surveyed areas.*

Table 1 shows how many of the wadi villages and PCAs yielded sherds of each of the pre-Islamic periods. This is a "ubiquity" or "presence or absence" analysis. It shows that, without any doubt, almost all the villages were already occupied by the Umm an-Nar period and that, whilst occupation appears to have ceased or diminished drastically at most villages during the Wadi Suq period, they were almost all reoccupied by the Late Iron Age.

If we accept that the amount of pottery picked up from each period in the PCAs will be a rough reflection of the amount of settlement activity in those periods — in other words, that it can be used as a "proxy" for settlement activity — then Figures 7-9 show the broad pattern of change in the amount of settlement activity through time in this area and in these wadi villages. However crude, this is already a very useful set of data presenting a quantifiable and comparable yardstick with which we can begin to take a more systematic approach to changes in

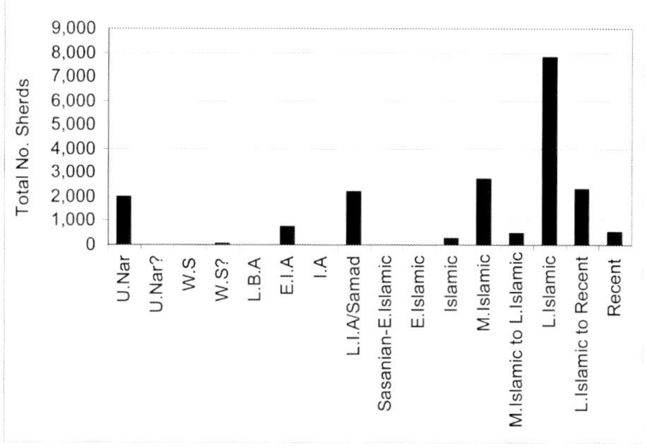

FIGURE 7. *A graph showing the total number of sherds by period from the whole survey.*

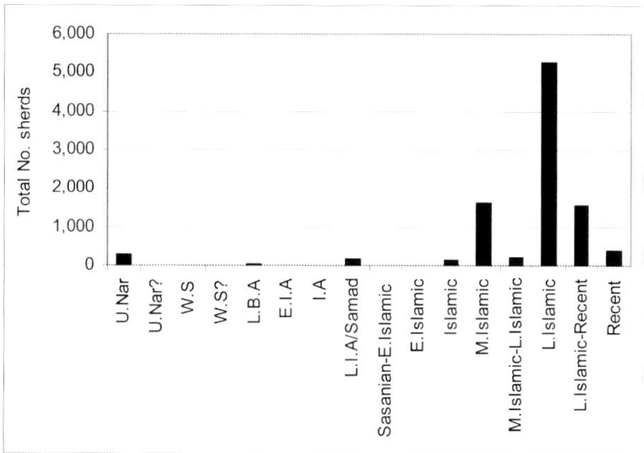

FIGURE 8. *A graph showing the sherd count by period from all the Pottery Collection Areas within the wadi villages.*

the amount of activity in this archaeologically difficult environment. It should be noted that the pattern within each wadi village is only relative. That is to say that the amount of pottery is not an absolute quantification of the amount of activity in any particular period, but only a number which can be roughly compared to other archaeological periods, so that it is possible to say, for example, that there was considerably more Umm an-Nar activity than there was Wadi Suq activity at a particular location. At a broader level, beyond individual wadi villages, the data can be used in an absolute sense, in that it can be stated, for example, that only one out of six wadi villages shows any evidence of settlement activity during the Wadi Suq period.

These initial conclusions rely upon the fact that pottery was in common use during all of the periods under

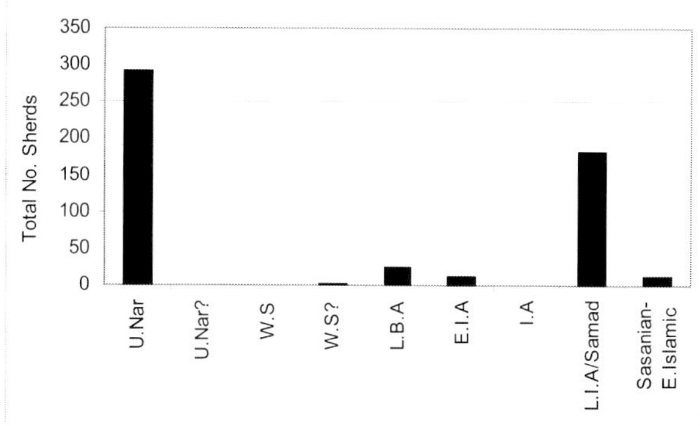

FIGURE 9. *A graph showing the total number of sherds of the pre-Islamic and early Islamic periods from all the Pottery Collection Areas within the wadi villages.*

consideration, that it was of a consistent, robust quality, and that there were no major fluctuations in the amount of pottery that was produced or used at any time. There is increasing evidence from excavations elsewhere in the region that this was indeed the case. It is of course possible that there may have been some fluctuation in the amount of pottery that was produced and used by individual groups at a very localised level, and that such fluctuations may be partly responsible for the changes in pottery deposition that have been detected using this methodology. Such issues remain to be resolved but can only be investigated though the collection and quantification of pottery from both survey and excavation.

The pattern is complicated by tombs, which appear to indicate a slightly different trend. Tombs of the Umm an-Nar, Wadi Suq, and Iron Age periods can be found in and around many of the wadi villages as well as in the surrounding areas, although they can be difficult to date and many have been reused much later than their original construction. Table 6 shows the total number and percentage of sherds by period from all types of sites: PCAs, tombs, and other types of structures. It makes clear a very important point, which is that, compared to other periods, a very high proportion of the pottery for the Wadi Suq and Early Iron Age periods is associated with tombs, whereas very few of the sherds from these two periods come from probable settlement locations such as PCAs.

The evidence for the continued use of tombs during the Wadi Suq period is intriguing. All of these tombs are located on the fringes of the wadi villages that the PCA evidence suggests had been largely abandoned during this period. The most likely explanation for this seems to be that these tombs continued to be used, either by very small residual communities who have left hardly

Period	Total number of wadi villages yielding pottery from PCAs	Proportion of wadi villages yielding pottery from PCAs
U.Nar	5	83 %
W.S.	1	17 %
L.B.A.	1	17 %
E.I.A.	2	33 %
L.I.A./Samad	5	83 %
Total	6	

Table 1. *Counts of wadi villages yielding pottery from PCAs.*

Period	PCAs	Tombs		Total sherds
U.Nar	292 (20.1%)	630 (43.4%)	531 (36.5%)	1453
W.S.	3 (12.5%)	18 (75%)	3 (12.5%)	24
L.B.A.	25 (100%)	0	0	25
E.I.A.	12 (3.3%)	271 (74%)	83 (22.7%)	366
L.I.A./ Samad	182 (31.4%)	180 (31%)	218 (37.6%)	580

Table 2. *The number and percentage of sherds by period from PCAs, all tombs (most of which come from the "surrounding surveys"), and "surrounding surveys" (including some tombs) (% based on the total number of sherds by period).*

any trace in the archaeological record, or by nomadic or semi-nomadic populations who continued to use the old abandoned settlements as camp sites and cemeteries. This might indicate some sort of cultural attachment to ancestral lands, or it might simply indicate that these locations continued to be attractive due to the natural resources they offered, or for other reasons. Whatever the explanation, the evidence indicates at least some degree of continuity through a period of very low settlement intensity.

Clearly much more could be done with these data and a fuller analysis will be presented in the forthcoming PhD thesis of N.S. al-Jahwari. The intention here has simply been to demonstrate the potential of the method through illustration of a detailed case study.

Interpretation

The patterns of change that emerge from the Wadi Andam data serve to confirm and add detail to the general understanding of cultural and economic changes that have affected the Oman peninsula through time. For the pre-Islamic period particularly, a number of interesting and important points emerge.

For example Tables 1 and 2 show that there is a large amount of evidence of the Umm an-Nar period from both PCAs and tombs and that, when both PCAs and tombs are taken into consideration, all modern wadi villages have yielded evidence of the Umm an-Nar period. This indicates that the Umm an-Nar period was one of the most intensive periods of occupation, and also that the study area was extensively inhabited during this period for the first time.

Most of the evidence comes from agriculturally viable locations suggesting a sedentary way of life. With the exception of a few Hafit period beehives/cairns surrounding some of the wadi villages, the Umm an-Nar material is the earliest evidence for the occupation of these villages, suggesting that it was at this time that these settlements first came into existence. If this pattern is shown to be true elsewhere in the Oman peninsula, then it suggests that a fundamental change in settlement and economy took place at the beginning of the Umm an-Nar period, with widespread sedentary occupation being accompanied by the emergence of a single distinctive culture over the whole region as well as specialized production of pottery and other artefacts. Since this time, settlements have remained largely in the same locations suggesting that more or less the same constraints affected settlement location in the Umm an-Nar period as they have done for much of the past. Since the Umm an-Nar period these settlements have only really varied in the intensity of occupation from one period to the next.

By contrast, the PCA evidence indicates a significant decline in both the intensity of occupation during the Wadi Suq period, and also in the number of settlement locations that were in use. As has been noted above, this may reflect a significant decline in the population or a move towards nomadism, or perhaps both. Of course, it may also reflect a change in the way that pottery was used and deposited, although evidence from Wadi Suq period settlements elsewhere in the region, such as Kalba and Tell Abraq, suggests that this was not the case.

A decline in activity during the Wadi Suq period has long been debated by archaeologists, based on an assessment of the number of sites that are known from the literature and the fact that Wadi Suq layers are absent from a number of key sites (e.g. Cleuziou 1981). The data presented here are the first to give a quantifiable indication of the relative scale of this decline at the lowest level of the settlement hierarchy. A much clearer picture, possibly showing regional variations, would emerge were further studies of this kind to be undertaken more widely across the peninsula.

At present it is difficult to give an explanation for the Wadi Suq decline. It has been argued that it might be related to a change in climate at the end of the third millennium BC (Brunswig 1989: 37–38) but radiocarbon evidence from playa lake beds indicates that the peninsula witnessed progressive aridity from as early as the end of the fourth millennium BC (e.g. McClure 1988; Parker *et al*. 2006: 474). It has also been argued that the decline of the wealth of the Oman peninsula during the first part of the second millennium BC was a result of changes in the economy of the Arabian Gulf at that time (Crawford 1996; 1998). However, whether these events can be linked to changes in settlement intensity in areas such as the Wadi Andam has still to be demonstrated.

The PCA evidence from the Wadi Andam Survey supports the idea that there was an increase in settlement intensity at the beginning of the Iron Age after the Wadi Suq decline. In addition, a relatively large amount of Early Iron Age pottery has been found from the "surrounding surveys" and control surveys outside the wadi villages, suggesting that activity may have emerged in these areas for the first time during this period. This material may result from Iron Age sites in defensive locations of the type that are known from elsewhere in the region at this time. It has already been argued that this period is one of increasing population and a developing social hierarchy and that the intensification in settlement might be related to the introduction of a *falaj* system (Wilkinson JC 1983: 177–194; Potts 1990: 354; al-Tikriti 2002: 117–140; Magee 1998: 51–54; 2004: 41; 2005: 225–228; Häser 2004: 417–419).

The evidence suggests that the Late Iron Age/Samad period saw a continuation of the revival of settlement intensity, reaching levels that were, perhaps, not far below those that had been achieved during the Umm an-Nar period. A decline in activity during the Sasanian period, followed by an increase in activity throughout the Islamic period has already been argued elsewhere (Kennet 2002; 2007).

There is unfortunately no space here for further discussion of these data and the trends that they suggest, but it is hoped that enough has been said to demonstrate the usefulness of this method of survey and the relevance of the data that it can yield to current debates.

Conclusion

To conclude, it can be argued that the methodology presented here, which is based on large-scale surface pottery collection, can be shown to be effective in providing quantifiable data on settlement activity and intensity that has a greater degree of statistical validity than data collected in a traditional, non-probabilistic fashion. The methodology also allows a more reliable comparison between sites and regions to be made and potentially provides a degree of detail and insight that would be missed by other survey techniques. The method takes into consideration the nature of the geographical environment as well as post-depositional processes such as traditional agricultural techniques. On the down side, the method is very time-consuming and labour-intensive as it depends on the collection of large quantities of pottery that require study, catalogue, and storage.

It seems sensible to suggest that this methodology might best be used judiciously to support traditional survey techniques in a way that will allow more detailed and robust conclusions to be drawn without creating an undue strain on project resources.

Acknowledgements

Thanks are due to Sultan Qaboos University, the Historical Association of Oman, and the Society for Arabian Studies in London for their participation in funding the Wadi Andam Survey. Grateful thanks are also extended to Dr Jürgen Schreiber, Mr John Martin, Mr Nasser al-Hinaei, Mr Yaboob Al-Rahbi, Mr Ali Al-Mahroqi, Mr Christian Velde, and Mr Salah al-Masrori for their kind help, and to Dr Peter Magee for reading and commenting on a draft of this paper.

Notes

1. For a fuller outline of the survey methodology see the forthcoming PhD thesis by N.S. al-Jahwari to be submitted to the Department of Archaeology, Durham University.

2. U.Nar = Umm an-Nar; W.S. = Wadi Suq; L.B.A. = Late Bronze Age; E.I.A. = Early Iron Age; I.A. = general Iron Age; L.I.A./Samad = Late Iron Age/ Samad.

References

Adams R.McC.

1965. *Land Behind Baghdad: a History of Settlement on the Diyala Plains.* Chicago: University of Chicago Press.

1981. *Heartland of Cities: Surveys of Ancient Settlement and Land Use on the Central Floodplain of the Euphrates*. Chicago: University of Chicago Press.

Bintliff J. & Sbonias K. (eds)

1999. *The Archaeology of Mediterranean Landscapes 1: Reconstructing Past Population Trends in Mediterranean Europe*. Oxford: Oxbow.

Brunswig Jr.R.H.

1989. Cultural History, Environment and Economy as seen from an Umm an-Nar Settlement: Evidence from Test Excavations at Bāt, Oman, 1977/78. *Journal of Oman Studies* 10: 9–50.

Cleuziou S.

1981. Oman Peninsula in the Early Second Millennium BC. Pages 279–293 in M. Taddei (ed.), *South Asian Archaeology*, 1979. Berlin: Dietrich Reimer Verlag.

Costa P.M. & Wilkinson T.J.

1987. The Hinterland of Sohar. *Journal of Oman Studies* 9: 79–88.

Crawford H.

1996. Dilmun, victim of World Recession. *Proceedings of the Seminar for Arabian Studies* 26: 13–22.

1998. *Dilmun and its Gulf Neighbours*. Cambridge: Cambridge University Press.

de Cardi B., Collier S. & Doe D.B.

1976. Excavations and Survey in Oman, 1974–1975. *Journal of Oman Studies* 2: 101–199.

de Cardi B., Doe D.B. & Roskams S.P.

1977. Excavation and Survey in the Sharqiyah, Oman, 1976. *Journal of Oman Studies* 3/1: 17–33.

de Cardi B., Kennet D. & Stocks L.

1994. Five Thousand Years of Settlement at Khatt, UAE. *Proceedings of the Seminar for Arabian Studies* 24: 35–95.

Doe D.B.

1977. Gazetteer of Sites in Oman, 1976. *Journal of Oman Studies* 3/1: 35–58.

ElMahi A.T. & al-Jahwari N.S.

2005. Tombs at Mahleya in Wadi Andam (Sultanate of Oman): A View of a Late Iron Age and Samad Period Death Culture**.** *Proceedings of the Seminar for Arabian Studies* 35: 57–69.

Francovich R., Patterson H. & Barker G. (eds)

2000. *The Archaeology of Mediterranean Landscapes 5: Extracting Meaning from Ploughsoil Assemblages*. Oxford: Oxbow Books.

Häser J.

2000. Formation and Transformation Processes of Oasis Settlements in the Sultanate of Oman: Preliminary Report on a New Field Project. *Proceedings of the Seminar for Arabian Studies* 30: 115–118.

2003. Archaeological Results of the 1999 and 2000 Survey Campaigns in Wādī Banī ʿAwf and the Region of al-Hamrāʾ (Central Oman). *Proceedings of the Seminar for Arabian Studies* 33: 21–30.

2004. Prehistoric Agricultural Water-Management on the Oman Peninsula. Pages 415–421 in J. Häser & H-D. Bienert (eds), *Orient-Archäologie 13: Men of Dikes and Canals, the Archaeology of Water in the Middle East*. Rahden: Deutsches Archäologisches Institut Orient-Abteilung.

Hastings A., Humphries J.H. & Meadow R.H.
1975. Oman in the Third Millennium BCE. *Journal of Oman Studies* 1: 9–55.
Humphries J.H.
1974. Harvard Archaeological Survey in Oman: II — Some Later Prehistoric Sites in the Sultanate of Oman. *Proceedings of the Seminar for Arabian Studies* 4: 49–77.
Ibrahim M. & Gaube H.
2000. *Oasis Settlement in Oman: Pilot Study 1999–2000.* [Unpublished Report].
Kennet D.
2002. The Development of Northern Ra's al-Khaimah and the 14th-century Hormuzi Economic Boom in the Lower Gulf. *Proceedings of the Seminar for Arabian Studies* 32: 151–164.
2007. The Decline of Eastern Arabia in the Sasanian period. *Arabian Archaeology and Epigraphy* 18: 86–122.
McClure H.A.
1988. Late Quaternary Palaeogeography and Landscape Evolution of the Rub al-Khali. Pages 9–13 in D.T. Potts (ed.), *Araby the Blest: Studies in Arabian Archaeology*. (Carsten Niebuhr Institute Publications, 7). Copenhagen: The Carsten Niebuhr Institute.
Magee P.
1998. Settlement Patterns, Polities and Regional Complexity in the Southeast Arabian Iron Age. *Paléorient* 24/2: 49–60.
2004. The Impact of Southeast Arabian Intra-Regional Trade on Settlement Location and Organization during the Iron Age II Period. *Arabian Archaeology and Epigraphy* 15: 24–42.
2005. The Chronology and Environmental Background of Iron Age Settlement in Southeastern Iran and the Question of the Origin of the Qanat Irrigation System. *Iranica Antiqua* 40: 217–231.
Meadow R.H., Humphries J.H. & Hastings A.
1976. Exploration in Oman, 1973 and 1975: Prehistoric Settlements and Ancient Copper Smelting with its Comparative Aspects in Iran. Pages 110–129 in F. Bagherzadeh (ed.), *Proceedings of the IV Annual Symposium of Archaeological Research in Iran 3rd–8th November 1975*. Tehran: Iranian Center for Archaeological Research.
Orchard J. & Stanger G.
1994. Third Millennium Oasis Towns and Environmental Constraints on Settlement in the Al-Hajar Region. *Iraq* 56: 63–100.
1999. Al-Hajar Oasis Towns Again! *Iraq* 61: 89–119.
Parker A.G., Goudie A.S., Stokes S., White K., Hodson M.J., Manning M. & Kennet D.
2006. A record of Holocene climate change from lake geochemical analyses in southeastern Arabia. *Quaternary Research* 66/3: 465–476.
Potts D.T.
1990. *The Arabian Gulf in Antiquity*. i. Oxford: Clarendon Press.
Pullar J.
1974. Harvard Archaeological Survey in Oman, 1973: I — Flint Sites in Oman. *Proceedings of the Seminar for Arabian Studies* 4: 33–48.
Schreiber J.
2004. Archaeological Reconnaissance at Izki and the Jebel Akhdar: Transformation Processes of Oasis Settlement in Oman 2004, Third Stage: A Preliminary Report. *Occident & Orient* 9/1–2: 6–11.
2005. Archaeological Survey at Ibra in the Sharqiyah, Sultanate of Oman. *Proceedings of the Seminar for Arabian Studies* 35: 255–270.
2007. "Transformation processes in oasis settlements in Oman" 2005 archaeological survey at the oasis of Nizwā: a preliminary report. *Proceedings of the Seminar for Arabian Studies* 37: 263–275.
Al-Tikriti W.Y.
2002. The South-East Arabian Origin of the Falaj system. *Proceedings of the Seminar for Arabian Studies* 32: 117–140.

Weisgerber G.
1980. "... und Kupfer in Oman" — Das Oman-Projekt des Deutschen Bergbau-Museums. *Der Anschnitt* 2–3, 32: 62–110.
1981. Mehr als Kupfer in Oman: Ergebnisse der Expedition 1981. *Der Anschnitt* 5–6, 33: 174–263.
Wilkinson J.C.
1983. The Origins of the Aflaj of Oman. *Journal of Oman Studies* 6/1: 177–194.
Wilkinson T.J.
1974. Agricultural Decline in the Siraf Region. *Paléorient* 2/1: 123–132.
2003. *Archaeological Landscapes of the Near East*. Tucson, AZ: The University of Arizona Press.
Yule P.
1993. Excavations at Samad Al Shān 1987–1991: summary. *Proceedings of the Seminar for Arabian Studies* 23: 141–153.
2001. *Die Gräberfelder in Samad al Shān (Sultanat Oman), Materialien zu einer Kultergeschichte*. Rahden: Verlag Marie Leidorf GmbH.
Yule P. & Kazenwadel B.
1993. Toward a Chronology of the Late Iron Age in the Sultanate of Oman. Pages 251–277 in U. Finkbeiner (ed.), *Materialien zur Archäologie der Seleukiden- und Partherzeit im sudlichen Babylonien und im Golfgebiet*. Tubingen: Deutsches Archäologisches Institut Abteilung Baghdad.
Yule P. & Weisgerber G.
1988. *Samad Ash-Shan: Excavations of the Pre-Islamic Cemeteries, Preliminary Report 1988*. Selbstverlag des Deutschen Bergbau-Museums. [Unpublished Report].

Authors' addresses
Nasser Said al-Jahwari, Department of Archaeology, College of Arts & Social Sciences, Sultan Qaboos University, P.O. Box 42, 123 Al-Khoud, Muscat, Sultanate of Oman.
e-mail buraimi75@hotmail.com

Derek Kennet, Department of Archaeology, Durham University, Durham DH1 3LE, UK.
e-mail derek.kennet@durham.ac.uk

Proceedings of the Seminar for Arabian Studies 38 (2008): 215–230

From prehistoric landscapes to urban sprawl: the Maṣnᶜat Māryah region of highland Yemen

Krista Lewis & Lamya Khalidi

Summary

The site of Maṣnᶜat Māryah in highland Yemen was a booming metropolis during the Himyarite era (first century BC–sixth century AD). Perched on the edge of the highland escarpment, its inhabitants overlooked roads, paths, and trade networks across the highlands and down to the Red Sea coast. Recent research has not only clarified these systems of early historic interaction but also revealed striking new evidence for the prehistoric antecedents of these patterns. This paper discusses the findings of several seasons of survey in and around Maṣnᶜat Māryah exploring long-term human use of the landscape. The Himyarite site of Māryah is well preserved with coherent urban planning evident from its streets, structures, and internal diversity. Māryah also lies at the centre of a network of distinctive contemporary satellite sites all oriented to face the urban centre. Prehistoric lithic materials recovered from the Māryah area deepen our perspective on long-term human resource exploitation in the region. We have also documented an important previously unsampled obsidian source nearby (Jirab al-Sawf) that was utilized from prehistoric to Islamic times. The prehistoric remains in the area are more than simply a prelude to Himyarite occupation, however. Megalithic monuments in visually prominent locations at Māryah are echoed by the similar placement of later special Himyarite structures, strongly suggesting an intentional continuity in symbolic manipulation of the landscape over time. From prehistoric utilisation of the landscape to the development of urbanism, this study underscores the importance of employing long-term perspectives to explore the more intriguing human dimensions of key cultural developments in ancient Arabia.

Keywords: Yemen, highlands, Himyarite, prehistory, obsidian

Introduction

The highland archaeological site of Maṣnᶜat Māryah is well known in the corpus of early historic sites in Yemen, mainly because of its large size, extensive well-preserved building remains, and *in situ* inscriptions. Until recently, however, the site and its surrounding landscape remained relatively uninvestigated. Several seasons of survey and excavation have now provided a much more detailed picture of land use and chronological development for the area. Our work has revealed complex strategies of urban and regional planning and resource extraction for the early historic Himyarite occupation, and confirmed human use of the area as early as the mid-Holocene.

Over several seasons of intensive survey in the area we have recorded additional key sites and landscape features and sampled a significant natural obsidian source. Our detailed mapping of Maṣnᶜat Māryah itself affords an insight into Himyarite urban planning strategies, architectural patterns, and relationships to other ancient towns. Here we discuss the implications of these findings for the highland archaeological record and for their insight into highland-lowland interaction spheres in southern Arabia.

The Maṣnᶜat Māryah study area

Ancient Māryah was an impressive urban centre, covering 36 ha in total. Māryah's scale is unparalleled by any other early historic site in the highlands, covering a much larger area than even the Himyarite capital city of Zafar. The extensive ruins that comprise the site of Maṣnᶜat Māryah occupy a prominent elongated plateau on the extreme western edge of the Yemeni highlands. The site overlooks fertile agricultural plains and valleys to the east and a dramatic drop in elevation plunging towards the Tihamah coast to the west. From its location at the edge of the highlands, Māryah guards a major pass through the escarpment edge mountain chain that was probably part of a major ancient route between the Tihamah and the

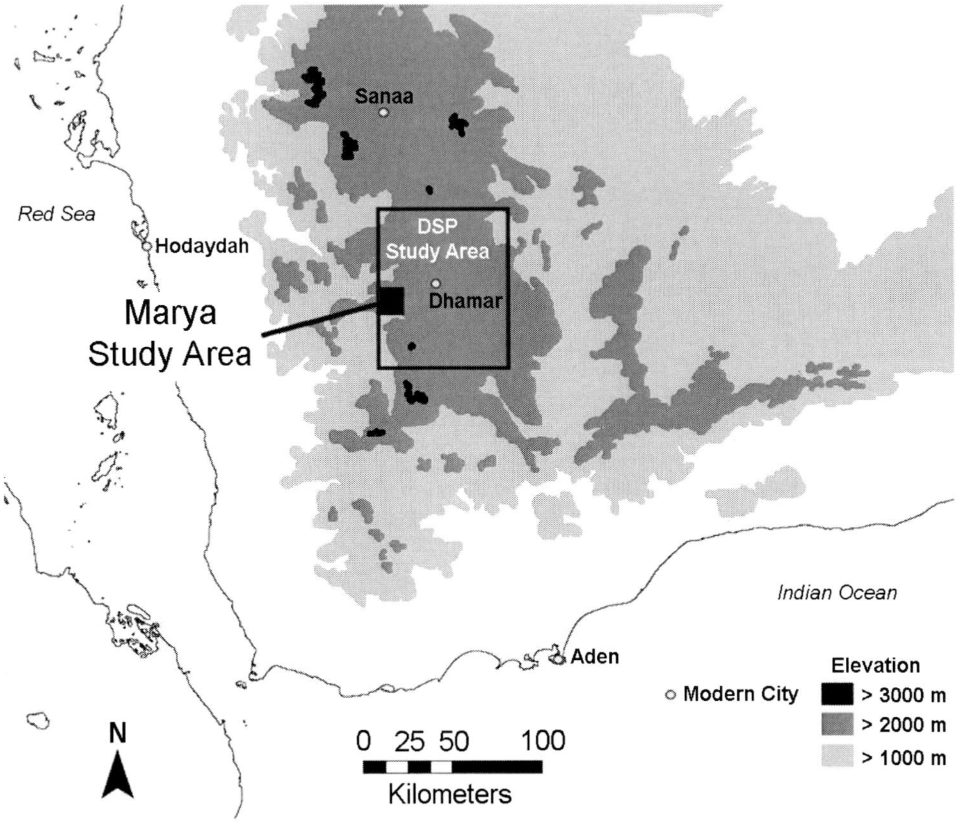

FIGURE 1. *The location of the Maṣnᶜat Māryah study area in south-west Arabia.*

highlands.

An Ancient South Arabian inscription at Māryah's West Gate mentions the Himyarite year 434 (Müller 1978). Current estimations place the beginning of the Himyarite era at 110 or 115 BC (Hoyland 2002: 72), placing this date at the end of the first quarter of the fourth century AD. This date likely refers to a flourishing period of residence and commerce in the city rather than its initial foundations; the archaeological evidence indicates the site was inhabited from well before that date. The site appears to have been completely abandoned at some point probably during later Himyarite or early Islamic times, since little evidence for Islamic remains can be found on the surface of the site.

The Maṣnᶜat Māryah study area lies approximately 13 km south-west of the modern city of Dhamār. (Fig. 1) This area is archaeologically dominated by the large Himyarite town of Maṣnᶜat Māryah (DS3) and four monumental Himyarite agricultural dams. This study area is part of the larger Dhamār Survey Project (DSP), a long-term research project in the central Yemeni highlands originally initiated by a team from the University of Chicago's Oriental Institute. Over the years, the DSP has developed into a multi-faceted collaborative research project involving scholars from a number of universities and institutions including most prominently Durham University, the University of Arkansas at Little Rock, the University of Chicago, the American Institute for Yemeni Studies, and the General Organization for Antiquities and Museums, Yemen (Barbanes 2000; Davies 2006; Edens 1999; Edens & Wilkinson 1998; Edens, Wilkinson & Barratt 2000; Gibson & Wilkinson 1995; Lewis 2005*a*; 2005*b*; 2006; Wilkinson 1997; 1998; 1999; 2003; Wilkinson & Edens 1999; Wilkinson, Edens & Gibson 1997).

Previous research at Maṣnᶜat Māryah

The archaeological site of Maṣnᶜat Māryah was first noted by Benardelli and Parrinello in 1970 and later revisited by Bayle des Hermens in 1976 (Benardelli & Parrinello 1970; Bayle des Hermens 1976*a*). Māryah's most famous feature, a fourteen-line Ancient South Arabian

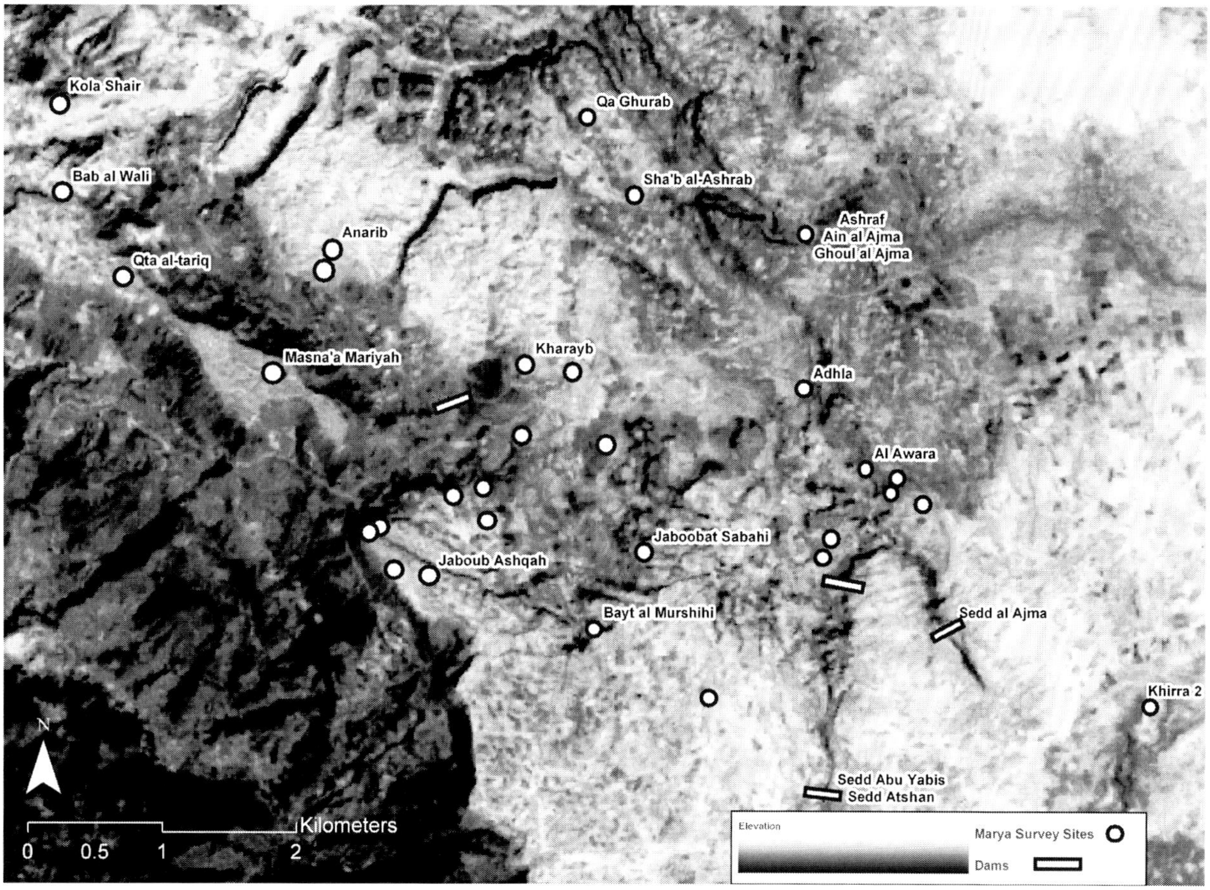

FIGURE 2. *A satellite image of the Maṣnᶜat Māryah study area indicating the locations of the surveyed sites of all periods, and major Himyarite dams.*

inscription carved into a natural rock face, was translated and published by Müller (1978). Despite continued visits to the site by many archaeologists, focused research on the archaeological remains of Maṣnᶜat Māryah and of the Dhamār province in general did not begin until the initiation of the DSP in 1994. Maṣnᶜat Māryah was one of the first sites visited by the DSP team, which earned it the site number DS3 in the register of the now more than 400 recorded sites.

Recent research

The archaeological landscape in the Māryah area provides a rich case study of Himyarite settlement, politics, and economy. Although the DSP team recorded the existence of the prominent archaeological sites and landscape features in the area many years ago, this early work did not extend to detailed examination of those remains or a comprehensive survey of Māryah's hinterland. Due to the importance of the archaeological record in and around Maṣnᶜat Māryah, it is towards those goals that we have directed our recent research.

Over the course of four field seasons from 2001 to 2006, the authors conducted an archaeological landscape survey in the Māryah area focused on documenting the contemporary Himyarite political and agricultural landscape surrounding the Maṣnᶜat Māryah and to identify any surviving earlier archaeological remains in the area. We have been very successful in meeting both of these goals: our fine-grained walking survey of over 18 km^2 of the landscape surrounding Maṣnᶜat Māryah has allowed us to record not only the major early historic sites but also more subtle evidence for land use, economic activities, and prehistoric occupations. To date, in the Māryah study area we have recorded thirty-two major archaeological sites and hundreds of significant archaeological landscape

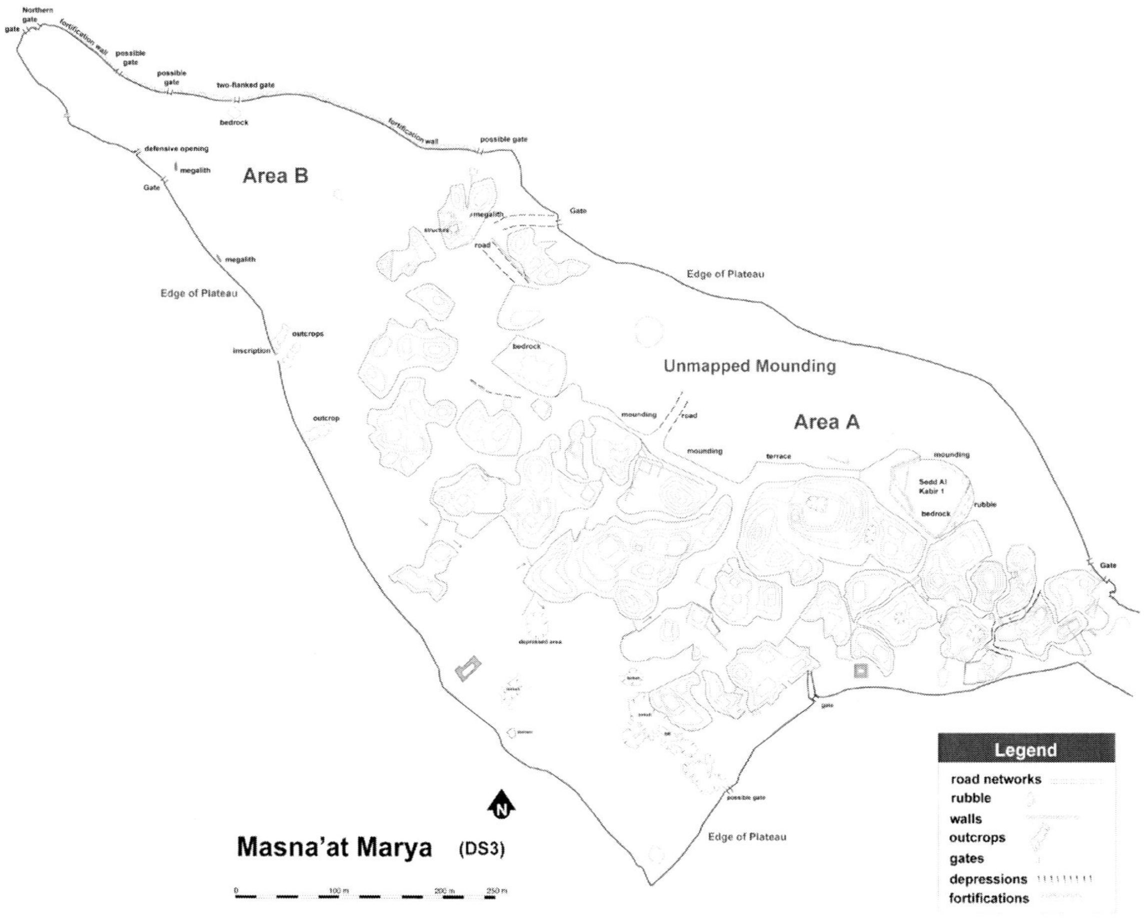

Figure 3. *A partial map of archaeological remains in the fortified portion of the Himyarite site of Maṣnᶜat Māryah in Dhamār Province, Yemen.*

features (Fig. 2). We have also begun the creation of a town plan for the site of Maṣnᶜat Māryah itself (Fig. 3), a task that will be completed in forthcoming seasons. In the following discussion, we will address three major categories of results from this ongoing research: the Himyarite landscape surrounding Maṣnᶜat Māryah, the remains of the urban centre itself, and evidence for prehistoric occupation in the study area.

The Himyarite landscape

Besides Maṣnᶜat Māryah, the area contains eleven other prominent sites of Himyarite date including two contemporary village-sized sites: al-Aḏlaᶜ (DS20) and Jabubah al-Ṣabaḥi (DS379). The second largest site in the study area is the 4 ha Himyarite period settlement of al-Aḏlaᶜ. Excavations in domestic contexts conducted in 2001 uncovered a pottery midden instrumental in refining the highland ceramic chronology and radiocarbon dates ranging from the first to the fifth centuries AD (Lewis 2005*a*). A concentration of about a dozen buildings makes up the settlement site of Jabubah al-Ṣabaḥi (DS379), the third largest Himyarite site in the Māryah area.

Architectural style, town plans, and consistent surface ceramic assemblages attest that all three towns were occupied at least roughly contemporaneously. It seems likely that the villages of al-Aḏlaᶜ and Jabubah al-Ṣabaḥi were politically and economically tied to, or under the administrative control of, the rulers of Māryah. The most striking evidence for interrelationships between the inhabitants of these three neighbouring settlements, however, comes from a unique network of buildings in

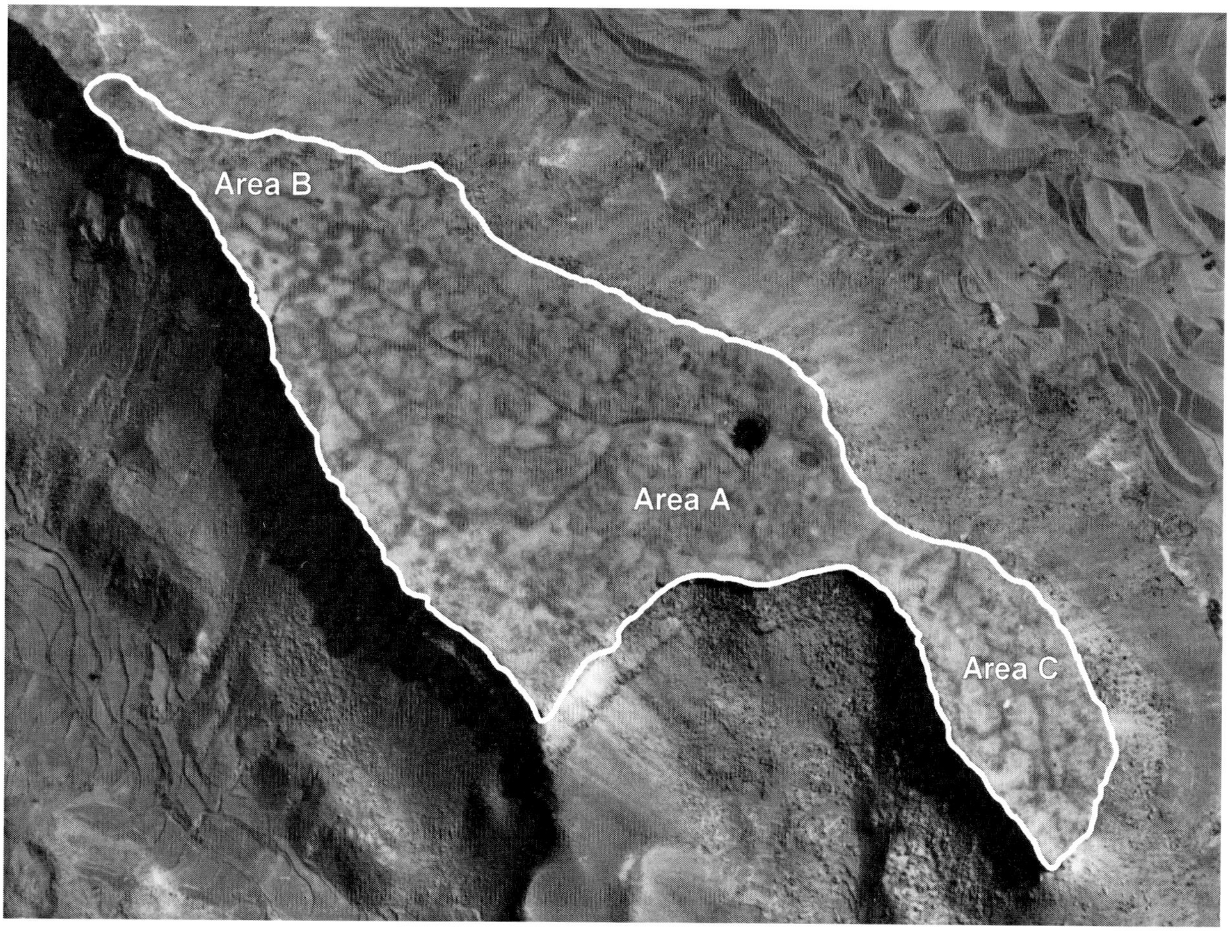

FIGURE 4. *An aerial photograph of the Maṣnᶜat Māryah plateau. The dark areas indicate streets and water cisterns, and the lighter areas stone rubble mounding.*

the survey area that visibly links these sites together.

The most remarkable building at Jabubah al-Ṣabaḥi stands slightly separated from the main cluster of domestic dwellings, on the protruding tip of an elevated rock outcrop overlooking the agricultural plain to the north. This building is situated facing and with a clear view of the Maṣnᶜat Māryah plateau. It is rectangular in plan, with characteristic Himyarite well-constructed double-faced walls built of medium to large rectangular stones. It has a formal wide-stepped entranceway, apron porches, and a courtyard on the south side of the structure.

The distinctive stepped building at Jabubah al-Ṣabaḥi closely echoes the plan of six other very similar structures found throughout the study area. There is a comparable building at al-Aḍlaᶜ, located slightly apart and at a higher elevation than the residential quarters. Three of the additional stepped buildings exist as isolated structures not associated with settlements (DS372, DS375, and DS390) and two are located together as a pair (DS62). The structures are not identical, but share a general size, plan, and architectural aesthetic. Each rectangular building displays wide shallow stepping paralleling the long axis of the structure, which probably lent a slightly ziggurat-like visual effect. All are located on promontories ringing the agricultural plain between the settlements of al-Aḍlaᶜ and Māryah. Each of these buildings is situated so that it has far-reaching views, but is oriented to point towards and view (or be viewed from) the central city of Maṣnᶜat Māryah.

The style of these stepped buildings contrasts with the common domestic architecture of the region, and all are located on high promontories with clear lines of sight towards the larger contemporary town of Maṣnᶜat Māryah. Throughout the study area, the similarity in style, location, and associated material culture for each of these buildings strongly suggests that they were constructed as a network to serve related purposes and to exist as a system of sites in conjunction with the Himyarite settlements of the region. The buildings may have served as temples or other administrative or public buildings. Alternatively, their locations on promontories with far-reaching views may have been intended to provide a defensive or security advantage. A fire burning or smoke rising from any of these locations would have been readily seen from a lookout point at Māryah and thus carry warnings or other messages. Whether these structures had administrative, military, religious, or some other function is a question we will continue to explore further in future seasons of work, but the existence of this network of features is a critical aspect of the landscape and underscores the importance of intensive survey for revealing important interlocking details of past human landscape use.

Other types of Himyarite features in the Māryah area include terraces, threshing floors, activity areas, an obsidian source (see below), isolated structures, round tombs, and a rock-cut tomb. The Māryah study area is particularly remarkable for its impressive Himyarite agricultural system, including four major dams, as well as an array of other features related to agricultural production and water management. Water cisterns are plentiful throughout the study area. The largest of these cisterns is over 100 m in diameter and is constructed of large cut stones in the distinctive Himyarite architectural style.

Many segments of ancient roads and paths lead to and between the Himyarite sites in the area providing additional clues for tracing socio-economic interaction networks. Ancient roads in the area are pathways bordered by stone walls, thoroughfares constructed of paved stone steps, and streets within towns. The recovery and mapping of the remnants of the Himyarite road system in the area is an extremely important component of our research, particularly in light of the text of the monumental *musnad* inscription at Maṣnᶜat Māryah. The text of this well-known fourteen-line inscription discusses the building of roads leading to the territories of neighbouring tribes and villages as well as pathways within the town itself (Müller 1978).

Maṣnᶜat Māryah: a Himyarite urban centre?

The chosen location for this Himyarite city atop a large plateau exemplifies traditional highland concerns for visual prominence and defensibility, as well as a Himyarite preference for symbolic control over topographically divided territory and routes of travel. Those who settled in this naturally defensible site, protected especially on the west by sheer stone cliffs, supplemented the locational advantages of their choice with the construction of a monumental fortification wall around the city. Traces of this wall can still be seen around the perimeter of the site. Māryah's town wall rises out of the topography and rock outcrops so smoothly that in places it is difficult to determine where the natural plateau-top ends and the human constructed fortification wall begins.

The overall town plan of ancient Māryah is quite clear from the extant surface remains and can be discerned in aerial photographs (Fig. 4), but only with our programme of intensive survey and mapping of the city have the essential details for understanding the site's character begun to emerge. The archaeological remains on the Māryah plateau can be generally grouped into three main parts. Two of these lie within the city walls: a crowded, central high-mounded "downtown" (Area A in Figs 3 & 4), and a more open area with a much lower density of architectural remains (Area B in Figs 3 & 4). The third division of the site lies on a separate appendage of the plateau connected to the main site only by a narrow neck of land (Area C in Fig. 4). The buildings and features there contrast sharply with the architecture of "downtown" Māryah (Area A), and include megalithic elements which resemble earlier sites elsewhere in Yemen and in the wider Near East.

The gates of Māryah

Māryah's inhabitants and visitors entered the city through three major (and at least ten secondary) gates and entryways ringing the town. The entryways that are described here as major gates deserve that attribution not for their size but for their formal elaboration and apparent importance to the planning strategies employed in the town. Those entering the city via the East Gate first had to climb up a 2–3 m wide stone paved roadway winding up the eastern slopes of the plateau. Wide steps and flanking walls of well-cut long slabs of stone mark this entry into the central downtown area of large buildings. The North Gate of the city and its associated pair of probable guardhouse structures were similarly constructed of meticulously dressed stones of megalithic proportions and overlook a rock-cut gorge that bisects the plateau.

Unlike these two gates, the West Gate shows no evidence of a formal built structure but consists of a corridor cut through the natural stone of the plateau edge. Māryah's famous *musnad* inscription flanks this cut-stone passage; the lines of text carved into the natural rock outcrop face out over the scenic and rugged terrain of the escarpment as it plunges down toward the Red Sea coast. The remaining entrances into the ancient town are less elaborate than the three gates described above and vary in size from wide openings, probably used to bring goods or crops into the town, to small staircases or rock-cut incisions just large enough for a single person to slip through.

Inside the walled city

The most impressive part of the site within the walls of Māryah is an approximately 18 ha area of densely concentrated stone rubble mounding. Structural remains here reach up to over 3 m in height. Individual buildings, streets, courtyard areas, and a large number of water cisterns can be distinguished despite the abundant rubble. Remnants of intact architecture of high-quality cut stones frequently peek through the large heaps of debris. Both architecture and artefacts indicate that this was the main public and commercial centre of Māryah during the Himyarite era.

The largest buildings at Māryah are clustered around a large triangular water cistern, which appears on the air photograph as a distinct black spot not only because of its great size (approximately 80 m across) but also because it still holds water almost all year round (Fig. 4). Māryah's main street runs from this cistern between the largest buildings on the site and then winds all the way through the town to the West (inscription-bearing) Gate.

The single largest structure at Māryah stands immediately west of this cistern and south of the east end of the main street. This massive structure consists of a rectangular mound 90–100 m across enclosing a large depression. A looter's hole on top reveals part of a flight of smooth plaster steps leading down into a central courtyard space. Future excavations will determine if this was a public congregational ritual space, a restricted palatial zone, or something else entirely, but the surface survey and mapping conducted so far emphasize the social importance not only of this structure, but also the other large structures and building complexes in this central area of "downtown" Māryah.

Within the central mounded zone, the further from these largest structures and the massive town cistern, the smaller the buildings. Judging from surface evidence, the buildings in the outer perimeter of the high-mounded district were probably domestic dwellings. Many of these structures have associated enclosed and relatively rubble-free private courtyard areas. Given the size and architectural elaboration of these structures compared to homes at contemporary sites such as al-Aḏlaᶜ, they were probably the residences of elite Himyarites.

Himyarite artisans worked in iron, copper, bronze, gold, and silver (Glanzman 2002: 114–115). Swords and other weaponry were apparent Himyarite specialities (Daum 1988: 15–16), as well as metal fittings of equine tack (Yule *et al.* 2007: 541–543). South Arabian excellence in metalworking was lauded by their contemporaries and in local inscriptions from the early centuries AD (Daum 1988: 15–16). Two concentrations of ironworking waste provide evidence for craft production at Māryah. An iron dagger from excavations at nearby al-Aḏlaᶜ provides an example of local tool use and may have been produced at the ironworking facilities at Māryah.

Beyond the central high-mounded district but still within the city walls, lies a relatively open and rubble-free zone containing only occasional scattered buildings. The structures in this part of the site are heavily weathered, mainly visible as sparse foundation stones, and lack the high rubble signature of "downtown" Māryah. These building remains either represent a different type of structure to those in the high-mounded part of the site, date to an earlier time period, or were intensively stone robbed for construction of later buildings. In considering the inhabited spaces of the Himyarite city, it does not suffice to simply dismiss these buildings as an earlier settlement phase. This intriguing space is not only included within the city's fortification and formal boundary, but is also entered via the monumental North Gate with its two formal flanking guardhouse buildings.

Perhaps this more open area of Māryah originally contained ephemeral structures that are not apparent from surface evidence today. Thus it might have been used as a market space, served as a place to keep animals, or used for the cultivation of special garden crops. A combination of some or all of these (and other) uses is certainly also possible. A defensive reading of the inclusion of such open space within the city's fortification system might suggest that this area was used for bringing supplies, animals, and non-residents, possibly allies from nearby towns, into a safe location in times of attack. On the other hand, this space may have simply been set aside for possible future expansion of the settlement that was never realized.

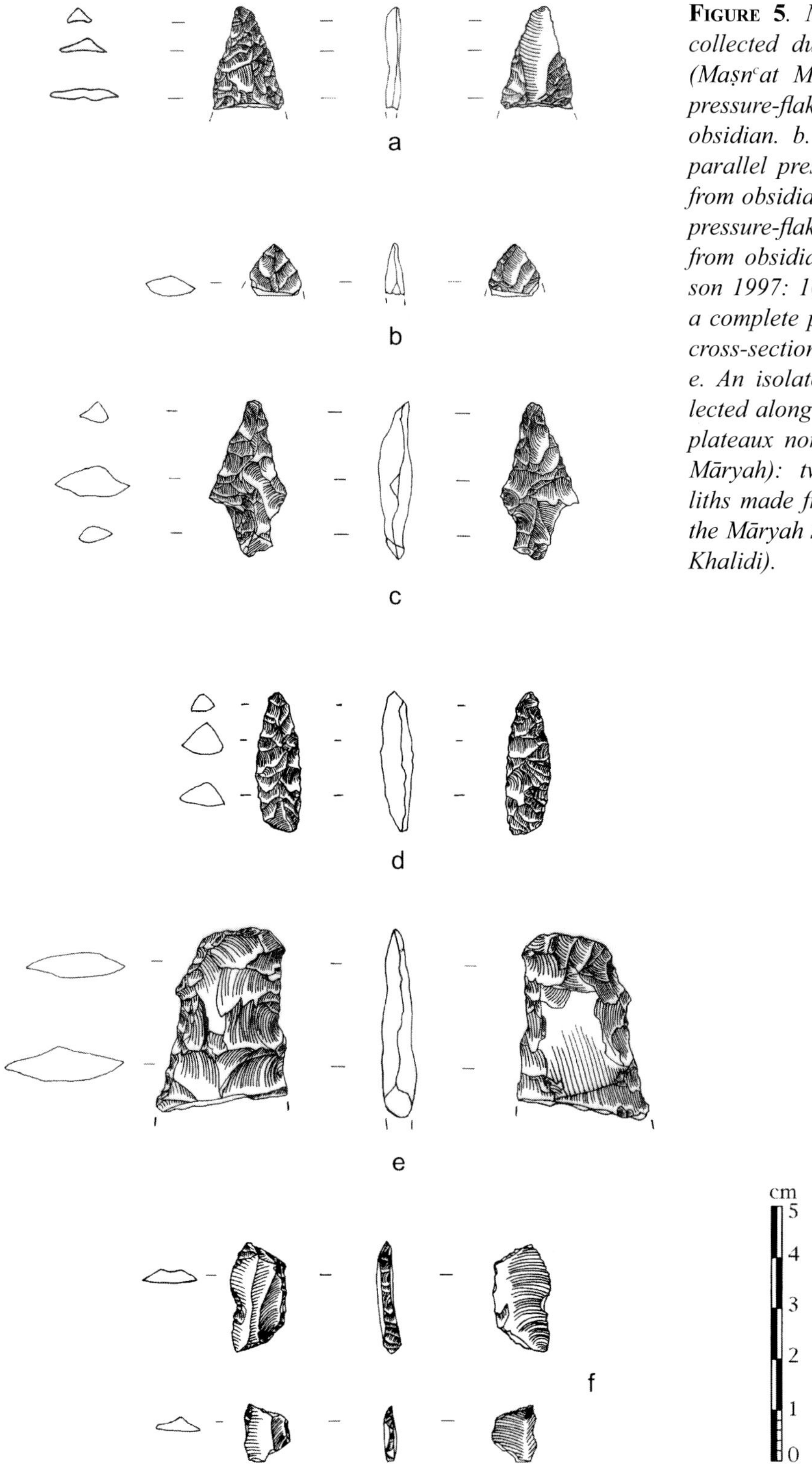

Figure 5. *Māryah survey area lithic tools collected during the 2007 season. a. DS3 (Maṣnᶜat Māryah): a fragmentary parallel pressure-flaked bifacial projectile made from obsidian. b. DS15 (Ashraf): a fragmentary parallel pressure-flaked bifacial point made from obsidian. c. DS 15 (Ashraf): a complete pressure-flaked tanged bifacial point made from obsidian (cf. Wilkinson, Edens & Gibson 1997: 109, fig. 5/1). d. DS409 (Anarib): a complete parallel pressure-flaked trihedral cross-sectioned biface made from obsidian. e. An isolated red jasper rough biface collected along the deeply dissected low eroded plateaux north of Māryah. f. DS3 (Maṣnᶜat Māryah): two trapezoid geometric microliths made from obsidian and collected from the Māryah southern appendix. (Drawn by L. Khalidi).*

Megalithic Māryah

The third major part of the Māryah cityscape poses the most difficult challenge of interpretation. The southernmost appendage of the plateau upon which Māryah sits is partitioned by long alignments of roughly shaped basalt megaliths. The area is also dotted with occasional scattered buildings and possible funerary structures. These structures have a completely different architectural style and archaeological signature than that of the high-mounded structures in the central part of Māryah.

This southern extension of the site consists mainly of building foundations constructed of large basalt stones with very little or no associated rubble. The entire space of approximately 5 ha appears to be designed as a single coherent megalithic complex, with the central area divided into long parallel arcades suggestive of processional ways. Although these parallel alignments are not currently capped with stone slabs, they may in fact be the long double alignment of partly covered large standing stones that Bayle des Hermens noted at the site of Māryah in 1976 (1976*a*).

In addition to the southern appendix of Māryah, which was constructed with an entirely different ethos and in differing proportions to the structures of the adjacent mounded Himyarite city, the edge of the larger Māryah plateau is dotted with megalithic elements. Solitary sunken chambers capped by large stone slabs, dolmen-like tables, and monoliths can be found dispersed along the perimeter of the site. Bayle des Hermens distinguished between two types of isolated megalithic elements on the site (1976*a*). The first are the horizontal stone slabs, propped onto small stones and the second a solitary dolmen-like chamber that was reused as a shepherd's hut. Braemer, Cleuziou and Steimer-Herbet do not consider the stone slabs to be dolmens "...because they are not associated with cists or funerary structures" (2003). While they are not in fact dolmens, their placement, along with large uprights, was predetermined within the landscape and not "...abandoned during their transportation from a quarry area..." as the authors speculate.

Like the Bronze Age tradition of placing tombs and large stone markers in prominently visible locations with a view over the surrounding territory (Khalidi 2006*a*; in press), these monuments are neither arbitrary nor do they fall into the hewn-stone tradition of the Himyarites. Their placement is strategic and possibly marks spaces that have been deemed territorial and sacred for millennia. It is thus of no surprise that the Himyarite stepped buildings occupy the same position within the landscape that such features do (Lewis 2005*b*). Currently three oblong upright stones, two dolmen features, and two horizontal table slabs occupy the perimeter of the site of Māryah, overlooking the landscape below.

Until further research at the site can be undertaken, the date of construction and the possible meanings of these features remain difficult to assess. The seemingly megalithic tradition at Māryah calls to mind the large stones used in structures and complexes of the late prehistoric period elsewhere in Yemen (Bayle des Hermens 1976*b*; Braemer, Cleuziou & Steimer-Herbet 2003; de Maigret & Antonini 2005; Doe 1971; Giumlia-Mair *et al.* 2000; Keall 2005; Khalidi 2006*b*; in press; Phillips 1998; Rougeulle 1999; Steimer-Herbet 2004; Vogt 1997).

Looking further afield, the tradition of using large stone slabs in funerary structures such as dolmens or cairn chambers and using large oblong uprights as orthostats or as isolated monuments, is found in the African Horn (Joussaume 1976; 1995) and throughout the Near East. In Saudi Arabia and Syro-Palestine, these monuments tend to date to the Chalcolithic and Bronze Age periods.

Lithic evidence from the Māryah study area

The lithic assemblages of sites in the Māryah study area complement what is most likely to be a late prehistoric architectural vernacular expressed in the variable use of large stones. Notable lithics include geometric microliths collected from the southern appendix at Māryah (Fig. 5/f). These are made from obsidian and almost certainly date to the Bronze or Iron Ages. While the occurrence of geometric microliths and *pièces esquillées* at the sites of DS76A and DS86 was tentatively assigned by the DSP to a possible aceramic Neolithic (Wilkinson, Edens & Gibson 1997), the simultaneous presence of these two tool types is a well-documented Bronze Age tradition on the African and Arabian Red Sea coasts (Callow & Wahida 1981; Crassard in press; Inizan & Francaviglia 2002; Joussaume 1995; Khalidi 2006*a*; 2007; Zarins 1989; Zarins & al-Badr 1986) and an Iron Age one in the desert fringe and Ḥaḍramawt (Bawden, Edens & Miller 1980; Caton Thompson 1944; Crassard 2007; de Maigret & Antonini 2005; Inizan & Francaviglia 2002; Sedov 1996). A more precise understanding of the role that the highlands played in inter-regional interactions can be elucidated by ascertaining the chronological time span of the introduction and lifespan of these two industries in the highlands in relation to that of the coastal lowlands to the west (third–second millennium BC) and the desert lowlands to the east (first millennium BC).

In addition, we can now report the discovery of Neolithic materials, proof of an extremely long time span for occupation in the study area. The recovery of a fragmentary bifacial parallel pressure flaked obsidian projectile (Fig. 5/a) (1) from the eroding deposits atop the southern appendix of the Māryah plateau is the first indication to date of a Neolithic presence on the site. Two technologically comparable bifacial projectiles, also made from obsidian, were recovered at the Iron Age site of Ashraf (DS15), which overlooks the Māryah plain from the east (Fig. 5/b–c). One tanged bifacial projectile was recovered from this site in an earlier season of the DSP (Gibson & Wilkinson 1995: 165) suggesting that the site may in fact have a significant Neolithic presence. Bifacial tools were also found in the deeply dissected low eroded plateaux north of Māryah (Fig. 5/d–e).

These findings are important because despite the fact that it has been well documented from ancient lake sediments in the highlands (and across the Arabian Peninsula) that the early to mid-Holocene period had a much wetter, more vegetated, stable environment than today (Davies 2006; DiBlasi 1997; Fedele 1985; 1990; Lézine *et al.* 1998; Marcolongo & Palmieri 1992; Munro & Wilkinson 2007; Sanlaville 1992; Wilkinson 1997), there is little evidence in the highlands of human occupation during this time (Wilkinson, Edens & Gibson 1997). Currently, the recorded DSP highland Neolithic sites number only seventeen out of a total of over 400 sites recorded. The difficulty of recording early sites is certainly a product of taphonomic processes such as erosion, burial, and later human manipulation of the landscape, as well as likely low population densities in the period. Many of the previously known highland Neolithic sites are in proximity to known ancient Holocene lakes. The evidence from the Māryah study area also follows this pattern. The al-Aḍla^{c} lacustrine basin to the south-east of Māryah has produced a very early date of 10,000 BC calibrated (Parker, Davies & Wilkinson 2006: 247–248).

The Māryah area obsidian source in context

The presence of bifacial projectiles made from obsidian is significant given the presence of an obsidian source in the immediate region. The obsidian source is located on the eastern slopes of the Kowlat Shaīr volcano, which looms immediately to the north-west of the Māryah plateau. Two flows from the source of Jirab al-Sawf (DSF06-030A-B) were sampled in 2006 and sent for petro-chemical analyses. The source is a volcanic pyroclastic tephra sequence with cobbles of obsidian embedded in it. The obsidian cobbles, which can be seen to be eroding out of the ash bed, range from gravel-sized to nodules larger than 30 cm across. In addition to the natural cobbles eroding from the feature, varied worked obsidian occurs scattered over the area, suggesting long-term exploitation of the source.

Based on the presence of a number of obsidian bifaces in the same micro-region, it can be presumed that humans extracted obsidian from this source as early as the Neolithic. In addition, dense obsidian manufacturing areas dating to all periods including the Islamic, are found at the source. Of the total of thirty-two sites recorded in the Māryah area, the majority have moderate to dense obsidian presumed to originate from this local source. Future survey work aims to deal in more detail with the obsidian's *chaîne opératoire* and determine whether what appears to be a local exploitation and distribution of the material is as Wilkinson, Edens and Gibson suggest, "…a relatively limited circulation of material from each source, with moderately steep drop-off with distance from the sources" (1997: 122).

The source's location on the very edge of the escarpment and along the watersheds of two of the larger western wadi systems (wadi Rima' and wadi Zabīd) further emphasizes its importance in the larger scope of prehistoric highland-lowland interaction and exchange. It may have served as a source to the people inhabiting the escarpment and interior coastal plain in addition or as an alternative to the large sources in the eastern highlands (namely Jebel Isbil and Lisi) (de Maigret 1985; 1990; Francaviglia 1990; Wilkinson, Edens & Gibson 1997) or across the Red Sea.

Conclusions

From obsidian trade to Himyarite roadways, the Maṣn^{c}at Māryah area has clearly been a critical nexus in wide interaction networks. Our study of the archaeological remains of Maṣn^{c}at Māryah has laid a solid foundation for extrapolating Himyarite sociocultural networks and urban planning strategies; a task that we continue to pursue with ongoing work at the site and in the region. In addition to clarifying the Himyarite socio-political universe, the Māryah study area has also proved to be an important location for understanding prehistoric occupation in the central Yemeni highlands. We have worked backwards chronologically here to illustrate how we have solved the common problem of later exploitation of the landscape obscuring earlier evidence. Fine-grained archaeological surveys fill in very important and often missed dimensions to our understanding of these spaces. Not only was the Māryah area inhabited for millennia, strategic places within the landscape were seemingly reused in similar symbolic and strategic ways. This is not to assert that prehistoric megalithic monuments and formal Himyarite stepped buildings with far-reaching views, for instance, had identical cultural meanings, but their similarities over time offer intriguing clues about what this landscape meant to the people who lived there.

Acknowledgements

Funding sources for the fieldwork and analysis presented here include: the American Institute for Yemeni Studies, IIE Fulbright, and the American Association of University Women. We would also like to express our appreciation to institutions and individuals that have provided support to this research; GOAM, CEFAS, the University of Chicago, Ali Sanabani, Dr Yusuf Abdullah, Tony Wilkinson, Vincenzo Francaviglia, and McGuire Gibson. Thanks are also due to the other team members who participated in fieldwork including Ahmed Mosabi, Joseph Daniels, Abdullah Masoudi, Ahmed Haidara, Dan Mahoney, Muslih al-Qubati, Saleh al-Faqi, Basel Khalil, Amin al-Mowri, and Tawfiq al-Ashwal.

Notes

1 A channel flake may have been removed from the point of this projectile, on the ventral face. Such a removal can also occur from impact of the point or can be the result of a knapping accident. While fluting was previously known as a technique indigenous to America, it is now well documented as an isolated occurrence in parts of south-east Arabia (Charpentier & Inizan 2002; Crassard 2007; Crassard *et al.* 2006). In each of these cases the assemblage is dominated by such a technique and a single occurrence in the highlands leans more favourably towards an explanation involving a "point of impact" or "knapping accident" scenario.

References

Barbanes E.
2000. Domestic and defensive architecture on the Yemen plateau: eighth century BCE–sixth century CE. *Arabian Archaeology and Epigraphy* 11: 207–222.

Bawden G., Edens C. & Miller R.
1980. Preliminary Archaeological Investigations at Tayma. *Atlal* 4: 69–106, pls 60–69.

Bayle des Hermens R.
1976*a*. Première mission de recherches préhistoriques en République arabe du Yémen. *l'Anthropologie* 80: 5–37.
1976*b*. Vue d'ensemble des résultats obtenus et civilisations préhistoriques rencontrées. *l'Anthropologie* 80: 35–37.

Benardelli G. & Parrinello A.E.
1970. Note su alcune localita archeologiche del Yemen. *Annali dell'Istituto Orientale di Napoli* 30: 117–120.

Braemer F., Cleuziou S. & Steimer-Herbet T.
2003. Dolmen-like structures: some unusual funerary monuments in Yemen. *Proceedings of the Seminar for Arabian Studies* 33: 169–182.

Callow P. & Wahida G.
1981. Fieldwork in Northern and Eastern Sudan, 1976–1980. *Nyame Akuma: Bulletin of the Society of Africanist Archaeologists* 18: 34–36.

Caton Thompson G.
1944. *The Tombs and Moon Temple of Hureidha (Hadhramaut).* xiii. Oxford: Oxford University Press.

Charpentier V. & Inizan M-L.
2002. Fluting In The Old World: The Neolithic Projectile Points of Arabia. *Lithic Technology* 27/1: 39–46.

Crassard R.
2007. *Apport de la Technologie Lithique à la Définition de la Préhistoire du Hadramawt, dans le Contexte du Yémen et de L'Arabie du Sud.* i & ii. PhD thesis, Université Paris 1 — Panthéon — Sorbonne. [Unpublished].
(in press). Obsidian lithic industries from al-Midamman (Tihama coast, Yemen). In E.J. Keall (ed.), *Pots, Rocks and Megaliths*. (British Archaeological Reports, International Series). Oxford: Archaeopress.

Crassard R., McCorriston J., Oches E., Bin 'Aqil A.A., Espagne J. & Sinnah M.
2006. Manayzah, early to mid-Holocene occupations in Wadi Sana (Hadramawt, Yemen). *Proceedings of the Seminar for Arabian Studies* 36: 151–173.

Daum W.
1988. From the Queen of Saba' to a Modern State: 3,000 years of civilization in southern Arabia. Pages 9–31 in W. Daum (ed.), *Yemen: 3000 Years of Art and Civilization in Arabia Felix*. Innsbruck: Pinguin Verlag.

Davies C.P.
2006. Holocene paleoclimates of southern Arabia from lacustrine deposits of the Dhamar highlands, Yemen. *Quaternary Research* 66/3: 454–464.

de Maigret A.
1985. Archaeological Missions (Yemen): Archaeological Activities in the Yemen Arab Republic, 1985. *East and West* 35: 337–375.
1990. *The Bronze Age Culture of Hawlan at-Tiyal and al-Hada (Republic of Yemen).* xxiv. Rome: ISMEO.

de Maigret A. & Antonini S.
2005. *South Arabian Necropolises: Italian Excavations at Al-Makhdarah and Kharibat al-Ahjur (Republic of Yemen).* iv. Rome: IsIAO.

DiBlasi M.
1997. Pollen-analytical approaches to the study of Late Holocene environmental history and human ecology on the Shire Plateau of northern Ethiopia. Pages 45–80 in K. Bard (ed.), *The Environmental History and Human Ecology of Northern Ethiopia in the Late Holocene: Preliminary Results of Multidisciplinary Project*. (Studi Africanistici — Serie Etiopica, 5). Naples: Istituto Universitario Orientale.

Doe B.
1971. *Southern Arabia*. London: Thames and Hudson.

Edens C.
1999. The Bronze Age of Highland Yemen: Chronological and Spatial Variability of Pottery and Settlement. *Paléorient* 25/2: 103–126.

Edens C. & Wilkinson T.J.
1998. Southwest Arabia During the Holocene: Recent Archaeological Developments. *Journal of World Prehistory* 12/1: 55–119.

Edens C., Wilkinson T.J. & Barratt G.
2000. Hammat al-Qa and the roots of urbanism in southwest Arabia. *Antiquity* 74 (286): 854–862.

Fedele F.G.
1985. Research on Neolithic and Holocene paleo-ecology in the Yemeni highlands. *East and West* 35: 369–373.
1990. Man, land and climate: Emerging interactions from the Holocene of the Yemen Highlands. Pages 31–42 in S. Bottema, G. Entjes-Nieborg & W. Van Zeist (eds), *Man's Role in the Shaping of the Eastern Mediterranean Landscape. Proceedings of the Inqua/Bai Symposium on the Impact of Ancient Man on the Landscape of the Eastern Mediterranean Region and the Near East.* Rotterdam/Brookfield, VT: A.A. Balkema.

Francaviglia V.M.
1990. Obsidian sources in ancient Yemen. Pages 129–134 in A. de Maigret (ed.), *The Bronze Age Culture of Khawlan at-Tiyal and al-Hada (Yemen Arab Republic).* Rome: IsMEO.

Gibson McG. & Wilkinson T.J.
1995. The Dhamar Plain, Yemen: A Preliminary Study of the Archaeological Landscape. *Proceedings of the Seminar for Arabian Studies* 25: 159–183.

Giumlia-Mair A., Keall E., Stock S. & Shugar A.
2000. Copper-based implements of a newly identified culture in Yemen. *Journal of Cultural Heritage* 1: 37–43.
Glanzman W.D.
2002. Arts, Crafts, and Industries. Pages 110–116 in St J. Simpson (ed.), *Queen of Sheba: Treasures from Ancient Yemen*. London: The British Museum Press.
Hoyland R.
2002. Kings, Kingdoms and Chronology. Pages 67–72 in St J. Simpson (ed.), *Queen of Sheba: Treasures from Ancient Yemen*. London: The British Museum Press.
Inizan M-L. & Francaviglia V.M.
2002. Les périples de l'obsidienne à travers la mer Rouge. *Journal des Africanistes* 72/2: 11–19.
Joussaume R.
1976. Les dolmens Éthiopiens. *Annales d'Éthiopie* 10: 41–52.
1995. Les premières sociétés de production. Pages 15–63 in R. Joussaume (ed.), *Tiya — l'Éthiopie des Mégalithes: Du biface à l'art rupestre dans la Corne de l'Afrique*. Poitiers: P. Oudin.
Keall E.J.
2005. Placing al-Midamman in time. The work of the Canadian Archaeological Mission on the Tihama coast, from the Neolithic to the Bronze Age. Pages 87–99 in *Archäologische Berichte aus dem Yemen*. (Deutsches Archäologisches Institut San'a', Band 10). Mainz am Rhein: Verlag Phillip Von Zabern.
Khalidi L.
2006*a*. *Settlement, Culture-Contact and Interaction Along the Red Sea Coastal Plain, Yemen: The Tihamah cultural landscape in the late prehistoric period, 3000–900 BC*. PhD thesis, University of Cambridge. [Unpublished].
2006*b*. Megalithic Landscapes: The development of the late prehistoric cultural landscape along the Tihama coastal plain. Pages 359–375 in A.M. Sholan, S. Antonini & M. Arbach (eds), *Sabaean Studies. Archaeological, Epigraphical and Historical Studies in Honour of Yūsuf M. ᶜAbdallāh, Alessandro de Maigret, Christian J. Robin on the Occasion of Their Sixtieth Birthdays*. Naples: Yemeni-Italian Centre for Archaeological Researches/Ṣanaᶜāᵓ: University of Ṣanaᶜāᵓ and Centre français d'archéologie et de sciences sociales de Ṣanaᶜāᵓ.
2007. The formation of a southern Red Seascape in the late prehistoric period: Tracing cross-Red Sea culture-contact, interaction, and maritime communities along the Tihamah coastal plain, Yemen in the third to first millennium BC. Pages 35–43 in J. Starkey, P. Starkey & T. Wilkinson (eds), *Natural Resources and Cultural Connections of the Red Sea: Proceedings of Red Sea Project III.* (Society for Arabian Studies Monographs, 5). (British Archaeological Reports, International Series, 1661). Oxford: Archaeopress.
(in press). The late prehistoric landscapes of the Tihamah coastal plain, Yemen (3000–900 BC): the domestication of space and the construction of human-landscape identity. *Revue des Mondes Musulmans et de la Méditerranée* (REMMM).
Lewis K.
2005*a*. The Himyarite site of al-Aḍlaᶜ and its implications for economy and chronology of Early Historic highland Yemen. *Proceedings of the Seminar for Arabian Studies* 35: 129–141.
2005*b*. *Space and the Spice of Life: Food, Politics, and Landscape in Ancient Yemen*. PhD thesis, University of Chicago. [Unpublished].
2007. Fields and Tables of Sheba: Food, Identity, and Politics in Early Historic Southern Arabia. Pages 192–217 in K.C. Twiss (ed.), *The Archaeology of Food and Identity*. xxxiv. Carbondale, IL: Center for Archaeological Investigations, Southern Illinois University.
Lézine A-M., Saliege J-F., Robert C., Wertz F. & Inizan M-L.
1998. Holocene Lakes from Ramlat as-Sab'atayn (Yemen) Illustrate the Impact of Monsoon Activity in Southern Arabia. *Quaternary Research* 50: 290–299.
Marcolongo B. & Palmieri A.M.
1992. Paleoenvironment and Settlement Pattern of the Tihamah Coastal Plain (Republic of Yemen). Pages 117–123 in *Yemen: Studi archeologici, storici e filologici sull'Arabia meridionale.* i. Rome: Istituto Italiano per il Medio ed Estremo Oriente.

Müller W.W.
1978. Die Sabäische Felsinschrift von Masna'at Māriya. Pages 137–148 in R. Degen, W.W. Müller & W. Röllig (eds), *Neue Ephemeris für semitische Epigraphik*. iii. Wiesbaden: Harrassowitz.

Munro R.N. & Wilkinson T.
2007. Environment, Landscapes and Archaeology of the Yemeni Tihamah. Pages 13–33 in J. Starkey, P. Starkey & T. Wilkinson (eds), *Natural Resources and Cultural Connections of the Red Sea*. (Society for Arabian Studies Monographs, 5). (British Archaeological Reports, International Series, 1661). Oxford: Archaeopress.

Parker A., Davies C. & Wilkinson T.
2006. The early to mid-Holocene moist period in Arabia: some recent evidence from lacustrine sequences in eastern and south-western Arabia. *Proceedings of the Seminar for Arabian Studies* 36: 243–255.

Phillips C.S.
1998. The Tihamah *c.* 5000 to 500 BC. *Proceedings of the Seminar for Arabian Studies* 28: 233–237.

Rougeulle A.
1999. Coastal settlements in southern Yemen: the 1996–1997 survey expeditions on the Hadramawt and Mahra coasts. *Proceedings of the Seminar for Arabian Studies* 29: 123–136.

Sanlaville P.
1992. Changements climatiques dans la Péninsule Arabique durant le Pléistocene supérieur et l'Holocène. *Paléorient* 18/1: 5–26.

Sedov A.V.
1996. On the Origins of the Agricultural Settlements in Hadramawt. Pages pp. 67–86 in C. Robin (ed.), *Arabia Antiqua: Early Origins of South Arabian States*. lxx/1. Rome: Istituto Italiano per il Medio ed Estremo Oriente.

Steimer-Herbet T.
2004. *Classification des sépultures à superstructure lithique dans le Levant et l'Arabie occidentale (IVe et IIIe millénaires avant J.-C.)*. Oxford: Archaeopress.

Vogt B.
1997. La fin de la préhistoire au Hadramawt. Pages 30–33 in C. Robin (ed.), *Yémen: Au pays de la reine de Saba*. Paris: Flammarion/Institut du Monde Arabe.

Wilkinson T.J.
1997. Holocene environments of the high plateau, Yemen, recent geoarchaeological investigations. *Geoarchaeology* 12: 833–864.
1998. Human environment interactions in the highlands of Yemen. Pages 291–302 in C.S. Phillips, D. Potts & S. Searight (eds), *Arabia and its Neighbours: Essays on prehistorical and historical developments presented in honour of Beatrice de Cardi*. Turnhouts: Brepols.
1999. Settlement, soil erosion and terraced agriculture in highland Yemen: a preliminary statement. *Proceedings of the Seminar for Arabian Studies* 29: 183–191.
2003. The organization of settlement in highland Yemen during the Bronze and Iron Ages. *Proceedings of the Seminar for Arabian Studies* 33: 157–168.

Wilkinson T.J. & Edens C.
1999. Survey and Excavation in the Central Highlands of Yemen: Results of the Dhamar Survey Project, 1996 and 1998. *Arabian Archaeology and Epigraphy* 10: 1–33.

Wilkinson T.J., Edens C. & Gibson McG.
1997. The Archaeology of the Yemen High Plains: A preliminary chronology. *Arabian Archaeology and Epigraphy* 8: 99–142.

Yule P., Franke K., Meyer C., Nebe G., Robin C. & Witzel C.
2007. Zafar, Capital of Himyar, Ibb Province, Yemen First Preliminary Report: 1998 and 2000, Second Preliminary Report: 2002, Third Preliminary Report: 2003, Fourth Preliminary Report: 2004. *Archäologische Berichte aus dem Yemen* 11: 477–548.

Zarins J.
1989. Ancient Egypt and the Red Sea trade: The case for obsidian in the predynastic and archaic periods. Pages 339–368 in A. Leonard Jr. & B.B. Williams (eds), *Essays in Ancient Civilization presented to Helene J. Kantor*. Chicago, IL: University of Chicago, SAOC 47.

Zarins J. & al-Badr H.
1986. Archaeological Investigation in the Southern Tihama Plain II (Including Sihi, 217–107 and Sharja, 217–172) 1405/1985. *Atlal* 10: 36–57.

Authors' addresses
Dr Krista Lewis, Assistant Professor of Anthropology, University of Arkansas at Little Rock, 2801 S. University Ave., Little Rock, AR 72204, USA.
e-mail kalewis1@alumni.uchicago.edu

Dr Lamya Khalidi, Chercheur, Centre d'Études Préhistoire, Antiquité, Moyen Age (CEPAM — UMR 6130 — CNRS), Université de Nice, Sophia Antipolis (UNSA), 250 rue Albert Einstein, Sophia-Antipolis, F–06560 Valbonne, France.
e-mail lamya.khalidi@gmail.com

Proceedings of the Seminar for Arabian Studies 38 (2008): 231–250

Women's inscriptions recently discovered by the AFSM at the Awām temple/Maḥram Bilqīs in Marib, Yemen

Mohammed Maraqten

Summary
The recent excavations of the AFSM at the Awām temple, modern Maḥram Bilqīs, have yielded over 500 inscriptions. Although the majority of the texts recovered from the temple are dedicatory, we also have legal, religious, and literary inscriptions as well as texts dedicated by, or referring to, women. Only about fifteen inscriptions refer to women making dedications to the god Almaqah, lord of Awām. This paper gives a general report on the women's inscriptions and their content as well as the epigraphic evidence for the study of Sabaean women. In addition to their role in the family, their health, several aspects of their status as women, including their economic and cultic role in Sabaean society, are briefly discussed. In addition, two recently discovered inscriptions are published here.

Keywords: women, Sabaʾ, Yemen, epigraphy, South Arabian

Excavations at the Awām temple/Maḥram Bilqīs by the AFSM (American Foundation for the Study of Man), under the direction of Mrs Merilyn Phillips-Hodgson, have yielded over 500 inscriptions (Figs 1 & 2). (1) The majority of the texts recovered from the temple are dedicatory. However, legal, religious, and literary texts as well as inscriptions dedicated by women have been found. These new inscriptions not only increase our knowledge of the Sabaic language in general, but also contain important data on the cultural, social, and political history of ancient Yemen (Maraqten 2004; 2006). Of the several hundred Sabaean inscriptions, those by, or concerning, women form only a small group (2005), but they provide good data about the status of women in South Arabian society and insights into its social structure.

The purpose of this paper is to give a general statement about the content of inscriptions that mention dedications by women, as well as an overview of some other inscriptions mentioning women. After a review of some of the women's inscriptions discovered by the AFSM in the 1950s, some information from those recently discovered at the Awām temple will be presented. However, it is not within the scope of this paper to discuss the status of women in South Arabia in general or Sabaʾ in particular. It simply aims to present the contribution of the epigraphic data from Maḥram Bilqīs to the study of the history of Sabaean women, as well as some aspects of the roles of women within Sabaean society. Several aspects will be discussed here such as marriage and the family, women's economic and cultic role, as well as the health care of women. Two recently discovered women's inscriptions will be also presented.

Sources for the study of the status of women in ancient South Arabia: the contribution of the inscriptions of Maḥram Bilqīs

Our knowledge of the status of women in ancient Yemen is still very limited (Beeston 1979: 120–122; 1983; Stiegner 1989; Frantsouzoff 1999). With a few exceptions the history of women in ancient Yemen, like that of their contemporaries elsewhere in the ancient Near East and Mediterranean region (e.g. Marsman 2003: 43ff.; Harris 1994), has been largely neglected by scholars. At present, little information is available about women in the Old Sabaean period (eighth century to second century BC). (2) The Maḥram Bilqīs inscriptions, which are dated to the Middle Sabaean period (first century BC to the fourth century AD), constitute the most important source for women's status in ancient Yemen. The study of these texts provides information on women in the family and their activities as legally and economically active persons.

Figure 1. *The Awām temple.*

However, there are still gaps in our knowledge and these texts do not permit a more complete and coherent picture of the lives of women in Sabaʾ.

In addition to the inscriptions discovered at Maḥram Bilqīs by the AFSM, there are also several women's inscriptions, which were recently discovered by the German Archaeological Institute at the Maḥram Bilqīs/Awām cemetery. These inscriptions are primarily engraved on limestone funerary stelae. Some of them have carved alabaster heads of women fixed in niches carved in these stelae and most have short inscriptions, which mainly give their names and filiations (Nebes 2002). (3) Moreover, there are a number of women's inscriptions which have been found in unscientific excavations but which according to their contents seem to have originated from Maḥram Bilqīs (e.g. YM 441 = CIAS I: 87–89, 39.11/r 1). Sabaic texts engraved on wood (primarily on palm-leaf stalks) also add useful information about the role of women in everyday life and business affairs. (4) Any study of the status of women in ancient Yemen should take into account this new category of Sabaic texts.

Several categories of inscriptions can be distinguished, namely dedicatory, legal, expiation, and confession texts (e.g. Ja 525). There are also texts that show that women themselves organized the construction of their houses (YMN 19, Wādī as-Sirr 1) or their graves (DJE 10, Müller 1972: 81f.; CIH 21). Some inscriptions mention that a man and his wife carried out the construction, possibly of a house (Nāmī 66).

Women are primarily mentioned in the dedicatory inscriptions, of which two groups can be distinguished, viz. (a) inscriptions dedicated by women themselves; and (b) inscriptions which mention women in their roles as mothers, daughters, wives, or servants, as well as in a legal context etc. The first group is the most significant because these inscriptions show the initiative of women

FIGURE 2. *The Awām temple, Area A.*

themselves, by expressing their wishes and revealing their personalities. We refer to this group as "women's inscriptions". These form a relatively small proportion of the Maḥram Bilqīs inscriptions found in the 1950s, about twenty texts or approximately 5 % of the total number of inscriptions discovered at that period.

Among the recently discovered inscriptions are some fifteen dedications to the god Almaqah made by women. This forms approximately 4 % of the inscriptions found in the recent campaigns. Among these are five so-called confession and expiation texts (e.g. MB 2004 S I-22, MB 2005 I-26, MB 2005 I-121), and several recently discovered inscriptions mention women in their roles as wives, daughters etc. (5)

The inscriptions discovered in the 1950s in which women were the dedicants of offerings are the following: Ja 686, 706, 717, 721, 722, 731, 742, 743, 751, 764; Ir 24, 34; ZI 24; CIAS I: 87–89, 39.11/r1; CIAS II: 49–53, 39.11/o3 no. 8; CIAS II: 75–77, 39.11/o5 no. 3; while the following are examples from the recent campaigns: MB 2004 I-85, MB 2004 I-109, MB 2004 I-172, MB 2005 I-20, MB 2005 I-34, MB 2005 I-62.

The South Arabian epigraphic sources mention more than 600 women by name and filiation. In her dissertation on women's names in Ancient South Arabian inscriptions, Sholan (1999: 30–42) lists 545 names. (6) More than 400 are Sabaic and the rest are Qatabanic, Minaic, and Hadhramitic. Moreover, of these 400 names, some 300 are from the inscriptions of Maḥram Bilqīs, a fact which proves the importance of the Awām temple in the life of Sabaean women, and the recent AFSM excavations at the Awām temple have added a couple of new women's names.

Women are mentioned in the Sabaean inscriptions in different terms. The common Sabaean terms for women are *ʾṯt/ʾnṯt* "woman, female, wife"; *ḥs^2kt* "wife" and *s*^{2}ʿ*t* "(female) spouse, marital partner"; ʾ*ḫt* "sister"; ʾ*m* "mother"; *bnt* "daughter"; *ḡlmt* "unmarried girl"; *mr*ʾ*t* "daughter, lady", ʾ*mt* (pl. ʾ*mh*) "(female) servant, slave"; *mlkt* "queen"; *rs*^{2}*yt* "priestess" (MB 2005 I-39/1, Maraqten 2005: 378); *mqtwyt* "an administrative position", *b*ʿ*lt* "an administrative position in the temple", *ḫdmt* "(female) servant"; and *qrs*^{2}*t* "a woman has an administrative position" (as "herdsman?" in SD 107; Sholan 1999: 22f. translates this term as "Hirtin"). (7) The plural terms ʾ*wld*/ʾ*lwd* and the collective *wld* (< sg. *wld*), are used for children regardless of sex. The term *b*ʿ*l* "master, lord" is also used in the sense of "husband". Other terms for husband are ʾ*s*^{1}, ʾ*ys*^{1}, and *mr*ʾ. The word *byt* is used for "family, lineage, clan, and village". (8)

Both groups of inscriptions from Maḥram Bilqīs — the AFSM discoveries of the 1950s and those found in recent campaigns — are broadly of the same types and contents. All are dedicatory or have a dedicatory character. The offerings were usually female statues. The inscriptions deal primarily with everyday themes such as safety and help in childbirth. Among both groups are several which deal with women's health issues, such as giving birth, giving thanks for having children, or recovery from sickness or distress. Some record information about the status of the women, such as that she was ʾ*mt/mlkn* "a servant of the king". Thus the newly discovered inscriptions add new insights into the position of women in Sabaean society.

The following are some examples of the content of these texts. A woman makes a dedication to Almaqah for the safety of her husband and her children (ZI 24); a woman makes an offering for the safety of her children (Ja 742); a woman thanks Almaqah for granting her both male and female children (Ja 742); another woman, called Magdḥalak, makes a dedication to Almaqah for granting her male and female children (Ja 743). The inscriptions frequently mention that women made successive dedications because Almaqah granted them children (Ja 686, 721, 764). Women in their role as mothers occur several times, such as taking care of their daughters and making dedications for their safety: for instance a woman dedicated a female statuette in thanks for her daughter's safe delivery of a baby girl (YM 2403, Nāmī 22, cf. also Haram 35 = RES 3956).

We have good information about children from the Maḥram Bilqīs texts (Preißler 1994: 223–229). Male children were preferred to female, and the inscriptions of Maḥram Bilqīs mention several times that people wish for children with *kwkbt/ṣdqm* "stars of Fortune", e.g. a person wishes ʾ*wldm* / ʾ*ḏkrm* / *hn*ʾ*m* / *ḏ-kwkbt* / *ṣdqm* "healthy male children with lucky stars" (Ja 703/5–6; see also Ja 567/23; 655/12–13; RES 4938/15–17; and Ryckmans J 1975). The same formula occurs in a recently discovered inscription from Maḥram Bilqīs (MB 2004 S I-62/11).

Women are also mentioned many times in dedications made by men. Thus, men thanked Almaqah for the safety of their daughters (Ja 694/6; 690/7), or their wives (e.g. RES 4938; MB 2004 I-33/7; MB 2004 I-81/3; MB 2004 I-86/15; MB 2004 I-122/20). The inscription CIAS I: 79–81, 39.11/o 6 no. 4 = YM 440 is a dedication by a man and his wife for their safety. In another fragmentary inscription, a man makes an offering to the goddess ʿUzzayān/al-ʿUzzā for the healing *lbthw* / ʾ*mt*ʿ*zyn* / *k-ḥlẓ[t..]* "of his daughter Amatʿuzzayān from the disease from which she suffered" (CIH 558/ 6–7). Two men thanked Almaqah for the safety of their "maidservants and wives" (Ja 594/8). As another example, a man and his children made their dedication for their safety, and the children mentioned that this was also for the safety of their mother (Ja 719/1–7). A man and his wife thanked Almaqah in their inscription because he helped them in a successful lawsuit (Hamilton 9). Another man thanked Almaqah for granting children to his wife (Ir 29 §2). In yet another inscription, a man and his brother made their dedication because they had had a child *bn* / ʾ*ṯthmw* "from their wife", i.e. the wife of one of them (e.g. Ja 738/9), (9) and another text mentions that two men thanked Almaqah for five children whom their wife had born (Müller 1). This text has been considered as evidence for polyandry (see below). Another man and his brother made a dedication and asked for children of either gender, but the god granted them a son, for which they made the dedication. The passage reads: ^{6}...*wldm* / ʾ*s*^{1}*m* / *f*ʾ*w* / ʾ*ṯt* ^{7}*m* "children both males and females" (CIAS II: 75–77, 39.11/o 5 no. 3). Men made dedications because their wives had born them children: *ḥs*^{2}*kthw* "his wife" (e.g. Ir 29 §2), ʾ*ṯthw* "his wife" (e.g. Ja 655/7) and ʾ*ṯthmw* "their wife" (e.g. CIAS II: 75–77, 39.11/o 5 no. 3; MB 2004 S I-44/7). The inscriptions do not provide any information about the wives of kings or their desire to have children. The only reference is to the wife of the Yadaʿʾīl Yaluṭ, king of Ḥaḍramawt (see below).

Women are also mentioned in legal texts as well as in the so-called expiation and confession inscriptions (Ja 525; CIAS I: 87–89, 39.11/r 1 = YM 441). (10) These texts are an important source for understanding the cult and rituals in the Awām temple as well as the regulations for visiting the temple. Moreover, among the Sabaean legal inscriptions there are the so-called texts of transfer, dealing with property. Three Sabaean monumental inscriptions mention the transfer of clients, including women (Fa 76, Fa 3, RES 3960), from one party to another, and there is one text on a palm-leaf stalk dealing with the transfer of women from one tribe to another (Stein 2003).

The following are some examples of the contents of the newly discovered texts. A woman and her daughter made a dedication to Almaqah for their safety and that of their children (MB 2005 I-93). We have another inscription recording the dedication by a priestess of the temple Ḥarūnum to Almaqah, because he had protected her when she gave birth to a boy (MB 2005 I-39). (11) Dedications were made as thanks for the safety of a woman in childbirth (MB 2004 I-109) and thanks for the life of sons and the birth of a boy (MB 2005 I-62). A woman thanked Almaqah for her delivery from sickness (MB 2005 I-20). Another inscription is a dedication by four women in gratitude for their recovery from distress (MB 2004 I-85). A further dedication from a man and his wife was for delivery from an epidemic (MB 2005 I-34). Another man thanked Almaqah for granting his daughter children (MB 2004 I-120/6), and an offering by a man to Almaqah was made in gratitude for the marriage of his two sisters (MB 2005 I-56, see below). Women are also mentioned in these texts in relation to purity (e.g. MB 2005 I-88).

Among the recently discovered documents are four of the so-called expiation and confession texts dealing with women. In one of them a man was punished by the god Almaqah because he abused his female servants (*w-s^{1}bṯhw*, MB 2006 I-73/7). One of these inscriptions mentions that a man made an offering because he had violated his wife (MB 2006 I-46). A penitential text refers to a dedication to Almaqah and mentions the Mother Goddess Umm ʿAṯtar in the context (MB 2004 S I-59); while another penitential inscription records the dedication by a woman and her daughter to Almaqah. These women designate themselves as *ʾmh* / *ʾmʿṯtr* "worshippers or maidservants of (the goddess) Umm ʿAṯtar" (MB 2004 S I-22). (12)

Women are also mentioned among the captured persons in military reports, e.g. the Sabaeans after occupying a city and slaughtering many of the inhabitants *w ʾys^{1}byw / kl / ʾwld / wʾnṯhw* "took captive all its children and women" (Ja 576/7). (13) In another recently rediscovered inscription, which reports on a war carried out against several cities in Ḥaḍramawt, including Šibām, many camels and small cattle etc. were captured and *ḫms^{1}y / ws^{1}ṯ / mʾtm / ʾwldm / wʾnṯm / s^{1}bym* "650 children and women were taken as captives" (Sh 32 = MB 2004 I-126/23). (14)

Figure 3. *An inscription mentioning a dedication from a woman, where she thanks Almaqah for the life of a son and the birth of a boy (MB 2005 I-62).*

Thanks for the life of a son and the birth of a boy

MB 2005 I-62

This text was found reused in the pavement of the Peristyle Hall, close to the north of the western row of inscriptions. Measurements: 28×20 cm, text: 26×20 cm. It can be dated according to the palaeography to around the second or third century AD (Fig. 3).

Text:

1. *r[fʾ]nʿṯt / ḏt / bhṯm / ʾḏm*
2. *rtn / ḥwrt / hgrn / mrḥbm / ʾ*
3. *dm / bny / grt / hqnyt / ʾlmqhṯhwnb*
4. *ʿl / ʾwm / ṯwrn / ḏhbn / ḏs^{2}ftt / ʾl*

5. *mqh / lḥyw / ws*^{1}*twfyn / bnwhy / s*^{2}*r[ḥ]*
6. *m / bkn / wldt / ġlmn / wḥmdt*
7. *ʾlmqh / bḏt / ḥyw / hwt / ġlmn / wl*
8. *wzʾ / ʾlmqh / ḫmrhy / ʾwldm / wʾṯm*
9. *rm / hnʾm / wls*^{1}*ʿdhmw / ḥẓy / wr[ḍ]*
10. *w / ʾmrʾhmw / bny / grt / ws*^{2}*ʿb[hmw]*
11. *s*^{1}*mhrm / bʾlmqhbʿlʾwm*

Translation

1. Ra[faʾ]nāʿaṯt of the family of Bahiṯum the Aḏmirite
2. [from Ḏamār], resident of the city of Marḥabum,
3. client of the Bany Gurrat, dedicated to Almaqah Ṯahwān,
4. lord of Awām, a (statue of a) bull made of bronze, which she had promised
5. Almaqah for the life and protection of her son Šāriḥum
6. and because she gave birth to a child; and she praised
7. Almaqah because this male child survived. And may Almaqah
8. continue to grant her children and good fruits
9. and may He (Almaqah) grant them the favour and good will of their lord
10. of their lords, the Banī Gurrat and their people
11. Sumharum. By Almaqah, lord of Awām.

Commentary

The personal name *r[fʾ]nʿṯt* "ʿAṯt has saved me" or "save me ʿAṯt" is constructed from three elements: *rfʾ*, the pronominal suffix of the 1st person singular or plural (Sholan 1999: 27) and the theophoric element *ʿṯt*, an abbreviation of the divine name *ʿṯtr*. The reconstruction of the name *r[fʾ]nʿṯt* is quite certain, cf. *rfʾnṯhw* "Ṯahw (epithet of Almaqah) has saved me" or "save me Ṯahw" (1999: 143). The word *ʾḏmrtn* is a *Nisbah*-form from the name of the city *ḏmr*, modern Ḏamār, south of Ṣanʿāʾ. Ḏmr is attested several times in Sabaic inscriptions (al-Sheiba 1987: 29). This appears to be the first mention of *mrḥbm* as a city, although it is known as a tribal name (Ir 30 §1, 31 §1, Ja 743/1). Bull statues given as offerings to Almaqah are attested many times (Sima 2000: 146–151, 153) and may have been symbols of fertility.

The status of women in the light of the Maḥram Bilqīs inscriptions

South Arabian civilization consisting of the Sabaean, Qatabanian, Ḥaḍramī, and Minaean traditions was patriarchal in its structure throughout its long history, from the beginning of the first millennium BC until the end of the sixth century AD (Beeston 1979: 120–122). Although women are commonly depicted in Sabaean art, there seems little doubt that their position was generally lower than that of men at all levels of society. The true role played by women has to be evaluated with some caution when using the records of their husbands, fathers, brothers, sons, and lords. However, the case is different with the small numbers of women's documents which survive, particularly those from Maḥram Bilqīs. These texts were, of course, commissioned by the women mentioned in them, and were not written by the women themselves. It seems to be that the scribes of the texts were men and as yet there are no South Arabian texts that can be said with certainty to have been written by women. All these facts make it difficult to reconstruct the status of women. In the following sections, several aspects of women's status in ancient South Arabia will be briefly presented.

Family and marriage

There is no term in Sabaic that corresponds precisely to the modern nuclear family consisting of father, mother, and children. The closest approximation is found in the word *byt* "house; village, estate; temple; clan, family, dynasty" (SD 34). This term, which is frequently translated as "family", had more the meaning of "clan" or "lineage" (Beeston 1972: 257f.). The Sabaean family was patriarchal in character and organization and its foundation was marriage. Several kinds of marriage were known in South Arabia: monogamy was the most common, but instances of polygamy, including both polygyny (*ʾḥs*^{2}*kthw* "his wives", Ry 520/5–6), *ʾḥs*^{2}*kthmy* "their wives" (Gar NIS 3/2–3), (15) and polyandry have been recorded, as well as examples of temporary marriage (CIH 581; Beeston 1978). (16) Polyandry is a form of marriage in which one woman is married to more than one man. The existence of this in ancient Yemen has been proved by Sabaic inscriptions (Wādī as-Sirr 1; YMN 19; Müller 1; Ryckmans J 1986; Avanzini 1991; Frantsouzoff 1999) (17) but it should be stressed that it was only rarely practised in ancient Yemen.

Figure 4. *A dedication for Almaqah from a man as thanks for the wedding of his two sisters (MB 2005 I-56).*

There is no precise term for marriage or a marriage contract in any of the ancient South Arabian languages, (18) and since we have no marriage contracts we do not know for certain what they would have been like or even whether contracts of this sort existed in a culture which can be described as very strictly collective. A.F.L. Beeston drew attention to the fact that marriage was a "union between two families" and not, as in Western culture, a partnership between two individuals (1979: 121), and this is absolutely correct. The Sabaean culture can be described as collectivism, i.e. a society in which people from birth onwards are integrated into strong, unified in-groups, which throughout a person's lifetime continue to protect them, in exchange for unquestioning loyalty. Collectivist cultures place great emphasis on groups and think in terms of "we", as opposed to individualist cultures that stress the individual "I". This explains why, when the Sabaeans speak of married women in the clan, they always use the plural form such as *ʾṯthw / ḥ*s^2*kthmw* "their (i.e. the clan's) wife" and *ʾwldhmw* "their children".

Newly married couples did not establish their own residence but instead became part of an existing household. While Sabaean marriage was primarily patrilocal, there is also evidence of some matrilocal or uxorilocal residence. It should also be noted that there is some epigraphic evidence of matrilineality in ancient Yemen, as has been observed by several scholars (e.g. Fa 76; Ja 700; see Beeston 1983; Ryckmans J 1986; Avanzini 1991; Korotayev 1995). (19)

After consummation of the marriage, the legal status of both parties was transformed, or at least clarified. Once married, the woman became a full member of her husband's clan and took on its affiliation, expressed by the designation *ḏt* "she of (the clan)" plus the name of her husband's clan. A variation is the formula *ḏt / byt* "she of the family" plus the name of her husband's family. There was thus a clear distinction between married and unmarried women. For instance *ʿmrlt / ḏt /* s^2*rḥm* "ʿAmrlāt of the clan Šarḥum" (Ja 721/1) was a woman who had married into the clan Šarḥum; and s^2*ḫḫ / ḏt / byt / hlkʾm* "Šaḫāḫ of the family Halʾakum" was one who had married into the family Halakʾum (Nāmī 27/1). An unmarried woman is designated as *bnt* X "daughter of X" in the inscriptions. (20) Sometimes the affiliation of the woman consists of the name of her own clan *and* the name of her husband's clan, for instance *ḡnmm / bnt / ʿzmm / ḏt / ʾlʾl / ʾḥnkt* "Ḡanīmum, daughter of ʿAzmum, she of [married into] the clan ʾAʾal, [the] Ḥankite" (CIH 450/1–2). There is one case of divorce in the Sabaic inscriptions (YMN 19; see Beeston 1997: 1–4).

Although we have no marriage contracts, we have some information about the marriage formulas that can help us understand some of the formulae in the arrangement of a marriage (RES 4233/9–10; Beeston 1981: 28; see also MAFRAY -Quṭrā 1/3–6). Another two good examples of the arrangement of marriages are the inscriptions Ir 24 §1–4 and MB 2005 I-56 (see below).

Dedication by a man in gratitude for the marriage of his two sisters

MB 2005 I-56

This text was discovered in area A. Measurements: 32×16×13 cm. This inscription can be dated to the middle of the third century AD (Fig. 4).

Text

1. *tbʿkrb / ḏṣryhw / tbʿ*
2. *krb / bn / krbm / hqny / ʾ*
3. *lmqhṯhwnbʿlʾwm / ṣlmn / ḏ*
4. *ḏhbn / ḏ*s^2*fthw / ḥmdm / ḏḫmr*
5. *hw / ʾlmqh /* s^1*twfyn / w*s^1*tkmln*
6. *ʾtwt / ʾḫtyhw /* s^1*mḥlk / ʿdy / b*
7. *yt / r* s^2*yn / wgdʿl / ʿdy / byt / k*
8. *rbm / wlḏḫmrhw / ʾlmqh / hʿ*
9. *nnhmw / bn / ḥlẓ / ḥlẓ / hʾ / w*
10. *ʾṯthw / blt / ḏt / krbm / wlw*
11. *zʾ / ʾlmqh / hʿnnhmw / bn / bʾ*
12. s^1*tm / wnkytm / wtlfm / wnḍʿ / w*
13. s^2*ṣy /* s^2*nʾm / wlḫmrhmw / ʾlmqh*
14. *ḥẓy / wrḍw / mrʾyhmw / ʾl* s^2*rḥ / y*
15. *ḥḍb / wʾḫyhw / yʾzl / byn / mlk*
16. *y /* s^1*bʾ / wḏrydn / bny / frʿm / ynhb /*
17. *mlk /* s^1*bʾ / bʾlmqhbʿlʾwm*

Translation

1. Tubbaʿkarib, who is protected by Tubbaʿ
2. karib of the family Karibum, dedicated to
3. Almaqah Ṯahwān, lord of Awām, the bronze statue,
4. which he had promised him in gratitude because
5. Almaqah granted him the safe accomplishment of
6. the marriage of both his sisters: Sumuḥalak into
7. the family Rašyān and Gaddʿalā into the family
8. of Karibum, and because Almaqah granted them and delivered
9. them from a sickness they have suffered,

[namely] he and his
10. wife Balat of the family Karibum, and
11. may Almaqah continue to aid them
12. against evil, mischief, perishing, harm,
13. malice of an enemy, and may Almaqah
14. vouchsafe them the favour and good will of their lord ʾIlšaraḥ
15. Yaḥḏub and his brother Yaʾzul Bayn, king of
16. Sabaʾ and Ḏū-Raydān, both sons of Fariʿum Yanhub
17. King of Sabaʾ. By Almaqah, lord of Awām.

Commentary

The personal name *tbʿkrb* "Tubbaʿ has blessed" is well attested in Sabaic (Tairan 1992: 88). The affiliation of the dedicator *tbʿkrb* is not indicated in the text but instead there is included the expression *ḏ-rṣy-hw*, which means literally "who has protected". The root *ṣry* means "protect", cf. *ḏ-ṣry-hw* "protector" (SD 145). This phrase indicates that *tbʿkr*b is a client. The protector has the same name and family name as the client, *tbʿkrb / bn / krbm*. The formula, personal name + *ḏ-ṣry-hw*, is attested several times in Sabaic inscriptions (e.g. Ja 589/1–4, 703/1–2). (21) The object dedicated was *ṣlmn / ḏ-ḏhbn* "a statue made of bronze", which is the most often attested offering at the Awām temple (Sima 2000: 307 ff.).

The most significant part of this text is the marriage formula: [4]*...bḏt / ẖmr* [5]*hw / ʾlmqh /* s^1*twfyn / w-* s^1*tkmln* [6]*ʾtwt / ʾẖtyhw /* s^1*mḫlk / ʿdy / b* [7]*yt / r* s^2*yn / w-gdʿl / ʿdy / byt / k* [8]*rbm / w-l-ḏ-ẖmrhmw* "in gratitude because Almaqah granted him the safeguard and accomplishment [i.e. the safe accomplishment] of the wedding ceremony of both his sisters: Sumuḥalak into the clan Rašyān and Gaddʿalā into the family of Karibum" (lines 4–8). The best parallel for our text is an inscription from Maḥram Bilqīs discovered by the AFSM in the 1950s (Ir 24). This inscription contains a formula that reads:

rbʿṯt / yġnm / bn / ṣʿqn / wtzʾd / w-nhmn / hqny / ʾlmqh / ṯhwn / bʿlʾwm / ṣlmn / ḏ-ḏhbn / ḏ-s^2*fthw / ḥmdm / bḏt / ẖmr / ʾlmqh / ṯhwn / bʿlʾwm / ʿbdhw / rbʿṯt / yġnm / bn / ṣʿqn / wtzʾd / w-nhmn / bʾmlʾ / wtb* s^2*r /* s^1*tmlʾ / wtb* s^2*rn / bʿmhw / k-y* s^1*tkmln / w-* s^1*twfyn / lhw / ʾwln / whkrbn / w-hklln / mrʾtn / ḏ-t* s^1*tmyn / tḥyʾl / bt / bny / grfm / w-ṣʿqm / ʿdy / bythmw / byt / tzʾd*

"Rabʿaṯt Yaġnum of the family Ṣaʿqān, Tazʾad and Nahmān dedicated to Almaqah Ṯahwān, lord of Awām, this statue made of bronze, which he promised him in gratitude because Almaqah Ṯahwān, lord of Awām, granted his servant Rabʿaṯt Yaġnum of the clan Ṣaʿqān, Tazʾad and Nahmān the requests and the good news which he besought and asked from him, the safeguard and success to bring home, to marry and wed the woman who is named Taḥīʾīl of the family Banū Girāfum and Ṣaʿqum, into their own family Tazʾad" (Ir 24 §1). (22)

The verbal root *hkrb* means "to make a contract of marriage". It was translated by the SD (79) as "unite a bride with one's own family". The term *hkll* in Ir 24 is translated by the SD (76) as "marry a wife". However, it seems that the expression for "to marry" is *hkrb*, as was suggested by A.F.L. Beeston (1983: 11), and *hkll* seems to have been the term for the wedding ceremony. Beeston translates *hkll* as "bring home a bride" (1983: 11).

The root ʾTW in our text is the key word to understanding this marriage formula. It is an expression for the wedding procession. The Sabaic root ʾTW literally means "come, come back". The term *ʾtwt* in our text can be compared with Sabaic *ʾtwt* which designates the "royal accession" (Ir 18 §1). Moreover, the term *ʾtyt* is used instead of *ʾtwt* with the same meaning in another inscription from Maḥram Bilqīs (Sh 18 = MB 2004 I-38/13). (23) This inscription reports the accession of the king Šāʿirum Awtar in the royal palace of Salḥīn in Mārib.

The two women in our text left their family house to join the households of their husbands, s^1*mḫlk / ʿdy / b* [7]*yt / r* s^1*yn* "Sumuḥalak to [her new home] the family Rašyān" and *gdʿl / ʿdy / byt / k* [8]*rbm* "Gaddʿalā to [her new home] the family of Karibum". The family name of these women prior to their marriage is not mentioned. However, following marriage these two girls became full members in the families *r*s^2*yn* and *krbm* and used the designation *ḏt*. The Sabaean clan *r*s^2*yn* is known from other Sabaic inscriptions (Ir 34/3, RES 4815/3,4). The *bny / krbm* are mentioned in an inscription from Maḥram Bilqīs (CIAS II: 13f., 39.11/o2 no. 3/23). Both names of the women s^1*mḫlk* and *gdʿl* are attested here for the first time in Ancient South Arabian inscriptions. *S*^{1}*mḫlk* is a compound name consisting of the theophoric element s^1*m* "(his) name" and *ḫlk* "to give" and may be translated as "Sumu (His name) has given", cf. *mlkḫlk* (Sholan 1999: 133). The name *gdʿl* consists of the theophoric element *gd* "luck, fortune" and the verbal form *ʿl*, root ʿLY "to be exalted, high".

In line 10, the wife of the dedicator Tubbuʿkarib is mentioned as *blt / ḏt / krb*. The personal name *blt* is found here for the first time in the Ancient South Arabian inscriptions. It may be interpreted according to the Sabaic root BLT "send, despatch (someone) on a mission" (SD 29). Although the dedicator Tubbᶜkarib is mentioned without his family name, his wife is mentioned with the name of the family into which she has married, namely *ḏt / krbm*. This is the family name of her husband's protector. The king ᵓIlšaraḥ Yaḥḍub and his brother Yaᵓzul Bayn, kings of Sabaᵓ and Ḏū-Raydān reigned together *c.* AD 236–260.

The role of women in the family

The primary roles of Sabaean women were within the family. According to the available information on the lives of women which is available in various South Arabian sources, i.e. excavated artefacts, works of art such as reliefs and sculptures, as well as the epigraphic evidence, the primary role of the Sabaean woman was centred on the home, the family, and childcare. There are several examples in the inscriptions of a mother taking care of her daughter (e.g. Ja 731).

Economic and administrative roles

Although women were mostly outside the political or administrative hierarchies, they were able to participate in certain spheres of life beyond the home. The political and social structure of Sabaᵓ was dominated by the male élite (Beeston 1978; Korotayev 1996: 73ff.) and women were given very few obvious opportunities to play a part in the administration or in public ceremonies.

The inscriptions inform us about some posts held by women. Two women are described as *bᶜlty* (feminine of *bᶜl* "lord"), a high, possibly administrative, position in the area of Mārib (CIH 373). Another inscription (CIH 95) records that a woman had a high administrative position. Service was rendered by a man to a woman who had *wrṯt-hw* "inherited him" (Beeston 1983: 7). Some women held positions in the administration of temples (*bᶜlt*, see below), while two other women are recorded as having had the post of *mqtwyt* "an administrative position" (Nāmī 14/2; CIH 289/6).

One text mentions that a woman bears the title *mlkt / ḥḍrmwt* "queen of Ḥaḍramawt" (Ir 13/7). This woman was the wife of ᵓIlᶜazz Yaluṭ, king of Ḥaḍramawt. This text proves that royal marriages existed in ancient Yemen. Although we are not informed about women of the royal family, this woman was the daughter of the Sabaean king ᶜAlhān Nahfān (end of the second century AD) and sister of the Sabaean king Šāᶜirum Awtar (beginning of the third century AD). Otherwise, we are not informed about the wives of the kings, who must have been rich and influential given their high social position.

Sabaean women were able to hold property in their own name; they appear as builders of houses, and sometimes with their menfolk as paying for the construction of their own tombs with their own money (Beeston 1983; Robin 1996: 1196f.; Breton 1999: 97–100), and as businesswomen in some transaction documents which survive on palm-leaf stalks (Maraqten 2002: 82).

Cultic roles of women at Maḥram Bilqīs

It is clear from Sabaean texts and artistic monuments that both men and women could take an active part in demonstrating their piety, whether by making regular offerings to Almaqah, dedicating statues, or more devotedly by playing sacred roles inside the Awām temple. From the Middle Sabaean period there are testimonies to the involvement of women in various practices in the religious life. A woman usually designates herself in the dedicatory inscriptions as *ᵓmt* "worshipper, servant, devotee" of Almaqah (e.g. Ja 706/5; 751/11). Women used to make pilgrimages to this temple in the same way as men. The active role of women at the Awām was thus the visit to the temple and the performance of the offering. In one inscription Sabaean individuals promised Almaqah that if he would grant them a child that survived, they would not only make an offering but also *wlhwfrnn / ᵓṯthmw / wbnhmw / ᶜdy / mḥrmn / lḥmdnn / mqm / ᵓlmqhw* "they would let their wives and their sons perform a pilgrimage to the temple (i.e. Awām) to praise the power of Almaqah" (Ja 669/15–17).

It seems that the participation of women as worshippers is hidden behind common male language. Furthermore, their expressions of belief were recorded less often than those of men, both in texts and iconography. However, there is evidence from Maḥram Bilqīs for the participation of women in cult rituals. It is to be noted that in the inscriptions, the offerings made by women are primarily female bronze statues while men dedicated male statues. (24) In addition, there are stelae representing women giving an offering to the divinity (e.g. YM 386).

Meanwhile, there are many Old Sabaic inscriptions which mention the dedication of persons to several deities, among them Almaqah, and inscriptions of this type have been discovered at the Awām temple. (25) The duty of these persons was to perform the services at the temple. The majority of those mentioned are men, although women are occasionally cited (e.g. RES 4808).

This means that women were not really involved in temple service in this period. (26)

In general, women did not play an important role in the administration of Maḥram Bilqīs and according to the records so far discovered none of the women appear to have been priestesses of Almaqah at Awām. However, in a recently discovered inscription at Awām a woman bears the title *rs^{2}yt ḥrwnm* "priestess of (the temple) Ḥarūnum". This temple must be located in the city of Mārib (MB 2005 I-39, Maraqten 2005: 378f.). In the official religion, a Sabaean woman did not stand back while a male mediated between her and the deity. Sabaean women received their oracles from Almaqah like the menfolk. There were women who were associated with sorcery and witchcraft according to an inscription from Maḥram Bilqīs (Ja 735; Müller 1988: 450–452). (27) This inscription records a prayer for rain and mentions the role of women in the rituals carried out in this prayer. One group of women is designated as *bnt mrb* "daughters of Mārib". Another two groups are *rqt* "female magicians" (Ja 735/9) and *ᶜṭwf* "female invocators" (Ja 735/9). (28) There is evidence for the sacred marriage in ancient Yemen (Müller 1993: 15–28) but there is no clear evidence of such a ritual associated with the Awām temple.

There were also two women who were religious specialists in the temple of the Sun-goddess Ḏāt Baᶜdān (Nāmī 74/6; Müller 1988: 449–450). One of them had the position *bᶜlt* "an administrative position in the temple" and the other was *ḥlmt* "interpreter of dreams" (Nāmī 74/6).

All countries of the ancient Near East shared the belief that one had to be pure to approach a deity. This was an important rule at the Awām as is proved by recently discovered epigraphic material. With regard to women, their vaginal discharge was considered impure in ancient Yemen and in particular in the Awām temple. In fact we have some good information about this from the so-called confession and expiation inscriptions and prescriptions. In particular, we have evidence from the texts found in the Awām dealing with the cultic impurity of women. (29) A woman made a dedication *...b-ḏ-bhʾt / m [8]ḥrmhw / wʾlbs^{1}hw / ʾ [9]l / ẓy* "because she entered his temple [i.e. Awām] while her clothes were not pure" (YM 441= CIAS I: 87, 39.11/r1). (30)

In one recently discovered prescription we read: [2] *…w-ḏ-ybhʾn / w-ʾl / ẓy / w-ʾl / tr [3]ḥḍ*... "and whoever enters [i.e. the Awām temple] [ritually] impure and without the ritual washing..." (MB 2005 I-58). This person, either a man or a woman, should be punished as the inscription states in the first line: "let him be aware of [his crime] and let him perform expiation". If they did not follow the rules for visiting this temple, women and men could be punished by the wrath of Almaqah through sickness etc. There is no evidence of cultic prostitution in ancient Yemen, and sexual intercourse was forbidden in the Awām temple. In the same prescription we read: [1] *...l-yḥḏrn / w-l-ynḏrn / ḏ-ys^{3}yfn / ʾnṯtm / bws^{1}ṭ / mḥr [2]mn* " ... let him be aware of [his crime] and let him perform an expiation: whoever has sexual intercourse with a woman inside the temple [i.e. Awām]" (MB 2005 I-58/1–2). (31) The verb *s^{3}yf* in this text is to be understood as "have sexual intercourse with a woman". This interpretation is based on the Arabic root SWF, cf. Arabic *sāwafa l-marʾata = ḍājaᶜa-hā* "He slept with the woman in, or on, one bed" (Lane 1469). To give the meaning of *sāwafa* as *ḍājaᶜa* "have sexual intercourse with a woman" makes the meaning *s^{3}yf* in this context quite certain.

Three categories of divinities seem to have existed in ancient South Arabia. The first were the official divinities, i.e. the national deities such as Almaqah, the state and national god of the Sabaeans. The second category included the tribal or local deities such as Taʾlab, the god of Sumᶜy, north of Ṣanᶜāʾ. The third category comprised the household and personal deities, and these represented popular religion. All three categories were worshipped by women in ancient South Arabia.

All women's inscriptions discovered at Maḥram Bilqīs are dedicated to Almaqah. This was because of his power as a god of fertility. Women who worshipped other deities and who lived in Mārib or in other regions such as the highlands of Yemen still used to come to Awām and make dedications to Almaqah.

It seems that women in ancient South Arabia, and particularly in Sabaʾ, preferred to worship specific deities, such as the Banātʾīl "Daughters of ʾĪl", i.e. the three goddesses Al-Lāt, al-ᶜUzzā, and Manāt; or Bitayʾīl "the two daughters of ʾĪl", i.e. Al-Lāt and al-ᶜUzzā, who were known in both North and South Arabia (Robin 2000: 113ff.). The South Arabian "Daughters of ʾĪl" are part of a low-ranking class of divinities belonging to popular religion. These female deities are particularly invoked by women and were preferred by them, as we can see from the amulets on which the names Al-Lāt (South Arabian *ltn*) and al-ᶜUzzā (South Arabian *ᶜzyn*) are inscribed (Ryckmans J 1980; Maraqten 1999).

The goddess Umm ᶜAṯtar "Mother of ᶜAṯtar" seems to have played the role of a Mother Goddess and was also a favourite deity of women (CIH 544). Two new confession inscriptions regarding women dedicated to the god Almaqah and mentioning Umm ᶜAṯtar have recently been discovered (MB 2004 S I-59; MB 2004 I-22). The term *ᵓmh*, plural of *ᵓmt* in this text, seems to refer to a kind of service or administration which the two women carried out. Meanwhile, dedications by women were also offered to the South Arabian supreme deity Aṯtar (Nāmī 14; CIH 289). A divinity which seems to have appealed to women is the vulture deity Nasr/Naswar, *ns¹r / ns¹wr* (Müller 1994). Further dedications of women were submitted to the goddess *nws²m* (Robin-Itwa 1, Robin 1982, i: 59).

A favourite deity of women was *bᶜl / bytn* "lord of the house". He is mentioned several times in relation to women or women's dedications (e.g. YM 2403), *bᶜlbythmw* "lord of their house" (Nāmī 22/2–6, CIH 179). A personal god seems to have been very popular in the everyday life of the Sabaeans. It is known primarily as *s²ymn* "the patron god" in Sabaic texts, especially on the inscribed sticks. *S²ymn* appears frequently in the greetings formula in Sabaic letters by both women and men. Sometimes goddesses are preferred, such as the sun-goddess D̲āt Ḥamīm (ᶜAbdallah 1996: 18ff.). Women also made dedications to what is called *ᵓlhhw* "her (personal) god" (YM 2402/2, see Sholan 2005: 51ff.).

Researchers have observed that the names given to women in ancient South Arabia were of special types and forms (Sholan 1999: 27–29). Women's composite personal names contain the names of specific goddesses, which would suggest that these goddesses were preferred by women. Many of these names express the private piety of women. For instance, names composed with Almaqah or his epithets have been found. The only personal name composed with Almaqah's name is the woman's name *ᵓmtᵓlmqh* "servant of Almaqah" (1999: 97). Otherwise, his name seems to have been considered taboo for use in personal names. However, his epithet Ṯahwān (*ṯhwn*) and the abbreviations of it, *ṯhw* and *ṯwn*, are used frequently in the women's names found in the inscriptions of Maḥram Bilqīs, e.g. *ᵓm<t>ṯwn* "servant of Ṯawn", *hnᵓṯwn* "fortune of Ṯawn", *rfᵓnṯhw* "Ṯahu has saved us/me" (1999: 99, 118, 143). There is only one name of a woman that is composed with *ᵓwm* and this is *kmlᵓwm* "Awām is complete" (1999: 128).

Although we lack any accurate data about the religious status of women in ancient Yemeni society, women seem to have had an important role in popular religion. This can be seen in their worship of various household and personal deities. These deities appear to have included those that protected women, including at times of childbirth.

Women's health care

Several dedicatory inscriptions by women provide information about their state of health. For instance, a woman named Amatalmaqah made a dedication to Almaqah for the healing of another woman named Naḍi.-rat "from a sickness that affected her eyes" (*bn / mrḍ / mrḍt / ᶜynhw*, Ja 706/6–7). Another woman made her dedication on behalf of her daughter because Almaqah had cured "her daughter Rabībatgawbān from the sickness she suffered" (*bnthw / ⁶[r]bbtgwbn / bn / kl / ⁷ᵓmrḍ / mrḍt*, Ja 731/5–7). (32)

The purification of women after childbirth and hygiene during menstruation was demanded in Sabaean society (see above); having sexual intercourse with a woman immediately after childbirth or during menstruation was not only considered an abomination and a perversion but was punished by the deity, to judge by several penitential inscriptions (e.g. Haram 40 = CIH 523, Ryckmans J 1972). However, we are informed about a woman who seems to have been affected by a disease during pregnancy. This woman, who bears the name Abḥalak, made an offering to Almaqah *bḏt / s²rḥ / wmtᶜn ⁶grbhw / bhry / hryt / bẖr ⁷f / s¹mhkrb / bn / ᵓbkrb / b[k] ⁸n / ḥmdt / bn / ẖbṯn / kwn / b ⁹hwt / ẖrfn* "in gratitude because he [Almaqah] protected and delivered her person when she became pregnant in the month of Sumhukarib, son of Abkarib — and for that she gave praise — from an epidemic that was spread in that year" (Ja 751/5–9; Preißler 1979: 273f.). (33) The woman here remained healthy throughout an epidemic and made this offering as a thanksgiving. No data about midwives are available and their work may have been carried out by old women or the women's mothers, as in more recent times.

In an offering by a woman to Almaqah in the Awām temple, which is located near Ṣanᶜāᵓ, the main motivation is stated to be *bḏt / s²w ⁸[f] / wwfyn / wmtᶜn / ᵓlmqhbᶜlᵓwm / grb / ᵓmthw / l[t]⁹wf / bt / btᶜ / bn / mwld / wldt / ġlmm / ḏkrm / myt[m] / ¹⁰ġyr / qllt / mwnn / bmḥgl / whᶜnhw / ws²rḥ / grbh ¹¹[w] / ᵓlmqhbᶜlᵓwm / bn / hwt / mrḍn* "in gratitude because Almaqah, lord of Awām saved, protected and delivered the body of his worshipper Litwaf the Bataᶜid from a [hard] confinement in which she gave a birth to a male child [which subsequently] died, [and] the moaning of giving the birth in the chamber of confinement was not little [and] Almaqah, lord of Awām protected her body from that sickness" (CIAS II: 49f., 39.11/o3, no 8/7–11 = Ja 2109, Preißler 1994: 227). (34)

The epigraphic material from Maḥram Bilqīs proves

that the majority of inscriptions by women concerning their health have been found in this temple and the dedications were made to Almaqah as a healing deity. Among the newly discovered inscriptions from Maḥram Bilqīs are several texts which mention that the reason for the dedications by women was because Almaqah had cured them or their daughters from sickness. Others deal with women's healthcare in general. In one inscription thanks are given for the safety of a woman in childbed. It states that this dedication was in gratitude [2]*...lwldt / hʾ / ʾṯtn / bḥrlt / ḏt / ʿḏr* [3]*n / ḡlmm / mytm* … "because she, that woman Baḥrlāt of the family ʿAḏrān, has born a dead boy" and she had survived the birth, even though the child died (MB 2004 I-109/2–3). In another dedication by a woman as thanks for delivery from sickness we read that this was [4]*bḏt / rbẖt / bn / ḥlẓ / ḥlẓ* [5]*t* "in gratitude because she had been cured from a sickness she suffered" (MB 2005 I-20/4).

The desire to have children was very strong in ancient Yemen, as in other parts of the ancient Near East. The large number of infant deaths through disease, birth defects, and accidents, together with the need to increase the labour force, as well as to provide heirs to facilitate the orderly transmission of property, made it necessary to have large families. For instance, in one case a woman had no surviving children. She made a votive offering to Almaqah because she promised him that whenever He would vouchsafe her children, she would make a dedication for him. Almaqah has now vouchsafed to her the life of two sons, so she made the offering as a fulfilment of her vow. She states in her inscription as follows: *wr* [8]*ʾ / ẖmrhw / ẖyw / bnyhw* [9]*ṯwbʾl / wʿmrm* "and now he [Almaqah] has vouchsafed to her the life of two sons Ṯawbʾīl and ʿAmrum" (Ja 717/7–9).

Acknowledgements

I would like to express my gratitude to Mrs Merilyn Phillips-Hodgson, President of the AFSM for her endeavours in directing the Maḥram Bilqīs project. I gratefully acknowledge the help of Dr ʿAbdallah Bawazir, President of the General Organization of Antiquities and Museums and his representatives in Mārib.

Notes

1 Several papers have been delivered to the Seminar for Arabian Studies about these discoveries and published in the *Proceedings of the Seminar for Arabian Studies* (e.g. Glanzman 2002).

2 A woman bearing the name *gḥmt* is mentioned in the Old Sabaic inscriptions of Yalā (cited by Sholan 1999: 35, 60).

3 These stelae are still unpublished although some were exhibited in the Yemen exhibition at the British Museum and elsewhere and published in the accompanying catalogues (e.g. Daum *et al.* 1999: 296; Simpson ed. 2002: 198ff.). A. Sholan considered these texts in her dissertation (1999).

4 These texts were discovered in unscientific digging, primarily in the Yemeni Jawf. There are several thousands of these texts (see Ryckmans, Müller & Abdallah 1994). For instance, one mentions a contract with a woman dealing with raising animals (ʿAbdallah 1994: 1–12). Y. ʿAbdallah (1996) published a letter from a woman. Another text — a receipt — mentions a woman repaying a debt (Maraqten 2002: 82). The author of the present paper is currently working on the publication of the collection in the National Museum of Ṣanʿāʾ and has published several articles on this subject. In addition, P. Stein is working on the collection of the Bayrische Staatsbibliothek, Munich (see Stein 2006). However, here it is not possible to consider the information gained from the inscribed sticks, since this is not within the scope of this paper.

5 Three recently discovered women's inscriptions have been published by the author. These are MB 2005 I-39, MB 2005 I-93, MB 2004 I-113 (Maraqten 2005). Apart from these inscriptions and the two others (MB 2005 I-62, MB 2005 I-56) published here, all MB inscriptions cited in this paper are unpublished.

6 Although this work is a philological analysis of the names, the author gives some valuable information about the contexts of the occurrences of the women's names (Sholan 1999: 42–88).

7 More recent evidence of *qrs²t* has been discovered (Dār al-Šukr/3,4,6,7, YM 17189/3; Bron & Gajda 2005: 116ff. translates *qrs²t* as "trésorière").

8 The translations of these terms follow the SD (cf. also Sholan 1999: 12–24).

9 For another text mentioning a dedication made by a man and his wife, see Ja 750.

10 There are other expiation and confession inscriptions by women relating to the god Ḏū-Samāwī, see Haram 33 = CIH 532, Haram 34 = CIH 533, Haram 35 = RES 3956, Haram 36 = RES 3957, Haram 40 = CIH 543, Haram 56 = CIH 568.

11 This text has been published (Maraqten 2005).

12 This divinity is known only from two other inscriptions (CIH 554, Nāmī 19, republished in Daum *et al.* 1999:

304). On the goddess Umm ᶜAṯtar, see Höfner (1970: 275–277) who suggests that she may have been a sun-goddess.

13 There is good information about the capture of women in pre-Islamic times in the so-called *Ayyām al-ᶜarab*. This title, which literally means "the days of the Arabs", denotes the battles and raids between the Arab tribes in the period before the rise of the Islam (see Lichtenstädter 1935: 20–38).

14 This inscription was published as a fragmentary text by Šarafaddīn (2004: 353f.). Fortunately, it was rediscovered in the 2004 season of AFSM excavations. The inscription is complete and contains thirty-two lines.

15 These two examples of polygyny are uncertain since the word *ʾḥs²kt* (pl. of *ḥs²kt*) "wives" can be a general indication or a collective designation for their wives, like "their sons", in the clan.

16 Classical Arabic sources mention that several kinds of marriage were known among the Arabs before Islam (Smith 1903: 67, 276f.).

17 See also the critical view of J. Ryckmans (1986: 413).

18 The Akkadian term for a marriage contract is *riksātum* or *riksū* (see Westbrook 1988: 29).

19 See also the discussion in Frantsouzoff 1999. There is more evidence from the inscriptions recently discovered at Maḥram Bilqīs.

20 On the evidence for women and their filiations, see Sholan 1999: 9–20.

21 *ḏ-ṣry-hw* was understood by Jamme (1962: 96) as a family name.

22 Beeston (1981: 27) translates the passage *kys¹tkmln / w- s¹twfyn / lhw / ʾwln / whkrbn / w-hklln / mrʾtn / ḏt- s¹tmyn / tḥʾl / bt / bny / grfm / w-ṣᶜqm / ᶜdy / bythmw / tẓʾd* as "that it should have been successfully achieved for him, to *ʾwl* and *hkrb* and *hkll* the lady TḤʾL of GRFM-ṢᶜQM into their own house, that of TẒʾD" (Ir 24 §1). Beeston translates the three verbs in this passage as "bring home (the bride)" (cf. *tʾwl* "return home" in a military context), "tie the marital knot" (Arabic *ᶜaqd al-nikāḥ*), and "consummate (the marriage)" (cf. also Beeston 1979: 121).

23 This inscription was rediscovered in the 2004 season. It contains twenty-two lines.

24 On references to female and male bronze statues in the published Sabaic inscriptions from Maḥram Bilqīs, see Sima 2000: 307ff.

25 A woman named Ẓūrᶜadan (*ẓwrᶜdn*) who was dedicated for the service of Mutabnaṭyān, the city deity of Haram, is mentioned in one inscription (Haram 6/4 = CIH 514/4). On these texts see Höfner 1970: 333f.

26 In an inscription from the Barʾān temple (DAI Barʾān 1988 1/B) a woman named Farᶜat (*frᶜt*) was dedicated to Almaqah to carry out services at the Barʾān temple. This siglum is cited according to a personal communication in Sholan 1999: 58 as an unpublished inscription (see below). However, the name of a woman *frᶜt* occurs in other inscriptions engraved on altars from Barʾān (DAI Barʾān 1988-2, DAI Barʾān 1994-5, DAI Barʾān 1996-1, published in Nebes 2005: 119) and seems to be the same person as above. N. Nebes (2005: 11) considers *frᶜt* to be a person or an altar. However, it should be considered as a name of a person since such category inscriptions are known from several inscriptions.

27 This inscription is engraved on two stone blocks. Fortunately, the recent AFSM excavations have brought to light the stone bearing the lower part of the text, which allows us to correct the previous reading.

28 The SD (22) translates this word as "support, escort" and considers the meaning as uncertain.

29 The matter of purity is attested in several expiation and confession inscriptions dedicated to the god Ḏū-Samāwī. In one text, a woman bearing the name *ʾḫyt* / (Uḫayyat) made a dedication "because she went out to his courtyard and she was not pure" (*bḏt / wḏʾt / ᶜ ⁶dy / mwṭnn / ḡyr / ṭh ⁷rm*, Haram 33/5–7 = CIH 532/5–7). Also, see the women's dedications to Ḏū-Samāwī regarding impurity (Haram 40 = CIH 523, Haram 35 = RES 3956, Haram 36 = RES 3957; see also Ryckmans J 1972).

30 In a similar inscription a woman was punished with sickness in her breast for nine months because she visited an Awām temple of Almaqah located near Ṣanᶜāʾ, while wearing unsuitable clothes (NAM 2494 = CIAS II: 41–44, 39.11/o3 no. 6).

31 The verb *s³yf* is attested in Sabaean in a penitential text from Maḥram Bilqīs (Ja 702/15–16) and in another fragmentary text possibly of a penitential nature (Ja 570/5). However, the SD (140) does not give a translation of these two examples. See also the discussion by N. Nebes 1995: 31f. and his translation of the phrase *whʾ / f-l / s³y ¹⁶f / ḥwlm / mykbt / bhw* as "und er (*sc.* ʾAlmaqah) möge den Traum gewähren, in dem es eine Orakelentscheidung gibt" (Ja 702/15). We have other expiation and confession inscriptions that inform us about men who made a sin-dedication because they had had sexual intercourse with women in a temple, see Daum *et al.* 1999: 290, München

94–317880, cf. also CIH 533.

32 Many of these inscriptions simply give general information such as *ḥmdm / b* [4]*d̲t / mt*ᶜ / ᵓ*mthw* / s^{2}*f* [5]*nqyn / d̲t /* s^{1}*ṭrn / bn / ḥ* [6]*lẓ / ḥlẓt* "in gratitude because he (the lord of the house) delivered his worshipper Šāfnāqayn of the family *d̲t* s^{1}*ṭrn* from a sickness that she suffered" (from Nāᶜiṭ, Nāmī 22).

33 Another text by a woman who was afflicted with an epidemic disease is CIH 557.

34 The SD's (89) translation of the term *mwnn* as "provision, food" is not satisfactory, but it may derive from the root ᵓNN, cf. the Arabic verb *anna* "He moaned; or uttered a moan, or moaning, or prolonged voice of complaint; or said, Ah! " (Lane 103), and the nouns *annah*, *anīn* "a moan, moaning or prolonged voice of complaint ... or a cry" (Lane 111).

Sigla

DAI Barᵓān 1988 1/B	Inscription in Robin & Vogt 1997: 144, 233 = Simpson ed. 2002: 164, fig. 58.
CIAS	Inscriptions in *Corpus des inscriptions et antiquités sud-arabes*. Louvain: Peeters, 1977–1986.
CIH	Inscriptions in *Corpus inscriptionum semiticarum* Pars IV. Paris: Reipublicae Typographeo, 1889–1932.
DAI	Deutsches Archäologisches Institut.
Dār al-Šukr	Inscriptions published in Bron & Gajda 2005: 116ff.
DJE 10	Inscription discovered by the Deutsche Jemen-Expedition, and published in Müller 1972.
Fa 3	Höfner 1976.
Fa 76	Inscription discussed in Korotayev 1995.
Gar NIS 3	Inscription in Garbini 1973.
Hamilton 9	Inscription in Brown & Beeston 1954.
Haram	Inscriptions from Haram in Robin 1992.
Ir	Inscriptions in al-Iryānī 1990.
Ja 550–851,	Inscriptions in Jamme 1962.
Ja 525	Inscription in Jamme 1955.
Lane	Lane 1863–1893.
MAFRAY-Quṭra 1	Inscriptions published in Robin 1979, republished in Müller 1983, and discussed in Kropp 1998.
MB	Registration siglum of inscriptions discovered by the AFSM excavations at Maḥram Bilqīs.
Müller 1	Inscription in Müller 1974.
Nāmī 14, 19, 22, 27, 74	Inscriptions in Nāmī 1943.
Ry 520	Inscription in Ryckmans G 1954.
RES	*Répertoire d'épigraphie sémitique*. Paris: Imprimerie nationale, 1900–1968.
Robin-Itwa 1	Inscription in Robin 1982.
SD	Beeston *et al.* 1982.
Sh	Šarafaddīn 2004.
Wādī as-Sirr 1	Inscription in Stiegner 1981.
YM	Inscriptions in the Yemen Museum.
YM 2402	Inscription in Sholan, Antonini & Arbach 2005.
YM 2403	Inscription in Daum *et al.* 1999: 282–283.
YMN 19	Inscriptions in ᶜAbdallah 1990 and republished in Beeston 1997.
YM 17189/3	Inscriptions published in Bron & Gajda 2005: 116ff.
ZI 24	Inscription in ᶜInān 2003.

For further sigla see Kitchen 2000.

References

ᶜAbdallah, Y.M.

1990. Mudawwanat al-nuqūš al-yamanīyat al-qadīmah. *Al-Iklīl* 8/1,2: 76–78.

1994. Ein altsüdarabischer Vertragstext von den neuentdeckten Inschriften auf Holz. Pages 1–12 in N. Nebes (ed.), *Arabia Felix. Beiträge zur Sprache und Kultur des vorislamischen Arabien. Festschrift Walter W. Müller zum sechzigsten Geburtstag*. Wiesbaden: Harrassowitz.

1996. Risālah min imraᵓah bi-ḫaṭṭ al-zabūr. *New Arabian Studies* 3: 18–28. [Arabic section].

Avanzini A.

1991. Remarques sur le „matriarchat" en Arabie du Sud. Pages 157–161 in C. Robin, L'Arabie antique de Karib'îl à Mahomet. Nouvelles données sur l'histoire des Arabes grâce aux inscriptions. *Revue du Monde musulman et de la Méditerranée* 61/3.

Beeston A.F.L.
1972. Kingship in Ancient South Arabia. *Journal of the Economic and Social History of the Orient* 15: 256–268.
1978. Temporary marriage in pre-Islamic South Arabia. *Arabian Studies* 4: 21–25.
1979. Some features of social structure in Saba. Pages 115–123 in A.T. al-Ansary, A.M. Abdalla, S. al-Sakkar & R.T. Mortel (eds), *Studies in the History of Arabia. 1. Sources for the History of Arabia. Proceedings of the First International Symposium on Studies in the History of Arabia, 23rd–28th of April 1977.* (University of Riyadh, 2 /1). Riyadh: University of Riyadh Press.
1981. Two epigraphic South Arabian roots: HYᶜ and KRB. Pages 21–34 in R.G. Stiegner (ed.), *Al-Hudhud, Festschrift Maria Höfner zum 80. Geburtstag.* Graz: Karl-Franzens Universität Graz.
1983. Women in Saba. Pages 7–13 in R.L. Bidwell & G.R. Smith (eds), *Arabian and Islamic Studies. Articles presented to R.B. Serjeant*. London: Longman.
1997. YMN 19: A Sabean Divorce case? Pages 1–4 in R.G. Stiegner (ed.), *Aktualisierte Beiträge zum 1. Internationalen Symposion Südarabien interdisziplinär an der Universtät Graz mit kurzen Einführungen zu Sprach- und Kulturgeschichte. In Memoriam Maria Höfner*. Graz: Leykam.
Beeston A.F.L., Ghul M.A., Müller W.W. & Ryckmans J.
1982. *Sabaic Dictionary*. Louvain-la-Neuve: Peeters/Beirut: Librairie du Liban.
Breton J-F.
1999. *Arabia Felix. From the time of the Queen of Sheba. Eighth century B.C. to the first century A.D.* Notre Dame, IN: University of Notre Dame Press.
Bron F. & Gajda I.
2005. Un texte juridique fragmentaire de Šibām al-Ḡiras. Pages 115-123 in A.M. Sholan, S. Antonini & M. Arbach, *Sabaean Studies. Archaeological, epigraphical and historical studies in honour of Yusuf M. ᶜAbdallah, Alessandro de Maigret, Christian Robin on the occasion of their sixtieth birthdays*. Naples/ Ṣanᶜāʾ: University of Ṣanᶜāʾ, Yemeni-Italian centre for Archaeological Researches.
Brown W.L. & Beeston A.F.L.
1954. Sculptures and inscriptions from Shabwa. *Journal of the Royal Asiatic Society* 1954: 43–62.
Daum W., Müller W.W., Nebes N. & Raunig W.
1999. *Im Lande der Königin von Saba: Kunstschätze aus dem antiken Jemen, 7. Juli 1999 bis 9. Januar 2000.* Munich: Staatliches Museum für Völkerkunde.
Frantsouzoff S.
1999. Die Frau im antiken Südarabien. Pages 151–169 in W. Daum, W.W. Müller, N. Nebes & W. Raunig, *Im Lande der Königin von Saba: Kunstschätze aus dem antiken Jemen, 7. Juli 1999 bis 9. Januar 2000.* Munich: Staatliches Museum für Völkerkunde.
Garbini G.
1973. Nuove iscrizioni sabee. *Annali dell'Istituto Orientale di Napoli* 33: 31–46.
Glanzman W.D.
2002. Some Notions of "Sacred Space" at the Maḥram Bilqīs in Marib. *Proceedings of the Seminar for Arabian Studies* 32: 187–201.
Harris R.
1994. Women (Mesopotamia). Pages 947–951 in D.N Freedman (ed.), *The Anchor Bible Dictionary*. vi. New York: Doubleday.
Höfner M.
1970. Die vorislamischen Religionen Arabiens. Pages 234–402 in H. Gese, H. Höfner & K. Rudolph (eds), *Religionen Altsyriens, Altarabiens und der Mandäer.* (Die Religionen der Menschheit, 10/2). Stuttgart: Kohlhammer.
1976. *Inschriften aus Ṣirwāḥ, Ḫaulān.* (II. Teil). *Mit einem Anhang von W.W. Müller*. (Sammlung Eduard Glaser, 12). (Österreichische Akademie der Wissenschaften, Phil.- hist.- Klasse, Sitzungsberichte, 304/5). Vienna: Österreichische Akademie der Wissenschaften.
ᶜInān Z.
2003. *Tārīḫ ḥaḍārat al-yaman al-qadīm*. Cairo: Dār al-āfāq al-ᶜarabīyah. [Reprint of the 1976 edition].
al-Iryānī M.
1990. *Fī tārīḫ al-yaman. Nuqūš musnadīyah wa- taᶜlīqāt*. (Second edition). Ṣanᶜāʾ: Markaz al-dirāsāt al-yamanīyah.

Jamme A.
1955. Inscriptions sud-arabes de la collection Ettore Rossi. *Rivista degli Studi Orientali* 30: 103–130.
1962. *Sabaean Inscriptions from Maḥram Bilqīs (Mârib)*. (Publications of the American Foundation for the Study of Man, 3). Baltimore, MD: Johns Hopkins Press.
Kitchen K.A.
2000. *Documentation for Ancient Arabia*. Part II. *Bibliographical Catalogue of Texts*. Liverpool: Liverpool University Press.
Korotayev A.V.
1995. Were there any Truly Matrilineal Lineages in the Arabian Peninsula? *Proceedings of the Seminar for Arabian Studies* 25: 83–98.
1996. *Pre-Islamic Yemen. Socio-political Organization of the Sabaean Cultural Area in the 2nd and 3rd Centuries AD*. Wiesbaden: Harrassowitz.
Kropp M.
1998. Free and bound prepositions: A new look at the inscription Mafray/Quṭra 1. *Proceedings of the Seminar for Arabian Studies* 28: 169–174.
Lane E.
1863–1893. *An Arabic-English Lexicon*. London: Williams & Norgate.
Lichtenstädter I.
1935. *Women in the Aiyâm al-ᶜArab. A study of female life during warfare in preislamic Arabia*. (Prize Publication Fund, 14). London: The Royal Asiatic Society.
Maraqten M.
1999. Ein Schutzamulett der altarabischen Göttin al-Lāt. Pages 148–150 in W. Daum, W.W. Müller, N. Nebes & W. Raunig, *Im Lande der Königin von Saba: Kunstschätze aus dem antiken Jemen, 7. Juli 1999 bis 9. Januar 2000*. Munich: Staatliches Museum für Völkerkunde.
2002. Altsüdarabisch Inschriften auf Holzstäbchen. Eine wichtige Quelle zur Erforschung der Sprache und Kultur des antiken Jemen. *Beiruter Blätter* 8–9: 80–84.
2004. The Processional Road between the Old Mārib and the Awām Temple in the light of a recently discovered inscription from Maḥram Bilqīs. *Proceedings of the Seminar for Arabian Studies* 34: 157–163.
2005. Three recently discovered Sabaean women inscriptions from Maḥram Bilqīs. Pages 377–385 in A.M. Sholan, S. Antonini & M. Arbach, *Sabaean Studies. Archaeological, epigraphical and historical studies in honour of Yusuf M. ᶜAbdallah, Alessandro de Maigret, Christian Robin on the occasion of their sixtieth birthdays*. Naples/Ṣanᶜāʾ: University of Ṣanᶜāʾ, Yemeni-Italian centre for Archaeological Researches, Ṣanᶜāʾ.
2006. Legal documents recently discovered by the AFSM at Maḥram Bilqīs, near Marib, Yemen. *Proceedings of the Seminar for Arabian Studies* 36: 53–67.
Marsman H.J.
2003. *Women in Ugarit and Israel: their social and religious position in the context of the ancient Near East*. (Old Testament Studies, 49). Leiden: Brill.
Müller W.W.
1972. Epigraphische Nachlese aus Ḥāz. Pages 75–85 in R. Degen, W.W. Müller & W. Röllig, *Neue Ephemeris für Semitische Epigraphik* 1. Wiesbaden: Harrassowitz.
1974. Sabäische Texte zur Polyandrie. Pages 125–138 in R. Degen, W.W. Müller & W. Röllig, *Neue Ephemeris für Semitische Epigraphik* 2. Wiesbaden: Harrassowitz.
1983. Altsüdarabische Dokumente. Pages 268–82 in O. Kaiser (ed.), *Texte aus der Umwelt des Alten Testaments*. i/3. *Dokumente zum Rechts- und Wirtschaftsleben*. Gütersloh: Mohn.
1988. Altsüdarbische Rituale und Beschwörungen. Pages 438–452 in O. Kaiser (ed.), *Texte aus der Umwelt des Alten Testaments*. ii/3. *Religiöse Texte*. Gütersloh: Mohn.
1993. "Heilige Hochzeit" im antiken Südarabien. Pages 15–28 in A. Gingrich, S. Haas, G. Paleczek & T. Fillitz (eds), *Studies in Oriental Culture and History. Festschrift for Walter Dostal*. Frankfurt-am-Main: Lang.
1994. Adler und Geier als altarabische Gottheiten. Pages 91–107 in I. Kottsiepe (ed.), *„Wer ist wie du, Herr, unter den Göttern?" Studien zur Theologie und Religionsgeschichte Israels, für Otto Kaiser zum 70. Geburtstag*. Göttingen: Vandenhoeck & Ruprecht.

Nāmī Ḫ.Y.

1943. *Našr nuqūš sāmīya qadīma min janūb bilād al-ᶜarab.* Al-Qāhirah: Maṭbaᶜat al-maᶜhad al-faransī lil-āṯār aš-šarqīyah.

Nebes N.

1995. *Die Konstruktionen mit/FA-/im Altsüdarabischen. Syntaktische und epigraphische Untersuchungen.* (Veröffentlichungen der Orientalischen Kommission der Akademie der Wissenschaften und der Literatur — Mainz, 40). Wiesbaden: Harrassowitz.

2002. Die „Grabinschriften" aus dem ᵓAwām-Friedhof. Vorbericht über die Kampagnen 1997 bis 2001. Pages 161–164 in *Archäologische Berichte aus dem Yemen.* 9. Mainz: von Zabern.

2005. Zur Chronologie der Inschriften aus dem Barᵓān Tempel. Pages 111–125 in *Archäologische Berichte aus dem Yemen.* 10. Mainz: von Zabern.

Preißler H.

1979. Die mittlesabäische Weihinschrift Jamme 751. *Altorientalische Forschungen* 6: 273–274.

1994. Kinder in mittlesabäischen Inschriften. Pages 223–229 in N. Nebes (ed.), *Arabia Felix. Beiträge zur Sprache und Kultur des vorislamischen Arabien. Festschrift Walter W. Müller zum sechzigsten Geburtstag.* Wiesbaden: Harrassowitz.

Robin C.

1979. Mission archéologique et épigraphique française au Yémen du Nord en automne 1978. *Comptes rendus de l'Académie des Inscriptions et Belles-Lettres*: 174–202.

1982. *Les Hautes-Terres du Nord-Yémen avant l'Islam.* (2 volumes). i. *Recherches sur la géographie tribale et religieuse de Khawlân Qudâ'a et du Pays de Hamdân.* ii. *Nouvelles inscriptions.* (Publications de l'Institut historique-archéologique néerlandais de Stamboul, 50). Leiden: Nederlands Historisch-Archaeologisch Instituut te Istanbul.

1992. *Inventaire des Inscriptions sudarabiques.* i. *Inabbaᵓ, Haram, al-Kāfir, Kamna et al-Ḥarāshif.* Paris: de Boccard/Rome: Herder.

1996. Sheba. 2. Dans les inscriptions d'Arabie du Sud. Columns 1047–1254 in J. Brend, E. Cothenet, H. Cazelles & A. Feuillet (eds), *Supplément au Dictionnaire de la Bible.* xii. Paris: Letouzey.

2000. Les «Filles de Dieu» de Sabaᵓ à La Mecque: réflexions sur l'agencement des panthéons dans l'Arabie ancienne. *Semitica* 50: 113–192.

Robin C. & Vogt B.

1997. *Yémen au pays de la reine de Saba.* Paris: Flammarion.

Ryckmans G.

1954. Inscriptions sud-arabes. Onzième série. *Le Muséon* 67: 99–119.

Ryckmans J.

1972. Les confessions publiques sabéennes: le code sud-arabe de pureté rituelle. *Annali dell'Istituto Orientale di Napoli* 32: 1–15.

1975. Une expression astrologique méconnue dans les inscriptions sabéennes. In Miscellanea in honorem Josephi Vergote. *Orientalia Lovaniensia Periodica* 6/7: 521–529.

1980. ᶜUzzā et Lāt dans les inscriptions sud-arabes: à propos de deux amulettes méconnues. *Journal of Semitic Studies* 25: 193–204.

1986. A three generations' matrilineal genealogy in a Hasaean inscription: matrilineal ancestry in Pre-Islamic Arabia. Pages 407–417 in H.A. Al Khalifa & M. Rice (eds), *Bahrain through the Ages: The Archaeology.* London: Kegan Paul International.

Ryckmans J., Müller W.W. & Abdallah Y.

1994. *Textes du Yémen Antique inscrits sur bois.* (Publications de l'Institut Orientaliste de Louvain, 43). Louvain-la-Neuve: Institut Orientaliste.

Šarafaddīn A.

2004. *Tārīḫ al-yaman al-ṯaqāfī.* (4 volumes). Ṣanᶜāᵓ: Jāmiᶜat Ṣanᶜāᵓ. [Reprint of the first edition, al-Qāhirah: 1967].

al-Sheiba A.

1987. Die Ortsnamen in den altsüdarabischen Inschriften. Pages 1–61 in *Archäologische Berichte aus dem Yemen.* 4. Mainz: von Zabern.

Sholan A.

1999. *Frauennamen in den altsüdarabischen Inschriften.* (Texte und Studien zur Orientalistik, 11). Hildesheim:

Olms.
2005. Dirāsah taḥlīlīyah li-naqš saba'ī jadīd min al-matḥaf al-waṭanī bi-ṣanᶜā'. Pages 51–63 in A.M. Sholan, S. Antonini & M. Arbach (eds), *Sabaean Studies. Archaeological, epigraphical and historical studies in honour of Yusuf M. ᶜAbdallah, Alessandro de Maigret, Christian Robin on the occasion of their sixtieth birthdays.* Naples/Ṣanᶜā': University of Ṣanᶜā', Yemeni-Italian centre for Archaeological Researches.

Sholan A.M., Antonini S. & Arbach M.
2005. *Sabaean Studies. Archaeological, epigraphical and historical studies in honour of Yusuf M. ᶜAbdallah, Alessandro de Maigret, Christian Robin on the occasion of their sixtieth birthdays.* Naples/Ṣanᶜā': University of Ṣanᶜā', Yemeni-Italian centre for Archaeological Researches.

Sima A.
2000. *Tiere, Pflanzen, Steine und Metalle in den altsüdarabischen Inschriften. Eine lexikalische und realienkundliche Untersuchung.* (Veröffentlichungen der Orientalischen Kommission der Akademie der Wissenschaften und der Literatur — Mainz, 46). Wiesbaden: Harrassowitz.

Simpson St J. (ed.)
2002. *Queen of Sheba: Treasures from Ancient Yemen*. London: British Museum Press.

Smith W.R.
1903. *Kinship & marriage in early Arabia*. London: Black.

Stein P.
2003. The Inscribed Wooden Sticks of the Bayerische Staatsbibliothek in Munich. *Proceedings of the Seminar for Arabian Studies* 33: 267–274.
2006. The Ancient South Arabian Minuscule Inscriptions on Wood. A new Genre of Pre-Islamic Epigraphy. *Ex Oriente Lux* 39: 181–199.

Stiegner R.G.
1981. Altsüdarabische Fragmente. Wādī al-Sirr (N-Jemen) 1978. Pages 325–346 in Stiegner R.G. (ed.) *Al-Hudhud, Festschrift Maria Höfner zum 80. Geburtstag*. Graz: Karl-Franzens Universität Graz.
1989. Zur Stellung der vorislamischen Frau bestätigen Inschriften Aussagen des Koran und muslimischer wie antiker Autoren? Pages 80–84 in A. Janata (ed.), *Jemen. Im Land der Königin von Saba.* Vienna: Museum für Völkerkunde.
1997. (ed.) *Aktualisierte Beiträge zum 1. Internationalen Symposion Südarabien interdisziplinär an der Universtät Graz mit kurzen Einführungen zu Sprach- und Kulturgeschichte. In Memoriam Maria Höfner.* Graz: Leykam.

Tairan S.A.
1992. *Die Personennamen in den altsabäischen Inschriften.* (Texte und Studien zur Orientalistik, 8). Hildesheim: Olms.

Westbrook R.
1988. *Old Babylonian marriage law.* (Archiv für Orientforschung, Beiheft 23). Horn: Ferdinand Berger.

Author's address
Dr Mohammed Maraqten, Orient-Institut Beirut der Deutschen Morgenländischen Gesellschaft, Rue Hussein Beyhum, Zokak el-Blat, P.O.B. 11-2988, 11072120 Riad El Solh, Beirut, Lebanon.
e-mail maraqten@staff.uni-marburg.de, maraqten@online.de

Proceedings of the Seminar for Arabian Studies 38 (2008): 251–264

A history of the Ziyadids through their coinage (203–442/818–1050)

AUDREY PELI

Summary

The history of the Ziyadids, from the eponymous founder of the dynasty, the ᶜAbbāsid general Muḥammad b. Ziyād b. ᶜUbayd Allāh b. Ziyād who officially built his capital Zabīd in 204/820, to their Ethiopian slaves, the Najahids, who took power at the beginning of the fifth/eleventh century, is essentially known from the lost work of Jayyāš, the Najahid ruler and son of the eponymous founder of this dynasty, which inspired ᶜUmāra. But the history of the Ziyadids is also known from the coins minted in their capital city from the beginning of the fourth/tenth century. Comparisons between the genealogy given by the sources and that given by the coins led us to assume that fierce power struggles followed the death of Ishāq b. Ibrāhīm and that Jayyāš b. Najāḥ rewrote their history by omitting some of the events. Moreover, the names of several Ethiopian slaves appeared during the rule of the last Ziyadid, leading us to think that the Ziyadids nominally kept ruling over the Tihāma, but under the effective power of the Ethiopian wazirs. Economic aspects can also be deciphered through the study of the die-links and the metrology with the help of the textual sources.

Keywords: Yemen, Zabīd, Ziyadid, coins, minting

Introduction

The history of the first independent Islamic dynasties of the Yemen has been known, for a long time, from the local chronicles and above all from ᶜUmāra's *al-Mufīd fī akhbār ṣanᶜāᵓ wa zabīd*. This work remains our only textual source for the history of the Ziyadids, who settled in Tihāma at the beginning of the third/ninth century. It was used by later Yemeni historians and gives the detailed genealogy of the Ziyadids (Bosworth 1996: 98, no. 41; Smith 1988: 138; 2004). It is inspired by the now lost work of Abū al-Ṭāmī Jayyāš b. Najāḥ, one of the sons of Najāḥ. This last was an Ethiopian wazir in the service of the last Ziyadid who founded the Najahid dynasty. He came to power during the second quarter of the fifth/eleventh century in Zabīd (ᶜUmāra 1985: 46 l. 10–47 l.1; Daghfous 1992–1993: 33).

But the study of the coins minted by the Ziyadids gives a totally different history. Almost all the known coins are now in Samir Shamma's collection (Album 1999) and come from a hoard that appeared in the 1960s. Their precise provenance is unknown but they were reported to have come from "south-western Arabia". At that time, Stephen Album called it the "ᶜAṣir hoard" (1999: xiii; Shamma 1971). Ziyadid coins are also to be found in public collections (Bibliothèque nationale de France, British Museum, University of Tübingen, and National Museum of Ṣanᶜāᵓ), but they are not yet published apart from some articles (Casanova 1894: 200; Lane-Poole 1877: 139; Lowick 1976). The coins minted by the Ziyadids, of which 98 % are dinars, represent 48 % of the mint production of Zabīd from the Abbasid period to the arrival of the Ayyubids in Yemen in 569/1172–1173 and date mostly from the reign of Isḥāq b. Ibrāhīm. However, the foundation and the beginnings of the Ziyadid dynasty are only known from ᶜUmāra.

Beginnings of the dynasty

After receiving a letter about the revolt of the Tihāma tribes ᶜAkk and Ashāᶜir in 202/817–818, the Abbasid caliph al-Maᵓmūn (198–218/813–833) sent Muḥammad b. Ziyād b. ᶜUbayd Allāh b. Ziyād, who claimed to be a descendant of the Umayyads, as amir to subdue the rebels (ᶜUmāra 1985: 51 l. 2; Smith 1988: 130). Ibn Ziyād conquered the Tihāma in 203/818–819 and founded the round city of Zabīd (1) in Shaᶜbān 204/January 820 (ᶜUmāra 1985: 50–51 l. 7). It is situated mid-way between the mountains and the sea in the Tihāma, between Wādī Zabīd, which gives its name to the city, and Wādī Rimaᶜ (Ibn al-Daybaᶜ 2006*a*: 275 ll. 1–4; Chelhod 1978: 49; Keall 1983; Sadek 2004) (Fig. 3).

Muḥammad b. Ziyād is said to have given the city its first wall (Yaḥyā b. al-Ḥusayn 1968, i: 151 l. 3; Chelhod

لا إله إلا
الله وحده
لا شريك له
محمد رسول الله

بسم الله ضرب هذا الدرهم بزبيد

المطيع
لله إسحاق
بن إبرهيم

جاء الحق و زهق الباطل إن الباطل
كان

1.1: AR 13,5 mm / 0,34 g **Isḥāq b. Ibrāhīm, Zabīd, no date** (University of Tuebingen 93.38.23)

لا إله إلا
الله وحده
لا شريك له
محمد رسول الله
بسم الله ضرب هذا الدينار بزبيد سنة
ثلث و ستين و ثلثمائة

المطيع لله
أمير المؤمنين
على بن إبرهيم

جاء الحق و زهق الباطل إن الباطل
كان زهوقا و نتزل من القرآن

1.2: AV 24,5 mm / 2,85 g **ʿAlī b. Ibrāhīm, Zabīd, 363/973-4** (University of Tuebingen BC8C4)

لا إله إلا الله
وحده لا شريك له
محمد رسول الله

جاء الحق و زهق الباطل إن الباطل
كان زهوقا

القادر بالله
أمير المؤمنين
حسين

بسم الله ضرب هذا الدرهم بالكدرة

1.3: AR 14.5 mm / 0.23 gr **al-Ḥusayn b. Salāma, al-Kadrā, no date (**University of Tuebingen 94.53.144)

لا إله إلا
الله وحده
لا شريك له
محمد رسول الله

بسم الله ضرب هذا الدينار بزبيد سنة
سبعين و ثلثمائة

الطائع لله
أمير المؤمنين
المظفر بن علي

جاء الحق و زهق الباطل إن الباطل
كان زهوقا و نتزل من القرآن

1.4: AV 24 mm / 2,82 gr **al-Muẓaffar b. ʿAlī, Zabīd, 370/980-1 (**University of Tuebingen BC8D1)

Figure 1. *Ziyadid coins.*

1978: 54), but, according to Ibn al-Daybaᶜ, it may have been constructed by another ruler, Ḥusayn b. Salāma, an Ethiopian slave who was wazir of the young Ziyadid placed on the throne (Ibn al-Daybaᶜ 2006*a*: 282 ll. 3–4; 2006*b*: 39 ll. 2–3; Chelhod 1978: 59). Whatever the case, al-Muqaddasī, who died around 380/990 (Miquel 1991: 492), tells us that Zabīd was fortified (*ḥiṣn min al-ṭīn*), so we can assume that Zabīd had its first wall during the Ziyadid dynasty and not during the Najahid period as suggested by Ibn al-Mujāwir's map (1951–1954, i: 77, pl. 3; al-Muqaddasī 1906: 84 l. 14; Chelhod 1978: 54, 58; Keall 1984: 52).

ᶜUmāra attributes to Muḥammad Ibn Ziyād the extension of Ziyadid territory to the major part of Yemen, i.e. to all the coastal territories from the south, between Ḥaḍramawt and Aden, and to the north, along the Red Sea coast as far as Ḥali, now in Saudi Arabia (ᶜUmāra 1985: 53–54). This ruler reigned until his death in 245/859–860 (Ibn al-Daybaᶜ 2006*a*: 275; Yaḥyā b. al-Ḥusayn 1968: 158 l. 14) and his first descendants, who are only known through the chronicles, were his son Ibrāhīm b. Muḥammad, who reigned for thirty-eight years (Ibn al-Daybaᶜ 2006*a*: 275 ll. 14–15; Yaḥyā b. al-Ḥusayn 1968: 158 l. 15), (2) his grandson Ziyād b. Ibrāhīm about whom almost nothing is known, and his great-grandson Ibrāhīm b. Ziyād about whom the sole account of al-Masᶜūdī testifies to his rule around 332/943–944 (1966–1979, i: 233 ll. 15–16) and, in consequence, reduces the length of Isḥāq b. Ibrāhīm's reign. (3)

This last ruler was succeeded by his nephew, Ibrāhīm b. Ziyād. He is the only Ziyadid known from written sources (ᶜUmāra 1985: 55 l. 4) as well as numismatic material. The first Ziyadid coinage really begins during his reign in the middle of the 340s/950s. Some years before, a few dinars were struck in Zabīd but in the name of the Abbasid without any mention of the Ziyadid ruler. (4)

Ziyadid coinage in the name of the Abbasids

The first coin minted in Zabīd during the Ziyadid period was struck in the name of the Abbasid caliphs without any mention of the Ziyadid ruler. The first coin may date from 307/919–920: this dinar, which bears the name of the Abbasid caliph al-Muqtadir billāh (295–320/908–932), is nevertheless isolated and the reading of the date is not certain (Album 1999: 71). From his successor al-Muttaqī (329–333/944–946), only dirhams are extant (Ilisch 2006: no. 1049; Album 1999: 72, 73) and they show a great similarity to Abbasid coin styles, while the dinars of al-Muṭīᶜ's reign (334–363/946–974) (Album 1999: 74, 75) follow the scheme and style of the coins minted in Baysh and ᶜAththar (5) (1999: pls 1–2, 15–19).

Isḥāq b. Ibrāhīm

The first dinars of Isḥāq b. Ibrāhīm's reign date back to the year 346/957. While the style of the inscriptions is close to the dinars of al-Muṭīᶜ's reign, they present a new organization of the legends: two margins surround the obverse field, the inner one gives the mint and the date while the outer one is inscribed with Qurᵓān 30:3–4. (6) On the reverse, the field inscriptions give the name of the caliph al-Muṭīᶜ lillāh (334–363/946–974) and that of Isḥāq b. Ibrāhīm (7) while the margin is filled with another quranic verse (17:83–84). (8) The dinar production is quite homogeneous: dates are known from 346/957–958 to 362/973. (9) Some *sudaysī* dirhams are also known from his reign (Darley-Doran 1986: no. 78; Tübingen 93.38.23) (Fig. 1/1). (10)

At the end of Isḥāq's rule, several rulers declared their independence at the expense of the Ziyadis: the Yuᶜfirids at Ṣanᶜāᵓ, (11) the Zaydī al-Hādī in northern Yemen, (12) and Sulaymān b. Ṭarf at ᶜAththar, along the Red sea coast (13) (ᶜUmāra 1985: 55–64; Chelhod 1978: 56). The territory of Abū al-Jaysh was then reduced from Adan to Sharja and from Ghulāfiqa to the surroundings of Ṣanᶜāᵓ (ᶜUmāra 1985: 64 ll. 6–7).

The sources attribute to Isḥāq b. Ibrāhīm an exceptional longevity of eighty years of reign. They say that he died in 371/981–982 (1985: 65 l. 3) or in 391/1001 (Ibn ᶜAbd al-Majīd 1985: 28 l. 4) and that he left an infant child whose name was ᶜAbd Allāh, Ziyād, or even Ibrāhīm, who ruled under the authority of his sister Hind and the Ethiopian slave Rushd (ᶜUmāra 1985: 65 ll. 3–5). But as we can see on the coins, the name of Abū al-Jaysh Isḥāq b. Ibrāhīm disappears in 363/974 when it is replaced by the name of his brother or the son of his nephew, ᶜAlī b. Ibrāhim. From then on, the Ziyadid rulers are only known from the numismatic material. These coins are mostly badly engraved and the reading of the dates is ensured by the names of the Abbasid caliph, which give known regnal dates.

ᶜAlī b. Ibrāhīm

From this ruler, we know four dinars: they are dated 363/974 (Album 1999: 140; Tübingen BC8C4: fig. 1/2), 366/977 (Album 1999: 141) and [3]68/[9]78–[9]79 (Darley-Doran 1999: no. 348). The style of the inscriptions

أمر به الأمير
المظفر
ابن على

جاء الحق و زهق الباطل إن الباطل
كان زهوقا و نتزل من القرآن

لا إله إلا الله
محمد رسول الله
القادر بالله

بسم الله ضرب هذا الدينار بزبيد سنة
ثمان و ثمانين

2.1: AV 24,5 mm / 2,56 g **al-Muẓaffar b. ʻAlī, Zabīd, [3]88/998** (British Museum 1980.6.5.1)

أمر به الأمير
المظفر
ابن علي

جاء الحق و زهق الباطل إن الباطل
كان زهوقا و نتزل من القرآن

لا إله إلا الله
محمد رسول الله
القادر بالله

بسم الله ضرب هذا الدينار بعثر سنة
خمس و تسعين

2.2: AV 24 mm / 2,64 gr **al-Muẓaffar b. ʻAlī, ʻAṯṯar ?, [3]95/1004-5 (**University of Tuebingen BC8C6)

أمر به الأمير
علي بن المظفر
المؤيد نجاح نصر
الدين

جاء الحق و زهق الباطل إن الباطل
كان زهوقا و نتزل من القرآن

لا إله إلا الله
محمد رسول الله
القائم بأمرالله

بسم الله ضرب هذا الدينار بزبيد سنة
سبع / تسع و ثلثين و أربع

2.3: AV 23 mm / 2,37 gr **ʻAlī b. al-Muẓaffar & al-Mua'yyad Najāḥ Naṣr al-dīn, Zabīd, 437/1045-6 or 439/1047-8** (Bibliothèque nationale de France 1972.1075)

ناصر
أمير المؤمنين
أمر به الأمير
على بن المظفر
السلطان

جاء الحق و زهق الباطل إن الباطل
كان زهوقا و نتزل من القرآن

المعار
لا إله إلا الله
محمد رسول الله
القائم بأمر لله
رشد

بسم الله ضرب هذا الدينار بزبيد سنة
سبع / تسع وثلثين و ثلثمائة

2.4: AV 18,5 mm / 1,74 g **ʻAlī b. al-Muẓaffar, Zabīd, 437/1045-6 or 439/1047-8** (British Museum 1890.11.1.25)

Figure 2. *Ziyadid coins.*

is quite close to that from the last dinars of Isḥāq's reign but the obverse bears only one margin and the title of the caliph appears with the name of the Ziyadid on the field reverse. ᶜAlī b. Ibrāhīm is however unknown from the textual sources and the precise dates of his reign are still unknown.

Then, two other names appear on the coins minted in Zabīd: al-Muẓaffar b. ᶜAlī and ᶜAlī b. al-Muẓaffar. For a long time, these coins, the reading of which is particularly difficult, were thought to have been minted by the Najahid dynasty (Bikhazi 1970: 114, no. 288; Lowick 1976). But by 1983, Nicholas Lowick, Lutz Ilisch, and Gerd-Rüdiger Puin, whose work on the Ziyadids still remains unpublished, reattributed these coins to the last Ziyadids (Album 1999: viii, no. 7).

Al-Muẓaffar b. ᶜAlī

Only four dinars minted in Zabīd in the name of al-Muẓaffar b. ᶜAlī bear a decipherable date. The first one, preserved in the Tübingen University collection (BC8D1), is dated 370/980–981: its date is so close to the dirhams from ᶜAlī b. Ibrāhīm' reign that we can assume that al-Muẓaffar b. ᶜAlī is ᶜAli b. Ibrāhīm's son (Fig. 1/4). Another coin was struck in the year [3]84/[9]94 (National Museum of Ṣanᶜāʾ M. I. 4967), a third one in 386/996 (Tübingen BC8D2), and a fourth in [3]88/[9]98 (British Museum 1980.6.5.1) (Fig. 2/1).

The first coins struck during al-Ṭāʾiᶜ's reign (363–381/974–991) follow the preceding specimen. But the coins minted during the reign of the caliph al-Qādir (381–422/991–1031) are different. Most of them bear the year 418/1027, which we can consider a "frozen" date because of the stylized inscriptions. The name of the caliph is relegated to the field obverse while on the field reverse is inscribed "Has ordered al-ʾamīr / al-Muẓaffar / b. ᶜAlī", giving a more important place to the name of the Ziyadid and to his title that appears here for the first time. However, the sources say that it was conferred by the Abbasid caliph on Muḥammad b. Ziyād (ᶜUmāra 1985: 51 l. 2). A dinar, which bears the same legends, was perhaps struck at ᶜAththar, the capital of the Ṭarfid family (Tübingen BC8C6: fig. 2/2), in [3]95/1004–1005. The reading of the mint is not certain but it is certainly not Zabīd. This coin would be the first known Ziyadid coin minted in this city.

ᶜAlī b. al-Muẓaffar

After al-Muẓaffar b. ᶜAlī, his son ᶜAlī b. al-Muẓaffar became ruler. Two dinars (Qedar 1985: no. 508; National Museum of Ṣanᶜāʾ 4969) give the name of this ruler alone, following the type his father introduced. All the other coins of ᶜAlī b. al-Muẓaffar give several other names, identified with the Ethiopian slaves who were in the service of the Ziyadids.

The first ones give the name of Najāḥ: the obverse field bears the same formula as the coins of ᶜAlī's predecessor but with the name of the Abbasid al-Qāʾim biʾamr illāh (422–467/1031–1075). Changes appear on the reverse: after the formula "Has ordered the amīr ᶜAlī b. al-Muẓaffar" the field bears the name of Najāḥ and his two titles *al-Muʾayyad Naṣr al-dīn* which were conferred on him by the Abbasid caliph (ᶜUmāra 1985: 77 l. 6; Ibn al-Mujāwir 1951–1954, i: 72 l. 13). (14) One of these dinars is dated 423/1032 (Album 1997: no. 91), another is from [4]34/1042–1043 (Tübingen BC9A6), two others give the year 437/1045–1046 or 439/1047–1048 (Bibliothèque nationale de France 1972.1075 [Fig. 2/3] and Popp 1996: no. 786; Lowick 1976: no. 2), while a dinar from the National Museum of Ṣanᶜāʾ is clearly from the year [4]39/[10]47–[10]48 (M.I. 4968). A dinar minted in the year 434/1042–1043 bears the name of al-Faḍl b. al-Muʾayyad who is certainly one of Najāḥ's sons as his father is identified by his title (Album 1997: no. 59). (15)

From 438/1046–1047 (Album 1999: 146), 437/1045–1046 or 439/1047–1048 (Qedar 1985: no. 509), and 442/1050–1051 (Album 1999: 147), three dinars of ᶜAlī b. al-Muẓaffar bear the name of Rushd on the obverse. New titles appear on coins minted in [4]34/1042–1043 (Tübingen BC8D4), in 437/1045–1046 or 439/1047–1048 (British Museum 1890.11.1.25 (Fig. 2/4); Bikhazi 1970: no. 288; Lowick 1976: no. 3) and in 440/1048–1049 (Lowick 1976: no. 4): the obverse field bears a word read as *al-maᶜār* by N.M. Lowick (1976: no. 3) (16) and, in the reverse field, the titles *Nāṣir ʾamīr al-muʾminīn* ("Helper of the Commander of the Faithful") and *al-Sulṭān* make a border around the legend "Has ordered the ʾamir / ᶜAlī b. al-Muẓaffar". As Lowick has pointed out, the title of *al-Sulṭān* is the "earliest attested numismatic occurrence of the term" (1976: 549–550) (17) but we do not know if it designates Najāḥ, as Lowick proposed, Rushd, or more probably the Ziyadid ruler, since this title does not appear in the textual sources. However, in the historical context, it would have been used only in reference to the head of state, the immediate deputy of the caliph in the provinces. So here, *al-Sulṭān* certainly designates ᶜAlī b. al-Muẓaffar, while his power is crumbling and is in the hands of his Ethiopian minister. On the other hand, the title of *al-*

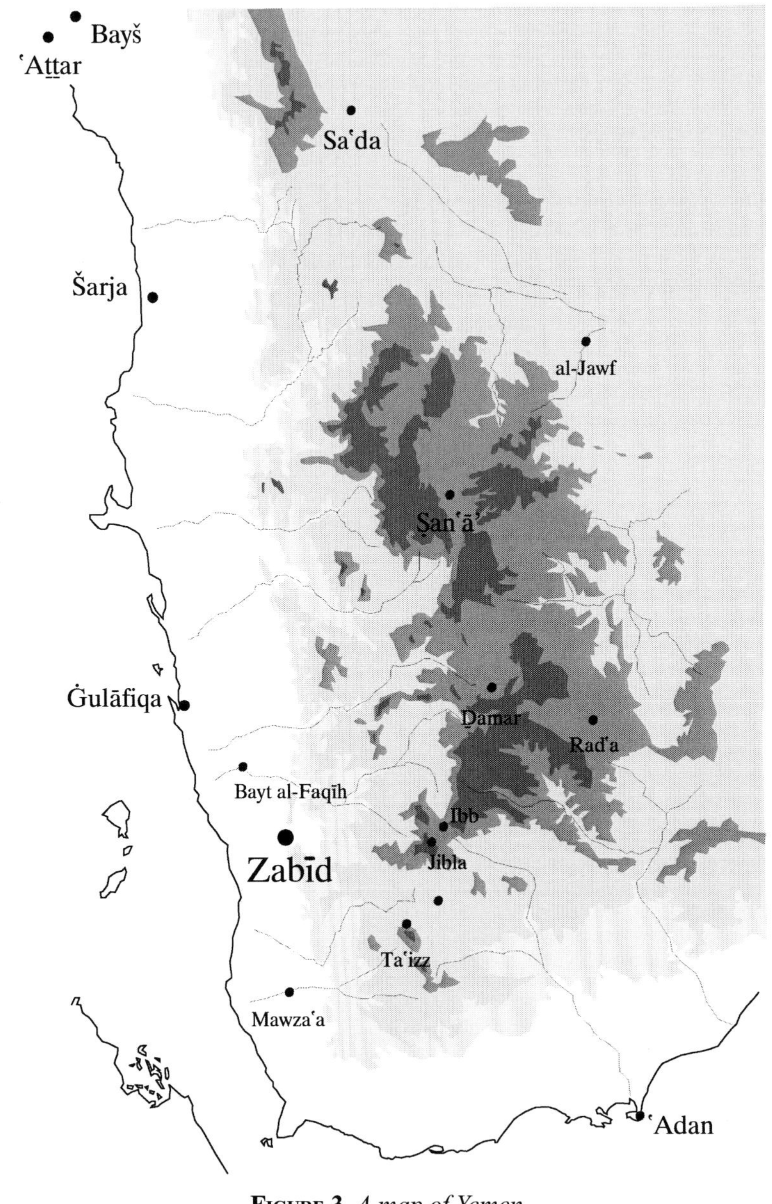

Figure 3. *A map of Yemen.*

Nāṣir was conferred earlier on Najāḥ by the caliph and this new title of *Nāṣir ʾamīr al-muʾminīn* could have been an additional honour. But we could also surmise that it designates ᶜAlī b. al-Muẓaffar, if we consider that all the inscriptions on the reverse field only refer to one person. During this period, the sources tell of the emergence of a new political and religious power: in 439/1047–1048 ᶜAlī b. Muḥammad al-Ṣulayḥī began to proclaim the Ismāᶜīlī *daᶜwā* in the name of the Fatimid caliph al-Mustanṣir billāh (427–487/1036–1094) in the mountainous region of Masār in the Ḥarāz (Ibn ᶜAbd al-Majīd 1985: 39 ll. 5–6; Ibn al-Daybaᶜ 2006*a*: 208 l. 2; ᶜImād al-Dīn 2002: 3; Yaḥyā b. al-Ḥusayn 1968, i: 247). This new power would have been seen as an immediate danger for the last Ziyadid and the emerging Najahid. The title of *Nāṣir ʾamīr al-muʾminīn* inscribed on the coins would perhaps have been a response to this new power, which also used propaganda weapons since *sudaysī* dirhams, which only bear the name and title of al-Mustanṣir, were minted in Zabīd (see e.g. Tübingen 93.98.2).

ᶜUmāra, a contradictory source

ᶜUmāra actually mentions the two Ethiopian slaves, Rushd and Najāḥ, but in a totally different way. For him, Rushd (18) was in the service of Abū al-Jaysh and he was in charge, for only a short time, of Isḥāq b. Ibrāhīm's son, ᶜAbd Allāh, also called Ibrāhīm or even Ziyād, (19) and of his sister Hind after Isḥāq's death (ᶜUmāra 1985: 65 l. 5).

When Rushd died his Ethiopian *mawla*, named Ḥusayn b. Salāma, took care of the two Ziyadids (1985: 65 l. 7). While the sovereignty of the Ziyadid was crumbling, he was able to reinforce and to rule over the initial Ziyadid territory for thirty years (1985: 65–66). (20) We owe him several foundations, such as the city of al-Kadrā, a considerable number of constructions on the two roads from Ḥaḍramawt to Mecca (1985: 67–73), the foundation of the Great Mosque of Zabīd, and that of the Ashāᶜir (Ibn al-Daybaᶜ 2006*b*: 39 l. 4; Chelhod 1978: 59).

After his death in 402/1011–1012, ᶜAbd Allāh or Ibrāhīm, another Ziyadid heir, was placed on the throne, and one of Ḥusayn's Ethiopian slaves (*ᶜabd ᵓustādh*), called Marjān, took care of him (ᶜUmāra 1985: 66 l. 4). Marjān had two Ethiopian slaves, Nafīs and Najāḥ, who fought each other for power (1985: 75–76). Nafīs walled in the Ziyadid heir and his aunt alive. (21) He is said to have struck coins in his own name (1985: 76 ll. 13–14), but no coins have been recorded so far. Najāḥ, founder of his eponymous dynasty, then took power after having given the last Ziyadids a decent burial, and executed Nafīs and Marjān in the same way as they had murdered the heir and his aunt (1985: 77 ll. 4–5). The Ziyadid dynasty would have ended after 198 years of rule.

As we can see, the genealogy of the Ziyadids provided by Jayyāsh b. Najāḥ and transmitted by ᶜUmāra does not fit with the names and dates given on the coins (Figs 4 & 5). First of all, he completely avoids mentioning the direct successor of Ziyād b. Ibrāhīm, Ibrāhīm b. Ziyād, who is only cited by al-Masᶜūdī (see above). In this way, he increases the importance of Isḥāq b. Ibrāhīm's reign, which was marked by the raising of Ethiopian slaves, of whom Jayyāsh b. Najāḥ is a descendant. Then, the Najahid author only mentions the infant descendant of Isḥāq b. Ibrāhīm. But how could a man over eighty years old leave a child as the head of state? On the contrary, the numismatic material offers us a more plausible genealogy, from Isḥāq's brother, ᶜAlī b. Ibrāhīm (see Figs 2 & 3). Jayyāš does not even mention them, which allows him to give more importance to the Ethiopian slave Ḥusayn b. Salāma, who may have — according to him — increased Ziyadid power and consolidated its territory. Moreover, he passes over the figure of Rushd by attributing to him by far less importance than to his father Najāḥ, who would have been the worthy successor of the Ziyadids, having given a decent burial to the last Ziyadid heir after his murder. But the coins leave no doubt: on the last

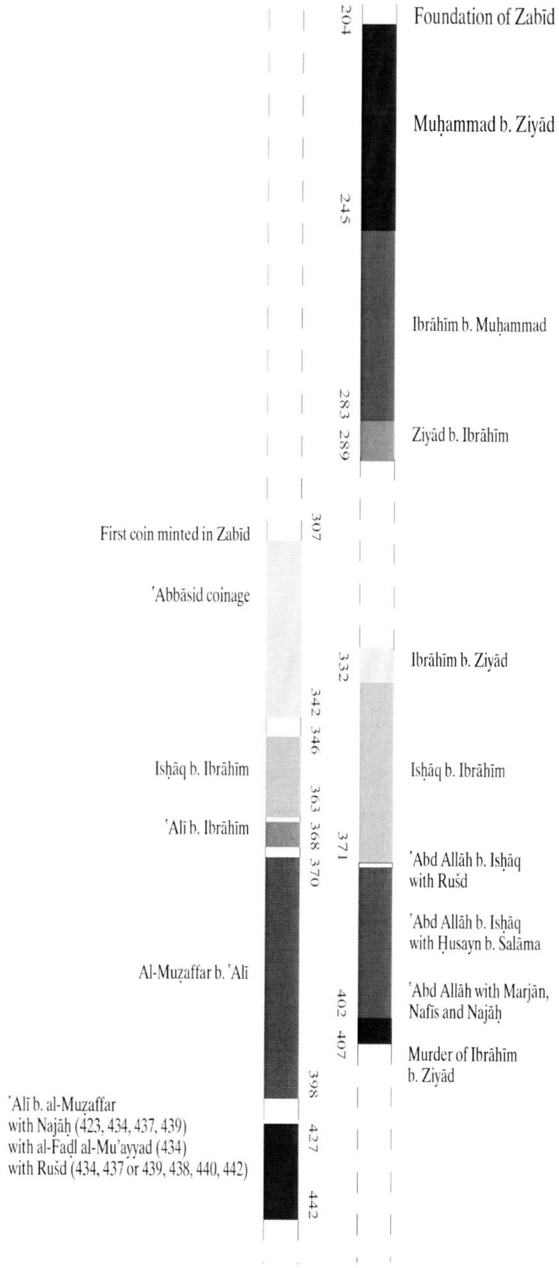

FIGURE 4. *The chronology of the Ziyadids from the historical sources (right) and the coins (left).*

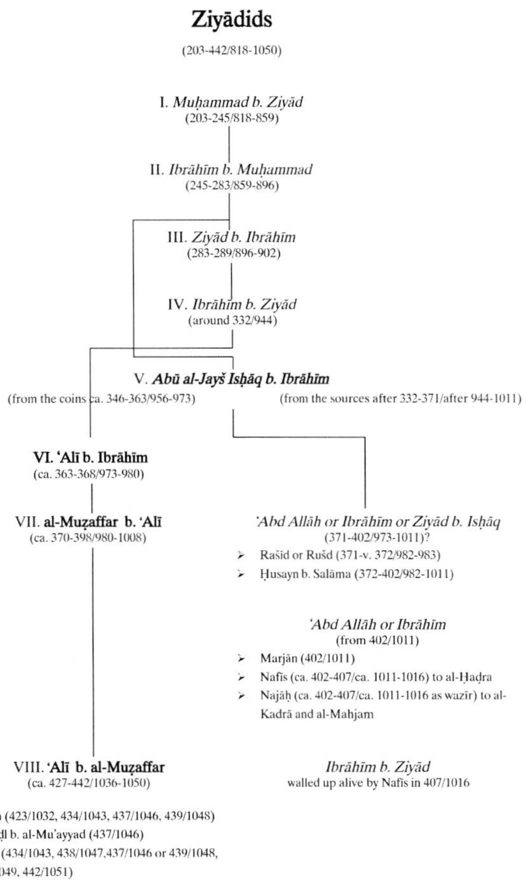

Figure 5. *The genealogy of the Ziyadids as told by the chronicles (in italic character) and by the coins (in bold character).*

Ziyadid known coin, struck in 440/1048 (Lowick 1976: no. 4), Rushd is the only figure to be mentioned with ᶜAlī b. al-Muẓaffar and the Abbasid caliph. Moreover, no coin struck in the name of Najāḥ alone has been recorded so far. After the Ziyadids, coins were struck in Zabīd in the name of the *shīᶜī* Sulayhids (from 445/1053–1054 to 451/1059) and then by the Najahid Jayyāsh b. al-Muᵓayyad (from 465/1073). Finally, as coins were minted at least until 442/1050–1051 in the name of the Ziyadid ᶜAlī b. al-Muẓaffar, we would have to suppose that the dynasty of the Ziyadids nominally ruled over Tihāma for at least forty years after the date given by Jayyāš, and that the Ethiopian wazirs were the real sovereigns. The reason why Jayyāsh b. Najāḥ manipulated the history of his predecessors would perhaps have to be seen as a search for legitimacy. No coins have been recorded in the name of Najāḥalone, who is presented by ᶜUmāra as the founder of the Najahid dynasty, apart from the coins minted by the Ziyadids where his name appears. Must we suppose then that Jayyāsh b. Najāḥ was a usurper and wrote his history in order to give himself legitimacy? As well as raising an interesting case of "historical manipulation" and giving a new image of the Ziyadid genealogy and of the history of the Yemeni Tihāma, coins are also rich in technical information that raise economic questions.

Technical aspects of the Zabīd mint and economic context

Whereas several mines of gold and silver are known to have been exploited in Yemen during the course of the third/ninth and fourth/tenth centuries, sources of Ziyadid gold remain mostly unknown. Al-Hamdānī mentions that, "in the land of the Banī Madhḥij, a mine of silver [existed] in the provinces of Ibn Ziyād, the lord of Zabīd" (2003: 127 ll. 5–6). Furthermore, gold was exploited in Wādī Baysh, in the ᶜAṣir region that belonged for a time to the Ziyadids before being absorbed in the Tarfid territory (Yāqūt 1957, i: 528).

During the excavations conducted by the Royal Ontario Museum in Zabīd, traces of a workshop from the fourth–sixth/tenth–twelfth centuries were found and Edward Keall suggests that it may have produced copper coin blanks (1989: 66). This is the only archaeological evidence of a mint in Zabīd. For the moment, no copper coins minted in Zabīd have been recorded, except a debased dirham struck in the name of the Najahid Jayyāsh b. al-Muᵓayyad (Tübingen 93.18.114). Keall also suggests that this area was the "government quarter of the town since at least the time of the Ayyubid conquest of the Yemen" (1989: 66).

One of the characteristics of the Ziyadid coinage, and more generally of the Yemeni coinage, is its low weight. However, some of the first dirhams minted during the Abbasid period follow the standard weight. But they still remain rare and are only found in foreign contexts, which could indicate that they were minted for trading purposes (Album 1999: 72; Ilisch 2006: no. 1049). The dinars minted by the Ziyadids in their own name weigh around 2.80 gm, which is a third less than the Abbasid standard. Although the material is variable in quantity under the different reigns, it shows a relative constancy in weight during the reigns of Isḥāq and ᶜAlī b. Ibrāhīm, with an average of 2.80 gm. The weight of the dinars then falls to around 2.60 gm during al-Muẓaffar b. ᶜAlī's rule and to 2.45 gm during ᶜAlī b. al-Muẓaffar's government. A sample of four Ziyadid coins from the National Museum of Ṣanᶜāᵓ (M.I. 27003, 27004, 27015, and 27018) were recently analysed by X-Ray fluorescence last spring by Florian Téreygeol (Centre National de la Recherche Scientifique). The first results show that the coins minted during the reign of al-Muẓaffar b. ᶜAlī are of a quite good quality (from 80 to 75 % of gold), but are rather less crude during the reign of his successor ᶜAlī b. al-Muẓaffar (around 65 % of gold). (22)

Another characteristic of Zabīd coinage during the Abbasid period and during Isḥāq's reign is the conservation of the reverse die from the preceding year (Album 1999: pls 4–6) (Fig. 6). Indeed, the same reverse die was used for minting dinars between the years 349/960–961 and 350/961. This phenomenon recurs during the years 352/963 and 353/964, and then in 354/965 and 355/966. From one year to another, the obverse die has to be modified, since it bears the mint year, but the reverse die can be used again as its inscriptions, i.e. the name of the caliph and of the Ziyadid ruler, do not change. Furthermore, the same reverse die was used during three consecutive years, in 360/971, 361/972, and 362/973 (1999: 135–137). From the point of view of technical fabrication, the die used for minting these three dinars was tougher than the obverse die, so we can assume that the reverse die was on the pile, (23) and was good enough to be used for the three years. As al-Hamdānī tells us in his *Kitāb al-jawharatayn*, the dies are made of iron and the end that bears the inscriptions is reinforced by the process of quenching (2003: 234 l. 4–235 l. 2; Toll 1970–1971: 131). Moreover, the dies wear out less in striking gold coins than silver or copper, since gold is more malleable. The minter can thus strike more dinars than dirhams with a similar tool. (24) However, since the die was used for a longer time than the preceding years, we can also assume that fewer dinars were struck during these three years than before. But as we do not have any more information on the Ziyadid economy, we cannot really draw any conclusion from these facts.

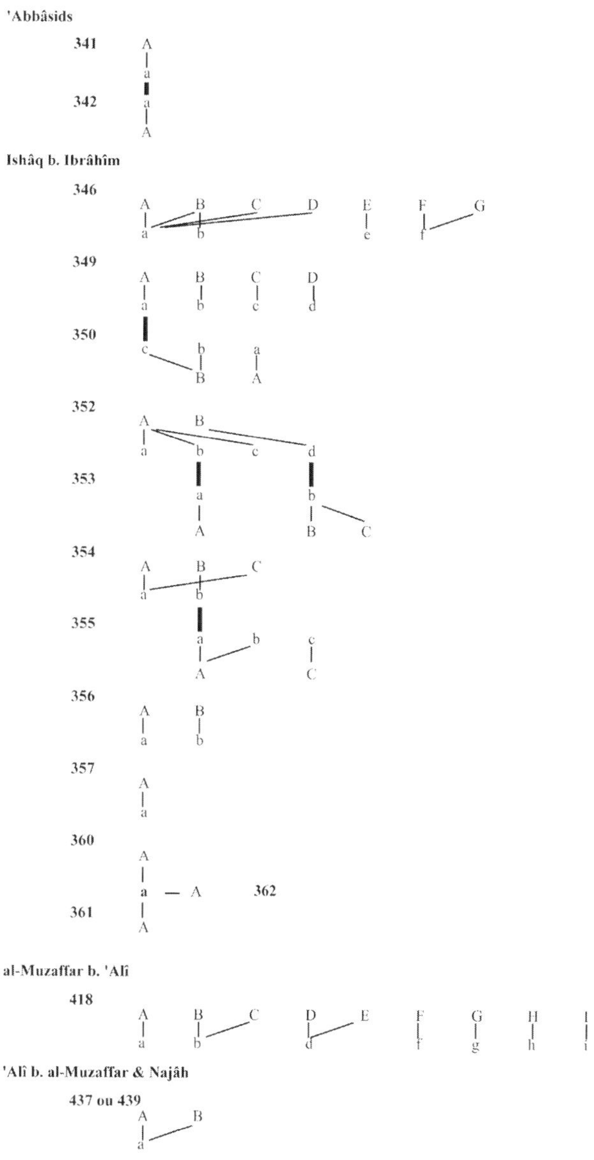

FIGURE 6. *Die-links of the Ziyadid coins minted in Zabīd (the bold links represent reused dies).*

ᶜUmāra and Ibn Ḥawqal are the only authors who give an idea of the economic resources of the Ziyadid state at this period. Indeed, the first says that he "saw the total of the revenues from the provinces of Ibn Ziyād for the year 366/976–977 [i.e. during ᶜAlī b. Ibrāhīm's reign], which amount reaches a million *ᶜaththarī* dinars" (25) (ᶜUmāra 1985: 64 l. 7–65 l. 2; Chelhod 1978: 59; Vallet 2006: 87) that were struck to a standard of just about 2.80 gm and are of a surprising uniformity (Album 1999: ix), which is not the case of the dinars minted in Zabīd. He then mentions that the Ziyadids collected taxes levied on the ships that came from India, on the amber collected on the Yemeni coasts, on the pearl fishing, and on the master of the Dahlak islands. Ibn Ḥawqal gives a similar account, but with different amounts that we cannot however take into consideration, as the copying of numbers is often a source of errors in manuscripts (Ibn Ḥawqal 1939: 23 l. 15–24 l. 7). He however insists on presenting "the descendant of Isḥāq b. Ibrāhīm" as the most powerful ruler of the region. Lastly, al-Masᶜūdī mentions that, even at the time of Ibrāhīm b. Ziyād, commercial links between Zabīd and Abyssinia were strong enough to allow a peace union between the two powers (al-Masᶜūdī

1966–1979, ii: 128 ll. 1–4). These accounts testify to the important commercial activity of the Ziyadids with India and Abyssinia. Unfortunately no Ziyadid coins have ever been discovered in these territories.

Conclusion

The study of the coins compared with the textual sources shows that the history of the Ziyadids was largely rewritten by their only historian, Jayyāsh b. Najāḥ. Fierce struggles for power may have arisen at the end of the Ziyadid dynasty, between the different Ethiopian wazirs who occupied important political positions. These struggles ended in taking control of the capital city, and in eliminating the last Ziyadid heir. These events raise the question of the presence of these Ethiopian slaves: Ethiopia and Tihāma were in contact before Islam, but what was the significance of the Ethiopian presence during the fourth/tenth century? Were they attracted by the economic conditions in Yemen? Did they form part of the gifts sent by the Ethiopian ruler, and then become high dignitaries?

Another question remains about the use of the coins minted by the Ziyadids. They were most probably struck for economic and trading purposes but for the moment, such coins have not been recorded in the regions in contact with Yemen during these periods, mostly Ethiopia and India. However, we probably have to put this fact down to the lack of excavations in these regions, and to the difficulty of identifying these coins.

Acknowledgements

I would like to thank my supervisors A. Northedge and P. Benoit (Université de Paris I – Panthéon Sorbonne). This study, which is based on the reading of the coins kept in the European public collections, would have been impossible without the kind help of the curators at the British Museum, Joe Cribb and Vesta Curtis, and at the Bibliothèque nationale de France, Michel Amandry and François Thierry, whom I especially thank for giving me permission to publish one of the coins in the Cabinet des Médailles. I am particularly grateful to Lutz Ilisch for giving me access to the coins of the University of Tübingen and to unpublished sources of information, and for sharing his knowledge with me.

I would also like to thank ᶜAbd al-ᶜAzīz al-Jandarī, director of the National Museum of Ṣanᶜāᵓ, and Florian Téreygeol (CNRS), with whom I undertook a project of studying, analysing, and publishing the Islamic coins kept in the museum. Last but not least, I want to express my gratitude to the Centre Français d'Archéologie et de Sciences Sociales de Ṣanᶜāᵓ and its director, Jean Lambert, and specially to Mounir Arbach (CEFAS), Rémy Audouin (Unesco), and Eric Vallet (Université de Paris 1 – Panthéon Sorbonne) who strongly supported me during my stay in Ṣanᶜāᵓ in April-May 2007.

Notes

1. According to al-Hamdānī and Ibn al-Mujāwir, settlements existed before the official foundation of the city of Zabīd on a site called Ḥuṣayb (al-Hamdānī 1990: 96 l. 4; Ibn al-Mujāwir 1951–1954, i: 65 ll. 1–2; Chelhod 1978: 53–54). This statement was confirmed by the excavations conducted by the team of the Royal Ontario Museum (Keall 1984: 52; 1989: 65).
2. According to al-Khazrajī, Ibrāhīm b. Muḥammad may have died in 279/892 (cited in Ibn al-Daybaᶜ 2006*a*: 275, n. 4).
3. According to the textual sources, Zabīd may have been sacked by the Qarāmiṭa several times during his reign: in Jumādā II 293/April 906, in 297/910, and in 300/912 (Ibn al-Daybaᶜ 2006*b*: 38 l. 12; Yaḥyā b. al-Ḥusayn 1968, i: 201, 203; Chelhod 1978: 56; Van Arendonk 1960: 141, 245).
4. According to ᶜUmāra, we know that the preaching of the Friday prayer, one of the two Islamic prerogatives of the sovereign along with minting, was made during Muḥammad b. Ziyād's reign in the name of the Abbasids (1985: 55 l. 1). The dinars and dirhams minted in Ṣanᶜāᵓ during the rule of the Yuᶜfirids, a local dynasty who settled in the Yemeni capital from 232/846–847, mentioned only the Abbasid caliph, as did the dinars minted by the Tarfid amirs who settled in ᶜAththar at the end of the third/ninth century.
5. ᶜAththar, capital city of the Tarfid rulers, is now in ruins: it is situated on a headland that lies on the bank of the red Sea, close to Mansiya on the river opposite Ras Tarfa (Zarins & Zahrani 1985).
6. "To Allah is the command in the former case and in the latter and on that day believers will rejoice in Allah's help to victory."
7. It is interesting to note that, on most of the coins minted by the Ziyadids, the name Ibrāhīm is written Ibrahīm, that the name of the city Zabīd is engraved Zabid and that the name of the Ethiopian slave Rashīd appears as Rashid, read by N. Lowick as Rushd (Lowick 1976: 548).
8. "And say: Truth has come and falsehood has vanished away. Verily falsehood is ever bound to vanish." See

Lowick 1976: 550–551 for a hypothesis on the use of this verse of the Qur'ān for revolutionary purposes.

9 Dinars from the years 347/958, 348/959, 351/962, and 358/969 are however unknown for the moment.

10 The *sudaysī* dirhams were struck with a weight corresponding to a sixth (*suds*) of the standard weight. They were probably used for local low-value transactions.

11 According to the sources, the ruler of Ṣanʿā' struck coins in the name of the Ziyadid (Ibn Ḥawqal 1939: 23; al-Muqaddasī 1906: 84; ʿUmāra 1985: 57; al-Wuṣābī 2006: 33 ll. 4–6) but, for the moment, such coins are not recorded. ʿUmāra tells us about dirhams but only dinars are known to have been struck in the name of the Abbasids during this period in Ṣanʿā'.

12 Dinars were minted in Ṣaʿda in the name of the Zaydī ruler from the year 297/910 (Sotheby's 18–19/04/94 no. 405). Most of them are dated the year of his death (298/911) (see e.g. Album 1999: 188).

13 The sources tell us that the amir of ʿAththar struck coins in the name of Ibn Ziyād (ʿUmāra 1985: 64 ll. 1–2). However, from 317/929 or 319/931 to 350/961, when the rulers of ʿAththar began to strike dinars in their own name (Album 1999: 373 ff.), dinars were minted in ʿAththar in the name of the Abbasids without any mention of the Tarfids or of the Ziyadids (Album 1999: 312–372; Album 1997: no. 74).

14 On the coins, the title appears as *Naṣr* but there could be a defective letter for *Nāṣir*.

15 According to the sources, Najāḥ had several children, of whom Saʿīd, Muʿārik, al-Dhakhīrah, Manṣūr, and Jayyāsh, the author of the Ziyadid history, are known (ʿUmāra 1985: 77 ll. 8–9).

16 R. Bikhazi proposed another reading: *abū ʿAlī* in the place of *al-maʿār*. He attributed the coin to a certain Nāṣir b. ʿAlī b. al-Muẓaffar (1970: 188). But this does not fit well with the names known from the other coins. However, the term as read by Lowick does not make any sense, although its root *ʿayn yā rā* deals with the idea of "standard". G.R. Puin reads *al-muʿīn* (personal communication from G.R. Puin to L. Ilisch, 1/6/1985), for which I did not find any meaning.

17 Indeed, Maḥmūd of Ghazna would have been the first sovereign to receive this title, from the Abbasid caliph al-Qādir (381–422/991–1031) (Bosworth *et al.* 1997: 885). At the same time, Ṭughril Beg (429–455/1038–1063) assumed this title on his own coinage from 438/1046–1047 onwards (Hennequin 1985).

18 According to ʿUmāra, his name was Rashīd (1985: 65 l. 5).

19 The various names are given by ʿUmāra. The same situation occurs for the successor of this child, son of Isḥāq b. Ibrāhīm, also called ʿAbd Allāh.

20 Three *sudaysī* dirhams could be attributed to him: they mention the Abbasid caliph al-Qādir billāh (381–422/991–1031) and were minted in al-Kadrā (Tübingen 93.18.113; 94.53.144 [Fig. 1/3] and 90.28.91). They unfortunately bear no date.

21 Ibn al-Mujāwir is the only author to give the child's name: according to him, he was called Ibrāhīm b. Ziyād (Ibn al-Mujāwir 1951–1954, i: 71 ll. 14–15).

22 The definitive results of these analyses will be published soon in the catalogue of the Islamic coins of the National Museum of Ṣanʿā' that I am preparing with ʿAbd al-ʿAzīz al-Jandarī, director of the museum, and Florian Téreygeol, chargé de recherche at the Centre national de la Recherche scientifique (Paris).

23 The pile is the lower die, which is stuck in the block, whereas the trussel is the upper die, which is held by the worker.

24 M. Bompaire notes for example that in Burgundy, around the year 1420, about 14,000 coins were struck with a pair of dies, and that usually the die used as the pile breaks three times less frequently than the die used as the trussel (Bompaire & Dumas 2000: 529).

25 They bear the name of the town of ʿAththar, the capital of an important opponent to Ziyadid power, the Tarfid family, who struck dinars from the middle to the end of the fourth/tenth century in their own name. Al-Muqaddasī (1906: 99) says that the dinar *ʿaththarī* is two thirds of a *mithqāl*. Indeed, the weight of the *mithqāl*, i.e. the legal dinar, was settled at 4.25 gm after ʿAbd al-Malik's reform in 77/696 (Miles 1962: 305), the dinars struck in ʿAththar weigh around 2.80 gm.

References

Album S.

1997. *Coins of the Islamic world (an important collection of gold, silver and copper coinage of the Arabian peninsula and Yemen)*. New York: Stack's.

1999. *Sylloge of Islamic coins in the Ashmolean*. x. Oxford: Ashmolean Museum.

Bikhazi R.J.
1970. The coins of al-Yaman, 132–569 A.H. *al-Abhath* 23/1–4: 3–127.

Bompaire M. & Dumas F.
2000. *Numismatique médiévale, monnaies et documents d'origine française*. (L'atelier du médiéviste, 7). Brepols: Turnhout.

Bosworth C.E.
1996. *The New Islamic dynasties*. Edinburgh: Edinburgh University Press.

Bosworth C.E., Schumann O., Kane O. & Kramers J.H.
1997. Al-Sulṭān. Pages 884–889 in *L'Encyclopédie de l'Islam*. (New edition). ix. Leiden: Brill.

Casanova P.
1894. Dinars inédits du Yémen. *Revue numismatique* (3rd series) 12: 200–220.

Chelhod J.
1978. Introduction à l'histoire sociale et urbaine de Zabīd. *Arabica* 25: 48–88.

Daghfous R.
1992–1993. La dynastie des Ziyadides à Zabīd (204–407/819–1016). *Cahiers de Tunisie* 162–163: 33–69.

Darley-Doran R.
1986. *Important collection of Islamic coins*. Zürich: Spink, Auction 18.
1999. *Islamic coins*. Dubai: Baldwin, Emirates Coins, Auction 1.

al-Hamdānī, Abū Muḥammad al-Ḥasan b. Aḥmad/ed. M. b. ᶜA. al-Akwaᶜ
1990. *Ṣifat Jazīrat al-ᶜArab*. Ṣanᶜāʾ: Maktabat al-Irshād.
2003. ed. Y.M. ᶜAbd Allāh. *Kitāb al-jawharatayn al-ᶜatiqatayn al-māʾiᶜatayn min al-ṣafrāʾ wa'l-bayḍāʾ*. Ṣanᶜāʾ: Maktabat al-Irshād.

Hennequin G.
1985. *Asie pré-mongole: les Saljuqs et leurs successeurs*. (Catalogue des monnaies musulmanes de la Bibliothèque nationale, 5). Paris: Bibliothèque nationale de France.

Ibn ᶜAbd al-Majīd, ᶜAbd al-Bāqī/ed. M. Ḥijazī & I. al-Haḍrānī
1985. *Tārīkh al-yaman al-musamma bahjat al-zamanfī tārīkh al-yaman*. Beirut: Dār al-ᶜAwdat.

Ibn al-Daybaᶜ, Abū ᶜAbd Allāh ᶜAbd al-Raḥmān
2006*a*. ed. M. b. ᶜA. al-Akwaᶜ. *Kitāb qurrat al-ᶜuyūn bi-akhbār al-yaman al-mayʾmūn*. Ṣanᶜāʾ: Maktabat al-Irshād.
2006*b*. ed. ᶜA.A. al-Ḥabshī. *Bughyat al-mustafīd fī tārīkh madīnat zabīd*. Ṣanᶜāʾ: Maktabat al-Irshād.

Ibn Ḥawqal, Abū'l-Qāsim Abū ᶜAlī al-Naṣībī/ed. J.H. Kramers
1939. *Kitāb Ṣurat al-ʾArḍ* Leiden: Brill.

Ibn al-Mujāwir, Jamāl al-Dīn Abū'l-Fatḥ Yūsuf/ed. O. Lögfren
1951– 1954. *Tārīkh al-mustabṣir. Descriptio Arabiae Meridionales*. (2 volumes). Leiden: Brill.

Ilisch L.
2006. *Antike — Islam*. Frankfurt: Peus, Auction 386.

ᶜImād al-Dīn, Idrīs/ed. A.F. Sayyid
2002. *The Fatimids and their successors in Yaman: the history of an Islamic community*. London: I.B. Tauris/ Institute of Ismaili Studies. [Arabic edition and English summary of ᶜImād al-Dīn's *ᶜUyūn al-akhbār*, volume 7].

Keall E.J.
1983. Zabid and its hinterland: 1982 report. *Proceedings of the Seminar for Arabian Studies* 13: 53–69.
1984. A preliminary report on the architecture of Zabid. *Proceedings of the Seminar for Arabian Studies* 14: 51–65.
1989. A few facts about Zabid. *Proceedings of the Seminar for Arabian Studies* 19: 61–69.

Lane-Poole S.
1877. Inedited Arabic Coins. Third notice. *Journal of the Royal Asiatic Society of Great Britain and Ireland*. [N. S.] 9: 135–143.

Lowick N.M.
1976. Coins of the Najahids of Yemen: a preliminary investigation. Pages 543–551 in *Actes du 8e Congrès International de Numismatique, 1973*. Paris: Association internationale des Numismates professionnels.

al-Masᶜūdī, Abūʾl-Ḥasan ᶜAlī/eds C. Barbier de Meynard & A. Pavet de Courteille

1966–1979. *Murūj al-dhahab wa maᶜādin al-jawhar*. Read and corrected by C. Pellat. (7 volumes). Beirut: Publications de l'Université libanaise.

Miles G.C.

1962. Dīnār. Pages 305–307 in *L'Encyclopédie de l'Islam*. (New edition). ii. Leiden: Brill.

Miquel A.

1991. al-Muqaddasī. Pages 492–493 in *L'Encyclopédie de l'Islam*. (New edition). vii. Leiden: Brill.

al-Muqaddasī, Shams al-dīn Abū ᶜAbd Allāh Muḥammad/ed. M. J. de Goeje

1906. *Aḥsan al-taqāsīm fī maᶜrifat al-aqālīm*. Leiden: Brill.

Popp V.

1996. *Antike — Islam*. Frankfurt: Peus, Auction 349.

Qedar S.

1985. *Islamic Coins*. Zürich: Leu.

Sadek N.

2004. Zabīd. Pages 370–371 in *The Encyclopaedia of Islam*. (New edition). xi. Leiden: Brill.

Shamma S.

1971. A hoard of fourth century dinars from Yemen. *American Numismatic Society Museum Notes* 17: 235–239.

Smith G.R.

1988. The political history of the Islamic Yemen down to the first Turkish invasion (1–945/622–1538). Pages 129–139 in W. Daum (ed.) *Yemen, 3000 years of art and civilisation in Arabia Felix*. Innsbruck/Franckfurt-am-Main: Pinguin Verlag/Umschau-Verlag.

2004. Ziyadids. Page 523 in *The Encyclopaedia of Islam*. (New edition). xi. Leiden: Brill.

Toll C.

1970–1971. Minting Technique according to Arabic Literary Sources. *Orientalia Suecana* 19–20: 125–139.

ᶜUmāra, Abū Ḥamza b. ᶜAlī/ed. M. b. ᶜA. Al-Akwaᶜ

1985. *Tāʾrīkh al-yaman al-musammā al-mufīd fī akhbār ṣanᶜāʾ wa zabīd, wa-shuᶜarāʾ mulūkihā wa aᶜyānihā wa udabāʾihā*. Ṣanᶜāʾ: Maktabat al-Yamaniyya.

Vallet E.

2006. *Pouvoir, commerce et marchands dans le Yémen rasulide (626–858/1229–1454)*. PhD thesis, Université de Paris 1 – Panthéon Sorbonne. [Unpublished].

Van Arendonk C./French transl. J. Ryckmans

1960. *Les débuts de l'fimāmat zaydite au Yémen*. (Publications de la Fondation de Goeje, 18). Leyden: E.J. Brill.

al-Wuṣābī, ᶜAbd al-Raḥman b. Muḥammad al-Hubayshī/ed. ᶜA.A. M. al-Ḥabshī

2006. *Tārīkh wuṣāb al-musamma al-iᶜtibār fī al-tawārīkh waʾl-āthār*. Ṣanᶜāʾ: Maktabat al-Irshād.

Yaḥyā b. al-Ḥusayn, Ibn al-Qāsim/ed. S.ᶜA. al-F. ᶜAshūr & M.M. Ziyāda

1968. *Ghāyat al-ᶜamānī fī akhbār al-quṭr al-yamanī*. (2 volumes). Cairo: Dār al-kātib al-ᶜarabī lil-ṭabaᶜat waʾl-nashar.

Yāqūt al-Rūmī/ed. F. Wüstenfeld

1957. *Muᶜjam al-buldān*. Beirut: Dār Ṣādir.

Zarins J. & Zahrani A.

1985. Recent Archaeological Investigations in the Southern Tihama Plain (the Sites of Athar and Sihi, 1404/1984). *Atlal* 9: 65–107.

Author's address

Audrey Peli, (Université de Paris 1 – Panthéon Sorbonne and Laboratoire «Islam médiéval» UMR 81 67) 29 rue Championnet, 75018 Paris, France.

e-mail audrey.peli@noos.fr

Proceedings of the Seminar for Arabian Studies 38 (2008): 265–276

Sadd al-Khanaq: an early Umayyad dam near Medina, Saudi Arabia

SAAD BIN ABDULAZIZ AL-RĀSHID

Summary
Sadd al-Khanaq or Sadd Muᶜāwiyah is an early Umayyad dam situated about 15 km east of Medina. The dam was built in a very narrow gorge or passage in Wādī al-Khanaq. The wadi runs from the south-east of Medina to the north-west where its water floods into a natural basin caused by the lava flows and earthquakes that hit the region of Medina and Hijaz in successive years (654/1256, 690/1291, 727/1326 and 734/1333). At the narrowest part of the wadi a massive dam was erected, forming a large lake. This main dam was built to block the course of the wadi flooding through the gorge. A second dam appears to act as a support to catch the surplus water running through a small branch of the wadi. The wall of the main dam rises from the level of the wadi bed to the highest spot on both shoulders of the rising mountain. Two sections of the main dam remain intact while its central bulk has been badly damaged, perhaps because of the pressure of the water against the wall of the dam and also as a result of earthquakes and volcanic eruptions. The second dam is located west of the main dam behind a high mountain. Its central section is also damaged, leaving two remaining segments showing the original construction. Our inspection of the two dams led to the discovery of an inscribed stone fixed on the highest spot of the wall of the main dam. It contains very valuable information regarding the date of the building of the dam by the Umayyad caliph Muᶜāwiyah bin Abi Sufyan (41/661–60/679). The registration of the dam and the recovery of the inscription provide us with valuable knowledge of an early masterpiece of water engineering, which will lead to the study of several existing dams in the Hijaz province.

Keywords: Sadd al-Khanaq, dam, Muᶜāwiyah, Saudi Arabia

Introduction

About 15 km to the east of al-Madīnah al-Munawwarah lies an ancient dam locally known as Sadd Wādī al-Khanaq (now identified as Sadd Muᶜāwiyah). It is located at 39° 55' 520" longitude and 24° 26' 400" latitude, some 10 km south-east of Medina airport. In fact, it is not one dam but two dams situated in the same locality.

The two dams were built on two narrow passages in the Wādī al-Khanaq (Fig. 1). The word al-Khanaq means "narrow neck in a valley" or "bottle neck". The water reached this particular area through Ḥaḍawḍāʾ (حضوضاء), a lowland area or depression where rainwater and floods gather from higher mountains, as well as a plateau of basalt towards both east and west. A stream of floodwater passed through Wādī al-Khanaq. This wadi is one of the most important wadis in Medina. It varies in length and width while passing through the mountains, rising 900 m above sea level. The most famous of these are Jibāl Ḥaḍawḍāʾ (جبال حضوضاء), al-Ġubay (الغبي), Jibāl al-Sadd (جبال السد), and Jibāl Ṭayy (جبال طي).

The water gathered into Wādī al-Khanaq which wound its course towards a nearby depression located north-east of Medina. This is called Sadd al-ᶜAqūl, and is a natural dam created by volcanism and lava eruption. The twin dams of al-Khanaq were built at the junction of two narrow water spillways that left the main wadi. They created a large artificial lake covering a wide area about 1600 m in length and 350 m in width, with a reservoir capacity of up to 560,000 m^3. The two dams

FIGURE 1. *A view of the first dam (right) and second dam (left) at Sadd al-Khanaq.*

together cover an area of about 3 km from north to south.

During our inspection we noted that in the area surrounding the complex, to the north of Ḥarrat Rahat and along the stream of Wādī al-Khanaq, there are many low depressions where rain and floodwater gathered and formed natural pools, which facilitated the development of fertile lands suitable for cultivation. It is evident that such locations near Medina and in the Hijaz region were utilized in the early Islamic period for establishing dams and digging wells for agricultural activities.

The first dam

The first dam was built on the narrowest passage of the wadi (Figs. 2 and 3). This is the main prominent dam on which we discovered a monumental stone with a Kufic inscription giving the date of construction of the dam.

The dam runs from east to west. The remains of the dam are a masterpiece of engineering and consist of two massive sections still perched on the edge of the rock foundations, while the central part of the dam has collapsed and was subsequently removed by strong floods. The two remaining portions of the dam give us a clear example of the techniques of engineering and construction. The wall of the dam is faced with cut stones whereas the core is composed of basalt rocks mixed with strong mortar and gravel. The dam is about 13.90 m wide and 17 m high. The southern façade of the dam is lined with courses of fired bricks from the top to the lowest part and rendered with strong plaster, while the northern façade of the dam is lined with large stones.

FIGURE 2. *The first dam at Sadd al-Khannaq.*

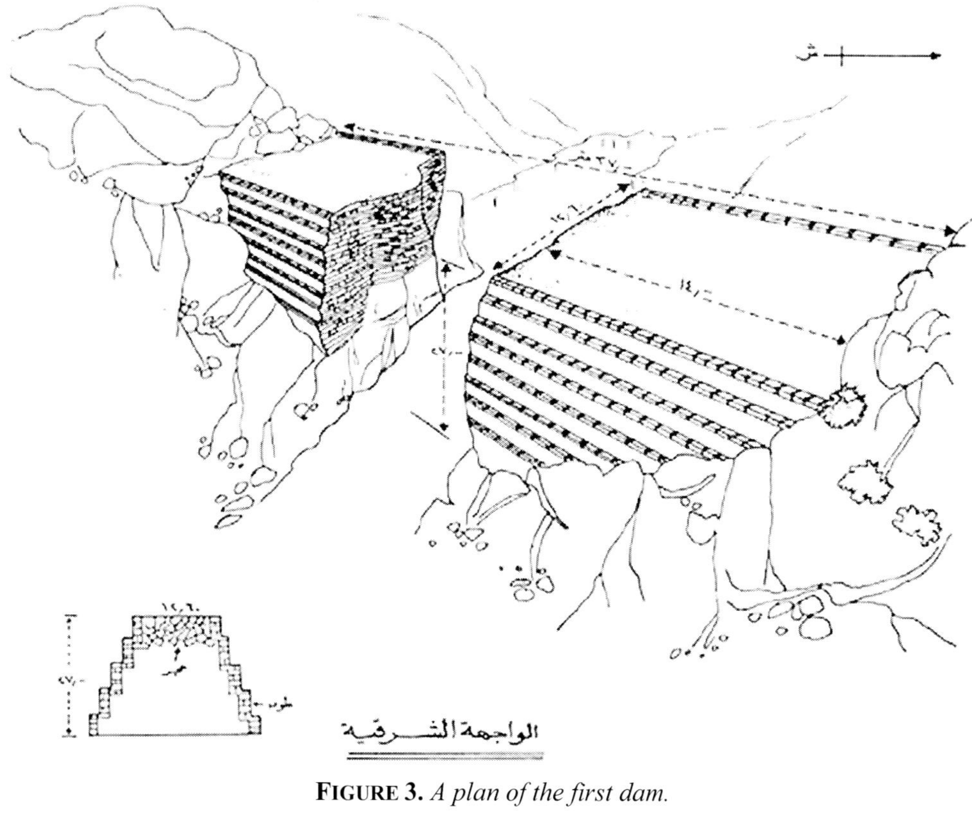

FIGURE 3. *A plan of the first dam.*

FIGURE 4. *The second dam at Sadd al-Khannaq.*

The two main extant areas of the dam survived because the structure was built on the shoulders of the mountain and the floodwater only affected the central portion. I should add that the dam did not collapse because of flood pressure but as a result of earthquake and volcanic activity.

The engineers who designed and built this dam did an excellent job. In order to provide extra resistance against the strong rush of floodwater, which at times may have risen above the highest level of the dam, they protected the dam with strong plaster so that the water could not penetrate the inner core of the wall. The plaster was applied in the form of long strips along the entire length of the wall in the shape of semi-steps. Moreover, the wall was built like a pyramid, being widest at the base and rising gradually in an oblique direction until it joined the adjacent mountain side. Thus the dam is widest at the base (17 m) and narrowest at the top (12.70 m); the length of the dam was about 43 m. The missing central part of the dam measures between 10 and 15 m across.

The second dam

This dam was built to the west of the first dam, and dominated a narrow passage where the surplus water returned and made its course towards the weakest spot in the offshoot of the valley (Fig. 4). Here also one must appreciate the engineers for their skill, scientific understanding of the environment, topography, balance of the water level, and the way in which they managed to built a supporting dam to control and properly use the excessive water.

FIGURE 5. *The foundation stone on the first dam, showing its location (left) and details of the inscription (right).*

The distance between the two dams is around 300 m. The second dam is oriented north–south. The central part of this dam has also been destroyed and about 29 m of its middle part has fallen down while the debris has been driven away by severe floods throughout the centuries. Two large segments of the dam are still very well preserved. The northern wall of the dam is 15 m long while the southern part is 12 m. The construction of the dam is similar to that of the main dam. The façade of the dam towards the lake is plastered with strong thick layers in long strips, while the other side of the wall has been strengthened by large basalt stones. The entire length of the dam is 56 m, with a width of 11 m at the base and 6 m at the top.

The irrigation system

It is evident from the construction of the first dam (i.e. the main dam) and the other supported dam, and from their massive building structure, thickness, and height that these were built on this particular location in order to create a large artificial lake with huge water capacity to serve for a long time. However, we were not able to find out how the water was distributed. No distributaries or irrigation conduits are preserved. The complex must have been provided with water outlets to control the flow and distribution of water for irrigation and drinking, and in case of an emergency to ease the strong pressure on the walls of both dams during strong floods. It is also evident that the land closer to the complex must have been used for farming and agriculture. There are also several wells in the vicinity of the dams and in the nearby settlement area, the ruins of which are still visible on the site. The water level in the wells usually rises during annual rain and floods, and while the dams preserved water for a long time their water capacity may have decreased in some less rainy seasons. The wells in such cases provide water even when there is a drought. Underground artisan channels could have linked these wells and retained water for a long period.

The industrial area

During survey of the area to the north-west of the two dams, on the edge of the depression, we found the remains of burnt bricks and quarries where stones were cut for the construction of the dams, in addition to large pieces of furnace used for making and preparing white mortar. Scattered on the site are red bricks and discarded brick moulds, which had been used several times so that their original colour has changed to black due to high and excessive temperature. Slag was found covering and attached to baked bricks on both sides. The site gives the impression that it was an industrial area for preparing building materials for the construction of this huge project. We also noted an area where stones were cut in the *ḥarrah* (basalt) plain and in the depression. A few potsherds have also been found that could be attributed to the same period as the dams.

The dating of the dam

As I have mentioned earlier, the dam is dated on the basis of a foundation stone installed on the top of the wall located in the south-western section of the dam. Surprisingly most historical and geographical sources do not mention the dam, despite its importance and prominent location on a route linking Medina with the ancient gold mine of Maᶜdin Banū Sulaym. This road was well known and used by the Abbasid caliph Hārūn al-Rašīd on his journey between Mecca and Medina.

Al-Ḥarbi (died 285/898), mentioned that Muᶜāwiyah built a dam along this road. He listed the three stoppages on the road from Medina to Maᶜdin Banū Sulaym along which Hārūn al-Rašīd used to travel on his journey to Mecca. The mileage given by al-Ḥarbi on this section of the road as follow:

Madīnah to Sadd Muᶜāwiyah	20 miles
Sadd Muᶜāwiyah to al-Arhadiyyah	32 miles
Al-Arhadiyyah to al-Malīḥah	21 miles
Al-Malīḥah to Maᶜdin Banū Sulaym	29 miles

(al-Ḥarbi, al-Manāsik: 329–330)

Al-Ḥarbi wrote that the dam held plenty of water retained in the lake behind the dam and that other stations also contained abundant water, except for the station of al-Malīḥah which sometimes lacked water (al-Ḥarbi: 330–331). Al-Ḥarbi is usually accurate when listing pilgrim routes and their stations in the early Abbasid period, but unfortunately he does not mention details of this dam, and neither does he give information regarding the wadi on which the dam was built.

Al-Samhūdi recounts that the dam is situated in an area called Ḥazm Banī ᶜAwal: by this perhaps he meant that the dam was passed by Caliph Hārūn al-Rashīd on his way from Medina to Maᶜdin Banī Sulaym. According to al-Asadi, al-Samhūdi said that the dam collected a large amount of water in the wadi bed "šaᶜib", and that it was built by Muᶜāwiyah to preserve water in the form of a large lake (al-Samhūdi 1374/1955, iv: 1232). Probably "šaᶜib" on which the dam was built is the same dam (Wādī Qanāt or "Wādī Šazat"). Al-Samhūdi also wrote that a valley close to Medina called "Wādī Qanāt" (i.e. canal) was formed by natural eruption of the lava flow of Ḥarrat al-Nār (i.e. fire) and is called *šazat* (al-Samhūdi 1374/1955, iii: 1074). It is likely that al-Samhūdi may be referring to the "Nār al-Ḥarrah" which occurred in 654/1256 when the region of Medina was hit by earthquakes and volcanism, and which according to Ibn Kaṯīr obstructed the flow of traffic along the pilgrim road from Iraq. The lava blocked Wādī Šazat and created a large natural dam (*ḥibs* – حبس), and the water could not pursue its natural course towards Medina beyond this natural dam (Ibn Kaṯīr, iii: 187–193).

Al-Samhūdi states that according to early historians, floodwater was retained behind this natural dam in order to form a large lake that looked like a huge sea as far as the eye could see. It was compared with the river Nile when in full flood. Al-Samhūdi also wrote that water passed through an opening in this natural dam in 690/1291 and that the water continued along the wadi towards Medina throughout the year. According to Al-Samhūdi, floodwater collected behind this natural dam every year and in 727/1326 and 734/1333 the floodwater even reached the centre of Medina (Al-Samhūdi 1374/1955, iii: 1074–1075). Local historians do not refer to the dam of Muᶜāwiyah but they recorded the natural formation of the dam (Sadd al-ᶜAqūl) which was created by the lava flow and accordingly formed a lake measuring about 5×1 km. This natural dam has been reinforced in recent years (ᶜAlī Ḥāfiẓ, 345–347). The well-known historian al-ᶜAyyāši mentioned Wādī Qanāt and the natural dam formed by the flow of lava (al-ᶜAyyāši 1414/1994: 456) but unfortunately he did not mention Sadd Muᶜāwiyah which is located in an area not far away to the south of Sadd al-ᶜAqūl (1414/1994: 462–474).

ᶜAbd al-Quddūs al-Ansary referred to Sadd al-Khanaq as one of several dams built in the arable lands in Mecca, Medina, and Taif, but although al-Ansary knew about the dam he did not specify its exact location (al-Ansary 1971: 28). ᶜAtīq al-Bilādi gives a description of Wādī Qanāt, which passes between Medina and the Uhud Mountain. He mentions that rain- and floodwater collected in this wadi originated from the upper highlands of Najd and pushed into Wādī al-Khanaq and then towards al-ᶜAqūl dam (al-Bilādi 1398–1404/1978–1984, vii: 165).

From the available sources we can say that the Muᶜāwiyah dam has been mentioned by two reliable sources, namely Al-Ḥarbi (d. 285/898) and Al-Samhūdi (d. 911/1505). These two references confirm the existence of the Muᶜāwiyah dam in the third/tenth century but we do not know why later historians do not mention it. Perhaps the dam was not functioning and was not in a good state of repair; by contrast the al-ᶜAqūl dam located in the same area became the best known in the region.

The foundation stone

The foundation stone with an inscription is laid on the highest spot of the northern façade of the wall of the dam (Fig. 5). The text is inscribed on grey basalt stone. The dimensions of the stone are 46×65×14 cm. The text consists of ten lines and the letters were incised with the utmost precision. There is synchronisation between the length of the lines and the size of the letters. The lines vary in length between 27 and 44 cm. (1) The text reads as follows:

1. بسم الله الرحمن الرحيم
2. هذا السد لعبد الله
3. معوية أمير المؤمنين
4. اللهم برك له فيه رب
5. السموت والأرض
6. بنيه أب رداد مولى
7. عبد الله بن عباس بحو
8. ل الله وقوته
9. وقام عليه كثير بن
10. الصلت و أبو موسى

Transliteration

1. bism illāh ar-raḥmān ar-raḥīm
2. hāḏa al-Sadd li ᶜabdullāh
3. muᶜāwiyah ᵓamīr al-muᵓminīn
4. allāhumma bārik lahu fīhi rabb
5. al-samawāt wa al-ᵓarḍ
6. banāhu abū raddād mawlā
7. ᶜabdullāh bin ᶜabbās bi-ḥawl
8. li-allāh wa-quwwatih
9. wa-qām ᶜalayhi kaṯīr bin
10. l-ṣalt wa-abū mūsā

Translation

1. In the name of Allah The Compassionate the Merciful
2. This dam is for ᶜAbdullāh
3. Muᶜāwiyah commander of the faithful
4. O Allah bring blessing for him, The Lord
5. of sky and earth
6. Built by Abu Raddād (mawlā) the adherent
7. (For) ᶜAbdullāh b. ᶜAbbās with the strength
8. And power of Almighty God
9. (built) under the supervision of Kaṯīr bin
10. l-Ṣalt and Abū Mūsā

It is clear from this text that Muᶜāwiyah bin Abī Sufyān built this dam for his own benefit as is evident from the phrase *bārik lahu fīhi* "bring blessing for him". The name of Muᶜāwiyah appears in lines 2–3 with his honorific title Amīr al-Muᵓminīn, which is very clear evidence that the dam was built after Muᶜāwiyah became caliph. In addition to the name of Muᶜāwiyah other names are mentioned in the text.

Names mentioned in the text

Muᶜāwiyah bin Abī Sufyān

According to the text of the inscription the dam was built for ᶜAbdullāh Muᶜāwiyah the commander of the faithful. The expression ᶜAbdullāh which is written before the original name as a form of modesty (meaning "the slave of God") is normally linked with the title of caliph. It means that the dam was built when Muᶜāwiyah was the Umayyad Caliph. Muᶜāwiyah is a well-known figure in Islamic history. He was one of the companions of the Prophet Muḥammad (pbuh) and also became one of the few specialists who wrote the Holy Qurᵓān during the revelation. Muᶜāwiyah was renowned as a leader and administrator. He accepted Islam (before his father became a Muslim) in year 7 of the Hijra, participated in several battles, and during the Caliphate of ᶜUmar became the Governor of Bilād al-Shām (Syria) and remained in this position during the Caliphate of ᶜUmān. He became the first Umayyad Caliph and continued to rule until his death in 60/679. His Caliphate lasted for nineteen years, three months and twenty days (al-Ṭabari, v: 323–325).

Abū Raddād (Mawlā ᶜAbdullāh bin ᶜAbbās)

This name is mentioned in lines 6–7. Abū Raddād was the supervisor of the project on behalf of Muᶜāwiyah. According to sources, his name was Raddād but he was known as Abū Raddād. He was a *ḥijāzi*, i.e. from the Hijaz. He was a (*rāwiyah*) *ḥadiṯ* transmitter (Ibn Ḥajar, i: 249; iii: 270–271). Abū Raddād was lucky to live close to the Prophet Muḥammad (pbuh) and thus became a narrator of the Prophet's sayings for which he was quoted in later periods (Ibn al-Aṯīr 1970, vi: 109).

A final remark may be added here regarding Abū Raddād who is mentioned as *mawlā*. The term *mawlā* does not necessarily mean an emancipated war captive or slave. In Islamic history there are *mawālī* adherents or clients that come as a result of *muᶜāhadah*, a treaty of friendship which take place between two tribes or a person who puts himself under the patronage of a man who has a high status and position in the society (Maṣri 1408 /1988).

ᶜAbdullāh bin ᶜAyyāš

This name has been mentioned in connection with Abū Raddād who supervised the building of the dam. We read the name as ᶜAbdullāh bin ᶜAyyāš. He was born in Abyssinia, and was renowned as the most knowledgeable person in the reading of the Holy Qurʾān. He was a *madīnī* (i.e. from Medina) and a *tabiᶜi* (second follower) as a student and considered as a reliable source in Ḥadīṯ (Aḏ-Ḏahabi [n.d.]: 148–161; Ibn al-Jawzi, vi: 72–75). He may have died either in Medina in the year 64/683 or in Sajistan in 78/697.

Another person mentioned in the text is ᶜAbdullāh bin ᶜAyyāš bin al-ᶜAlqami who was granted land in Wādī al-ᶜAqīq in Medina in the year 41/661. We doubt if this person was involved in the building of the dam, as he has never been mentioned in other sources (Al-Samhūdi, 1374/1955, vol. iii: 1044; al-Fairūzabādi, 343). One might dispute the reading of the name because there are similarities in the calligraphy and engraving in ᶜAbbās and ᶜAyyāš. When there are no dots under or above the letters the formation of the letters *ba* and *ya* is identical.

A very well-known learned person, ᶜAbdullāh bin ᶜAbbās was the cousin of the Prophet Muḥammad (pbuh); he died in Taif in the year 68/687 but was never attached to any administrative work and devoted his life to learning and teaching. As he was a well-known and famous person he might have been mentioned here owing to his relationship with Abū Raddād (Aḏ-Ḏahabi [n.d.]: 148–161; Ibn al-Jawzi, VI: 72–75).

Kaṯīr bin al-Ṣalt

This name is mentioned in lines 9–10 as the person who was in charge of the construction of the dam. He is a well-known figure in historical sources. His full name was Kaṯīr bin al-Ṣalt bin Maᶜdi Karib al-Kindi. According to Ibn Saᶜd his original name was Qalīl which means "little", but Caliph ᶜUthmān renamed him Kaṯīr which means "plentiful". Kaṯīr was born in Medina at the time of the Prophet Muḥammad (pbuh). He was a man of nobility and wealth and owned a large house in Medina. It is also reported that he became the clerk scribe for Caliph ᶜAbdulmalik (bin Marwān). He died between 71/690 and 80/699. Ibn Kaṯīr recorded his death in the year 77/969 (Ibn Saᶜd, v: 14; al-Ḥarbi: 404; Ibn al-Aṯīr 1970, iv: 460; Adh-Dhahabi [n.d.]: 513–514; Ibn Kaṯīr, vol.ix, 21).

Abū Mūsā

This name is mentioned in line 10 of the text as a joint participant in the building of the dam. We do not know anything about this person. It seems that he was well known to the extent that the writer of the text did not write his full name and was satisfied by writing only his surname (*kunyah*) as Abū Mūsā. There are many persons with this title who are known among the companions of the Prophet and his followers (Ibn Ḥajr, xii: 251–252; Ibn al-Aṯīr, 1970, vi: 306–308).

Analysis of the text

This text was executed with great skill and accuracy as seen in the uniformity of the lines, words, and sentences both at the beginning and at the end of each line. The letters are incised in a cursive angular shape with no ornamentation. The words and names are written without excessive extension of letters either in the middle or at the end of the words, as can be seen in the following words and names:

al-Samawāt (السموات), *bārik* (برك), *Muᶜāwiyah,* (معوية)

This style is similar to the calligraphy of early quranic scripts. The text does not include letters with diacritical marks (dots) except one letter in the name *al-Ṣalt* in line 5, where two dots appear above the letter *ta*. If we compare this text with the inscription located at the Muᶜāwiyah dam built near Taif and dated 58/677, we find many words associated with diacritical marks (dots). For example Muᶜāwiyah *banāhu, ṯaman, mataᶜ, al-muʾminīn*). (المؤمنين،متع،ثمن،بنيه،معوية) The inscription located in Medina on Sadd al-Khanaq is distinguished by the writing of the *basmalah* (the invocation), unlike the text in Taif, which was written without the *basmalah*. While both the inscriptions in Medina and Taif have a similar introductory or starting pattern, i.e. (هذا السد لعبد الله معوية أمير المؤمنين) *hāḏā al-Sadd li ᶜAbdillāh muᶜāwiyah amīr almuʾminīn.* Starting words are dedicated to the Caliph, the prayer words in each text, on the other hand, are different and have no similarities.

The Taif text contains the name of one single person who supervised the construction of the dam ᶜAbdullāh bin Ṣaḫr, (عبد الله بن صخر) while the text in Medina includes three names (Kaṯīr bin al-Ṣalt, Abū Mūsā and Abū Raddād) (أبو رداد ، أبو موسى ، كثير بن الصلت).

The text in Medina does not indicate the name of the inscriber, while the Taif inscription mentions the name ᶜAmr bin Ḥabbāb or Janāb. ((عمرو بن حباب (جناب)

The Taif inscription consists of six lines and thirty words while in the Medina text we have ten lines and thirty-two words. (2)

It is interesting to note that the inscription on Muᶜāwiyah's dam in Taif was placed on a large natural rock lying on an elevated area overlooking the dam, while the inscription in Medina was placed on a specially prepared cut stone and fixed on the last set of stones on top of the wall of the dam as a coronation stone.

The historical value of the Medina inscription

The foundation inscription of Sadd al-Khanaq or Muᶜāwiyah is a valuable source of information. It is a document recording a masterpiece of water engineering in Medina, and evidence of the facilities provided by Caliph Muᶜāwiyah. The text indicates the title of Amīr al-Muʾminīn (the commander of the faithful). The name of Muᶜāwiyah together with his title as caliph is tangible evidence for the accurate dating of the dam, in addition to the names of prominent figures who are known in early Islamic period and the beginning of the Umayyad caliphate, such as Abū Raddād (al-Layṯi) and Kaṯīr bin al-Ṣalt. These names and the comparative analysis of letters in the text, the construction technique of the dam, its architectural design, and other archaeological evidence such as pottery sherds and inscriptions all give us a coherent conclusion of the history of this water project.

Writing a specific text on a large cut stone and having it fixed on the wall of the dam after its completion represented a clever policy of the Umayyad caliphs, engineers, administrators, and those who supervised the work. The coronation stone was fixed in the wall of the main dam perhaps at the last moment on the completion of the project, and an opening ceremony might have been organized for the occasion, either in honour of the Caliph himself or of someone on his behalf.

The documentary text of Sadd al-Khanaq is the second official record bearing the name of Caliph Muᶜāwiyah in the region of Hijaz. The first documentary text is the inscription located on the Muᶜāwiyah dam near Taif (Sadd Saisad) dated 58/677.

It must be emphasized that these two recorded texts are of great historical value since they show how Umayyad caliphs were keen to record their development and architectural projects such as palaces, water installations, road constructions, religious buildings etc. In this respect they followed the same customs and traditions of pre-Islamic early kingdoms in Arabia such as the numerous building inscriptions from public buildings in South Arabia (Doe 1983: 189–202).

Similarly, most of the agricultural installations during the reign of Caliph Muᶜāwiyah had foundation stones like those found on the two dams in Medina and Taif. Al-Samhūdi, for example, mentions that Muᶜāwiyah instructed the Governor of Medina, Marwān bin Muḥammad, to build a palace on the outskirts of Medina. Marwān appointed al-Nuᶜmān bin Bašīr to supervise the project. Al-Samhūdi adds that an inscribed coronation stone was fixed on the palace.

The text reads as follows:

li ᶜabdullāh muᶜāwiyah amīr al-muʾminīn mimmā ᶜamila al-nuᶜmān bin bašīr

"so it is evident that the work was executed by al-Nuᶜmān bin Bašīr for ᶜAbdullāh Muᶜāwiyah the Commander of the Faithful" (Ibn al-Aṯīr 1970, v: 326–329).

It is not surprising that Muᶜāwiyah had established a great dam in Medina. According to historical sources he paid special attention to agricultural development, wells, *qanāts*, canals, and dams. He owned arable lands in Hijaz and Yamāmah where he benefited financially from their production, such as dates, grapes, and wheat. Muᶜāwiyah appointed several superintendents to supervise and run his business, including ᶜAbd ul-Raḥmān bin Abī Aḥmad bin Jaḥš, al-Naẓīr, Ibn Minaʾ, and Saᶜd.

According to historians Muᶜāwiyah earned from his farms in Medina and its environs 150,000 camel loads (*wasaq*) per year of wheat alone (al-Samhūdi 1374/1955, i: 129). It is said that Muᶜāwiyah purchased a farm from Bani Sulaym that consisted of date palms and vineyards never before seen in size and pleasant scenery:

وكان أعنابا ونخلا لم ير مثله

The farm contained several houses and wells while the natural topography and land was very picturesque and fertile and enriched with pasture for raising animals that brought wealth to its owners:

وبها منازل و بئار كثيرة ، وهي ذات عضاة وآكام تنبت ضروبا من الكلاء، صالحة للمال

(al- Samhūdi 1374/1955, iii: 1067).

Muᶜāwiyah once planted 5000 palm trees in one farm near Medina (al-Balāḏuri, 132–133). There are many stories related to the use of land and development of farms by Muᶜāwiyah (al-Zubayr bin Bakkar, 365; Yāqūt, IV: 12).

In conclusion I would like to suggest that this initial brief research report on Sadd al-Khanaq could mark the beginning of major scientific studies on agricultural developments in the early Islamic periods. Future studies should deal with the geology, water resources, capacity of the dam, water distribution system, and how far the water reached from this dam. All water projects and irrigation systems implemented during the Muᶜāwiyah and Umayyad Caliphates should be studied in detail. The authentic dating of Sadd al-Khanaq may lead us to the study of other early dams such as Sadd al-Bint, Sadd al-Ḥaṣīd, and many other dams, wells, canals, and the remains of early Islamic settlements.

Notes

1 The stone has been recovered from robbers and is now stored in the National Museum in Riyadh.

2 For details on the Muᶜāwiyah dam in Taif see Grohmann 1971: 52–58, pls 8, 1/12, z68).

References

Arabic sources

al-ᶜAyyāši, Ibrāhīm bin ᶜAli

1414/1994. *Al-madīna bayn al-mādi wal-ḥāẓir.* (Second edition). (Maktabat al-Ṯaqāfah) Medina.

Al-Ansary, ᶜAbd al-Quddūs

1971. *Bayn al-tārīkh wa al-aṯār.* (Second edition), Beirut

1393/1973. *Āṯār al-madīna al-munawwarah.* (Third edition). Medina:

Al-Balāḏuri, Aḥmad Bin Yaḥya.

1400/1979. *Ansāb al-Ašrāf*, ed. Iḥsān ᶜAbbās, Beirut.

Al-Bilādi, ᶜAtīq bin Ġaiṯ

1398–1404/1978–1984. *Muᶜjam maᶜlim al-ḥijāz.* (10 volumes). (Dar makkah li al-našr wa al-tawzīᵓ) Mecca.

Al-Ḏahabi, Abu ᶜAbdullāh bin Aḥmad/ed. ᶜUmar ᶜAbd al-Salām

[n.d.] *ᶜUṯmān, tārīkh al-islām wa wafiyyat al-mašāhīr wa l-aᶜlām, tadmuri.* (17 vols.) (Dār al-Kitāb al-Arabi), Beirut:

Ḥāfiẓ, ᶜAli.

1405H. *Fuṣūl min Tārīkh al-Madīnah al-Munawwarah.* (Šarikat al-Madīnah Li al-Ṭibāᶜah wa al-Našr), 2nd edition, Jiddah.

Al-Ḥarbi, Ibrāhīm Bin Isḥāq.

1389/1969. *Kitāb al-Manāsik wa-Amākin Ṭuruq al-Ḥajj wa-Maᶜlim al-Jazīrah*, ed. Ḥamad al-Jāsir, (Dār al-Yamāmah). Riyadh.

Ibn al-Aṯīr, Abu l-ḥasan ᶜAlī bin Muḥammad/ed. Muḥammad Ibrāhīm al-Banna.

1970. *Asad ul-ġābah fi maᶜrifat al-Ṣaḥābah.* (7 volumes). Cairo: (al-Šaᶜb.)

Ibn Ḥajr, Abu l-Faḍl Aḥmad Bin ᶜAli.

1327H. *Tahḏīb al-Tahḏīb.* (12 Vols.) Ḥaydar Abād.

Ibn al-Jawzi, Abu l-Faraj

1412/1992. *Al-muntaẓam.* (Dār al-Kutub al-ᶜilmiyyah). Beirut.

Ibn Kaṯīr, Abu l-Fidāᵓ, al-Ḥāfiẓ Bin Ismāᶜīl.

1979-1980. *Al-Bidāyah wa al-Nihāyah*, 14 vols. (Maktabat al-Maᶜārif). Beirut.

Ibn Saᶜd, Muḥammad.

1389/1978. *At-Ṭabaqāt al-Kubra*, 8 vols. (Dār Bayrūt). Beirut.

Al-Maṣri, Jamīl ᶜAbdullāh.

1408/1988. *Al-Mawāli wa-Mawqif al-Dawlah al-Umawiyyah Minhum.* (Dār Umm al-Qura), ᶜAmmān.

al- Rāshid, Saad bin Abdul Aziz

1400/1980. Al-āṯār al-islāmiyyah fi al-jazīrah al-ᶜarabiyyah fi ᶜahd al-rasūl (pbuh) wa l-ẖulafāᵓ al-rāšidīn. *Dirāsāt fi tārīẖ al-jazīrah al-ᶜarabiyyah* 3/2 (King Saud University, Riyadh): 146–152.

1414/1993. *Zubaydah: ṭarīq al-ḥajj min al-kūfah ila makkah al-mukarramah "dirāsah aṯāriyyah".* Riyadh: Dār al-Waṭan.

1421/2000. *Dirāsāt fi al-aṯār al-islāmiyyah al-mubakkirah bi al-madīna al-munawwarah.* (Muᵓassasat al-Ḥuzaimi). Riyadh.

Al-Samhūdi, Nūr ad-Dīn ᶜAli bin Aḥmad/ed. Muḥyi ad-Dīn ᶜAbd al-Ḥamīd

1374/1955. *Wafaᵓ al-wafaᵓ bi ᵓaẖbār dār al-muṣṭafa.* (4 volumes). (Matbaᶜat al-Saᶜādah) Cairo.

Other sources

Doe B.
1983. *Monuments of South Arabia.* Naples/New York: Falcon-Oleander.

Grohmann A.
1971. *Arabische Paläographie.* Part II. *Das Schriftwesen. Die Lapidarschrift.* (Österreichische Akademie der Wissenschaften, Philosophisch-historische Klasse, Denkschriften 94/ii). Vienna: Herman Böhlaus Nachf.

Hamidullah M.
1939. Some Arabic Inscriptions of Madinah of the Early Years of Hijrah. *Islamic Culture* 13/4: 427–439.

Khan M. & al-Mughannam A.
1982. Ancient Dams in Taif Area 1981 (1410). *Atlal* 6: 125–136, pls 105–123.

Author's address
Prof. Saad bin Abdulaziz al-Rashid, P.O. Box 85518, Riyadh 11612, Saudi Arabia.
E-mail salrashid@yahoo.com

Proceedings of the Seminar for Arabian Studies 38 (2008): 277–282

The jinn in Ḥaḍramawt society in the last century (1)

Mikhail Rodionov

Summary

This paper intends to characterize certain attitudes and practices of the local population with respect to a class of supernatural beings traditionally regarded as an integral part of human society. Using oral and written sources the author presents the human-jinn relations not in terms of folklore or magic but as the everyday practice of conflicts and alliances. The modern demonology of South Arabia is addressed by many scholars yet, as has been admitted more than once, much still remains to be done.

Keywords: jinn, Ḥaḍramawt, al-Quʿayṭī periodicals

The jinns as a category of reasonable beings created by God along with angels and humans are extensively covered in Islam and in Islamic studies. Usually seen as the richest demonological areas of the Islamic world, southern Arabia and northern Africa provide us with diverse data in this respect (Rodionov 1993; Frantzousoff 1993). For Yemen in general and Ḥaḍramawt in particular, we have the famous account of seventh-eleventh-century Arabia in Ibn al-Mujāwir's *Tāʾrīkh al-Mustabṣir* introduced and commented by G. Rex Smith (1985; 1988; 1990; 1995). In 1995 a number of articles edited by Anne Regourd appeared in *Quaderni di Studi Arabi* (vol. 13) under the title "Divination, magie, pouvoirs au Yemen". In her article Silvaine Camelin (1995) depicts various contacts between traditional social groups of the town of al-Shiḥr in Ḥaḍramawt, on the one hand, with the world of jinns on the other; the latter world seems to our author to be totally separated from that of the humans. In the local belief system, however, these two worlds form a rather integral entity. Oral narratives and written texts allow us to present the human-jinn relations not in terms of folklore or magic, but as the everyday practice of conflicts and alliances.

Whereas the written sources are limited, the relevant field information — abundant as it may be — often appears oblique and/or ambiguous. Indeed local people treat this topic reluctantly and with a specific mixture of laughter and apprehension. Nevertheless, some personalities are reputed to have regular connections with jinns. Among them is a friend of mine, al-sayyid Ḥusayn Bin Shaykh Bū Bakr, a miller and a petty landowner of Khuraykhar, Jidfirah, and al-Quzah, which are three villages in Wādī Dawʿan (Fig. 1). For twenty-five years he has been extraordinarily helpful to the Russian scientific mission in Yemen: it was he who noticed in 1983 some rough stones which appeared to be the stone tools of the Olduvai men settled in a cave near al-Quzah; it was he who discovered in 1989 near Khuraykhar a hoard of more than 500 copper pre-Islamic local coins, and it was Ḥusayn who provided me with valuable information on bee-keeping, folk medicine, ibex-hunt rituals, etc.

His neighbours maintain that Ḥusayn started his relations with jinns after recovering from a serious illness during his pilgrimage to Mecca. They are almost certain that he uses jinns at least for delivering mail and some goods. He is said to pay the jinns in cash for their services, "asking them to do so-and-so in a language which is neither Arabic, nor English" and letting a banknote glide into the air: if it disappears, the jinns will run errands for him.

Collective tradition believes that alliances and cooperation between jinns and humans (mostly from the *sādah* and *mashāyikh* social strata) are less frequent than conflicts. Half a century ago some of these conflicts were covered in the local periodicals.

On 23 Rabīʿ al-Awwal 1373/30 November 1953 in issue 11 of the monthly *majallah al-Akbār*, the official edition of the al-Quʿayṭī sultanate published in al-Mukallā by sayyid Ḥusayn Muḥammad al-Bār in 1953–1954, the most important foreign news was the demise of the

FIGURE 1. *Al-Sayyid Ḥusayn Bin Shaykh Bū Bakr.*

٦

العدد الحادى عشر — الأخبار — السنة الاولى

رئيس تحريرها المسؤل
حسين محمد البار
العنوان ادارة النشر بالمكلا
لا تعاد الرسائل لأربابها
نشرت أم لم تنشر

الأخبار
مجلة شهرية
لسان حال الحكومة القعيطية
بحضرموت

الأشتراك السنوى
فى الداخل ٨ شلن
الخارج ١٢
الأعلانات يتفق بشأنها
مع الأدارة

المكلا ٢٣ ربيع اول سنة ١٣٧٣ هـ موافق ٣٠ نوفمبر سنة ١٩٥٣ م

الذكرى الخالدة

احتفلت بلاد العالم الأسلامى فى هذا الشهر بذكرى مولد الرسول الأعظم محمد بن عبدالله (ص) تلك الذكرى الخالدة التى تحمل إلى أقطار الأسلام فى كل عام نفحات عطرة من انفاس النبوة التى حررت العالم من العبوديات . وطهرت الأنسال من الأوشاب والأرجاس . وسمت بعقله وفكره وعقيدته إلى مقام كريم . واحتفلت هذه البلاد فى الداخل والساحل والقرى والمدن بهذه الذكرى العظيمة . التى إتخذت منها الدولة القعيطية عيداً من اعيادها الرسمية . تعطل فيه المصالح والمدارس . وترفع الأعلام . ويقوم الجيش النظامى بجولاته لأستعراضية فى طول المدينة وعرضها . وقد أقيمت للمناسبة العسكرية عدة حفلات أهمها حفلة القصر السلطانى التى حضرها كبار رجال الدولة وعلى رأسهم مولانا صاحب العظمة سلطان البلاد . وقد اقيمت كالمعتاد فى ساحة القصر وهرعت العاصمة كلها لشهودها . وافتتحت بقراءة برنامجها من قبل عزة الشيخ مسلم بن عوض بلعلا ثم قراءة ماتيسر من آى الذكر الحكيم . تلاها الشيخ صالح سلوم ثم تلاوة قصة المولد النبوى من قبل الشيخ عبد الرحمن باعشن وبعد ذلك تبارى الخطباء فافتتح الكلام فضيلة رئيس القضاة الشرعيين الشيخ عبدالله بن عوض بكير بكلمة جامعة وتلاه فضيلة الشيخ محمد عبد الله باجنيد بكلمة تحدث فيها عن (نشأة الرسول قبل البعثة) وتلاه السيد الأديب احمد محمد العطاس فتحدث عن حياة الرسول فى الفتره الواقعه بين البعثة والهجرة والشيخ عبدالله سعيد باعنقود وكان حديثه عن حياة الرسول منذ الهجره إلى الوفاة وقد اختتم هذا الحفل شاعر الدولة الشيخ عبدالله احمد الناخبى

FIGURE 2. *The front page of Al-Akbār, No. 11, 23 Rabīᶜ al-Awwal 1373/30 November 1953.*

"falcon of Arabia", King ᶜAbd al-ᶜAzīz Āl Saᶜūd (Fig. 2). Among the domestic information one can read about new regulations on district administrative councils commented by the prolific scholar Muḥammad ᶜAbd al-Qādir Bā Maṭraf. Most of the readers also discussed a short article on page 12 (Fig. 3). It reads as follows:

"A mischievous ᶜIfrīt in Ḥajr intimidates the village Miḥmidah

Nowadays the people of the Ḥajr district are talking only about a malicious ᶜIfrīt who brought fear and anxiety not only to the Miḥmidah section but to all sections of the Ḥajr district (*liwā*ᵓ) in general. The locals cannot compare these bizarre happenings with anything that has taken place either recently or in the remote past. Reports from trustworthy sources, both official and private, agree that the ᶜIfrīt has left his jar in order to get hold of the house of two sheikhs, Muḥammad and ᶜAbdallāh, sons of ᶜAlī Bā ᶜAbdallāh al-ᶜAmūdī, not with the object of using it as a residence, as it is the case with many oppressors of this kind, but rather to eradicate the family and to oust it from their mansion where they have been living quite properly for a long time.

Thus a war between both sides started with the military actions of shelling the inhabitants of this peaceful house with stones, fire and filth. And blood was shed: children were scared and the hearts of women trembled. Men of the house and men of the village rose against oppression to repulse the invasion. But he rebuffed all their efforts with weird tricks and dances at the thresholds of rooms, acting out of his invisible world and waging the war on. The Mārid [= the ᶜIfrīt] took possession of females' jewellery, dresses and utensils and threw them outside from windows and the roof. He added filth into food and beverages. The inhabitants of the house, the village and the entire district failed to resist and to stop the Mārid's evil deeds. Finally the family deserted their house and appealed to the authorities of their region. At the meeting attended by the sultan's representative ᶜAbd Ḥamad, the police lieutenant Muḥammad Nāṣir and the villagers, all of them at last made a complaint to the sultan's representative at Ḥajr from the depth of their souls asking for help and to restore justice. Meanwhile they got from the Mārid nothing but choleric laughter and stones launched at them as if it was petrified rain. People returned and made their reports to the office of the Secretary of State. The family asked for a mental examination seeking peaceful agreement between the village and the Mārid. That is the news from the Miḥmidah section of Ḥajr, and that is the most bizarre thing that took place in this country. Experts in mental problems say they have no information about such a phenomenon but there is a connection [between this incident] and the strange and exciting stories told by the inhabitants of Wādī al-Khaṣīb."

An external reader may take this article for nothing more than a joke deriding superstition either in a positivist Western outlook of the 1950s or a modernist Islamic trend of the local Irshādī movement. However my Ḥaḍramī informants, including ᶜAbdallāh al-Bār, a literary critic and a son of the first editor of *al-Akhbār*, took the article rather seriously, saying that up to the present day Miḥmidah has been notorious for such incidents (Fig. 4).

The rivalry between the naughty cunning demon (*ᶜifrīt*), also called in the article a rebel giant (*mārid*), and the *mashāyikh* al-ᶜAmūdī may be explained by the fact that the Ḥajr district is populated by Ḥajūr, an ethno-social group of African origin who still retain some African demonological traditions even today, whereas the al-ᶜAmūdī clan is proud that their ancestor Sheikh Saᶜīd brought Sufism to Ḥaḍramawt as a disciple of Abū Madyan al-Maghribī (d. 592/1195-96). One may also suppose that houses and land in Miḥmidah are rather valuable since the village is situated in a cultivated valley — as is also the case with Wādī al-Khaṣīb ("the fertile wadi") mentioned in the article and Wādī Duhr, a summer residence of the Zaidi imams. The Austrian scholar Andre Gingrich remarked that, in contrast to the Sunni-Shāfiᶜī of the south, the Zaidis of the north were less tolerant of beliefs in the jinn world (1995: 200). In a way the Yemeni poet and scholar ᶜAbdallāh al-Baradūnī contradicts this when he talks about the imam Yaḥyā's relationship with the jinns (Taminian 2000: 220–226). According to him, the imam declared that a tribe of jinns residing at Jabal Nuqum (another area of the jinns is Wādī ᶜAbqar somewhere in the south) was among his subjects and when their sheikh was declared to have been

ص — ١٢ — الأخبار السنة الأولى

* بلغ عدد الكائن في منطقة القطن وحدها مايزيد على ٦٥ مكينة . وقد أقبل الناس على شراء هذه الآلات حتى بلغت الطلبات المقدمة إلى قائم القطن ٣٠ طلبا لثلاثين آلة رافعة ويقدر ماتستهلكه الكينة في البذر ١٢٠ مكيا لاً من القمح
* عقد الأستاذ قحطان الشعبي ناظر الزرعة في منطقة الداخل مؤتمراً زراعياً حضره أعضاء المجالس المحليه في المنطقتين القعيطية والكثيرية . وقدشرفه بالحضور سكرتير الدوله الكثيرية بالنيابة . ونائب السكرتير . ونائب لواء شبام وقائم القطن . وقد القى فيه الأستاذ الشعبي تفاصيل وافيه عماقام به من التجاريب الزراعية . وعرض فيه المحرات الحديث الذى جاء به اخيراً وتحدث حديثا مسهباً عن هذا الحرات وعدم تكاليفه بالنظر إلى مايصرفه الزارعون على فلاحة الأرض جريا على سابق عادتهم . وقد عقد مقارنة وافية بين طريقة استعماله . وبين الطريقة العتيقة في أعمال الفلاحة انتهى منها إلى تعداد محاسنها . وضرورتها للاعمال التقدمية في زراعة البلاد .

العفريت الساخر في حجر

ينشر الرعب بقرية محمده

* لاحديث للناس في لواء حجر بهذه الأيام الاحديث ذلك العفريت الخطير ـ الذى نشر الرعب والقلق في مقاطعة محمده . بل وفي جميع مقاطعات لواء حجر نظراً للاعمال الغريبه التي قام بها والتي لم يشهد أهالي هذه البلادلها مثيلا في تاريخهم القريب اوالبعيد . فقد تضافرت الأنباء الوارده من عدة مصادر موثوق بها رسمية وغير رسميه بان العفريت قد انطلق من القمقم ليحتل منزل الشيخين محمد وعبدالله ابني على باعبد الله العمودى . لابقصد السكنى كما يحدث لكثير من امثاله ابناء الظلام ولكن ليقتلع جذور هذه الأسرة الهادئة من منزلها الذى عاشت فيه زمنا طويلا دون ان يحدث مايعكر اصفاءه
* وتبدأ الحرب بين الطرفين وتبدأ عمليات قذف افراد السكان سكان المنزل الوادع بالحجاره . والنار . وبالقاذورات . فتسيل الدماء . ويهلع الأطفال وتنخلع قلوب النساء . ويهب رجال المنزل ورجال من القريه للانقاذ أولرد العدوان فيقابل الارد كل ذلك بضحكات ساخره يرسلها ورقصات على أعتاب الحجرات يقوم بها من عالمه غير المنظور وتتطور الحرب فيعمد المارد الى حلى النساء وملابسهن والى اثاث المنزل فيقذفها إلى خارج المنزل من النوافذ والسطوح ويعمد الى القاذورات فيضعها في الطعام والشراب وهنا تكون المقاومة مقاومة سكان المنزل ـ وسكان القريه وسكان اللواء كله قد عجزت عن إيقاف المارد عند حده . فتهجر الأسره منزلها وتتصل بالرجال المسؤلين في المقاطعه فيحضر قائم الدوله عبد حمد ويحضر الملازم الشرطي محمد ناصر ويحضر معهم رجال من القريه ويحضر بعد كل هؤلاء وأولئك نائب الدوله بحجر على صيحات الأستغاثه الصادره من الأعماق للنجده وللتحقيق فلايظفرون من المارد بغير الضحكات الصفراء وبغير الحجاره يقذفهم بها كالمطر المنهمر . فيعود القوم أدراجهم . ويرفع النبا الى سكرتارية الدوله وتتجه الأسرة الى البحث عن روحاني يعقد صلحاً بين القريه والمارد . هذه الأنباء من مقاطعة محمده بحجر وهى اغرب ماشهدته تلك البلاد نشرها ليقول علماء الأرواح ما عندهم حول هذه الظاهره وهل لها علاقة بقصة غريبه مثيره يتحدث بها سكان الوادى الخصيب

الأخبار
مجلة شهرية لسان حال الحكومة القعيطية بحضرموت
الإشتراك السنوى في الداخل ٨ شلن الخارج ١٢
العنوان إدارة النشر بالمكلا حضرموت .

FIGURE 3. *Al-Akbār, No. 11, p. 12.*

killed, the imam ordered the citizens of Ṣanaᶜāᵓ to tar the front doors of their homes and to dye their faces when going outside in order to protect themselves against the jinns. During the civil war of 1962–1970, the Republican poet al-Dhahbānī wrote a satirical poem on this topic. In the aforementioned Wādī Duhr a house spirit behaved himself exactly in a manner depicted in the cited article from "al-Akhbār". By hook or by crook the house spirit tried to throw a certain merchant al-Masᶜūdī out of his house. The conflict was solved only when the imam sent to the jinns a team of respectable arbitrators comprising ᶜAbd al-Karīm al-Muttahar, the editor of the first Yemeni newspaper "al-Imān", and the imam's son al-Ḥasan as the Commander-in-Chief of the Royal armed forces.

It is not my task to discuss the factual authenticity of the incidents in Miḥmidah in the south and Wādī Duhr in the north. In both cases a conflict between the world of humans and the world of the jinns was approached by the traditional technique of mediation (*wisāṭah*) in order to demonstrate the power of a human government. As applied by the al-Quᶜayṭī sultan's authorities, it failed,

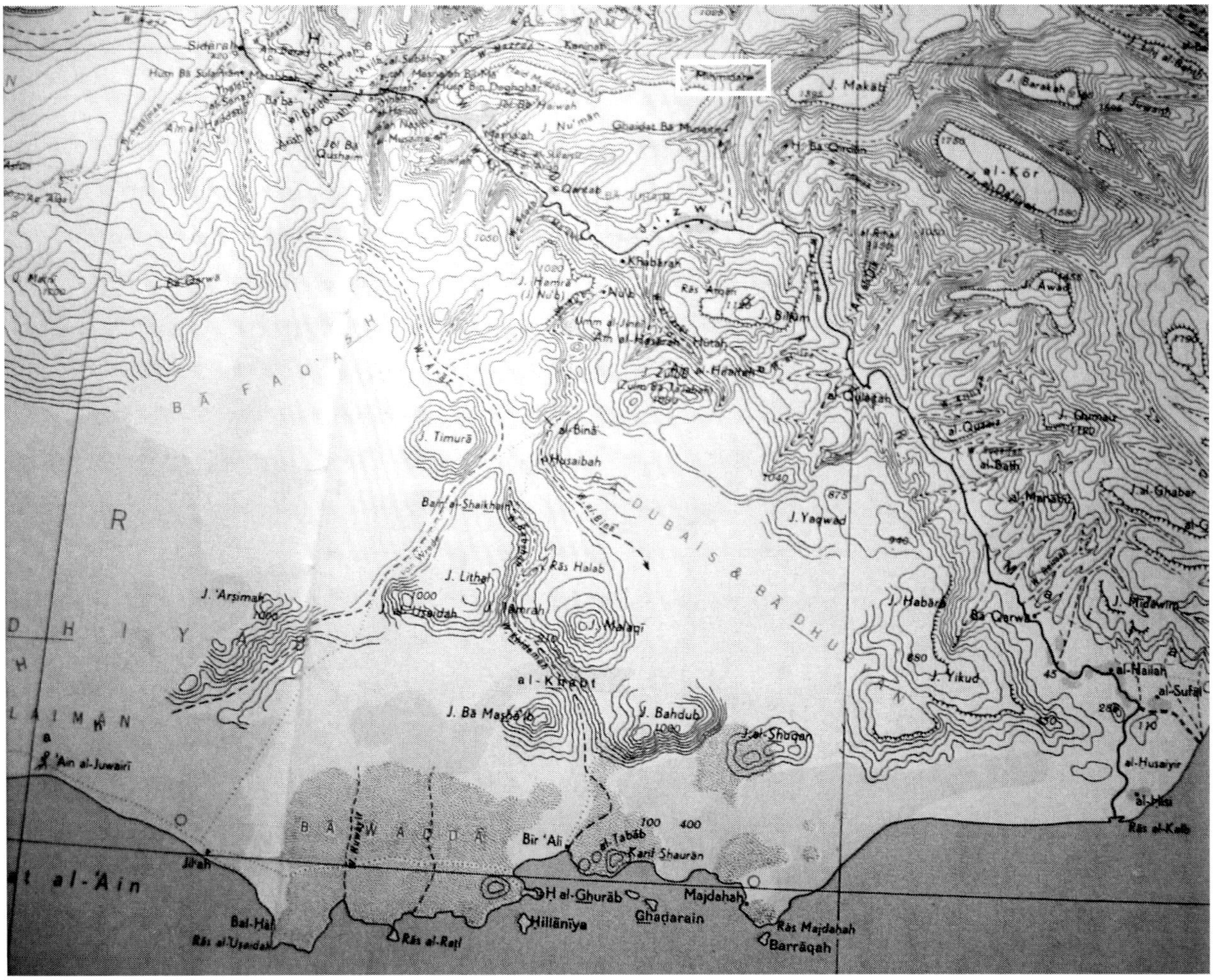

Figure 4. *The village of Miḥmidah (denoted by white rectangle). Map source: H. von Wissmann South Arabia. Part of Aden Protectorate from Shuqra to al-Shihr and Baihan to Hadramaut. Published by the Royal Geographical Society. 1957-1958.*

but as applied by the imam Yaḥyā's arbitrators it was a success, at least for a while.

One can ignore these narratives of the last century or label the jinns as poltergeists, etc. For many Ḥaḍramī people, however, the jinns formed a part of their everyday life. In that sense of cultural cosmos, including the worlds of angels, humans and jinns are real as far as our collective imagination is a part of social reality.

Note

1 This paper was supported by the 2007–2009 INTAS grant; project "Elucidation of features of pre-Islamic religion in modern rites and beliefs of Yemen".

References

Camelin S.
1995. Croyance aux jinns et possession dans le Hadramaout. Pages 159–180 in A. Regourd (ed.), Divination, magie, pouvoirs au Yemen. *Quaderni di Studi Arabi* 13.

Frantzousoff S.
1993. Superstitions and Sorcery Rites in South Arabia 13th to 15th centuries. Pages 7–19 in M. Rodionov & M. Serebryakova (eds), *Traditional World Outlook of the Peoples of Western Asia*. Moscow: Vostochnaya Literatura. [In Russian].
Gingrich A.
1995. Some remarks on the Connotation of Jinn in North-Western Yemen. Pages 199–212 in A. Regourd (ed.), Divination, magie, pouvoirs au Yemen. *Quaderni di Studi Arabi* 13.
Rodionov M.
1993. Pages 3–6 in M. Rodionov & M. Serebryakova (eds), *Traditional World Outlook of the Peoples of Western Asia*. Moscow: Vostochnaya Literatura. [In Russian].
Smith G.R.
1985. Ibn al-Mujāwir on Dhofar and Socotra. *Proceedings of the Seminar for Arabian Studies*. 15: 79–93.
1988. Ibn al-Mujāwir's 7th/13th century Arabia — the wondrous and the humorous. Pages 111–125 in A.K. Irvine, R.B. Serjeant & G. R. Smith (eds), *A Miscellany of Middle Eastern articles — in memoriam Thomas Muir Johnstone 1924–83*. Harlow: Longman.
1990. Ibn al-Mujāwir's 7th/13th guide to Arabia: the eastern connection. *Occasional Papers of the School of Abbasid Studies* (St Andrews) 3: 71–89.
1995. Magic, jinn, and the Supernatural in Medieval Yemen: examples from Ibn al-Mujāwir's 7th/13th century guide. Pages 7–18 in A. Regourd (ed.), Divination, magie, pouvoirs au Yemen. *Quaderni di Studi Arabi* 13.
Taminian L.
2000. *Yemeni Sana'ani Poetry*. PhD dissertation, Ann Arbor, MI. [Unpublished].

Author's address
Mikhail Rodionov, Tul'skaya Street 8, app. 2, St. Petersburg, 191124, Russia.
e-mail mrodio@yandex.ru

Proceedings of the Seminar for Arabian Studies 38 (2008): 283–288

The Indian ships at Moscha and the Indo-Arabian trading circuit

Eivind Heldaas Seland

Summary

Periplus Maris Erythraei, the first-century AD merchant's guide written in Greek, mentions ships sailing from India calling at Moscha Limên, which is generally identified as Sumhuram/Khor Rori in modern Oman. These ships are said to have spent the winter at Moscha "because of the late season" (*Periplus* 32), and modern commentators have considered them to be Indian ships on their way home after trading voyages to Arabia. While this is probably true, it might not be the whole truth. There should be no need to spend two sailing seasons for a return trip from India to Arabia, and different passages in the *Periplus* and other classical literature, combined with later Arab and European experiences with Indian Ocean navigation, build a case for these ships being ready to set out on the last leg of a wider Indian Ocean circuit. This sheds new light on the maritime contacts of the Arabian Peninsula in antiquity and on the economy of the port of Moscha/Khor Rori.

Keywords: Indian Ocean, navigation, Khor Rori, monsoon trade, *Periplus of the Erythraean Sea*, Arabia

In its description of the Arabian coast, the first-century Roman merchant's guide *Periplus Maris Erythraei* describes the port of Moscha Limên. The port has generally been identified with the site of Khor Rori in the Dhofar region of modern Oman. (1) Khor Rori was discovered by Theodore Bent in 1895. The site was first excavated by the American Foundation for the Study of Man in the early 1950s and since the 1990s has been the focus of investigations by the Italian Mission to Oman directed by Professor A. Avanzini.

In the *Periplus* (sec. 32), Moscha is described as a "designated harbour (*hórmos apodedeigménos*) for loading the Sachalite frankincense", "Sachalitês" being the name of the region. Still, the settlement does not figure among the major ports of call in the commerce between southern Arabia and the Mediterranean, unlike Muza on the Red Sea coast or Kanê near modern Bir Ali, and neither is it described as a stopping place on the route from Egypt to India, as are Okêlis at the straits of Bab el-Mandeb and Eudaimôn Arabia (modern Aden). Instead we learn that Moscha was frequented by "some vessels ... customarily sent to it from Kanê; in addition those sailing by (*parapléonta*) from Limyrikê or Barygaza that passed the winter (*paracheimásanta*) because of the season being late (*opsinoîs kairoîs*)". These ships "take on a return cargo (*antiphortízousin*)" of local frankincense in exchange for cloth, grain, and oil.

Limyrikê was the Greek name for the Malabar Coast and Barygaza was an important market near modern Broach in Gujarat. The *Periplus*, however, only reports that the ships sailed by from these places, and there is no textual reason to conclude that they were Indian, Arabian, or Roman. The question has received only limited attention in the past, but that does not mean that it is unimportant. While modern labels of nationality and ethnicity may be of little help when describing the origins and cultural identities of the people involved in a cosmopolitan Indian Ocean trade, sea-going ships were complex and involved expensive technology, and they had to be built, equipped, financed, owned, and operated from somewhere. An investigation into the origin of the ships at Moscha can help us determine the role of that enigmatic port in a wider context than the frankincense trade to which it is normally connected.

Commentators and translators have assumed that these ships were either Arabian or Roman ships returning home from India (Schoff 1995: 35; Warmington 1995: 342, n. 2; Wheeler 1955: 144; Albright 1982: 9) or Indian ships that were delayed on the last leg of their homeward journey. Lionel Casson, in favour of the last view, seems to have a valid point when he writes that "there was no reason for returning Arab craft to stop and winter at Moscha; winter was precisely the time when they did return from India, not only to Arabia, but to anywhere west of it" (Casson

1989: 172–173).

Casson's argument is based on the well-known fact that any sailing on the Indian Ocean is determined by the monsoon system. The monsoons provide stable and strong winds from the south-west in the summer and from the north-east in the winter. This offers the opportunity for passage from all ports of the Arabian Sea and back again in the course of a year. The periods of changing and weak winds between the monsoons, sailing against the wind and along the coasts offer some alternatives, but the main sailing seasons are determined by the monsoons. This applied to ancient shipping regardless of ships being Indian, Arabian, or Roman just as much as it did to later Arab and European navigation in the Indian Ocean. Combining the information in the *Periplus* with later Arab and European experiences of Indian Ocean navigation enables us to shed light on how the Indian ships ended up in Moscha and what they were doing here. This opens a window on areas of the ancient monsoon trade wider than simply trade between the Roman Empire, India, and Arabia, and diversifies our impression of the economy of Moscha/Khor Rori.

Ancient sources provide a straightforward set of rules for using the monsoons. The *Periplus* recommends leaving Egyptian ports in July for all destinations in the Indian Ocean (sec. 14, 39, 49, 56). As with later Arab and British practice (see below) they would probably not start their Indian Ocean crossing until August. In this way they would avoid the worst storms of the south-west monsoon in June and July, when in later periods, ports were closed both in India and Arabia (Thornton 1703: 30; Tibbetts 1981: 226, 227–228, 230). Pliny (6.106) reports that ships set out on the return voyage from India between the start of December and mid-January. By doing this they would arrive at the mouth of the Red Sea in time to catch favourable southerlies there in January and February (NIMA 2001: January–February). The report that the ships at Moscha had sailed out from Indian ports, combined with the statement that the ships "wintered" (*paracheimásanta*) at Moscha, would thus exclude the possibility that the ships were from Roman Egypt and makes it very unlikely that they were from Arabia, this supports Casson's conclusion (1989: 173). Albright (1982: 9) rightly points out that "winter" is hardly the same in Dhofar as it is in the Mediterranean and suggests that *paracheimásanta* should be read simply as "lay over there". While this is certainly conceivable, the sailing schedule described above gives us no reason not to take the text at face value. In conclusion: if ships wintered in Dhofar, they were probably from India and that means that they were on their way home when they called at Moscha.

Why did these ships have to spend the winter in Dhofar? Later texts from the Indian Ocean give some hints. For the voyage from India to the west, Ibn Majid's famous navigational handbook from the late fifteenth century recommends sailing from India (Gujarat and Konkan) to all western destinations from 18th October onwards or day 330 of the navigational year based on the Persian calendar (Tibbetts 1981: 361–362). Ships going from Malabar waited until March (100th–130th day) due to heavy rain (1981: 230–231). This would bring Indian ships to Arabia, Socotra, Somalia, and the Red Sea any time during the winter. For their return voyage Ibn Majid recommends using the start of the south-west monsoon, called by him "the end of the sailing season" until 11th May (Tibbetts 1981: 225) because the full strength of the south-west monsoon closed the ports on the Malabar and Konkan coasts (1981: 226). During this period Ibn Majid advises any sensible man to stay ashore (1981: 227–228). Another window opened for the passage from Arabia to India from the 280th–300th day of the navigational year (29th August–18th September) (1981: 226), using the end of the south-west monsoon, representing "the beginning of the sailing season" to Ibn Majid (1981: 226). After this it was difficult to sail from Arabia (and the western coasts of the Arabian Sea) to India until April–May of the next year. In short this means that Indian ships, e.g. from Malabar, waiting until January (Pliny) or February–March (Ibn Majid) would have had a hard time catching the "end of the sailing season" opportunity to return to India before 11th May, and would have had to use the "beginning of the sailing season" in August–September. This is why the late or unlucky sailor might have had to winter in Arabia.

Ibn Majid gives little information on the August–September passage from Arabia to India, but his report can be corroborated by the experiences of European navigators of the seventeenth and nineteenth centuries.

Carsten Niebuhr took passage on a British ship from Mokha to Bombay in 1763. His ship left on 23rd August, entered the Arabian Sea through Bab el-Mandeb on 25th August and arrived in Bombay on 11th September, sailing by way of Cape Guardafui, which he passed around 30th August. On 23rd August, Niebuhr's ship was the last of all the Indian and English ships leaving that year, and Niebuhr's captain, J. Martin, would have left earlier if he could, because the winds were changing (Niebuhr 1774: 447–452).

John Thornton was a former captain and navigator of

the East India Company. In 1703 he published the third volume of his *English Pilot*, dealing with the routes to Indian Ocean destinations. Thornton includes his own experiences in his accounts of the Indian Ocean routes, and gives us several interesting pieces of information with regard to the passage between Arabia and India.

Thornton recommends using the end of the south-west monsoon, just as the ship Niebuhr travelled on did, and he writes that the monsoon lasts until the start of September (1703: 31). He also recounts his own experience from the end of August 1690, when he was on a ship bound for Muscat, but lost his passage and had to winter in Dhofar before going from there to India (1703: 31). Adding eleven days — as England was still on the Julian calendar at this time — this brings us to approximately the time when Carsten Niebuhr was already arriving in Bombay in the last ship of the 1763 season. The warnings issued by Ibn Majid (Tibbetts 1981: 227), Thornton (1703: 31), and Niebuhr (1774: 447–448) about missing the passage to India indicate that this was no infrequent occurrence.

Thornton had to spend the winter in Dhofar, and he did that for a reason. Ibn Majid states that if you were held up on your way to India and were able to wait out the north-east monsoon at al-Shihr or Fartak you would only have to wait for four months, but if you wintered in Yemen, and by that he includes both a number of Red Sea ports and Aden, you would have to wait for a full year (Tibbetts 1981: 227). So the further east you were able to winter, the better off you were. This must have been a strong motivation to winter in the Dhofar region. In 1703 Thornton reports that, "About 8 or 10 leagues to the eastwards of Dofar lies Maribatt, where many ships have gone when they have lost their passage" (sic). This brings us very close to Khor Rori, which is situated between modern Maribat and modern Salalah, and which must have been an excellent, sheltered harbour, if the inlet, which is now blocked by a sandbar, was more accessible in the ancient period than it is today.

So Dhofar was an attractive place to wait out the north-east monsoon in the late seventeenth century, in the late fifteenth century, and to believe the *Periplus* account of Moscha, even in the first century. This should not surprise us, as the basic conditions laid down by the monsoons were the same. This tells us that Moscha was not the isolated outpost that the *Periplus* describes it as but — at least under certain circumstances — a natural port of call on the Indian Ocean circuit. If we can assume that at least some Indian ships lost their passage every year, their annual presence at Moscha must have had an influence on the local economy.

But why would Indian ships risk losing the passage home to India, thus involving several months' involuntary stay in Dhofar when they could easily have done the Arabia to India circuit in the winter–spring, using the start of the south-west monsoon for their return as Ibn Majid recommends (Tibbetts 1981: 225–226)? I suggest that Moscha was among the last stops on a larger circuit that required more time.

The *Periplus* reports Indian shipping or trade with India, either in the writer's own time or as a thing of the past, at Socotra (sec. 31), ports in northern Somalia (sec. 14), Adulis in Eritrea (sec. 6), Muza (sec. 21), Aden (sec. 26), and finally Moscha (sec. 32). The considerable finds of Indian pottery at Berenikê opens the possibility that Indian merchants also frequented Egyptian ports (Sidebotham & Wendrich 1999: 452–453; Begley & Tomber 1999).

The Indian Ocean Directory by A.G. Findlay incorporates British navigation experience until the transition from sail to steam, but the fourth edition from 1882 is still for the most part geared towards sail technology. For the India–Aden/Red Sea passage Findlay recommends a route just north of Socotra during most of the north-east monsoon (1882: 174, map facing p. 155) and just south of Socotra in the March–April transitional period (1882: 170, 174). While English merchants found little of interest in Socotra (Thornton 1703: 7), it would be a convenient first stop on a trading circuit for ships sailing out from India, as attested both by the *Periplus* (sec. 31) and by Thornton (1703: 7). From there ships could continue to the Somali ports, visited both by ships sailing "principally to these ports of trade" and by those following the coast and taking on "whatever cargo comes their way", as the *Periplus* reports (sec. 14). The next leg would be up the Red Sea, which was available during the whole north-east monsoon. If the Indian ships arrived in the Red Sea in the spring, say March–April, which was the last advisable time according to Thornton (1703: 30), they would have a hard time returning through the straits to the Arabian Sea before Ibn Majid's "end of the sailing season" in May (Tibbetts 1981: 225–226). Heading for the Arabian Sea at Ibn Majid's "beginning of the sailing season" (1981: 226) in August and September, ancient navigators would run the same risk of losing their passage as Thornton and Niebuhr did in the eighteenth century. As demonstrated above, Dhofar and Moscha would then be an attractive place to spend the winter.

Seen against this general background of Indian Ocean

navigation, the case of the Indian ships at Moscha allows us to draw three conclusions about Moscha and one about the ancient Indian Ocean trade:

- Moscha/Khor Rori was integrated in an Indian Ocean–Red Sea trading circuit which provided the settlement with subsistence goods like cloth, oil, and grain (*Periplus* 32).
- Dhofar was an attractive region for the mooring of ships that had lost their passage to India. Moscha/Khor Rori was the only major settlement in Dhofar in this period. Its harbour would provide ships with safe mooring and its walls and warehouses would give sailors necessary safety for life and property.
- Security normally comes at a price. The presence of wintering ships in Dhofar could provide additional motivation for the Ḥaḍramī kings to establish and maintain the settlement at Moscha/Khor Rori, although frankincense production is likely to have been the primary motivation.
- The old notion that only Greek and Roman ships dared to sail the passage with the south-west monsoon (Hourani 1995: 27–28; Raschke 1978: 655–657; Casson 1989: 290–291) should be discarded. If the Romans left their Egyptian harbours in July, they would hardly enter the Indian Ocean from the Red Sea much earlier than the English did in the seventeenth and eighteenth centuries. The Indian ships wintering at Moscha in the first century were certainly using the same south-west monsoon as Roman ships and as the British ships in risk of losing their passage in the eighteenth century.

Notes

1 The identification was first proposed by Bent (1895: 125) and has since been supported by the archaeological missions working on the site (Albright 1982: 7; Avanzini 2002: 20); but see also von Wissmann (1977), Groom (1995: 184–186), and Costa (2002: 24–25) who object to this identification.

Sigla

NIMA	National Imagery and Mapping Agency.
Periplus	The *Periplus Maris Erythraei* in the edition of Casson 1989.

References

Albright F.P.
1982. *The American Archaeological Expedition in Dhofar, Oman.* (Publications of the American Foundation for the Study of Man, 6). Washington, DC: American Foundation for the Study of Man.

Avanzini A. (ed.)
2002. *Khor Rori Report I.* (Arabia Antica, 1). Pisa: Edizioni Plus.

Begley V. & Tomber R.
1999. Indian Pottery Sherds. Pages 161–182 in S.E. Sidebotham & W.Z. Wendrich (eds), *Berenike 1997. Report of the 1997 Excavations at Berenike and the Survey of the Egyptian Eastern Desert, including Excavations at Shenshef.* Leiden: Universiteit Leiden.

Bent T.J.
1895. Exploration of the Frankincense Country, Southern Arabia. *Geographical Journal* 6/2: 109–133.

Casson L. (ed. and transl.)
1989. *The Periplus Maris Erythraei.* Princeton: Princeton University Press.

Costa P.M.
2002. The South Arabian Coast and the Ancient Trade Routes in light of recent exploration and a discussion of the written sources. Pages 19–27 in L. Healy and V. Porter (eds), *Studies on Arabia in Honour of Professor G. Rex Smith.* Oxford: Oxford University Press.

Groom N.
1995. The Periplus, Pliny and Arabia. *Arabian Archaeology and Epigraphy* 6: 180–195.

Hourani G.F.
1995. *Arab Seafaring.* (Second edition). Princeton: Princeton University Press.

Findlay A.G.
1882. *A Directory for the Navigation of the Indian Ocean.* (Fourth edition). London: Richard Holmes Laurie.
National Imagery and Mapping Agency (NIMA)
2001. *PUB 109 Atlas of Pilot Charts for the Indian Ocean.* (Fourth edition). Culver City, CA: National Imagery and Mapping Agency.
Niebuhr C.
1774. *Carsten Niebuhrs Reisebeschreibung nach Arabien und andeen umliegenden Ländern.* Copenhagen: Friedrich Perthes/Hamburg: Nicolaus Möller.
Pliny/ed. and transl. H. Rackham
1997–2001. *Natural History.* (Loeb Classical Library). Cambridge, MA: Harvard University Press.
Raschke M.G.
1978. New Studies in Roman Commerce with the East. Pages 604–1361 in H. Temporini & W. Haase (eds), *Aufstieg und Niedergang der Römischen Welt* 2.9.2. Berlin: Walter De Gruyter.
Schoff W.H.
1995. *The Periplus of the Erythraean Sea — Travel and trade in the Indian Ocean by a merchant of the first century.* Delhi: Munshiram Manoharlal [Reprint of the 1912 edition].
Sidebotham S.E. & Wendrich W.Z. (eds)
1999. *Berenike 1997. Report of the 1997 Excavations at Berenike and the Survey of the Egyptian Eastern Desert, including Excavations at Shenshef.* Leiden: Universiteit Leiden.
Thornton J.
1703. *The English Pilot, the third book.* London: John Thornton.
Tibbetts G.R.
1981. *Arab Navigation in the Indian Ocean Before the Coming of the Portuguese being a translation of Kitāb al-Fawā'id fī uṣūl al-baḥr wa'l-qawā'id of Aḥmad b. Mājid al-Najdī.* London: The Royal Asiatic Society of Great Britain and Ireland. [Reprint of the 1971 edition].
Warmington E.H.
1995. *The Commerce Between the Roman Empire and India.* New Delhi: Munshiram Manoharlal. [Reprint of the 1974 edition].
Wheeler M.
1955. *Rome Beyond the Imperial Frontiers.* (Second edition). Middlesex: Penguin Books.
Wissmann H. von
1977. *Das Weihrauchland Sa'kalan, Samarum und Moscha.* (Sitzungsberichte der Österreichische Akademie der Wissenschaften, Hist.-Phil. Klasse 324). Vienna: Akademie der Wissenschaften.

Author's address
Eivind Heldaas Seland, Department of Archaeology, History, Cultural Studies and Religion (AHKR), University of Bergen, P.O. Box 7805, N-5020 Bergen, Norway.
e-mail eivind.seland@ahkr.uib.no

Proceedings of the Seminar for Arabian Studies 38 (2008): 289–300

The Red Sea Tihami coastal ports in Saudi Arabia

Mohammed A.R. al-Thenayian

Summary
The main aim of this paper is to present the preliminary results of our survey conducted in 1991 along the eastern coast of the Red Sea in Saudi Arabia. This survey was confined to collecting samples of surface potsherds from the following five archaeological Islamic sites (from north to south): al-Sirrayn, ᶜUlyab (Ḥamdānah), Ḥaly, ᶜAṯṯar, and al-Šarjah which are all located on the eastern coastal sandy strip (Tihāmah) of the Red Sea in Saudi Arabia. (1)

Keywords: Islamic, pottery, Tihāmah, Red Sea, ports

Introduction

The following paper is a brief review of the geographic and historical context of the following five archaeological sites: al-Sirrayn, ᶜUlyab (Ḥamdānah), Ḥaly (b. Yaᶜqūb), ᶜAṯṯar, and al-Šarjah (Fig. 1). The importance of studying the pottery from these sites stems from the fact that all these sites were commercial coastal towns (ports) which used to receive imports as well as local products. In addition, they played a prominent historical role as sea and inland pilgrim way stations on the Yemeni and Omani pilgrim routes. (2)

The site of al-Sirrayn (Fig. 2)

The archaeological site of al-Sirrayn is located *c.* 40 km to the south of al-Liṯh city (40° 37' E, 19° 40' N). It is believed that the name (al-Sirrayn is a dual form of Sirr) is derived from the root *s-r-r* in the Ancient South Arabian Sabaic language (Beeston *et al.* 1982: 128). This interpretation conforms to the site's geographical layout where the two wadis of ᶜAlyab and Ḥalyah (Ḥaly) converged and the meaning accords with the mediaeval historian al-Fāsī's statement (1985, vi: 60) where he refers to al-Sirrayn by calling it "the two wadis" (*alwādiyayn*):

> *..., and he granted al-Sirrayn to his two brothers, Muǧāmis and Mubārak, he means that place which is well-known by the name of al-wādiyayn.*

In addition to its location on the Yemeni coastal and middle routes (*al-jāddah al-sulṭāniyyah*), the importance of al-Sirrayn stems from the fact that it was under the authority of Mecca's ruler and a main harbour for the regions of al-Ḥijāz and al-Sarāwāt (al-Yaᶜqūbī 2002: 154–155; Ibn Ḫurrdāḏabah 1889: 147–148; al-Ḥakamī 1985: 72). During the fourth/tenth centuries, the local economy of al-Sirrayn was mainly based on taxes (*mukūs*) levied by its ruler on ships loaded with goods, including slaves imported from or exported to Yemen (Ibn Ḥawqal [n.d.]: 33).

We may deduce from al-Maqdisī's description (1906: 69–70, 86) of al-Sirrayn during the last quarter of the fourth/tenth century that it was then a small walled town with a fort (*ḥiṣn*) containing the city's Friday mosque (*jāmiᶜ*), and a reservoir adjacent to its main gate. Furthermore, the city's administrative affairs were linked to ᶜAṯṯar. During the same century, al-Sirrayn appears as a major Red Sea harbour on Ibn Ḥawqal's map ([n.d.]: 28–30) of the Arabian Peninsula, along with other major harbours which he lists as follows: Aylah (al-ᶜAqabah), ᶜAynūnah, al-Jār, Jeddah, Ḥaly, al-Ḥamaḍah, ᶜAṯṯar, al-Šarjah, al-Ḥardah, Ǧulāfiqah, Mocha, Aden and Sāḥil Ḥaḍramawt. Before the end of the fifth/eleventh century, we understand that al-Sirrayn, including its harbour, was transformed into a large developed walled city with many markets (*aswāq*), baths (*ḥamāmāt*), and a Friday mosque constructed on the coast (al-Bakrī 1977: 48). Al-Sirrayn's prosperity continued throughout the following three centuries (i.e. from the sixth–eighth/twelfth–fourteenth centuries) and it became a secure fortified centre for merchants. Its fort and Friday mosque were noted by the

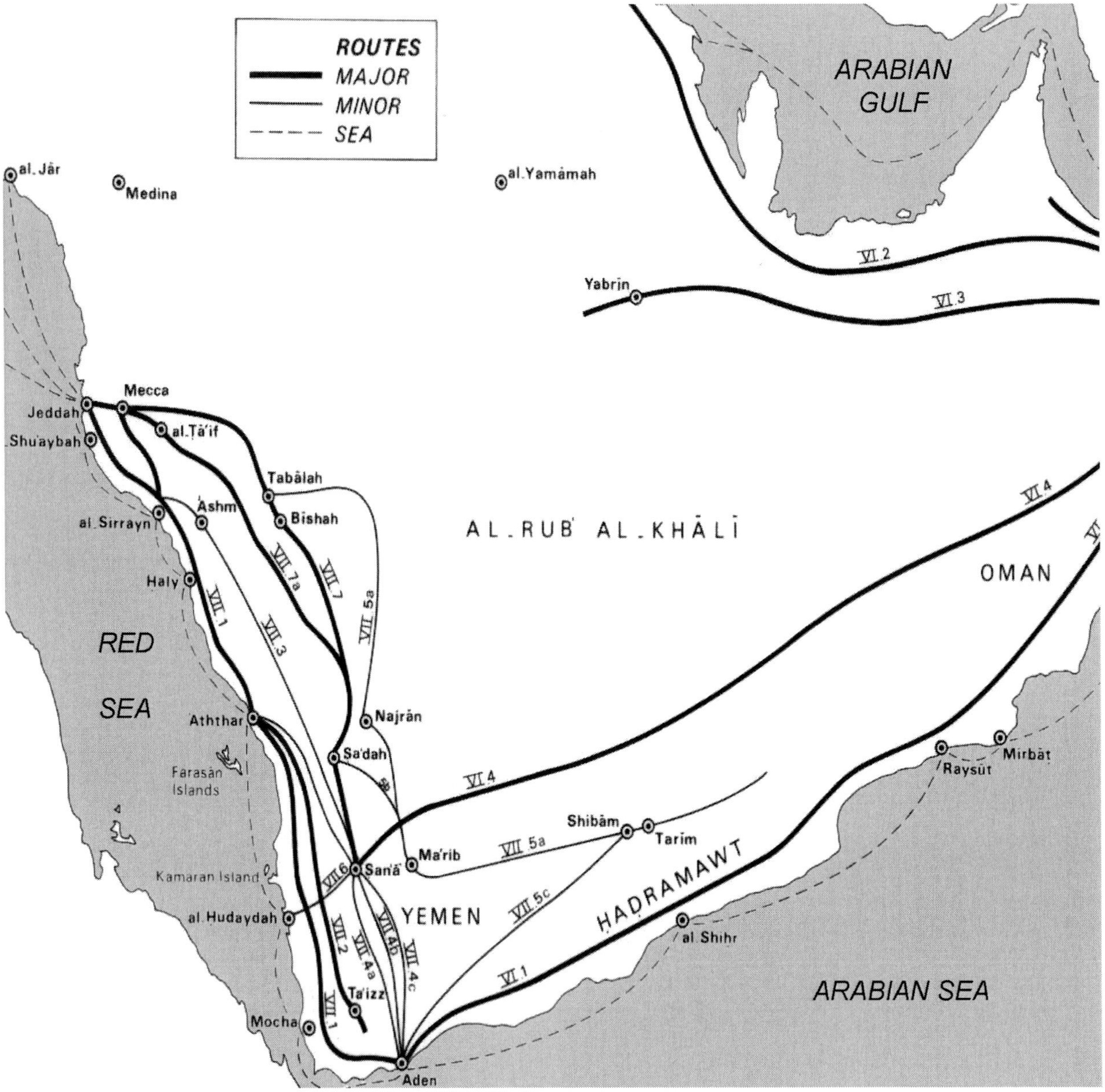

Figure 1. *A map of Arabia showing the sites discussed.*

early Arab geographers as architectural landmarks on the coast of the Red Sea (al-Idrīsī 1989, i: 132, 137–138, 145; cf. Mortel 1985: 94, 177).

As far as we are aware, there are no solid historical or archaeological data concerning the end of al-Sirrayn. Nevertheless, this must have occurred in the ninth/fifteenth century as it is absent from later historical chronicles.

Today a large part of the archaeological site of al-Sirryan is covered entirely with shifting sands. In addition to traces of construction clusters, archaeological mounds (tells) and the city's cemetery, the site's surface is littered with potsherds and broken fragments of red bricks. The city's cemetery includes dated and undated tombstones; the dated ones were executed in the years 331–593/942–1196 (al-Rashid *et al.* 2003: 207; al-Dāirah al-Iʿlāmiyyah 2000*a*: 311–312).

Figure 2. *The site of al-Sirrayn.*

The site of ᶜUlyab (Ḥamdānah) (Fig. 3)

ᶜUlyab (or Ḥamdānah as it is called locally) is sited in a wadi bearing the same name (ᶜUlyab); it is located approximately 9 km to the west of a small village called al-Ṣahawah, and approximately 8 km to the south-east of the archaeological site of al-Sirryan. It seems possible that its name is derived from the Ancient South Arabian Sabaic language (*ᶜ–l-b*) which means either *ᶜalb* trees (*Zizyphus spina Christi*) or the land which is cultivated with *ᶜalb* (Beeston *et al.* 1982: 15).

As far as we are aware, the earliest reference to the wadi ᶜAlyab is included in a historical statement concerning the emergence of the Yemeni false prophet, al-Aswad al-ᶜAnasī, in 11/632 (al-Ṭabarī [n.d.]: 496). During the first and second/seventh and eighth centuries ᶜAlyab is mentioned by some of the early Arab poets such as Durayd b. al-Ṣamah (d. 8/629), ᶜAbd Allah b. al-Aḥwaṣ (d. 105/723) and Abū Dahbal al-Jumaḥī (d. 126/743–744). From the beginning of the third/ninth century ᶜUlyab became an active pilgrim way station on the Yemeni coastal pilgrim route (al-Yaᶜqubī 2002: 155), and is recorded by a number of early Arab geographers such as al-Ḥarbī (1969: 647), Ibn Ḫurrdāḏabah (1889: 149) and Qudāmah (1889: 192). By the mid-sixth/twelfth century, al-Idrīsī (1989, i: 148) describes ᶜUlyab as "a sizable and populated village". A century later, in 742/1341, ᶜUlyab witnessed the arrival of the Rasulid king, al-Sulṭān al-Mujāhid ᶜAlī b. al-Muᵓayyad Dāūd b. Yūsif b. Rasūl, during his journey to Yemen after performing the hajj of this year (al-Thenayian 2000: 130, 151–152). It seems likely that ᶜUlyab continued to serve as a pilgrim way station until the beginning of the tenth/sixteenth century.

The recent archaeological investigations indicate that the archaeological site of ᶜUlyab consists of a cemetery, a well, and an archaeological mound (tell). The cemetery includes a number of dated and undated inscribed tombstones: the dated examples fall between the first quarter of the fifth century (416/1025) and the end of the eighth century (900/1494–1495), whereas

Figure 3. *The site of ᶜUlyab (Ḥamdānah).*

undated inscribed tombstones should be dated according to their palaeography between the third and fifth/ninth and eleventh centuries (al-Zaylaᶜī 1995: 7–36).

The site of Ḥaly (Ḥaly b. Yaᶜqūb)(Fig. 4)

Ḥaly (or Ḥaly b. Yaᶜqūb), which is known locally as Ḥaly Qadīm, is located approximately 4 km to the north-east of a small hamlet called Maḫshūsh and *c.* 30 km to the south of the village of al-Qawz (41° 32' E, 18° 45' N). It seems plausible that its name is derived from the Ancient South Arabian Sabaic *ḥ-l-y* which means "donation", "goods", or "movable property" (Beeston *et al.* 1982: 68). This meaning accords with Ibn al-Mujāwir's interpretation (1986: 53) of the same name, despite the fact that his statement has no substantial historical confirmation.

Along with other ports on the eastern coast of the Red Sea such as al-Sirrayn, Ḥaly acted from the beginning of the third/ninth century as a sea and inland pilgrim way station on the coastal routes (Ibn Ḥawqal [n.d.]: 28–30; Ibn Ḫurrdāḏabah 1889: 147–148; Qudāmah 1889: 192). In the industrial field, Ḥaly was famous for producing wooden or glass bowls (*aqdāḥ*) which were named after the site (*aqdāḥ ḥaly,* "bowls of Ḥaly") (al-Maqdisī 1906: 98). Ḥaly was described in the fourth/tenth century as a well-built populated coastal town, and it belongs to the region of ᶜAṯṯar (1906: 86, 69–70). During this century, its Friday mosque was constructed by the order of the Ziyādī commander al-Ḥusyan b. Sallāmah (d. 402/1011). The existence of the foundation stone of this mosque is recorded by the Yemeni historian ᶜUmārah al-Ḥakamī (1985: 76–80). In the fifth/eleventh century, according to al-Bakrī (1977: 49), Ḥaly became an immense developed city, full of well-built houses and fortified palaces, and its inhabitants used to draw their water from dug wells. During the sixth/twelfth century, the city of Ḥaly was known as Alḥiṣn and it is often connected historically with al-Sirrayn. At that time, it seems likely that the development of Ḥaly was limited, so it is described as a small town. However, its harbour remained very active (al-Idrīsī 1989, i: 137–138, 148; al-Ḥakamī 1985: 66, 76–80). At the end of the seventh/thirteenth century Ibn al-Mujāwir (1986: 53) visited Ḥaly and described it thus: "it is a town with a big mosque and a lighthouse [*manārah*]".

Due to the activities of its harbour, Ḥaly regained its past glory and it developed to such an extent that it was described by Ibn Baṭūṭah (1981, i: 271), who visited

Figure 4. *The site of Ḥaly (b. Yaᶜqūb).*

it in the year 729/1328, as a very well developed large city, and the architecture of its mosque was the best in the region. Ibn Baṭūṭah's information is echoed by the Yemeni historian al-Janadī (1983, ii: 210), who added that Ḥaly belongs to the Arabs of Kinānah who are renowned in helping pilgrims and doing good deeds for them. In the mid-eighth/fourteenth century (742/1341), the Rasulid king al-Sulṭān al-Mujāhid stopped twice at Ḥaly during pilgrimages to and from Mecca (al-Thenayian 2000: 128, 130). During the second half of the eighth/fourteenth century and the following two centuries, Ḥaly was selected as a safe haven by some of the amirs of Mecca, including Rumayṯah and Ḥumayḍah, who had fled Mecca following brutal assaults by the Mamluk army, and was adopted as a permanent residential home by other amirs who were either dismissed from power or decided to retire from political affairs (al-Ḫazrajī 1911/1914, i: 407–410; al-Fāsī 1985, iv: 96, 235, 406–407; vi: 70–71; vii: 122–123; Mortel 1985: 139, 148, 153–154, 164). During the eleventh/seventeenth century, Ḥaly was mentioned frequently as a stopping place for the Yemeni pilgrimage caravan. This happened during the hajj seasons of 1058/1648 and 1082/1671 (al-Wazīr 1985: 122, 154, 248, 282). References to Ḥaly as a maritime and inland stopping-place for Yemeni pilgrims continued during the first half of the thirteenth/nineteenth century (Jaḥāf 2004: 387; al-Thenayian 2000: 62–63).

Apart from two isolated hills covered with scattered potsherds, the entire archaeological site of Ḥaly, including its famous mosque, is today covered by a modest village called Ḥaly Qadīm (al-Zaylaᶜī 1986: 23–24; al-Dāirah al-Iᶜlāmiyyah 2000*a*: 199–201).

The site of ᶜAṯṯar (Fig. 5)

The archaeological site of ᶜAṯṯar is situated approximately 40 km to the north-west of the present modern city of Jāzān (42° 15' E, 17° 08' N). Like the ports of al-Sirrayn and al-Šarjah, ᶜAṯṯar was subject to the Yemeni false prophet in 11/632. This event is the first reference to ᶜAṯṯar in Islamic history. Along with al-Sirrayn, ᶜAṯṯar was one of Mecca's dependencies. However, in addition to being a major pilgrim way station, its port actively served the entire Hijazi region. By the fourth/tenth century, ᶜAṯṯar had reached its heyday and become the chief city of its region. Consequently, the other inland towns and sea

Figure 5. *The site of ᶜAṯṯar.*

ports such as al-Sirrayn, Ḥaly, and Bayš were connected with it.

ᶜAṯṯar appears on Ibn Ḥawqal's map of the Arabian Peninsula ([n.d.]: 32) as a main port located on the eastern coast of the Red Sea. During this period, it is described as a large and important city of the region, and the port of Ṣanᶜāʾ and Ṣaᶜdah. It had a well-organized market (*sūq*), a Friday mosque and public bath, and was well known for producing sesame oil (al-Maqdisī 1906: 69–70, 86, 98).

Additionally, there were two mints *(dār ḍarb al ᶜumlah)*, one in ᶜAṯṯar and the other in the city of Bayṣ. Their minting of golden coins (dinars) was named after ᶜAṯṯar (*al-dinār al-ᶜaṯṯr-ī* or *al-ᶜaṯṯriyyah)*. As far as we are aware, all of the coins found so far which were struck in ᶜAṯṯar date to the fourth/tenth century (al-Sharᶜān 1997: 118–121; Bikhazi 1970: nos 1–4, 51–52, 73–74; Darley-Doran 1988: 182–201). ᶜAṯṯar survived during the following centuries and was mentioned in the sixth/twelfth century as a sea and an inland pilgrim way station (al-Idrīsī 1989, i: 137; al-Ḥakamī 1985: 76–80).

The only surviving source to mention the end of ᶜAṯṯar is a statement by the Yemeni historian al-Janadī (1983, ii: 327), where he refers indirectly to the destruction of ᶜAṯṯar (*ẖarāb ᶜaṯṯar*) by saying that: "it was destroyed a long time ago" (*qad ẖuribat munḏū zaman ṭawīl*). Bearing in mind that al-Janadī's death occurred in the years 730–732/1329–1331, the destruction of ᶜAṯṯar might have taken place during the second half of the seventh/thirteenth century. Although this statement is unsupported by other historians, this date coincides with the shifting of the capital of the Sulaymānī Miẖlāf from ᶜAṯṯar to the Upper Jāzān (Jāzān al-ᶜUlyā) (al-Zaylaᶜī *et al.* 2003: 110).

The site of al-Šarjah (Fig. 6)

The archaeological site of al-Šarjah is situated on the sea coast of al-Mūwassam, in the far south-western corner of the province of Jāzān (42° 49' E, 16° 23' N). It seems reasonable that its name derived from the Ancient South Arabian Sabaic word *š-r-j* which means "the watercourse" (Beeston *et al.* 1982: 134). It might have got this name because of its location at the end of a broad wadi called Ḥaraḍ. Like the other nearby coastal towns and ports, al-Šarjah was subject to the control of the Yemeni false prophet in 11/632.

Figure 6. *The site of al-Šarjah.*

Al-Šarjah's history has close similarities with its neighbouring towns and ports. Its history as a main sea port and inland pilgrim way station, and its commercial connection with the Yemeni, Hijazi, and African sea ports, is mentioned by some of the early Arab geographers, including al-Yaᶜqūbī (2002: 155–156), Ibn Ḫurrdāḏabah (1889: 143), and al-Ḥakamī (1985: 76–80). During the fourth/tenth century, al-Šarjah was described as a sizeable town with a Friday mosque (*jāmiᶜ kabīr*) looking over the sea coast, with many storage facilities for keeping sorghum (*ḏurah*) which was exported to Aden and Jeddah (al-Maqdisī 1906: 69–70, 86; al-Hamdānī 1974: 68). In 729/1328, Ibn Baṭūṭah (1981, i: 271) arrived in al-Šarjah on his voyage to the Yemen from Ḥaly and described it as a small town inhabited by Yemeni merchants. In 742/1341 the Rasulid king al-Sulṭān al-Mujāhid ᶜAlī b. al-Mūʾayyad Dāūd b. Yūsif b. Rasūl halted at al-Šarjah on his return from performing the hajj (al-Thenayian 2000: 127, 139).

Recent archaeological fieldwork conducted at al-Šarjah resulted in the discovery of four Mamluk coins dating between 648 and 792/1250 and 1389 (Zarins & al-Badr 1986: 68). To sum up, the results of the archaeological work carried out at al-Šarjah's archaeological site indicate that it should date to between the seventh and eighth/thirteenth and fourteenth centuries (al-Dāirah al-Iᶜlāmiyyah 2000*a*: 325).

A summary of the pottery assemblages

An attempt was made during the survey of the five sites to collect a selection of diagnostic sherds of each type represented on the surface. These are briefly reviewed below as space prevents a longer discussion.

Alkaline blue and green wares

The types of alkaline wares found at al-Sirrayn, Ḥaly,

ᶜAṯṯar, and al-Šarjah are as follows:

- alkaline blue and green wares
- alkaline green wares with underglaze colour
- alkaline monochrome green wares
- alkaline green wares

Different types of so-called alkaline glazed wares have been found in great quantities at a number of Islamic archaeological sites situated in the northern, north-western, western, and southern regions of Saudi Arabia, as well as in Yemen. The recent archaeological research indicates that the alkaline wares found at these sites may date to between the second and fifth/eighth–eleventh centuries (Gilmore, al-Ibrahim & Murad 1982: 19, pl. 33/b; Ghabban 1988: 429–430, pls 193–195; al-Zaylaᶜī *et al.* 2003: 102–103, 110; al-Rashid 1986: 104–105, figs 167, 171–172; Rougeulle & Benoist 2001: 209, fig. 5/1–3, 211; Rougeulle 2003: 295).

Lustre wares

Al-Sirrayn and ᶜAṯṯar are the only sites at which lustre wares were found. These belonged to two types, viz. monochrome and polychrome. Monochrome and polychrome lustre wares dating to the period between the second and fourth/eighth–tenth centuries have been found elsewhere in Saudi Arabia and Yemen (Zarins & Zahrani 1985: 84; Gilmore *et al.* 1985: 117, pl. 101; al-Rashid 1986: 105–106, figs 168–170, 176; 1993: 435–437; Lane & Serjeant 1948: 110).

Chinese celadon wares

Glazed and unglazed fragments of Chinese celadon sherds were collected from two sites (al-Sirrayn and ᶜAṯṯar). This type was discovered in the north, north-west, and south of the Arabian Peninsula. The preliminary archaeological reports date it to between the fourth and eighth/tenth–fourteenth centuries (Lane & Serjeant 1948: 123–129; Whitcomb 1988: 188, 202, fig. 22; Hardy-Guilbert & Rougeulle 1995: 32–35; Zarins & al-Badr 1986: 65–66; Gilmore *et al.* 1985: 77).

Sgraffito and splashed wares

These were discovered at the sites of al-Sirrayn and ᶜAṯṯar. It is likely that sgraffito wares are more common at Islamic sites compared with the splashed ones: whereas the former were found at many sites within Saudi Arabia and Yemen, the latter have not been discovered, as far as the author is aware, at sites in Yemen. Both types date to between the fourth and sixth/tenth–twelfth centuries (al-Rashid 1993: 439–440; 1986: 105; Ghabban 1988: 428–429, pls 191–192; Hardy-Guilbert 2001: 70, fig. 4; Hardy-Guilbert & Rougeulle 1995: 32, fig. 2/16; Keall 1983: 384–385, fig. 4/9; Gilmore *et al.* 1985: pl. 102; Zarins, Kabawi & Murad 1983).

Tin-glazed wares

These were represented by a single fragment recovered from the surface of the site of al-Sirrayn. Certain examples of tin-glazed wares were found in excavations of Islamic sites located in the west and south-west of Saudi Arabia and southern Yemen. They have been dated to between the third and fifth/ninth–eleventh centuries (Zarins & Zahrani 1985: 84; Zarins & al-Badr 1986: 65–66; al-Rashid 1986: 105, fig. 165, 174; 1993: 437–438).

Over/underglaze-painted wares

Overglaze-painted wares were collected from al-Sirrayn while underglaze-painted ware was recovered from ᶜAṯṯar. The recent archaeological work in Saudi Arabia reveals the presence of over/underglaze-painted wares at sites located in the north, north-west, and south-west parts of the kingdom. According to the available published reports, this type of pottery dates to between the fourth and fifth/tenth and eleventh centuries (al-Rashid 1986: 105; 1993: 439–440; Ghabban 1988: 428–429, pls 191–192; al-Dāʾirah al-Iᶜlāmiyyah 2000*b*: 295–296).

Ḥaysī monochrome glazed wares

The sites of ᶜUlayb (Ḥamdānah) and Ḥaly are the only ones where Ḥaysī glazed wares were discovered. It has been observed that the surface of ᶜUlayb has more fragments of this type of pottery compared with the latter site. The Ḥaysī monochrome glazed wares were found at only certain sites situated in the western and southern parts of Yemen. Due to its limited distribution, a specific dating has not yet been recorded (Keall 1983: 385; Whitcomb 1988: 190, figs 10/o, p, r–x, fig. 12/w–ee; Hardy-Guilbert & Rougeulle 1995: 36–37, figs 5/3, 5/9–12, 14).

Tihami monochrome and blue glazed wares

Very few samples of this type of pottery were found at ᶜUlyab (Ḥamdānah) and Ḥaly, and none were found elsewhere. It is believed that the blue Tihāmah ware is a Yemeni product, as were Ḥaysī wares. Their distribution beyond Yemen is very limited and the site of al-Šarjah is the only locality within Saudi Arabia where this type was found. The result of the archaeological fieldwork indicates that the blue Tihāmah wares date to between the sixth and tenth/twelfth–sixteenth centuries (Keall 1983: 383, fig. 4/8; Whitcomb 1988: fig. 12/r, u; Hardy-Guilbert & Rougeulle 1995: 35–37, figs 5/3, 6; Zarins & al-Badr 1986: 65–66).

Chinese porcelain wares

Chinese porcelain wares were only discovered on the surface of ᶜUlyab (Ḥamdānah), but were very abundant here. This type of Chinese ceramic has also been discovered at certain sites located in the south and south-west of Yemen but as far as we are aware, there are no reports of its presence at any Islamic sites in Saudi Arabia. This type could date to between the ninth and thirteenth/fifteenth–nineteenth centuries (Keall 1983: 385; Whitcomb 1988: fig. 22/b; Hardy-Guilbert & Rougeulle 1995: 37, 40).

Notes

1 This research, as far as we are aware, is the first of its kind in shedding some light on the surface pottery types of the archaeological sites under scrutiny. More future collective research of this subject is needed.

2 We should point out that the history, archaeology and epigraphy of these archaeological sites, except al-Šarjah site, was the subject of an unpublished Ph.D. thesis.

References

al-Bakrī, Abū ᶜUbayd Allah ᶜAbd Allah b. ᶜAbd al-ᶜAzīz/ed. ᶜA.A. al-Ghunaym
1977. *Al-mamālik wa-ᵓl-masālik*. Kuwait: Dhāt al-Salāsil.

Beeston A.F.L., Ghul M.A., Muller W.W. & Ryckmans J.
1982. *Sabaic Dictionary*. Louvain & Beyrouth: Peeters.

Bikhazi R.J.
1970. Coins of al-Yaman 132–569 A.H. *Al-Abhath* 23/1–4: 3–127.

al-Dāᵓirah al-Iᶜlāmiyyah
2000*a*. *Al-ṯaqāfah al-taqlīidiyyah fīal-mamlakat al-ᶜarabiyyah al-saᶜūdiyyah: al-mawāqᶜ al-āṯriyyah*. ii. Riyadh: The Circle for Publishing & Documentation.
2000*b*. *Al-ṯaqāfah al-taqlīidiyyah fīal-mamlakat al-ᶜarabiyyah al-saᶜūdiyyah: al-āthār*. i. Riyadh: The Circle for Publishing & Documentation.

Darley-Doran R.E.
1988. Examples of Islamic Coinage from Yemen. Pages 182–203 in W. Daum (ed.), *Yemen: 3000 Years of Art and Civilisation in Arabia Felix*. Frankfurt-am-Main: Pinguin.

al-Fāsī, Taqī al-Dīn Muḥammad b. Aḥmad/ed. F. Said
1985. *Al-ᶜaqd al-ṯhamīn fī tāriẖ al-balad al-amīn*. Beirut: al-Rislah.

Ghabban A.I.
1988. *Introduction à l'étude archéologique des deux routes syrienne et égyptienne de pélerinage au nord-ouest de l'Arabie Saoudite*. Thèse de doctorat, Université de Provence Aix-Marseille. [Unpublished].

Gilmore M., al-Ibrahim M. & Murad A.
1982. Preliminary Report on the Northwestern and Northern Regions Survey 1981. *Atlal* 6: 7–21 [Arabic section], 9–38 [English section].

Gilmore M., Ibrahim M., Mursi J. & al-Talhi D.
1985. A Preliminary Report on the First Season of Excavations at Al-Mabiyat, An Early Islamic Site in the Northern Hijaz. *Atlal* 9: 113–123 [Arabic section], 109–125 [English section].

al-Ḥakamī, ᶜUmārah, Najm al-Dīn b. ᶜAlī/ed. M. al-Akwaᵓ.
1985. *Tāriẖ al-yaman, (al-musammah) al-mufīd fī aẖbār ṣanᶜāᵓ wa-zabid*. Ṣanᶜāᵓ: al-Maktabah al-Yamaniyyah.

al-Hamdānī, al-Ḥasan b. Aḥmad b. Yaᶜqūb/ed. M. ᶜA. al-Akwaᶜ
1974. *Ṣifat jazīrat al-ᶜarab*. Riyadh: Manshut Dār al-Yamāmah.

al-Ḥarbī, Ibrāhīm b. Isḫāq/ed. H. al-Jasir
1969. *Kitāb al-manāsik wa-āmākin ṭuruq al-ḥajj wa-maᶜālim al-jazīrah.* Riyadh: Manshut Dār al-Yamāmah.
Hardy-Guilbert C.
2001. Archaeological research at al-Shihr, the Islamic Port of Hadramawt, Yemen (1996–1999). *Proceedings of the Seminar for Arabian Studies* 31: 69–79.
Hardy-Guilbert C. & Rougeulle A.
1995. Archaeological Research into the Islamic Period in Yemen: Preliminary Notes on the French Expedition, 1993. *Proceedings of the Seminar for Arabian Studies* 25: 29–44.
al-Ḫazrajī, ᶜAlī b. al-Ḥasan/ed. M.B. Asal
1911/1914. *Al-ᶜuqūd al-luʾluʾiyyah fī tāriḫ al-dawlah al-rasūliyyah.* (2 volumes). Cairo: al-Hilāl Press.
Ibn Baṭūṭah, Abū ᶜAbd Allah Muḥammad b. ᶜAbd Allah/ed. ᶜ A.M. al-Kattani
1981. *Tuḥfat al-nuḍḍār fī ġarāʾib al-amsār wa ᶜajāʾib al-asfār.* (2 volumes). Beirut: al-Rislah.
Ibn Ḥawqal, Abū al-Qāsim al-Naṣībī
[n.d.]. *Kitāb ṣūrat al-arḍ*. Cairo: Dār al-Kiṭb al-Islami.
Ibn Ḫurrdāḏbah, Abū al-Qāsim ᶜUbayd Allah/ed. M.J. de Goeje
1889. *Kitāb al-masālik wa-ʾl-mamālik.* Leiden: Bibliotheca Geographorum Arabicorum/E.J. Brill.
Ibn al-Mujāwir, Jamāl al-Dīn Abū al-Fatḥ Yūsuf b. Yaᶜqūb ed. O. Lofgren
1986. *Ṣifat bilād al-yamman wa-makkah wa-baᶜḍ al-ḥijāz, (al-musammāh) tāriḫ al-mustabṣir.* Beirut: Manshurāt al-Madinah. [Reprinted].
al-Idrīsī, Abū ᶜAbd Allah Muḥammad
1989. *Kitāb nuzhat al-muštāq fī iḫtirāq al-ā fāq.* (2 volumes). Beirut: ᶜAlam al-Kutub.
Jaḥāf, Luṭf Allah b. Aḥmad/ed. Ibrahim b. Ahmad al-Maqhafi
2004. *Durar nuḥūr al-hūrr al-ᶜaīn bi-sirat al-imām al-manṣūr ᶜalī wa-aᶜlām dawlatih al-mayāmīn (1189–1224/1775–1809).* Ṣanᶜāʾ: Maktabat al-Irshād.
al-Janadī, Abū ᶜAbd Allah Bahā al-Dīn/ed. M. al-Akwaᶜ
1983. *Al-sulūk fī ṭabaqāt al-ᶜulamāʾ wa-ʾl-mulūk.* (2 volumes). Beirut: Bisāt Press.
Keall E.J.
1983. The dynamics of Zabid and its hinterland: the survey of a town on the Tihamah plain of North Yemen. *World Archaeology* 14/3: 378–392.
Lane A. & Serjeant R.B.
1948. Pottery and Glass Fragments From the Aden Littoral, with Historical Notes. *Journal of the Royal Asiatic Society*: 108–133.
al-Maqdisī, Šams al-Dīn Muḥammād b. Aḥmad/ed. M.J. de Goeje
1906. *Kitāb aḥsan al-taqāsim fī maᶜrifat al-āqālim.* Leiden: Bibliotheca Geographorum Arabicorum, Lugduni Batavorum/E.J. Brill.
Mortel R.T.
1985. *Al-aḥwāl al-siyāsiyyah wa-ʾl-iqtiṣādiyyah bi-makkah fī al-ᶜaṣr al-mamlūkī.* Riyadh: King Saud University Press.
Qudāmah, b. Jaᶜfar al-Baġdādī/ed. M.J. de Goeje
1889. *Nubḏhah min kitāb al-ḫarāj wa-ṣ anᶜat al-kitābah.* Leiden: Bibliotheca Geographorum Arabicorum/E.J. Brill.
al-Rashid, Saᶜad b. ᶜAbd Alᶜzīz
1986. *Al-Rabadhah: a Portrait of Early Islamic Civilisation in Saudi Arabia.* Riyadh: King Saud University Press.
1993. *Darb Zubaydah: the Pilgrim Road from Kufa to Makkah.* Riyadh: Dār al-Watan. [In Arabic].
al-Rashid, Saᶜad b. ᶜAbd Alᶜzīz; al-Zaylaᶜī, Aḥmad b. ᶜUmar; al-Hārthī, Nāsir b. ᶜAlī; al-Fiᶜr, Muḥammad b. Fahad; Iskubī, Khālid b. Muhammad; ᶜAli, Jamāl al-Dīn Surāj
2003. *Āthār manṭaqat makkat al-mukkaramah slisilah āthār al-mamlakat al-ᶜarabiyyah al-saᶜudiyyah.* Riyadh: Ministry of Education/Deputy Ministry of Antiquities & Museums.
Rougeulle A.
2003. Excavations at Sharmah, Hadramawt: the 2001 and 2002 seasons. *Proceedings of the Seminar for Arabian Studies* 33: 287–307.

Rougeulle A. & Benoist A.
2001. Notes on pre- and early Islamic harbours of Hadramawt (Yemen). *Proceedings of the Seminar for Arabian Studies* 31: 203–214.
al-Sharᶜān, Nāyf b. ᶜAbd Allah
1997. *Nuqūd umawiyyah wa-ᶜabāsiyyah ḍarb al-ḥijāz wa-najd wa-tihāmah.* M.A. thesis, Dept. of Archaeology, Faculty of Arts, King Saud University, Riyadh. [Unpublished].
al-Ṭabarī, Muḥammad b. Jarīr/ed. Abu Suhayb al-Karmi
[n.d.]. *Tāriẖ al-umam wa-al-mulūk (tāriẖ al-ṭabarī).* Riyadh: International Ideas Home.
al-Wazīr, ᶜAbd Allah b. ᶜAlī/ed. M. Jazim
1985. *Tāriẖ ṭabaq al-ḥ alwa wa-ṣiḥāf al-mann wa-ᶜl-salwa.* Ṣanᶜāᵓ: Markaz al-Dirāsāt wa-l-Buhuth.
Whitcomb D.
1988. Islamic Archaeology in Aden and Hadhramaut. Pages 177–252 in D.T. Potts (ed.), *Araby the Blest: Studies in Arabian Archaeology.* (Carsten Niebuhr Institute Publication, 7). Copenhagen: Museum Tusculanum.
al-Yaᶜqubī, Aḥmad b. Abī Yaᶜqūb b. Waḍāḥ al-Kātib/ed. M. Dannawi
2002. *Kitāb al-buldān.* Beirut: Dār al-Kutub.
Zarins J. & al-Badr H.
1986. Archaeological Investigation in the Southern Tihamah Plain II (Including Sihi, 217-107 and Sharja, 217-172) 1405/1985. *Atlal* 10: 43–69 [Arabic section], 36–57 [English section].
Zarins J. & Zahrani A.
1985. Recent Archaeological Investigations in the Southern Tihama Plain: The sites of Athar and Sihi. *Atlal* 9: 69–111 [Arabic section], 65–106 [English section].
Zarins J., Kabawi A. & Murad A.
1983. Preliminary Report on the Najran/Ukhdud Survey and Excavations: 1402/1982. *Atlal* 7: 21–39 [Arabic section], 22–40 [English section].
al-Zaylaᶜī, Aḥmad b. ᶜUmar
1986. *Al-mawāqiᶜ al-islāmiyyah al-mundaṯirah fī wādi ḥaly (3–9/9–15 centuries), ḥawliyyah kuliat al-ādāb.* Kuwait: Academic Publication Council, Kuwait University.
1995. *Nuqūsh islāmiyyah min ḥamdānah bi-wādī ᶜulyab.* Riyadh: King Fahad National Library.
al-Zaylaᶜī, Aḥmad b. ᶜUmar; al-Khalifah, Khalifah b. ᶜAbd Allah; al-Sharikh, ᶜAbd Allah b. Muhammad; al-Zahrani, ᶜAbd Allah b. Salim; al-Turki, Shakir b. Jasim
2003. *Āṯār manṭaqat jāzān: slisilah athār al-mamlakat al-ᶜarabiyyah al-saᶜūdiyyah.* Riyadh: Ministry of Education/Deputy Ministry of Antiquities & Museums.

Author's address
Mohammed A.R. al-Thenayian, Faculty of Tourism & Archaeology, Department of Archaeology, King Saud University, PO Box 2627, Riyadh 12372, Saudi Arabia.
e-mail ghadahabu@hotmail.com; mtheny@gmail.com

Proceedings of the Seminar for Arabian Studies 38 (2008): 301–310

Šālôm (Sālim) al-Šabazī's (seventeenth-century) poem of the debate between coffee and qāt

Yosef Tobi

Summary
Šālôm (Sālim) al-Šabazī (1619–after 1680) was the most important Jewish poet in Yemen. Although he was well versed in Jewish tradition and expressed more than any other Jewish-Yemeni poet the national feelings of his coreligionists and their longing for their homeland, Šabazī's verse should be considered and examined as an integral part of Yemeni poetry in general. This is because more than half of his huge poetical production, about 830 poems, is in Arabic, even though he wrote them and they were further copied in Hebrew script (Judaeo-Arabic); also, a significant part of his verse is coloured with typical Yemeni literary qualities, particularly the double-girdled *muwaššaḥ* and the entire linguistic and literary features of the *ḥumaynī*. In many respects, his Arabic verse followed the Muslim Yemeni poetry that flourished in the sixteenth century.

A considerable number of Šabazī's poems do not betray any genuine Jewish background, such as the debate poems, of which we have at least ten. Two of them are between *qāt* and *qahwah* (coffee), two prestigious plants "revealed" in Yemen, which constitute a noteworthy component in Yemeni history and culture. No wonder that Šabazī who lived in southern Yemen, not far from the town of Taʿizz, the original land of *qāt* and coffee, devoted two of his poems to this topic. One of these poems is very well known and has been published in Hebrew, European, and Arabic publications. The other is published here for the first time, based on several manuscripts, with an English translation and a comprehensive discussion about Yemeni debate poems.

Keywords: Yemen, Jewish poetry, Šabazī, debate poems, *qāt,* coffee

The earliest known Yemeni-Hebrew poetry, from the eleventh century, displays a clear link first with the ancient Palestinian school of Hebrew liturgical poetry (fifth–tenth centuries) and later with the Spanish Hebrew school of poetry (950–1150), which in turn was largely based on the poetical principles of mediaeval Arabic oriental and Andalusian verse. The affinity with the ancient Hebrew school faded out, while the similarity with the Spanish school, especially in terms of scanning and rhyming, increased to the point where, by the end of the fifteenth century, Yemeni-Hebrew verse might be defined as a branch of it (Tobi 1991: 18–26).

But during that century the Yemeni-Muslim school of the *ḥumaynī* was founded, an event generally ascribed to Aḥmad ibn Falītah al-Ḥakamī (d. around 1330) and ʿAbd Allah al-Mazzāḥ (d. around 1426) (ʿAmrī 2001: 1231).[1] Yemeni-Jewish poets revealed a very liberal openness to this new school in respect of language, prosody, and content. Significant change took place during the second half of the sixteenth century, as revealed in the poems of Yôsēp ben Yiśrâʾēl, who lived in the region of Šarʿab in lower Yemen (ʿAmir 2000). He was the first Yemeni-Jewish poet whose verse should be unequivocally classified as a unique new poetical school, heavily shaded with local Yemeni characteristics whereby it plainly differs from all Hebrew verse written in any other country since then.

Yet the most noteworthy step was taken by Šālôm (Sālim) al-Šabazī (1619–*c.* 1680), a younger relative of Yôsēp ben Yiśrâʾēl, unquestionably the most prominent figure in Yemeni-Jewish poetry. He gained this popularity and the highest standing among his Jewish coreligionists in Yemen, and recently also among scholars of Hebrew verse generally, due to his large poetic output and variety and the powerful Jewish national feelings he expressed. But little is known about one significant aspect of his verse, which has drawn sparse attention: his being the most important poet to paint Yemeni-Jewish poetry in abundant local colours even though he was not the first Yemeni-Jewish poet who contributed in this regard. A large amount of his poetry might be considered simply as a Jewish manifestation of the *ḥumaynī*. The close affinity of

Šabazī's verse to the *ḥumaynī* has already been observed by some Israeli scholars: Piamenta (1997), Semah (1988; 1989) and myself (Tobi 2006*a*; 2006*b*), and by the American scholar M.S. Wagner (2004*a*; 2004*b*; 2006). Obviously, meaningful comparative research cannot be done before we have a comprehensive critical edition of Šabazī's verse. This consists of about 830 poems, most of them in Arabic and very long. However, as a by-product of this heavy assignment, in which I have been immersed in recent years, I would like to present in this paper a limited comparative study.

Most of Yemeni-Jewish poetry prior to Šabazī, in Hebrew or in Arabic, dealt mainly with the national theme of exile and redemption or the ethical-philosophical theme of body versus soul and repentance. Šabazī was the first to expand the content of Yemeni-Jewish poetry far beyond these traditional concerns. The new ones were plainly taken from the *ḥumaynī* poetry, which itself had deviated from the traditional "genres" (*aḡrāḍ*) of the mono-rhyme *qaṣīdah*. Thus the rather solemn panegyric (*madḥ*) or epistolary poems, constituting a significant component of the chronological writings, are written as *qaṣāᶜid* (sg. *qaṣīdah*), for instance, the *dīwān* of Šawkānī (1986) or the recently published work by M. Zabārah (1998). Sharply different is the *ḥumaynī* divided into two major sections: on the one hand are religious spiritual, allegorical Sufi poems praising Muḥammad and his family. Many of them open with the theme of love, abundantly found, for example, in the *dīwān* of al-Saqqāf (b. 1513). On the other hand there is *hazl*, humorous and scornful poetry, such as that of Ḫafanjī (d. 1766–1767) (Wagner MS 2004*b*.[2] The *ḥumaynī*, especially the allegorical love poems (*ghazaliyyāt*), was not welcomed by Zaydī scholars, such as Ṣāliḥ al-Maqbalī (1631–1696), who approvingly quoted Ibn Ḫaldūn's opinion that monistic works, including those by Ibn al-ᶜArabī and most of ᶜUmar ibn al-Fāriḍ's poetry, should be destroyed (Homerin 1994: 77). This was not the case with Yemeni-Jewish allegorical poetry, in particular that of Šabazī, which became an admired and respected model imitated by other poets.

Yemeni-Jewish poetry did not adopt the *hazl* style of the *ḥumaynī* but it did adopt some fairly light poetical themes, the most popular of which was the *Rangstreit* (debate about rank) poems, i.e. poems in which two or more personified things, such as towns, writing implements, or seasons of the year, argue as to which is the most important. This literary genre was already known by the term *munāẓarah* (or *mufāḫarah*, or *munāfarah*) in mediaeval Arabic and Hebrew poetry, especially in the *maqāmah* works.[3]

The most two famous debate poems in Yemeni-Jewish verse are between cities in Yemen: (a) *qālat taᶜizz al-ᶜudaynah jannat al-awṭān yā man rasūlī ilā ṣanᶜāᵓ bi-dhā al-ᶜilwān* (Taᶜizz of ᶜUdaynah, the paradise of the homelands, said: who will be my messenger to Ṣanᶜāᵓ with this message), a debate between the capitals of Šāfīᶜī in southern Yemen and Zaydī in central Yemen (ḤuḤ 115b–117a; ḤḤ, *šīrōt*: 443–446);[4] (b) *qāl al-muḫā yā ᶜadan ᵓismaᶜ wi-tfakkar* (Mokha said: Behold and reflect, O you, Aden) by a certain ᶜAwāḍ al-Nahīki is a debate among the four leading cities in Yemen: the capitals Ṣanᶜāᵓ (Yazāl) and Taᶜizz and the ports of Mokha and Aden (ḤuḤ 114a–115b).[5]

Šabazī also wrote at least ten poems of this kind, two in Hebrew, one in Arabic and Hebrew, and four in Arabic.[6] The two Hebrew poems are: (a) *nẹ̄fẹ̄š we-śeḵẹl šāᵓalū lī ᵓêzêh meᵓôd mithālelī* (Soul and Mind asked me, which of them is more praiseworthy), a philosophical issue about the relationship between the two spiritual entities in a human being (ḤḤ, *šīrōt*: 279);[7] (b) *ᶜayīn welēb yaḥad merībīm / bên ha-kerūḇīm sōbebīm* (Eye and Heart debate together among the Cherubim, they turn around them), another philosophical issue on who is responsible for the sins of a human being, both being attracted to worldly material delights (ḤḤ, *šīrōt*: 406–407).[8] The poem in Arabic and Hebrew is (c) *tanādamū rūḥī wa-ᶜaqlī / sviyyā we-ᶜōfer bābelī* (My Soul and my Mind debated/ a gazelle and a Babylonian fawn), a debate in which the author explicitly sides with Soul and unequivocally draws back from Mind (Hallevy 1998–2003, i: 255–256; ii: 833–834).

The four other poems by Šabazī have completely different themes: (d) *al-šābb wa-l-šaybah tanādū / fī raᵓyhum yitrādadū* (the Youth and the Old man debated / they express their thoughts over and over). Its title (*ᶜunwān*) is *munādamat afkār al-nāṭiqah* (a debate poem about the thoughts who witness themselves) (only in MSS); (e) *al-ᶜazab wa-l-muzawwaj ajmaᶜīn / ᵓawṣalū ᶜindanā mitšāriᶜīn* (the bachelor and the married man together / came to us asking for judgment), a debate about whose life is better (ḤḤ, *šīrōt*: 96–99);[9] (f) *tinādam al-mašmūm- bi-bustānoh kull fann min makānoh* (the scented plant argued in its garden / each delight deserves its state), a debate between the various scented plants in the garden (ḤuḤ 119a–120b); (g) *tinādam al-aṭyāb ᶜindī ᵓayn ḫawāṣ zāᵓidī* (the scents debated before me / about where the high virtues are), a debate about whose aroma is more pleasant (only in MSS); (h) *sālim qāl allah rabbī maqṣūdī / lammun fī yawmun qad jāz ᵓilā ᶜindī* (Sālim said: God my Lord is my aspiration / when once one day [Tobacco and Coffee] approached me), a debate about whose delights are better (only in MSS).[10]

In two of Šabazī's poems the two contending parties are *qāt* and *qahwah*: (i) *al-qāt wa-l-qahwah yisʾalūnī / mā taḥkumū ʾayn afḍal al-funūnī* (Qāt and Coffee ask me: / what is your opinion, where is the best pleasure?) (ḤuḤ 71a–b);[11] (j) *al-qāt wa-l-qahwah tinādam / quddām ahlayn al-ḥikam* (Qāt and Coffee jointly debate / in the presence of people of knowledge) (only in MSS, see below). It should be pointed out that, according to a popular Yemeni legend, *qāt* and coffee were first grown in the same place, the town of al-ʿUdayn on the slopes of Mount Ṣabur (Varisco 2007: 245).[12]

As already noted by Bacher, Šabazī's Arabic debate poems are completely different in their non-Jewish spirit and mood from his Hebrew debate poems (and we may add from the Hebrew-Arabic poems): "Auch diese letzteren Gedichte sind ganz frei von jüdischen Elementen und schließen sich wahrscheinlich ähnlichen Erzeugnissen der weltlichen arabischen Poesie an, während sich zwei andere, in hebräischer Sprach verfaßte, hieher gehörige Poesien Schibzis [...] den ähnlichen Poesien der klassischen neuhebräischen Dichtung anreiht".[13]

There are at least three other Judaeo-Arabic debate poems between *qāt* and coffee: (a) by a poet known only by his first name, Šelōmōh: *hāt al-qalam yā ṣāfī al-ḏāt / ša-ktub niẓāmī fī ṯabāt / al-qāt wa-l-qahwah bi-rannāt / yatanādamū bayn al-ruwāt* (Bring the pen, you whose essence is pure / I shall write down my scanned verse with firmness of purpose / Qāt and Coffee with ringing sounds / debate with each other in the company of teachers); (b) by one Abū Mūsā: *abū mūsā yaqūl ṣaḥīḥ man qāl min al-marāqiḥ wa-l-šurūḥ al-alwān* (Abū Mūsā says: Approved is he who speaks verses about fine foods and entertainment); (c) by an anonymous poet: *al-qāt wa-l-qahwah yatanādamū quddāmanā / al-qāt qāl fī ḏā al-zamāna* (Qāt and Coffee debate with each other in our presence. / Qāt said: at that time). Although we can say nothing about the chronological relation between Šabazī and the authors of the two other poems, Šabazī was apparently the first Yemeni-Jewish poet to write in this genre and the three other poems were written as an imitation of his verse. This conjecture correlates what is already well known about Šabazī as the great inventor of poetical genres in Yemeni-Jewish poetry, often derived from the *ḥumaynī* Muslim poetry, and his central role as a poet who shaped classical Yemeni-Jewish poetry in all its features. Thus, Šelōmōh, author of the third poem, borrowed its opening line from one of Šabazī's known poems: *hāt al-qalam yā ṣāfī al-dhāt / wa-ḥḍir li-ḥibrī wa-l-dawāt* (Bring the pen, you whose essence is pure / and fetch my ink with the inkwell). There is no question about Šabazī's direct connection with Yemeni-Muslim poetry, while later Yemeni-Jewish poets were probably impacted indirectly by Muslim poetry through his work. However, Šabazī was not the first to write about the merits of *qāt*; this distinction goes to Yôsēp̄ ben Yiśrâʾēl, Šabazī's relative of the preceding generation, in his poem *yaqūl al-šāʿir al-nāḍim* (the versifier poet says): *ghuṣūn al-qāt fī ʿadnān / ṣufāt afnān / yaslī ḫāṭir al-makrūb* (the branches of *qāt* in Paradise / the choicest of pleasures / it diverts the heart of the distressed).

Of all five above-mentioned debate poems between Coffee and Qāt, the first one by Šabazī ((i) above: *al-qāt wa-l-qahwah yisʾalūnī*) is the best known and most common in the Jewish written *dawāwīn* (sg. *dīwān*), in manuscripts, and in print. It was also published in Arabic characters and translated into Hebrew and German (see n. 11). The four other poems are known only in a few manuscripts. The present paper focuses on Šabazī's other unpublished poem ((j) above), and is compared with other Judaeo-Arabic poems on the same subject, and with Muslim-Yemeni verse on the *qāt*. But first let us examine the Judaeo-Arabic text of the hitherto unpublished poem, in transcription and with its translation. The text is found in at least four handwritten *dawāwīn*: (a) MS Ben Zvi Institute, Jerusalem, no. 3286, ff. 65b–67a (BZ1); (b); MS Ben Zvi Institute, Jerusalem, no. 1238, ff. 111–112 (BZ2); (c) MS Tobi Collection, Jerusalem, ff. 478–479 (T);[14] (d) MS Raṣon Hallevy Collection, Tel Aviv, *šîrôt*, no. 337 (R).[15] The following text is generally based on MS BZ2, but in some places I have preferred the version of the other MSS.[16] In the transcription I have usually followed the vocalization in MS BZ2, based on the Judaeo-Arabic Yemeni pronunciation.

al-qāt wa-l-qahwah tnādam
quddām ahl al-ḥikam

al-qāt ajāb mā miṯl fannī
kullēn li-ghuṣnī yimtanī
ḥīn askun al-bustān mudnī
kammun fatā lī mumtanī
man hū siʿīd yiltaḏḏ li-ghuṣnī
al-muštahar, niʿam al-hanī
al-fātiḥah ʿindī tunaẓẓam
wa-l-ḏikr li-lah wa-l-qasam

jawwabathū al-qahwah bi-ʾifṣāḥ
najmī qablak qad alāḥ
ḥīn yḥaḍḍrūnī waṣṭ al-aqdāḥ
li-l-marqaḥah li-kull ṣabāḥ

yā rubb sikhī al-kaff samāḥ
yuqrab jihātī fī jināḥ
man d̲āqanī basmal wa-sallam
wa-l-fātiḥah awwal niẓām

al-qāt ajāb ᵓamrī muṣarraḥ
bayn ahl al-afnān qad ṣalaḥ
lī tūn wa-hayᵓah minnak aṣlaḥ
rad̲wān šayh̲ī qad nafaḥ
wa-ayd̲ā al-ah̲d̲ar šaykhī al-muṣarraḥ
yawm al-sarārah wa-l-faraḥ
wa-nawbatī fī al-ẓuhr tuḥakkam
wa-ᵓusāmir ahlēn al-niᶜam

jawwabathū al-qahwah twaqqaf
lī šayh̲ mit̲lak muᶜarraf
al-šādhilī šayh̲ī al-mušarraf
nūr al-jawāmiᶜ wa-l-ᶜukaf
dāᵓim fnūnī lā t̲h̲ālaf
man lad̲d̲anī tuwwah waqaf
fī kull ḥīn fannī muqaddam
wa-aṭīb fī ḥayt̲ al-karam

al-qāt ajāb kafā al-maᶜātib
kut̲r al-maḥāfah lā yajib
lī ᶜahd wa-lī mit̲āq wājib
kullēn mujālasatī yiḥibb
kamm lī anā kamm min rawātib
fī kull maᶜnā antasib
qālat ṣabur ghuṣnī tijassam
lā yaltaḥiẓ fīhū wa-kamm

jawwabathū al-qahwah tsāriᶜ
ifham kalāmī wi-stamiᶜ
li-l-jism amrī ṣaḥḥ muṭbiᶜ
man lad̲d̲ afnānī qiniᶜ
lammayt al-arbaᶜ al-ṭabāiᶜ
ᶜind al-ṭabīb al-mubtadiᶜ
ṣafrā wa-dam sawdā wa-balġam
lā yilḥaẓū minnī alam

al-qāt ajāb fannī muzayyad
mašhūr anā fī kull ḥadd
jāᵓ al-tutun li-l-qāt yišhad
wa-qāl lahū mā lak ᶜanid
ᵓiblīs šayh̲ak lā twarrid
man ammanak jīt al-balad
qad ṣāḥ ᶜalayk ibn al-muᵓayyad
wa-ajāz ḥarīqak bi-l-ᶜamad
wallā al-tutun mā zād tkallam
li-l-šād̲iliyyah aḥtakam

al-h̲amr awṣal jā bi-himmah
qāl mā lakum fī mah̲ṣumah
al-kull dhū naqḥah wa-niᶜmah
qad ṣaḥḥ lakum al-taqdimah
qad istah̲ād̲ūkum bi-ḥikmah
afnānakum mutlāᵓimah
yawm al-surūr al-kull niltamm
nijlī al-mhimmah wa-al-haram
sālim yaqūl akmalt šiᶜrī
wa-anā li-rabbī šākirī
d̲ī minhū tadbīr amrī
muᶜawwid̲ man kān ṣābirī
hū ᶜizzatī hū d̲āt naṣrī
yaslī min al-hamm h̲āṭrī
li-l-ᶜilm alqannī wa-afham
anẓum wa-anquš bi-l-qalam

Variations:

3 *mā* – BZ1: *lā*. 7-8 missing in BZ1 & T. 12 *qablak* – T: *qubālak*. 15 *yā* – T missing. 17 *basmal* – T: *bi-al-saml.* 16 T: *wa-d̲ikr li-allah wa-al-qasam.* 21 *lī tūn* – BZ2: *lī tayn*; T: *laytoh. aṣlaḥ* – BZ2: *ašraḥ*; T*: anšaraḥ*. 22 *qad* – BZ1: *lī*. 23 *muṣarraḥ* – BZ2, T: *al-mufad̲d̲al*. 24 *al-sarārah* – BZ1: *al-sarāᵓir*. 25 *fī al-ẓuhr* – BZ1: *bi-l-ẓuhr*. 26 BZ1: *wa-aṭīb fī ḥayt̲ al-karam*; *wa-ᵓusāmir* – T: *wa-ᵓasmār*. 27–34 in BZ1 after l. 42. 31 *t̲h̲ālaf* – BZ1, BZ2: *tuh̲allif.* 32 *tuwwah* – BZ1: missing. 33 *muqaddam* – BZ1: *yuqaddam*; T: *muzayyad.* 35 *al-maᶜātib* – BZ1: *al-ᶜātib*. 36 *al-maḥāfah* – T: *maḥānah*. 37–38 T: missing. *mujālasatī* – BZ2: *li-majlisatī.* 41 *qālat ṣabur* – BZ1: *rūs al-jibāl*; T: *wa-qāt ṣabur*; *ghuṣnī* – BZ2: *ghabnī*; *tijassam* – T; *jisim*. 42. *fīhū* – BZ1: *fannī*; BZ2: *fīhā*. 43–44 T: missing. 48. *al-mubtadiᶜ*: BZ1: *al-muh̲tariᶜ*; T: *al-mubtariᶜ*. 49. *wa-dam sawdā* – BZ2: *wa-sawdā dam.* 50 *yilḥaẓū* – BZ1: *yaltaḥiẓ*; *minnī* – BZ1: *fīnī*; *alam* – T: *al-hamm*. 51 *fannī* – BZ1: *fīnī*. 52 *ḥadd* – BZ1,T: *aḥad*. 53 *li-l-qāt* – T: *li-qāt*. 54 *wa-qāl* – BZ1, T: *qālat*. 57–58 BZ1: missing. 59 *zād* – BZ1: *ᶜād*; T: *zid*. 60 *li-l-šād̲iliyyah* – BZ1: *li-l-šuhād liyyah*; T: *li-al-šād̲ilah*; *aḥtakam* – BZ2: *muḥtakam*. 63 *naqḥah* – BZ1: *hayᵓah*. 68. *al-haram* – T: *al-hadam*. 71 BZ2: *tadbīr amrī hū li-rabbī*; *minhū* – BZ1: *munhij*. 72 BZ2: *muᶜīd̲ kammin ṣābirī*. 73 *naṣrī* – *šarrī*. 74 *yaslī* – BZ1: *yuslī*; T: *yajlī*. 75 *li-l-ᶜilm* – BZ2: *li-l-malam*; *alqannī* – BZ1: *wāfaqnī*.

Translation:

Qāt and Coffee are joined in debate,
In the presence of knowledgeable people.

Qāt said: There is no pleasure like mine
All desire my branch
As I dwell humble in the garden

So many youths desire me
The lucky one shall delight in my branch,
The famous, the graces of the pleasant.
The *fātiḥah* was composed for me
And the *ḏikr* and the oath for God[17]

Coffee answered him eloquently:
My star has risen before yours
While I am served in cups
As a fine beverage every morning
Often the generous and the bountiful
Come close to me, proximate
He who tastes me will be grateful and bless[18]
And the *fātiḥah* is the best verse

Qāt said: My name is renowned
Among people of pleasure it is known
I have a garb and appearance sounder than yours
My Sheik *Raḍwān*[19] diffuses fragrance
And so *al-Aẖḍar*[20] is my celebrated Sheik
In the day of delight and rejoicing
My turn at noon will happen
And I shall entertain of an evening with people of grace

Coffee answered him: Hold!
I have a recognized Sheik like yours
Al-Šāḏilī[21] is my esteemed Sheik
The luminosity of the mosques and the retreats
My pleasure never ends
He who tastes me stopped there
Every time my pleasure is served
And I am content in the place of nobility

Qāt said: Cease rebuking
Excess anxiety is not needed
I have a contract, I have a binding pact
One and all wish for my banquet
How many gatherings I have
I am related to every matter
(Mount) Ṣabur[22] said: My branch has increased
If mind is turned to it, and much more

Coffee answered him: Hasten,
Comprehend my words and listen
My statement is a lesson for the body
He who has delighted in my bliss is content
I have collected all four humours
From the Excellent Doctor (God)
The yellow bile and the blood, the black bile and the phlegm
No one shall see any pain from me

Qāt said: My pleasure excels
I am recognized everywhere.
(Now) Tobacco came to give evidence against Qāt
He told him: Why you are stubborn?
The Devil, your Sheik, has not come.
Who trusted you and let you come to town
Ibn al-Muʾayyad has shouted at you
And let you be burned in al-ʿAmad.[23]
Tobacco turned away and spoke no more
Requesting the judgment of the adherents of al-Šāḏilī[24]

Wine enters eagerly
He says: Why you are in a quarrel?
All is right and has good life
You have got payment in advance
You have been forcibly taken by God's Will
Your pleasures suit each other
On the day of happiness we shall all assemble
We shall dispel worry and sorrow
Sālim says: I have completed my verse
And I praise my God
Who directs me to arrange my speech
He recompenses him who is patient
He is my glory, He constitutes my victory
He diverts all worries away from my heart
He bestowed on me knowledge and let me comprehend,
How to compose verses and inscribe with the pen.

The quarrel between *qāt* and coffee seemingly ends with the intervention of wine, making peace between the two parties. A similar solution of making peace is presented by Šabazī in his other poem: *jamʿatkum ʿīzāz ʿindī / wa-maṭlabī fīkum wa-sirr qaṣdī* / [...] *al-kull yā afnān tuʿjibūnī* (You are both dear to me / you are my desire and what I aim for / [...] your pleasures both make me content). But immediately after that, Šabazī does not fail to determine the superiority of wine: *wa-sīdakum ẖamr al-zabīb ṣāfī / muzhī al-maqām ḍīq al-qulūb šāfī* (your master is raisin wine, pure / who makes the company bloom and cures the distress of hearts). However, in our poem peace is made only after *qāt* is severely attacked and criticized by tobacco, who says that one scholar, Ibn al-Muʾayyad, ruled that it should be burned. In fact we see here the tension between two contradictory tendencies regarding *qāt*: its popularity, particularly among the higher social strata who could afford it, while religious scholars generally forbade it due to its narcotic effect.

I could not identify a Muslim scholar named Ibn al-Muʾayyad. Still, many famous Yemeni scholars and writers, like the aforementioned Ṣāliḥ al-Maqbalī, and Muḥammad al-Šawkānī (1760–1834), forbade the use of *qāt*,[25] while many poets and Sufi scholars adopted a highly positive attitude to it and wrote about it with great enthusiasm. Such are the renowned Zaydī Imām Šaraf al-Dīn Yaḥyā (1473–1557/8) and his sons ᶜAbd Allah (*c.* 1510–1565), and ᶜAlī (1521–1570), and the Sufi Muḥammad al-ᶜUqayl al-Yamanī (d. 1602), who were the first to recount the virtues of the *qāt* (Schopen 1978: 187–200). But it is related that Imam Šaraf al-Dīn Yaḥyā banned the consumption of *qāt* as well as coffee (Serjeant & Lewcock 1983: 173; Varisco 2007: 245).[26] In general, the religious scholars during the first generations after the "revelation" of *qāt* did not tend to ban it and it became a subject of debate only from the second half of the sixteenth century (Varisco 2007: 252).[27] However, reality was always much more vigorous than any religious or health arguments (Wagner MS 2005: 122–127), although up to the mid-nineteenth century it was mainly consumed by rich people because of its high price (Varisco 2007: 250).

Chewing *qāt* was not as common among the Jews in Yemen as it was among their Muslim neighbours; and it was more common among the Jewish communities in the southern area of Šarᶜab than among the Jews of Ṣanᶜāʾ. A rabbi of the Jewish community of Radāᶜ in the second quarter of the twentieth century actually ruled that it was prohibited by religion. This accords with the widespread Yemeni-Jewish maxim: *al-qāt wulᶜat al-muslimīn, wa-al-ᶜanab wulᶜat al-yahūd* (*qāt* is the pleasure of the Muslims and grapes [wine or araq] is the pleasure of the Jews).[28] This maxim, expressing the strong attraction of the Muslims in Yemen to *qāt*, corresponds to Wagner's very instructive conclusion: "Many poems devoted to coffee and *qāt* drew from the classical Arabic *ẖamriyyah* [wine poem. Y.T.] in their libertinism and eroticism" (Wagner MS 2005: 121; see also pp. 130, 132–133). This was not the case with Yemeni-Jewish poetry in which versifying about *qāt* was limited to *munādamāt* without any libertine or erotic overtone. In any case, Yemeni-Jewish poetry — in Hebrew or Arabic — featured no real debate about the adverse effects of chewing *qāt*, but only indirectly referred to it in the *munādamāt*, with the challenge by coffee. The final result of the debate, the poetical solution, is no winner or two winners: each of the debaters is legitimately accepted and its significant contribution to happiness is highly esteemed.

I could find only one Yemeni-Muslim debate poem between *qāt* and coffee, of the kind discussed in this paper: a *qaṣīdah* by ᶜAbd al-Karīm ibn Aḥmad Muṭahhar (d. 1946), but I would not take this as conclusive. An earlier literary debate between coffee and *qāt* in *maqāmah* (rhymed prose) form is presented in *Tarwīḥ al-awqāt fī al-mufāḫarah bayn al-qahwah wa-l-qāt* by Muḥammad al-Muᶜallimī (d. 1861–1862) (Ḥibšī 1987: 357–378). Other literary expressions of the keen social and religious tension between *qāt* and coffee are well known in Yemeni-Muslim literature since the sixteenth century to the present day (Wagner MS 2005; Weir 1985: 76–78). The similarity of the praises of the *qāt* in Šabazī's and other Jewish poets' verse is well illustrated by two lines from a poem by ᶜAbd Allah ibn Aḥmad ibn Isḥāq (d. 1777–1778), depicted by Wagner as "a poet who seems to have been a fence-sitter in the debate between coffee and *qāt*" (Wagner MS 2005: 131):

mā fī al-marāqiḥ miṯl al-qāt marqaḥah
yahdī ilā kull qalb minhi afrāḥan
hayhāt hayhāt mā l-ṣahbāʾ tuqās bihi
wa-law udīrat ᶜalā l-nidmān aqdāḥan

Translation:

Among the intoxicants there is none like *qāt*
To guide happiness to every heart
What a difference! What a difference! Red [wine] cannot compare to it
Even if it is passed around to the boon-companions in flagons.[29]

Note too that twentieth-century popular verse of the Arabian Peninsula contains some debate poems between coffee and tea.[30] Nevertheless, we can conclude that Sālim Šabazī was, like many other Jewish poets in Yemen who were indeed Yemeni poets, unquestionably connected with Yemeni-Muslim verse; but for reasons having to do with their separate spiritual and social legacy, they developed their distinctive poetry. We can say that the impressive number of debate poems in Šabazī's verse (10) is due to his relation to Hebrew poetry, in which this genre of debate poems is already known from the ancient Palestinian liturgical school.

Notes

1 For a detailed study on the *ḥumaynī* see Ghānim 1972; for a collection of *ḥumaynī* poems see ʿAmrī 2001.

2 On *hazl* in Arabic poetry see Sadan 1983; Van Gelder 1991.

3 For a general study on *Rangstreit* literature see Steinschneider 1908 (a list of more than 160 pieces, briefly reviewed with many additions by Rescher [1925]). On the Arabic mediaeval *munāẓarāt* see Ḥasnāwī 1999; Mattock 1991; Van Gelder 1991; 1987 (Pen versus Sword); Heinrichs 1991 (Rose versus Narcissus); on the Hebrew mediaeval poems see Haberman 1943; Turniansky 1982; Van Bekkum 1991. On the tenth-century roots of the *munāẓarāt* (or *munāfarāt*) about philosophical or scientific issues, generally held in the presence of ruler or vizier who acted as an arbiter, see Kraemer 1992: 179–180.

4 See also Bacher 1909: 138–132.

5 See also Bacher 1909: 143–146. For debate poems between cities in Arabic literature, like Mecca versus Medina, see Wagner E 1963: 14–17. The *munāẓarah* between cities or towns in Yemeni-Muslim literature is known in the *maqāmah* (rhymed prose) style, e.g. ʿAbd Allah al-Wazīr's (d. 1734–1735) *maqāmah* on Bīr al-ʿAzab and al-Rawḍah, the two garden localities close to Ṣanʿāʾ (Wazīr 1986). For other works of that kind see Wagner MS 2005: 145, n. 5.

6 Six of them are listed by Bacher (1910: 83, no. 16).

7 See also Steinschneider 1908: 57–58, no. 104.

8 See also Steinschneider 1908: 22, no. 4; Bacher 1909: 131–132. For a debate of the Heart-versus-Eye-poem by the ʿAbbāsī poet ʿAbbās ibn al-Aḥnaf see Wagner E 1963: 18–19. Wagner believes that Ibn al-Aḥnaf borrowed this theme from Jewish literature.

9 See also Bacher 1909: 132–133.

10 See also Bacher 1909: 133–134. For a debate of Rose versus Narcissus in Muslim Arabic verse see Heinrichs 1991.

11 This poem was republished by Qāfiḥ 1961: 224–225 (2002: 295–297) (with a Hebrew translation); Schopen 1978: 201–205, 242–245 (in Arabic characters with a German translation); Ḥibšī 1981–1982: 197–199 (partial text in Arabic characters); Klein-Franke 1987: 280, 297. See also Bacher 1909: 134–138. For a short note see Weir 1985: 240.

12 The legend wrongly explains the literary meaning of ʿUdayn as two twigs, but in fact it is the diminutive form of *ʿadan*.

13 Bacher 1910: 39 (underlined words in original text); compare Wagner E 1963: 4, n. 1.

14 This manuscript, of more than 1300 pages, was copied by my father Ḥayyim Tobi in the late 1930s, after his immigration from Ṣanʿāʾ to Jerusalem in 1935; it is one of the largest Judeo-Yemeni *dawāwīn*.

15 This manuscript and MS BZ 1238, copied by Yiḥyê ʿIrāqī during the 1930s and the 1940s in Tel Aviv, after his immigration from the north of Yemen, are the largest Judeo-Yemeni *dawāwīn* known to me.

16 I could not consult MS R as it had been sold to an unknown person or institute.

17 *Fātiḥah* and *ḏikr* are two Muslim religious terms that Šabazī has no difficulty using. The first occurs again in this poem, and in Šabazī's other debate poem on *qāt* and *qahwah*. The second term can mean the Qurʾān but in this case is taken to refer to the Sufi chanting of the name of God.

18 In the original text *basmal wa-sallam*, two typical Muslim verbs.

19 I have no idea of the identity of this person, but it may be the nickname of something connected with *qāt*.

20 See note 19.

21 According to Yemeni tradition, ʿAlī ibn ʿAmr al-Šāḏilī, the patron saint of Mocha (d. 1418), discovered coffee and distributed it all over the country (Wagner MS 2005: 122), and thus it took the place of *qāt* (Weir 1985: 76). Sheik Šāḏilī is mentioned in Šabazī's other poem too. After him the Šāḏiliyyah is used as a metonym for coffee, twice in Šabazī's other poem, and also in other debate poems. In certain Yemeni sources the import of coffee to Yemen is ascribed to some other Sufi scholars, such as Aḥmad ibn ʿAlwān (d. 1267) (Varisco 2007: 245). In Yemeni-Jewish folktales Ibn ʿAlwān figures as the mystical adversary of Šabazī.

22 Not far from Taʿizz, where there where extensive plantations of high-quality *qāt* were situated. Compare Qāt's words in Šabazī's other poem: *jabal Ṣabur suknī* (Mount Ṣabur is my dwelling). Jabal Ṣabur, especially the area of Hadanān on its slopes, is one of the principal and most famous *qāt*-growing places, as mentioned both by Yemeni poets and scholars and by foreign travellers (Varisco 2007: 230, 245–247). In the area of Hadanān *qāt* is picked three times a year, while in other areas only twice (2007: 243).

23 A town in southern Yemen, apparently mentioned here only for the rhyme.

24 See n. 21.

25 In accordance with his ruling, the "Šawkānī Publishing House" (*Dār al-Šawkānī li-l-Maṭbaᶜah wa-l-Našr*) published a collection of religious documents to support the prohibition of *qāt* (Mismār 1998).

26 The contradiction between Imam Yaḥyā's poem and his ruling is discussed by M.S. Wagner (2005: 145–146, n. 21).

27 For a comprehensive study on the debate about the *qāt* see Varisco 2004.

28 David Šemûᵓēl Karasso, the Jewish merchant of Salonica, who lived in Yemen from 1875 to 1880, reports on *qāt* chewing by the local population at coffee shops at noon, when all shopkeepers close their business, but nothing is said about Jews (Karasso 1880: 92–93, 107 [a Hebrew translation of the second part of this very rare source in Judeo-Spanish is included in Tobi 1976: 121–190]; Tobi 1976: 132–133, 143).

29 For other Yemeni-Muslim poems praising *qāt* see Wagner MS 2005: 130–137.

30 Serjeant 1951, Arabic section: 38–53 (Ḥaḍramawt); Holes 1996 (Bahrain). I have to thank my colleague Prof. Mikhail Rodionov for informing me about the Ḥaḍramī poem and about a collection of *ḥumaynī* Ḥaḍramī verse on tea and coffee collected by his Ḥaḍramī friend Šayẖ ᶜAlī Bā Rajāᵓ. See also Wagner E 1963: 3–5.

Sigla

ḤḤ *Ḥāpeṣ Ḥayyim* in Muqayṭun 1955.
ḤuḤ *Ḥuppat Ḥatānîm* in ᶜAwād & Co. 1925.

References

ᶜAmir Y.
2000. *Šîrātō šel r. Yôsēp ben Yiśrâᵓēl*. PhD thesis, Ramat Gan, Bar Ilan University. [Unpublished].

ᶜAmrī M./ed. Ḥ. al-ᶜAmrī.
2001. *Safīnat al-adab wa-l-taᵓrīẖ*. iii. *Min al-adab al-yamanī (al-naṯr wa-l-ḥumaynī)*. Beirut: Dār al-Fikr al-Muᶜāṣir.

ᶜAwāḍ M. & Co.
1925. *Ḥuppat Ḥatānīm* [a collection of Jewish-Yemeni poems]. Aden: M. ᶜAwāḍ & Co.

Bacher W.
1909. Zur Rangstreit-Literatur aus der arabischen Poesie der Juden Jemens. Pages 131–147 in G. Maspero (ed.), *Mélanges Hartwig Derenbourg*. Paris: Ernest Leroux.
1910. *Die hebräische und arabische poesie der Juden Jemens*. Strasbourg: Karl J. Trübner.

Ghānim M.A.
1972. Verse used in Ṣanᶜānī songs. *Al-Abhath* 25: 17–326.

Haberman A.M.
1943. Rešîmāh šel šîrê vikkuᵓaḥ le-maᶜalōt be-ᶜiḇrît. Pages 59–62 in D. Frankel (ed.), *Sēfer ha-yôvēl li-ḵvôd Prof. Alexander Marx*. New York: ᶜAlîm.

Hallevy R.
1998–2003. *Šîrat yiśrâᵓēl be-tēmān — mi-miḇḥar ha-šîrâh ha-Šabazīt ha-têmânît*. i–ii. Qiryat Ōnô: Māḵôn Môšêh; iii. Tel Aviv: Afikim.

Ḥasnāwī R.J.A.
1999. *Al-munāẓarāt al-laghawiyyah wa-l-adabiyyah fī al-ḥaḍārah al-ᶜarabiyyah al-islāmiyyah*. Amman: Dār Usāmah li-n-Našr wa-l-Tawzīᶜ.

Heinrichs W.
1991. Rose versus narcissus. Observations on an Arabic literary debate. Pages 179–198 in Reinink & Vanstiphout 1991.

Ḥibšī ᶜA.
1981–1982. Al-qāt fī al-adab al-yamanī. Pages 173–202 in *Al-qāt fī ḥayāt al-yaman wa-l-yamaniyyīn: raṣd wa-dirāsāt wa-taḥlīl*. Ṣanᶜāᵓ: Markaz al-Dirāsāt wa-l-Buḥūṯ al-Yamanī.
1987. *Majmūᶜ al-maqāmat al-yamaniyyah*. Ṣanᶜāᵓ: Maktabat al-Jīl al-Jadīd.
1986. *Al-adab al-yamanī: ᶜaṣr ẖurūj al-atrāk al-awwal min al-yaman 1635–1879*. Beirut: Al-Dār al-Yamaniyyah.

Holes C.
1996. The dispute of coffee and tea: A debate-poem from the Gulf. Pages 302–315 in J.R. Smart (ed.), *Tradition and Modernity in Arabic Language and Literature.* Richmond: Curzon.

Homerin T.E.
1994. *From Arab Poet to Muslim Saint: Ibn al-Fāriḍ, His Verse, and His Shrine.* Columbia, SC: University of South Carolina.

Karasso D.S.
1880. *Zikrôn têmân: La istoria de los judeos de la parti de teman.* Constantinople: Il Tiempo.

Klein-Franke A.
1987. The Jews of Yemen. Pages 265–280 & 297–299 in W. Daum (ed.), *Yemen: 3000 Years of Art and Civilization in Arabia Felix.* Innsbruck: Pinguin-Verlag.

Kraemer J.L.
1992. *Humanism in the Renaissance of Islam.* Leiden: E.J. Brill.

Mattock J.A.
1991. The Arabic Tradition: Origin and Development. Pages 153–163 in Reinink & Vanstiphout 1991.

Mismār ᶜA.
1998. *Šahādat al-ṯiqāb ᶜalā aḍrār al-qāt.* [Ṣanᶜāᵓ].

Muqayṭun Š (ed.).
1955. *Ḥāpeṣ Ḥayyim* [a collection of Jewish-Yemeni poems]. Jerusalem: Š. Muqayṭun

Piamenta M.
1997. Al-jamāl al-ḥissī wa-l-jismānī fī balāghat al-šiᶜr al-yamanī al-mudarrij ᵓilā al-ᶜammiyyah (dirāsah laghawiyyah). *Al-Karmal* 18–19: 93–114.

Qāfiḥ Y.
1961. *Halikôt têmân.* Jerusalem: Ben Zvi Institute. [Reprinted under the same title but with new pagination, 2002].

Reinink G.J. & Vanstiphout H.L.J. (eds).
1991. *Dispute poems and Dialogues in the Ancient and Mediaeval Near East.* Leuven: Department Orientalistiek.

Rescher O.
1925. Zu Moritz Steinschneider "Rangstreitliteratur". *Der Islam* 14: 397–401.

Rodionov M.
2005. Spor dvukh napitkov (iz poezii Hadramauta). Pages 380–384 in A.V. Sedov & I.M. Smilianskaya (eds), *Arabia Vitalis. Festschrift for the 60th anniversary of V.V. Naumkin.* Moscow: Russian Academy of Science, Institute of Oriental Studies.

Sadan J.
1983. *Al-adab al-ᶜarabī al-hāzil wa-nawādir al-ṯuqalāᵓ.* Tel Aviv: University of Tel Aviv.

Šawkānī A./ed. Ḥusayn al-ᶜAmrī.
1986. *Dīwān al-šawkānī islāk al-jawhar.* Damascus: Dār al-Fikr (second edition).

Schopen A.
1978. *Das Qāt: Geschichte und Gebrauch des Genussmittels Catha Edulis Forsk. In der arabischen Republik Jemen.* Wiesbaden: Franz Steiner Verlag.

Semah D.
1988. The poetics of *ḥumaynī* poetry in Yemen. *Jerusalem Studies in Arabic and Islam* 11: 220–239.
1989. Li-mqôrôtâb ha-ṣūrāniyyim šel šîr ha-ēzôr ha-têmânî. *Tarbiz* 58: 239–260.

Serjeant R.B.
1951. *South Arabian Poetry, I: Prose and Poetry from Ḥaḍramawt.* London: Taylor's Foreign Press.

Serjeant R.B. & Lewcock R.
1983. *Ṣanᶜāᵓ: An Arabian Islamic City.* London: World of Islam Festival Trust.

Steinschneider M.
1908. *Rangstreit-Literatur: Ein Beitrage zur Vergleichenden Literatur- und Kulturgeschichte.* Vienna: Osterreichische Akademie der Wissenschaften.

Tobi Y.
1976. *Yehūdē têmân ba-mēʾâh ha-yôd-têt.* Tel Aviv: Afikim.
1991. *Aḇrāhām ben ḥalfôn: šîrîm.* Tel Aviv: Afikim.
2006*a*. Yemeni Jewish and Muslim *Muwaššḥāt.* Pages 319–327 in E. Emery (ed.), *Muwashshahaat: Proceedings of the Conference on Arabic and Hebrew Strophic Poetry and its Romance Parallels, School of Oriental & African Studies, London, 8-10 October 2004.* London: RN Books.
2006*b*. The *Ḥumaynī* poetry of the Yemeni-Jewish poet Shalom Šabazī. Pages 168–182 in Y.E. Berezkin, I.A. Alimov, M.I. Vasilenko, M.N. Souvorov & S.A. Frantzouzov (eds), *Arabian culture in Asian Context, Mikhail Rodionov Festschrift.* St Petersburg: Peterburgskoe vostokvedenie. [In Russian].

Turniansky Ch.
1982. Šîr ha-vikkūʾaḥ ha-yehūdī ve-gilgūlô be-aškenaz. *Ha-Sifrūt* 32: 2–12.

Van Bekkum W.J.
1991. Observations on the Hebrew debate in medieval Europe. Pages 77–90 in Reinink & Vanstiphout 1991.

Van Gelder G.J.
1987. The conceit of pen and Sword: on an Arabic literary debate. *Journal of Semitic Studies* 32: 329–360.
1991. Arabic debates of jest and earnest. Pages 199–211 in Reinink & Vanstiphout 1991.

Varisco D.M.
2004. The elixir of life or the devil's cud: the debate over *qāt* (*catha edulis*) in Yemeni culture. Pages 101–118 in R. Coomber & N. South (eds), *Drug Use and Cultural Context: Traditions, Change and Intoxicants beyond "The West".* London: Free Association Books.
2007. Turning over a new leaf: the impact of the *qāt* (catha edulis) Yemeni horticulture. Pages 239–256 in M. Conan & W.J. Kress (eds), *Botanical Progress, Horticultural Innovation and Cultural Change.* Washington, DC: Dumbarton Oaks Research Library and Collection.

Wagner E.
1963. *Die Arabische Rangstreitdichtung und ihre Einordnung in die allgemeine Literaturgeschichte.* Wiesbaden: Franz Steiner Verlag.

Wagner M.S.
2004*a*. *The Poetics of* Ḥumaynī *Verse: Language and Meaning in the Arab and Jewish Vernacular Poetry of Yemen.* PhD thesis, New York University. [Unpublished].
2004*b*. Changing visions of the tribesman in Yemeni vernacular literature. *Al-Masar* 5: 3–30.
2005. The debate between Coffee and Qāt in Yemenī literature. *Middle Eastern Literatures* 8: 121–149.
2006. Arabic influence on Šabazian poetry in Yemen. *Journal of Semitic Studies* 51: 117–136.

Wazīr ᶜA./ed. ᶜA. al-Ḥibšī.
1986. *Aqrāṭ al-ḏahab fī al-mufākharah bayn al-rawḍah wa-bīr al-ᶜazab.* Ṣanᶜāʾ: Al-Dār al-Yamaniyyah li-n-Našr wa-l-Tawzīᶜ.

Weir S.
1985. *Qat in Yemen: Consumption and Social Change.* London: The British Museum.

Zabārah M.
1998. *Ḫulāṣat al-mutūn fī abnāʾ wa-nubalāʾ al-yaman al-maymūn.* Richmond, VA: Yemeni Heritage & Research Center.

Author's address
Prof. Yosef Tobi, Hebrew & Comparative Literature, University of Haifa, Haifa, Israel 31905.
e-mail tobiy@research.haifa.ac.il

Proceedings of the Seminar for Arabian Studies 38 (2008): 311–318

The Azd migrations reconsidered: narratives of ᶜAmr Muzayqiya and Mālik b. Fahm in historiographic context

Brian Ulrich

Summary

The migration of the Azd tribes from western Arabia to ᶜUman has occupied a central place in the history of the pre-Islamic Persian Gulf. This paper takes a tradition critical approach in examining the narratives of these migrations independently of each other. The author argues that ᶜAmr Muzayqiya and Mālik b. Fahm were not originally part of the same complex, and that whereas the former clearly dates from the early Islamic period, the latter may go back to pre-Islamic Arabia. There is, however, no good evidence with which to fix a date for any migration into ᶜUman recalled in the Mālik b. Fahm stories.

Keywords: Azd, Oman, Samad, Ibn al-Kalbī, Arab tribal history

The Azd were one of the most important Arab tribal groups during the Umayyad period, prominent in such places as Basra, the Jazira, Azerbaijan, Khurasan, and parts of the Arabian Peninsula. In the literary sources, their origin story is "The Scattering of al-Azd", which tells of their flight from the bursting of the Maʾrib dam and subsequent migrations, with groups remaining behind in different areas. The story of the Azd migrations represented an important component of mediaeval Islamic conceptions of pre-Islamic history, one which has also been invoked by modern scholars of the period. Some of the latter, especially J.C. Wilkinson, have seen in them literary representations of long-term developments (1977: 128). In this paper I shall attempt to deepen our understanding of these sources by adopting a tradition critical approach, examining the Azd migration traditions both in the context of the historiographical milieu of the early Abbasid period and within the oeuvre of the writers to which they are attributed.

The tradition of the Azd migrations can be neatly separated into two parts, one concerning the flight of ᶜAmr Muzayqiya from the Sayl al-ᶜArim and the "Scattering of the Azd", and the other involving Mālik b. Fahm's migration from south-western Arabia to become Oman's first Arab settler. Colonel S.B. Miles noted that al-Azkawī's account of Mālik b. Fahm's journey and the Battle of Salūt (al-Azkawī 1985: 211–224) does not mention the bursting of the Maʾrib dam (Miles 1919: 16–17). Al-Azkawī's account is almost identical to that in the *Ansāb al-ᶜArab* and both are sourced to an al-Kalbī, certainly Hishām b. Muḥammad Ibn al-Kalbī (al-ᶜAwtabī 1984, ii: 265–282). The *Ansāb* author, in turn, ties this account in with an earlier account of the flight from Maʾrib led by ᶜAmr Muzayqiya by means of a brief tradition from Abū Ḥātim al-Sijistānī which tells of Mālik's decision to leave the Sarāt Mountains following a dispute over the treatment of a man under his protection, a tradition which in a few brief clauses mentions the scattering of the Azd and the flood as events prior to Mālik's residence in Sarat. In *Taʾrīkh al-Mawṣil*, al-Azdī has a very similar story recounted through a different chain of authorities, these seemingly local to the Jazira, which omits Maʾrib altogether; al-Azdī himself mentions it fleetingly in his introduction to the report (1967: 96–97). Meanwhile, of the ᶜAmr Muzayqiya traditions, those in al-Balādhurī's *Futūḥ al-Buldān* and al-Hamdānī's *al-Iklīl* make no mention of Mālik b. Fahm, while that in *Ansāb al-ᶜArab* mentions only his name alongside that of ᶜAmr Muzayqiya as leading the Azd from Maʾrib (al-ᶜAwtabī 1984, ii: 189) and again as the leader of the Azd ᶜUmān in a stylized list of all the Azd groups (al-ᶜAwtabī 1984, ii: 193).

This split is also seen in the classical genealogical scheme largely associated with Ibn al-Kalbī. Al-Azd had several sons, but the two most important were Māzin and Naṣr. Māzin, sometimes called Ghassān, was the ancestor of ᶜAmr Muzayqiya, who links together a number of prominent groups such as the Ghassānids and Anṣār. What is striking is that, of these groups, only the

Muhallabids and their relatives among the B. ᶜImrān seem recognizably Azdi during the Umayyad period. The other significant Azd groups, the Azd ᶜUman, Azd Sārah, and Azd Shanūᵓah, are descendants of Naṣr. (Caskel & Strenziok 1966, i: tables 176, 210).

The traditions surrounding ᶜAmr Muzayqiya as we have them clearly belong to the Islamic period, and were usually deployed to promote the Anṣār by linking them with pre-Islamic Arabian kings. One piece of evidence for this is Muḥammad b. Ḥabīb's genealogical work, available in manuscript in the British Library, where Ibn al-Kalbī is quoted as saying that "The Anṣār are said to be Imruᵓ al-Qays" (Ibn al-Kalbī: f. 247. Caskel noted that in the same manuscript the Anṣār occupied the same place in the Yamani genealogy as the Quraysh did for the Nizaris (Caskel & Strenziok 1966, i: 92). The Azd, Ghassān, and Anṣār also immediately follow Qaḥṭān in a Rajip Pasha manuscript which is also from Ibn Ḥabīb (1966, i: 99–101), though I have been unable to examine it to see how closely its presentation compares with the British Library version. Other sources also emphasize the Anṣāri connections to southern Arabia through the ᶜAmr Muzayqiya tradition. In *Futūḥ al-Buldān*, al-Balādhurī incorporates it into his account of the history of Medina, concluding that the Anṣār tribes became great during the Jāhiliyyah so that they could later support Muḥammad (1866: 18). It also figures into the poetic corpus of Ḥassān b. Thābit, Muḥammad's "poet laureate", as well as one al-Nuᶜmān b. Bashīr al-Ansārī (Caskel & Strenziok 1966, ii: 32).

ᶜAmr Muzayqiya's connection to al-Azd was slight enough that in his *al-Iklīl*, al-Hamdānī doesn't even mention the two together. He describes ᶜAmr's older brother ᶜImrān b. ᶜĀmir as a king and a *kāhin* who possessed knowledge of the religion of Sulaymān. ᶜImrān warned people that they would be scattered throughout the land, but was not heeded. When he died at age 400 [sic], he summoned ᶜAmr and predicted both the breaking of the dam and the Ethiopian invasion as God's wrath. He also added, however, that a new blessing would come in the form of a prophet Muḥammad al-Tihāmī. He also bids his brother marry Ṭurayfah bt. al-Khayr al-Hajuriyya, who was the inheritor of his knowledge (al-Hamdānī 1940: 217–218).

In his *al-Ishtiqāq*, Ibn Durayd largely follows Ibn al-Kalbī in using ᶜAmr Muzayqiya to link together diverse groups. Although it goes unmentioned in the text, modern scholars have linked the work to the *shuᶜubiyya* controversy because it was written to refute those who claimed Arab names had no meaning (Ibn Durayd [1958]: 4; Toorawa 2005: 85). According to Ibn Durayd, ᶜAmr Muzayqiya got his byname because he tore up his clothes every day so that no one could wear them after him. Among his sons, Jafnah was the ancestor of the Ghassānids, and his name came perhaps from a vine, perhaps a sword, or perhaps a famous person. Ibn Durayd agrees with other sources, however, in claiming that the name Ǧassān derives from a watering hole. Al-Ḥārith was called "Muḥarriq" because he was the first to torment people with fire. (1) Thaᶜlabah, ancestor of the Anṣār, was called al-ᶜAnqaᵓ because of his long neck. Ḏuhl is the ancestor of the bishops of Najrān who sent a delegation to the Prophet. A final son, Kaᶜb, was the ancestor of Samawᶜal b. Ḥayya, a Jew who ruled Taymāᵓ and became arabicized. Al-Hārith's descendants included another Jew, al-Fiṭyawn, who was King of Yathrib before being killed by the Ansar; some of his descendants fought at Badr (Ibn Durayd [1958]: 435–436).

The longest extant version of the ᶜAmr Muzayqiya narrative is found in the *Ansāb al-ᶜArab* attributed to al-ᶜAwtabī, a text the provenance of which has been the subject of some commentary. Wilkinson believed all extant copies stemmed from a single incomplete, defective, and probably edited parent, though he did not know about the Krakow manuscript. He also suggested that its author was a Salmah b. Muslim who lived in the early eleventh century and was the grandson of the *Ḍīyāᵓ* author (Wilkinson 1976: 153). Part of his evidence was that the *Ansāb* author claimed to have met a Shīrāzī who had met the son of Ibn Durayd (1976: 161 n. 9). Hassan Naboodah has argued convincingly that its author is not in fact an al-ᶜAwtabī, but rather an unknown writer of the mid-tenth century. The attribution to al-ᶜAwtabi appears only in the work of the nineteenth-century author as-Sālimī. Not only are there stylistic and political differences between the *Ansāb* and other works attributed to al-ᶜAwtabī, but all sources used by the author date before the tenth century. The author's own claim is that he had covered everything up until 345/956, and this reflects the work's actual content, which refers to events past that date in only a few brief instances, which Naboodah explains as later additions by copyists (2006: 141–167). Naboodah also notes that most of the work's sources were Iraqi, suggesting that he had studied in Basra at some point (2006: 164–166, see also al-Rawas 2000: 7). One implication of this is that the *Ansāb al-ᶜArab* is not a strictly Omani source, but rather a work within the broader early Islamic cultural milieu which has an Omani emphasis.

This pseudo-ᶜAwtabī's account of ᶜAmr Muzayqiya is sourced to an Abū ᶜAbdallāh al-Mawṣilī, coming via Wahb b. Munabbih and Ibn al-Kalbī. I have not been able to identify this al-Mawṣilī, though parts of his text are identical to the parallel account in al-Masᶜūdī (2) (1966, ii: 318–333). It begins with Sabā, his progeny, and the prosperity of Maʾrib, including a detailed description of the dam. When the people forsook God, they were warned of an impending catastrophe by ᶜImrān, as in al-Hamdānī. Before his death, he summoned his brother and urged him to marry the *kāhinah* Ṭurayfah, of the people of Radamān from Ḥimyar. One day Ṭurayfah divines the imminent bursting of the dam and warns her husband. ᶜAmr's first instinct is to conceal the fact and sell his property in the region, but he then fears people might think ill of him if he did that. Instead, he invites the people of Maʾrib to a feast, where by prior arrangement he quarrels with one of his sons who winds up striking him. This leads the shocked people to want to buy his property, in the expectation that he will soon leave because of the insult. His property thus sold, he departs with his sons, accompanied by Mālik b. Fahm and the Azd.

The Azd then travelled north passing through several countries, in each of which they fought against the inhabitants and left behind some of their number. ᶜAmr Muzayqiya died early on, and was replaced as king by his son Thaᶜlabah. Finally the Azd reached Mecca, where they drove out the Jurhum before scattering in different directions in search of better lands, leading to the different groups being linked as al-Azd in the genealogies, such as the Ghassānids and Khuzāᶜah. In some ways, this represents a second distinct "scattering". Thaᶜlabah's own descendants, Aws and Khazraj, come to occupy Yathrib, where in early Islamic times they become the Anṣār.

This account displays several features that date it to the early Islamic period. The most obvious is the prominence given to Mecca and Medina, as well as the Anṣār. In addition, it is a perfect example of the *iftirāq* theme identified by Werner Caskel as a means by which tribes were linked into a unified people through recourse to a common ancestor, whose descendants were then scattered throughout the peninsula (Caskel & Strenziok 1966, i: 41–44). As Yamanis, the ᶜAmr Muzayqiya group traced themselves back to the ancient South Arabian kingdoms, exemplified in the person of Sabā, one of the descendants of Qaḥṭān.

It is extremely difficult to reconstruct a chronology for the development of the ᶜAmr Muzayqiya accounts. Caskel posits some ideas culminating with the end of the Sufyānid period; however, his evidence consists entirely of snatches of poetry (Caskel & Strenziok 1966, ii: 32–33). Whether we accept the application of the Parry-Lord thesis of oral formulaic composition to such early Arabic poetry or Gregor Schoeler's model of written composition for oral performance with the acceptance of further development by rāwīs the attribution of verses to certain poets cannot be taken as binding for attitudes present in their lifetime. (3) In the case of Ḥassān b. Thābit, Walid Arafat has also suggested that his name became attached to the work of later poets glorifying the Anṣār, singling out those which emphasize their genealogy (Ḥassān b. Thābit 1971, i: 28–29).

We can, however, suggest a hypothesis regarding the material's context. In the introduction to his rendition of Ibn Isḥāq's life of the Prophet, which contains several poems referring to the ᶜAmr Muzayqiya tradition, A. Guillaume calls attention to the massacre of Ḥusayn and his followers at Karbala and the sack of Medina in which 10,000 Anṣār were killed at the start of the Second *Fitnah*, and suggests the poetry in Ibn Isḥāq's biography belongs to a world shaped by those events: "Its aim is to set forth the claims of the Anṣār to prominence in Islam not only as men who supported the prophet when the Quraysh opposed him, but as men descended from kings" (Guillaume 1955: xxvii). James Monroe claimed the poetry supported an alleged Shiᶜism on Ibn Isḥāq's part and that the Anṣār were inextricably bound to this movement (Monroe 1983: 371).

It is true that Hishām b. Muḥammad al-Kalbī was based in Kufa, a city which was an early centre of proto-Shiᶜism as well as Jāhiliyya history (Kilpatrick 2003: 15–16), and his father, Muḥammad b. al-Sāʾib al-Kalbī, was said to be an extremist Shiᶜite (Scholler 2000: 18–19). The main elements of the proto-Shiᶜite movement during the eighth century, however, are not well understood, and in any case the Anṣār are only played up in the versions attributed to Ibn Ḥabīb rather than the Escorial manuscript identified as Ibn al-Kalbī's actual *Nasab al-Kabīr*, and which matches the description of the book's contents found in Ibn al-Nadīm's *Fihrist* (1871: 97–98). (4) We would be better off saying merely that the traditions are designed to glorify the Anṣār, and by extension the Yamani grouping to which they are linked.

Shorn of its tenuous links to the migration of ᶜAmr Muzayqiya and his descendants, the account of Mālik b. Fahm includes little of what one might expect if it had early Islamic literary origins. One of the oldest narrative accounts is found in Abū Zakariyya al-Azdī's *Taʾrīkh al-Mawṣil*, an early tenth-century local history from the Jazira. It features under the year 129 AH as part of a special history of the leading Azd clans in the region, all of whom traced their descent to Mālik b. Fahm, and it comes via sources from that area. In this version, the Azd Shanūʾah lived in the Sarah area and multiplied, after which some of them went to Oman and became the Azd ʿUman. Mālik b. Fahm was the first of these, and the reason for his migration was the disrespect shown to his neighbour by the people of an unnamed brother in the matter of that neighbour's dog (al-Azdī 1967: 97). He was eventually killed by his son Sulaymah (1967: 99–100).

Genealogically, al-Azdi's Mālik b. Fahm had fourteen sons, of whom Jadhīmah was the eldest and the one who gave Mālik his *kunyah*. One important aspect of this presentation is that eight of the sons are grouped according to three mothers, from Ṭayʾ, ʿAbd al-Qays, and Kindah (al-Azdī 1967: 98–99). I can find no reason why those tribes would stand out prominently in either Mosul or in Basra, where many of the Mālik b. Fahm groups were before coming to Mosul. They do, however, make sense as important tribes in Oman (al-Rawas 2000: 31; Wilkinson 1977: 244–247). This suggests that the idea of a Mālik b. Fahm grouping goes back at least to Marwānid Oman, and that other elements of the story may do so as well. We might also tentatively accept Asad Ahmed's view that the importance of matrilineal ties declined during the Abbasid period (2007: 280, n. 202). One further note is that "Fakhidh al-Kalbah", the toponym ostensibly explained by the dog story, seems unlikely to be an Iraqi development. (5) The al-Azdī version is also similar to what was very briefly summarized by al-Yaʿqūbī in his *Tārīkh*, including the identification of the Azd ʿUman as originally Azd Shanūʾah (1883, i: 332–333). Pseudo-ʿAwtabī's version comes from Ibn al-Kalbī and is primarily focused not on the migration, but rather on the Battle of Salūt against the Persians. Following the dog quarrel, Mālik b. Fahm passes to Oman by way of Ḥaḍramawt. His followers include not only Azd, but Quḍāʿah, with Mālik and ʿAmr b. Fahm b. Taymallāh listed as among their leaders. Mālik b. Fahm al-Azdī seeks land from Oman's ruler, a *marzubān* under Dārā b. Dārā b. Bahman, and winds up having to win two major battles against them — one against the *marzubān*, and the other against an invasion force sent by Dārā. Mālik reigned as king for seventy years.

One interpretation of Mālik b. Fahm's place in the development of the Azd during the Umayyad period comes from Werner Caskel, who did not address the question of an Azd migration as such, but argued that the Azd of the garrison towns were actually two tribes with the same name (Caskel & Strenziok 1966, ii: 41). He also claims that the Mālik b. Fahm tribes were not originally Azd, but instead added while in Basra to the Daws, who allegedly dominated the Basran Azd prior to their arrival. Wilkinson, however, was unable to find evidence of any Daws group in an important position during the period in question (1969: 55). Caskel cites Julius Wellhausen's assertion that the Ḥuddān, the leaders of the Azd in early Basra, were Daws (Wellhausen 1902: 249). This contention contradicts all the genealogical literature I have examined, including Caskel's own charts (Caskel & Strenziok 1966, i: tables 210–216). Despite this flaw in argumentation, Caskel's justified status as a frequent tribal reference work means his views continue to be cited on this matter. (6)

Wilkinson, on the other hand, sees the story of Mālik b. Fahm as representing genuine historic links between Oman and western Arabia over a period extending from the late Achaemenid period up until the eighth century. He supports this early date by accepting both Dārā b. Dārā as a memory of an Achaemenid presence from when the first Azd arrived and South Arabian artefacts discovered at Mleiha in Sharjah, including an inscription in a South Arabian language as opposed to the Hasaitic inscriptions usually found along that coast (1977: 128–129, 135 n. 6). An attempt to date early Azd migrations with reference to Dārā b. Dārā, however, runs into a problem. It would be remarkable if the local tribal tradition had preserved the same name for a distant monarch's memory as the literary tradition of the garrison towns, and the name Dārā b. Dārā b. Bahman was probably supplied by Ibn al-Kalbī himself. The key to this addition lies in his story of the Tanūkh migrations. Wilkinson himself dealt with these traditions, which he saw as important to developing the ties between the Quḍāʿah and Azd as part of a broader Yamani identity (1969: G4–G7). More recently, they have been studied in depth by Jan Retso. In Ibn al-Kalbī's version, the Tanūkh were a group of tribes that included parts of Maʿadd, Quḍāʿah, and Azd which allied and migrated from Tihāmah to Baḥrayn; among their leaders were the Mālik and ʿAmr b. Fahm b. Taymallāh b. Asad b. Wabarah. One of ʿAmr's descendants, Mālik b. Zuhayr, invited Jadhīmah b. Mālik b. Fahm al-Azdī to dwell with him, and married him to his sister Lamīs bt. Zuhayr, after which the Azd and Tanūkh became allies. The Tanūkh then migrated to Iraq, with Jadhīmah going with them and becoming the first to rule in Iraq as king (Retso 2003:

474–476; al-Ṭabarī 1879–1901, i: 744–750).

Ibn al-Kalbī's Tanūkh material has them leaving Ḥīrah for Syria in the days of Ardashīr b. Bābak (al-Ṭabarī 1879–1901, i: 821–822). From this he could have calculated that the Tanūkh were in Baḥrayn during the Parthian period, which may also have been clear from his sources. The early rulers of Tanūkh included Jadhīmah, who by the seventh century was listed as a son of Mālik b. Fahm. For Ibn al-Kalbī the true Persian rulers were the descendants of Bahman b. Asfandiyār, whose two sons were Dārā, equivalent to Darius I, and Sāsān, ancestor of the Sasanids. In this he followed the official Sasanid court histories, which cast that dynasty as restorers of the Persian Empire of the ancients. The Sasanids denigrated the Arsacids, portraying them as a product of Alexander the Great's plans and not true Iranian rulers (Yarshater 1983: 474). For Ibn al-Kalbī the Seleucid and Parthian era is the age of the "party kings", described, according to Moshe Perlmann's translation from al-Ṭabarī, with the words: "Each of them had only a small domain with castles and structures surrounded by a ditch. Nearby enemies were similarly established, and they would raid one another, only to retreat suddenly" (al-Ṭabarī 1987: 129). For that reason, when confronted with a tradition about conflict between Mālik b. Fahm and a Persian ruler, he had to anchor it chronologically at the end of the Achaemenid period.

The name Dārā b. Dārā in the story of the Battle of Salūt is, therefore, unreliable evidence for chronologically fixing the migrations of those who became the Azd. We are left with a tradition, reported by Ibn al-Kalbī, that brings newcomers into Oman via a southern migration route, who then establish dominance over the country and wage at least two distinct campaigns against Persian forces, one involving a local governor, and the other an invasion from overseas. This gives us little about which we can be more specific, especially since Mālik b. Fahm's kingship may be exaggerated and the two individual campaigns against the Persians may themselves incorporate multiple historical conflicts; a parallel example would be the way Afghan oral accounts of the British wars in Afghanistan frequently merge them into a single event (Dupree 1967: 60–70). Furthermore, we cannot discount the possibility that inhabitants of the area prior to any immigration from the west became incorporated into the Mālik b. Fahm grouping, adding their own historical memories to the general account.

Paul Yule has written that the Samad archaeological culture of Late Iron Age Oman did not evolve out of the Early Iron Age Lizq/Rumaylah culture in south-eastern Arabia (2005: 303). He has also argued that it represents the Azd migrations, based largely on a lack of other known candidates who might have entered Oman around 300 BC, which he takes as both the start of the Samad period and the time of early Azd penetration based on the mention of Dārā b. Dārā by Ibn al-Kalbī (Yule 1999: 123–124). The dating of the beginning of the Samad culture is also complicated due to a paucity of tells, improbable radiocarbon dating results, and the paucity and uncertainty of artefactual comparisons (Yule 2007: 5–8). That said, Jürgen Schreiber's unpublished results from ᶜIbra suggest that the Samad period definitely followed the Early Iron Age, although there could have been a gap between them (Yule 2005: 310). In any case, if the above argument about the literary sources is correct, establishing a connection between the Samad culture and al-Azd must rely on the relationship of that culture with other areas of the Arabian Peninsula associated with them. Scholars should also remain open to the possibility that it represents a group such as the Mahrah whose traditions were preserved only in part or not at all by the early Islamic historians (Dostal 1989: 27–36).

Other archaeological finds have also occasionally been linked to Ibn al-Kalbī's account of the Azd migrations. The Mleiha stele used by Wilkinson is interesting, but also unique. Mohammed Bhacker and Bernadette Bhacker see the account of the Azd migrations as supporting a picture of persistent South Arabian penetration to Oman as revealed in excavations such as those at Khor Rori in Dhofar, though it is unclear from their discussion whether the South Arabian script they refer to is being used for the South Arabian language, as well as whether their evidence supports the presence of actual South Arabians as opposed to something like a transit point for South Arabian goods (Bhacker & Bhacker 2004: 23–25).

My conclusions regarding the accounts of Mālik b. Fahm and ᶜAmr Muzayqiya might contribute to pessimism as to whether early Islamic historians passed down any useful information for reconstructing pre-Islamic Arabian history. This is not my position. Those using this material, however, must take account of the milieu in which it was produced in its extant form, as well as how it fits into the broader views of history of which it frequently forms part. Most Muslim historians of the eighth, ninth, and tenth centuries were not mere collectors, but scholars concerned with the past for a variety of reasons which affected what they chose to preserve and the context in which they preserved it. Understanding these reasons and their effects on the transmission of information, as well as beliefs current when they worked, can help us determine how they worked and thus what to make of their products.

Acknowledgements

I would like to thank the University of Wisconsin Medieval Studies Program for funding a 2005 research trip to Cairo, the University of Wisconsin Department of History for funding a 2006 research trip to London, and the George L. Mosse Program in History for the two-year fellowship that allowed me the leisure to complete this research. My advisor, Michael Chamberlain, has be
en invaluable as a source of support and suggestions, while Michael Lecker generously loaned items from his personal collection while sharing his considerable knowledge of the sources on early Arab tribal history. Paul Yule patiently explained the chronological issues surrounding the Samad culture. Jűrgen Schreiber, Scott Savran, Michael Zwettler, David Morgan, and Christine Kepinski also helped clarify issues that arose in the course of research relevant to this paper, while Larry Thomas provided technical assistance with the genealogical tables. All errors are the sole responsibility of the author.

Notes

1 Although we do not expect these etymologies to be real, the passive form of the noun makes this one especially puzzling.

2 There was an Abu Abdullah al-Mawṣilī in the time of al-Mustarshid in the twelfth century, but if it is the same figure then he must not have had much impact on the content of what he passed down, as al-Maᶜsūdī's parallel version was written in the tenth century (Ibn ᶜAsākir 1995–2001, v. 52: 330–332).

3 For a discussion of issues surrounding the transmission of Arabic poetry, the implications for its content, and relevant references, see James Montgomery's introduction to a recent translation of a selection of Schoeler's articles (Montgomery 2006: 20–23).

4 I have not been to Escorial, and this paper was written based on a copy in the possession of Michael Lecker.

5 Pseudo-ᶜAwtabī names the place "Najd al-Kalbah".

6 Caskel also suggests the Azd used Mālik b. Fahm in order to link themselves to Jadhīmah and the Tanūkh (Caskel & Strenziok 1966, ii: 42). This involves a separate complex of issues, which there is not space to address here.

References

Ahmed A.Q.

2007. *Between the Acts: The Hijazi Elite and the Internal Politics of the Umayyad and Early Abbasid Empires.* PhD thesis, Princeton. [Unpublished].

al-ᶜAwtabī, Salamah ibn Muslim./ed. Anonymous

1984. *al-Ansāb*. (2 volumes). ᶜUmān: Wizārat al-turāth al-qawmī wa-al-thaqāfah.

al-Azdī, Abū Zakariyyāᵓ Yazīd b. Muḥammad/ed. A. Ḥabībah

1967. *Taᵓrīkh al-Mawṣil*. Cairo: Da\r al-taḥrīr lal-ṭabrᶜ wa-al-nashr.

al-Azkawī, Sirḥān b. Sᶜaīd/ed. Aḥmad al-ᶜUbaydlī

1985. *Kashf al-ghummah al-jamiᶜ li-akhbār al-ummah*. Nicosia: Dilmun.

al-Balādhurī, Aḥmad b. Yaḥyā/ed. M.J. de Goeje

1866. *Futūḥ al-Buldān*. Leiden: E.J. Brill.

Bhacker M.R. & Bhacker B.

2004. Qalhat in Arabian History: Context and Chronicles. *Journal of Oman Studies* 13: 11–55.

Caskel W. & Strenziok G.

1966. *Ğamharat an-Nasab. Das genealogicische Werk des Hisam Ibn Muhammad al-Kalbi*. (2 volumes). Leiden: E.J. Brill.

Dostal W.

1989. Mahra and Arabs in South Arabia: A Study in Inter-ethnical Relations. Pages 27–36 in Moawiyah M. Ibrahim (ed.), *Arabian Studies in Honor of Mahmoud Ghul: Symposium at Yarmouk University December 8–11, 1984*. Wiesbaden: Otto Harrassowitz.

Dupree L.
1967. The Retreat of the British Army from Kabul to Jalalabad in 1842: History and Folklore. *Journal of the Folklore Institute* 4/1: 50–74.

Guillaume A.
1955. *The Life of Muhammad: A Translation of Ishaq's Sirat Rasul Allah*. Karachi: Oxford University Press.

al-Hamdānī, Ḥasan b. Aḥmad/ed. N.A. Faris
1940. *Al-Iklīl VIII*. Princeton: Princeton University Press.

Ḥassān b. Thābit/ed. W.N. Arafat
1971. *Dīwān*. (2 volumes). London: Messrs. Luzac and Company, Ltd.

Ibn ᶜAsākir, Abū al-Qāsim ᶜAlī/eds ᶜUmar al-ᶜAmrawī and ᶜAlī Shīrī
1995–2001. *Taʾrīkh madinat Dimashq*. (80 volumes). Beirut: Dār al-fikr.

Ibn Durayd, Abū Bakr Muḥammad b. al-Ḥassān/ed. ᶜAbd al-Salām Muḥammad Hārūn
[1958.] *al-Ishtiqāq*. Cairo.

Ibn al-Kalbī, Hishām b. Muḥammad.
[n.d.] *Jamharat al-nasab*. British Library, Or. Add. 23297.
[n.d.] *Kitāb an-nasab al-kabīr*. Escorial, Arabe, 1698.

Ibn al-Nadīm, Abū al-Faraj Muḥammad b. Isḥāq/ed. G. Flugel
1871. *Kitāb al-Fihrist*. Leipzig: F.C.W. Vogel.

Kilpatrick H.
2003. *Making the Great Book of Songs: Compilation and the author's craft in Abu l-Faraj al-Isbahani's Kitab al-aghani*. London: RoutledgeCurzon.

al-Masᶜūdī, Abū al-Ḥassān ʾAlī b. al-Ḥusayn/ed. C. Pellat
1962-1967. *Murūj al-Dhahab wa-Maᶜādin al-Jawāhir*. (7 volumes). Beirut: Manshurat al-Jamiᶜa al-Lubnaniya.

Miles S.B.
1919. *The Countries and Tribes of the Persian Gulf*. London: Harrison and Sons.

Monroe J.
1983. The Poetry of the Sirah Literature. Pages 368–373 in A.F.L. Beeston, T.M. Johnstone, R.B. Serjeant and G.R. Smith (eds), *The Cambridge History of Arabic Literature: Arabic Literature to the End of the Umayyad Period*. Cambridge: Cambridge University Press.

Montgomery J.E.
2006. Editor's Introduction. Pages 1–27 in J.E. Montgomery (ed.), *The Oral and the Written in Early Islam*. London: Routledge.

Naboodah H.M.A.
2006. Kitab al-Ansāb li-l-ᶜAwtabī: iškālāt fī ʾl-nasbah wa-ʾl-taʾalīf. *Majallah dirāsāt al-Khalīj wa-ʾl-Jazīrah al-ᶜArabiyyah* 32: 139–172.

al-Rawas I.
2000. *Oman in Early Islamic History*. Reading: Ithaca Press.

Retso J.
2003. *The Arabs in Antiquity: Their history from the Assyrians to the Umayyads*. London: RoutledgeCurzon.

Scholler M.
2000. Sira and Tafsir: Muhammad al-Kalbi on the Jews of Medina. Pages 18–48 in H. Motzki (ed.), *The Biography of Muhammad: The Issue of the Sources*. Leiden: Brill.

al-Ṭabarī, Abū Jaᶜfar Muḥammad b. Jarīr/eds M.J. de Goeje *et al.*
1879–1901. *Taʾrīkh al-rusul wa-l-mulūk*. (19 volumes). Leiden: Brill.
1987. ed. and trans. M. Perlmann. *The History of al-Tabari Volume IV: The Ancient Kingdoms*. (Series editor E. Yar-Shater). Albany, NY: State University of New York Press.
1987. ed. and trans. M. Perlmann. *The History of al-Tabari Volume IV: The Ancient Kingdoms*. (Series editor E. Yar-Shater). Albany, NY: State University of New York Press.

Toorawa S.M.
2005. *Ibn Abi Tahir Tayfur and Arabic Writerly Culture: A ninth-century bookman in Baghdad*. London: RoutledgeCurzon.

Wellhausen J.
1902. *Das Arabische Reich und sein Sturz.* Berlin: Georg Reimer.

Wilkinson J.C.
1969. *Arab Settlement in Oman: the origins and development of the tribal pattern and its relationship to the Imamate.* PhD thesis, Oxford. [Unpublished].
1976. Bio-bibliographical Background to the Crisis Period in the Ibadi Imamate of Oman. *Arabian Studies* 3: 137–164.
1977. *Water and Tribal Settlement in Southeast Arabia: A Study of the Aflaj of Oman.* Oxford: Clarendon Press.

al-Yaᶜqūbī, Aḥmad ibn ᶜAlī/ed. M.T. Houtsma
1883. *Taʾrīkh.* (2 volumes). Leiden: Brill.

Yarshater E.
1983. Iranian National History. Pages 359–477 in E. Yarshater (ed.), *The Cambridge History of Iran, Vol. 3(1): The Seleucid, Parthian and Sasanian Periods.* Cambridge: Cambridge University Press.

Yule P.
1999. The Samad Period in the Sultanate of Oman. *Iraq* 61: 121–46.
2005. The Samad Culture — Echoes. *Proceedings of the Seminar for Arabian Studies* 25: 303–315.
2007. *Sasanian Presence and the Late Iron Age Samad in Central Oman, Some Corrections.* Paper received July 16, 2007. [Unpublished].

Author's address
Brian Ulrich, PhD Candidate, Department of History, University of Wisconsin, 3118 Humanities Building, 455 North Park Street, Madison WI 53706, USA
e-mail bjulrich@wisc.edu

Proceedings of the Seminar for Arabian Studies 38 (2008): 319–326

British policy on Arabia before the First World War: an internal argument

Abdol Rauh Yaccob

Summary
It is a difficult task to be able to measure the importance to the British of Arabia in general and south-west Arabia in particular prior to the First World War. Early history of imperial expansion in the area, which was punctuated by constant conflicts and involved a considerable amount of diplomacy and intrigue with the indigenous population, may suggest that south-west Arabia was considered as important as other areas within the British Empire. It may be observed, however, that from the beginning of the twentieth century, south-west Arabia was considered something of a backwater by the British. This was initially prompted by the non-intervention policy of 1906 which can be interpreted as a reversal of the previous active policy, reviving therefore the traditional function of Aden alone, and so eliminating the competition for supremacy with other powers, notably the Ottomans in the hinterland. Historically, from 1839 to the 1870s British policy had been one of non-intervention in tribal affairs. The only relations that existed following the occupation of Aden were in the form of friendship treaties. This policy apparently sufficed for the security of Aden and the sea route to India and the East. The rulers of the neighbouring tribes had been independent of the Ottomans and the Zaydi imam since the early eighteenth century. However, when the tribes were threatened by the presence of the Ottomans in 1872 they began to seek other assistance, notably from the British at Aden, and subsequently an interventionist policy in tribal affairs was put into effect. The intervention policy later proved costly and led to a military commitment that diverted attention from the traditional function of Aden. The argument against intervention won the day when the Liberals came to power in 1905. On 4th May 1906 the new Secretary of State for India, Lord Morley, reversed the policy of expansion that had been carried out since the 1870s.

Keywords: British, Aden, Arabia, politics

Introduction

Firstly it must be considered that after the occupation of Aden in January 1839, British policy was one of non-intervention in Arab affairs. However, a number of friendship treaties were made with neighbouring Arab tribes immediately after occupation. These were apparently dictated by the need to secure the sea route between England and India as well as a desire to secure the safety of the settlement and its supplies. An area in the hinterland behind and near Aden was strictly controlled, kept free from interference by any other powers, and bound by mutual friendship towards and interest in the British. The first treaty of this kind was made with the Abdali sultan on 31st January 1839 immediately following the occupation of Aden. This was followed by a treaty with the chief of Waht, another sub-tribe of the Abdali on 2nd February 1839, the chief of Aqrabi on 4th February, the chiefs of Subayhi on 18th February, and the sultan of Lower Yafai on 21st February. A second batch of similar treaties was made with the chief of Hawshabi on 14th June and the Fadli on 8th July that year. In June of that year an agreement of a more binding nature was made with the Abdali sultan by which the sultan not only engaged to maintain peace and friendship with the British Government but was also to receive an annual subsidy of 6500 Maria Theresa dollars. Although the policy was declared as non-interventional, the British effectively engaged with the neighbouring Arab tribes under the pretext of friendship treaties. This policy of non-intervention was reaffirmed in June 1871 when C.U. Aitchison, the Government of India Foreign Secretary, rejected the proposals of Wedderburn, Acting Secretary to the Government of Bombay, to take over the entire Abdali area so that any foreign state could be prevented from taking up a position manifestly antagonistic or injurious to British interests, which had been enlarged by the opening of the Suez Canal.

Secondly, only after the arrival of the Ottomans in Yemen in 1872, was the proposal made in 1873 to bring all the Arab tribes in the Aden hinterland — who previously had had treaties with the British — under British protection. Initially this proposal was not approved but after Ottoman pressure intensified protectorate treaties were sanctioned. This was the beginning of a policy of real intervention and was followed by a number of affirmative commitments including the demarcation of a boundary with the Ottomans, the introduction of troops, and the establishment of a political officer in the Aden hinterland.

The 1906 policy of non-intervention

Officially the intervention policy came to an end when the Liberals came to power in Britain. Indeed, many believed that the non-intervention policy was initiated by W. Lee Warner,[1] a member of the Indian Council, when it caught the eye of the new Secretary of State for India, Lord Morley. A change of government in Britain did not normally affect foreign policy, especially in and around Aden. As an outpost of the Bombay authorities, Aden was under the control of the Government of India and administratively too remote to concern anyone except, as Gavin described, only "Indian experts", defence planners, and representatives of shipping interests (Gavin 1975: 232). However at the time the Liberals came to power in 1905, debate on foreign and defence policy of the British Empire was at its height and the Aden policy did not escape the new atmosphere. Following the request of the Bombay Government for a general policy review over the murder of a postal runner in the Aden Protectorate, Warner noted that:

> " …looking to the great difficulty of increasing our military force at Aden, the powerlessness of the Turks who are not likely to encroach with hostile intent, and the extreme desirability of not encouraging the tribes or sub-tribes to look to our intervention in case of quarrels with each other, we should lay down the following principles:
>
> 1. The main object of the delimitation is achieved by our possession of a line beyond which Turkish troops or agents cannot advance without protest.
> 2. Accidental advances beyond that line should not be exaggerated and our first resort in the event of any deliberate or continued advance would be by diplomatic action at Constantinople.
> 3. The suggestion is made as a matter for consideration that round Aden and within the Protectorate a general line should be drawn within which even internal disturbances would ordinarily call for vigilance, and any acts of violence on British territory would, of course, be punished at once. But beyond the line of vigilance our agent should be careful to take no action that could draw us into political or military entanglements without express sanction of the Government of India.
> 4. A railway line to Dhala or a cantonment there are beyond the present contemplation of H.M. Government. Even the permanent retention of an agent there must be viewed as experimental.
> 5. The disarmament of the tribes in the nine cantons is out of question, but there is no objection to the tribesmen being deprived of our arms on arrival in British territory.
> 6. The dispatch of postal runners or agents of British Government into the interior is to be avoided as much as possible, so that the tribesmen may not have the opportunity of attacking them or of misunderstanding our intentions.
> 7. Any punitive expedition for offences committed during the demarcation and not then and there punished is to be avoided.
> 8. No demonstration along the demarcated frontier is needed, and the tribes on the frontier should settle their own affairs with their neighbours over frontier as far as possible".[2]

Warner's note greatly impressed the new Secretary of State for India, Lord Morley, who took office on 11th December 1905 and adopted all of the principles of Warner's argument within his own policy of non-intervention on 4th May 1906. This new policy was communicated to the Government of India to coincide with the appointment of a new Resident, Major-General E. De Brath.[3] The new policy laid down principles that reversed those of his predecessors and it also made reference to the traditional role of Great Britain within Arabia. For this reason Morley adopted the interpretation of the former Foreign Secretary, Lord Lansdowne, over the responsibilities and obligations of Great Britain following the new frontier demarcation with the Ottoman Government and that there should be no desire to interfere with the internal and domestic affairs of the tribes.[4] The new policy did not change the traditional role of Aden as he stated that:

"The security and strength of Aden, one of the

main posts and fortresses that guard the lines between England and India, must always be a standing object in national policy. That strength will obviously be impaired and not augmented by quarrels with tribes, by intervention in their disputes, by locating troops at a distance from the fortifications of Aden, or by any excessive readiness to resort to expeditions out of all proportion, whether immediate or indirect, to either the occasions for them or to any clear advantage to be gained by them."[5]

On the basis of these principles, the new orders were introduced. Firstly, frontier trespasses should not be exaggerated, and should a protest be required, it would naturally be by way of action at Constantinople. Secondly, the area where active intervention by local authorities would be permitted was specified. Thirdly, troops and other schemes outside the defined area were withdrawn. Fourthly, the Political Officer at Dhala was also to be withdrawn. The dispatch of postal runners or agents of the British government into the interior was to be avoided. Any project for disarming the tribes in the nine cantons should be dismissed from serious consideration. Punitive expeditions for offences committed during the demarcation, and not punished then and there, were now out of the question. No demonstrations along the frontier whether demarcated or not, were needed, and finally, no fresh treaties were to be concluded without referring to the Foreign Secretary.[6]

This new 1906 non-intervention policy was not welcomed by British officials, especially those in India and Arabia. Indeed, the new policy caused surprise not only in India, Bombay, and Aden but also among individuals at the India Office in London, including Sir Hugh S. Barnes who had served as Indian Foreign Secretary under three successive viceroys and who was now a member of the Political Committee.[7]

The new policy was not, however, immediately put into effect. The officials in Aden, Bombay, India, and London were discussing any serious and damaging effects that could arise, and initially they were not inclined to accept the policy. Contra views and arguments of the Aden Residency were defended by the Government of Bombay and India. Minto,[8] the new Viceroy expressed his anxiety as to the new policy. He wrote to Morley stating that, "I am afraid you have given us a great deal of anxiety as to the Aden Hinterland question and the proposed withdrawal from Dhala … I confess the withdrawal appears to me very full of difficulties ...".[9] Although his arguments were declined, Minto did not yet regard the secret dispatch of the policy as binding orders. He thought that there was an opportunity for the Bombay Government and the Resident of Aden to comment on whether any serious danger or difficulty would arise if the new policy was put into effect. He accordingly wrote to Bombay in order to furnish a full statement of the views of the Resident at Aden and the Governor in Council on the new policy. He again received a statement from Morley that he had no option but to implement it. He did not lose hope however. He wrote privately to Morley to persuade him in the first place to review the opinions of the Resident and the Government of Bombay.[10] The new Resident at Aden, Major-General E. De Brath forwarded his views to Minto stressing two aspects, one political and the other military. Politically he argued that a complete withdrawal from the hinterland would be shortly followed by a resurgence in tribal fighting, lawlessness, and acts of violence along the trade routes, and furthermore by an increase in the illicit traffic in arms and by intrigue on the part of the Turkish frontier officials. Militarily "our withdrawal from Dhala, must be regarded as wholly disadvantageous due to the unhealthy climate of Aden in contrast with a good climate and exceptionally healthy one of Dhala". Moreover the presence of British at Dhala provided moral support to the amir of Dhala. The Resident further argued that the British departure from the hinterland would afford the Ottomans unlimited opportunities for intrigue and for furtherance of their pan-Islamic programmes. Finally the Resident believed that the new policy would increase the illicit traffic in arms and ammunition owing to the inability to watch and check its development on the spot.[11]

In August 1906, Minto forwarded these views from local officials in Aden and Bombay in a last attempt to convince Morley of the need for change. He explained that the Government of India had no desire to extend their responsibility and entangle themselves in purely tribal affairs, but that the question of policy in the hinterland was one on which they attached vital importance. The presence of troops and of the political officer was to augment the strength of that fortress commanding the main trade routes between Aden and the hinterland and also as an important position on the line of communications between Aden and Yemen. He further argued that the present policy of concentrating British naval forces in European waters might easily leave the command of the Arabian Sea in the hands of foreign powers. The withdrawal affected British reputation among the Arabs and there would be a real danger, as they would be confronted by an independent

Arabia that had lost faith in the ability or willingness of the British to keep their promises to their friends.[12]

At the India Office, on receiving the views of the Viceroy, Lee Warner drafted a dispatch on Arabian policy to Morley. He repeated the previous views by stating that, "we are embarking on an entirely new policy outside the fortress of Aden, which will require an Agent and more troops in order to maintain an unpopular Amir in his throne, to combat a pan-Islamic programme in Yemen, to settle tribal disputes, and to maintain our reputation among the Arabs". He considered the arguments from the Government of India to be inconclusive; Aden was said to be unhealthy but the Government of India produced no figures, no complaint was made over the problem of training at Aden; and as to arms traffic, it was certain that a garrison at Dhala could have no influence upon the matter owing to the long line of frontier and the Turkish landing places at Shaykh Sa'id.[13]

However, Lee Warner did not carry all the council members with him. In a note to Morley, Hugh Barnes argued that the Government of India and the local authorities were correct. In general Barnes considered that, "we ought not to forbid, as, I understand, the Despatch of 4th May did forbid even the limited amount of interference and control which experience shows us we have usefully exercised in the past". He further argued that, "there is no intention of prohibiting such limited interference as the Residents have successfully exercised in the past to keep open the trade routes and adjust intertribal quarrels".[14]

Morley, however, adopted Lee Warner's views, which had been approved by the Political Committee at the India Office, and on 5th October 1906 an explanation was made by London of the disadvantages of local interests in comparison with imperial interests. Morley stated that, "British interest at Aden mainly centred in the British territory and fortress at Aden, and the prime object of recent arrangements with the Ottoman Porte was to reduce the risk of international complications by arriving at a definite understanding as to the outer boundary of the tribal country in political relations with the British Settlement".[15] Morley also believed that the pan-Islamic programme in Yemen, which haunted the Residency at Aden, could not be controlled without undesirable meddling in the internal and domestic doings of the tribes. Furthermore the stemming of religious tides had never hitherto been regarded as a desirable or even tolerable element in Indian policy. The possibility of the emergence of an independent Arabia, which was the subject of warnings by the Viceroy, was regarded by Morley as a subject of imperial policy and not to be decided by considerations of Indian interest alone. Other arguments put forward by the Government of India to support local interests — for instance that Aden was unhealthy and therefore troops could not be trained there, or the prevention of the arms traffic — were regarded by Morley as secondary issues.[16] The view of the Government of India was therefore seen to suit local needs only. Meanwhile the India Office placed more emphasis on diplomatic and international relations of the Empire. The Resident was instructed to act strictly in a spirit of non-intervention.

After September 1906, the policy of non-intervention in Arab affairs was strictly observed by the India Office. The Aden Residency was in a dilemma, facing political instability in the Protectorate territory while observing the policy of non-intervention, and consequently pressed for active intervention. The new policy was seen as difficult to implement with respect to relations with the Ottoman authorities in Yemen. Under the new policy, the Aden authorities had no discretion to settle boundary disputes, but had to have approval from the India Office and the Foreign Office. The situation grew worse before the Aden authorities were authorized to take action, but in the end they were finally given permission to intervene in hinterland affairs. The situation could have been avoided if the Aden authorities had been given discretion to settle locally and furthermore if a British officer and troops had been present in the hinterland to prevent the occurrence of disputes before they matured. It was also argued that the Aden Residency was cut off from news of the hinterland except through agents of the sultan and Arab news correspondents in the hinterland. The information provided by them was sometimes unreliable and this situation could also have been avoided if British officers had been present.

The policy of non-intervention was also seen as making it difficult to follow new developments in Yemen, especially concerning the movement of the imam in Yemen and in the north-east of the Aden Protectorate. As a result of the change of policy, the Aden Residency was authorized to raise matters relating to the imam with the Ottoman officials but as the imam was on good terms with the Ottomans, his position must have been naturally protected, and the protected tribes were made to bear all the blame and were immediately called to Aden to clarify the situation, notably on the occasion of the alleged Imamic-Yafai relations.

Conclusion

It may be observed that the policy of non-intervention was introduced not merely because of the change of government in Britain at that time, but other circumstances also played a part. There had been a number of reasons that led Morley, a new Secretary of State for India, to adopt the policy. The British government was at that time reviewing their foreign and defence policy. Aden and Arabian policy therefore naturally came under review.

The arguments forwarded by Morley and Lee Warner at the India Office in London, however, emphasized other factors. The first of these was that the Government had already settled their boundary disputes with the Ottomans through the Anglo-Turkish Commission of 1902–1905. The India Office argued that the primary objective of the intervention policy was achieved through the above-mentioned Commission. This principle can be traced in Morley's argument when he referred to the interpretation of the Secretary of State for Foreign Affairs, Lansdowne, in 1903, concerning the responsibility of the Government following the settlement of the boundary with the Ottomans. This argument appears to be accurate as the settlement had been observed by the Ottomans although the agreement was only ratified later, in 1914. Furthermore, it was a fact that the Ottomans were no longer a threat to British interests in South Arabia after their boundary settlement with the British. The policy of intervention had begun when the threat of the Ottomans appeared to be at its height. The Protectorate treaties with Arab tribes around Aden took place when the Ottomans moved to the area and supported the rival of the Abdali sultan, and this quite apart from their constant claim of the whole of Yemen. The Anglo-Turkish Commission was seen by the India Office as settling this dispute. These circumstances had supported Lee Warner's argument that the Ottomans would not move towards the Aden protectorate because of their powerlessness, and things did not actually happen as anticipated even after the withdrawal of troops from the area.

However, closer to the scene, the India-Aden authorities interpreted the boundary settlement as extending their responsibility, not only to secure the new arrangement but also to support the new protected chiefs following the boundary demarcation. They also argued that as the Ottomans and the Zaydi imam were fighting, they should follow the events closely in order to report on or control the possible intervention of the imam in the Aden Protectorate. In London, the India Office did not consider the emergence of the Zaydi imam as an urgent factor that required intervention, and furthermore the matter should not be decided by the Indian-Aden authorities alone. Another reason for the India Office policy was that the new policy was partly formed to avoid British interference in purely tribal matters. London's argument on the role of Aden as a coaling station was safeguarded through various treaties with the neighbouring tribes. London's argument over the role of Aden indicates the emphasis of the policy of non-intervention, as this arrangement would suffice to protect coaling without any further interference in tribal affairs.

The new policy was not only opposed by Barnes, a member of the council at the India Office, but also by Minto, the new Viceroy, Lord Lamington, the Governor of Bombay, and De Brath, the new Resident at Aden. Throughout the years 1906 to 1914, the Aden Residency opposed the policy of non-intervention and sought to modify it. The Residents at Aden, first De Brath and then Bell, and other officials such as Jacob continued to press London to modify the policy in order to allow local authorities limited intervention such as the settlement of disputes involving the Ottomans, the Yemenis, and the protected chiefs, the conclusion of fresh treaties with the tribes, and the assistance to the Zaydi imam. At the beginning of the policy, Minto, the Governor General of India from November 1905 to November 1910, supported the opposition of the local officials, but subsequently accepted the change and his successor, Hardinge, was cautious in seeking any modification. While Morley was at the India Office there was no breach of the policy. His successor, Crewe, upheld the policy of non-intervention in principle but was more willing to tolerate minor exceptions, notably in the episode of the treaties with Bayda and the Awdhali in 1911. The political secretaries in India and London, McMahon and Hirtzel respectively, were also inclined to accept minor modifications and supported the initiative to conclude fresh treaties with the sultans of Bayda and 'Awdhali.

The damaging effect of the policy of non-intervention was, according to local officials, considerable. The withdrawal of the troops indirectly encouraged the Ottomans and the imam alike to extend their influence into the Protectorate. The advance of the Ottomans into Lahej in 1915 during the First World War was seen as a direct result of the policy of non-intervention. The policy had changed the role of the Abdali sultan and after the new policy was put into effect, the Aden Residency relied mostly on him as mediator between the government and the Arab tribes, and also in his role as a British informant. This policy undoubtedly increased the influence of the Abdali sultan in the Protectorate. The dependence on the Abdali sultan, who had his own interests to consider, had an injurious effect on the British position with other Arab tribes. The policy that loosened the ties with those tribes encouraged them to look towards the imam and the Ottomans for assistance in settling tribal matters. This situation had a damaging effect on British prestige in the Protectorate before, during, and after the war.

Notes

1 Sir William Lee Warner who served for a long time in Bombay, Calcutta, and London, was educated at Rugby School and St John's College, Cambridge. He joined the Bombay Civil Service in 1867. He held the highest post as Secretary to the Government of Bombay from 1887 to 1895. In September 1895 he retired from the Civil Service and was then appointed Secretary to the Political and Secret Department, the India Office, from September 1895 to November 1902, and became a member of the Council of India from November 1902 to November 1912.

2 L/P&S/10/74 note by Lee Warner 27/3/1906.

3 Major General E. De Brath was due to arrive in Aden on 19th April 1906.

4 The previous Foreign Secretary's statement in the House of Lords on 30th March 1903 was cited:

With regard to the responsibility for these territories, I do not see why what has taken place should make any difference in these responsibilities. We have never desired to interfere with the internal and domestic affairs of the tribes. On the other hand, we have throughout made it perfectly plain that we should not tolerate the interference of any other Power with them.

5 L/P&S/10/74, Secretary of State for India to Viceroy 4/5/1906.

6 L/P&S/10/74, Secretary of State for India to Viceroy 4/5/1906.

7 Barnes was not in London when the dispatch of 4th May was drafted and he was also absent from the discussions in the committee, which preceded its formulation.

8 Gilbert John Elliot Murray Kynlynmound (1845–1914), 4th Earl of Minto, served in the army in the Russo-Turkish War in 1877, in Afghanistan in 1879, and in Egypt in 1882. From 1883 to 1886 he was Military Secretary to the 5th Marquess of Lansdowne, Governor General of Canada. From 1898 to 1904 he was Governor General of Canada, and from November 1905 to November 1910, Viceroy of India.

9 Minto Papers, MS 12735 Minto to Morley 7/6/1906.

10 Minto Papers, MS 12735 Minto to Morley 20/6/1906.

11 R/20/A/1102, Resident to Government of Bombay 1/7/1906.

12 Minto papers, MS 12636 Government of India to the Secretary of State for India 9/8/1906.

13 L/P&S/10/74 note by Lee Warner 29/8/1906.

14 L/P&S/10/74 note by Hugh Barnes 5/9/1906.

15 R/20/A/1102, India Office to Viceroy 5/10/1906.

16 R/20/A/1102, India Office to Viceroy 5/10/1906.

References

Gavin R.J.
1975. *Aden under British Rule 1839–1967*. London: Hurst.

Sources of documents

British official documents at the India Office Library in London

L/P&S/10	Political and Secret Department, the India Office
R/20/A	Settlement of Aden 1839–1937 and the Protectorate affairs, 1837–1928
R/20/E	Political and Secret Department, Government of Bombay

Private papers of British officials

The Minto Papers at the National Library of Scotland, Edinburgh
The Private Papers of Charles, Baron Hardinge of Penshurst at Cambridge University Library

Author's address
Abdol Rauh Yaccob, Islamic University of Sultan Sharif Ali, Jalan Tungku Link, Gadong, Brunei Darussalam, BE1410, Brunei.
e-mail rauh@ipishoas.ubd.edu.bn

Proceedings of the Seminar for Arabian Studies 38 (2008): 327–340

The Peristyle Hall: remarks on the history of construction based on recent archaeological and epigraphic evidence of the AFSM expedition to the Awām temple in Mārib, Yemen

Zaydoon Zaid & Mohammed Maraqten

Summary

The Awām temple (modern Maḥram Bilqīs) is located near the ancient Sabaean capital of Mārib, about 160 km to the east of the Yemeni capital Ṣanaʿāʾ. Previous work here included investigations by the American Foundation for the Study of Man (AFSM) expedition in 1952 led by Wendell Phillips, and the more recent AFSM excavations under its president Merilyn Phillips, which together have exposed one of the most significant architectural complexes in ancient South Arabia. The main concern of this paper is the presentation of the different architectural phases of construction in relation to the Peristyle Hall and to set these phases within the time frame presented by the occupational history of the Awām temple.

Keywords: Awām temple, history of architecture, Yemen, Sabaʾ, South Arabia

The architectural components of the Awām temple complex present a high quality of style and techniques. Based on architectural styles as well as archaeological and epigraphic data, this temple can be divided into different architectural phases of construction. The temple complex consists of several major architectural components (Figs 1–2):

- The Oval Wall, enclosing most of an open-air Oval Precinct
- The Peristyle Hall with thirty-two pillars surrounding a large courtyard
- The Annex Area along the north-east side of the Peristyle Hall and parallel to the eight monumental pillars
- The large courtyard area, Area A, building 1, paved passage and staircases
- The mausoleum adjacent to the south-east exterior of the Oval Wall
- The cemetery to the south-west of the Oval Wall.

The excavations and architectural analysis of the Awām temple indicate that its construction and alteration were undertaken over a long period that started at least towards the beginning of the first millennium BC; it is recorded in inscriptions at the end of the seventh century BC and it continued until the end of the fourth or the beginning of the fifth century AD.

The excavated data are insufficient to present a comprehensive view of the construction history of the temple complex, yet they do enable a reconstructed sequence of occupation history into which most of the temple components can be integrated. Throughout this period of long occupational history of the site, Awām went through many changes and alterations until it attained its final shape. These constant changes and enlargements of the Awām sanctuary demonstrate, along with the monumental inscriptions, that Awām was one of the most important monuments of the Sabaean period, which doubtless composed the religious centre of the city of Mārib and of ancient South Arabia as a whole.

The Peristyle Hall is the main concern of this paper: it was first excavated in the 1950s under Wendell Phillips (Albright 1958; Glanzman 1998) and completely cleared during the two 2004 seasons of AFSM excavations, with investigations continuing into the 2006 season. It has the plan of a truncated rectangle orientated north-west to south-east. Its walls have headers and stretchers in the manner of a casemate, which are very similar to the construction methods used for the Oval Wall. Remains of the headers and stretchers can be seen above the flat sides adjoining the false windows on the interior wall of the Peristyle Hall.

One question of considerable interest concerns the date of the Peristyle Hall. In the early stages of research, the assumption was made that the Peristyle Hall is an

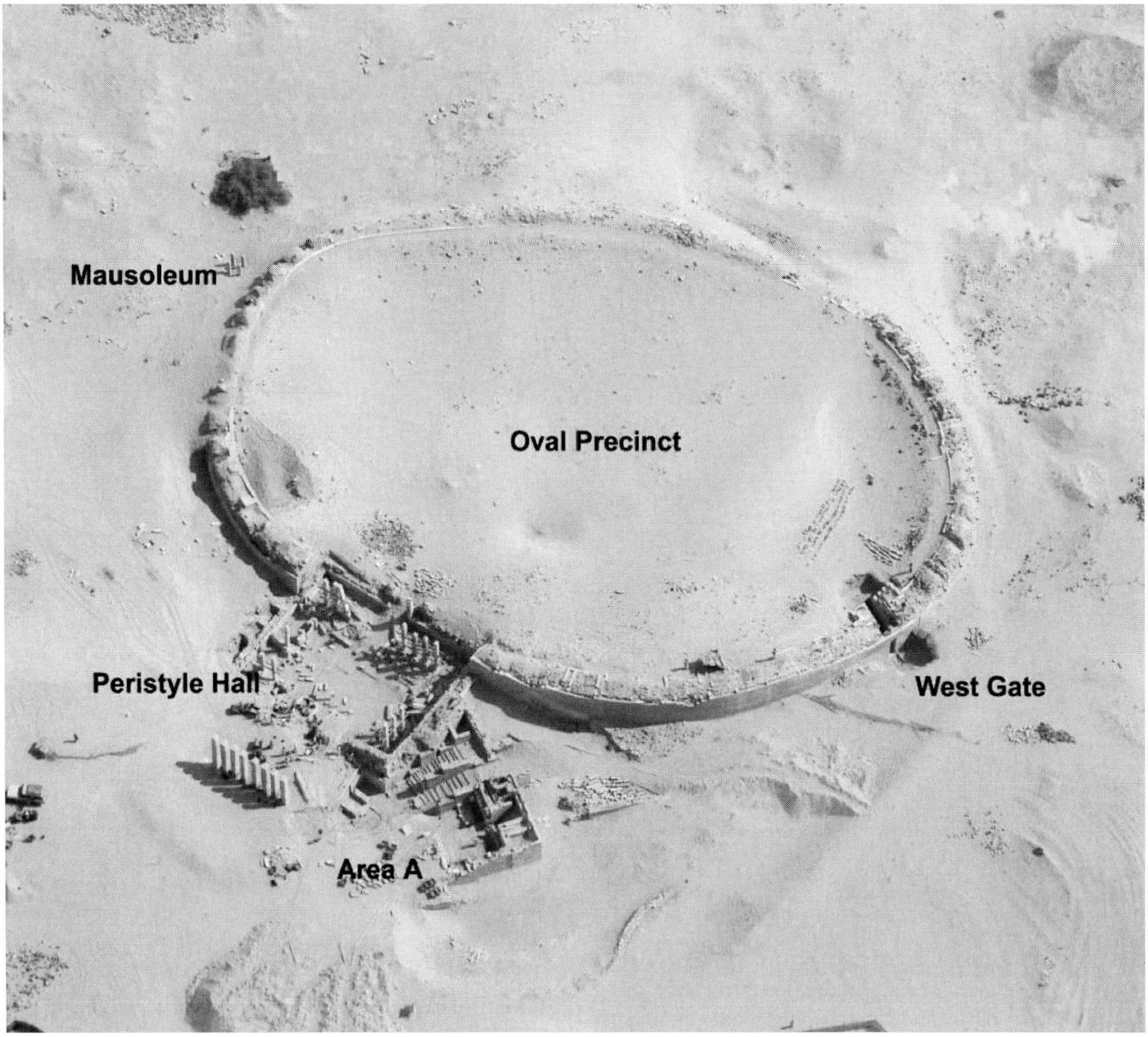

Figure 1. *A view of the Awām temple in 2004.*

architectural addition which was added to the temple complex in one of its latest phases of construction (Albright 1958: 231). In the absence of particular inscriptions related directly to the construction of the Peristyle Hall, we have to rely on further data to clarify its accurate date. Nevertheless, the discovery of more than 300 inscriptions in the Peristyle Hall, which are primarily *in situ* or reused in pavements or other small structures, would provide the general time frame for the Peristyle Hall. In addition, the architectural sequences of Awām as well as the direct relationship between the Peristyle Hall and the Oval Wall are important sources for the dating.

One of the earliest building phases of the Awām temple is certainly the construction of the Oval Wall, which existed as a sacred place. This is evident by the rediscovery of a number of inscriptions on the exterior of the Oval Wall. These inscriptions, which spanned several generations, chiefly record the temple's building activities and document the construction of the temple from at least the seventh century BC to the first century AD (MB 2001 I-16 = CIH 957; Ja 500–557; CIH 373).

With regard to the earliest phases of construction, the inscription MB 2001 I-16 (CIH 957 = Glaser 484; Müller & Rhodokanakis 1913: 46, 137) is of great interest.

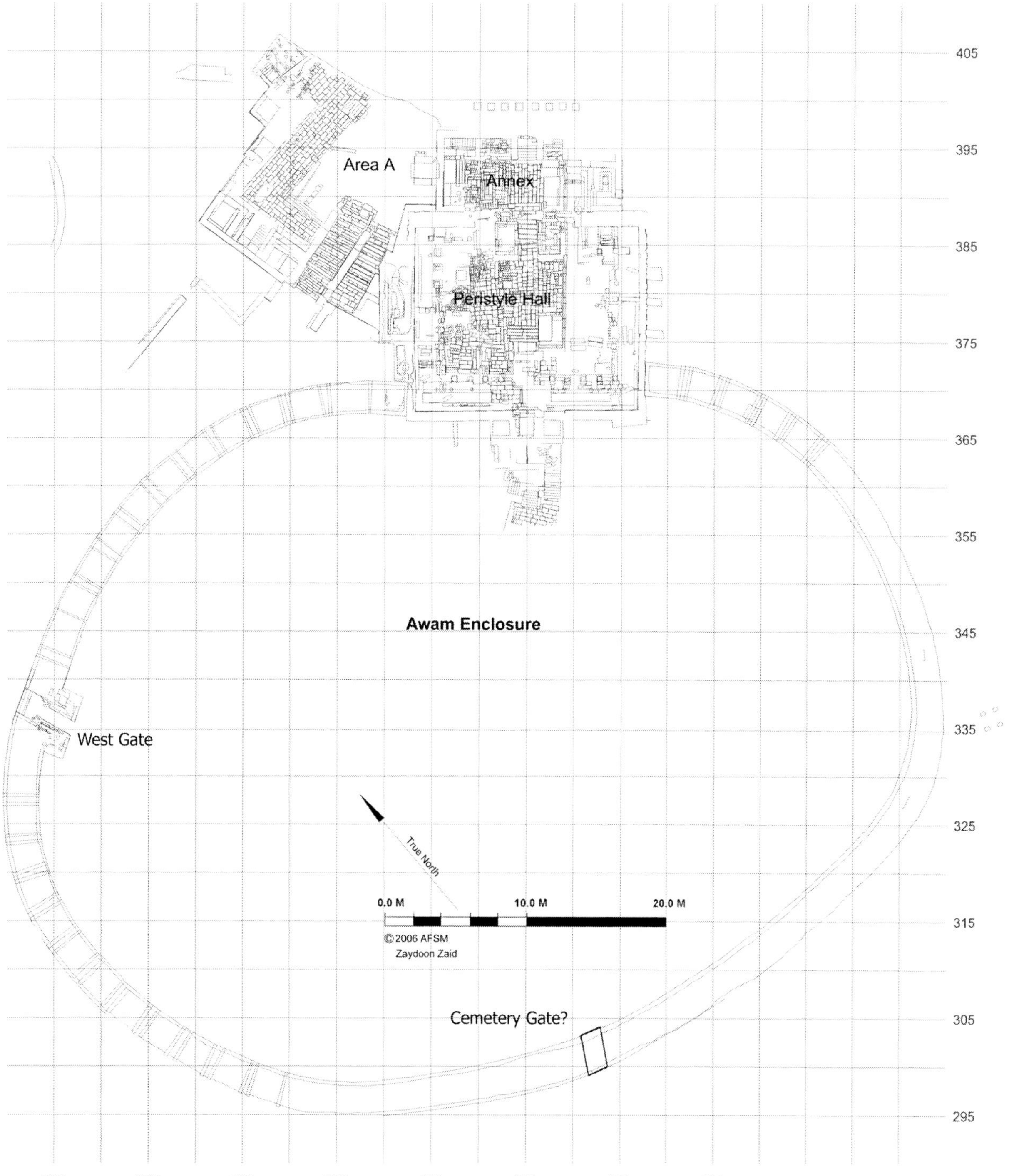

Figure 2. *A master plan of the Awām temple showing the different areas.*

FIGURE 3. *Monumental architecture elements, including staircases and the paved floor excavated inside the area adjacent to the Peristyle Hall entrance to the Awām enclosure.*

This inscription, which was discovered in the 2001 AFSM season, was discussed by W.D. Glanzman and M. Maraqten in the following year (Glanzman 2002; Maraqten 2002). It is engraved on the twenty-eighth course from the top (Glanzman 2003: 191). The translation of this inscription implies that the founder and initiator of Awām is Yada^{c}ʾīl Ḏarīḥ, the *mukarrib* of Saba (Maraqten 2002). However it does not confirm that this ruler built the entire complex. Moreover, the analysis of the archaeological data showed that the building of the Oval Wall was not the work of one phase. Research on different sections of the wall demonstrate that at least parts of it, particularly the south-west section, went through different stages of repair throughout the lifespan of the temple complex. These are evident through the placement of the wall segment construction as well as the style of the masonry dressing. The segments of the wall showed a change in masonry style indicating different phases of construction (Glanzman 1999: 77–82). The Oval Wall seems to have had at least three phases of construction, the earliest of which predates the seventh century BC with the latest in the mid-first century AD. The latest date of reconstruction is indicated by an inscription engraved on the thirteenth course from the top of the Oval on the east side (CIH 373 = Glaser 483; Glanzman 2003: 191) and which mentions Karibʾīl Watar Yuhan^{c}im (*c.* 45–60 AD) in connection with building activities associated with the Oval Wall.

The seventh century BC appears to present the start of a construction project which began by increasing the height of the Oval Wall (Wissmann 1982: 183–185; Glanzman 2003). This project included the massive gateway, the north-west portion of the Oval Precinct, and most importantly the creation of the original plan of the Peristyle Hall.

FIGURE 4. *Inscription MB 2004 S I-20 excavated in one of the rooms adjacent to the staircase in the north-east part of the Peristyle Hall.*

The north-west entrance to the Oval Precinct was excavated in 2004 by Carl Phillips and consisted of an interior and exterior doorway enclosing a narrow passage. This passage had originally been roofed with timbers that were subsequently burned, but the grain of the wood was still clearly visible. Rows of holes extending down either side of the doorway indicate that some type of metal strips or panels had once framed the door. A five-course panel was preserved above this doorway, the upper two courses of which were bonded into the Oval Wall. This doorway was later reduced to a small entrance measuring 80 cm in width, as opposed to the original width of 2.70 cm. This is documented in two monumental inscriptions on the exterior facade of the gate, which were rediscovered in 1998. These are Ja 553 (top) and Ja 552 (bottom). These inscriptions belong to the same person and inform us of the construction of this gate that might be dated as early as the end of the fifth century BC. The three-line inscription (Ja 552) that was cut into the panel is a summary of Ja 553 (Wissmann 1982: 343–345). In addition, three newly discovered inscriptions from the pavement and debris inside the gate prove that this gate was used until the fourth century AD.

The addition of the main gate into the Oval Precinct replaced the earlier entrance to the temple from the west. This earlier entrance was simply a large gap in the west side of the Oval Wall. While the earlier entrance provided access to the temple, its reduced size restricted entry. It is difficult to imagine that a great temple such as Awām would have been entered through a narrow gate only 80 cm across, hence our assumption that the north-west gate had lost its function as a public entrance and instead changed its function possibly to an entrance used by high-ranking citizens, priests, or royalty. By doing so, the main

Figure 5. *Excavations in the west and east rear wall of the Peristyle Hall.*

Figure 6. *The eastern corner of the Peristyle Hall rear wall with the eastern edge of the Oval Wall.*

FIGURE 7. *Three different types of floor identified in the Peristyle Hall.*

access of movement was shifted towards the area in front of the eight pillars, i.e. the Peristyle Hall. As the date of the north-west gate indicates, this shift occurred at the end of the sixth or the beginning of the fifth century BC. This controlled and changed access into the temple to one main axis of movement, namely from north to south. By so doing, a new arrangement was necessary within the temple in order to cope with these developments. In its early stage this included both the area inside the Oval Wall and the area in front of the pillars.

In 2005, M. Ibrahim conducted excavations in front of the southern Peristyle Hall pylons with the aim of clarifying the architecture and the occupational sequence, and of locating the initial Oval Precinct flooring. Ibrahim's excavations in this part of the temple complex are very significant. The data provided by the excavation greatly helped to establish an initial layout of the area adjacent to the Peristyle Hall entrance (Ibrahim 2006). M. Ibrahim found a very early bronze plaque *in situ* (MB 2005 I-134, unpublished) and dated by M. Maraqten to the fifth to seventh centuries BC (Ibrahim 2006), as well as a sequence of building phases including rooms, staircases, and a very well preserved stone pavement (Fig. 3). According to Ibrahim, the construction in this area started as early as the eighth century BC and continued throughout the fifth century AD (2006: 210). The eighth-century date is evident from the discovery of an inscription (MB 2005 I-106) found within the fill of a doorway excavated in front of the entrance to the Peristyle Hall (2006: fig. 19). Other eighth-century BC inscriptions were also found in other parts of the temple. Among those is inscription MB 2004 S I-20 (Fig. 4), which was excavated in one of the rooms in the north-east part of the Peristyle Hall. This inscription has been dated according to the palaeography. It is a fragmentary dedicatory inscription of parts of a building, and two blocks of the inscription survive. It reads: *[m]ṣrʿy / wtḥth / s¹qfn / bʿṯtr / wḏmrʿly / hqny*. The reading of this inscription should be reconstructed as: *bʿṯtr / wḏmrʿly / hqny* […] *[m]ṣrʿy / wtḥth / s¹qfn* […] and translated as "Bi-ʿaṯtar and Ḏamarʿalī have dedicated … a door and beneath it a roof". The words *mṣrʿy* "leaf of door, door, gate" and *s¹qf* "roof of a building, roof,

Figure 8. *Basalt wall foundations excavated in Area A.*

Figure 9. *The basalt wall representing part of the foundation walls for the architectural arrangements in the Awām temple during the eighth century BC.*

FIGURE 10. *An original platform excavated inside the Peristyle Hall.*

roofing" are known in Sabaic (SD, 145, 127f.).

The 2005 excavations therefore cleared the architectural sequence in front of the Peristyle Hall entrance, whereas excavations the following year expanded this sequence and clarified the larger occupational area at the very entrance of the Oval area. As the outer back wall had never been previously defined, the clearing of areas to the west and east of the Peristyle Hall entrance helped shed light on the relationship of the Oval Wall to that of the rear wall of the Peristyle Hall (Fig. 5). The rear wall of the Peristyle Hall was built of plain cut limestone blocks with some drafting. It was filled with a rubble core, which faces the interior windows' walling. In the west, stone robbing created a sharp stepped appearance and the wall continued east to the pylon. Further west, the distinctive crenellated outer face of the Peristyle Hall gave way to a straight block wall set into the Oval Wall. The same arrangements were also noted at the other end of the rear wall, i.e. on the east side. However, the outer wall in the east side was not fully excavated and the rear wall was heavily robbed, revealing the core fill. Furthermore, the outer wall projected 2.35 m beyond the Oval Wall. The corner found at some depth also created an extension/tower, and not a simple 90° corner as seen in the west side.

Deeper excavation in this area also uncovered a possible doorway into the Peristyle Hall and gave a clear indication that the Peristyle Hall was cut into the Oval Wall (Fig. 6). Whereas those arrangements and the architectural sequence in the west side suggest that the pylon and the back wall were an integral architectural element in the upper levels of the Awām, a careful study of the architecture and stone sequencing on the eastern side suggests that the rear wall of the Peristyle Hall went through at least two phases of rebuilding, with the latest post-dating an earlier phase of the Oval Wall. In other words, the rear wall of the Peristyle Hall was cut into a pre-existing early-phase Oval Wall which itself precedes the second phase of the Oval Wall, which is dated to the seventh century BC. All of these arrangements of the Oval Wall and the architectural sequence in front of the hall entrance predetermined the main area available for

Figure 11. *An original platform excavated inside the Annex Area, with an inscription (MB 2005 I-138) engraved on it.*

the original layout of the Peristyle Hall. The assumption made here is that the original layout of the Peristyle Hall was planned and installed while the upper courses and the north-west gate of the Oval Wall were being built. This was imposed for functional reasons necessitated by the reconstruction at the end of the sixth or the beginning of the fifth century BC.

Another source for dating the Peristyle Hall is certainly the paved floor in the centre of the space created by the Peristyle Hall. A close study of the Peristyle Hall floor revealed three different floor types (Fig. 7). The latest floor, covering half of the total floor area, consisted of refitted and reused blocks. Some are of simple masonry, others are decorated, and yet others are reused Sabaean inscriptions. Another type of floor in the Peristyle Hall was of plaster and this lay under the portico floors in the area of the pillars. A third type of floor to the east of the main floor consisted of heavily compacted and possibly lightly smoothed earth. This type of floor was probably used during the early stage of the Peristyle Hall construction and was probably contemporary with the sixth-century arrangements in the complex. The Ground Penetrating Radar survey and excavations in the Peristyle Hall indicate earlier orientations of structures and floors beneath the surfaces related to the sanctuary's last major phase of use, but they did not suggest earlier flagged pavements (Moorman *et al.* 2001).

A small sounding in the south-east corner of the Peristyle Hall confirms the existence of layers of plaster floors reaching an earlier wall made of basalt. This basalt wall is very similar to ones excavated in Area A by Dr Abdu Othman (Fig. 8). It is also similar to the basalt walls excavated in the Barʾān temple, namely Temple I, which is dated to the late ninth century BC (Vogt 1999; Görsdorf & Vogt 2001). It may also correspond to the basalt wall excavated in Area A. These walls therefore may belong to the first phase in the occupational history of Awām. As in the Barʾān temple, the basalt walls represent an earlier phase prior to the architectural arrangements in the Awām temple during the eighth century BC, if not earlier (Fig.

9). Another interesting feature to be noted in the area of this sounding was the relation between the floors and the adjacent six-course foundation wall supporting the bases of the Peristyle Hall pillars. The floors are built against the outer surface of the foundation wall. There is no indication of any cut through the floor and consequently both may be placed within the same period.

A stone platform in the Peristyle Hall paved floor presents itself in a different way to the rest of the masonry floor blocks (Fig. 10). It is located on the eastern side of a bronze basin next to the steps leading to the portico in front of the main entrance to the Oval Wall (Albright 1958: 226). Two inscriptions were engraved on bronze plaques and attached to the bronze basin (Ja 831, 832) and dated by von Wissmann (1982: 188, 319–322) to *c.* 425 and 407 BC. However, these two inscriptions should now be dated to at least the sixth century BC (cf. Seipel 1999: 327f., nr. 254 = Ja 832 = YM 343; Ja 831 = BM 134834).

The platform was constructed of grey stone with polished surfaces. The same type of platform was also excavated inside the eastern side of the Annex Area (Fig. 11). Both platforms seem to be part of a phase earlier than the present floor of the Peristyle Hall. The date, at least for the Annex platform, is evident from the line of text observed on the upper part of the block: this inscription (MB 2005 I-138, Fig. 11) mentions the *mukarrib* Yadaʿʾʾīl Ḏarīḥ (*c.* 670 BC), who is the same Sabaean ruler who constructed the earliest part of the Oval Wall (see above). It was discovered *in situ* in the 2005 season and is the most recently discovered piece of evidence for dating the Peristyle Hall. The presence of these two platforms is very significant as it suggests the existence of a floor of an earlier entrance hall, as early as the seventh century BC. The extension of this earlier entrance hall seems to extend beyond the present one and included the area of the later Annex.

It seems that the most obvious architectural developments after the seventh century BC focused on the Peristyle Hall, which was enclosed within walls constructed of fine limestone ashlar facing an inner rubble core. Two levels of false windows decorated the inner faces of these walls and the same applied to the outside faces of the northern wall. As mentioned earlier, the dating of the Peristyle Hall is a matter of integrating the architectural sequence with the evidence supplied by the excavated inscriptions. The architectural sequence showed that the erection of the Peristyle Hall was necessitated by the extensive construction project that started in the seventh–sixth centuries BC. Van Beek was able to show that the dressing of the Peristyle Hall walls is identical with that of the upper courses of the north side of the Oval Wall (Van Beek 1958).

Other architectural arrangements inside the Peristyle Hall are dated to a later period. Among these are two rows of monumental inscriptions, which were found *in situ* along the western and eastern walls of the Peristyle Hall. The first row in the west is dated to the period between the first and third centuries AD whereas the eastern row is dated between the first century and the second half of the fourth century AD.

Architectural modifications were not limited to the area of the entrance but also included other areas of the temple complex. The Annex Area was newly organized and Area A added to the complex. In 2006 the far rear wall of the Annex was uncovered and cleared. A series of steps leading to the paved floor was exposed and revealed a new element to the Annex; a second staircase was revealed which was centred on the eight monumental pillars to the north. This staircase was later blocked, as in the case of the ʿAlhān Nahfān gate excavated in 2002 to the far west of the Annex wall and which dates to the end of the second century AD. An *in situ* bronze plaque was excavated at the base of the west pylon forming the gate. The latest floor of the Annex was already partially uncovered in 2005 and consists of reused inscriptions, plaques, and architectural blocks similar to those incorporated in the latest floor of the Peristyle Hall. A large formal drain known from earlier excavations and originating in the Peristyle Hall was found to turn east and enter the formal table area in the eastern part of the Annex. A subsidiary ablution area led to a plastered basin that also drained into the formal Peristyle Hall drain. The architectural plan of the Annex is thus virtually complete. The layout suggests an initial low staircase or portico surrounding the main pillars to the north on three sides. This was later remodelled with the addition of doorways and entrances leading from a number of different directions but which were themselves later blocked. The initial occupation and construction of the Annex suggest a mid-first-millennium BC date. The sanctuary attained its final state with the expansion of the whole complex to the west and the addition of new buildings in Area A.

The earliest material cultural remains excavated in the Awām complex date to the eighth century BC. Inscriptions mark the beginning of the history of occupation of the site (MB 2001 I-16 = CIH 957). A recently discovered but as yet unpublished inscribed block that served as the base of a statue, mentions a dedication by the Shaᶜb of Sabaʾ and is dated according to the Himyaritic era (i.e. 115 or 110 BC) to the late fourth century AD. It confirms the continuity of the main function of the temple as a sacred place. The dating formula in this inscription reads: *ḏ-l-ḫrfn / ḏlts*^{1c}*t / wṯmnyy* ^{8}*wʾrb*ᶜ */ mʾtm* "(dated) to the year of 489 Himyaritic = 374/379 AD)" (MB 2004 I-147/7–8). The architectural sequence for the Awām temple would therefore seem to span a period from the first millennium BC to the late fourth century AD.

Sigla

BM	British Museum
CIH	*Corpus inscriptionum semiticarum.* Pars iv. Paris: Imprimerie nationale, 1889–1932.
I	Inscription.
Glaser 484	= CIH 957, von Wissmann 1982: 183–85.
Ja	Inscription in Jamme 1962.
MB	Registration *siglum* of inscriptions discovered by the AFSM excavations at Maḥram Bilqīs.
S	September season 2004.
SD	See Beeston *et al.* 1982.
YM	Yemen National Museum.

References

Albright F.P.

1958. Excavations at Mārib in Yemen. Pages 215–268 in R. LeB. Bowen, Jr. & F.P. Albright, *Archaeological Discoveries in South Arabia.* (Publications of the American Foundation for the Study of Man, 2). Baltimore, MD: Johns Hopkins Press.

Glanzman W.D.

1998. Digging Deeper: the results of the first season of activities of the AFSM on the Mahram Bilqīs, Mārib. *Proceedings of the Seminar for Arabian Studies* 28: 89–104.

1999. Clarifying the record: the Bayt ʾAwwām revisited. *Proceedings of the Seminar for Arabian Studies* 29: 73–88.

2002. Some notions of sacred spaces at the Maḥram Bilqīs in Mārib. *Proceedings of the Seminar for Arabian Studies* 32: 187–201.

2003. An examination of the building campaign of Yadaᶜʾil Dharīḥ bin Sumuhᶜalay, mukarrib of Sabaʾ, in light of recent archaeology. *Proceedings of the Seminar for Arabian Studies* 33: 183–198.

Beeston, A.F.L., Ghul, M.A., Müller, W.W. Ryckmans, J.

1982. *Sabaic Dictionary.* Louvain-la-Neuve: Peeters/Beirut: Librairie du Liban.

Görsdorf J. & Vogt B.

2001. Radiocarbon Datings from the Almaqah Temple of Bar'an, Ma'rib, Republic of Yemen: Approximately 800 cal BC to 600 cal AD. Pages 1363–1369 in H.J. Bruins, I. Carmi & E. Boaretto (eds), Near East Chronology: Archaeology and Environment. (Proceedings of the 17th International C14 Conference, University of Arizona). *Radiocarbon* 43/3.

Ibrahim M.

2006. Report on the 2005 AFSM excavations in the Ovoid Precinct at Maḥram Bilqīs/Mārib. *Proceedings of the Seminar for Arabian Studies* 36: 199–216.

Jamme A.

1962. *Sabaean Inscriptions from Maḥram Bilqīs (Mārib).* (Publications of the American Foundation for the Study of Man, 3). Baltimore, MD: Johns Hopkins Press.

Maraqten M.

2002. Newly discovered Sabaean inscriptions from Maḥram Bilqīs, near Mārib. *Proceedings of the Seminar for Arabian Studies* 32: 209–216.

Moorman B., Glanzman W.D., Maillol J-M. & Lyttle A.L.

2001. Imaging beneath the surface at Maḥram Bilqīs. *Proceedings of the Seminar for Arabian Studies* 31: 179–187.

Müller D.H. & Rhodokanakis N. (eds).
1913. *Sammlung Eduard Glaser I. Eduard Glasers Reise nach Mārib*. Vienna: Alfred Hölder.
Seipel W. (ed.).
1999. *Jemen. Kunst und Archäologie im Land der Königin von Saba'*. Vienna: Kunsthistorisches Museum.
Van Beek G.W.
1958. Marginally Drafted, Pecked Masonry. Pages 287–295 in R. LeB. Bowen, Jr. & F.P. Albright, *Archaeological Discoveries in South Arabia*. (Publications of the American Foundation for the Study of Man, 2). Baltimore, MD: Johns Hopkins Press.
Vogt B.
1999. Der Almaqah-Tempel von Bar'an ('Arsh Bilqis). Pages 219–222 in W. Seipel (ed.), *Jemen. Kunst und Archäologie im Land der Königin von Saba'*. Vienna: Kunsthistorisches Museum.
Wissmann H. von/ed. W.W. Müller.
1982. *Die Geschichte von Sabaʾ II. Das Grossreich der Sabäer bis zu seinem Ende im frühen 4. Jh. v. Chr.* Vienna: Verlag der Österreichischen Akademie der Wissenschaften.

Authors' addresses
Dr-Ing. Zaydoon Zaid, c/o American Foundation for the Study of Man, P.O. Box 2136, Falls Church, VA 22042, USA.
e-mail zaydoon@web.de

Dr Mohammed Maraqten, Orient-Institut Beirut der Deutschen Morgenländischen Gesellschaft, Rue Hussein Beyhum, Zokak el-Blat, P.O. Box 11-2988 11072120 Riad El Solh, Beirut, Lebanon.
e-mail maraqten@staff.uni-marburg.de, maraqten@online.de

Proceedings of the Seminar for Arabian Studies 38 (2008): 341–344

Papers read at the Seminar for Arabian Studies held at the British Museum, London, on 19-21 July 2007

NB Papers published in this volume of PSAS are highlighted with an asterisk *

Session I	**Eastern Arabian Archaeology**
Manfred Boehme & Gerd Weisgerber	New research on the Bronze Age cemeteries at Bat, Oman
* Nasser Al-Jahwari	Wadi Settlement at Northern Oman: Towards a Model for Settlement Quantification
Crystal Fritz	Human Behaviour and Ceramic Correlates in SE Arabian Iron Age
Peter Magee	Excavations at Muweilah (Sharjah, UAE)
Peter Magee, Marc Handel, Don Barber, Margaret Uerpmann, Hans-Peter Uerpmann, Crystal Fritz & Sabah A. Jasim	Two seasons of research at al-Hamriya. Results of a joint Bryn Mawr College – University of Tubingen research project
Steffen Laursen	The Bahrain Burial Mound Project
Session II	**Yemeni Archaeology**
* Michael Harrower	Mapping Incipient Irrigation in Wadi Sana, Hadramawt
* Ueli Brunner	Ancient Irrigation in Wadi Jirdan, Yemen
* Christian Darles	Latest results, new dating and recent evidence for the fortifications of Shabwa (Hadhramawt)
* Krista Lewis & Lamya Khalidi	From Prehistoric Landscapes to Urban Sprawl: the Masna'at Maryah region of highland Yemen
* Zaydoon Zaid & Mohammed Maraqten	The complexity of the Peristyle Hall: Remarks on the history of construction based on recent archaeological and epigraphic evidence of the AFSM expedition to the Awam Temple in Marib, Yemen
* Mohammed Maraqten	Women's inscriptions recently discovered by the AFSM at the Awam Temple/ Mahram Bilqis in Marib, Yemen
* Yosef Tobi	Shalom (Salim) al-Shabazi. (11th Century) as a Yemeni Poet

Session III	**Defining the Palaeolithic of Arabia**
Special session organized by Jeffrey I. Rose	
* Adrian Parker & Jeffrey I. Rose	Demographic confluence and radiation in southern Arabia
Tomas Kivisild	Genetics and the southern route of dispersal
Abdullah Alsharekh	An early Lower Palaeolithic site from central Saudi Arabia
* Julie E. Scott-Jackson, Sarah Milliken, William B. Scott-Jackson & Sabah A. Jasim	Upper Pleistocene Stone-tools from Sharjah, UAE. Initial Investigations: Interim Report
* Ghanim Wahida, Walid Yasin & Mark Beech	Barakah: a Middle Palaeolithic Site in Abu Dhabi
Hans-Peter Uerpmann, Margarethe Uerpmann, Johannes Kutterer, Marc Handel, Sabah A. Jasim & Anthony E. Marks	The Stone Age Sequence of Jebel Faya in the Emirate of Sharjah (UAE)
* Rémy Crassard	A Middle Palaeolithic in South Arabia? Levallois and Wa'shah methods from Yemen
* Anthony E. Marks	Crossing the Rift: Technology of the Late, Middle and Upper Pleistocene in East Africa
Session IV	**The Arabian Neolithic**
* Vincent Charpentier	The Arabian Neolithic Chronology: a point of view from Ja'alan Oman
* Francesco Fedele	Wadi at-Tayyilah 3, a Neolithic settlement on the eastern Yemen Plateau and its archaeofaunal information
* Sophie Méry & Vincent Charpentier	A Neolithic settlement at Akab (Umm al-Quwayn, United Arab Emirates)
Session V	**North-Western Arabia**
Ricardo Eichmann	Architecture and stratigraphy in NW-Arabian oasis settlements (2nd millennium BC - 1st millennium AD)
Arnulf Hausleiter	Painted pottery groups in NW Arabia of the late 2nd/early 1st millennia BC
Abdul Kareem Al-Ghamdi	Antiquities of Jarash: Asir region, Kingdom of Saudi Arabia

* Saad al-Rashid	Sadd al-Khanaq: an Early Umayyad Dam Near Medina: Saudi Arabia
Session VI	**Ancient Seafaring**
Elizabeth Lambourn	Khutba & Khil'a: Networks of mercantile recognition and clientship between Calicut, Aden and Herat
* Eivind Heldas Seland	Indian ships at Moscha and the ancient Indo-Arabian trading circuit
Session VII	**Early Islamic History, Settlement, and Archaeology**
* Brian Ulrich	The Azd Migrations Reconsidered: Accounts of Malik b. Fahm and 'Amr Muzayqiya in their Historiographic Context
Khalifa Mohamed Omer	Muwatta' as a source for the economic and social history of Medina
* Audrey Peli	A history of the Ziyadids through their coinage (AD 203-442/818-1050)
* Mohammed Al-Thenayian	The Pottery of the Red Sea Tihami Coastal Ports in Saudi Arabia: Preliminary Notes
Harald Veldhuijzen	Rediscovery of a Fort: the Qasr al-Hosn of Abu Dhabi
* Alexandrine Guerin	Zekrit site: settlement patterns during the XIXth century in Qatar. Tribes and territory
Giovanna Ventrone Vassallo	Towards a comprehensive Catalogue of Islamic Religious Architecture of Yemen
Salma Samar Damluji & Tracy Thompson	Wadi Daw'an Project
Norbert Nebes	Gerrhaeans in Marib - A new fragment to a dated text
Session VIII	**Recent History and Linguistics**
* Abd Rauh Yaccob	British Policy in Arabia until the end of the First World War: Internal Disputes
* Yahya Asiri	Relative clauses in Rijal Alma' dialect (South-west Saudi Arabia)
* Mikhail Rodionov	The djinn and afarit in the South Arabian society of the last century

Poster Presentations

Alessandra Avanzini	MENCAWAR: Mediterranean Network for Cataloguing and Web Fruition of Ancient Artworks and Inscriptions
Afra S. Bin Sulaiman, Alia A. Malik, Hind D. Bin Dulmook, Mona F. Al Gurg & Nouf A. Dhmani	Ghleelah, Past, Present and Future: Architectural and Environmental analysis and re-design of Ghleelah community, Ras Al Khaimah, UAE
* Fabio Cavulli & Simona Scaruffi	Stone artifacts from KHB-1, a Holocene fisher-gatherer settlement in the Ja'lân region (Sultanate of Oman)
* An De Waele & Aurelie Daems	Human-Animal Relationships in Pre-Islamic Southeast Arabia: A View from the Camelid and Equid Burials
Steffen Terp Laursen & Kasper Lambert Johansen	The Bahrain Burial Mound Project
Carolyn Perry	The MBI al Jaber Foundation
Helen Walkington & Adrian G. Parker	The chronology and sedimentology of the Neolithic Graveyard and shell midden complex, Umm al-Qawain (UAQ2), United Arab Emirates